Turkish

Turkish: A Comprehensive Grammar has been extensively revised in this second edition to provide a complete reference guide to modern Turkish grammar, presenting an accessible description of the language with a thorough description of the sound system, intonation patterns, word structure and sentence structure of Turkish.

The book presents a stimulating analysis of the complexities of the language through detailed descriptions and illustrative examples. Relevant parts of the examples are highlighted for better understanding and are accompanied by grammatical glosses that will facilitate the parsing of the constructions. An extensive system of cross-referencing makes it easy for the reader to see the connection between topics.

The book is designed as a source for intermediate and advanced learners and users of Turkish and for students of linguistics. It can be used as a reference book and supplementary material in colleges, universities, and continuing education classes, both in Turkish courses and specialized linguistics classes.

Aslı Göksel is an independent researcher and former Professor of Linguistics at Boğaziçi University, Istanbul, Turkey

Celia Kerslake was University Lecturer and Emeritus Fellow of Turkish, St Antony's College, Oxford University, UK.

Routledge Comprehensive Grammars

Turkish

A Comprehensive Grammar

Second Edition

Aslı Göksel and Celia Kerslake

LONDON AND NEW YORK

Second edition published 2025
by Routledge
4 Park Square, Milton Park, Abingdon, Oxon, OX14 4RN

and by Routledge
605 Third Avenue, New York, NY 10158

Routledge is an imprint of the Taylor & Francis Group, an informa business

© 2025 Aslı Göksel and Celia Kerslake

The right of Aslı Göksel and Celia Kerslake to be identified as authors of this work has been asserted in accordance with sections 77 and 78 of the Copyright, Designs and Patents Act 1988.

All rights reserved. No part of this book may be reprinted or reproduced or utilised in any form or by any electronic, mechanical, or other means, now known or hereafter invented, including photocopying and recording, or in any information storage or retrieval system, without permission in writing from the publishers.

Trademark notice: Product or corporate names may be trademarks or registered trademarks, and are used only for identification and explanation without intent to infringe.

First edition published by Routledge 2005

British Library Cataloguing-in-Publication Data
A catalogue record for this book is available from the British Library

Library of Congress Cataloging-in-Publication Data
Names: Göksel, Aslı, author. | Kerslake, Celia, author.
Title: Turkish: a comprehensive grammar/Aslı Göksel and Celia Kerslake.
Description: Second edition. | Abingdon, Oxon; New York,
NY: Routledge, 2025. |
Series: Routledge comprehensive grammars | Includes bibliographical references and index.
Identifiers: LCCN 2024027331 (print) | LCCN 2024027332 (ebook) | ISBN 9781138350519 (hardback) | ISBN 9781138350533 (paperback) | ISBN 9780429435836 (ebook)
Subjects: LCSH: Turkish language–Grammar. |
Turkish language–Textbooks for foreign speakers–English.
Classification: LCC PL121 .G65 2025 (print) | LCC PL121 (ebook) |
DDC 494/.355–dc23/eng/20240921
LC record available at https://lccn.loc.gov/2024027331
LC ebook record available at https://lccn.loc.gov/2024027332

ISBN: 978-1-138-35051-9 (hbk)
ISBN: 978-1-138-35053-3 (pbk)
ISBN: 978-0-429-43583-6 (ebk)

DOI: 10.4324/9780429435836

Typeset in Times New Roman
by Deanta Global Publishing Services, Chennai, India

In memoriam, Celia Kerslake 1946–2023

Contents

Introduction to the second edition — *xxvii*
Introduction (first edition) — *xxix*
Abbreviations — *xxxviii*
List of conventions observed in this book — *xli*
The Turkish alphabet and writing conventions — *xliii*

PART 1
Phonology: The sound system — 1

1 Phonological units — 3
   1.1 Consonants and vowels 3
      1.1.1 Consonants 3
         1.1.1.1 Consonants and their allophones 4
      1.1.2 Vowels 10
         1.1.2.1 Vowels and their allophones 10
         1.1.2.2 Long vowels 12
   1.2 The distribution of consonants and vowels 13
      1.2.1 Consonant clusters 13

2 Sound changes produced in the word by suffixation — 14
   2.1 Alternations of voiceless/voiced consonants: 'p'/'b', 't'/'d', 'k'/'g', 'k'/'ğ', 'ç'/'c' 14
   2.2 Alternations of single consonants with doubled consonants 17
   2.3 Vowel/ø (zero) alternation 17
   2.4 Short/long vowel alternations 18
   2.5 œ/e Alternation 19
   2.6 Alternation of 'a', 'e', 'u' and 'ü' with 'ı' and 'i' 19

3 Vowel harmony — 21
3.1 Types of vowel harmony 21
3.2 Vowel harmony in suffixes and clitics 22
   3.2.1 Vowel harmony in I-type suffixes 22
   3.2.2 Vowel harmony in A-type suffixes 23
3.3 Vowel harmony in roots 24
3.4 Exceptions to vowel harmony 24

4 Stress in words and phrases — 26
4.1 Stress in words 26
   4.1.1 Regular words 26
   4.1.2 Irregular words 27
4.2 Stress in compounds 29
4.3 Stress and suffixes 29
   4.3.1 Stressable suffixes 30
   4.3.2 Unstressable suffixes 31
4.4 Phrasal stress 31
   4.4.1 Stress in verb phrases 32
   4.4.2 Sress in noun phrases 32
   4.4.3 Stress in postpositional phrases 33

5 Intonation and sentence stress — 34
5.1 The intonation contours of Turkish 34
5.2 Position of stress in the intonational phrase 36
   5.2.1 Primary stress 36
   5.2.2 Secondary stress 37
5.3 Sentences with more than one intonation contour 38

PART 2
Morphology: The structure of words — 39

6 Principles of suffixation — 41
6.1 The form of suffixes 41
   6.1.1 Vowel alternation in suffixes 41
   6.1.2 Consonant alternation in suffixes 42
   6.1.3 The attachment of a suffix to a stem: deletable vowels and consonants 42
6.2 Irregular changes under suffixation 44
6.3 The order of suffixation 45

7 Word classes, derivation and derivational suffixes 47
   7.1 Word classes 47
      7.1.1 Nominals 47
      7.1.2 Verbs 49
      7.1.3 Postpositions 49
      7.1.4 Conjunctions and discourse connectives 49
      7.1.5 Interjections 49
   7.2 Derivation 50
      7.2.1 Suffixes that attach to verbs 51
         7.2.1.1 Suffixes that attach to verbs to form nominals 51
         7.2.1.2 Suffixes that attach to verbs to form verbs 55
      7.2.2 Suffixes that attach to nominals 55
         7.2.2.1 Suffixes that attach to nominals to form verbs 55
         7.2.2.2 Suffixes that attach to nominals to form nominals 57
   7.3 The internal ordering of derivational suffixes 65
   7.4 Prefixation 65

8 Inflectional suffixes 66
   8.1 Nominal inflectional suffixes 66
      8.1.1 The plural suffix -lAr 67
      8.1.2 Possessive suffixes 67
      8.1.3 Case suffixes 68
      8.1.4 Other nominal inflectional markers 68
   8.2 Verbal inflectional suffixes 71
      8.2.1 Voice suffixes 72
         8.2.1.1 Causative 73
         8.2.1.2 Passive 73
         8.2.1.3 Reflexive 74
         8.2.1.4 Reciprocal 74
      8.2.2 The negative marker 74
      8.2.3 Tense, aspect and modality markers 75
         8.2.3.1 Position 1 76
         8.2.3.2 Position 2 77
         8.2.3.3 Position 3 77
   8.3 The copula 'be', copular markers and -DIr 81
      8.3.1 The copula 'be' 81
      8.3.2 The copular markers -(y)DI, -(y)mIş, -(y)sA 82

8.3.3 -DIr 83
8.4 Person markers 84
    8.4.1 Group 1 85
    8.4.2 Group 2 86
    8.4.3 Group 3 87
    8.4.4 Group 4 87
8.5 Subordinating suffixes 88
    8.5.1 Multi-functional subordinating suffixes: -DIK, -(y)AcAK, -mA, -mAK 88
        8.5.1.1 -DIK, -(y)AcAK 88
        8.5.1.2 -mA, -mAK 90
    8.5.2 Subordinating suffixes which have a single function 92
        8.5.2.1 -(y)An, -(y)Iş, -(y)AsI 92
        8.5.2.2 Subordinating suffixes which only form converbs 92

9 Reduplication and doubling 95
9.1 Emphatic reduplication 95
9.2 m-Reduplication 96
9.3 Doubling 97
    9.3.1 Doubling in lexical formations 98
    9.3.2 Doubling with -(y)A_2 99

10 Noun compounds 100
10.1 Bare compounds 101
    10.1.1 Noun-noun compounds 101
    10.1.2 Adjective-noun compounds 102
    10.1.3 Noun compounds with derived nominals 102
    10.1.4 Verb-verb compounds 103
10.2 -(s)I Compounds 103
    10.2.1 The functions of -(s)I compounds 104
    10.2.2 -(s)I compounds and words expressing nationality 105
10.3 Embedding compounds within other compounds 106
10.4 Separability of the constituents of compounds 107

11 Clitics 109
11.1 The clitics of Turkish 109
    11.1.1 The properties of individual clitics 110
        11.1.1.1 bile 110
        11.1.1.2 dA 110

   11.1.1.3 diye 111
   11.1.1.4 ki 112
   11.1.1.5 mI 113
   11.1.1.6 ya 116
   11.1.1.7 -(y)sA/ise 116
   11.1.1.8 Person markers 117
11.2 Clitics, unstressable suffixes and stress 118
 11.2.1 Unstressable suffixes and clitics in the same word or phrase 118
 11.2.2 Clitics in separate phrases 119
 11.2.3 The combination of clitics with the negative marker -mA 120

PART 3
Syntax: The structure of sentences   121

12 Simple and complex sentences   123
12.1 Constituents of a sentence: Subject and predicate 123
 12.1.1 Predicate 123
  12.1.1.1 Verbal sentences 124
  12.1.1.2 Nominal sentences 124
  12.1.1.3 The complementarity of -(y)- and var/yok with ol- 129
 12.1.2 Expression of the subject 131
12.2 Agreement of subject and predicate 132
 12.2.1 Person and number marking on the predicate 132
 12.2.2 Agreement of a 3rd person predicate with different types of plural subject 133
  12.2.2.1 Subject marked with the plural suffix 133
  12.2.2.2 Subjects containing determiners 135
  12.2.2.3 Pronominalized determiners as subjects 136
  12.2.2.4 Conjoined subjects 137
 12.2.3 Personal pronouns as subject complements 139
12.3 Complex sentences and subordination 139
12.4 Functional sentence types 141

13 The verb phrase   143
13.1 Constituents of the verb phrase 144
 13.1.1 The verb 144
 13.1.2 Complements of the verb 145

            13.1.2.1 Direct object 145
            13.1.2.2 Oblique object 146
        13.1.3 Adverbials 148
    13.2 Transitivity and voice 149
        13.2.1 Causative constructions 150
            13.2.1.1 Multiple occurrences of the causative
                      suffix 151
            13.2.1.2 Causatives of verbs of emotion 152
        13.2.2 Passive constructions 153
            13.2.2.1 Passivizing a transitive verb 153
            13.2.2.2 Expressing the agent in a passive
                      sentence 153
            13.2.2.3 Impersonal passives 155
            13.2.2.4 Double passive constructions 155
        13.2.3 Constructions with non-productive voice suffixes 156
            13.2.3.1 Reflexive constructions 156
            13.2.3.2 Reciprocal constructions 158
        13.2.4 Combinations of voice suffixes 158
    13.3 Auxiliary verbs 160
        13.3.1 Compound verb forms 161
            13.3.1.1 Compound verb forms containing bound
                      auxiliaries 161
            13.3.1.2 Compound verb forms containing free
                      auxiliaries 162
        13.3.2 Nominal-verb compounds 164

14 **The noun phrase**   **166**
    14.1 Structure of the noun phrase 167
        14.1.1 Items which can function as the head of a noun
               phrase 167
        14.1.2 Modifiers in the noun phrase 168
    14.2 Countability 168
        14.2.1 Uses of the indefinite article bir with noun phrases that
               do not denote discrete entities 169
    14.3 Nominal inflection 170
        14.3.1 Number 170
            14.3.1.1 Plural marking with -lAr 170
            14.3.1.2 Further uses of the plural suffix -lAr 172
            14.3.1.3 Transnumeral uses of the unmarked form 174
        14.3.2 Person (possessive suffixes) 175

                14.3.2.1 Marking possession in -(s)I compounds 177
        14.3.3 Case 178
                14.3.3.1 The non-case-marked noun phrase 178
                14.3.3.2 The accusative case marker 180
                14.3.3.3 The dative case marker 181
                14.3.3.4 The locative case marker 183
                14.3.3.5 The ablative case marker 184
                14.3.3.6 The genitive case marker 185
    14.4 The genitive-possessive construction 186
    14.5 Partitive constructions 189
        14.5.1 The bare-headed partitive construction with ablative-
                marked modifier 190
        14.5.2 The -(s)i-marked partitive construction with ablative-
                marked modifier 192
        14.5.3 The -(s)i-marked partitive construction with genitive-
                marked modifier 193
        14.5.4 Other features of partitive constructions 194

15 **Adjectival constructions, determiners and numerals**   **195**
    15.1 Functions of adjectivals 196
    15.2 Adjectives 197
        15.2.1 Forming adjectives by means of derivational suffixes
                and compounding 197
        15.2.2 Intensive forms 197
    15.3 Complex adjectivals 198
        15.3.1 Adjective + noun 198
        15.3.2 Locative-marked noun phrase 198
        15.3.3 Ablative-marked noun phrase 198
        15.3.4 Noun phrase marked with -lI 199
        15.3.5 Noun phrase marked with -lIk 199
        15.3.6 Locative-marked noun phrase + -ki 200
        15.3.7 Temporal adverbial + -ki 200
        15.3.8 Noun phrase + diye 200
        15.3.9 Relative clause 201
        15.3.10 Possessive-marked noun phrase + adjective
                (truncated relative clause) 201
    15.4 Modification of adjectives 201
        15.4.1 General modification 201
                15.4.1.1 By simple adverbials of degree 201
                15.4.1.2 By complex adverbials 202

15.4.2 Comparatives 202
15.4.3 Superlatives 204
15.5 Complementation of adjectives 205
15.6 Determiners 206
    15.6.1 Indefinite determiners 206
    15.6.2 Definite determiners 207
15.7 Numerals 207
    15.7.1 Cardinal numerals 207
    15.7.2 Ordinal numerals 209
    15.7.3 Distributive numerals 210
15.8 The enumerator tane and measure/type terms 210
15.9 The position of determiners and numerals within the noun phrase 211
    15.9.1 Numerals with determiners 211
    15.9.2 Determiners or numerals with adjectives 212
    15.9.3 Determiners or numerals with complex adjectivals formed with -DAn, -lI or -lIk 213
    15.9.4 Determiners or numerals with locative-marked complex adjectivals 214
    15.9.5 Determiners or numerals with adjectivals formed with -ki 214
    15.9.6 Determiners or numerals with relative clauses 215

16 Adverbial constructions   217

16.1 Types of adverbial construction 217
    16.1.1 Simple adverbs 217
    16.1.2 Adjectives used as adverbs 217
    16.1.3 Doubled forms 218
    16.1.4 Noun phrases without case marking 219
    16.1.5 Noun phrases with oblique case marking 219
    16.1.6 Noun or adjective suffixed with $-CA_1$ 219
    16.1.7 Constructions with -DIr 220
    16.1.8 Postpositional phrases 220
    16.1.9 Constructions with olarak 220
    16.1.10 Constructions with olmak üzere 221
    16.1.11 Truncated relative clauses as adverbials 222
    16.1.12 Adverbial clauses 222
16.2 Syntactic functions of adverbials 222
16.3 Modal adverbials 223

16.4 Circumstantial adverbials 226
    16.4.1 Time adverbials 226
        16.4.1.1 Location in time 227
        16.4.1.2 Duration 235
        16.4.1.3 Frequency 235
        16.4.1.4 Other time adverbials 236
    16.4.2 Place adverbials 238
    16.4.3 Manner adverbials 240
    16.4.4 Other types of circumstantial adverbial 241
16.5 Adverbials of quantity or degree 242
16.6 Adverbials of respect 244
16.7 Focus-sensitive adverbials 244
    16.7.1 Exclusive adverbials 244
    16.7.2 Particularizing adverbials 245
    16.7.3 The adverb tam 245
16.8 Modification of adverbs 246

17 Postpositional phrases   248
17.1 Structure of the postpositional phrase 248
17.2 Bare postpositions 249
    17.2.1 Postpositions taking non-case-marked or genitive complements 249
    17.2.2 Postpositions taking dative complements 252
    17.2.3 Postpositions taking ablative complements 254
17.3 Possessive-marked postpositions 256
    17.3.1 Group 1: spatial relations 257
        17.3.1.1 Group 1 possessive-marked postpositions with genitive complements 258
        17.3.1.2 Group 1 possessive-marked postpositions with non-case-marked complements 259
        17.3.1.3 Particular features of individual postpositions in Group 1 260
    17.3.2 Group 2: abstract relations 262
        17.3.2.1 Particular features of individual postpositions in Group 2 264
17.4 Syntactic functions of the postpositional phrase 265
    17.4.1 Adverbial function 266
    17.4.2 Adjectival function 266
    17.4.3 Predicative function 267

18 Pronouns and pronominal constructions — 268

- 18.1 Personal pronouns 268
  - 18.1.1 Simple personal pronouns 268
  - 18.1.2 kendi 270
    - 18.1.2.1 Bare form kendi 271
    - 18.1.2.2 Inflected kendi-: emphatic, reflexive, simple pronominal and resumptive usages 271
  - 18.1.3 kendi kendi- 277
  - 18.1.4 The reciprocal pronoun birbir- 'each other', 'one another' 278
  - 18.1.5 The omission and usage of personal pronouns 280
    - 18.1.5.1 Conditions under which personal pronouns are used 281
- 18.2 Demonstrative pronouns: bu, 'this (one)' şu 'this/that (one)', o 'that (one)' 285
- 18.3 Locative and directional pronouns 286
  - 18.3.1 Locative pronouns: bura- 'here', şura- 'here', 'over there' and ora- 'there' 286
  - 18.3.2 Directional pronouns 287
- 18.4 Pronominalized adjectives, numerals and determiners 288
- 18.5 Pronominal expressions with -ki 290
- 18.6 Other pronominal expressions 291
  - 18.6.1 Pronominal quantifiers 291
  - 18.6.2 insan 'one' 292
  - 18.6.3 şey 292

19 Questions — 293

- 19.1 Questions with mI 293
  - 19.1.1 Yes/no questions 293
    - 19.1.1.1 Direct yes/no questions 294
    - 19.1.1.2 Tag questions 295
  - 19.1.2 Alternative questions 297
  - 19.1.3 Positions for mI other than the end of the sentence 298
  - 19.1.4 The effect of placing mI after a particular phrase 299
  - 19.1.5 Yes/no questions in contrastive contexts 301
- 19.2 Wh-questions 301
  - 19.2.1 Wh-phrases 302
    - 19.2.1.1 kim 'who' 302
    - 19.2.1.2 ne 'what' 303
    - 19.2.1.3 nere- 'where' 304

         19.2.1.4 *hangi 'which'* 306
         19.2.1.5 *kaç 'how many'* 306
         19.2.1.6 *ne kadar 'how much'* 307
         19.2.1.7 *ne zaman 'when'* 309
         19.2.1.8 *neden, niye, niçin 'why'* 309
         19.2.1.9 *nasıl 'how'* 309
    19.2.2 *The position of wh-phrases in a sentence* 310
         19.2.2.1 *Position of wh-phrases in linking sentences* 311
    19.2.3 *Wh-phrases and stressed phrases* 312
    19.2.4 *Multiple wh-phrases* 313
19.3 *Echo questions* 313
    19.3.1 *Echo questions following a question* 313
    19.3.2 *Echo questions following a statement* 314
    19.3.3 *derken constructions*
19.4 *Questioning parts of subordinate clauses* 314
19.5 *Modal adverbs used in questions* 315
    19.5.1 *hani* 315
    19.5.2 *acaba* 316
    19.5.3 *yoksa* 316
    19.5.4 *bakalım* 317
19.6 *Rhetorical questions* 317

20 Negation   319

20.1 *-mA* 319
    20.1.1 *Negating clauses with simple verbs* 319
    20.1.2 *Negating clauses with compound verb forms* 320
    20.1.3 *-(y)Ip...-mA 'whether/if...(or not)'* 322
20.2 *değil* 322
    20.2.1 *Negating nominal sentences* 322
    20.2.2 *Negating verbal sentences* 323
    20.2.3 *değil in elliptical sentences* 324
20.3 *yok* 325
20.4 *The negative connective ne ... ne 'neither ... nor'* 326
20.5 *Expressions interacting with negation* 327
    20.5.1 *hiç 'never', 'ever', 'at all'* 328
    20.5.2 *hiçbir 'no', 'any', and expressions containing hiçbir and herhangi bir 'no', 'any'* 329
    20.5.3 *(hiç) kimse 'no one', 'anyone'* 330
    20.5.4 *Modifiers of negation markers* 331
         20.5.4.1 *asla 'never', katiyen 'never'* 331

20.5.4.2 *pek 'much', 'very', (pek) fazla 'much', 'too much'* 331
20.5.4.3 *o kadar 'so', 'such', 'all that'* 332
20.6 Expressions interacting with negation in subordinate clauses 332
    20.6.1 Expressions interacting with negation in noun clauses 332
    20.6.2 Expressions interacting with negation in relative clauses and adverbial clauses 333
20.7 *sakın 'be sure', 'mind (you don't)', 'I wonder if ...', 'I do hope...'* 333
20.8 Usage of *-mA* without negative meaning 334

21 Tense, aspect and modality   335
21.1 The expression of tense, aspect and modality 336
21.2 Tense 336
    21.2.1 Past tense 337
    21.2.2 Present tense 338
    21.2.3 Future tense 339
21.3 Aspect 341
    21.3.1 Perfective and imperfective 341
    21.3.2 Subdivisions of imperfective: progressive and habitual 342
    21.3.3 Events and states 344
    21.3.4 Aspect in nominal sentences 345
        21.3.4.1 The distinction between *oldu* and *-(y)DI/idi* or *vardı* 345
        21.3.4.2 Habitual aspect in nominal sentences 346
        21.3.4.3 Other meanings of *oluyor* 347
21.4 Modality 348
    21.4.1 Generalizations and hypotheses 348
        21.4.1.1 Statements of permanent or generalized validity 348
        21.4.1.2 The use of *-DIr* in formal communication 351
        21.4.1.3 Hypothetical and counterfactual situations 351
        21.4.1.4 Assumptions, conjectures and hopes 352
    21.4.2 Possibility and necessity 354
        21.4.2.1 The expression of possibility 354
        21.4.2.2 The expression of necessity/obligation 360

21.4.3 Evidentially marked statements with -mIş or
-(y)mIş 365
   21.4.3.1 Information-based evidential statements 365
   21.4.3.2 Result-based evidential statements 367
   21.4.3.3 Use of the evidential copula to express a newly discovered state of affairs 368
   21.4.3.4 Evidentiality in questions 368
21.4.4 Volitional utterances 369
   21.4.4.1 Wishes 369
   21.4.4.2 Commands 370
   21.4.4.3 Suggestions: 1st person optative forms -(y)AyIm, -(y)AlIm 372
   21.4.4.4 Deliberation about possible action: questions with -sAm, -sAk 372
   21.4.4.5 Requests and offers: 2nd person aorist interrogative 373
   21.4.4.6 Expression of commitment: first person aorist 373
21.5 Tense, aspect and modality in compound verb forms 374
   21.5.1 Compound forms in which the lexical verb is marked with -mIş 375
      21.5.1.1 The resultative usage of compound verb forms with -mIş 377
   21.5.2 Compound forms in which the lexical verb is marked with -(I)yor 377
   21.5.3 Compound forms in which the lexical verb is marked with -(y)AcAk 378
   21.5.4 Compound forms in which the lexical verb is marked with -(A/I)r or -mAz 378
   21.5.5 The addition of the past copula -(y)DI to compound verb forms 379

22 Definiteness, specificity and generic reference   381
22.1 Definite status 382
22.2 Indefinite status 383
   22.2.1 Specific and non-specific indefinites 384
22.3 Categorial status 388
22.4 Generic reference 390
   22.4.1 Generic reference by singular noun phrases 390
      22.4.1.1 The bare generic 390

22.4.1.2 *The indefinite generic 391*
22.4.2 *Generic reference by plural noun phrases 392*
22.4.3 *Generic noun phrases as direct objects 393*
22.5 *The effect of word order on referential status 394*
22.6 *The effect of stress on referential status 395*
22.7 *The effect of tense, aspect and modality on referential status 395*

23 Word order   398
23.1 *Unmarked sentences: word order and stress 398*
   23.1.1 *Verbal sentences 399*
      23.1.1.1 *The immediately preverbal position 400*
   23.1.2 *Nominal sentences 402*
      23.1.2.1 *Linking sentences 402*
      23.1.2.2 *Existential sentences 402*
23.2 *The unmarked order of major constituents 403*
   23.2.1 *Subjects and modal adverbs 403*
   23.2.2 *Objects 404*
   23.2.3 *Adverbial constructions 405*
23.3 *Word order variations 406*
   23.3.1 *The position of focused constituents: the pre-predicate area 409*
   23.3.2 *The position of background information: the post-predicate area 410*
   23.3.3 *The topic position 412*
      23.3.3.1 *Topic shifters 413*
23.4 *Dislocated constituents 415*
   23.4.1 *Dislocated adjectival constructions 415*
   23.4.2 *Dislocated constituents of genitive-possessive constructions 415*
   23.4.3 *Dislocated constituents of noun clauses 416*

24 Noun clauses   417
24.1 *Finite and non-finite noun clauses 418*
24.2 *Bare finite noun clauses (finite noun clauses without a subordinator) 418*
   24.2.1 *Subject or object of the verb de- 418*
   24.2.2 *Subject or object of a verb of perception or cognition 420*
   24.2.3 *Subject or object of the verb iste- 420*

24.3 Finite noun clauses with a subordinator 421
    24.3.1 Clauses formed with diye 421
    24.3.2 Clauses formed with ki 422
        24.3.2.1 Subject or object of the verb de- 423
        24.3.2.2 Subject or object of a verb of perception or cognition 423
        24.3.2.3 Subject or object of the verb iste- 425
        24.3.2.4 The combination of adjectival predicates with ki 425
    24.3.3 Clauses formed with gibi 425
24.4 Non-finite noun clauses 426
    24.4.1 Clauses formed with -mAK 426
        24.4.1.1 The non-case-marked form -mAk 427
        24.4.1.2 The accusative-marked form -mAyI 429
        24.4.1.3 The oblique case-marked forms -mAyA, -mAktA (-mAdA), -mAktAn 429
        24.4.1.4 Passive -mAK clauses subordinated to main verb iste-, çalış-, başla- 431
    24.4.2 Clauses formed with -mA 432
        24.4.2.1 -mA without possessive suffixes 432
        24.4.2.2 -mA with possessive suffixes 433
    24.4.3 Clauses formed with -DIK/-(y)AcAK 437
        24.4.3.1 Indirect statements 438
        24.4.3.2 Indirect questions 440
        24.4.3.3 Other functions of -DIK/-(y)AcAK clauses 441
    24.4.4 Clauses formed with -(y)Iş 442
    24.4.5 Overlapping uses of -mA, -DIK/-(y)AcAK, -(y)Iş 442
        24.4.5.1 As direct object of verbs of perception or cognition 442
        24.4.5.2 As oblique object of verbs of emotion 443
    24.4.6 Omission of genitive marking on the subject of clauses formed with possessive-marked -mA, -DIK/-(y)AcAK 444
    24.4.7 The use of auxiliary ol- in non-finite noun clauses 445
24.5 Small clauses 447
    24.5.1 Small clauses occurring with main clause transitive verbs 447
    24.5.2 Small clauses occurring with main clause intransitive verbs 449
    24.5.3 Tense/aspect and person marking 449

24.6 Noun clauses as modifiers in -(s)I compounds: phrasal compounds: 450

25 Relative clauses — 453

25.1 Principles of relativization 454
    25.1.1 Markers of non-finite relative clauses: the participle suffixes 455
        25.1.1.1 -(y)An 455
        25.1.1.2 -DIK/-(y)AcAK with possessive suffixes 458
        25.1.1.3 -DIK/-(y)ACAK without possessive suffixes 461
        25.1.1.4 Summary of strategies of relativization 463
    25.1.2 Relative clauses with embedded noun clauses 463
25.2 Restrictive and non-restrictive relative clauses 464
25.3 Pronominal relative clauses 466
25.4 The expression of tense and aspect in relative clauses 468
    25.4.1 The use of auxiliary ol- in relative clauses 469
        25.4.1.1 The omission of olan: truncated relative clauses 473
25.5 Other complex adjectival constructions 475
25.6 Finite relative clauses with ki 475
    25.6.1 ki in non-restrictive relative clauses 475
    25.6.2 ki in restrictive relative clauses 476
    25.6.3 Comment usage of ki 477

26 Adverbial clauses — 479

26.1 Finite adverbial clauses 480
    26.1.1 Clauses formed with diye 480
        26.1.1.1 Reason 480
        26.1.1.2 Purpose 481
        26.1.1.3 Precaution 481
        26.1.1.4 Understanding 481
    26.1.2 Clauses formed with ki 482
        26.1.2.1 Location in time 482
        26.1.2.2 Purpose 483
        26.1.2.3 Result 483
        26.1.2.4 Basis for deduction 483
    26.1.3 Clauses formed with madem(ki) 484
    26.1.4 Clauses formed with nasıl ki 484

26.1.5 Clauses formed with (sanki)...-mIş/-(y)mIş gibi 484
26.1.6 Clauses formed with -DI mI 485
26.1.7 Clauses formed with dA 486
26.1.8 Clauses formed with -(y)Adursun 486
26.2 Non-finite adverbial clauses: structural characteristics 486
    26.2.1 Genitive case marking or its absence in the subject of a non-finite adverbial clause 487
    26.2.2 Possibility of the adverbial clause having a separate subject from that of the superordinate clause 487
    26.2.3 Tense and aspect marking in non-finite adverbial clauses 489
26.3 Non-finite adverbial clauses: semantic classification 492
    26.3.1 Addition 492
    26.3.2 Agreement 493
    26.3.3 Concession 493
    26.3.4 Condition 494
    26.3.5 Conjunction 494
    26.3.6 Dismissal 494
    26.3.7 Information base for an utterance 495
    26.3.8 Manner 495
    26.3.9 Means 497
    26.3.10 Preference 498
    26.3.11 Proportionality 498
    26.3.12 Purpose 498
    26.3.13 Quantity or degree 499
    26.3.14 Reason 500
    26.3.15 Substitution 500
    26.3.16 Time 500
26.4 Converbial clauses used adjectivally 505
    26.4.1 Attributive function 505
    26.4.2 Predicative function 506

27 Conditional sentences 508
27.1 The grammatical marking of conditional clauses 509
    27.1.1 The verbal suffix -sA and the copular marker -(y)sA (or ise) 509
    27.1.2 The conditional conjunctions eğer and şayet 510
27.2 Predictive conditionals 511
    27.2.1 Aorist + -(y)sA 511
        27.2.1.1 Open conditionals 512

27.2.1.2 Generic and habitual conditionals 513
27.2.1.3 Compound forms with olursa 514
27.2.2 Open and habitual conditionals expressed without aorist marking 515
27.2.3 -sA 516
27.2.3.1 -sA used without past copular marking of the main clause 516
27.2.3.2 -sA used with past copular marking of the main clause 517
27.2.4 -sAydI 518
27.2.5 -sAymIş 519
27.2.6 Compound verb forms with olsa/olsaydı/olsaymış 520
27.3 Knowable conditions 522
27.4 Further uses of -sA and -(y)sA as subordinators 524
27.4.1 -sA...-sA 524
27.4.2 -sA and -(y)sA/ise with dA 525
27.4.2.1 -sA with dA 525
27.4.2.2 -(y)sA/ise with dA 526
27.5 Clauses with wh-phrases and conditional marking 527
27.5.1 Concessives 529
27.6 Conditional constructions without conditional suffixes 530
27.6.1 -DIğI takdirde, -mAsI durumunda/halinde 530
27.6.2 -DI mI 530

28 Conjunctions, co-ordination and discourse connection 531
28.1 The juxtaposition of two or more constituents 531
28.2 The subordinating suffixes -(y)Ip and -(y)ArAk 532
28.3 Conjunctions and discourse connectives 533
28.3.1 Additive 534
28.3.1.1 ve, -(y)lA/ile, dA 'and', dA 'too', bile 'even', ve de 'and what's more', bir de 'and also', ya 'and [...]?' 534
28.3.1.2 üstelik, üstüne üstlük, hem, hem (de), buna ek olarak, ayrıca, kaldı ki 'and (what's more)', 'also', sonra 'and then' 537
28.3.1.3 hatta, dahası 'even', 'indeed' 537
28.3.1.4 şöyle dursun/bir yana/bırak(ın) 'let alone' 538
28.3.2 Enumerating 538
28.3.3 Alternative 539

28.3.3.1 *ya da, veya, (ve) yahut (da), yoksa 'or', ya... ya (da) '(either...) or'* 539
28.3.3.2 *ister...ister, olsun...olsun, ha...ha, ama...ama 'whether...or'* 540
28.3.4 Adversative 541
28.3.4.1 *ama, fakat, ancak, yalnız 'but'* 541
28.3.4.2 *gene (de)/yine (de) '(and) yet', '(and) still', bununla birlikte/beraber, buna karşın/rağmen 'despite this', 'nevertheless'* 542
28.3.4.3 *ne (var) ki, gelgelelim, gel gör ki, mamafih 'however'* 542
28.3.4.4 *halbuki/oysa (ki), 'whereas', 'however'* 542
28.3.4.5 *dA, ya 'but', -(y)sA/ise 'as for', 'whereas'* 543
28.3.4.6 *gerçi/hoş 'it's true that', 'admittedly', 'actually', aslında* 544
28.3.4.7 *ki and ya* 544
28.3.4.8 *peki 'but'* 545
28.3.4.9 *yok 'but'* 546
28.3.5 Expansive 546
28.3.6 Causal 548
28.3.7 Inferential 549
28.3.8 Temporal 550
28.3.9 Conditional 550
28.3.10 Organizational 552
28.3.11 Corroborative 553
28.3.12 Reminding 553
28.3.13 Constructive 554
28.4 The effects of co-ordination and discourse connection 555
28.4.1 The elision of suffixes and clitics in co-ordinated constructions 555
28.4.1.1 Elision of copular markers and person markers 555
28.4.1.2 Elision of nominal inflectional markers 556
28.4.1.3 Elision of other items: -(y)ken, bile, mI, (subordinator) ki 557
28.4.2 The elision of phrases in co-ordinated constructions 557
28.4.2.1 The elision of noun phrases in co-ordinated constructions 558
28.4.3 The elision of noun phrases in other contexts 559

Appendix 1: Reduplicated stems 561
Appendix 2: Tense, aspect and modality markers 564
Glossary of grammatical terms 569
Bibliography 583
Index 588

Introduction to the second edition

In the twenty years since the publication of *Turkish, A Comprehensive Grammar* there have been many occasions where we have had to reevaluate our book. We have been fortunate enough to see it used by researchers, colleagues, students and a broader group of readers. Their suggestions, together with our own observations, lead to major revisions, reformulated descriptions and updated examples.

As we were embarking on the new edition, we were asked by some colleagues whether Turkish had changed during the last twenty years. This is a difficult question to answer since linguistic changes over short periods of time are not easy to pinpoint, but it certainly has become easier to find information thanks to the arrival of search engines. While in the first edition we mostly had to rely on our own insights and notes drawn from literary sources, we now have at our disposal online sources to check usages. Some of the changes we made are a result of having this access. One change concerns the words, which, in the first edition, we considered dated. Most of them are still in use today and we decided to remove the symbol we previously used to indicate that a form was decreasing in usage. We have also removed from this edition the symbol that referred to informal usage. Now we merely mention whether a form is formal or colloquial.

We have made major changes to Chapter 4 (Word stress and phrasal stress), Chapter 10 (Compounds), Chapter 11 (Clitics), Chapter 12 (Sentence structure), and Chapter 23 (Word order). In Chapter 4 we added new sections on phrasal stress and revised the section on unstressable suffixes, moving the main part to Chapter 11. Chapter 10 has been expanded to contain types of compound previously not included. We have expanded Chapters 12 and 23 to include additional examples of linking and existential sentences, thus shifting the focus from verbal sentences to achieve a more balanced coverage. We have added new sections to Chapter 15 (Adjectival constructions), 18 (Pronouns and pronominal constructions), Chapter 19 (Questions), Chapter 20 (Negation), Chapter 24 (Noun clauses), and Chapter 25 (Relative clauses). The revision of many subsections includes new examples, expanded descriptions and coverage of novel forms.

A large body of work on Turkish linguistics has been produced after the publication of the first edition. As in the first edition, the format of the publication does not allow references to the work of others in the text. In the revised bibliography, we confine ourselves to those that provide insights about the description of a particular item.

We became aware of various aspects of Turkish as they were presented in our book during discussions in linguistics conferences or in private conversations with colleagues and students. Their comments and questions are reflected in the revisions. We are grateful to Christian Bassac, Sinan Bayraktaroğlu, Monik Charette, Geoffrey Haig, Atakan İnce, Meltem Kelepir, Hakan Keser, Nihan Ketrez and Anthony E.R. Taylor for their contribution, whether they were aware of it or not. During the preparation of the first edition, we drew heavily on the expertise or grammaticality judgements of the following colleagues, students and friends: Didar Akar, Dimitris Antoniou, Ceyda Arslan, Öznur Ayman, Ercan Balcı, Cem Çakır, Georgia Catsimali, Monik Charette, Ruth Christie, Ann Denwood, Dilek Elçin, Gülen Ergin, Eser Erguvanlı-Taylan, Kate Fleet, Jorge Hankamer, Katerina Hardiman, Onat Işık, Atakan İnce, Meltem Kelepir, Elisabeth Kendall, Zeynep Kulelioğlu, Wilfried Meyer-Viol, Güneş Müftüoğlu, Mine Nakipoğlu, Mehmet Ölmez, A. Sumru Özsoy, Müfide Pekin, Andras Riedlmayer and Şükriye Ruhi. We are indebted to all these people for sparing the time to help us. We do not claim to have represented their ideas correctly and needless to say, any remaining errors are ours. We would also like to thank our editors at Routledge, Iola Ashby and Andrea Hartill for their efforts in providing us with an editable copy of the first edition and for their patience, and to our anonymous copy-editor for their comments and suggestions.

In this introduction I use the word 'we' with a heavy heart as my dear friend and co-author Celia Kerslake died on February 2023, more than a year before I submitted the manuscript. Prior to her death, Celia and I had gone over each chapter several times. I was left with many emails and notes to sift through, to organize and to implement. I hope I have done Celia's well-known diligence, high standards and scholarship justice. I shall remember her with love and gratitude.

Aslı Göksel
May 2024

Introduction (first edition)

Turkish and its speakers

Turkish belongs to the Turkic family of languages, which have been spoken for many centuries across a vast territory from the Balkans to China. Within this family, which includes such languages as Uighur, Uzbek, Tatar and Kazakh, Turkish forms part of the southwestern or Oghuz branch. Its closest relatives are Gagauz (spoken by less than 200,000 people of Orthodox Christian religion, mostly in southern Moldova), Azerbaijanian (spoken by up to 20 million people in Iran and Azerbaijan) and Turkmen (spoken by some 3 million people in Turkmenistan and by about 400,000 in Iraq).

Turkish itself is spoken predominantly in the Republic of Turkey, of which it is the official language. No statistics are available as to how many of Turkey's population of 70 million have Turkish as their first language. Most of the ethnic minorities have undergone considerable (in some cases, total) linguistic assimilation. In the largest ethnic minority, that of the Kurds (which is variously estimated to make up between 8 per cent and 20 per cent of the country's population), a large number of people are bilingual. A reasonable estimate would probably be that Turkish is now the first language of 55–60 million of Turkey's citizens, with another few million people speaking it with equal fluency to their native language.

Turkish speakers outside Turkey fall into two groups. The first consists of communities located in various lands that were formerly, for several centuries, part of the Ottoman Empire. There are populations of this kind in Bulgaria (760,000), Greece (115,000), Macedonia (80,000) and Romania (23,000). Cyprus, also a former Ottoman territory, has seen its Turkish-speaking population considerably enlarged by migration from Turkey since 1974. There may be as many as 150,000–200,000 Turkish speakers living in the Turkish Republic of Northern Cyprus at the time of writing.

The second group of Turkish speakers outside Turkey comprises those who, since the 1960s, have taken up residence in various western European countries, Australia and North America. The number in western Europe is nearly 4 million, of whom half live in Germany. The Australian Turkish community numbers some

40,000, and the number of Turkish speakers in North America is 50,000–60,000. Although in all these migrant communities there is a tendency for the use of Turkish to decline with each succeeding generation, it can probably be stated with reasonable certainty that Turkish is spoken as a first language or with native fluency by about 65 million people worldwide.

Break with the Ottoman past

The Turkish language underwent two kinds of radical change as part of the revolutionary reform programme launched by Mustafa Kemal (Atatürk) after the establishment of the Republic in 1923. The first was a sudden and comprehensive change in the medium in which it was written, with the introduction of a specially adapted form of the Latin alphabet in 1928, accompanied by a total prohibition on any further use of the Arabic script for teaching or publication in Turkish. The second affected the substance of the language itself, particularly its lexicon, and comprised a systematic campaign, launched by the official Turkish Language Foundation in 1932, to 'liberate' Turkish from its 'subjugation' to other languages, i.e. to Arabic and Persian. In order to give some indication of the significance of this change it will be necessary to say something about the Ottoman form of Turkish, the precursor of the modern language.

As a linguistic term, 'Ottoman' denotes the form of Turkic which became the official and literary language of the Ottoman Empire (1300–1922). This was, essentially, the variety of Oghuz Turkic which developed in Anatolia after that region was settled by Oghuz Turks in the eleventh to thirteenth centuries. It was written in the Arabic script, the form of writing adopted not only by the Oghuz but by all the Turkic-speaking peoples who, from about the tenth century onwards, had accepted the Islamic faith. The primacy accorded in Islam to the Arabic language itself, the language of the Qur'an, had a profound impact on the intellectual life of Ottoman society. The language of scholarship and of Islamic law, and the medium of instruction in the only schools available to the Muslim population before the nineteenth century, the *medreses*, was Arabic. In literature, on the other hand, the influence that was more directly felt was that of Persian, since it was the aesthetics of Persian poetry and ornate prose that provided inspiration for the Ottoman literati. A truly cultured Ottoman was expected to have a fluent command of 'the three languages', and many Turkish-speaking Ottomans did indeed write treatises in Arabic and/or poetry in Persian.

As far as Ottoman itself was concerned, the degree to which written texts reflected the spoken idiom varied greatly according to the level of education of the writer and the purpose and intended readership of the document. In any kind of sophisticated writing the Turkish structural base became all but submerged, surfacing mainly in the inflectional morphology and in other non-lexical items such as pronouns, determiners, and auxiliary verbs. Arabic and Persian borrowings were not confined to the lexicon, but included grammatical elements also. Arabic words were often used in their distinctive plural forms, and adjectives were made to agree with them in terms of gender, as they would in Arabic itself. A host of Arabic prepositional phrases, completely alien to Turkish syntax, were imported more or less as lexical units. A number of Persian constructions became particularly prevalent. One was the ubiquitous *izafet*, by which the head of a noun phrase was linked to the modifying noun or adjective that *followed* it (as in *asakir-i İslam* 'armies of Islam' or *memalik-i Osmaniye* 'Ottoman dominions'). Another was the compound adjective, used mainly for ornamental or rhetorical reasons, and often designed to rhyme with its head noun (as in *padişah-ı alem-penah*, 'world-sheltering monarch' or *vezir-i Asaf-tedbir* 'vizier wise as Asaf'). It should be noted that the majority of these imported elements were totally absent from the language of the unschooled Turkish-speaking masses. On the other hand, some common words of Arabic or Persian origin, such as *perde* 'curtain', *kitap* 'book', *namaz* 'ritual prayer', *cami* 'mosque', had become fully integrated into the general lexicon. The only significant foreign *grammatical* influence to be seen in the popular language was the Indo-European type of subordinate clause (introduced by a subordinating conjunction and having a finite verb. (See the clauses with *ki* discussed in Chapters 24–6 of this book.)

The term 'Ottoman' was not applied to the language of the Ottoman state until the mid-nineteenth century, when, as part of the reform movement known as the Tanzimat, attempts were made by the government to foster a sense of Ottoman identity that might save the ailing empire. Before then, when it was necessary to distinguish Turkish from any other language, it had been called precisely that (*Türki* or *Türkçe*), however impregnated it might have been with Arabic and Persian elements. It was in the Tanzimat period that Turkish (under the politicized name 'Ottoman') first began to be taught in schools, the new state schools designed to train soldiers, bureaucrats and technical experts for the service of a modernized state. There was now a clear need for the language to be defined and streamlined, through the production of grammars and dictionaries, in order to maximize its effectiveness as a means of public communication. A newly emerging class of Turkish intellectuals, who had access to Western writings and were full of new ideas that they wanted to convey to a wide public, shared the state's interest in regularizing and simplifying the language, although their standpoint – liberal and patriotic – was largely opposed to the government. The new genres of writing in which they were involved, principally journalism, drama and the novel, all played their part in the evolution of a modern form of Ottoman, shorn of much of its rhetorical opacity, and with a regularized, transparent sentence structure much closer to that of modern Turkish.

The closing decades of the life of the Ottoman Empire witnessed the emergence of a new sense of ethnic identity among the Turkish educated elite, which had hitherto defined itself only as Ottoman and Muslim. The discoveries of European Turcologists drew attention to the long-forgotten linguistic and cultural links existing between the Turks of the Ottoman Empire and other peoples spread out far across Asia. The first scholarly dictionary of Ottoman Turkish to be written by a Turk, the *Lehçe-i Osmani* (Ottoman Dialect) of Ahmet Vefik (1877), clearly identified Ottoman as just one branch of a much wider, 'Turkish' language.¹ This revolutionary idea was at the heart of an incipient Turkish national consciousness that gathered strength as the empire increasingly fell victim to internal disintegration and the predations of the European powers.

After the constitutional revolution of 1908 the politically dominant Committee of Union and Progress gave all but overt encouragement to the formation of a number of societies and publications devoted to the promotion of this new sense of Turkish nationhood, which was incompatible with the official ideology of Ottomanism. As the Ottoman state teetered on the brink of final collapse, the Turkish language became for many intellectuals and writers the key to unlocking the spirit of unity and common purpose that alone, they believed, would enable the nation (in some as yet unknown form) to survive.

This message was first clearly enunciated in 1911 in the journal *Genç Kalemler* (Young Pens), which called on young writers to put themselves in the service of the nation by creating a 'national literature' in a 'new language'. The rules of this 'new language' (*yeni lisan*) were defined quite precisely: no Arabic and Persian grammatical constructions were to be used, except in lexicalized phrases for which there was no available alternative; Arabic and Persian plural forms were to be avoided; Arabic and Persian words that were not current in the spoken language, and for which a Turkish equivalent was in common use, should similarly be rejected (e.g. for 'water' Arabic *ma* and Persian *ab* should both be abjured in favour of Turkish *su*). Already at this period there were extremists who wanted to see *all* Arabic and Persian loanwords, even those long integrated into the popular language, replaced by Turkish synonyms, if necessary, retrieved from old texts or imported from eastern 'dialects.' But at this stage the moderate view prevailed, and the 'new language' campaign was remarkably successful in its aims. By the period of the First World War the use of a natural, unadorned Turkish, close to the language of speech, had become the unquestioned stylistic imperative of literary writing. However, bureaucratic, legal and scholarly discourse remained more resistant to change, as evidenced even in the diction of Atatürk's famous six-day speech of 1927, the *Nutuk*.

The Kemalist language reform (*dil devrimi*) begun in the 1930s differed from all previous efforts in two important ways.² First, despite the nominally autonomous status of the Turkish Language Foundation (Türk Dil Kurumu, TDK), this was an openly state-sponsored campaign, funded by annual grants from the state budget and having at its disposal all the implementational apparatus of the bureaucracy, the education system and the state radio monopoly. Second, the aims and scope of this project were far more radical and ambitious than anything that had gone before. There was now an overt commitment to complete purification of the language, and any word that was deemed worthy of acceptance was designated

---

1 The Turkic/Turkish distinction is a recent terminological innovation of western origin.
2 For a recent study in English of the language reform movement see Lewis (1999).

öztürkçe 'pure Turkish'. This new lexicon included, in addition to native words already in general use, the following new categories: (1) words used in Anatolian dialects but not part of the current standard language of the urban elite; (2) obsolete Turkish words discovered by searching through relatively unpretentious texts from the early and middle Ottoman periods; (3) neologisms derived from Turkish roots and suffixes; (4) other more dubious coinages, often similar in form to European words, which were justified by pseudo-etymologies. It should be noted that there was very little antagonism to the quite conspicuous European borrowings (such as *otobüs, gazete, elektrik, demokrasi*) which had entered the language as part of the general process of modernization from the late eighteenth century onwards, predominantly from French.

The remarkable fact about the project of socio-linguistic engineering comprising the language reform is the enthusiasm with which it was embraced by a large majority of the Turkish educated class. This applies not only to first-generation Kemalists but also to their children, some of whom, in the 1960s and 1970s, were inspired as much by socialism as by nationalism. In the middle decades of the twentieth century the 'language question' was a subject of fierce controversy, with the Kemalists and leftists equally committed to the purist ideal, regarding it as representing all that was modern, secular and progressive, while conservatives fought a rearguard action in defence of the nation's cultural heritage, and the moral, emotional and aesthetic values attached to many of the words that had been consigned to disuse. Since the 1980s the heat has gone out of this debate, but this is due as much as anything to the fact that in large measure the aims of the reformers have been achieved, and that, for better or for worse, the lexicon of Turkish in the early twenty-first century is radically different from that of the early twentieth century.

Previous grammars of Turkish

The first comprehensive modern treatment of Turkish grammar was Jean Deny's monumental *Grammaire de la langue turque, dialecte osmanli* (Paris, 1921). This was a significant first step towards the creation of a terminology that would accurately reflect the features of the language without trying to assimilate them into Indo-European preconceptions. While Deny's main focus was on the standard spoken and written language of Istanbul at the time of writing (pre-1914), his work also encompasses current popular and dialectal forms and older Ottoman usages. A Turkish translation by Ali Ulvi Elöve, with useful additional notes, was published twenty years later by the Turkish Ministry of Education (*Türk Dili Grameri (Osmanlı Lehçesi)*, 1941).

Within Turkey itself, the change of alphabet and the language reform movement generated both a surge of interest in the structure of the language and a great pedagogical need for a new conceptualization and a new terminology. Tahsin Banguoğlu's *Ana Hatlariyle Türk Grameri* (Outlines of Turkish Grammar) (1940), was produced in response to a ministerial request for a work that might serve as a basis for school textbooks. Modern in its approach, and drawing on contemporary

French linguistics, Banguoğlu's book identified itself as a descriptive, not a historical grammar, and was rich in examples reflecting the spoken language. It was reprinted in 1974 with updated terminology, under the title *Türkçenin Grameri* (The Grammar of Turkish), and is still highly regarded. Ahmet Cevat Emre's *Türk Dilbilgisi* (Turkish Grammar) (1945) was the earliest comprehensive grammar to be published by the Turkish Language Foundation (TDK). It was less systematic than Banguoğlu's work, and was not reprinted, but it remains of considerable historical interest.

Muharrem Ergin's *Türk Dil Bilgisi* (Turkish Grammar) (1952), a historical grammar of Oghuz Turkic, is a very different kind of work and was written from a standpoint opposed to the radicalism of the TDK. It is highly traditional in its approach and concentrates almost entirely on phonological and morphological phenomena.

The next milestone in the description of Turkish was the grammar published in Russian by the Soviet Turcologist A. N. Kononov in 1956. This work, unfortunately not linguistically accessible to the present authors, is recognized as having provided a highly valuable and original synthesis of research on Turkish down to that date.[3] Four years later appeared the *Osmanisch-Türkische Grammatik* of H. J. Kissling (Wiesbaden, 1960). Despite its title (which was intended to emphasize the essential continuity between Ottoman and modern Turkish), this book was designed as a practical reference tool for German-speaking learners of Turkish.

The first Turkish grammar to be written from a theoretical-linguistic standpoint was Lloyd B. Swift's *A Reference Grammar of Modern Turkish* (Bloomington, Ind., 1963). This was a pioneering attempt to describe the grammatical phenomena of Turkish in structural terms, i.e. as a complete system, and it marked an important new beginning in conceptual terms. At about the same time, two further grammars of a broadly pedagogical nature appeared in Turkey. Haydar Ediskun's *Yeni Türk Dilbilgisi* (New Turkish Grammar) (1963), reissued as *Türk Dilbilgisi* in 1985 and regularly reprinted down to today, was designed as a university textbook for non-specialist students. It includes an introductory section on language in general, and on the Turkish language reform movement in particular. Tahir Nejat Gencan's clearly arranged and readable *Dilbilgisi* (Grammar), published by the TDK in 1964 and reprinted many times since, had the avowed objective of deriving the rules of Turkish from a wide-ranging assemblage of examples from admired writers (old and new), and from time-honoured usages such as proverbs.

The two grammars that are best known to English-speaking learners of, and researchers on, Turkish are those of Lewis (1967) and Underhill (1976). Geoffrey Lewis's philologically based *Turkish Grammar* (2nd edition 2000) is insightful and highly readable. The author uses examples drawn from mid-twentieth-century Turkish literary and journalistic texts, and devotes particular attention to the structures that are most alien to an English-speaking learner of Turkish. Robert

---

3 See Hazai (1978), 77; Johanson (1990), 152

Underhill's *Turkish Grammar* (Cambridge, Mass., 1976) is arranged as a coursebook. This means that pedagogical concerns determine the way in which the material is organized, and some space is allocated to vocabulary, exercises and matters of usage. Nevertheless, this work by a linguist from the generative tradition brought increased clarity to a number of topics and continues to be much in demand both as a teaching tool (particularly in the USA) and as a resource for linguists.

The influence of generative linguistics had already been seen in the concise survey of Turkish grammar published by Yüksel Göknel in 1974 under the title *Modern Türkçe Dilbilgisi* (Modern Turkish Grammar). This includes, as well as a description of Turkish phonology, morphology and syntax, a section in which linguistic theories, predominantly generative, are applied to the structures discussed. A more recent comprehensive grammar in Turkish, Mehmet Hengirmen's *Türkçe Dilbilgisi* (Turkish Grammar) (1995), which describes itself as a textbook for students and teachers, is also inspired by this approach. In addition to the sections on Turkish grammar, it has a chapter on the application of generative theories of syntax to Turkish, as well as a chapter on the Turkic languages.

Jaklin Kornfilt's volume *Turkish* (London, 1997), is the most recent comprehensive grammar to appear in English. It forms part of Routledge's Descriptive Grammars series, addressed mainly to linguists who seek data on specific points across languages. The structure of the book is determined by a research questionnaire that has been applied uniformly to all the languages covered in the series. Kornfilt's analyses are well supported by examples, some illustrating little discussed or hitherto unnoticed aspects of Turkish.

The last few years have also seen the appearance of pedagogical presentations of Turkish grammar in both French and German. Bernard Golstein's *Grammaire du Turc: ouvrage pratique à l'usage des francophones* (1997; second edition 1999) and Brigitte Moser-Weithmann's *Türkische Grammatik* (2001) are addressed respectively to French-speaking and German-speaking learners of Turkish. Despite their limitations of scope and analysis, the French-Turkish and German-Turkish comparative dimensions of these works furnish some interesting insights.

Scientific linguistic research on the structure and use of contemporary Turkish was a rare phenomenon before 1970.[4] The situation has, however, changed radically in the last three decades, as modern linguistic methodologies have increasingly made their impact. Already by the beginning of the 1980s there was sufficient research activity, both in and outside Turkey, for a series of biennial international conferences on Turkish linguistics to be launched, and the twelfth of these was about to take place as this book went to press. Attempting a scholarly description of Turkish grammar is no longer an isolated struggle. On the contrary, it requires an engagement with the collective achievement of an international body of scholars in a field that is increasingly well connected to the linguistic mainstream.

---

4 See Underhill (1986).

Aims and organizations of this grammar

What we have aimed to do in this book is to provide a description of the structure of contemporary standard Turkish that is both systematic and comprehensive. We have divided the book into three main parts, dealing respectively with phonology (the sound system), morphology (the structure of words) and syntax (the structure of sentences). We have paid particular attention to the distinction between morphology and syntax, in order to bring out as clearly as possible the systems in place at each level.

The chapters in Part 2 are concerned exclusively with the forms that words can take. In Turkish, because of its highly agglutinative structure, the description of word structure is largely a matter of identifying the different categories of suffixes, and the rules determining what kinds of stem they may attach to and in what order. All discussion of how words combine into phrases, clauses and sentences is confined to Part 3. This is also where semantic issues, i.e. the effects of structure on meaning, are discussed.

There is a hierarchy among the structures discussed in Part 3. For example, adjectival structures (Chapter 15) usually form part of noun phrases (Chapter 14). Noun phrases, for their part, can occur as complements within the verb phrase (Chapter 13), and/or combine with verb phrases to form clauses or sentences (Chapter 12). Furthermore, there is a parallelism between the phrasal structures described in Chapters 14–16 (having respectively a nominal, adjectival and adverbial function) and the clausal structures described in Chapters 24–6 (which follow the same sequence). The ample use that we have made of cross-references throughout the text serves in part to draw attention to the systematic links between different levels of the language. It also makes it possible to draw the reader's attention from one use of a particular form (e.g. a suffix or clitic) to others described in another part of the book, and in so doing to help readers both to connect and to distinguish between different functions of the one form.

The book is intended to be useful to a wide range of people interested in Turkish, first and foremost university students and other advanced learners of the language, but also teachers and translators of Turkish, and academic linguists. Our methodology has been informed by questions of concern to general linguistic scholarship, but we have taken care to make all our explanations accessible to those without a formal linguistic training. We have strictly avoided any involvement with theoretical issues, and have kept our terminology as simple and neutral as possible. Every point has been clearly illustrated with examples. All the examples are translated, and selective use has also been made of linguistic glosses, which indicate the grammatical functions of individual suffixes. It should be noted that in the examples which are thus glossed, the segmentation is morphological, not phonological, i.e. the hyphens show the boundaries between roots and suffixes, and between the suffixes in a sequence; they do not mark syllable boundaries (as required by the conventions of Turkish orthography). A glossary of grammatical terms has been provided at the end of the book, and terms that can be found in the glossary are shown in bold on their first occurrence in a chapter.

Limitations of space make any claim to totally comprehensive coverage unrealistic, and we have had to exercise a degree of selectivity with regard to forms or usages that have marginal currency. Arabic and Persian inflectional forms are no longer a productive part of the Turkish language, and we have therefore excluded them entirely.

It is very important to note that this is a descriptive, not in any sense a prescriptive, grammar. In other words, we have tried to record how the language is actually used at the present time, without offering any judgements as to what is 'right' or 'wrong'. We have sought to reflect *variety* of usage as well as regularity, and in this connection, we have had to indicate in some places that a particular construction is used only by some speakers and not favoured by others. Another kind of variation is that relating to register, i.e. to the formality or otherwise of the speech situation or text type. In our discussion of particular forms and constructions we have been careful to mention if there is any stylistic restriction on their use. Unless we have mentioned in the text that a particular form or construction is formal, informal, colloquial, etc., it can be assumed that it is in unrestricted use.

Most suffixes in Turkish are variable in form according to the rules of vowel harmony and consonant alternation, which are explained in Chapters 3 and 6 respectively. In this book any parts of a suffix that are subject to such variation are shown in capital letters, e.g. *-lAr*, *-sIn*, *-DI*. Similarly, many suffixes have an initial vowel or consonant that is dropped in certain contexts. Such deletable elements are shown in brackets when a suffix is cited, e.g. *-(y)mIş*.

The English translations of the example sentences have been made as idiomatic as possible. Where the structure of the idiomatic translation is so different from that of the Turkish as to make it possibly difficult to see how it was arrived at, we have added in brackets a literal translation of all or part of the sentence. Where translations are provided for individual words (e.g. in Parts 1 and 2) it should not be assumed that these represent the only meanings that these words can have.

July 2004

Abbreviations

ABL	ablative case
ACC	accusative case
ADJ	adjective/adjectival/adjectivizer
ADV	adverb/adverbializer
AOR	aorist
Ar.	Arabic
AT	attributive
AUX	auxiliary verb
C	consonant
CAUS	causative
CL	clitic
COM	comitative
COND	conditional
COND.COP	conditional copula
CONJ	conjunction/connective
COP	copula
crs.	corresponds to
CV	converb marker
DAT	dative case
DEF	definite
DER	derivational suffix
DET	determiner
EMPH	emphatic
ENUM	enumerator
EV.COP	evidential copula
EV/PF	evidential/perfective
Fr.	French
FUT	future
GEN	genitive case
GM	generalizing modality
IMP	imperative

IMPF	imperfective	
INDEF	indefinite	
INF	infinitival	
INFL	inflectional suffix	
INS	instrumental	
INT	interrogative	
INTR	intransitive	
LIT.	literally	
LOC	locative case	
N	noun	
NC	noun compound	
NCM	noun compound marker	
N.DER	noun-/nominal-deriving suffix	
NEG	negative	
NEG.AOR	negative aorist	
OBL	oblique case	
OBLG	obligative	
obs.	obsolete	
OPT	optative	
PART	participle	
PASS	passive	
P.COP	past copula	
PF	perfective	
PL	plural	
POSS	possessive	
POT	potentiality	
PROG	progressive	
PRON	pronominalizer	
PSB	possibility	
REC	reciprocal	
REF	reflexive	
RP	relative pronoun	
SG	singular	
s/he	she, he (also 'it', depending on the context)	
s.o.	someone	
s.t.	something	
s.w.	somewhere	
SUB	subordinator	
TAM	tense/aspect/modality	
TR	transitive	
V	vowel	
V.DER	verb-deriving-suffix	
VN	verbal noun marker	

Abbreviations

1 first person
2 second person
3 third person
Ø zero

List of conventions observed in this book

italics in the text or in lists are used for Turkish examples
italics in the text are used for highlighting a point in the text
italics in the English translations correspond to the highlighted parts in the Turkish examples
italics in the text are used for English examples cited for explanatory purposes
bold in the Turkish examples highlights the point which is being discussed
bold italics in the Turkish examples emphasize a particular part in a highlighted section
bold in the text (apart from headings) is used to highlight the key concepts under discussion in a chapter, and/or to indicate a term that is explained in the glossary
. (full stop) between two English words in the glosses indicates that the corresponding item in Turkish is either one word, or two (or more) words which do not have a word-for-word translation into English
' ' indicates a letter in the alphabet
' ' in the text indicates a mention of a part of a suffix, or one of the forms of a suffix
' ' indicates English translations of Turkish words, phrases and sentences
/ shows that either form is grammatical
/ / indicates the phonemic representation of a phonological unit
| indicates the boundary between two intonational phrases
[ ] indicates the phonetic realization of a phonological unit (i.e. the sound of a particular segment)
[ ] in the Turkish examples indicates a subordinate clause
[ ] in the translations indicates either (i) a word or phrase which is required for the grammaticality of the English translation or for stylistic reasons, but which does not occur in the Turkish example or (ii) in cases where a subordinate clause is marked in the Turkish example, a subordinate clause
( ) in a suffix indicates that the enclosed item is present only under certain morphophonological conditions
( ) in an example indicates that the item enclosed is optional
(…) indicates the omission or dislocation of a particular item
{ } is used selectively to mark the boundaries of a noun phrase

(hyphen) in front of a form indicates that it is a suffix
(hyphen) after a form indicates either that it is a verb (e.g. *gül-* 'laugh') or that it cannot occur without a suffix (e.g. *bura-* 'here')
(hyphen) in the Turkish glosses indicates suffix boundaries
~ indicates syllable boundaries
'A.' and 'B.' at the beginning of examples indicate different speakers
capital letters in the suffixes indicate variability
capital letters in the Turkish examples and English translations indicate stressed words or syllables
small capital letters in the Turkish examples indicate secondary stress
ˊ (acute accent) indicates stress within individual words
: (colon) after a vowel indicates that the vowel is long, and after a consonant it indicates delayed release
In the English translations, we refrained from using the pronouns they/them/their in their third person singular references, as this would have compounded the ambiguity of pronominal reference in Turkish. See e.g. p.176 (45-6).

The Turkish alphabet and writing conventions

The list below provides a rough guide to the pronunciation of the 22 consonants and 8 vowels in Turkish. Only the most prominent aspects of pronunciation are highlighted. The explanations are based on the speech habits of native speakers of British English and should be read in conjunction with Section 1.1.

Letter	Pronunciation
A, a	pronounced as *u* in 'c*u*p'
B, b	*b* as in '*b*it'
C, c	*j* as in '*j*am'
Ç, ç	*ch* as in '*ch*ip'
D, d	*d* as in '*d*eep'
E, e	*e* as in 't*e*n'
F, f	*f* as in '*f*it' or '*f*ull'
G, g	*g* as in '*g*et' or '*g*ull'
ğ	either lengthens the sound of the vowel preceding it or is silent between two vowels
H, h	*h* as in '*h*ope'; pronounced also in word medial and final positions and sometimes silent between two vowels
I, ı	pronounced as *a* in '*a*mong', '*a*lone'
İ, i	a shorter form of *ee* as in 'b*ee*t' or *i* as in 'b*i*t'
J, j	*s* as in 'lei*s*ure'
K, k	*k* as in '*k*ept', '*c*ure' and '*c*alf'
L, l	*l* as in '*l*amp', 'bu*ll*' or '*l*urid'
M, m	*m* as in '*m*ilk'
N, n	*n* as in '*n*o'
O, o	*o* as in '*o*ff'
Ö, ö	resembles the sound which is produced when *e* as in 'b*e*t' is pronounced with the lips rounded, as in the German sound 'ö'
P, p	*p* as in '*p*in'
R, r	produced with the tip of the tongue touching the alveolar ridge
S, s	*s* as in 'hi*ss*'

Ş, ş	*sh* as in '*sh*eep'
T, t	*t* as in '*t*ime'
U, u	*u* as in 'c*u*te' or p*u*t'
Ü, ü	resembles the sound which is produced when *i* as in 'b*i*t' is pronounced with the lips rounded, as in the German sound 'ü'
V, v	*v* as in '*v*ery'
Y, y	*y* as in '*y*ou'
Z, z	*z* as in '*z*igzag'

Circumflex

In the writing system, a circumflex '^' has different functions:

(i) It is sometimes placed over a vowel to indicate that it is long, e.g. *kâtil* [kʰaːtʰɪl] 'murderer', but this is neither regular nor a reliable means of identifying a long vowel (see 1.1.2.2).
(ii) In some words of Persian or Arabic origin, a circumflex may be placed on a vowel to palatalize the previous consonant, e.g. *kâr* 'profit' [cʰaɾ].
(iii) In words such as *hâlâ* 'still', the circumflex fulfils both functions by showing as long the vowels (in both syllables) and palatalizing 'l'.

In view of the functional ambiguity of the circumflex, and the fact that its use is not consistent in publications, it has been avoided altogether in this book except in the cases of *hâlâ* 'still', *kâr* 'profit', *kâh ... kâh* 'now... now', where its omission could lead to ambiguity.

Apostrophe

The apostrophe is used for separating a proper noun from its inflectional suffixes (Chapter 8), as in:

Semra'dan	'from Semra'
Hürriyet'te	'in *Hürriyet*' (a newspaper)

When the plural suffix *-lAr* or a derivational suffix (Chapter 7) is attached to a proper name, no apostrophe is used:

Türkler	'the Turks'
Ankaralılar	'the people of Ankara'
İngilizce	'English' (the language)
Atatürkçülük	'Kemalism'

If the proper name is a *-(s)I* compound (10.2) the apostrophe before an inflectional suffix is placed after *-(s)I* or *-lArI*:

Van Gölü'nden 'from Lake Van'
Amerika Birleşik Devletleri'nde 'in the United States of America'

(Note that the 'n' of the suffixes *-(s)I(n)* and *-lArI(n)* is placed after the apostrophe.)

An apostrophe is not used when adding suffixes of any sort to the names of political institutions (other than states) and commercial establishments:

Milli Eğitim Bakanlığına 'to the Ministry of National Education'
Ticaret Odalarının 'of the Chamber of Commerce'
Sheraton Otelinde 'in the Sheraton Hotel'

Proper names are spelt as in their bare form, even in cases where the addition of a suffix changes the pronunciation (2.1):

Ahmet'in [axmedín] 'Ahmet's'
Tarık'ın [tʰa:rí:n] 'Tarık's'

Syllabification and dividing a word at the end of a line

All syllables contain one vowel in Turkish. A vowel cannot be the first item in a syllable unless it is at the beginning of a word, that is, it always belongs to the same syllable as a preceding consonant if there is one:

a~ta~ma~dım 'I could not throw'
at~tım 'I threw'
park~tan 'from the park'

The silent consonant 'ğ' conforms to the conditions on consonants:

ba~ğı~ra~ma~ya~ca~ğım 'I will not be able to shout'

At the end of a line, a word can be divided at any syllable boundary, *irre- spective of* whether the division breaks up a single semantic unit (such as a stem or a suffix):

park 'park' *par~ka* 'to the park'
git- 'go' *gi~di~le~me~ye~ce~ği~ne* 'instead of [one] not being able to go [there]'

(Note that in the second example the verb root 'git', the passive suffix 'il' and the converbial suffix 'yeceğ' are broken up.)

Part 1

Phonology: The sound system

Chapter 1

Phonological units

Words are made up of sequences of distinct **phonological units** called **consonants** and **vowels**. Some consonants and vowels sound the same wherever they occur within a word and have a single pronunciation. Others have more than one way of being pronounced, depending on the surrounding sounds. The various pronunciations of a phonological unit conditioned by its position are called its **allophones**.

In 1.1 we discuss the consonants and vowels of Turkish and in 1.2 their distribution within a word.

In this chapter (and sometimes elsewhere in this book) phonological units are indicated by double slashes (/ /) and their allophones by square brackets ([ ]). The corresponding Turkish alphabetical symbols are indicated by inverted commas (' '). Consonants pronounced with a delayed release (i.e. doubled consonants) and long vowels are indicated by a following colon (:). Stress is indicated by an acute accent (́).

1.1 Consonants and vowels

1.1.1 Consonants

The consonants in Turkish differ from each other in terms of whether they are **voiced** or **voiceless**, their **point of articulation** and their **manner of articulation**. The voiced/voiceless contrast is the most prevalent one in processes involving phonology and word structure (2.1, 6.1.2).

DOI: 10.4324/9780429435836-2

Voiceless consonants	Voiced consonants
/p/	/b/
/t/	/d/
/k/	/g/
/tʃ/ ('ç')	/dʒ/ ('c')
/f/	/v/
/s/	/z/
/ʃ/ ('ş')	/ʒ/ ('j')
/h/	
	/m/
	/n/
	/l/
	/r/
	/j/ ('y')

/ɣ/ ('ğ') does not correspond to a consonantal sound (1.1.1.1).

1.1.1.1 Consonants and their allophones

The following factors affect the pronunciation of particular consonants in certain environments:

(i) **palatalization** (producing a consonant with the blade of the tongue against the hard palate) affects the velar consonants /k/, /g/, /t/ and the glottal consonant /h/ in front vowel environments

(ii) **aspiration** (producing a consonant with a forceful release of air) affects the voiceless plosives /p/, /t/, /k/ and the voiceless affricate /tʃ/

(iii) **bilabialization** (producing a consonant by bringing the lips together) affects the voiced labio-dental consonant /v/ and to a lesser extent, its voiceless counterpart /f/

The descriptions below regarding the pronunciation of consonants in 'word-final position' apply only to those cases where a word is followed by a pause or uttered in isolation. Otherwise, the pronunciation of a word-final consonant is, in most cases, conditioned by the initial sound in the following word. For example, /p/, which is described below as aspirated at the end of a word or before a vowel, sounds so in word-final position only if it is followed by a pause or a word beginning with a vowel. If it is followed by a word starting with a consonant, it is an unaspirated /p/. In other words, the 'p' of *tıpa* 'stopper', *Tıp Ansiklopedisi* 'Encyclopaedia of Medicine' and *tıp* 'medicine' (pronounced in isolation) are all aspirated, whereas the 'p' in *tıpkı* 'just like' or in *Tıp Dergisi* 'Journal of Medicine' is unaspirated.

Another point about pronunciation concerns two identical consonants that occur next to each other. Such **doubled consonants** are pronounced with a delayed release, as in *attım* [atʰːím] 'I threw [it]' (as opposed to *atım* [atʰím] 'my horse') and *kaç çocuk* [kʰátʃʰːodʒukʰ] 'how many children' (as opposed to *kaç okul* [kʰátʃʰokʰuɫ] 'how many schools').

The consonants of Turkish and their allophones are detailed below. Where the phonetic symbol is different from the orthography, the latter is indicated in brackets (e.g. /ʧ/ ('ç')).

/p/ [p]   *kapla-* 'cover', *şapka* 'hat', *kitapçı* 'bookshop', *iplik* 'thread'
     [pʰ] *parla-* 'shine', *pirinç* 'rice', *pırasa* 'leek', *kapak* 'cover', *ipek* 'silk', *top* 'ball', *ip* rope'

[p] is an unaspirated voiceless **bilabial plosive** which occurs before a consonant. [pʰ] is an aspirated voiceless bilabial plosive which occurs before vowels or in word-final position.

/b/ [b]   *bak-* 'look', *bebek* 'baby', 'doll', *bora* 'gale', *biz* 'we', *öbek* 'group', *abla* 'elder sister'

[b] is a voiced bilabial plosive. It does not occur in word-final position except in a few loanwords such as *rab* '(the) Lord', *rob* 'robe' and *ab* 'water'.

/t/ [t]   *katla-* 'fold', *saatçi* 'clockmaker', *etnik* 'ethnic', *atkı* 'scarf'
     [tʰ] *tara-* 'comb', *türev* 'derivative', *etek* 'skirt', *otuz* 'thirty', *it-* 'push', *inat* 'insistence'

[t] is a voiceless unaspirated **denti-alveolar** plosive which occurs before a consonant. [tʰ] is an aspirated dental plosive which occurs before a vowel or in word-final position.

/d/ [d]   *dışla-* 'exclude', *doğru* 'correct', *diz* 'knee', *ada-* 'dedicate', *badem* 'almond', *ödün* 'compromise', *adlı* 'named', *fidye* 'ransom'

[d] is a voiced denti-alveolar plosive. It does not occur in word-final position except in a few words such as *ud* 'lute', *had* 'limit' and *ad* 'name', most of which are borrowed.

/k/ [k]   *okşa-* 'caress', *bakla* 'broad beans', *sıkma* 'squeezed', *parkta* 'in the park'
     [kʰ] *katıl-* 'join', *sıkı* 'tight', *doruk* 'zenith', *sok-* 'push in', *kazak* 'sweater'
     [c]   *ikna (et-)* 'convince', *ekle-* 'add', *eksi* 'minus'
     [cʰ] *kemir-* 'gnaw', *kömür* 'coal', *iki* 'two', *sök-* 'dismantle', *bölük* 'squadron', *erk* 'power'

[k] is a voiceless unaspirated **velar** plosive which occurs between a **back vowel** (one of /ɪ/, /a/, /o/ or /u/) and a consonant. Its aspirated counterpart [kʰ] occurs before a back vowel or in word-final position following a back vowel. [c] and [cʰ] are voiceless **palatal** plosives which occur with **front vowels** (one of /e/, /i/, /ö/ or /ü/). [c] occurs between a front vowel and a consonant, and its aspirated counterpart [cʰ] occurs before a front vowel or in word-final position following a front vowel. The palatalization of [cʰ] is more pronounced when it follows /i/ or /ü/ and occurs at the end of a word, as in *delik* 'hole' or the final 'k' in *küçük* 'small'.

A slightly more palatalized version of [cʰ] occurs before back vowels in some loanwords, as in *kağıt* 'paper', *katip*, 'clerk, secretary', *mahkum* 'prisoner', *kufi* 'Kufic'. The vowels following 'k' in these words are alternatively spelt with a circumflex (^), e.g. *kâğıt, mahkûm*.

/g/	[g]	*gıdıkla-* 'tickle', *gırtlak* 'throat', *gaz* 'gas', *gocuk* 'duffle coat', *gaga* 'beak'
	[ɟ]	*gez-* 'stroll', *giy-* 'wear', *göç* 'migration', *Ege* 'Aegean'

[g] is a voiced velar plosive which occurs in syllables with the back vowels /ɪ/, /a/, /o/ and /u/. Its palatal counterpart [ɟ] occurs in syllables with the front vowels /i/, /e/, /ö/ and /ü/. /g/ does not occur in syllable-final or in word-final position except in loanwords such as *program* 'programme', *psikolog* 'psychologist', *katalog* 'catalogue', *lig* 'league'.

A slightly more palatalized version of the sound [ɟ] can also occur before a back vowel in loanwords, as in *yegane* 'only', *gavur* 'infidel' (derogatory), *dergah* 'dervish convent'. The vowels following 'g' in these words are alternatively spelt with a circumflex (^), e.g. *yegâne*.

/tʃ/ ('ç')	[tʃ]	*biçki* 'cutting out', *saçma* 'nonsense', *içmeler* 'spa'
	[tʃʰ]	*çene* 'chin', *çabuk* 'quickly', *çöp* 'rubbish', *uçuk* 'pale', *ölçü* 'measurement', *kılıç* 'sword', *ilgeç* 'postposition'

[tʃ] is a voiceless **post-alveolar affricate** which occurs before a consonant. Its aspirated counterpart [tʃʰ] precedes vowels or occurs in word-final position.

/dʒ/ ('c')	[dʒ]	*caz* 'jazz', *cebir* 'algebra', *cuma* 'Friday', *cins* 'type', *acı* 'pain', *böcek* 'insect'

[dʒ] is a voiced post-alveolar affricate. It rarely occurs in word-final position (e.g. *hac* 'pilgrimage' and *sac* 'sheet iron', mostly for purposes of distinguishing these words from words containing its voiceless counterpart /tʃ/, i.e. *haç* 'cross' and *saç* 'hair').

/f/	[Φ]	*ufuk* 'horizon', *küfür* 'curse', *kof* 'rotten', *örf* 'common usage', 'custom'
	[f]	*fakat* 'but', *nefes* 'breath', *defter* 'notebook', *lif* 'fibre'

[Φ] is a voiceless bilabial **fricative** which occurs in the pronunciation of some speakers before the rounded vowels /u/, /ü/, /o/ and /ö/ and to a lesser extent in word-final position following a rounded vowel. [f] is a voiceless **labio-dental** fricative which occurs elsewhere.

/v/   [ω]   *avun-* 'console (oneself)', *tavuk* 'chicken', *havuç* 'carrot'
         [β]   *vur-* 'hit', *vücut* 'body', *ov-* 'massage', *döv-* 'beat'
         [v]   *virgül* 'comma', *vatan* 'motherland', *ev* 'house', *tava* 'frying pan'

[ω] is a bilabial **glide** which occurs between two vowels where at least one of the vowels, usually the one following it, is rounded. [β] is a voiced bilabial fricative, which also occurs with rounded vowels but only when it is not intervocalic (i.e. when it is in word-initial or syllable-final position). The difference between [ω] and [β] is very slight and is not audible in the speech of some speakers. [v], the voiced labio-dental fricative, occurs elsewhere.

/s/   [s]   *somurt-* 'sulk', *sarı* 'yellow', *su* 'water', *süt* 'milk', *ısı* 'heat', *askı* 'hanger', *pas* 'rust'

[s] is a voiceless denti-alveolar fricative.

/z/   [z]   *zorla-* 'force', *zar* 'dice', 'membrane', *zehir* 'poison', *otuz* 'thirty', *doz* 'dosage', *uzun* 'long, tall', *azınlık* 'minority'

[z] is a voiced denti-alveolar fricative.

/ʃ/ ('ş')   [ʃ]   *şiş-* 'swell', *işlek* 'busy', *şarkı* 'song', *meşin* 'leather', *kaş* 'eyebrow', *güneş* 'sun'

[ʃ] is a voiceless post-alveolar fricative.

/ʒ/ ('j')   [ʒ]   *jüpon* 'underskirt', *jet* 'jet', *jilet* 'razor blade', *garaj* 'garage', *bej* 'beige', *Jülide* (a name), *ajan* 'agent', *ejderha* 'dragon'

[ʒ] is a voiced post-alveolar fricative. It occurs in words borrowed from Indo-European languages, in particular from Persian and French.

/ɣ/('ğ')   *soğuk* 'cold', *bağır-* 'shout', *eğik* 'bent', *dağ* 'mountain', *gittiğim* 'that I went'

The so-called 'soft-g' is pronounced as a velar fricative in some dialects but in standard Turkish, rather than having a consonantal sound, it affects the pronunciation of a word in a way that depends on its position in that word:

(i) The vocal omission of 'ğ' between identical vowels creates vowel sequences that are sometimes pronounced as long vowels within a single syllable and sometimes as vowels belonging to consecutive syllables: *uğur* [u:ɾ]/[uúɾ] 'good luck', *sığın-* [sı:n]/[sıín] 'take shelter', *sevdiğim* [sevdí:m]/[sevdiím] 'that I love'. Between identical front vowels 'ğ' may sound like a palatal glide (*düğün* [düjǘn] 'wedding', *eğer* [éjæɾ] 'if'.

(ii) Between rounded vowels 'ğ' is mostly inaudible but can also be pronounced as a bilabial glide: *soğuk* ([soúkʰ] or [soɯúkʰ] 'cold').

(iii) Between a rounded vowel and an unrounded vowel 'ğ' is mostly inaudible but can also be pronounced as a bilabial glide: (*soğan* [soán] or [soɯán] 'onion').

(iv) In word-final or syllable-final position, it lengthens a preceding back vowel (*dağdan* [da:dán] 'from the mountain', *sığ* [sı:] 'shallow'), but may be pronounced as a palatal glide [j] when following a front vowel (*eğlen-* [ejlǽn] 'have fun').

(v) 'a+ğ+ı' sequences are either pronounced as [aı] or like a long 'a' (*ağır* [aíɾ] or [a:ɾ] 'heavy').

(vi) 'ı+ğ+a' sequences, on the other hand, are only pronounced as [ıa] (*sığan* [sıán] '[one] which fits').

(vii) When 'ğ' occurs between an 'e' and an 'i' it is either inaudible or pronounced as a palatal glide [j]. Hence the sequences 'e+ğ+i' and 'i+ğ+e' can be pronounced as [ei] or [ie] respectively, or they can be pronounced as if they have an intervening 'y', as in *değil* [dejíl] 'not' and *diğer* [díjæɾ] 'other' (similar in pronunciation to words *written* with a palatal glide, e.g. *meyil* 'slope', *diyen* 'who says'). The sequence 'e+ğ+i' may also be pronounced as the long vowel [i:] and sometimes as two 'i' vowels belonging to consecutive syllables: *değil* [di:l]/[diíl] 'not', *eğil-* [i:l]/[iíl] 'bend'.

For the pronunciation of 'ğ' in forms containing the future/participle suffix *-(y)AcAK*, see 8.2.3.3. For the consonantal behaviour of 'ğ' when a suffix follows it, see 6.1.3.

/h/   [ç]   *his*len- 'become emotional', *hemen* 'immediately', *hürriyet* 'freedom', *ihtimal* 'possibility', *Salih* (a name)

      [x]   *ıh*lamur 'linden', *ah*şap 'wooden', *kah*ve 'coffee', *sabah* 'morning'

      [h]   *h*ala 'paternal aunt', *h*orla- 'snore', *ah*ır 'barn'

[ç] is a voiceless palatal fricative that occurs with front vowels in the following environments: before a front vowel, between a front vowel and a consonant, and after a front vowel in word-final position. When the vowel is /i/, the palatalization is more pronounced. [x], the voiceless velar fricative, follows a back vowel and precedes a consonant, or follows a back vowel in word-final position. [h], the voiceless glottal fricative, occurs before a back vowel. /h/ may be silent between two identical vowels, as in *pastahane* [pʰastʰa:nɛ́] 'cake shop' and *daha* [da:] 'more', or between a vowel (usually /a/) and a consonant, causing the preceding vowel to lengthen, as in *kahve* [kʰa:vɛ́] 'coffee' and *Ahmet* [a:métʰ].

/m/ [m] *masal* 'fairytale', *mine* 'enamel', *müzik* 'music', *emin* 'sure', *kumar* 'gambling', *kambur* 'hunchback', *tarım* 'agriculture'

[m] is a bilabial **nasal**.

/n/ [n] *nasıl* 'how', *nine* 'grandmother', *inek* 'cow', *ünlü* 'famous', *sorun* 'problem', *on* 'ten'
[ŋ] *bank* 'bench', *banka* 'bank', *yangın* 'fire', *mangal* 'brazier'
[ɲ] *renk* 'colour', *engin* 'boundless', *dingin* 'calm', *süngü* 'bayonet'

[n] is a dental nasal which occurs in all positions except when /n/ is followed by /k/ or /g/. In such cases /n/ is realized as a velar nasal [ŋ] following a back vowel and preceding a velar plosive, and as a palatal nasal [ɲ] following a front vowel and preceding a palatal plosive.

There is no audible difference between 'n' and 'm' when either of these occurs before a labio-dental fricative (/f/ or /v/). In such cases the vowel preceding 'n' or 'm' becomes slightly nasalized: *Enver* [ẽvǽɾ̥] (a name), *amfi* [ãfi] 'lecture room'.

/l/ [l] *leylek* 'stork', *lira* 'lira', *elli* 'fifty', *ölüm* 'death', *gül* 'rose'
[ɫ] *oluk* 'gutter', *kalın* 'thick', *bal* 'honey', *pul* 'stamp'

[l] is a palatalized post-alveolar **lateral** which occurs adjacent to front vowels, and [ɫ] is a velarized dental lateral which occurs adjacent to back vowels. /l/ generally gets assimilated with a preceding /n/ in fast speech, e.g. *kadınlar* 'women' may be pronounced [kʰadın:áɾ̥] *anla-* 'understand' as [an:á].

The palatal sound [l] can also occur adjacent to back vowels in loanwords such as *lale* 'tulip', *laf* 'word(s)', *ulufe* 'service pay in the Ottoman empire', *lokum* 'Turkish delight', *rol* 'role'. The vowels 'a' and 'u' following 'l' in these words are sometimes spelt with a circumflex (^), e.g. *lâle, ulûfe*.

/r/ [ɾ] *rahat* 'comfort', *renk* 'colour', *iri* 'big', *oruç* 'fasting', *karşı* 'against', *artık* 'waste'
[ɹ] *ört* 'cover', *kork-* '(be) afraid', *karşı* 'against', *artık* 'leftover'
[ɾ̥] *tür* 'type', *ger-* 'stretch', *iksir* 'elixir', *kar* 'snow', *var* 'there is/are', *mor* 'violet'

[ɾ] is a voiced alveolar **flap** produced with the tip of the tongue touching the alveolar ridge. It occurs in initial and intervocalic positions. The voiced alveolar **approximant** [ɹ] is used where /r/ is followed by a consonant in the same syllable. The pronunciation of /r/ in words where it is followed by a syllable (i.e. minimally a consonant-vowel sequence, as in *karşı* 'against' or *artık* 'leftover) varies between a flap and an approximant. The devoiced alveolar fricative [r̥] occurs in word-final position.

/r/ is sometimes deleted in colloquial speech, in particular in the imperfective suffix *-Iyor* (8.2.3.3) and in *bir* 'a', 'one'. In the case of *bir*, this usually occurs when it is not stressed (*bir ev* [bi év] 'a house'), but also sometimes when it is stressed (*bir daha* [bída:] 'again', *sadece bir ev* [sá:dedʒɛ bí ev] 'only one house'). See 15.6.1. for further examples.

/j/('y')   [j]   *ye-* 'eat', *yoğurt* 'yogurt', *yağ* 'oil', *ayak* 'foot', *oyun* 'game', *ayna* 'mirror', *kay-* 'slide', *huy* 'disposition'

[j] is a palatal glide. The sequence 'i + y' can be realized as a long vowel, as in *iyi* [i:] 'good' and *diyeceğim* [di:dʒæm] 'I will say'.

The **glottal stop** ('ʔ') survives mainly in the speech of some elderly speakers and is going out of usage. It is confined to words of Arabic origin and mostly to those in which it is intervocalic (*saat* [saʔátʰ] 'clock', 'watch', *fiil* [fiʔíl] 'verb', *teessüf* [tʰeʔes:üɸ] 'sorrow', *taarruz* [tʰaʔaɾ:úz] 'assault'). Note that an intervocalic glottal stop can also be pronounced as a long vowel (1.1.2.2).

1.1.2 Vowels

Turkish has a very symmetrical vocalic system, consisting of the eight vowels /a/, /e/, /ɯ/ ('ı'), /i/, /o/, /œ/ ('ö'), /u/, /y/ ('ü'). Here, the symbols ɯ/, /œ/ and /y/ of the International Phonetic Alphabet will be replaced by their counterparts in the Turkish orthography, /ı/, /ö/ and /ü/ respectively.

The eight vowels differ from each other in terms of the height of the tongue, the **rounded**ness of the lips and the **front**ness of the tongue involved in their articulation.

	High		Non-high (mid and low)	
	Rounded	Unrounded	Rounded	Unrounded
Front	ü	i	ö	e
Back	u	ı	o	a

In addition, Turkish has the long vowels /a:/, /u:/, /i:/ and /e:/ in loanwords of Arabic and Persian origin.

1.1.2.1 Vowels and their allophones

Vowels can occur at the beginning and end of words and between two consonants. In words of native origin, /o/ and /ö/ occur only in the first syllable (except for words which contain the imperfective suffix *-Iyor* (3.4 (vi) and 8.2.3.3).

The back vowels /a/, /o/ and /u/ are palatalized when following or preceding the palatal consonants [c], [ɟ] and [l], and /i/, /u/ and /ü/ are lowered in word-final position.

/a/ [a] *kara* 'black', *aşı* 'vaccination', *kurak* 'arid', *algı* 'perception', *banka* 'bank'
 [ḁ] *laf* 'word(s)', 'banter', *lapa* 'mush', *alfabe* 'alphabet', *kağıt* 'paper'

[a] is a low, back and unrounded vowel. Its **fronted** allophone [ḁ] occurs before or after the palatal consonants [c], [ɟ] and [l] in loanwords. An alternative spelling for words in which [ḁ] follows one of these consonants is with a circumflex on the vowel (^), e.g. *lâf*, *kâğıt*.

/e/ [e] *sevgi* 'love', *ekim* 'October', *bez* 'cloth', *senin* 'your'
 [ɛ] *ile* 'with', *küfe* 'large basket', *bale* 'ballet', *dene-* 'try'
 [æ] *gel-* 'come', *ver-* 'give', *ben* 'I', *sen* 'you', *gizem* 'mystery'

The non-high, front and unrounded vowel /e/ has three allophones. Going from the highest, that is, mid, to the lowest, these are: the mid, front, closed vowel [e], its lowered counterpart [ɛ], an open-mid, front vowel, and [æ], a low front vowel. [e] sounds like a shorter form of the vowel sound in the English word *late*, [æ] resembles a shorter form of the vowel sound in *bat* and [ɛ] is between the two, with a sound similar to the first vowel in *air* in English. [æ] occurs before /l/, /m/, /n/ and /r/ in instances where the sequences '*el*', '*em*' '*en*' and '*el*' are not followed by a vowel, as in *gerdi* 's/he stretched', *kent* 'town', *pergel* 'pair of compasses' and *iner* 's/he/it goes down'. [ɛ] occurs in word-final position. [e] occurs in all other places. All three occur in words such as *gezegende* [ɟezeɟændɛ] 'on the planet' and *perende* [perændɛ] 'somersault' (see also 2.5). Note that /e/ may be pronounced either as [e] or [æ] in a limited number of words before /l/, /m/ and /n/. Hence speakers may pronounce *el* 'hand', *kendi* 'self' and *hem* 'both' either with [e] or with [æ].

/i/ [i] *erik* 'plum', *iletişim* 'communication'
 [ɪ] *ilgi* 'interest', *deri* 'skin', *kedi* 'cat'

[ɪ] is a higher-than-mid, front, unrounded vowel which occurs in word-final position. Its pronunciation resembles the vowel sound in *bit* in English. [i], which occurs elsewhere, is a front, high, unrounded vowel, a shorter version of the vowel sound in *beat* in English.

/ı/ [ı] *asıl* 'real', *kışla* 'barracks', *ılık* 'lukewarm', *kırmızı* 'red'

[ı] is an unrounded, high, back vowel.

/o/ [o] **o** 'he/she/it/that', *b**o**l* 'abundant', *ot**u**r-* 'sit', *k**o**p-* 'snap', *protokol* 'protocol'
   [ǫ] *l**o**kum* 'Turkish delight', *r**o**l* 'role'

[o] is a mid, back, rounded vowel. Its palatalized counterpart [ǫ] occurs before or after /l/ in loanwords. A circumflex (^) is sometimes placed on the vowel in these words, e.g. *lôkum, rôl*. /o/ occurs only in the initial syllable in words of Turkic origin but it may appear in any syllable in loanwords.

/ö/ [ö] *göl* 'lake', *ölçü* 'measurement', *dökül-* 'be spilt', *sözlük* 'dictionary', *kuvöz* 'incubator', *şoför* 'chauffeur'

[ö] is a mid, front, rounded vowel. In loanwords /ö/ can occur in any syllable, but like /o/ it appears only in the first syllable in native words.

/u/ [u] *b**u**luş* 'finding', *ufak* 'small', *k**o**şul* 'condition'
   [ụ] *ulema* 'the learned (ones)', *bl**u**cin* 'denims', *l**u**gat* 'dictionary', *k**u**fi* 'Cufic'
   [ʋ] *b**u*** 'this', *k**u**t**u*** 'box', *ord**u*** 'army'

[u] is a rounded, high, back vowel which sounds like the vowel sound in the English word *hood*. [ụ] is its palatalized allophone, which occurs before or after the palatal consonants [c], [ɟ] and [l] in loanwords. An alternative spelling for some words in which [ụ] follows one of these consonants is with a circumflex (^) on the vowel, e.g. *lûgat, kûfi*. [ʋ] is more lowered than [u] and occurs in word-final position. It is pronounced in a similar way to the vowel in *put* in English.

/ü/ [ü] *üzüntü* 'sadness', *püre* 'mash', *süprüntü* 'rubbish', *ömür* 'life'
   [y] *üzüntü* 'sadness', *örgü* 'knitted', *sövgü* 'curse'

[ü] is a rounded, high, front vowel. [y] is more lowered than [ü] and occurs only in word-final position.

1.1.2.2 Long vowels

In addition to the long vowels created by 'ğ' above, words borrowed from Persian and Arabic can contain long vowels. Sometimes long vowels are indicated by a circumflex (^) in the orthography. The list below provides a few examples:

/a:/ *matbaa* 'press', *kira* 'rent', *mavi* 'blue', *arif* 'wise person'
/u:/ *mevzu* 'topic', *suret* 'copy', *buse* 'kiss', *Numan* (a name)
/i:/ *fiil* 'verb', *ilan* 'advertisement', *sine* 'bosom', *Didem* (a name)
/e:/ *teessüf* 'sorrow', *temin* 'acquisition', *tesir* 'effect'

For the effect of 'ğ' and 'h' on preceding vowels, see 1.1.1.1 and for vowel length under other circumstances, see 2.4

1.2 The distribution of consonants and vowels

In Turkish, roots are predominantly monosyllabic, that is, they contain a single vowel. The most common combinations of consonants (C) and vowels (V) in native Turkish roots are VC (*at* 'horse', *ol-* 'be', *in-* 'descend', *iş* 'work', *üç* 'three') and CVC sequences (*gel-* 'come', *bak-* 'look', *güz* 'autumn', *göl* 'lake'). There are also CV sequences such as *bu* 'this', *şu* 'that', *su* 'water', *ne* 'what', *de-*, 'say', but these are fewer in number and those which are nominals usually require an additional consonant ('n' or 'y') when they combine with suffixes (6.1.3). Other types are VCV sequences such as *ara-* 'look for', *ile* 'with', *öte* 'far side', and VCC and CVCC sequences such as *ört-* 'cover', *sert* 'hard', *genç* 'young'. There is a single occurrence of a root which consists only of a single vowel, the word *o* 'he, she, it, that'. This word requires a consonant when it combines with a suffix (6.2 (ii)).

In most cases, a root which contains more than one syllable in Turkish is a derived word (7.2). For the rules of syllabification in Turkish, see p. xlv.

1.2.1 Consonant clusters

Consonant clusters, that is, sequences of two different consonants, occur word-initially only in loanwords. Some speakers insert one of the vowels /i/ or/ɪ/ in or before the cluster:

	Alternative pronunciation
spor 'sport'	[ispʰóɾ, sipʰóɾ]
stil 'style'	[istʰíl, sitʰíl]°
stres 'stress'	[sitrés]
stüdyo 'studio'	[sütʰúdjo]
tren 'train'	[tʰirǽn]
psikoloji 'psychology'	[pʰiskʰoloʒí]/ [pʰisikʰoloʒí]
kral 'king'	[kʰɪráɫ]
grev 'strike'	[gɪrév]
plan 'plan'	[pʰilán]

Consonant clusters are frequently found in word-final position, as in *ilk* 'first', *alt* 'lower', *sark-* 'hang', *kork-* 'fear', *zamk* 'adhesive', *renk* 'colour', *kart* 'tough', *üst* 'top', *aşk* 'love', *baht* 'luck', *teyp* 'tape recorder', *genç* 'young', *felç* 'paralysis', *bronz* 'bronze', *şans* 'luck', *alarm* 'alarm'.

Chapter 2

Sound changes produced in the word by suffixation

There are a number of contexts where the addition of a suffix causes a change in the quality of the last consonant of a word. Some of these changes are confined to specific words, whereas others occur as part of general phonological processes in the language. Those which occur only in certain words are:

(i) A voiceless consonant alternating with its voiced counterpart, e.g. *kitap* 'book' but *kitabım* 'my book' (2.1)
(ii) A single consonant alternating with its doubled counterpart, e.g. *sır* 'secret' but *sırrım* 'my secret' (2.2)
(iii) A high vowel alternating with zero (i.e. absence of that vowel), e.g. *burun* 'nose' but *burnum* 'my nose' (2.3)
(iv) A short vowel alternating with a long vowel, e.g. *zaman* 'time' but *zamanım* [zama:nım] 'my time' (2.4)

The changes which are part of general phonological processes are:

(v) Final 'k' alternating with 'ğ' in nominals, e.g. *çocuk* 'child' but *çocuğum* 'my child' (2.1)
(vi) [æ] alternating with [e], e.g. *ben* [bæn] 'I' but *benim* [benim] 'mine' (2.5)
(vii) Final 'a', 'e', 'u' and 'ü' alternating with 'ı' or 'i', e.g. *de-* 'say' but *diyecek* 's/he will say' (2.6)

2.1 Alternations of voiceless/voiced consonants: 'p'/'b', 't'/'d', 'k'/'g', 'k'/'ğ', 'ç'/'c'

In some words ending in one of the voiceless consonants 'p', 't', 'k' and 'ç', this final consonant changes to its voiced counterpart before a suffix beginning with a vowel.

'p'	is replaced by	'b'
't'	is replaced by	'd'
'(n)k'	is replaced by	'(n)g'
'ç'	is replaced by	'c'
'k'	is replaced by	'ğ'

DOI: 10.4324/9780429435836-3

Some of these alternations take place in words borrowed from Arabic or Persian, where the word originally ends in a voiced consonant ('b', 'd', 'g' or 'c', as in *kitab* 'book'). The final segment is devoiced in the bare form (hence *kitap*) or in syllable-final position (i.e. when followed by a suffix beginning with a consonant, e.g. *kitaptan* 'from the book'). The original voiced consonant is retained where it is followed by a suffix beginning with a vowel (e.g. *kitabım* 'my book'). Alternations in voiceless/voiced consonants also occur in some words of Turkish origin or words borrowed from languages other than Arabic or Persian. Note that only some of the words which in their bare form end in a voiceless consonant are subject to change, and most of these words are nouns.

(i) final 'p' → 'b'

   dolap 'cupboard'   *dolaba* 'to the cupboard'
   cep 'pocket'   *cebim* 'my pocket'
   küp 'cube'   *kübik* 'cubic'

(ii) final 't' → 'd'

   kilit 'lock'   *kilidim* 'my lock'
   kanat 'wing'   *kanadı* 'its wing'
   yarat- 'create'   *yaradan* 'creator'

The class of nouns ending in a non-changing 't' includes the large number of Arabic borrowings which end in the Arabic feminine suffix *-et/at*, such as *cumhuriyet* 'republic' → *cumhuriyetin* 'of the republic' and French loanwords ending in 't', e.g. *bilet* 'ticket' → *biletim* 'my ticket', *ceket* 'jacket' → *ceketim* 'my jacket'.

(iii) final 'n' + 'k' → 'n' + 'g'

   renk 'colour'   *renge* 'to the colour'
   denk 'equal'   *dengi* 'his/her/its equal'

'k' alternates with 'g' only when it is preceded by 'n' (otherwise it alternates with 'ğ', see (v) below). Nouns of this form which have been borrowed in recent times from European languages do not normally undergo 'k'/'g' alternation:

   tank 'tank'   *tankı* 'his/her/its tank'
   bank 'bench'   *bankı* 'his/her/its bench'

(iv) final 'ç' → 'c'

   ağaç 'tree'   *ağacı* 'his/her/its tree'
   güç 'power'   *gücün* 'your power'
   taç 'crown'   *taca* 'to the crown'
   aç 'hungry'   *acık-* 'be hungry'

(v) While the scope of the aforementioned alternations is limited to particular words and is a lexical matter, the next alternation is a general rule which applies to nominals ending with 'k' when they are combined with a suffix beginning with a vowel. In such cases 'k' alternates with 'ğ'. Due to the pronunciation properties of 'ğ' (1.1.1.1) this process is also referred to as 'k'/Ø (zero) alternation.

final 'k'	→	'ğ'
yaprak 'leaf'		*yaprağı* 'its leaf'
gök 'sky'		*göğe* 'to the sky'
otomatik 'automatic'		*otomatiğin* 'of the automatic (switch)'

Note that only a final 'k' which is preceded by a vowel undergoes 'k'/'ğ' alternation. Final 'k' alternates with 'g' when preceded by 'n' (see (iii) above), otherwise it remains as 'k' (eg. *zamk* 'adhesive' and *zamkı* 'the adhesive' (ACC)). 'k'/'ğ' alternation also affects suffixes ending in 'k', such as -*DIK* (8.5.1.1), -*(y)AcAK* (8.2.3.3, 8.5.1.1) and -*mAK* (8.5.1.2):

| *gelecek* | 's/he's going to come' | *geleceğim* | 'I'm going to come' |
| *aldık* | 'we bought' | *aldığımız* | 'the one/that we bought' |

In the case of -*mAK*, 'k' also alternates with 'y':

| *almak* | 'to buy' | *almaya/almağa* | '(in order) to buy' (also pronounced [aɫmɪjá] or [aɫmá:]) |

'k'/'ğ' alternation does not affect words with long vowels (2.4). For example, *tebrik* 'congratulation(s)', where 'i' is originally long, does not undergo 'k'/'ğ' alternation, hence, tebriki [tʰebɾiːcʰí] 'his/her congratulation(s)'.

There are certain categories to which alternations of voiceless/voiced consonants do not generally apply:

(i) Most monovocalic words are not subject to these changes:

saç	'hair'	*saçım*	'my hair'
yük	'load'	*yüküm*	'my load'
top	'ball'	*topum*	'my ball'
at	'horse'	*atım*	'my horse'

(ii) The vast majority of verbal roots are not subject to these changes. A verbal root such as *kap-* 'snatch' retains its final consonant in suffixation, hence *kapın* 'snatch!', although this is not the case with nominals, e.g. *kap* 'container', but *kabın* 'your container'. Similarly the verb *ak-* 'flow' retains its final consonant under suffixation (e.g. *akan* 'flowing') but the adjective *ak* 'white' may not (cf. *ağar-* 'become white', but *akı* 'its white (part)'). There are only a few verbs that have a change in their final consonant when followed by a suffix beginning with a vowel:

et-	(auxiliary verb/'do')	*eder*	's/he does'
git-	'go'	*gidiyor*	's/he is going'
tat-	'taste'	*tadınca*	'upon tasting'

2.2 Alternations of single consonants with doubled consonants

In a small number of nouns ending in 'b', 't', 'd', 'k', 'l', 's', 'z', 'm' and 'n' the final consonant is duplicated when a vowel is attached to it. These are words borrowed from Arabic, which, in their original form, have geminates, that is, doubled consonants. In Turkish such words appear with a single consonant in their bare form or when followed by a suffix beginning with a consonant.

*ha*k 'right'	*hak*lar 'rights'	*hakk*ın 'your right'
his 'emotion'	*his*ten 'of the emotion'	*hiss*i 'emotional'
sır 'secret'	*sır*lar 'secrets'	*sırr*ımız 'our secret'
hat 'line'	*hat*lar 'lines'	*demiryolu hatt*ı 'railway line'
zıt 'opposite'	*zıt*sa 'if [it's] the opposite'	*zıdd*ı 'the opposite of it'

Some of these words keep their original double consonants in nominal-verb compounds where they combine with the auxiliaries *et-* 'do' and *ol-* 'be' (13.3.2): *hallet-* 'solve', *hallol-* 'be solved', *hisset-* 'feel'. Others appear in nominal-verb compounds with a single consonant: *hak et-* 'deserve'. It should be noted that since bare forms do not give any indication that they end in geminates, such words have to be learned individually.

2.3 Vowel/Ø (zero) alternation

There are a number of nouns in which the high vowel ('ı', 'i', 'u' or 'ü') of the final syllable in the bare form does not appear when a suffix beginning with a vowel is attached (e.g. *isim* 'name' but *ismi* 'his/her name'). Many of these are words of Arabic origin, which do not have a vowel in this position (e.g. the Arabic word *ism* 'name' does not contain a vowel between 's' and 'm'). In Turkish when such a word appears in its bare form an **epenthetic vowel** is inserted, hence the second 'i' in *isim*. It is important to remember that this is not a general phonological process. It occurs in some words of Arabic origin and in a few words of Turkish origin. When such words combine with a stressable suffix (4.3.1) containing a high vowel such as the accusative case marker *-(y)I*, there is invariably no epenthetic vowel in the inflected form. However, there may be variation among speakers regarding the inclusion of epenthetic vowels in words with a suffix containing a non-high vowel (such as the dative case marker -*(y)A*):

	ACC	DAT
karın 'belly'	*karnı*	*karna* or *karına*
şehir 'town'	*şehri*	*şehre* or *şehire*
izin 'permission'	*izni*	*izne* or *izine*

It is not possible to know whether the final high vowel in the bare form of a word is epenthetic or not. Words which look identical may differ in this respect:

koyun 'bosom'	→	*koynu* 'his/her bosom'
koyun 'sheep'	→	*koyunu* 'his/her sheep'
nehir 'river'	→	*nehri* 'the river' (ACC)
Nehir 'Nehir' (a name)	→	*Nehir'i* 'Nehir' (ACC)

If a word containing an epenthetic vowel is followed by an auxiliary verb beginning with a vowel (*et-* 'do' or *ol-* 'be' (13.3.2)), the epenthetic vowel does not appear, and the noun and verb coalesce into a single word:

| *sabır* 'patience' | *sabrı* 'his/her patience' | *sabret-* 'be patient' |
| *kahır* 'distress' | *kahrı* 'his/her distress' | *kahrol-* 'be damned' |

2.4 Short/long vowel alternations

In a number of words which have 'a', 'u' or 'i' in the final syllable, these vowels are replaced with their long counterparts /a:/, /u:/ and /i:/ when a suffix beginning with a vowel is attached:

meram 'plight'	*mera:mını* 'your/his/her plight' (ACC)
hukuk 'law'	*huku:ken* 'legally'
zaman 'time'	*zama:nım* 'my time'
zemin 'ground'	*zemi:ni* 'the ground' (ACC)

As in gemination (2.2) and in most cases of epenthesis (2.3), the alternation of short vowels with their long counterparts occurs in words of Arabic origin, in this case those which originally contain a long vowel. These words have to be learned individually, as there is no indication in the words that they contain a long vowel. This process can also take place across word boundaries when such words are followed by an auxiliary verb beginning with a vowel (*et-* 'do' or *ol-* 'be' (13.3.2)):

| *merak* 'curiosity' | *mera:k et-* 'be curious' |
| *emin* 'sure' | *emi:n ol-* 'be sure' |

Short/long vowel alternation does not affect proper nouns that are derived from common nouns with long vowels:

murat 'wish' → *mura:dı* 'his/her wish'
Murat 'Murat' (a name) → *Murat'ı* ([muratʰí] or [muɾadí]) 'Murat' (ACC)

2.5 æ/e Alternation

[æ], which is a lowered allophone of /e/, does not occur in environments where there is a following consonant-vowel sequence (1.1.2.1). In cases where a word (including words that contain suffixes) has [æ] but is followed by a consonant-vowel sequence as a result of (further) suffixation, this [æ] is replaced by [e]:

gel- 'come' [ɾæl]   [ɾældím] 'I came'   [ɾelíɾ] 's/he comes'
evler 'houses' [evlǽɾ] [evlærdɛ́] 'in (the) houses' [evleɾím] 'my houses'
sen 'you' [sæn]   [sændɛ́] 'on you'   [senín] 'your'

2.6 Alternation of 'a', 'e', 'u' and 'ü' with 'ı' and 'i'

In the spoken language, some suffixes which conjoin to a word by means of the consonant 'y' (6.1.3) may affect the pronunciation of a preceding 'a', 'e', 'u' or 'ü'. The presence of 'y' often causes these vowels to be pronounced as 'i'. Alternatively, 'a' and 'u' can be pronounced as 'ı'. The suffixes that most commonly cause such a change are the suffix *-(y)AcAK* (8.2.3.3, 8.5.1.1), the participle suffix *-(y)An* (8.5.2.1), the adverbial suffix *-(y)IncA* (8.5.2.2) and the combination of the optative suffix with the 1st person optative marker: *-(y)AyIm* (8.2.3.1, 8.4). In the case of the verbs *de-* 'say' and *ye-* 'eat', the change is reflected in the orthography:

de- 'say'   *di-yen* (say-PART) '(the one) who says'
ye- 'eat'   *yi-yecek* (eat-FUT) 's/he will eat'

In most cases, however, only the pronunciation is affected:

atla- 'jump'   *atlayan* (jump-PART) '(the one) who jumps', pronounced [atlaján], [atlɪján] or [atlijɑ́n]
özle- 'miss'   *özleyince* (miss-CV) 'upon missing', pronounced [özlejíndʒɛ] or [özlíːndʒɛ]
oku- 'read'   *okuyacak* 's/he is going to read', pronounced [okʰujdʒákʰ] or [okʰijdʒákʰ]
üşü- 'be cold' *üşüyeyim* 'let me be cold', pronounced [üʃíːm] or [üʃijejím]

Note that the effect of 'y' on a previous vowel can result in the violation of vowel harmony (e.g. [atlijánˈ] above).

Inflectional suffixes which end in 'a' or 'e' also tend to be affected by a following 'y'. For example, the vowel of the negative marker -*mA* is usually replaced in pronunciation with a high vowel when followed by a suffix beginning with 'y':

duyma- 'hear.NEG'   *duymayabiliyorum* (hear-NEG-PSB-IMPF-1SG)
'I [may or] may not hear', pronounced
[duymajabilíjorum]/[duymɪjabilíjorum]/
[duymijabilíjorum]

The imperfective suffix -*(I)yor* has a similar effect on the final 'a' or 'e' of the word it attaches to (8.2.3.3).

Chapter 3

Vowel harmony

Vowel harmony is a phonological process which determines the vowel in all but the first syllable of a word. In **roots** or **lexicalized stems** with more than one syllable, the second vowel harmonizes with the first one:

kabak 'marrow'   *etek* 'skirt'
uzak 'far'   *ipek* 'silk'

Similarly, **suffixes** harmonize with the vowel in the preceding syllable, irrespective of whether the root is of native or foreign origin:

kuş-lar 'birds'   *ev-ler* 'houses'
puma-lar 'pumas'   *otobüs-ler* 'buses'

After describing the types of vowel harmony in 3.1, we discuss how vowel harmony operates in suffixes (3.2) and in roots and lexicalized stems (3.3). In 3.4, exceptions to vowel harmony are given.

3.1 Types of vowel harmony

The properties of Turkish vowels are crucial for understanding how vowel harmony works (1.1.2). To summarize, the vowels are all combinations of three features which result from (i) the position of the tongue in the oral cavity, and then whether the tongue is (a) high or non-high, and (b) whether it is towards the front or towards the back, and (ii) the position of the lips (whether they are rounded or not). Only the first vowel of a native word is fully determined in terms of its features. The rest of the vowels in a word depend on the vowel in the first syllable (in roots) or in the preceding syllable (in all other stems and suffixes).

Vowel harmony in Turkish is a combination of two kinds of harmonization process. One of these is **fronting harmony** which is the assimilation of a vowel with the vowel in the preceding syllable in terms of frontness: when the vowel in a syllable is a front vowel, it passes on its frontness to the next syllable, yielding sequences of syllables with front vowels (e.g. *geç-ti* '[it] passed', *böl-üm* 'part', *düş-en-ler* 'the

DOI: 10.4324/9780429435836-4

ones that have fallen'). In a similar fashion, words can be composed of sequences of back vowels (e.g. *sor-u* 'question', *kuş-lar* 'birds', *aç-ıl-dı* '[it] was opened').

The other type of harmony process is **rounding harmony**, which is the assimilation of a vowel with the vowel in the preceding syllable in terms of roundedness. Like frontness, but narrower in its scope of application, roundedness is a property which is copied from the rounded vowel of the previous syllable (e.g. *üz-ül-dü-nüz* 'you became sad', *sor-ul-ur* 'it is asked', *öv-ün-dük* 'we boasted'). We expand on these below.

3.2 Vowel harmony in suffixes and clitics

A handful of exceptions aside (3.4), vowel harmony operates in all **suffixes** and **clitics**, irrespective of whether these are attached to words of native or foreign origin. In terms of vowel harmony, there are two types of suffix in Turkish, I-type and A-type. In this chapter, we use the term 'suffix' as a cover term for suffixes proper and clitics (Chapter 11).

3.2.1 Vowel harmony in I-type suffixes

The vowels of I-type suffixes are all high, but they get their other features (i.e. frontness and roundedness) from the preceding vowel. An I-type suffix appears as 'i', 'ı', 'ü', or 'u', but the choice of one or the other is determined by fronting and rounding harmonies.

When an I-type suffix is attached to a root or lexicalized stem:

'ı' is selected if the preceding vowel is 'ı' or 'a'	'i' is selected if the preceding vowel is 'i' or 'e'
kız-ın 'your daughter'	*diz-in* 'your knee'
baş-ın 'your head'	*el-in* 'your hand'
'u' is selected if the preceding vowel is 'u' or 'o'	**'ü'** is selected if the preceding vowel is 'ü' or 'ö'
burn-un 'your nose'	*yüz-ün* 'your face'
kol-un 'your arm'	*göz-ün* 'your eye'

Examples of I-type suffixes are the genitive suffix *-(n)ın, -(n)in, -(n)un, -(n)ün*, the accusative suffix *-(y)ı, -(y)i, -(y)u, -y(ü)* and the evidential/ perfective suffix *-mış, -miş, -muş, -müş*. Brackets indicate that the consonants and vowels in them are deletable (6.1.3). Capital letters indicate alternating sounds (6.1.2).

Stem	I-type suffix	Forms	Stem + I-type suffix
çay 'tea'	*-(I)m* (1SG.POSS)	*-m, -ım, -im, -um, -üm*	*çay-ım* 'my tea'
su 'water'	*-lI* (ADJ)	*-lı, -li, -lu, -lü*	*su-lu* 'watery'

güzel 'nice'	*mI* (INT)	-mı, -mi, -mu, -mü	*güzel mi* 'is it nice'
sor- 'ask'	*-DI* (PF)	-dı, -di, -du, -dü -tı, -ti, -tu, -tü	*sor-du* 's/he asked'

3.2.2 Vowel harmony in A-type suffixes

The vowels of A-type suffixes are unrounded and non-high, but they are variable in terms of whether they are back or front. The choice of the appropriate vowel in an A-type suffix depends on whether the vowel in the syllable preceding it is front or back. The roundedness or unroundedness of the preceding vowel does not affect it.

When an A-type suffix attaches to a root or lexicalized stem:

'a' is selected if the preceding vowel is 'a', 'ı', 'o' or 'u'	'e' is selected if the preceding vowel is 'e', 'i', 'ö' or 'ü'
hava-dan 'from the air'	*ev-den* 'from the house'
kız-dan 'from the girl'	*biz-den* 'from us'
yol-dan 'by the road'	*göl-den* 'from the lake'
şun-dan 'of this'	*tür-den* 'of the type'

Examples of A-type suffixes are the plural suffix *-lar, -ler*, the dative suffix *-(y)a, -(y)e*, the conditional suffix *-sa, -se* and the future marker *-(y)acaK, -(y)eceK*.

Stem	A-type suffix	Forms	Stem + A-type suffix
tür 'type'	*-lAr* (PL)	*-lar, -ler*	*tür-ler* 'types'
yık- 'destroy'	*-mA* (NEG)	*-ma, -me*	*yık-ma* 'don't destroy'
gelenek 'tradition'	*-sAl* (ADJ)	*-sal, -sel*	*gelenek-sel* 'traditional'

As a result of the two types of vowel harmony, Turkish has the following vowel sequences across syllables:

'a'	can only be followed by	'a' or 'ı'
'ı'	can only be followed by	'a' or 'ı'
'o'	can only be followed by	'a' or 'u'
'u'	can only be followed by	'a' or 'u'
'e'	can only be followed by	'e' or 'i'
'i'	can only be followed by	'e' or 'i'
'ö'	can only be followed by	'e' or 'ü'
'ü'	can only be followed by	'e' or 'ü'

3.3 Vowel harmony in roots

With only a few exceptions (3.4 (i)), fronting harmony occurs in all native roots. Rounding harmony affects the majority of native words as well but there are a few cases where the vowel in the second syllable is rounded despite the fact that the preceding vowel is not. This is usually the result of an intervening labial consonant ('p', 'b', 'f', 'v' or 'm'): *savun-* 'defend', *tavuk* 'chicken', *kabuk* 'shell', 'skin'.

3.4 Exceptions to vowel harmony

(i) A few native words, such as *anne* 'mother', *elma* 'apple' and *kardeş* 'sibling' are non-harmonic.

(ii) Compounds (some of which are written as a single word, Chapter 10) are non-harmonic: *bugün* 'today', *keçiboynuzu* 'carob', *Karagöz* (a shadow theatre character).

(iii) Loanwords often violate the rules of vowel harmony, e.g. *kitap* 'book', *kalem* 'pencil', *lale* 'tulip', *penaltı* 'penalty', *fasulye* 'bean(s)', *marul* 'lettuce', *masum* 'innocent', *jaluzi* 'Venetian blind', *lobi* 'lobby'.

(iv) The vowel of a suffix may get harmonized as a front vowel even where a loanword does not have a front vowel in the last syllable:

*hakikat-*si*z*	(truth-ADJ)	'disloyal'
bahs-i	(topic-ACC)	'the topic (ACC)'
harb-in	(war-GEN)	'of the war'
kalp-ler	(heart-PL)	'hearts'

This happens regularly in loanwords that end in a palatal 'l':

gol-ü	(goal-3SG.POSS)	'his/her goal'
etol-den	(scarf-ABL)	'from the scarf'
hal-im	(condition-1SG.POSS)	'my condition'

(v) Suffixes and prefixes of foreign origin are invariable:

-*izm*: *Şamani*z*m* 'Shamanism'
-*en*: *tamamen* 'completely'
anti-: **anti**demokratik 'antidemocratic'
bi-: **bi**haber 'unaware', 'ignorant'

(vi) A few native suffixes, or parts of suffixes, are invariable:

a. The second vowel in the bound auxiliaries -*(y)Abil*, -*(y)Iver*, -*(y)Agel*, -*(y)Adur*, -*(y)Akal*, -*(y)Ayaz* (8.2.3.2): *kalkabildi* 's/he managed to stand up'; the non-deletable vowel of the imperfective suffix *-(I)yor* (8.2.3.3): *görüyorum* 'I see'; the converbial marker *-(y)ken* (8.5.2.2): *bakmışken* 'having looked'

b. The vowels in some derivational suffixes (7.2.2.2):

-gen: *altıgen* 'hexagon'
-gil: *halamgil* 'my aunt and her family'
-(I)mtrak: *pembemtrak* 'pinkish'
-leyin: *sabahleyin* 'in the morning'

c. The suffix *-ki* (8.1.4) optionally undergoes vowel harmony after *gün* 'day' and *dün* 'yesterday': *dünki/dünkü* 'yesterday's'.

(vii) The clitics *bile, diye, ki, ya, ise* (11.1.1) are invariable: *baktım ki* 'upon seeing', *söyledim ya* 'but I have said [it]', *bunlar ise* 'as for these'.

Chapter 4

Stress in words and phrases

The term **stress** refers to the high pitch and/or loudness with which a syllable is pronounced relative to others in the same word or sequence of words. This chapter discusses the position of stress in isolated words and isolated phrases. The syllable which is stressed in an isolated word or phrase is the same one that is stressed when that particular word or phrase is the most prominent one within a sentence (Chapters 5 and 23). In this chapter an acute accent will be used to indicate a stressed syllable.

In section 4.1 we discuss the stress patterns in words, followed by the stress pattern in **compounds** in 4.2. The classification of suffixes according to their properties relating to stress is the topic of 4.3. In 4.4 we turn to the stress patterns in verb phrases, noun phrases and postpositional phrases. **Sentence stress** is discussed in Chapter 23.

4.1 Stress in words

4.1.1 Regular words

Most words have regular stress, that is, they are stressable on the final syllable:

kadín	'woman'
kalabalík	'crowd'
hastá	'ill'
kutú	'box'
öğrén-	'learn'
beklé-	'wait'
cumhuriyét	'republic'

In vocative forms, that is, forms of address, stress is removed from the final syllable and placed on the penultimate syllable:

DOI: 10.4324/9780429435836-5

Kádın!	'Hey woman!'
Çocúklar!	'Hey kids!'
Hüséyin!	'Hüseyin!'

Stress may also be removed from the final syllable and placed in a position at or closer to the beginning of a word to express enthusiasm when meeting a person:

Çócuklar!	'Kids!'
Múhittin!	'Muhittin!'

If a diminutive suffix (*-CIK* (7.2.2.2) or its inflected form *-CIğIm*) is added to a form of address, the stress remains in its original position:

Semrácığım 'Semra, darling!'

4.1.2 Irregular words

The following groups of words are irregular in that stress is on a position other than the final syllable:

(i) Adverbs are mostly stressable on the first syllable:

şímdi	'now'
bélki	'perhaps'
yárın	'tomorrow'
áncak	'only', 'only just'
mútlaka	'definitely'

Note that this rule does not apply to words which function primarily as adjectives (16.1.2) but to those that are adverbs in their primary function (16.1.1). Thus, in *Bunu koláy yaptım* 'I did this easily', the adjectival *koláy* 'easy' retains its regular stress position even though it functions as an adverb in this sentence. Adverbs that contain suffixes or clitics are usually stressed on the **stressable syllable** within the word, e.g. *kesinlíkle* 'definitely', 'for sure' (see 4.3.2 (i)). For some adverbs, the position of stress is variable, e.g. *öncedén/őnceden* 'before', 'formerly', *akşamá/ákşama* 'in the evening'.

(ii) Many nouns of foreign origin (in particular, those which are borrowed from a language other than Arabic or Persian) do not conform to the stress pattern of native words and are stressed on a syllable other than the final one:

lokánta (Italian)	'restaurant'
bánka (Italian)	'bank'
iskémle (French)	'chair'
táksi (French)	'taxi'
lóbi (English)	'lobby'
fútbol (English)	'soccer'
péncere (Persian)	'window'
politíka (Greek)	'politics'
iskéle (Greek)	'quay'
satsúma (Japanese)	'satsuma'

(iii) Place names are stressed on a syllable other than the final one:

Ánkara, İstánbul, Táksim, İngiltére, Fránsa, Afríka

Exceptions are place names ending in the suffix *-istan,* which are variably stressed on the last syllable or on the penultimate one:

Hindistán/Hindístan	'India'
Gürcistán/Gürcístan	'Georgia'

Note that the difference in stress is the only distinguishing factor between some place names and otherwise identical common nouns:

mısír 'maize'	*Mísır* 'Egypt'
ordú 'army'	*Órdu* (a city on the Black Sea coast of Turkey)
bebék 'baby'	*Bébek* (a district in Istanbul)

(iv) Question words are stressed on the first syllable:

hángi	'which'
násıl	'how'
níçin	'why'

(v) Words which have reduplicative prefixes (Chapter 9) and most of the words containing loan prefixes (7.4) are stressed on the (first syllable of the) prefix:

kápkara	'pitch black'
ásosyal	'antisocial'
ántidemokratik	'antidemocratic'

(vi) A small number of idiosyncratic words, e.g. *ánne* 'mother', *ábla* 'elder sister'.

(vii) Words that contain unstressable suffixes (4.3.2)

(viii) Words which are compounds (4.2).

4.2 Stress in compounds

Most compounds (Chapter 10) are stressed on (the stressable syllable of) the first element:

búgün   'today'
báşbakan   'prime minister'

This is also true of *-(s)I* compounds (10.2), irrespective of whether the two parts are written together or separately:

sokák lambası   'street light'
telefón rehberi   'telephone directory'
çáy bardağı   'tea glass'
dérs kitapları   'textbooks'
búzdolabı   'refrigerator'
kasímpatı   'chrysanthemum'
deréotu   'dill'

However, there are exceptions and some compounds are stressed on the final syllable:

alışveríş   'shopping'
bilgisayár   'computer'
kabakulák   'mumps'

In compound verb forms containing a verb and a free auxiliary (13.3.1.2) or in nominal-verb compounds (13.3.2) stress falls on (the stressable syllable of) the first word:

anlamíş ol-   'have understood'
bitiríyor gözük-   'seem [to] be finishing'
yardím et-   'help'
hastá ol-   'become ill'
şarkí söyle-   'sing'
karşí gel-   'oppose'
mecbúr kal-   'be obliged'

For stress in compound verb forms containing bound auxiliaries, see 4.3.1 (iii).

4.3 Stress and suffixes

In terms of stress, the suffixes of Turkish are divided into two classes: stressable and unstressable.

4.3.1 Stressable suffixes

The great majority of Turkish suffixes belong to this class. The effect of stressable suffixes on the position of potential word stress is as follows:

(i) When a stressable suffix is added to a regular word (4.1.1), the position of word stress moves to the new final syllable.

kitáp	'book'
kitap-lár	'books'
kitaplar-ím	'my books'
kitaplarım-dá	'in my books'
kitaplarımda-kí	'the one in my books'
kitaplarımdaki-lér	'the ones in my books'
kitaplarımdakiler-é	'to the ones in my books'
kır-	'break'
kır-íl	'be broken'
kırıl-acák	'it will be broken'
kırılacak-lár	'they will be broken'

(ii) When a stressable suffix is added to an irregular word (4.1.2) the position of stress remains on the stressed syllable of that word:

iskémle	'chair'
iskémle-ler	'chairs'
iskémleler-imiz	'our chairs'
iskémlelerimiz-de	'on our chairs'
iskémlelerimizde-ki	'the one on our chairs'
iskémlelerimizdeki-ler	'the ones on our chairs'
Afríka	'Africa'
Afríka-lı	'African'
Afríkalı-lar	'Africans'
Afríkalılar-ın	'of Africans'

Those pairs of common nouns and place names that differ from each other only in the position of stress have different stress patterns in their inflected forms as well:

mısırdakilér	'the ones in the maize'
Mísır'dakiler	'the ones in Egypt'

(iii) Some suffixes which are polysyllabic, e.g. *-(y)ArAk* (8.5.2.2), *-mAksIzIn* (8.5.1.2), *-sAna, -sAnIzA* (8.4), *-(I)yor* (8.2.3.3) and *-(y)Iver, -(y)Agel, -(y)Akal, -(y)Adur, -(y)Ayaz* (8.2.3.2, 8.5.2.2 (ii)), are stressed on their first syllable:

kaz-	'dig'	*kaz-árak*	'by digging'
bak-	'look'	*bak-máksızın*	'without looking'
gel-	'come'	*gel-íyor*	's/he is coming'
şaş-	'be astounded'	*şaş-ákal-dı-m*	'I was astounded'

The first syllable of these polysyllabic suffixes bears the word stress even when other stressable suffixes follow:

gel-íyor-lar 'they are coming'
tut-úver-miş 'apparently s/he suddenly took hold of [it]'

For the effects of multiple suffixation and cliticization, see 11.2.

4.3.2 Unstressable suffixes

There are a number of suffixes which do not take stress and place stress on the syllable before them. These are the derivational suffixes *-(A/I)cIK* (under *CAK₁*), *-CA₁*, (some of the words with) *CA₃*, *-CAcIK*, *-CAnA* *-CAsInA*, *-en*, *-lA*, *-leyin*, *-rA*, *-(y)In* (7.2.2.2), *-(y)lA* (8.1.4):

úfacık 'tiny'	*kadínca* 'womanly'
uçárcasına 'as if flying'	*tamámen* 'completely'
kíşın 'in winter'	*yáyla* 'plateau'
búraya '[to] here'	*órada* 'there'

There are other unstressable items, namely various person markers (11.1.1.8), the negative marker (8.2.2) and **clitics** (Chapter 11) that affect stress in words. For the combination of the negative marker and the aorist (*-(A/I)r/-z*), see 8.2.3.3. For the stress that the negative marker and clitics generate, see 5.2.1 and 11.2.3. For the interaction of unstressable suffixes and clitics, see 11.2.1.

4.4 Phrasal stress

Verb phrases (Chapter 13), noun phrases (Chapter 14) and postpositional phrases (Chapter 17) have their particular stress pattern when they are in isolation. They retain their stress pattern when they are the stressed constituents in a sentence. However, when a phrase is uttered inside a sentence it may not be stressed at all, or it may be stressed on a different syllable, e.g. for reasons of focusing. For the properties of sentence stress, see Chapters 5 and 23.

4.4.1 Stress in verb phrases

Stress falls on the stressable syllable of the complement in verb phrases if this complement does not have a case marker:

kitáp oku- 'read a book'
oyún seyret- 'watch a play'
túz ekle- 'add salt'

Where the complement has a case marker, stress can fall on the stressable syllable of the complement or, less commonly, of the verb:

kitabí oku- / *kitabı okú-*
'read the book'/ 'read the book'

oyunú seyret- / *oyunu séyret-*
'watch the play' / 'watch the play'

tuzú ekle- / *tuzu eklé-*
'add the salt' / 'add the salt'

4.4.2 Sress in noun phrases

Noun phrases can be stressed on the stressable syllable of their complements or of their heads. In a noun phrase that contains an adjective, stress falls on the noun or on the adjective unless this latter is itself modified (e.g. by *en* 'most' or *daha* 'more' (15.4, see also 5.2.2 (21), (22)):

{*eskí bir év*} / {*eskí bir ev*} 'an old house'
{*én eski ev*} 'the oldest house'

Where a noun phrase contains one of the quantifiers *birtakım* 'some', 'a number of', *biraz* 'a little' and *bir miktar* 'some', 'a certain amount of' (15.6.1 (ii)), but no adjectives, stress falls on the noun:

{*bir miktar şekér*} 'some sugar'

Where a noun phrase contains any of the other indefinite determiners in 15.6.1 (other than *bir* 'a(n)'), a definite determiner (15.6.2) or a numeral (15.7), this constituent is usually stressed:

{*sorusu olan HER öğrenci*} '*every* student who has a question'

4.4.3 Stress in postpositional phrases

Many of the bare postpositions (17.2) share properties with clitics (Chapter 11) in that they do not take stress. Postpositional phrases containing the postpositions *gibi* 'like', *için* 'for', 'in order (to)', *adına* 'for', 'in order (to)', 'in the name of', 'on behalf of', *kadar* 'as…as', 'until', 'as far as', *doğru* 'towards', *göre* 'according to', 'since', *karşı* 'against', 'towards', *karşın* 'in spite of', *başka* 'apart from', 'other than', *beri* 'since', 'for', *dolayı* 'because of', *itibaren* 'from', 'with effect from, are stressed on the stressable syllable of their complements:

bebeklér için 'for babies'
düné kadar 'until yesterday'
sınavdán dolayı 'because of the exam'

rağmen 'in spite of', *itibaren* 'with effect from', *önce/evvel* 'before' and *sonra* 'after' are usually stressed on the stressable syllable of their complements but they can also be stressed themselves:

havayá rağmen / havaya ráğmen 'in spite of the weather'
tatildén önce / tatilden ónce 'before the holiday'

bu yana 'since' can have stress on the stressable syllable of the complement or on *bu* 'this':

pazardán bu yana / pazardan bú yana 'since Sunday'

Among the postpositional phrases expressing spatial relations, whether they are concrete or abstract (17.3.1), those which have genitive complements are stressed on the case markers of both constituents:

kapının önüné 'to front of the door'
manavín karşısındá 'across from the greengrocer's'
kutunún içindén 'from (inside) the box'

Those with non-case-marked complements are stressed on the stressable syllable of their complements:

sevínç içinde 'in a joyful manner'
kurúl önünde 'in front of a committee'

Postpositional phrases expressing abstract relations are also stressed on the stressable syllable of their complements:

çocuğú uğruna 'for the sake of his/her daughter/son'
diplóması sayesinde 'thanks to his/her diploma'

Chapter 5

Intonation and sentence stress

Intonation refers to the rising and falling of the voice in terms of pitch. The continuous flow of speech may be seen as divided into consecutive sections known as **intonational phrases**. An intonational phrase, which may be as short as a single word, but usually consists of several, is the unit of speech within which a single primary **stress** and a single **intonation contour** occur. There may be pauses between intonational phrases. If a sentence contains more than one intonational phrase the stress which is the most prominent is called sentence stress.

In this chapter we describe the main intonation contours of Turkish (5.1) and the position of primary and secondary stress in unmarked sentences (5.2). The syllable which is acoustically the most prominent one in an intonational phrase is said to have primary stress, indicated by capital letters below. A syllable which is less acoustically prominent than the one which has primary stress but which still stands out among the others is said to have secondary stress, indicated below by small capital letters. Where an example consists of more than one intonational phrase, the boundary between them is shown by a vertical stroke. The effect of shifting the position of stress and the interaction of this with the order of constituents in a sentence are discussed in Chapter 23.

5.1 The intonation contours of Turkish

There are three types of intonation contour in Turkish:

(i) Slight rise followed by fall. This is the standard contour for statements (including negative statements) regarded by the speaker as complete and also for the last intonational phrase in more complex statements:

(1) O HER zaman yemek-ler-in-i loKANta-da ye-r.
    s/he every time meal-PL-3SG.POSS-ACC restaurant-LOC eat-AOR
    'S/he always eats in a restaurant.'

DOI: 10.4324/9780429435836-6

(ii) High rise followed by fall. This is the standard contour for yes/no questions (expressed with *mI* (19.1)):

(2) Dün çocuk-LAR okul-a git-Tİ mi?
yesterday child-PL school-DAT go-PF INT
'Did the children go to school yesterday?'

(iii) Slight rise, followed by fall-rise. This occurs in:

a. Questions involving a wh-phrase (e.g. *ne* 'what', *nere-* 'where', *kim* 'who' (19.2)):

(3) Her gün NEreye gid-iyor-SUN?
every day where go-IMPF-2SG
'Where do you go every day?'

b. An intonational phrase whose content is not complete in itself and needs continuation. Important examples are conditional clauses, other adverbial clauses, all but the last item in co-ordinated phrases or lists, and phrases with topic shifters:

(4) Eğer sokağ-a çık-mak isTİ-yor-SAN ...   (Conditional clause)
if street-DAT go.out-VN want-IMPF-COND.COP-2SG
'If you want to go out ...'

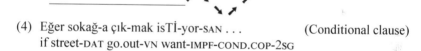

(5) Bugün Ziya-yla buluş-tuĞ-un zaMAN ...   (Adverbial clause
today Ziya-COM meet-CV-2SG.POSS time   of time)
'When you meet Ziya today ...'

(6) EVE gitTIM, ÇANtamı alDIM ...   (Co-ordinated items)
'I went home, took my bag ...'

(7) Ali'ye geLİNce   (Topic shifter)
'as for Ali'

5.2 Position of stress in the intonational phrase

5.2.1 Primary stress

In a simple sentence which is uttered as a single intonational phrase the unmarked position of primary stress is the stressable syllable (Chapter 4) of the word which is situated just before the predicate:

(8) Aydın bana çiÇEK getir-di.
    Aydın I.DAT flower bring-PF
    'Aydın brought me flowers.'

(9) Şu anahtarı HANginize vereyim?
    'Which of you shall I give this key to?'

(10) Dışarda bir köPEK var.
    'There's a dog outside.'

Two factors may cause a change in the position of stress:

(i) Clitics and the negative marker (see also 11.2.3):
When a clitic occurs in a sentence, primary stress is placed on the stressable syllable of the phrase before it:

(11) LONdra-ya **mı** gid-ecek-siniz?
    London-DAT INT go-FUT-2PL
    'Are you going to go to London?'
    (lit. 'Is it London you're going to go to?')

(12) Londra'ya gideCEK **mi**siniz?
    'Are you going to go to London?'

(13) Ahmet'TE **de** bunlardan bir tane var.
    'Ahmet has one of these, too.'

(14) Turgut nasıl bilSİN **ki**?
    'How on earth should Turgut know?'

The negative marker (8.2.2) causes primary stress to occur on the syllable before it:

(15) [Herkesin burada olduğun]-u BİL**mi**yordum.
    'I didn't know [everyone was here].'

(ii) Focusing a constituent:
Focusing a constituent may cause primary stress to appear on a constituent other than the one which immediately precedes the predicate:

(16) Ziya babasıNI onbeş yıldır görmüyormuş, annesini deĞiL.
'Ziya hasn't seen his FATHER for 15 years, not his mother.'

For a detailed discussion of the interaction of focusing and primary stress, see 23.3.1.

5.2.2 Secondary stress

Secondary stress occurs mainly on the following types of constituent (where it is indicated in small capital letters):

(i) The stressable syllable of subject and topic (23.3.3) noun phrases:

(17) Dün **Zeki-nin** ABla-sı iş-TEN ayrıl-mış.   (Subject)
yesterday Zeki-GEN sister-3SG.POSS work-ABL leave-EV/PF
'*Zeki's sister* left her job yesterday.'

(18) **Arkadaş-lar-**IMIZ-la BUrada buluş-acağ-ız.   (Topic)
friend-PL-1PL.POSS-COM here meet-FUT-1PL
'We're going to meet *our friends* here.'

(ii) Adverbs which are not in the immediately preverbal position (in which case they have primary stress), in particular *daha* 'more' and *en* 'most' (15.4, see also 4.4.2):

(19) Çamaşır-lar-ı **GEne** makina-nın iç-in-DE bırak-mış-ım.
laundry-PL-ACC again machine-GEN inside-3SG.POSS-LOC leave-EV/PF-1SG
'I seem to have left the laundry in the washing machine *again*.'

(20) Kitapları HEP yerDE bırakıyorsun.
'You *always* leave the books on the floor.'

(21) Bundan **daHA** uygun bir sözcük düşüNEmiyorum.
'I can't think of a *more* appropriate word than this one.'

(22) Bu hayvanların arasında **en** vahşisi kapLANmış.
'Apparently the *most* savage of these animals is the tiger.'

(iii) Most quantificational constituents, that is, determiners (15.6) such as *her* 'every', numerals (15.7), pronominalized determiners (18.4 (iv)) such as *bazısı* 'some [people]', *kimi* 'some [people]' and pronominal quantifiers (18.6.1) such as *herkes* 'everyone', *her şey* 'everything':

(23) Halk politikacıların **çoğuna** güVENmiyor.
'The people don't trust *most* politicians.'

5.3 Sentences with more than one intonation contour

Complex sentences containing an adverbial clause or a conditional clause have more than one intonation contour:

(24) Bugün buluş-tuğ-uNUZ   zaMAN | bana teleFON ed-in.
today meet-CV-2PL.POSS time   I.DAT telephone AUX-2PL.IMP
'When you meet up today give me a ring.'

(25) Biletleri alDIysan | içeRİ girelim
'If you've got the tickets, let's go in.'

Part 2

Morphology: The structure of words

Chapter 6

Principles of suffixation

In Turkish the vast majority of words which contain more than one syllable are complex. Processes of word formation create words that can be very long and sometimes correspond to whole sentences in English. The main word formation process in Turkish is **suffixation**, the formation of a new word by attaching an affix to a stem. This stem can be a root, a lexicalized stem, a derived or inflected word or a compound.

In 6.1 we describe the conditions that determine the vowels and the consonants in suffixes and the changes that take place at the boundaries between stems and suffixes. In 6.2 irregular alternations to the stem are discussed and in 6.3, the order of suffixation.

The rules that apply to suffixes also apply to **clitics** (Chapter 11).

6.1 The form of suffixes

Almost all suffixes in Turkish have more than one form. The initial consonant in some suffixes and the vowels in almost all suffixes depend on the consonants or vowels that precede them. For example, the plural suffix has two forms, *-lar* (as in *kuş-lar* 'birds') and *-ler* (as in *kedi-ler* 'cats'), with only the vowel alternating between 'a' and 'e', whereas the perfective suffix has eight forms, *-dı*, *-di*, *-du*, *-dü*, *-tı*, *-ti*, *-tu*, *-tü* (as in *kal-dı* 'remained' but *düş-tü* 'fell') where both the consonant and the vowel are subject to alternation. In this book, when a suffix is being discussed in the text (rather than used in an example) the alterable sounds within it are indicated by capital letters. Thus, the plural suffix is written as *-lAr* and the perfective suffix as *-DI* when these suffixes are being discussed in isolation.

6.1.1 Vowel alternation in suffixes

The vowel of a particular suffix is selected on the basis of the rules of vowel harmony, which are explained in 3.2. Some suffixes and clitics do not undergo vowel harmony (3.4).

6.1.2 Consonant alternation in suffixes

Some suffixes in Turkish begin with the voiceless/voiced pairs 'ç'/'c' (e.g. the nominal-deriving suffix -*CI* (7.2.2.2)), 't'/'d' (e.g. the locative suffix -*DA* (8.1.3)) or 'k'/'g' (e.g. the adjective-deriving suffix -*GAn* (7.2.1.1)). The selection of the voiced or voiceless variant depends on the last phonological unit in the stem. When a suffix beginning with one of these pairs is attached to a stem ending in any one of the voiceless consonants, the voiceless variant in the pair is used as the initial consonant of the suffix. Otherwise (i.e. when the stem ends in a vowel or a voiced consonant) its voiced counterpart is used.

To summarize:

'p', 't', 'k', 'f,' 'h', 'ç', 'ş', 's' are followed by 'ç', 't', 'k'
'b', 'd', 'c', 'v', 'l', 'm', 'n', 'j', 'r', 'z', 'y', 'ğ' and vowels are followed by 'c', 'd', 'g'

'C' stands for 'ç'/'c', 'D' for 't'/'d', and 'G' for 'k'/'g':

C: *süt-çü*	'milkman'	*posta-cı*	'postman'
D: *sokak-ta*	'in the street'	*oda-da*	'in the room'
G: *as-kı*	'hanger'	*diz-gi*	'print'

6.1.3 The attachment of a suffix to a stem: deletable vowels and consonants

In Turkish, vowels do not occur next to each other. Therefore, if a suffix beginning with a vowel is attached to a stem ending in a vowel, either the initial vowel of the suffix is deleted, or the consonant 'y' is added. As a result, suffixes are divided into two groups: those which can lose their initial vowel and those which can acquire the buffer consonant 'y'. All such vowels and consonants are shown in brackets when a suffix is being discussed in isolation.

Examples of the first type are the 1st person possessive suffix -*(I)m*, the aorist suffix -*(A/I)r* and the adjectival suffix -*(I)mtrak*. Most **derivational suffixes** (Chapter 7) are of this type.

*pul-**um*** 'my stamp'	but	*kafa-**m*** 'my head'
*gör-**ür*** 's/he sees'	but	*ara-**r*** 's/he searches'
*yeşil-**imtrak*** 'greenish'	but	*sarı-**mtrak*** 'yellowish'

Some examples of suffixes which take the consonant 'y' are the converbial suffix *-(y)IncA,* the dative suffix *-(y)A* and the future marker *-(y)AcAK.* Most **inflectional suffixes** (Chapter 8) are of this type.

gel-ince 'upon coming'	but	*dene-yince* 'upon testing'
Yusuf-a 'to Yusuf'	but	*Emine-ye* 'to Emine'
sor-acak 's/he will ask'	but	*atla-yacak* 's/he will jump'

A suffix beginning with a consonant is directly attached to a stem ending in a consonant, as is the case with the ablative suffix *-DAn,* the perfective suffix *-DI* and many others:

ev-den 'from the house'
git-ti 's/he left'

However, there are three exceptions. One of these is the genitive suffix (8.1.3), which has a deletable initial 'n'. Another is the 3rd person possessive suffix, which has a deletable initial 's'. Finally, the distributive suffix contains a deletable 'ş'. These consonants appear in order to avoid vowel sequences; otherwise, they are deleted. In this book, when such suffixes are discussed in isolation, their initial consonant is shown in brackets:

Genitive *-(n)In* (8.1.3):

Yusuf-un	(Yusuf's)	but	*Suna-nın*	(Suna's)
Selim-in	(Selim's)	but	*Emine-nin*	(Emine's)

3rd person possessive suffix *-(s)I(n)* (8.1.2):

ev-i	(his/her house)	but	*elbise-si*	(her/his dress)
kitab-ı	(his/her book)	but	*kafa-sı*	(his/her head)

For the *(n)* in *-(s)I(n),* see 6.2 (ii. b).

Forms which contain suffixes with deletable initial sounds can be ambiguous, as it may not always be clear which segment a particular vowel or consonant belongs to:

diz-im 'my knee' (*diz* 'knee'-1SG.POSS)
dizi-m 'my serial' (*dizi* 'serial'-1SG.POSS)

Note that a stem ending in 'ğ' (1.1.1.1) combines with the vowel-initial variant of a suffix:

dağ-ın 'of the mountain/your mountain'
bağ-ımız 'our vineyard'
iç-tiğ-im 'that I have drunk'

6.2 Irregular changes under suffixation

Apart from the sound changes described in Chapter 2, some stems and suffixes undergo additional changes when a suffix is added:

(i) The pronouns *ben* 'I' and *sen* 'you' become *bana* 'to me' and *sana* 'to you' when the dative suffix *-(y)A* (8.1.3) is added.
(ii) At the end of certain types of stems 'n' appears when particular suffixes are added:
  a. In the case of the 3rd person pronoun *o* (18.1.1) and the demonstrative pronouns (18.2), 'n' appears when the following are attached:

  the plural suffix *-lAr* (8.1.1)
  case suffixes (8.1.3)
  the adverbial suffix *-CA$_1$* (7.2.2.2)
  the adjectival suffix *-sIz* 'without' (7.2.2.2)

  Some examples are: *ona* 'to him/her/it', *onlar* 'they', *onca* 'according to him/her', *onsuz* 'without him/her/it', *bunu* 'this (one) (ACC)', *şunlar* 'those', *bunsuz* 'without this', *bunca* 'this much'.
  The same applies in the case of the colloquial usage in which the comitative/instrumental and conjunctive suffix *-(y)lA* 'with' (8.1.4) is affixed to the non-case-marked, rather than to the genitive-marked, form of these pronouns: *onla* 'with him/her' (crs. *onunla*), *bunla* 'with this' (crs. *bununla*).
  b. There are a number of other pronominal stems and two suffixes in which an 'n' appears when either case suffixes (8.1.3) or the adverbial suffix *-CA$_1$* (7.2.2.2) are attached. These are the following:

  The personal pronoun *kendi-* (in its 3rd person reflexive, simple pronominal and emphatic usages (18.1.3)): *kendinde* 'at/on him/her(self) (colloquial)', *kendince* 'according to him/her(self)'. *Kendi* behaves differently from the other two groups listed below in that in colloquial speech *-(y)lA* can also attach to it by means of an intermediary 'n': *kendinle* 'with him/her(self)'.

  The 3rd person possessive suffixes *-(s)I* (singular) and *-lArI* (plural) (8.1.2) and pronouns containing them: *kendisi* 'self', 's/he' (18.1.2), *kendi kendisi* 'self' (18.1.3), *birbiri/birbirleri-* 'each other' (18.1.4) and all of the pronominalized determiners listed in 18.4 (iv): *kendisine* 'to himself/herself', *birbirlerini* 'each other (ACC)', *bazılarından* 'from some of them', *hepsinde* 'in all of them', *birine* 'to one of them'.

  The suffix *-ki* in its pronominal usage 'the one ...' (18.5): *evdekinde* 'in/on/at the one in the house', *buradakinden* 'from the one which is here'.

(iii) In the case of just two words, *su* 'water' and *ne* 'what', 'y' appears at the junction with any of the following suffixes:

   a. the possessive suffixes, except the 3rd person plural
   b. the genitive suffix

   e.g. *suyum* 'my water', *suyun* 'your water', 'of the water', but *suları* 'their water(s)'; *neyimiz* 'what (of ours)', *neyi* 'what (of his/hers)' (also *nesi* 'what (of his/her/its)', but *neleri* 'what (of theirs)'). Note that the forms *nen* (and rarely *nem*) for *ne*+possessive can be used in colloquial speech, usually with the existential predicate *var* 'existent' (e.g. *Nen var?* 'Are you alright?' lit. 'What do you have?').

(iv) Surnames ending in *-oğlu:* Note that *-oğlu* 'son of' contains the 3rd person singular possessive suffix *-(s)I* (8.1.2), hence conforms to the pattern mentioned in (ii. b) above, as in *Senemoğlu'nu, Senemoğlu'ndan*. However, case suffixes (but not *-CA₁*) can also combine directly with such names without an intermediary 'n', as in *Senemoğlu'yu, Senemoğlu'dan*, etc. (but *Senemoğlu'nca*).

(v) Certain adjectives lose their final consonant ('k') when combining with derivational suffixes:

alçak 'low'	+ *-(A)l*	*alçal-* 'decline'
ufak 'small'	+ *-(A/I)cIK*	*ufacık* 'tiny'
küçük 'small'	+ *-mAn*	*küçümen* 'rather small'

   Others lose their final vowel in such circumstances:

kuru 'dry'	+ *-(A)K*	*kurak* 'arid'
sarı 'yellow'	+ *-(A)r*	*sarar-* 'fade'

(vi) There are some contractions that frequently occur in rapid or colloquial speech. The most regularly occurring example is the loss of the final vowel in the locative pronouns *bura-* 'here', *şura-* 'here', 'over there' and *ora-* 'there' (18.3.1) and the wh-phrase *nere-* 'where' (19.2.1.3) when a locative or ablative case marker is added:

bura- 'here'	+ *-DA*	*burda/burada* '(in) here'
nere- 'where'	+ *-Dan*	*nerden/nereden* 'from where'

6.3 The order of suffixation

In Turkish, a large number of suffixes and clitics can be added to a single item. In the overwhelming majority of cases, derivational suffixes (Chapter 7) precede inflectional suffixes (Chapter 8). Clitics (Chapter 11) occur after inflectional suffixes.

(1) Suç-lu-luk-la mı?
    crime-N.DER-N.DER-INS INT
    DER-DER-INFL CL
    'In a guilty manner?'

(2) diz-ge-ler-in-de
    arrange-N.DER-PL-3SG.POSS-LOC
    DER-INFL-INFL-INFL
    'on their systems'

(3) Yap-ı-laş-tır-ıl-ma-mış.
    build-N.DER-V.DER-CAUS-PASS-NEG-EV/PF
    DER-DER-INFL-INFL-INFL-INFL
    '[It] has not been built up.'

Note that the clitic *dA* 'also', 'and' (11.1.1.2), which regularly occurs after all the inflectional suffixes in a word, in colloquial usage may appear between the two segments of *-(y)Abil* (8.2.3.2):

(4) Gid-ebil-ir-im **de**. / Gid-e **de** bil-ir-im.
    go-PSB-AOR-1SG also / go-PSB also PSB-AOR-1SG
    INFL-INFL-INFL CL / INFL CL INFL-INFL-INFL
    '*And* I can [indeed] go.'

(5) Gör-üş-tür-ül-e-me-ye **de** bil-iyor mu-ydu-nuz?
    see-REC-CAUS-PASS-PSB-NEG-PSB also PSB-IMPFINT-P.COP-2PL
    'Did it *also* sometimes happen that you were not allowed to see each other?'

In speech, the interrogative clitic *mI* (11.1.1.5) can occur between the converb *-(y)I* (8.5.2.2 (ii)) and the bound auxiliary *-ver* 'give' (13.3.1.1) in the composite verb form *-(y)Iver*:

(6) Hükümlü-ler-i sal-ı **mı** ver-miş-ler?
    convict-PL-ACC release-CV INT give-PF-3PL
    'Have they released the convicts?'

The attachment properties of each suffix and clitic are described in the relevant sections of Chapters 7, 8 and 11. For the internal ordering of derivational suffixes, see 7.3.

Chapter 7

Word classes, derivation and derivational suffixes

This chapter discusses the word classes of Turkish and the means by which new words are formed by using **derivational suffixes**. Section 7.1 introduces the word classes of Turkish, such as noun, adverb and verb. 7.2 is on **derivation**, the formation of a new word by means of attaching a suffix to a **root**. In 7.2.1 and 7.2.2 we list the derivational suffixes that attach to verbs and nominals respectively and in 7.3 we discuss the ordering of derivational suffixes. 7.4 is on prefixation, a process which has a very limited range of application in Turkish. Throughout this book, we indicate verbs by a following hyphen (e.g. *kazı-* 'scrape' (verb) versus, *kazı* 'excavation' (noun)).

7.1 Word classes

A word in Turkish can belong to one of the following classes: nominal (noun, pronoun, adjective or adverb), verb, postposition, conjunction or discourse connective, or interjection.

7.1.1 Nominals

The group **nominal** contains four word classes: **noun, pronoun, adjective** and **adverb**. In Turkish the boundaries between noun, adjective and adverb are somewhat blurred. Many words and compounds are able to occur with the typical functions of more than one of these classes, although in almost all such cases one function or another is dominant in the actual usage of that particular lexical item. We call this its primary function. For example, the word *efsane* 'legend' can occur as an adjective in *efsane oyuncu* 'legendary actor', but its main function is as a noun. Similarly, *güzel* can occur as a noun in *güzelim* 'my beauty' (affectionate mode of address), or as an adverb, as in *Güzel konuştu* 'S/he spoke well'. But in by far the majority of its occurrences, the function of the word *güzel* is adjectival, as in *güzel bir köpek* 'a beautiful dog'. Below we describe the criteria for identifying the primary function of any specific word belonging to the nominal group.

DOI: 10.4324/9780429435836-9

(i) Nouns:
A noun is a word used for a thing (e.g. *ağaç* 'tree'), a person (e.g. *kadın* 'woman'), an abstract concept (e.g. *mutluluk* 'happiness'), or the proper name of a person (e.g. *Suzan*) or place (e.g. *Londra*). Nouns in Turkish can be inflected for **number** (8.1.1, 14.3.1), **person** (8.1.2, 14.3.2) and **case** (8.1.3, 14.3.3).

(ii) Pronouns:
A pronoun (Chapter 18) is a word which is substituted for a noun phrase in contexts where it is either not necessary to name the referent explicitly or where it is impossible to do so. Examples are *sen* 'you', *bu* 'this (one)', *başkası* 'another (one)', *ne* 'what', *kimse* 'anyone', 'no one'. Pronouns are inflected for number, person and case, e.g. *bunlar* 'these', *hepimiz* 'all of us', *şurada* 'here', 'over there'.

(iii) Adjectives:
An adjective (15.2) ascribes some property, quality or status to the entity denoted by a noun. Examples are *sarı* 'yellow', *yumuşak* 'soft' and *dürüst* 'honest'. Adjectives in Turkish can be modified by adverbials such as *çok* 'very', 'too', *son derece* 'extremely' and *oldukça* 'rather', as in *çok önemli* 'very important', *oldukça yumuşak* 'rather soft' (15.4.1.1). They can be expressed in comparative or superlative forms by the addition of the modifiers *daha* 'more' or *en* 'most', as in *daha dürüst* 'more honest' and *en yumuşak* 'softest' (15.4.2 and 15.4.3). **Determiners**, such as *bir* 'a/an', *her* 'each', *bütün* 'all' and *bu* 'this', 'these' (15.6) and **numerals**, such as *iki bin* 'two thousand', *üçüncü* '(the) third' (15.7) are functionally related to the adjective class.

Most lexical items which occur primarily as adjectives can also occur as nouns, taking plural, possessive and case suffixes as required, or they can function as adverbs, in particular as circumstantial adverbs of manner (16.4.3). An example of the first type is the word *küçük* 'small', which is primarily used as an adjective, as in *küçük kızlar* 'little girls', but which can also be used as a noun, as in *küçükler* '(the) little ones'. An example of the second type is the word *kötü* 'bad', as in *kötü yol* 'bad road', which, when placed immediately before the verb in a sentence, functions as an adverb meaning 'badly', as in *kötü yüzmek* 'to swim badly'.

(iv) Adverbs:
An adverb modifies, that is to say, provides further specification of the meaning of, a verb, an adjective, another adverb, or a whole sentence (Chapter 16). Adverbs that modify verbs typically provide information about the manner, time or degree of the occurrence of an event: *yavaşça* 'slowly', *hep* 'always', *çok* 'a lot'. Adverbs that modify adjectives or other adverbs specify the degree to which the concepts they denote apply, such as *biraz* 'somewhat' and *çok* 'very' in *biraz büyük* 'somewhat large', *çok sık* 'very often'. Examples of adverbs that modify a whole sentence are *belki* 'perhaps' and *maalesef* 'unfortunately'. Occasionally, words that occur primarily as adverbs can be inflected

as nouns. Thus *şimdi* 'now' can appear in the form *şimdilerde* 'nowadays', which includes number and case markers.

7.1.2 Verbs

A **verb** is a word which expresses an action, event, process or state, such as *koş-* 'run', *bit-* 'end', *ol-* 'be', 'become', *kal-* 'remain', 'stay' (indicated by a following hyphen). Verbs in Turkish are inflected for **voice** (8.2.1, 13.2), **negation** (8.2.2, 20.1), **tense**, **aspect** and **modality** (8.2.3, Chapter 21) and **person** (8.4, 12.2.1). Verb stems, derived or non-derived, are indicated in this book by a following hyphen.

7.1.3 Postpositions

Postpositions (Chapter 17) are words which take noun phrase complements and the postpositional phrase formed in this way typically functions as an adverbial (17.4). Examples are *karşı* 'against' (e.g. *bana karşı* 'against me'), *sonra* 'after' (e.g. *toplantıdan sonra* 'after the meeting') and *için* 'for', e.g. *kimin için* 'for whom'). Lexical items that occur primarily as postpositions (17.2) are not inflected when functioning as such. However, an important sub-class of postpositions (17.3) is formed from nouns by the addition of person (possessive) and case markers (e.g. *ön-ün-de* 'in front of' from *ön* 'front'). Some lexical items which function primarily as postpositions may also occur as nouns. For example, *karşı* can also be used meaning 'the other side' and in this case, it can be inflected like a noun, as in *karşıdan* 'from the other side'.

7.1.4 Conjunctions and discourse connectives

Conjunctions join two or more items which have the same syntactic function. Examples are *ve* 'and', *fakat* 'but', *dA...dA* 'both...and', as in *Hasan ve Hüseyin* 'Hasan and Hüseyin', *Git ama kalma* 'Go but don't stay [there]' and *Can da sen de* 'both Can and you'. **Discourse connectives** are used between, or sometimes inside, sentences for purposes of cohesion in discourse. Among other functions, they can introduce statements which are a further development of a previous statement, e.g. *hatta* 'moreover', *üstelik* 'and on top of that', or they can be used for expanding on a previous statement e.g. *yani* 'in other words', or for presenting a fact that appears to contradict what has just been said, e.g. *halbuki* 'whereas'. Conjunctions and discourse connectives constitute the only word class that cannot be inflected. They are discussed in detail in Chapter 28.

7.1.5 Interjections

These are words which express feelings, such as *ay* 'ouch!', *hay allah* 'oh dear!', *vah vah* 'what a shame!', *allah allah* 'good heavens!', or which are used to initiate conversation or to express the speaker's attitude towards the addressee, such as *yahu* 'hey'. A few interjections in Turkish can be used as nouns and can combine with inflectional suffixes (e.g. *ahlarımdan* 'from my sighs') or derivational suffixes (e.g. *ahla-* 'sigh').

7.2 Derivation

Derivation is the creation of a new **lexical item** (i.e. a form which would be found in a dictionary) from a stem. The vast majority of derivation in Turkish is achieved through suffixation. Prefixation is used, to a very limited extent, for **reduplication** (9.1) and in a few loanwords (7.4). **Compounding**, which is another type of word formation process, is discussed in Chapter 10. In very rare cases, word formation does not involve any of the above derivational processes; a stem can change its word class without any overt marker, as in the case of *kuru* 'dry' and *kuru-* '(to) dry'.

When a derivational suffix attaches to a stem it produces a new word connected in meaning to that stem. Some derivational suffixes change the class of the word they attach to. For example, the nominal-deriving suffix *-I* combines with verbal stems such as *kaz-* 'dig' and *güldür-* 'cause to laugh' to form the nouns *kazı* 'excavation' and *güldürü* 'comedy'. Other derivational suffixes create words of the same class as the stem to which they are attached. For example, the suffix *-lIk* can derive nouns from nouns, as in the case of *krallık* 'kingship', 'kingdom' from *kral* 'king'.

In most cases, the meaning of a word which contains a derivational suffix is not predictable by segmenting it into parts. For example, the words *kayık* 'boat', *kayak* 'ski' and *kaydırak* 'slide' are all derived from the verb *kay-*'slide' and although the suffixes themselves indicate that these words are nominals, they do not give an indication as to the exact meaning of the new words they form. Similarly, the particular suffix that a word can take is not predictable. For example, the suffixes *-lA*, *-lAş*, *-(A)l* and *-(A)r* can all change adjectives into verbs that express the process of changing state (i.e. become what the adjective denotes), but the adjectives they attach to are not chosen on the basis of a particular grammatical condition, as witnessed by the words *geniş-le-* 'widen', *kalın-laş-* 'broaden', *ince-l-* 'become thin' and *kaba-r-* 'swell'.

The roots that derivational suffixes attach to may not always be identifiable words in modern Turkish. Some derivational processes took place a long time ago and while the derived word is still in use, the root may have become obsolete (e.g. *yay* 'summer' (obs.) in *yay-la* 'plateau'). It may also be the case that the root of the word is still in use in some parts of Turkey but is not likely to be used in modern standard Turkish (e.g. *dil-* '(to) slice' in *dil-im* 'slice').

Productive derivational suffixes are those which regularly have particular meanings and can be used freely with a particular type of stem. For example, the suffix *-lI*, in one of its meanings, can be used freely with almost all place names, to indicate that a person comes from, or is a native of, the place specified, as in *Londralı* 'Londoner', *Kuzey İrlandalı* 'native of Northern Ireland', *oralı* '(person) from there'. The majority of derivational suffixes, however, are unproductive. This means that although they may be present in a number of words that are still in use, they are no longer perceived by speakers as items usable in the production of new words (e.g. the suffix *-gaç* in *utangaç* 'shy').

Derivational suffixes were widely used as a means of coining new words to replace their non-native counterparts during the language reform movement that was launched in the early 1930s. Words of mostly Arabic and Persian origin, but also some other loanwords, were replaced by new words made up by adding derivational suffixes to Turkish or Turkic roots. While most of the derivational suffixes employed were Turkish, a few were borrowed from other Turkic languages (e.g. *-tay* in *kurultay* 'conference'), and others were used in ways that were difficult to justify in terms of any naturally occurring precedents (e.g. *-sAl*). However, despite the scholarly opposition encountered by aspects of the word-creation process, many of the neologisms have effectively replaced their loan counterparts, or are in the process of doing so; others proved short-lived and yet others co-exist with their synonyms or near-synonyms of foreign origin, e.g. *teklif* (Ar.) and *öneri* 'proposal', *mesela* (Ar.) and *örneğin* 'for example', *teorik* (Fr.) and *kuramsal* 'theoretical'. In the examples given in this chapter, no attempt has been made to distinguish between naturally occurring words and coinages.

In the lists below, some suffixes may be composite (i.e. a combination of two or more suffixes).

7.2.1 Suffixes that attach to verbs

Suffixes that attach to verbs create new words which are either nominals (noun, adjective or adverb) or verbs.

7.2.1.1 Suffixes that attach to verbs to form nominals

Nominal-deriving suffixes that attach to verb stems mostly create words that function primarily as nouns. They may also create adjectives and in rare instances adverbs. Most suffixes of this type are unproductive.

-A	Forms nouns: *süre* 'time span', *yara* 'wound'. Less commonly, it forms adverbs: *geçe* 'past' as in *ikiyi çeyrek geçe* 'quarter past two'.
-(A)C	Forms nouns: *süreç* 'process', *kaldıraç* 'pulley', *bağlaç* 'conjunction'.
-(A)cAn	Forms adjectives: *sevecen* 'loving', *babacan* 'fatherly'.
-AğAn/-AgAn	Forms adjectives. The more frequently used form is the one containing 'ğ': *olağan* 'usual', *durağan* 'still', *gezegen* 'planet'. See also *-GAn* below.
-(A)K	Forms (i) nouns, usually denoting concrete objects: *elek* 'sieve', *adak* 'sacrifice', *kayak* 'ski': (ii) adjectives: *ürkek* 'timid', *korkak* 'cowardly'.

-(A)l	Forms (i) nouns: *okul* 'school', *kural* 'rule'; (ii) adjectives: *sanal* 'virtual'.
-(A)m	Forms nouns: *kuram* 'theory', *dönem* 'period', *anlam* 'meaning'.
-(A)mAK	Forms nouns: *basamak* 'step', *kaçamak* 'evasion'.
-(A)nAK	Forms nouns: *tutanak* 'minutes', *ödenek* 'subsidy', *görenek* 'custom'.
-(A/I)r	Forms: (i) nouns: *keser* 'adze', *yarar* 'benefit', 'use', *gelir* 'income' (ii) adjectives (within compounds): *çalar saat* 'alarm clock', *okuryazar* 'literate' (iii) adjectival clauses: *uzaktan farkedilebilir bir renk* 'a colour (which is) noticeable from far away'.
-(A)v	Forms nouns: *sınav* 'examination', *görev* 'duty', *türev* 'derived form', 'derivative'.
-(A)y	Forms: (i) nouns: *olay* 'event', *deney* 'experiment' (ii) adjectives: *yapay* 'artificial', *düşey* 'vertical'
-C/-InC	This pair of suffixes forms: (i) nouns: *direnç* 'resistance', *basınç* 'pressure' (ii) adjectives: *iğrenç* 'disgusting', *gülünç* 'ridiculous'. -*ç* is added to verbs ending in -*n*, otherwise -*Inç* is used.
-DI	Forms nouns: *uydu* 'satellite', *alındı* 'receipt', *çıktı* 'printout'.
-DIK	Forms: (i) nouns: *tanıdık* 'acquaintance' (ii) adjectives: *bildik* 'familiar', *tanıdık* 'familiar'. See also -*mAdIk* below. For a special adjectival usage, see 25.1.1.3.
-GA/-(A)lgA	Forms nouns: *dizge* 'system', *süpürge* 'broom', *çizelge* 'table' (i.e. tabulated information).
-GAC	Forms: (i) nouns: *süzgeç* 'sieve', *kıskaç* 'pincers', *yüzgeç* 'fin' (ii) adjectives: *utangaç* 'shy'.
-GAn	Forms: (i) nouns: *etken* 'factor', *sürüngen* 'reptile' (ii) adjectives: *konuşkan* 'talkative', *kaygan* 'slippery'.
-GI	Forms nouns, mostly denoting concrete objects: *silgi* 'eraser', *sürgü* 'bolt', but also abstract nouns such as *bilgi* 'knowledge', *sevgi* 'love'.
-GIC	Forms nouns: *dalgıç* 'diver', *başlangıç* 'beginning'.
-GIn	Forms: (i) nouns: *baskın* 'raid', *sürgün* 'exile' (ii) adjectives: *etkin* 'active', *durgun* 'calm'.

-(I)K	Forms: (i) nouns: *konuk* 'guest', *kayık* 'boat', *öksürük* 'caugh' (ii) adjectives: *soluk* 'faded', *kırık* 'broken', *donuk* 'frozen'.
-(I)lI	A composite of *-I* (below) and *-lI* (7.2.2.2), forms adjectives and adjectival phrases: *yazılı* 'written', (*kağıda*) *sarılı* 'wrapped (in paper)'.
-(I)n	Forms nouns: *basın* '(the) press', *yayın* 'publication', 'broadcast', *yığın* 'heap'.
-(I)ntI	Forms nouns: *söylenti* 'rumour', *girinti* 'indentation', *alıntı* 'quotation'.
-(I)r	Forms nouns: *yatır* 'shrine'.
-(I)t	Forms nouns: *geçit* 'crossing', 'pass', *yazıt* 'inscription', *umut* 'hope'.
-mA	Forms: (i) nouns: *basma* 'printed cloth', *kıyma* 'minced meat', *inme* 'paralysis', 'stroke' (ii) adjectives: *dökme* '(of metal) cast'.
-mAC	Forms nouns: *bulamaç* 'thick soup', *yırtmaç* 'slit'.
-mAcA	A composite of *-mA* and *-CA₁*, forms nouns: *bulmaca* 'puzzle', *koşmaca* 'tag (game)', *çekmece* 'drawer'.
-mAdIK	Forms adjectives. The form *-mAdIK* which contains the negative marker is a productive suffix, unlike its affirmative counterpart *-DIK* (see above). It can attach directly to verb stems or to their passive form: *kırmadık* 'unbroken', *görmedik* 'unseen', *görülmedik* 'unseen', 'unprecedented'.
-mAK	Forms nouns: *ekmek* 'bread', *çakmak* 'lighter', *yemek* 'food', 'meal'.
-mAn	Forms: (i) nouns indicating a person's occupation: *öğretmen* 'teacher', *danışman* 'adviser', *eleştirmen* 'critic' (ii) adjectives: *şişman* 'fat'. See also *-mAn* (7.2.2.2), the counterpart of this suffix which is added to nominals.
-mAz	Forms: (i) nouns: *açmaz* 'impasse', *tükenmez* 'ball-point pen' (ii) adjectives: *bitmez* 'endless', *anlaşılmaz* 'incomprehensible' (iii) adjectival clauses: *gözle görülemez* (*bir ayrıntı*) '(a detail) which is invisible to the [naked] eye'.
-mIK	Forms nouns: *kıymık* 'splinter', *kusmuk* 'vomit'.
-mIş	Forms nouns from intransitive verb stems: *geçmiş* '(the) past', *dolmuş* 'public car operating like a bus', *ermiş* 'saint'.
-sAK	Forms nouns: *tutsak* 'prisoner'. See also *-sAK* (7.2.2.2), the counterpart of this suffix which is added to nominals.
-sAl	Forms adjectives: *görsel* 'visual', *işitsel* 'aural'. See also *-sAl* (7.2.2.2), the counterpart of this suffix which is added to nominals.

-sI	Forms nouns: *tütsü* 'incense', *yatsı* 'ritual worship performed by Muslims two hours after sunset', *giysi* 'garment'.
-tay	Forms nouns denoting an institution or organized meeting: *Danıştay* 'Council of State', *çalıştay* '(academic) workshop'. See also *-tay* (7.2.2.2), the counterpart of this suffix which is added to nominals.
-tI	Forms nouns from two-syllable stems ending in *-l* or *-r*: *doğrultu* 'direction', *bağırtı* 'shout', *morartı* 'bruise'.
-(y)AcAK	Forms nouns: *yiyecek* 'food', *içecek* 'drink', *gelecek* 'future'. For a special adjectival usage, see 25.1.1.3
-(y)An	Forms nouns: *sıçan* 'rat', *bakan* 'minister'.
-(y)AsI, *-(y)AsIcA*	*-(y)AsI* forms adjectives which mean 'worthy of': *görülesi* 'worth seeing'. Both *-(y)AsI* and *-(y)AsIcA* form adjectives used in expressing ill-wishes: *kahrolası(ca)* 'damned', *lanet olası(ca)* 'cursed'.
-(y)AsIyA	Forms adverbs indicating the degree to which an action is performed, in terms of the imagined endpoint: *ölesiye* 'to the point of dying', *doyasıya* 'to the point of fulfilment/satisfaction'.
-(y)I	Forms: (i) nouns: *yazı* 'writing', *güldürü* 'comedy', *batı* 'west', *deyi* 'utterance' (ii) adjectives: *dolu* 'full', *duru* 'clear'.
-(y)IcI/-cI	Probably the most productive suffix in this category, this forms: (i) nouns expressing: 　a. a person practising a certain profession or having a certain occupation: *koruyucu* 'guardian', *öğrenci* 'student', *dilenci* 'beggar' 　b. a tool, machine or substance performing a particular function: *yazıcı* 'printer', *yatıştırıcı* 'sedative', *uyuşturucu* 'narcotic' (ii) adjectives denoting that the action of a verb is an inherent quality of the person or thing to which the adjective is applied: *yapıcı* 'constructive', *üzücü* 'distressing', *yorucu* 'tiring' (iii) adjectival clauses that mark an attribute which is regarded as an inherent property of the entity denoted by the noun that the adjectival construction qualifies. Some forms with *-(y)IcI* are complex adjectivals (25.5). The noun which is qualified (in parentheses below) is usually inanimate and is the understood subject of the verb: *nezleyi önleyici (ilaçlar)* '(medicines) that prevent the common cold', *endişelerimizi giderici (sözler)* '(words) that ease our worries'.

Note that the *-cI* form of this suffix occurs only after '-n' (see (i.a) above). See also *-CI* (7.2.2.2), the counterpart of this suffix which is added to nominals.

-(y)Im Forms nouns from underived verbal roots: *bölüm* 'department', 'chapter', 'part', *seçim* 'choice', 'election', *deneyim* 'experience', or from derived intransitives with *-(I)l/-n*: *gerilim* 'tension', *devinim* 'movement'.

-(y)Iş Forms nouns: *direniş* 'resistance', *giriş* 'entrance', *yürüyüş* 'walk', 'march'.

7.2.1.2 Suffixes that attach to verbs to form verbs

-(A/I)klA Indicates repetitive or intermittent action: *uyukla-* 'doze', *dürtükle-* 'prod continually'.

-AlA Indicates the suddenness of the onset of an action: *şaşala-* 'be bewildered', *durala-* 'suddenly stop (to reflect)'.

-(I)n In the vast majority of cases, this suffix, which is identical in form to the reflexive suffix (8.2.1.3), forms intransitive verbs: *sevin-* 'be happy', *görün-* 'appear', 'seem', *kaçın-* 'avoid', *tıkan-* 'be/become blocked', but it can also form transitive verbs: *edin-* 'acquire'.

-(I)ş This suffix, which is identical in form to the reciprocal suffix (8.2.1.4), indicates one or other of the following:
  (i) that the action denoted by the verbal root is performed in an unorganized manner: *koşuş-* 'run back and forth', *uçuş-* 'fly about'
  (ii) a shared act: *bölüş-* 'share', ↓*kırış-* 'share', *fısıldaş-* 'whisper among themselves'
  (iii) the intensity of a property of the verbal root: *kokuş-* 'give off a putrid smell', 'become rotten' (from *kok-* 'smell').

-(I)ştır A composite of *-(I)ş* and *-DIr* (reciprocal + causative, 8.2.1.4, 8.2.1.1)), it indicates intensive or repetitive action: *araştır-* 'investigate', *itiştir-* 'push back and forth'.

7.2.2 Suffixes that attach to nominals

Suffixes that attach to nominals create both verbs and other nominals (nouns, adjectives and adverbs).

7.2.2.1 Suffixes that attach to nominals to form verbs

-A Forms verbs from nouns: *kana-* 'bleed', *türe-* 'spring up', 'derive' and adjectives: *boşa-* 'divorce'.

-(A)l Forms intransitive verbs from adjectives of quality: *kısal-* 'become short(er)', *daral-* 'become narrow(er)', *incel-* 'become thin(ner)'.

-(A)r	Forms verbs from adjectives, particularly those denoting colour. The verbs thus created indicate the process of acquiring that colour or state: *karar-* 'turn black', *ağar-* (from *ak* 'white') 'turn white', *delir-* 'go mad'.
-(A)ş	Forms verbs from nouns: *yanaş-* 'approach'.
-(A)t	Forms verbs from nouns: *gözet-* 'safeguard'.
-DA(n)	Forms verbs mostly from onomatopoeic stems: *çatırda-* 'crack', *şakırda-* 'jingle', *kıpırda(n)-* 'move', 'fidget', *vızılda(n)-* 'hum', 'buzz', 'whinge'. The '*-n*' may be added only where the subject is human.
-GIr	Forms verbs from onomatopoeic stems that are not found in isolation: *fışkır-* 'spurt out', *püskür-* 'spray'.
-(I)K	Forms intransitive verbs from (i) adjectives: *acık-* 'become hungry' (from *aç* 'hungry'), *gecik-* 'be delayed' (from *geç* 'late') (ii) nouns: *gözük-* 'seem', 'appear'.
-(I)msA	Forms transitive verbs from adjectives: *azımsa-* 'underestimate', *özümse-* 'assimilate', 'make one's own'. Also used with the pronoun *ben* 'I': *benimse-* 'consider [s.t.] one's own'.
-lA	Forms verbs from: (i) nouns: *tuzla-* 'put salt on', *avla-* 'hunt', *bıçakla-* 'stab' (ii) adjectives: *akla-* 'acquit', *kurula-* 'dry (s.t.)' (iii) onomatopoeic stems indicating the sound produced by animals: *gıdakla-* 'crow', *miyavla-* 'miaow', *havla-* 'bark' (iv) onomatopoeic stems indicating the sound produced by humans: *üfle-* 'blow out (as in 'a candle')', *ahla-* 'sigh', *ofla-* 'huff'. The result of (i) and (ii) is most often a transitive verb, but there are cases where *-lA* can also create intransitive verbs: *çabala-* 'try hard', *şişmanla-* 'become fat', *zayıfla-* 'grow thin'.
-lAn	A composite of *-lA* and *-n* (passive/reflexive, 8.2.1.2, 8.2.1.3) forms verbs from: (i) adjectives: *kurulan-* 'dry oneself', 'be dried', *hazırlan-* 'get ready', (ii) nouns: *güneşlen-* 'sun-bathe', *hırslan-* 'get angry', *evlen-* 'get married'. Almost all of the verbs containing *-lAn* are intransitive. *-lAn* can combine with the causative suffix *-DIr* (e.g. *evlendir-* 'to marry (two people to each other)', *öfkelendir-* 'make [s.o.] angry'). This happens mainly where the nominal root is a noun.
-lAş	A composite of *-lA* and *-(I)ş* (reciprocal, 8.2.1.4) forms: (i) intransitive verbs from adjectives of quality. The verbs thus created indicate the process of attaining that particular quality: *güzelleş-* 'become beautiful', *koyulaş-* 'darken', 'thicken', *kırlaş-* 'turn white (of hair)'

	(ii) verbs from nouns to indicate mutual activity: *haberleş-* 'communicate with one another', *mektuplaş-* 'communicate with each other by letter', *e- mailleş-* 'e-mail (each other)'.
-lAt	A composite of *-lA* and *-t* (causative 8.2.1.1) forms transitive/causative verbs from adjectives: *kirlet-* 'make [s.t.] dirty', *serinlet-* 'make [s.o.] cool down', *genişlet-* 'expand [s.t.]'. Some of these verbs do not have a corresponding *-lA* form.
-sA	Forms:
	(i) transitive or intransitive verbs from nouns: *önemse-* 'consider important', *susa-* 'become thirsty'
	(ii) transitive verbs from adjectives: *garipse-* 'consider strange', *hafifse-* 'consider trivial'.

7.2.2.2 Suffixes that attach to nominals to form nominals

A few of these suffixes are of Arabic or Persian origin. Words containing Arabic and Persian suffixes are increasingly giving way to their synonyms of Turkish origin.

-(A)C	Forms adjectives from nouns: *anaç* 'motherly', *kıraç* 'infertile'.
-(A/I)cIK	See *-CAK₁*.
-(A)K	Forms adjectives from adjectives: *solak* 'left- handed', *kurak* 'arid'.
-(A)l	Forms adjectives from nouns: *yerel* 'local', *ulusal* 'national', *yasal* 'legal'. This suffix was introduced as part of the language reform movement alongside *-sAl* and has the same function.
-(A)n	Forms nouns from nouns or adjectives: *köken* 'origin', *düzen* 'system'.
-ane	A suffix of Persian origin (pronounced [a:nɛ́]) which forms adjectives from nouns borrowed from Arabic and Persian: *şairane* 'poetic', *dostane* 'friendly'.
-(A)rI	The spatial nominals *iç* 'inside' and *dış* 'outside' can be used in their bare form only as adjectives (e.g. *iç taraf* 'inner part', *dış kapı* 'outer door') (10.1.1 (v)). Otherwise they always have to have possessive marking (e.g. *evin içi* 'the inside of the house'). The addition of the derivational suffix *-(A)rI* allows these words to appear on their own and to be case-marked: *dışarı(ya) (çık-)* '(go) outside'.
-(A)t	Forms nouns or adjectives from nouns or adjectives: *özet* 'summary', *başat* 'dominant'.
-(A)y	Forms nouns or adjectives from nouns: *yüzey* 'surface', *güney* 'south'.

-baz	A suffix of Persian origin which forms nouns from nouns: *hokkabaz* 'magician', 'trickster', *düzenbaz* 'cheat'.

-CA₁	This is a productive and unstressable suffix (4.3.2) which:
	(i) forms adjectives
	   a. from nouns, meaning 'characteristic of a...', describing actions or attitudes: *çocukça* 'childish', *aptalca* 'idiotic'
	   b. from the pluralized form of a round numeral or of a measure expression, suggesting a large number or amount in an imprecise fashion: *binlerce* 'thousands of', *kilolarca* 'kilograms of', *hektarlarca* 'acres of'
	(ii) forms nouns, adjectives or adverbs denoting a language from nouns of nationality: *Japonca* '(in) Japanese', *İsveççe* '(in) Swedish' (16.1.6)
	(iii) forms adverbs: *kolayca* 'easily', *ailece* 'as a family' (16.1.6). Also combines with the verbal noun suffix *-mA*. See *-mAcA* (7.2.1.1).

-CA₂	Reduces the intensity of adjectives: *güzelcé* 'prettyish', *hızlıcá* 'quite fast', *küçükçé* 'rather small'. This suffix is usually stressable.
-CA₃	A diminutive suffix which expresses (sometimes figuratively) a smaller version of the entity denoted by the noun it attaches to: *tarihçe* 'short history', *günce* 'diary'. The words formed by *-CA₃* are stressed unpredictably on the suffix or on the syllable preceding it (4.3.2).
-CAcIK	This unstressable suffix (4.3.2) combines with adjectives and adverbs usually with the effect of emphasizing the quality expressed by the adjective or adverb: *yakíncacık* 'close by', *hémencecik* 'immediately'.
-CAK₁, -CAğIz, -CIK, -(A/I)cIk	These are all diminutive suffixes which are used for expressing intensification of diminutiveness, and/or endearment and pity. The choice of the appropriate suffix is not predictable: *yavrucak* 'the poor child', *çocukcağız* 'the poor/dear child', *kuşcağız* 'the little birdie', *kedicik* 'the poor/dear little cat'. In the same way, the unstressable suffix *-(A/I)cIK* (4.3.2) is added to adjectives to intensify the degree of diminutiveness they express. The words thus derived are stressed on the first syllable: *dáracık* 'very narrow', *ázıcık* 'very little', *kúçücük* 'tiny'.
-CAK₂	This suffix forms: (i) adjectives from adjectives (synonymous with adjectival (stressable) *-CA₂*): *büyücék* 'rather large' (from *büyük* 'large') (ii) nouns from nouns: *oyuncak* 'toy'

	(iii) (in colloquial registers) adverbs from nouns *évcek* 'the whole household together', *mahallécek* 'as a neighbourhood' (as in 'We acted as a neighbourhood.')
	(iv) occasionally adverbs from adverbs indicating haste: *çábucak* 'very quickly' (from *çabuk* 'quickly').
	When -*CAK₂* derives adverbs, stress falls on the stressable syllable of the root. Adverbs thus derives are colloquial alternatives to those derived by -*CA₁* (e.g. *mahallécel mahallécek* 'as a neighbourhood').
-*CAnA*	Colloquial and unstressable form (4.3.2) of adverbial -*CA₁* where the root is an adjective: *güzélcene* 'nicely', *yaváşçana* 'slowly', *koláycana* 'easily'.
-*CAsI*	A composite of -*CA* and 3rd person possessive, this unproductive composite suffix forms modal adverbs (16.3) and discourse connectives (28.3.10 (ii)): *açıkçası* 'frankly', *kısacası* 'in short'. See also -*sI* (below).
-*CAsInA*	A composite and unstressable (4.3.2) suffix, forms manner adverbs from adjectives with a negative connotation: *aptalcasına* 'stupidly', *salakçasına* 'like a twit'. See also *-(A/I)rcAsInA/-mIşçAsInA/-(y)mIşçAsınA* (8.5.2.2 (ii)).
-*CI*	A productive suffix which forms:
	(i) nouns indicating a person associated with a profession: *güreşçi* 'wrestler', *lokantacı* 'restaurant owner', *Almancacı* 'German teacher'. Also occurs in the question word *neci* used to inquire about someone's occupation.
	(ii) nouns or adjectives indicating ideological adherence to a person, cause or idea: *Atatürkçü* 'Kemalist', *devrimci* 'revolutionary', *gerici* 'reactionary'
	(iii) nouns indicating a person engaged in a particular activity: *yolcu* 'traveller', *kapkaççı* 'snatch-and-run thief'
	(iv) nouns indicating one who likes or is in the habit of consuming a particular type of food or drink: *içkici* 'boozer', *tatlıcı* 'someone with a sweet tooth'
	(v) adjectives indicating the habitual involvement of a person with the entity denoted by the root: *palavracı* 'liar', 'lying', *şüpheci* 'sceptical'
	See also -*(y)IcI*, the counterpart of -*CI* which is added to verbs (7.2.1.1).
-*CIl*	Forms adjectives and nouns from nouns, and it indicates love or affinity towards what is denoted by the root: *insancıl* 'humane', 'philanthropic', *evcil* 'domesticated'. It is also added to the pronoun *ben* 'I': *bencil* 'selfish'.
-*DA*	An unproductive suffix which forms nouns and adjectives from nouns: *gözde* 'favourite'.

-DAm	Forms nouns from nouns: *gündem* 'agenda', *yöntem* 'method'.
-DAn	Forms adjectives and nouns from adjectives and nouns: *sıradan* 'ordinary', *neden* 'reason', *içten* 'sincere', *toptan* 'wholesale'.
-dan	A suffix of Persian origin which forms nouns from nouns and denotes some kind of container: *şamdan* 'candlestick', *cüzdan* 'wallet'.
-dar	A suffix of Persian origin which, when attached to nouns forms (i) nouns: *kasadar* 'cashier' (ii) adjectives: *dindar* 'religious'.
-Daş/-Deş	Forms nouns form nouns and denotes possessors of a shared attribute: *yandaş* 'supporter', *kardeş* 'sibling' (from *karın* 'abdomen'), *meslektaş* 'colleague' (i.e. person of the same profession)'.
-en	An unstressable suffix (4.3.2) of Arabic origin which forms adverbs from nouns: *şahsen* 'personally', *hakikaten* 'really'.
-engiz	A suffix of Persian origin which forms adjectives from nouns: *esrarengiz* 'mysterious', *dehşetengiz* 'terrifying', 'awesome'.
-gen	Forms names given to geometric figures from numerals: *dörtgen* 'quadrilateral', *altıgen* 'hexagon'.
-gil	This suffix indicates group membership, especially when referring to species of animals or plants, and is used with the plural suffix in this function: *baklagiller* 'legumes', *turunçgiller* 'citrus fruits'. In non-standard usage it may also refer to human groups when attached to: (i) proper names: *Ahmetgil* 'Ahmet and his family/group' (ii) nouns indicating family members, in which case *-gil* is preceded by a possessive suffix: *amcasıgil* 'his/her uncle (and his family)'.
-(h)ane	The word *hane* 'house', borrowed from Persian and pronounced [a:né]), appears as a suffix in words denoting places: *hastane* 'hospital', *pastane* 'cake shop', *kayıkhane* 'boathouse'.
-I	Forms adverbs of time from the pluralized form of nominals denoting recurrent time locations: *sabahları* 'in the morning(s)', *önceleri* 'formerly'. (16.4.1.1). See also *-lArI*.
-(I)msAr	Forms adjectives from adjectives: *iyimser* 'optimistic', *karamsar* 'pessimistic'.
-(I)msI	Forms adjectives expressing similarity to the thing or quality denoted by the root when dttached to nouns or adjectives: *barakamsı* 'shed-like', *meyvamsı* 'fruity', *yeşilimsi* 'greenish'. See also *-sI* below.
-(I)mtraK	Forms adjectives from colour and taste denoting adjectives and expresses approximation to what that adjective denotes: *mavimtrak* 'bluish', *ekşimtrak* 'sourish'.

Word classes, derivation and derivational suffixes   61

-(I)ncI Forms ordinal numbers from cardinal numbers: *ikinci* 'second', *yüzüncü* 'hundredth' (15.7.2). Also used with the question word *kaç* 'how many' to inquire about the number of a particular item in an ordered list: *kaçıncı (gün)* 'which (day)', and with *son* 'last': *sonuncu* '(the) last (one)'.

-istan A Persian suffix which forms names of countries or regions: *Macaristan* 'Hungary', *Arabistan* 'Arabia'.

-(I)t Forms adjectives and nouns from nouns: *eşit* 'equal', *karşıt* 'opposite'.

-iye A suffix of Arabic origin which forms nouns from Arabic stems: *maliye* 'public finance', *Harbiye* 'Military Academy'.

-iyet A suffix of Arabic origin which forms nouns from Arabic stems: *maliyet* 'cost', *medeniyet* 'civilization'.

-(I)z Attaches to numerals to indicate (a member of) a group of siblings born in a single birth: *dördüz* 'quadruplet(s)', *ikiz* 'twin(s)'.

-kâr A suffix of Persian origin pronounced [cʰaɾ] and sometimes written without a circumflex (^), forms nouns indicating a person associated with a profession or occupation: *sanatkâr* 'artist', *hizmetkâr* 'servant'.

-lA Attaches to nouns to designate a place associated with the concept in the root: *yayla* 'plateau' (from *yay* (obs.) 'summer'), *tuzla* 'salt mine'. This suffix is unstressable (4.3.2) and stress remains on the root.

-lAm Forms nouns from nouns: *boylam* 'meridian', *denklem* 'equation', *önlem* 'precaution'.

-lAmA Forms nouns or adverbs from nouns: *gözleme* 'pancake', *şekerleme* 'crystallized fruit', 'nap', *balıklama (atla-)* '(dive) head-first'.

-lArI(n) Forms adverbials from terms denoting days, recurrent time locations and seasons: *yazları* 'in (the) summers', *salıları* 'on Tuesdays'. See also *-leyin* and *-(y)In* below.

-leyin An unstressable suffix (4.3.2) which forms adverbials from terms denoting times of the day: *sabahleyin* 'in the morning', *geceleyin* 'at night'. See also *-lArI(n)* and *-(y)In*.

-lI This a productive suffix which forms:
   (i) nouns and adjectives where the entity described possesses, is characterized by, or is provided with the object or quality expressed by the stem:
      a. from nouns and adjectives: *atlı* 'horseman', 'horse-drawn', *sevgili* 'lover', 'dear', *akıllı* 'clever', *mavili* 'in blue', *hızlı* 'rapid'. Also occurs in the question word *neli*, used to inquire about the attribute of something (e.g. *neli dondurma* 'what kind of ice cream').

        b. from nouns of place and locative pronouns (18.3.1) to indicate or describe a person belonging to or coming from that place: *üniversiteli* 'university student', *Londralı* 'Londoner', *köylü* 'villager', *buralı* 'from here'. Also occurs in the question word *nereli* 'from where', used to ask about a person's country (or town, etc.) of origin.

        c. from numerals to indicate groups comprising that number of entities: *üçlü* 'threesome', 'trio', *altılı* 'sextet'

(ii) adjectival phrases from noun phrases, which express that the entity described possesses, is characterized by, or is provided with the object or quality expressed by the noun phrase: *kısa saçlı* 'short-haired', *dört çocuklu* 'with four children', *mavi elbiseli* 'in a blue dress', *bindokuzyüzlü yıllar* 'the nineteen hundreds'. For deriving such adjectival phrase from *-(s)I* compounds, see 15.3.4.

(iii) The double usage of this suffix, *-lI...-lI*, produces adjectives: *kızlı oğlanlı (bir grup)* '(a group) of girls and boys', or adverbs: *geceli gündüzlü (çalış-)* '(work) day and night'.

-lIğInA   A composite suffix that is attached to noun phrases containing a numeral, it forms adverbs of time: *sekiz aylığına* 'for eight months'.

-lIK   This productive suffix forms:

(i) nouns from nouns, adjectives or adverbs to indicate:

    a. the state relating to a particular concept: *krallık* 'kingship', *sağırlık* 'deafness', *iyilik* 'goodness', *çabukluk* 'speed'

    b. an application, embodiment or institutionalization of the concept in question: *krallık* 'kingdom', *iyilik* 'good deed', *askerlik* 'military service'

    c. an object or garment associated with a body part: *gözlük* 'spectacles', *başlık* 'headgear'

    d. a storage place or container for a particular type of object: *odunluk* 'woodshed', *kitaplık* 'bookcase', *ayakkabılık* 'shoe rack'

    e. a place where the entity denoted by the root is found collectively: *zeytinlik* 'olive grove', *mezarlık* 'cemetery'

    f. a person whose relationship is analogous to the blood relationship indicated by the root: *analık* 'stepmother', *evlatlık* 'child servant'

    g. a banknote: *onluk* 'tenner'.

(ii) adjectives which indicate:
    a. when added to nouns, suitability for the type of entity denoted by the stem: *dolmalık* 'for stuffing (vegetables)', *elbiselik* 'for a dress', *karakolluk* 'requiring police intervention'
    b. when added to nouns, a place where the item denoted by the root is found in abundance: *kayalık* '(a) rocky (place)', *kumluk* '(a) sandy (place)'
    c. when added to nouns denoting periods of time, recurrent production or occurrence: *günlük* 'daily', *aylık* 'monthly'
    d. when added to numerals, the approximate age of a person: *ellilik* 'in (his/her) fifties', or the value or price of something: *yüz milyonluk* 'worth a hundred million'

(iii) adjectival phrases from quantitative expressions of the form numeral+noun, which according to the meaning of this noun can express weight, length, capacity, duration, value, price, etc.: *beş kiloluk* 'weighing five kilos', *üç saatlik* 'three-hour', *iki kişilik* 'suitable for two people', *beş yüz milyon liralık* 'worth five hundred million lira'.

-mAn   Forms adjectives and nouns with idiosyncratic meanings: *sarman* 'ginger' (used of cats), *toraman* 'sturdy', *katman* 'layer'. See also *-mAn* (7.2.1.1), the counterpart of this suffix which is added to verbs.

-rA   An unstressable suffix (4.3.2) which forms the locative pronouns *ne* 'what', to *bura-* 'here', *ora-* 'there', *nere-* 'where' (18.3.1) from demonstrative pronouns. In some dialects these can appear on their own, but in modern standard Turkish they must combine with at least one of the nominal inflectional suffixes (the plural suffix, case and possessive suffixes).

-sAK   Forms nouns: *tümsek* 'mound', *bağırsak* 'intestine'. See also *-sAk* (7.2.1.1), the counterpart of this suffix which is added to verbs.

-sAl   A suffix introduced as part of the language reform to replace the suffix *-(v)i* of Arabic origin (see below), it attaches to nouns to form adjectives that express the notion of relationship to the concept denoted by the root: *tarihsel* 'historic(al)', *yapısal* 'structural', *küresel* 'global'. In rare cases, it also forms nouns: *kumsal* 'sandy beach'. See also *-sAl* (7.2.1.1), the counterpart of this suffix which is added to verbs.

-sI   Like *-(I)msI* and *-(I)mtrak*, this suffix expresses similarity. Forms from nouns
(i) adjectives: *kadınsı* 'feminine', *çocuksu* 'childlike', 'naïve'
(ii) modal adverbs and discourse connectives: *doğrusu* 'frankly', *dahası* 'and what's more'. See also *-CAsI* above.

-sIl	Forms adjectives: *yoksul* 'poor', *varsıl* 'wealthy'.
-(s)InA	A composite of *-(s)I(n)* and *-A* suffix which forms adverbs: *inadına* 'out of spite', *üçyüz lirasına* 'for three hundred liras' (this latter used in betting or trading contexts).
-sIz	This productive suffix is added to: (i) nouns to form adjectives denoting that the entity described lacks whatever is expressed by the root or stem: *parasız* 'penniless', 'free (of charge)', *eşsiz* 'unequalled', *sınırsız* 'unlimited', *güvenliksiz* 'unsafe', 'unmonitored' (ii) nouns and pronouns to form adverbs denoting the non-involvement in an event of whatever is expressed by the root or stem: *arabasız* 'without a/the car', *parasız* 'free of charge', 'without paying', *sensiz* 'without you' (iii) nouns to form nouns (a rare usage): *aynasız* (slang) 'police officer', *telsiz* 'wireless', 'walkie-talkie', *Hamursuz* 'Passover'.
-(ş)Ar	This productive suffix forms distributive numerals from cardinal numbers (15.7.3): *üçer (kişi)* 'three (people) each', *onaltışar (kitap)* 'sixteen (books) each', and to the question word *kaç* 'how many': *kaçar* 'how many each'. When combining with *yarım* 'half', the initial consonant remains: *yarımşar* 'half each'.
-tay	Forms nouns denoting an institution from nouns: *Yargıtay* 'Supreme Court'. See also *-tay* (7.2.1.1), the counterpart of this suffix which is added to verbs.
-tI	Added to onomatopoeic stems to form nouns: *gıcırtı* 'squeak', *takırtı* 'rattle', *gürültü* 'noise'.
-vari	A suffix of Persian origin (pronounced [vaːɾí]or [vaːɾíː]) which is going out of usage: *gangstervari* 'gangsterlike', *Amerikanvari* 'American-style'.
-(v)i	A suffix of Arabic origin (pronounced [viː]) which forms adjectives: *milli* 'national', *resmi* 'official', *hukuki* 'legal', *ananevi* 'traditional'.
-(y)A₁	A suffix of Arabic origin which indicates feminine gender: *müdire* 'female director'. Also appears in names given to women: *Aliye*, *Semiha*.
-(y)A₂	Forms adverbs from identical nouns by attaching to the second one: *üst üste* 'on top of each other', *yan yana* 'next to each other', *kız kıza* 'as two girls'. See also (9.3.2).
-(y)at	A suffix of Arabic origin which forms nouns, some of them with plural meaning: *tahkikat* 'investigation', *ihracat* 'exports', *maddiyat* 'material things'.
-(y)In	An unstressable suffix (4.3.2) forms adverbs from nouns denoting seasons, deriving adverbials: *yazın* 'in (the) summer', *kışın* 'in (the) winter'. See also *-lArI(n)* and *-leyin* above.

-zade	A suffix of Persian origin which forms nouns that refer to a (male) child: *şehzade* 'son of a sultan', *haramzade* 'villain'.
-zede	A suffix of Persian origin, which when added to nouns forms nouns indicating the victim of some catastrophic event: *depremzede* 'earthquake victim', *felaketzede* 'victim of a (certain) disaster'.

7.3 The internal ordering of derivational suffixes

There are no clear-cut rules governing all combinations of derivational suffixes. However, there are a few points which apply to the majority of cases:

(i) Unproductive derivational suffixes tend not to co-occur.
(ii) Suffixes which are unproductive tend to precede productive ones (although it may be very difficult in many cases to decide which category a suffix belongs to). For example, the productive noun-deriving suffix *-lIK* follows the unproductive *-(h)ane*:

    hasta- 'patient' + *-(h)ane* → *hastane* 'hospital' + *-lIk* → *hastanelik* 'in a state suitable for hospitalisation'.

But the same suffix *-lIk* can occur before or after an equally productive one, e.g. the noun-deriving suffix *-CI*:

    göz 'eye' + *-lIK*→ *gözlük* 'spectacles' + *-CI* → *gözlükçü* 'optician'
    göz 'eye' + *-CI* → *gözcü* 'guard' + *-lIK* → *gözcülük* 'being a guard'

It can also recur in the same word:

    göz-lük-çü-lük 'the profession/business of an optician'

7.4 Prefixation

Apart from the reduplicative prefixes discussed in 9.1 and 9.2, the only other prefixes in Turkish are of foreign origin:

    antidemokratik 'antidemocratic'
    postmodern 'postmodern'
    gayrimüslim 'non-Muslim'
    bihaber 'unaware', 'ignorant'
    namütenahi 'infinite'

With the exception of *anti-*, which has some degree of productivity, these prefixes occur only with loanwords. Most of the words thus formed are stressed on the (first syllable of the) prefix.

Chapter 8

Inflectional suffixes

Inflectional suffixes indicate how the constituents of a sentence relate to each other and express functional relations such as **number, case, person** and **tense**. In this chapter, a description of the forms and attachment properties of these suffixes is provided; for the meaning and usage of each suffix, the reader is referred to the relevant chapters in Part 3.

In section 8.1 we discuss the inflectional suffixes that attach to nominals and in section 8.2 those that attach to verbs. Sections 8.3 and 8.4 focus on **copular markers** and **person markers**. Section 8.5 explains the attachment properties of suffixes which form subordinate clauses.

8.1 Nominal inflectional suffixes

The suffixes that attach to nominals are those marking number, person (expressed by possessive suffixes) and case. The only number suffix is the plural suffix *-lAr*. The order in which nominal inflectional suffixes appear on the stem is number-person-case:

(1) çocuk   -lar   -ım   -a
    child   -PL   -1SG.POSS   -DAT
              NUMBER   PERSON   CASE

   'to my children'

For an exception, see Chapter 14 (38).

These forms can further be combined with the copular markers (8.3.2), *-DIr* (8.3.3) and person markers (8.4) to form predicates (12.1.1.2):

(2) Ev   -ler   -imiz   -de   -ymiş   -ler.
    home -PL   -1PL.POSS   -LOC   -EV.COP   -3PL
    'Apparently they are/were at our homes.'

8.1.1 The plural suffix -lAr

The suffix -*lAr* (14.3.1.1) is used primarily to indicate plurality: *köpekler* 'dogs', *sular* '[glasses, etc. of] water', *şunlar* 'these', *sarılar* 'the yellow [ones]'. For other functions see 14.3.1.2. This suffix should not be confused with the 3rd person plural marker -*lAr* which appears, as at the end of example (2) above, on predicates to indicate subject agreement (8.4 and 12.2.1-2).

8.1.2 Possessive suffixes

The forms of the possessive suffix are:

1st person singular		-(I)m	'my'
2nd person singular	(familiar)	-(I)n	'your'
	(formal)	-(I)nIz	'your'
3rd person singular		-(s)I(n)	'his', 'her', 'its', 'their'
1st person plural		-(I)mIz	'our'
2nd person plural		-(I)nIz	'your'
3rd person plural		-lArI(n)	'their'

Examples:

ev-**im**	'my house'	araba-**m**	'my car'
ev-**in**	'your house' (familiar)	araba-**n**	'your car' (familiar)
ev-**iniz**	'your house' (formal)	araba-**nız**	'your car' (formal)
ev-**i**	'his/her/their house'	araba-**sı**	'his/her/their car'
ev-**imiz**	'our house'	araba-**mız**	'our car'
ev-**iniz**	'your house'	araba-**nız**	'your car'
ev-**leri**	'their house(s)'	araba-**ları**	'their car(s)'

For the number ambiguity in the 3rd person forms see 14.3.2 and 14.4.

Apart from indicating the possessor in a noun phrase (14.3.2, 14.4), possessive suffixes are also added to the subordinating suffixes -*DIK*, -*(y)AcAK*, -*mA* and -*(y)Iş* (8.5.1) to mark the subject of the subordinate clause: *ilgilendiğimiz* (*konular*) '(the topics) that we are interested in', *gidecekleri* (*ülke*) '(the country) that they will go to', *anlamanız* (*için*) 'so that you understand', (*kitabı*) *okuyuşu* 'his/her reading the book'. For a full discussion see Chapters 24–6.

Possessive suffixes can be followed by case markers: *odamda* 'in my room', the marker -*(y)lA/ile* 'with', 'by', 'and' (8.1.4): *annemle* 'with my mother', 'my mother and...' and to a limited extent by the adverbial suffix -*CA₁* (7.2.2.2): *kanımca* 'in my opinion'.

The 3rd person singular form -*(s)I(n)* appears as -*(s)I* when no other suffix follows it: *tepesi* 'its summit/top', *yüzü* 'his/her face'. When it is followed by a case suffix or by the adverbial suffix -*CA₁*, it appears as -*(s)In*: *tepesinde* 'at its summit/ top', *yüzüne* 'to his/her face', *fikrince* 'in his/her opinion'. Similarly, the 3rd person plural form -*lArI(n)* appears as -*lArI* when no other suffix follows it. However, when there is a case suffix or -*CA₁* following it, it appears as -*lArIn*: *elbiselerine* 'to their dress(es)'. For the ambiguity of words containing the 3rd person plural possessive form, e.g. *ev-lerin-e* 'to their house(s)' and words containing the plural suffix + 3rd person singular possessive marker, e.g. *ev-ler-in-e* 'to his/her houses', 'to their houses' see 14.3.2. In this book, for reasons of simplicity, we use the forms -*(s)I* and -*lArI* when referring to these suffixes.

The suffix -*(s)I* has a number of functions in addition to those that it shares with the other possessive suffixes:

(i) It marks the head of a noun compound: *düğün pastası* 'wedding cake' (10.2, 24.6).
(ii) It occurs in some composite suffixes: *anlamazmışçasına* 'as if uncomprehending' (26.3.8 (ii)).
(iii) It marks the head of a partitive construction: *kitaplardan üç tanesi* 'three of the books' (14.5.2–3).
(iv) It forms pronominals from a variety of word classes: *burası* 'this place', *içerisi* 'the inside', *eskisi* 'the old one', *hiçbiri(si)* 'none of them' (18.3–4).
(v) It appears on (impersonal) verbal nouns which contain -*mA*: *okuması zor* '[it] is difficult to read' (24.4.2.2).

8.1.3 Case suffixes

Turkish has five case suffixes:

-*(y)I*	Marker of the **accusative** case: *sarayı* 'the palace (ACC)', *suyu* 'the water (ACC)', *küçüğü* 'the small one (ACC)'
-*(y)A*	Marker of the **dative** case: *Kars'a* 'to Kars', *dereye* '(in)to the river', *masaya* 'on (to) the table', *size* 'to you'
-*DA*	Marker of the **locative** case: *radyoda* 'on the radio', *evde* 'at home', *sepette* 'in the basket'
-*Dan*	Marker of the **ablative** case: *okuldan* 'from/out of (the) school', *sonuçtan* 'from the result', *sisten* 'from the fog'
-*(n)In/-Im*	Marker of the **genitive** case: *çocuğun* 'the child's', *Fatma'nın* 'Fatma's', *bahçenin* 'of the garden'. -*Im* attaches only to 1st person pronouns: *benim* 'my', *bizim* 'our'

The function of these suffixes is discussed in 14.3.3.

8.1.4 Other nominal inflectional markers

-*(y)lA/ile* This marker can have comitative, instrumental or conjunctive meaning. In all of these functions it appears predominantly in the suffixal form *-(y)lA* and less commonly as the separate form *ile*. The comitative/instrumental marker forms postpositional phrases (17.2.1 (iii)). Like the dative, locative and ablative case markers it attaches to noun phrases enabling them to function as oblique objects (13.1.2.2) or adverbials (13.1.3 (v)). However, unlike case suffixes, it is unstressable (4.3.2): *Ahmét'le* 'with Ahmet' (comitative), *kalémle* 'with a pen/pencil' (instrumental), *baltáyla* 'with an axe' (instrumental). This marker also functions as a noun phrase conjunction: *Ahmet'le Mehmet* 'Ahmet and Mehmet', *kedimle köpeğim* 'my cat and my dog' (28.3.1.1 (ii)).

In the standard language, *-(y)lA* attaches to the genitive-marked forms of the following pronouns (the **genitive-attracting pronouns**), except where the plural suffix *-lAr* is also present (17.2.1):

(i) simple personal pronouns (18.1.1): *benimle* 'with me'
(ii) demonstrative pronouns (18.2): *şununla* 'with this/that one'
(iii) *kim* 'who' (19.2.1.1): *kiminle* 'with whom'

The free-standing form *ile* is not used with genitive-attracting pronouns. In everyday colloquial speech, *-(y)lA* may be attached directly to pronouns without an intervening genitive case marker: *benle* 'with me', *şunla* 'with this/that one' (6.2 (ii.a)), *kimle* 'who with', and in even more informal contexts 'l' may be pronounced as [n] with the marker itself sometimes followed by [n]: *Fatma'ynan, şunnan, kimnen*.

-ki(n) This is a stressable suffix whose vowel is invariable except that, in some cases, it harmonizes with a preceding 'ü': *evdeki* '(the one) in the house', *oradaki* '(the one) over there', *sizinki* 'yours', *kızınki* 'the one belonging to the girl', *suyunki* 'the one belonging to (the) water'. When it follows *dün* 'yesterday' and *gün* 'day' and words containing *gün*, it is sometimes pronounced and written with 'ü': *bugünkü/bugünki* 'today's', *dünkü/dünki* 'yesterday's'. In all other cases where it follows 'ü' it is more likely to be pronounced as 'i': *gülünki* 'that of the rose'. The consonant 'n' appears only when *-ki* is followed by a case suffix or *-CA₁*: *evdekinde* 'in/on/at the one in the house' (6.2 (ii.b)). In this book, for reasons of simplicity, we refer to this suffix as *-ki*. (The suffix *-ki* should not be confused with the clitic *ki* (11.1.1.4)).

-ki has two main functions: to form attributive adjectival phrases (15.3.6–7) and to form pronominal expressions (18.5). These are formed in the following ways:

(i) By attaching *-ki* directly to adverbials which express a location in time: *yarınki (gazete)* 'tomorrow's (newspaper)', *bu seneki (portakallar)* 'this year's oranges', *her zamanki* 'the usual (one)', *salıki toplantı* 'Tuesday's meeting'. Note that the only other days of the week that can directly combine with -*ki* are *pazar* 'Sunday' and *cuma* 'Friday'. All days of the week, including the above three, can combine with -*ki* in the form of a -*(s)I* compound where the compound marker is deleted before the affixation of -*ki*: *salı günkü (programlar)* 'Tuesday's (programmes)', *çarşamba günkü konuşmamız* 'our conversation on Wednesday'.

(ii) By attaching -*ki* to noun phrases and postpositions which contain the locative suffix: *sokak**taki** araba* 'the car on the street', *önünüz**deki*** 'the one in front of you'.

(iii) By attaching -*ki* to noun phrases which contain the genitive suffix: *sen**inki*** 'yours', *adam**ınki*** 'the man's [one]', *odan**ınki*** 'the one belonging to the room'. Expressions formed in this way are pronominal only.

Any *pronominal* form containing -*ki* can be further inflected by adding:

(i) The plural suffix -*lAr*: *masadaki**ler*** 'the ones on the table', *masanınki**ler*** 'the ones which belong to the table'. As a result, words which contain -*ki* can sometimes have more than one plural suffix: *masa**lar**daki**ler*** 'the ones on the tables'.

(ii) A case suffix, which can be added to a singular or plural form: *bendeki**ne*** 'to the one that I have', *mutfağınki**leri*** 'the ones belonging to the kitchen (ACC)', *bahçedeki**nden*** 'of/from the one in the garden'. As a result, words which contain -*ki* can sometimes have more than one locative or genitive marker: *anneminki**nin** (rengi)* '(the colour) of my mother's one', *evdeki**lerde*** 'at/on/in the ones in the house'.

(iii) One of the markers -*(y)lA/ile* (see above), -*CA₁* 'according to', 'by' (7.2.2.2, 16.1.6) or -*sIz* 'without' (7.2.2.2). The combination with -*(y)lA/ile* is regular: *sokaktaki**yle*** 'with the one on the street', *mutfaktakiler**le*** 'with the ones in the kitchen', *arabanınki**yle*** 'with the one belonging to the car', *perdeninkiler**le*** 'with the ones belonging to the curtain'. On the rare occasions when -*ki* combines with -*CA₁* or -*sIz*, these attach to the plural form: *Amerika'dakiler**ce*** 'by the ones in America', *bahçedekiler**siz*** 'without the ones in the garden'.

-*ki(n)* can combine with a genitive or locative form that already contains -*ki(n)*:

*ev-de-**ki**-ler-in-**ki*** (house-LOC-Kİ-PL-GEN-Kİ)   'the one belonging to those at home',

*masa-nın-**kin**-de-**ki*** (table-GEN-Kİ-LOC-Kİ)   'the one in the table's' (where "the table's" could refer e.g. to a drawer)

8.2 Verbal inflectional suffixes

There are two distinct types of verb form in Turkish: **finite** and **non-finite**.

(i) Finite verb forms:
The inflectional suffixes that can appear in finite verb forms are the following:

> Voice suffixes (8.2.1)
> The negative marker (8.2.2)
> Tense, aspect and modality markers (8.2.3)
> Copular markers (8.3)
> Person markers (8.4)

A finite verb form in Turkish obligatorily contains a **person marker** from Groups 1–4 (8.4), which indicates the subject:

(3) Otur-acağ-ım.
 sit.down-FUT-1SG
 'I'm going to sit down.'

Note that a 3rd person singular subject is indicated by the *absence* of any person marker, except where the relevant group is Group 3 or 4:

(4) Şu anda evden çık-tı.
  leave-PF
 'S/he has just left the house.'

In all forms except the imperative forms and the 3rd person optative, a verb must contain one of the **tense**, **aspect** and **modality** suffixes from Position 3 and may contain tense, aspect and modality suffixes from the other positions (8.2.3):

(5) Yüz-**üyor**-uz.
 swim-IMPF-1PL
 'We're swimming.'

Voice suffixes, the **negative marker** and **copular markers** may also occur in finite verb forms:

(6) Yık-**ıl-ma**-mış-tı.
 demolish-PASS-NEG-PF-P.COP
 'It had not been demolished.'

The order in which the suffixes appear in a finite verb form is:

STEM-VOICE-NEGATION-TENSE/ASPECT/MODALITY-COPULAR MARKER-PERSON
MARKER-*DIr*

(7) Döv-üş -tür -t -ül -me -yebil-iyor -muş -sunuz -dur.
    beat -REC-CAUS-CAUS-PASS -NEG -PSB-IMPF -EV.COP -2PL -GM
    'It is presumably the case that you (two) were not always made to fight against each other.'

Irregular combinations are explained in the description of individual suffixes.

(ii) Non-finite verb forms:
The inflectional suffixes that can appear in non-finite verb forms are the following:

Voice suffixes (8.2.1)
The negative marker (8.2.2)
Tense, aspect and modality markers from positions 1–2 (8.2.3.1–2)
Subordinating suffixes (8.5)
Nominal inflectional suffixes (8.1)

Non-finite verb forms obligatorily contain a **subordinating suffix** (also called a **subordinator**). Because these are **nominalized forms**, most of them can be followed by some or all of the nominal inflectional suffixes described in 8.1. For details see 8.5.

(8) sev-***mek***-le
    like-SUB-INS
    'by loving [him/her/it]'

The order of the suffixes in a non-finite verb form is the following:

STEM-VOICE-TENSE/ASPECT/MODALITY-NEGATION-SUBORDINATING SUFFIX-NOMINAL INFLECTIONAL MARKERS

(9) yaz -dır -a -ma -dığ -ım -dan
    write -CAUS -PSB -NEG -SUB -1SG.POSS -ABL
    (i) 'because I was unable to have [it] written'
    (ii) 'of the one I was unable to get written'

8.2.1 Voice suffixes

These are the **causative**, **passive**, **reflexive** and **reciprocal** suffixes. Voice suffixes come immediately after the verbal stem preceding all other suffixes. The only exception to this is the combination of the passive suffix with -*(y)Iver* (8.2.3.2). For the effect a voice suffix has on the structure of a clause see 13.2 and for the ordering of voice suffixes see 13.2.4.

8.2.1.1 Causative

The causative suffix attaches to **transitive** and **intransitive verb** stems. It has the following forms:

- *-DIr*   *yaptır-* 'make/let [s.o.] do/make/build [s.t.]', *koydur-* 'have/make [s.o.] put [s.t.] [s.w.]', *öldür-* 'kill', *doldur-* 'fill [s.t.]'
- *-t*   *kapat-* 'close [s.t.]', *daralt-* 'narrow down', 'reduce', *uyut-* 'make/let [s.o.] sleep'
- *-It*   *sarkıt-* 'dangle [s.t.]', *ürküt-* 'scare', *korkut-* 'scare'
- *-Ir*   *düşür-* 'drop', *bitir-* 'finish [s.t.]', *duyur-* 'announce'
- *-Ar*   *çıkar-* 'extract', *gider-* 'remove'
- *-Art*   *çökert-* 'crush'

The form of the causative suffix occurring with any particular verb stem is predictable, at least in part, from the form of the stem. Around thirty mono- syllabic stems, most of which are intransitive, combine with one of these forms: *-It, -Ir, Ar* or *-Art*.

Polysyllabic stems ending in a vowel, 'l' or 'r' combine with *-t*. In all other circumstances, *-DIr* is used.

It is possible for more than one causative suffix to appear simultaneously on a single verb stem. Such combinations conform to the rules given above. Thus *-t* follows *-DIr, -Ir* or *-Ar* (as these suffixes end in 'r') and *-DIr* follows *-t* or *-Art*: *bit-ir-t-tir-di* 's/he arranged for it to be finished'. For the syntactic properties of multiple causativization see 13.2.1.1.

Some intransitive verbs do not combine with the causative suffix and instead have unrelated transitive counterparts. For example, the transitive counterpart of *gir-* 'enter' is *sok-* 'insert' (also 'allow to enter'). These can be further causativized (as in *soktur-*). Another irregular verb is *em-* 'suck', for which the transitive form is *emzir-* 'breastfeed'. Some verbs which contain a form that looks like a causative suffix are not derived directly from an existing non-causative root, e.g. *getir-* 'bring', *götür-* 'take', *kaldır-* 'raise' (derived from *kalk-* 'rise'), none of which contain identifiable roots.

8.2.1.2 Passive

The passive suffix *-Il/(I)n* (can be attached to transitive and intransitive stems. It turns a transitive verb into an intransitive one, as in *sev-* 'love' → *sevil-* 'be loved' or an intransitive verb into a subjectless predicate (13.2.2.3–4).

The passive suffix has the following forms:

- *-n*   *aran-* 'be searched (for)', 'be rung up', *yıkan-* 'be washed'
- *-In*   *bilin-* 'be known', *delin-* 'be punctured/perforated'
- *-Il*   *yapıl-* 'be done/made/built', *görül-* 'be seen'

-*n* is attached to stems ending in a vowel, -*In* is attached to stems ending with the consonant 'l' and -*Il* is attached to stems ending with all other consonants.

8.2.1.3 Reflexive

The reflexive suffix -*(I)n* is an unproductive suffix. It attaches to transitive verbs, to form an intransitive verb denoting an action that one can perform on or for oneself, and combines only with a few stems, given below:

- *(I)n*   *giyin-* 'get dressed', *yıkan-* 'have a bath/shower', *kurulan-* 'dry oneself', *taran-* 'comb one's hair', *örtün-* 'cover oneself', *sarın-* 'wrap oneself (in)'

For the syntactic effects of reflexivization, see 13.2.3.1. For the non-reflexive usage of the suffix -*(I)n*, see 7.2.1.2.

Note that the reflexive suffix shares a form with the passive suffix. As a result, the reflexive and passive forms of some verbs are identical, e.g. *yıkan-* can mean 'be washed (by someone)' or 'have a bath/shower', depending on the context.

8.2.1.4 Reciprocal

The reciprocal suffix -*(I)ş* combines with only a few transitive and intransitive stems and indicates mutual involvement in an action. When it combines with a transitive stem it usually indicates the reciprocity of an action (i.e. A does x to B and B does x to A):

-*(I)ş*   *araş-* 'ring each other', *öpüş-* 'kiss each other', *seviş-* 'make love', 'love each other', *görüş-* 'see/meet up with each other'

Stems containing the reciprocal suffix tend not to combine with the similar-sounding verbal noun suffix -*(y)Iş* (8.5.2.1). Instead, they combine with -*mA* (8.5.1.2). Some verbs that seem to have a segment identical to a reciprocal suffix are not transparently related to a non-reciprocal stem, e.g. *konuş-* 'speak'. (See also -*(I)ş* (7.2.1.2) and -*lAş* (7.2.2.1.).)

8.2.2 The negative marker

The negative marker -*mA* is situated between voice suffixes and tense/ aspect/modality markers. There are irregularities in the combination of the negative marker with:

(i) the aorist -*(A/I)r/-z* (8.2.3.3)
(ii) the possibility suffix -*(y)A* (8.2.3.1)
(iii) the non-premeditative suffix -*(y)Iver* (8.2.3.2)

Inflectional suffixes   75

The vowel of the negative marker becomes a high vowel ('ı' or 'i') when it is followed by -(I)yor (8.2.3.3), -(y)AcAk (8.2.3.3) and a few other suffixes beginning with 'y' (2.6). In the case of the -mA + -(I)yor combination, the vowel also undergoes vowel harmony like an I-type suffix (3.2.1), which is reflected in the orthography: *anlamıyor* 's/he does not understand', *görmüyor* 's/he does not see'. For other examples see 2.6.

The negative marker is unstressable and causes the syllable before it to receive stress: *anlámadık* 'we did not understand', *anlaşílmasın* 'let it not be understood'. An exception to this rule is its combination with most forms of the aorist suffix where it becomes stressable: *anlamáz* 's/he does not understand'. For other examples see 8.2.3. For its effects on stress in combination with other items and sentence intonation, see 11.2.3 and 5.2.1 (i).

The negative marker occurs in composite suffixes such as *-mAdAn* and *-mAzdAn* (8.5.2.2). For its occurrence in compound verb forms, see 20.1.2.

8.2.3 Tense, aspect and modality markers

Most of the suffixes falling into this group have more than one function and may simultaneously mark tense, aspect and/or modality. The syntactic and semantic properties of these suffixes are discussed in detail in Chapters 21 and 27, and are summarized in Appendix 2.

When tense, aspect and modality markers co-occur, they appear in the order given below:

1	2	3	4	5
-(y)A (possibility)	-(y)Abil (possibility)	-DI (perfective)	*Copular markers*	-DIr
	-(y)Iver (non-premeditative)	-mIş (perfective evidential)	-(y)DI (past copula)	(generalizing modality)
	-(y)Agel	-sA (conditional)	-(y)mIş (evidential copula)	
	-(y)Ayaz	-(A/I)r/-z (aorist)	-(y)sA (conditional) copula)	
	-(y)Akal	-(y)AcAK (future)		
	-(y)Adur	-(I)yor (imperfective)		
		-mAlI (obligative)		
		-mAktA (imperfective)		
		-(y)A (optative)		
		-(y)AsI (desiderative)		

The following points should be noted:

(i) Suffixes which are in the same column cannot co-occur on a single stem.
(ii) Finite verbs (except for imperative forms (8.4.4) and 3rd person optative forms (8.4.3)) obligatorily contain a suffix from Position 3:

(10) Geç-**ti**-n.
　　　pass-PF-2SG
　　　　　3
　　　'You've pass*ed*.'

(11) itir-e-me-**miş**-tir.
　　　finish-PSB-NEG-PF-GM
　　　　1　　3　　5
　　　'S/he *has* probably not be*en* able to finish [it]'.

(12) Oku-yabil-**ecek**-miş.
　　　read-PSB-FUT-EV.COP
　　　　2　　3　　4
　　　'Apparently, s/he *will* be able to read [it].'

(iii) The markers in Positions 4–5 can also attach directly to a subject complement, to *değil* or to the existential expressions *var/yok* in nominal sentences (8.3, 12.1.1.2).

(13) Yazın Paris-te-**ydi**-k.
　　　　　　Paris-LOC-P.COP-1PL
　　　　　　　　　　4
　　　'We *were* in Paris during the summer.'

(14) O rehber değil-**miş**.
　　　　　　not-EV.COP
　　　　　　　4
　　　'Apparently, s/he is not a tour guide.'

(15) Mutlaka zamanı var-**dır**.
　　　　　　　　existent-GM
　　　　　　　　　　5
　　　'I'm sure s/he has the time.'

(iv) Non-finite verb forms obligatorily contain a subordinating suffix (8.5), but they can also contain suffixes from Positions 1–2.

(16) otur-**abil**-mek
　　　sit-PSB-VN
　　　　2
　　　'to *be able to* sit [down]'

8.2.3.1 Position 1

-(y)A　The possibility suffix *-(y)A* appears only in negative verb forms. It is the only tense/aspect/modality suffix that precedes the negative marker: *bakamayız* 'we cannot look', *göremiyordur* 's/he probably

can't see'. It can co-occur with the possibility suffix *-(y)Abil* from Position 2: *bakamayabiliriz* 'we may/might not be able to look'.

8.2.3.2 Position 2

The suffixes in this group are composite, consisting of one of the verb roots *bil-* 'know', *ver-* 'give', *gel-* 'come', *yaz-* 'make a mistake (obs.)', *dur-* 'stay' and *kal-* 'remain', here functioning as bound auxiliaries (13.3.1.1), preceded by the converbial suffix *-(y)A* or *-(y)I*. (8.5.2.2 (ii)). All of these suffixes except for *-(y)Abil* are stressed on the first syllable (4.3.1 (iii)). They occur with one of the suffixes in Position 3.

-(y)Abil   The possibility suffix *-(y)Abil* can occur with any of the suffixes in Position 3: *gide**bile**ceğim* 'I shall be able to go', *göre**bil**diğim* '(the one) that I can see'. See also *-(y)A* above.

-(y)Iver   This suffix can occur with all the suffixes in Position 3 except for *-mAktA*: *bitiri**ver**miş* 'apparently s/he finished [it] without effort', *pişiri**ver**irdim* 'I would just have cooked it'. It can either follow or, less commonly, precede the negative marker: *yap**may**ıverdi* 's/he simply didn't do [it]', *yap**ıver**medi* 's/he refrained from simply doing [it]'. Although it follows voice suffixes in general, it may precede the passive suffix: *yapılı**ver**di/yap**ıver**ildi* 'it was suddenly done'.

-(y)Agel, *-(y)Adur*, *-(y)Ayaz*, *-(y)Akal*
   These markers mostly occur in (semi-)lexicalized forms: *yap**agel**mişizdir* 'we have gone on doing [it]', *düş**eyaz**dım* 'I almost fell'. The most productive one is *-(y)Adur*: *oku**yadur*' 'go on reading' (13.3.1.1).

8.2.3.3 Position 3

-DI   The **perfective** suffix can be followed by a person marker from Group 1, one of the copular markers *-(y)DI* or *-(y)sA*, but not by *-(y)mIş* or *-DIr*: *olduk* 'we became', *gittiydin* 'you had left' (see *-(y)DI* (8.3.2)), *beklediysen* 'if you have waited'.

-mIş   The **evidential/perfective** suffix can be followed by a person marker from Group 2, any one of the copular markers and by *-DIr*. When it is *not* followed by another tense/aspect/modality marker, *-mIş* indicates both evidentiality and perfectivity: *koşmuş* '(apparently) s/he ran/has run', *unutmuşum* 'I seem to have forgotten'. When it is followed by a copular marker or *-DIr*, it indicates only perfectivity: *başlamıştık* 'we had started', *anlamamışsa* 'if s/he has not understood', *görmüşlerdir* 'they must have seen [it]'. Similarly, when *-mIş* is followed by an auxiliary verb in compound verb forms (13.3.1.2) it indicates only perfectivity: *yapmış olduk* 'we have done [it]', *görmüş bulunuyorum* 'I have seen [it]'.

-sA	The **conditional** suffix can be followed by a person marker from Group 1 or by *-(y)DI* or *-(y)mIş*, but not by *-(y)sA* or *-DIr*: *düşünsen* 'if you thought/were to think', *hazırla-masaydın* 'if you had not prepared [it]'. In colloquial speech *-sA* can be replaced by the optative suffix *-(y)A* (see below) when followed by a copular marker: *arasaydın/arayaydın* 'if (only) you had rung', 'you should have rung'.
-(A/I)r/-z	The **aorist** suffix is phonologically irregular, as it displays a variation between six vowels, 'ı', 'i', 'ü', 'u', 'a' and 'e'. It is also the only suffix that has a different form (*-z*) when used with the negative marker. The aorist suffix may be followed by a person marker from Group 2 or any one of the copular markers, but not by *-DIr*: *okurum* 'I read', *gülerdin* 'you used to/would laugh'.

The distribution of the different forms is as follows:

(i) *-(I)r* attaches to polysyllabic stems: *konuşur* 's/he speaks', *koparır* 's/he breaks [it]' and to monosyllabic stems which already contain a suffix: *ye-n-ir* 'it is eaten' (but *yen-er* 's/he beats [s.o]').

(ii) Monosyllabic verbs ending in 'l' or 'r' are unpredictable in terms of which form they combine with. Of the forty-odd monosyllabic stems that end in 'l' or 'r', the following combine with *-Ir*: *al-* 'take', *bil-* 'know', *bul-* 'find', *dur-* 'stop', *gel-* 'come', *gör-* 'see', *kal-* 'stay', 'remain', *ol-* 'be', *öl-* 'die', *var-* 'reach', *ver-* 'give', *vur-* 'hit': *bilir* 's/he knows', *kalır* 's/he stays', *görür* 's/he sees', *bulur* 's/he finds'. Other stems ending in 'l' or 'r' combine with *-Ar*: *örer* 's/he knits', *kurar* 's/he establishes'.

(iii) Monosyllabic verbs ending in any other consonant combine with *-Ar*, with the exception of *san-* 'imagine': *sanırım* 'I think'.

(iv) The way in which the aorist suffix combines with the negative marker *-mA* is highly irregular:

    a. The suffix itself takes a completely different form, *-z*, when it follows *-mA* in verb forms inflected for the 2nd and 3rd persons: *anlamazsın* 'you wouldn't understand', *gitmez* 's/he doesn't/won't/ wouldn't go'.

    b. *-z* is deleted before the 1st person singular and plural markers. In the 1st person singular form, the person marker *-(y)Im* is replaced by *-m*: *yemem* 'I won't/ wouldn't eat'. In the 1st person plural form, the person marker is placed immediately after the negative marker: *kalmayız* 'we won't/wouldn't stay'. This means that, in these particular forms, the aorist is expressed by the *absence* of a distinct suffix.

Inflectional suffixes 79

c. Unlike the negative marker in other contexts (8.2.2), the combination *-mA-z* is *stressed*. When it is followed by the 3rd person plural marker *-lAr*, *-mA-z* may or may not be stressed: *koşmazlár/koşmázlar* 'they will/do not run'. When the possibility suffix *-(y)A* precedes *-mA-z*, the former is stressed: *koşámaz* 's/he cannot run'.

The table below shows the negative aorist forms of the verb *bak-* 'look', both with and without the presence of a copular marker. In the second column the past copula *-(y)DI* is used as an example of a copular marker.

	Negative + aorist	*Negative + aorist + copular marker*
1SG	bak-**má**-m	bak-**má**-z-dı-m
2SG	bak-**má**-z-sın	bak-**má**-z-dı-n
3SG	bak-**má**-z	bak-**má**-z-dı
1PL	bak-**má**-yız	bak-**má**-z-dı-k
2PL	bak-**má**-z-sınız	bak-**má**-z-dı-nız
3PL	bak-**ma**-z-lár/ bak-**má**-z-lar	bak-**ma**-z-lár-dı/ bak-**má**-z-lar-dı

-(y)AcAK The future suffix may be followed by a person marker from Group 2, any one of the copular markers or by *-DIr*: *geleceğim* 'I shall come', *sileceKtiniz* 'you were going to erase [it]', *bulacaktır* 'I'm sure s/he'll find [it]'. Despite being written with 'a' or 'e', the initial syllable of the future suffix is often pronounced like an I-type suffix (3.2.1): *kalacak* 's/he will stay' [kʰahdʒákʰ], *dönecek* 's/he will return' [dönüdʒécʰ]. When this suffix is followed by a person marker starting with a vowel, the final 'k' is replaced by 'ğ' (1.1.1.1). In formal speech, the inflectional sections of forms such as *seveceğim* 'I will love' and *alacağım* 'I am going to take [it]' are pronounced as two consecutive vowels with stress on 'ce' or 'ca': [sevedʒéim] or [sevidʒéim], [atʰadʒáım] or [atʰıdʒáım]. But in everyday colloquial speech the combination of the future marker with person markers has a contracted version, as shown for the verb *in-* 'go/come down'. For a general discussion of the effect of the initial *-(y)* of a suffix on a preceding vowel see also 2.6.

Future marker *-(y)AcAk* + person marking:

	Formal	*Colloquial*
1SG *ineceğim*	[inedʒéim]/[inidʒéim]	[inidʒæm]
2SG *ineceksin*	[inedʒécsin]/[inidʒécsin]	[inidʒæn]
3SG *inecek*	[inedʒécʰ]/[inidʒécʰ]	[inidʒécʰ]
1PL *ineceğiz*	[inedʒéiz]/[inidʒéiz]	[inidʒæz]
2PL *ineceksiniz*	[inedʒécsiniz]/[inidʒécsiniz]	[inidʒæːníz]

3PL *inecekler* [inedʒeclæɾ]/[inidʒeclæɾ] [inidʒeclæɾ]

In the case of colloquial forms with back vowels, the [æ] in the future suffix is replaced by [a]: [jazɪdʒán] 'you are going to write', etc.

-(I)yor The **imperfective** suffix *-(I)yor* contains the obsolete verb stem *yor-* which is invariable. Except where the negative marker is present (8.2.2), *yor-* assigns stress to the preceding vowel, whether this vowel is *-(I)* or the final vowel of the stem that *-(I)yor* attaches to: *koşúyor* 's/he runs', *korúyor* 's/he protects'.

-(I)yor combines regularly with stems ending in a consonant: *satıyor* 's/he sells/is selling', *görüyor* 's/he sees'. Stems ending in a vowel combine with the component 'yor'. In the case of stems ending in a high vowel ('i', 'ı', 'ü' or 'u') '*yor*' is added directly to the stem: *eriyor* 'it melts/is melting', *kuruyor* 'it dries/is drying'. However, where a stem ends in 'a' or 'e', the combination with '*yor*' causes this vowel to become high (see 2.6). This high vowel is then subject to vowel harmony (3.2.1):

anla- 'understand' → *anlıyor* 's/he understands'
okşa- 'caress' → *okşuyor* 's/he caresses/is caressing'
bekle- 'wait' → *bekliyor* 's/he waits/is waiting'
özle- 'miss' → *özlüyor* 's/he misses'

The same situation occurs when *-(I)yor* is attached to the negative marker:

saklama- 'not hide' → *saklamıyor* 's/he doesn't hide/ is not hiding'
söyleme- 'not tell' → *söylemiyor* 's/he doesn't tell/ isn't telling'

-(I)yor may be followed by a person marker from Group 2, any one of the copular markers or by *-DIr*: *çalışıyorum* 'I work/am working', *arıyordu* 's/he was looking for [it]', *anlıyorsa* 'if s/he understands [it]', *gidiyordur* 's/he's probably going'. In colloquial speech the 'r' at the end of the suffix is often not pronounced when it is followed by a suffix beginning with a consonant: *gidiyorsun* 's/he goes/is going' [ɟidíjosun]/ [ɟidíjoɹsun], *ödüyorduk* 'we were paying' [ödǘjodukʰ]/ [ödǘjoɹdukʰ] or when it is at the end of a word: *sarıyor* 's/he wraps' [saríjo]/[saríjoɾ]. 'r' is retained when it is followed by a suffix beginning with a vowel: *seviyorum* 'I love/like' [sevíjorum].

-mAlI The obligative suffix may be followed by a person marker from Group 2 or by any one of the copular markers: *oturmamalısın* 'you must not sit', *anlattırmalıydılar* 'they should have made [him/her] tell [the story]'. In formal texts it can also be followed by *-DIr* when

the verb is in the 3rd person singular or plural form: *gitmelidir(ler)* 's/he/(they) should go', *yapılmamalıdır* 'it should not be done'.

-mAktA This is an **imperfective** suffix which is mostly used in formal contexts. It may be followed by a person marker from Group 2 or any one of the copular markers: *okumaktasın* 'you are (in the process of) reading', *bitirmekteydim* 'I was (in the process of) finishing'. It can also be followed by *-DIr* when the verb is in the 3rd person singular or plural form: *dönmektedirler* 'they are (in the process of) returning', *görülmemektedir* 'it is not seen/observed'.

-(y)A The **optative** suffix occurs mostly in the 1st person singular and plural forms: *gideyim* 'let me go', 'I'll go', *oturalım* 'let's sit (down)'. It may also occur in the 2nd person singular and plural forms, usually in adverbial clauses of purpose with the subordinator *diye* or *ki* (26.1.1.2, 26.1.2.2): *gösteresin (diye)* '(so that) you [can] indicate'. Apart from the person markers in Group 3, *-(y)A* may be followed by *-(y)DI* or *-(y)mIş*: *gideydim* 'if (only) I had gone'. In these combinations with copular markers *-(y)A* is a colloquial alternative to the conditional suffix *-sA* (see above).

-(y)AsI The **desiderative** suffix indicates an intention, inclination or temptation to perform an action. It is used rarely and with a few verbs: *gidesiyim* 'I feel like going'. It more often occurs with the auxiliary verb *ol-*: *gidesi oldum* 'I attempted to go' (21.5.3).

8.3 The copula 'be', copular markers and *-DIr*

The copular markers in Position 4 are composite. They are made up of the copula *-(y)-* and the suffixes *-DI*, *-mIş* and *-sA*.

8.3.1 The copula 'be'

The copula, which in most cases corresponds to the verb 'be', has different forms. These are:

(i) *-(y)-*: This appears in *-(y)DI*, *-(y)mIş*, *-(y)sA* and in the converbial form *-(y)ken* (8.5.2.2 (ii), 26.3.16 (iii)). The segment 'y' in these markers should not be confused with the consonant which occurs at the beginning of many suffixes for purposes of attachment (6.1.3). The markers containing the copula *-(y)-* are unstressable (4.3.2). *-(y)-* is the contracted form of *i-* below.

(ii) *i-*: This is a stem which appears in the now seldom used forms *idi*, *imiş*, *ise* and *iken*, e.g. *seviyor idiysen* 'if (as you imply) you loved [him/her]'. In the limited cases in which they are used in verbal forms, the form containing *i-* are most often the stressed word within the whole sentence and they are stressed on their second syllable. This is because they are used primarily for purposes of emphasizing the tense or modality that a particular copular marker expresses, especially by contrast to another tense or modality expressed in the preceding utterance. For example, in a context where someone makes a statement to the effect that Ahmet likes horror films, whereas the addressee believes that Ahmet used to like horror films but no longer does, s/he could respond by saying:

Sever i*di.*
'He *used* to.'

(iii) *ol-* (see 12.1.1.2–3).

8.3.2 The copular markers -(y)DI, -(y)mIş, -(y)sA

These markers are the contracted forms of *idi, imiş* and *ise* (8.3.1 (ii)). They attach to:

(i) Verbs containing one of the suffixes in Position 3 (for exceptions see the description of individual suffixes): *bırakmıştı* 's/he had left', *yürümekteymişler* 'they are/were apparently walking', *koşuyorsak* 'if we are running', *bitirmiş olacaklardı* 'they were supposed to have finished [it]'
(ii) Nominals (7.1.1) to form nominal predicates (12.1.1.2): *hastaydı* 's/he was ill', *evdeymişler* 'apparently they are/were at home', *heveslivsek* 'if we are enthusiastic'

Note that the component *-(y)-* (the copula proper) is omitted following a consonant: *satıyorduk* 'we were selling [it]', *yemişti* 's/he had eaten', *oynarsan* 'if you play'. *-(y)DI* and *-(y)sA* are followed by person markers belonging to Group 1 and *-(y)mIş* by person markers belonging to Group 2 (for details and exceptions see 8.4). The copular markers are unstressable and place stress on the (stressable) syllable before them (4.3.2).

-(y)DI The **past copula** can attach to:
(i) All suffixes in Position 3 on a verb stem: *koşuyordu* 's/he was running', *kalkmalıydı* 's/he should have got up'. The forms *-DIydI* and *-mIştI* are identical in meaning, but the former is restricted to colloquial or regional registers: *geldiydi* 's/he had arrived', *gelmişti* 's/he had arrived'. Note that *-(y)DI* can sometimes occur *after* a person marker which is attached to the perfective marker *-DI* (8.2.3.3): *gittimdi* 'I had been [there]', as well as before it: *gittiydim.*
(ii) Nominals: *öğretmenimdiniz* 'you were my teacher', *buradaydım* 'I was here', *hastaydık* 'we were ill'.

-(y)mIş	For the combination of the past copula with the conditional copula see *-(y)sA* below.
	The **evidential copula** can attach to:

- (i) All suffixes in Position 3 on a verb stem except for *-DI*: *anlıyormuşsun* 'you apparently understand/understood', *otursaymışlar/otursalarmış* 'apparently, if they had sat...'
- (ii) Nominals: *öğretmenmiş* 'apparently s/he is/was a teacher', *evimmiş* 'it is/was apparently my house'

For the combination of the evidential copula with the conditional copula see *-(y)sA* below.

-(y)sA   The **conditional copula** can attach to:

- (i) All suffixes in Position 3 except for *-sA*: *görmüşse* 'if s/he has (apparently) seen', *seviyorsan* 'if you love [him/her]'. Note that *-(y)sA* can also occur *after* a person marker which is attached to the perfective marker *-DI* (8.2.3.3): *gittimse* 'if I have gone [there]', as well as before it: *gittiysem*.
- (ii) Nominals: *şoförse* 'if s/he is a driver', *yaşlıysa* 'if s/he is old', *evdeysem* 'if I am at home'
- (iii) The copular markers *-(y)DI* and *-(y)mIş*. When *-(y)sA* combines with these other copular markers, *-(y)sA* usually follows them: *gidiyorduysan* 'if (as you imply) you were going', *bakıyormuşsan* 'if (as you say/as is claimed) you were looking'. However, some speakers use the reverse order with *-(y)DI*: *gidiyorsaydın*.

In nominal predicates, the free-standing forms *idiyse* and *imişse* can also be used: *masada idiyse* 'if it was on the table', *kiracı imişseler* 'if they are/were tenants'.

8.3.3 -DIr

The **generalizing modality marker** *-DIr*, also unstressable, follows the person markers of Group 2 (8.4.2), except in the case of the 3rd person plural suffix *-lAr*, which it may precede or follow:

1SG		*gid-iyor-um-**dur***	'I'm presumably going'
2SG	(familiar)	*gid-iyor-sun-**dur***	'you're presumably going'
	(formal)	*gid-iyor-sunuz-**dur***	'you're presumably going'
3SG		*gid-iyor-**dur***	's/he's presumably going'
1PL		*gid-iyor-uz-**dur***	'we're presumably going'
2PL		*gid-iyor-sunuz-**dur***	'you're presumably going'
3PL		*gid-iyor-lar-**dır**/gid-iyor-**dur**-lar*	'they're presumably going'

-*DIr* occurs in:

(i) Verbal forms which already contain one of the Position 3 suffixes *-mIş*, *-(y)AcaK*, *-(I)yor*, *-mAlI*, *-mAktA*: *anlamışlardır* 'they've probably understood', *unutacağızdır* 'we will almost certainly forget', *sanıyor-dur* 's/he's probably assuming', *bilmelidir* 's/he must know', *gitmekte-dir* 's/he is going'. In the case of *-mAlI* and *-mAktA*, combinations with *-DIr* occur mainly in the 3rd person singular and plural forms

(ii) Verbal forms which have the combination *-(I)yormuş* (the imperfective suffix followed by the evidential copula). This occurs only in colloquial speech: *bitiriyormuştur* 's/he must have been finishing [it]'

(iii) Nominal predicates: *yırtıcı bir kuştur*, 'it's a bird of prey', *güzelsindir* 'you are definitely pretty', *burdadır* 's/he's probably here', *vardır* 'there is/must be'

(iv) Expressions denoting a period of time: *bunca zamandır* 'for all this time' (16.1.7, 16.4.1.2 (iii.b), Chapter 19 (85))

When *-DIr* is attached to an indefinite noun phrase which is the subject or object in a sentence, it emphasizes the scale of the event described: *Bir curcunadır gidiyordu* 'There was pandemonium', *Bir inattır tutturdu* 'S/he is being totally unreasonable'.

8.4 Person markers

Person markers are attached to both verbal and nominal predicates to indicate the (grammatical person of the) subject. In most cases they follow all other suffixes: *kaçsan* 'if you ran away', *çalışıyoruz* 'we're working', *bakayım* 'let me see', *gidin* 'go!', *odamdayım* 'I'm in my room'. In the following contexts, however, person markers optionally or obligatorily precede another suffix:

(i) 1st and 2nd person forms which contain *-DIr* (8.3.3)
(ii) Verb forms with *-DI* followed by *-(y)DI* or *-(y)sA* (8.4.1)
(iii) The 3rd person plural suffix *-lAr*: When this suffix occurs in a form which contains a Position 3 suffix and a copular marker, its preferred position is between these two, but it may also come at the end:

kat-sa-**lar**-dı/kat-sa-ydı-**lar**	'if they had added [it]'
bak-acak-**lar**-mış/bak-acak-mış-**lar**	'apparently they are/were going to look'

In nominal predicates the 3rd person plural suffix normally follows a copular marker:

öğrenci-ydi-**ler**	'they were students'
hasta-ymış-sa-**lar**	'if they are/were ill'
mimar değil i-di-yse-ler	'if they aren't/weren't architects'

However, there are two exceptions:

a. When suffixed to a locative-marked noun phrase -*lAr* may precede a copular marker, although this is less common:

orada-ydı-lar (or *orada-lar-dı*)	'they were there'
evde-yse-ler (or *evde-ler-se*)	'if they are at home'

b. When suffixed to one of the negation markers *değil* or *yok* (20.2–3), -*lAr* normally precedes a copular marker, although the reverse order is also possible:

öğrenci değil-ler-di (or *değil-di-ler*)	'they were not students'
evde yok-lar-mış (or *yok-muş-lar*)	'apparently they are/were not at home'

A non-case-marked subject complement to which the 3rd person plural predicate marker -*lAr* has been added should not be confused with a noun phrase containing the number suffix, that is, the plural marker -*lAr*. In the former case -*lAr* is unstressable, whereas in the latter case it is stressable (see also Chapter 22 (39)):

Öğretménler. 'They are teachers.'	(3rd person plural predicate marker)
öğretmenlér '(the) teachers'	(number suffix)

For the circumstances under which the 3rd person plural predicate marker can be used or omitted, see 12.2.1–2. The conditions that apply to the usage of the familiar and formal 2nd person singular forms in the groups below are the same as those described for the selection of the 2nd person singular pronouns *sen* 'you' (familiar), *siz* 'you' (formal) or *sizler* (formal) in 18.1.1.

There are four groups of person markers that occur in predicates. Most of these person markers are stressable. For the unstressable ones, see 11.1.1.8.

8.4.1 Group 1

1st person singular	-*m*
2nd person singular (familiar)	-*n*
(formal)	-*nIz*
3rd person singular	-
1st person plural	-*k*
2nd person plural	-*nIz*
3rd person plural	(-*lAr*)

The 3rd person singular is expressed by the absence of any suffix: *geldi* 's/he has arrived', *kalsa* 'if s/he were to stay', *yazmıştı* 's/he had written'.

The markers in this group are used after:

(i) The Position 3 verbal suffixes -*DI* and -*sA*: *çekildiniz* 'you retreated', *baktılar* 'they looked', *bıraksak* 'if we were to leave [it]', *uyusan* 'if you slept', *kaldılar* 'they stayed'
(ii) The copular markers -*(y)DI* and -*(y)sA*: *çekilirdiniz* 'you used to retreat', *bırakıyorsak* 'if we are leaving [it]', *evdeydik* 'we were at home', *hastaysalar* 'if they are ill'
(iii) The negative marker in 1st person singular negative aorist verb forms: *koşamam* 'I cannot run', *tekrarlamam* 'I will not repeat [it]'

When a verb form contains -*DI* followed by -*(y)DI* or -*(y)sA*, the person markers can occur either after -*DI* or after the copular marker: *geldinizse/ geldiyseniz* 'if you have arrived', *baktıydık/baktıktı* 'we had looked'.

8.4.2 Group 2

1st person singular	-*(y)Im*
2nd person singular (familiar)	-*sIn*
(formal)	-*sInIz*
3rd person singular	-
1st person plural	-*(y)Iz*
2nd person plural	-*sInIz*
3rd person plural	(-*lAr*)

The 3rd person singular is indicated by the absence of any suffix: *okuyormuş* 'apparently s/he's reading', *bakacak* 's/he's going to look' or*ada* 's/he's there'.

The markers in this group are used after:

(i) The Position 3 verbal suffixes -*mIş*, -*(A/I)r/-z*, -*(y)AcAK*, -*(I)yor*, -*mAlI*, -*mAktA*, -*(y)AsI*: *unutmuşsun* 'you seem to have forgotten', *biliriz* 'we know', *hatırlamalıyım* 'I must remember', *gideceğim* 'I shall go', *ilgilenmemişler* 'apparently they did not take any notice'
(ii) The copular marker -*(y)mIş*: *çalışmalıymışız* 'apparently we have to work', *söylüyormuşsunuz* 'apparently you've been saying'.
(iii) Nominals which are part of nominal predicates: *okuldayım* 'I'm at school', *hastasınız* 'you're ill', *buradalar* 'they're here'.
(iv) The negative marker -*mA* in 1st person plural negative aorist verb forms: *gitmeyiz* 'we will not go'

In colloquial speech the 's' in the forms -*mIşsIn(Iz)* (evidential/perfective suffix + 2nd person singular/plural) and -*(y)mIşsIn(Iz)* (evidential copula + 2nd person singular/plural) can be deleted, reducing these forms to -*mIşIn(Iz)* and -*(y)mIşIn(Iz)*: *satmışın* 'I hear you've sold [it]', *bitiriy-ormuşunuz* 'I gather you're finishing [it]'. The combination of Group 2 person markers with the future suffix also has a colloquial version (see - *(y)AcAk*, 8.2.3.3).

8.4.3 Group 3

1st person singular	-*yIm*
2nd person singular (familiar)	-*sIn*
(formal)	-*sInIz*
3rd person singular	-*sIn*
1st person plural	-*lIm*
2nd person plural	-*sInIz*
3rd person plural	-*sIn(lAr)*

All of the person markers above except the 3rd person forms attach to the optative suffix -*(y)A* (8.2.3.3) or the desiderative suffix -*(y)AsI*: *bakayım* 'let me see', *oynayabilesiniz* '[so that] you would be able to play', *kaçalım* 'let us escape', *yiyesiyim* 'I feel like eating'. The 3rd person forms -*sIn* and -*sInlar* do not attach to the optative suffix (or to any other Position 3 suffix) but conjoin directly with the verb (which may contain a suffix from Position 2): *kalkmayıversin* 'let him/her just not get up', *bitirebilsinler* '[so that] they are able to finish [it]'.

8.4.4 Group 4

2nd person singular (familiar)	-, -*sAnA*
(formal)	-*(y)In*, -*(y)InIz*, -*sAnIzA*
3rd person singular	-*sIn*
2nd person plural	-*(y)In*, -*(y)InIz*, -*sAnIzA*
3rd person plural	-*sIn(lAr)*

These are person markers used in imperative forms. They attach directly to the verb stem: *okutun* 'make [him/her/them] read', *gel* 'come here!'. Note that the 3rd person singular and plural forms are identical with those in Group 3 and may express either wishes or instructions: *geçmiş olsun* 'may it (your present or recent trouble) soon be over/not return', *gitsin* 'let him/her/it go', *beklemesinler* 'tell them not to wait'. The 2nd person is expressed by the absence of a suffix and the persuasive imperative forms, used mostly in informal speech, -*sAnA* and -*sAnIzA*, are composite forms containing the conditional suffix, the 2nd person markers from Group 1 and the harmonized interjection *A*. These two person markers are mostly used for expressing suggestions rather than orders: *otursanıza* 'why don't you sit down', *oturun* 'sit down!' (21.4.4.2).

8.5 Subordinating suffixes

Suffixation is the primary means of forming subordinate clauses in Turkish. Subordinating suffixes are nominalizing suffixes. Apart from a few which can attach also to nominal stems (8.5.2.2), subordinating suffixes combine with verb stems to form nominals, some of which can be inflected with the plural suffix (8.1.1), the appropriate possessive marker (8.1.2) to refer to the subject of the subordinate clause, a case suffix (8.1.3) and *-(y)lA* or *-ki* (8.1.4). Any verb form which contains a subordinating suffix is **non-finite**. Non-finite verb forms are of the three following types:

(i) **verbal nouns**: these are non-finite verbs of **noun clauses** (Chapter 24)
(ii) **participles**: these are non-finite verbs of **relative clauses** (Chapter 25)
(iii) **converbs**: these are non-finite verbs of **adverbial clauses** (Chapter 26)

Some examples are:

(17) [Sorun **yarat-*acağ-ı***] belli.   (Verbal noun)
problem create-VN-3SG.POSS clear
'It is clear [*that s/he/it will create* problems].'

(18) [Sorun **yarat-*an***] kuruluş-lar uyar-ıl-dı.   (Participle)
problem create-PART organization-PL admonish-PASS-PF
'The organizations [*that were creating* problems] were admonished.'

(19) [Sorun **yarat-*maktansa***] sonuç-lar-ı kabullen-di. (Converb)
problem create-CV consequence-PL-ACC accept-PF
'[*Instead of creating* problems] s/he accepted the consequences.'

The majority of subordinating suffixes in Turkish form only one of the three types of non-finite verb. However, certain subordinators, namely *-DIK*, *-(y)AcAK*, *-mA* and *-mAK* can form more than one type of subordinate clause. In this section we describe the attachment properties and morphological characteristics of each subordinating suffix. For a full discussion of their functions see Chapters 24–7. Note that where person marking is obligatory in a particular non-finite form, this is indicated below by the 3rd person singular form.

8.5.1 Multi-functional subordinating suffixes: -DIK, -(y)AcAK, -mA, -mAK

8.5.1.1 -DIK, -(y)AcAK

-DIK and *-(y)AcAK* form all three types of subordinate clause. They can be followed by possessive suffixes and case suffixes. Where they function as participles in pronominal relative clauses (25.3), they can be followed by all of the nominal inflectional suffixes described in 8.1, including the plural marker, *-(y)lA* and *-ki*: *sattıklarımınki* 'the one belonging to those that I sell/sold'.

-DIK: This suffix usually expresses present or past time. It forms:

(i) Verbal nouns: *gitti**ği**ni* (*bil-*) '(know) that s/he has left', *kıskandır**dığ**ınızı* (*anla-*) '(understand) that you are making/have made [s.o.] envious' (24.4.3).
(ii) Participles: *göreme**diğ**im* (*film*) '(the film) that I was not able to see', *öpüş**tüğ**ü* (*kız*) '(the girl) (whom) s/he has kissed/is kissing' (25.1.1.2).
(iii) Converbs: *bak**tığ**ımızda* 'when we look/looked', *anla**dığ**ımdan* 'because I understand/(have) understood'.

-DIK has a converbial function when it occurs in one of the following combinations (26.2–3), some of which involve postpositions (Chapter 17):

> *-DIğIndA*: *yürü**düğ**ümde* 'when I walk'
> *-DIkçA*: *koş**tuk**ça* 'the more [s.o.] runs'
> *-DIğIndAn* (*beri/dolayı/ötürü*): *gel**diğ**imizden beri* 'since we arrived'
> *-DIğI* (*için/zaman/sırada/anda/halde/kadarıyla/takdirde/gibi/sürece/nispette*): *bakma**dığ**ım için* 'because I haven't looked/am/was not looking', *gör**düğ**üm anda* 'the moment I saw [it]'
> *-DIğInA* (*göre*): *isteme**diğ**inize göre* 'since you don't/didn't want [it]'
> *-DIktAn* (*sonra/başka*): *al**dık**tan sonra* 'after taking [it]', *anla**dık**tan başka* 'in addition to understanding'

-(y)AcAK: This subordinator indicates (relative) future time and forms:

(i) Verbal nouns: *anla**yacağ**ımı* (*san-*) '(imagine) that I would understand', *ite**ceğ**ini* (*düşün-*) '(think) that s/he would push' (24.4.3)
(ii) Participles: *oku**yacağ**ım* (*kitap*) '(the book) that I am/was going to read', *seveme**yeceğ**im* (*bir kişi*) '(a person) that I shall/would not be able to like', *görü**şeceğ**i* (*doktor*) '(the doctor) whom s/he is/was going to see' (25.1.1.2)
(iii) Converbs: *öğrene**ceğ**ine* 'instead of learning', *isteye**ceğ**imden* 'because I am going to want'

-(y)AcAK has a converbial function when it occurs in one of the following combinations (26.2–3), some of which involve postpositions (Chapter 17):

> *-(y)AcAğI* (*için/zaman/sırada/anda/halde/gibi*): *kalka**cağ**ın zaman* 'when you are going to get up', *oturmaya**cağ**ı için* 'because s/he isn't/wasn't going to stay', *gide**ceğ**i gibi* 'in addition to the fact that s/he is/was going to go'
> *-(y)AcAğIndAn* (*dolayı/ötürü*): *satmaya**cağ**ından ötürü* 'on account of the fact that s/he is/was not going to sell [it]'
> *-(y)AcAğInA* (*göre*): *içmeye**ceğ**ime göre* 'since I am/was not going to drink [it]'
> *-(y)AcAk* (*kadar/derecede*): *sakla**yacak** kadar* 'to the point of hiding [it]'

Note that words containing the subordinating suffix *-(y)AcAK* have a different stress pattern and pronunciation from finite verbs containing the future marker *-(y)AcAK* (8.2.3.3). The finite forms which contain the future marker *-(y)AcAK* combine with the unstressable person markers (8.4.2, 11.1.1.8,) and have short vowels, whereas the non-finite forms which contain the subordinator *-(y)AcAK* are followed by stressable possessive markers (8.1.2). However, in the colloquial contracted forms that occur in non-finite as well as finite future verbs, this distinction in stress is neutralized in the 1st and 2nd person singular and plural forms. (Compare the table below with that given for the same verb *in-* 'go/come down' in 8.2.3.3.)

Subordinator *-(y)AcAk* + possessive marking:

	Formal	*Colloquial*
1SG *ineceğim*	[inedʒeím]/[inidʒeím]	[inidʒǽ:m]
2SG *ineceğin*	[inedʒeín]/[inidʒeín]	[inidʒǽ:n]
3SG *ineceği*	[inedʒeí]/[inidʒeí]	[inidʒǽ:]
1PL *ineceğimiz*	[inedʒeimíz]/[inidʒeimíz]	[inidʒæ:míz]
2PL *ineceğiniz*	[inedʒeiníz]/[inidʒeiníz]	[inidʒæ:níz]
3PL *inecekleri*	[inedʒeclerí]/[inidʒeclerí]	[inidʒeclerí]

8.5.1.2 -mA, -mAK

Both *-mA* and *-mAK* form verbal nouns and converbs. These two suffixes differ in respect of which nominal inflectional markers they can combine with. The plural suffix attaches to *-mA* only: (*evden*) *kaçmalar* 'incidents of running away (from home)'. Combinability with possessive suffixes is the most significant difference between the two subordinators. While *-mA* is often followed by one of the possessive markers, *-mAK* cannot combine with them:

-mA
koşmam (için)
'(in order for) me to run'

-mAK
koşmak (için)
'(in order) to run'

These forms can be inflected for case:

gitmenizi (bekliyor)
's/he expects you to leave'

gitmeyi (bekliyor)
's/he expects to leave'

şarkı söylemene (bayılıyor)
's/he loves [the way] you sing'

şarkı söylemeye (bayılıyor)
's/he loves singing'

koşmamda (ısrar etti)
's/he insisted that I run/ran'

koşmakta (ısrar etti)
's/he insisted on running'

konuşmamdan (korkuyor)   *konuşmaktan (korkuyor)*
's/he is scared that I might talk'   's/he is scared of talking'

-mA can also combine directly with the genitive case-marker, whereas *-mAK* cannot: *üniversiteye git**menin** (anlamı)* '(the significance) of going to university'. Some speakers attach the locative case marker directly to *-mA*: *cevap ver**mede** (geciktim)* 'I am/was late in responding', but forms where the locative suffix is attached to *-mAK* are more widespread: *cevap ver**mekte** (geciktim)* 'I am/was late in responding'.

Note that when *-mAK* combines with a suffix beginning with a vowel, as in the case of the accusative and dative suffixes, the resulting form is spelt and pronounced more commonly nowadays as *-mayı, -meyi* (ACC) and *-maya, -meye* (DAT), rather than *-mağı, -meği* (ACC) and *-mağa, -meğe* (DAT). Since a case marker can also attach to *-mA* directly without an intervening possessive marker (as seen above in the case of the genitive and locative case markers), it may not always be clear whether the accusative or dative case marker has attached to *-mA* or to *-mAK*. In this book we adhere to the new spelling of these forms (with 'y' rather than 'ğ') and consider these forms as a combination of *-mAK* + ACC/DAT.

-mAK: This subordinator forms:

(i) Verbal nouns: *al**mak** (iste-)* '(want) to buy', *sev**meyi** (öğren-)* '(learn) to love', *ağla**maya** (başla-)* '(start) crying' (24.4.1)
(ii) Converbs: *iç**meksizin*** 'without drinking'

-mAK has a converbial function when it occurs in one of the following combinations (26.2–3), some of which involve postpositions (Chapter 17):

-mAk (üzere/için/yerine/suretiyle/şartıyla): *ver**mek** için* 'in order to give'
-mAklA (birlikte): *okuyabil**mekle** birlikte* 'although able to read'
-mAksIzIn (formal): *dön**meksizin*** 'without returning'
-mAktAn (öte/başka/gayrı): *sat**maktan** öte* 'apart from selling [it]'
-mAktAnsA: *bitir**mektense*** 'rather than finishing [it]'.

-mA: This subordinator forms:

(i) Verbal nouns: *anla**mamamı** (iste-)* '(want) me not to understand' (24.4.2)
(ii) Converbs: *yazıl**ması** için* 'in order for it to be written'

-mA has a converbial function when it occurs in one of the following combinations (26.2–3), some of which involve postpositions (Chapter 17):

-*mAsI* (*için/halinde/durumunda/yüzünden*): *öksür**mesi** halinde* 'in the event of his/her coughing'

-*mAsIndAn* (*itibaren/önce/sonra/ötürü/başka/dolayı*): *seçil**mesinden** önce* 'before s/he was elected', *istememe**mizden** ötürü* 'because we don't/ didn't want [it]'

-*mAsInA* (*rağmen/karşın*): *anlaş**manıza** rağmen* 'in spite of your getting along well together'

8.5.2 Subordinating suffixes which have a single function

8.5.2.1 -(y)An, -(y)Iş, -(y)AsI

-*(y)An*   This suffix forms participles: *okuyan (çocuk)* '(the child) who studies/is studying' (25.1.1.1). When it occurs in pronominal relative clauses (25.3) it can be followed by all of the nominal inflectional suffixes described in 8.1: *okuyanlarımıza* 'to the ones among us who study/are studying'.

-*(y)Iş*   This suffix can combine with the plural marker, possessive suffixes and case suffixes. It forms verbal nouns: *oturuşumu (beğen-)* '(like) my way of sitting', *duruşunuz* 'the way you stand', 'your stance' (24.4.4).

A subordinating suffix highly restricted in its usage is *-(y)AsI*. It is mostly used with the predicate *yok* (non existent): *yiyesim yok* 'I don't feel like eating'.

8.5.2.2 Subordinating suffixes which only form converbs

The following suffixes form converbs (26.2–3). With the exception of *-(y)mIşÇAsInA*, none of these suffixes combine with person markers:

(i) Suffixes containing the negative marker -*mA* or its combination with the negative aorist -*z* (-*mA-z*):

-*mAdAn* (*önce/evvel* 'before'): The forms containing -*mA* are stressed on the syllable preceding the negative marker, e.g. *yıkıl**madan*** 'before being demolished'.

-*mAzdAn* (*önce/evvel* 'before'): The forms containing -*mA-z* occur with *önce* or *evvel* 'before'. They are stressed on the case suffix following the negative marker, e.g. *yıkıl**mazdán** önce* 'before being demolished'. The form -*mAzdAn önce* is slightly more formal than -*mAdAn önce*.

(ii) Other converbial suffixes:

-(y)A Occurs with the auxiliary usage of the verbs *bil-, dur-, kal-, gör-, yaz-* to form Position 2 suffixes (e.g. *-(y)Abil, -(y)Adur*): *oku**yabil*- 'be able to read', *koşadur-* 'continue running'.

-(y)I Occurs with the auxiliary usage of *ver-* to form the Position 2 suffix *-(y)Iver*: *yürü**yüver-* 'suddenly walk', *koş**uver-* 'suddenly run'.

-(y)IncA *yüz**ünce* 'when [s.o.] swims/swam', *kalkma**yınca* 'when [s.o.] doesn't/didn't get up'.

-(y)ArAk *koş**arak* 'running', *büyü**yerek* 'growing up', *çalış**arak* 'by working'. Also (colloquial) *-(y)ArAktAn*: *bakaraktan* 'looking'.

-(y)AlI (beri) *düşün**eli (beri)* 'since thinking about [s.t.]', *gel**eli beri* 'since arriving', 'since [s.o.] arrived'. Colloquial form of *-DIğIndAn beri*.

-(y)IncAyA (kadar/değin/dek)/-(y)AnA (kadar).
    *gid**inceye* kadar 'until/by the time [s.o.] goes/went'.
    -(y)AnA is a colloquial version: *otur**ana* kadar 'until/by the time [s.o.] sits/sat down'.

-(A/I)r/-(y)AcAk/-mIş/-(y)mIş/-(I)yor gibi.
    *kalk**acak* gibi 'as if about to get up', *anl**ar* gibi 'as if understanding', *içki içm**iş* gibi 'as if having drunk alcohol'.

-(A/I)rcAsInA/-mIşçAsInA/-(y)mIşçAsInA.
    *hissed**ercesine* 'as if feeling'. With the form *-(y)mIşçAsInA* there is the possibility of adding person marking: *konuşuyor**muşumcasına* 'as if I was talking'. *-(y)mIşçAsInA* can also be added to nominal stems: *öğretmen**mişçesine* 'as if s/he was a teacher', *sonsuz**muşçasına* 'as if (it) was endless.

-(y)Ip *koş**up* *al-* 'run and get', *gir**ip* *otur-* 'enter and sit down'. Because of its conjunctive function, this suffix is discussed in 28.2.

-(y)ken The segment *-(y)-* is the copula (8.3.1). Because of this, *-(y)ken* attaches not directly to the verb stem but instead to a Position 3 verbal suffix or to a nominal (8.3.2, 26.2.3 (iv)): *bakar**ken* 'when/while ([s.o.] is/was) watching', *çocuk**ken* 'when/as a child', 'when [s.o.] was a child', *sokakta**yken* 'while in the street', *bizim**ken* 'when [s.t.] is/was ours'. Unlike the other copular markers it cannot combine with person markers, except optionally with the 3rd person plural suffix *-lAr*: *gider(ler)**ken* 'as they go/

went'. It is invariable (i.e. its vowel does not undergo vowel harmony (3.4 (vi)).

A few converbial forms are made up of pairs of suffixes added to adjacent verbs. All forms except for the first pair are used in colloquial contexts:

-(A/I)r...-mAz   Added to identical verb stems without any person marking: *yer yemez* 'as soon as [s.o.] eats/ate', *gider gitmez* 'as soon as [s.o.] leaves/left'.

-DI...-(y)AlI   Added to identical verb stems in colloquial speech. The first stem has person marking: *duydum duyalı* 'ever since I heard [it]', *baktırdın baktıralı* 'ever since you had [it] checked', *alındı alınalı* 'ever since it was bought'.

-(y)A...-(y)A   Added to identical or similar verb stems or to semantically contrasting ones: *baka baka* 'staring', *yedire yedire* 'continuously making [s.o.] eat', *bağıra çağıra* 'at the top of his/her voice', *gide gele* 'going back and forth', *bata çıka* 'sinking and rising'. For further discussion see (26.3.8 (i)).

-(y)An...-(y)AnA   Added to identical verb stems and used to express the unexpectedly large number of people involved in a particular activity (in colloquial speech): *Konsere giden gidene* 'Masses of people went to the concert'. *Şu saçma dergiyi de alan alana!* 'Everyone's buying this ridiculous magazine!'

Chapter 9

Reduplication and doubling

Reduplication is the repetition of part of a word. The following are the two types of reduplicative process in Turkish:

(i) Emphatic reduplication: *kıpkırmızı* 'stark red' (9.1)
(ii) *m*-reduplication: *çirkin mirkin* 'ugly, or anything like that' (9.2)

Doubling is the repetition of a whole word, with or without the addition of various suffixes. The following are a few of the forms of doubling:

(iii) Doubling a word: *yavaş yavaş* 'slowly' (9.3)
(iv) Doubling a word with the suffix *-(y)A*: *yan yana* 'next to each other' (9.3.2)

There are also some lexicalized constructions where a word is coupled with a similar sounding stem:

(v) *eğri büğrü* 'crooked' (9.3.1)

9.1 Emphatic reduplication

Emphatic reduplication is used for accentuating the quality of an adjective or adverb:

uzun 'long'   →   *upuzun* 'very long'
güzel 'pretty'   →   *güpgüzel* 'very pretty'

It occurs mainly with underived adjectives and occasionally with adverbs.

In emphatic reduplication, a prefix is attached to the stem. If the stem begins with a vowel the prefix consists of this vowel plus the reduplicative consonant 'p':

ince 'thin'   →   *i* + **p** + *ince*   →   *ipince* 'very thin'
eski 'old'   →   *e* + **p** + *eski*   →   *epeski* 'very old'

DOI: 10.4324/9780429435836-11

If the stem begins with a consonant, the prefix consists of this consonant, the vowel following it and one of the reduplicative consonants 'p', 's', 'r' or 'm':

sarı 'yellow'	→	*sa* + **p** + *sarı*	→	*sapsarı* 'bright yellow'
katı 'hard'	→	*ka* + **s** + *katı*	→	*kaskatı* 'hard as a rock'
temiz 'clean'	→	*te* + **r** + *temiz*	→	*tertemiz* 'clean as a pin'
siyah 'black'	→	*si* + **m** + *siyah*	→	*simsiyah* 'pitch black'

In some cases, the reduplicated segment contains the additional segments *-A*, *-Il* or *-Am*.

(i) *-A*:

gündüz 'daytime', 'by day'	*gü* + **p** + **e** + *gündüz* 'in broad daylight'
sağlam 'in good condition'	*sa* + **p** + **a** + *sağlam* 'in very good condition'
yalnız 'alone'	*ya* + **p** + **a** + *yalnız* 'all alone' (also *yapyalnız*)

(ii) *-Il* or *-Am*:

çıplak 'naked' *çı* + **r** + **ıl** + *çıplak* 'stark naked' (also *çırçıplak*)
parça 'piece' *pa* + **r** + **am** + *parça* 'torn to shreds', 'smashed to pieces'

The occurrence of a particular reduplicative consonant is, to a degree, predictable, in that it cannot be the same as the first consonant of the stem. For a list of stems which can undergo emphatic reduplication, see Appendix 1.

Words which undergo emphatic reduplication are stressed on the initial syllable (e.g. *kápkara*, *sápasağlam*, *ápaçık*) except when the reduplicated form contains *-Il* or *-Am*, in which case this latter syllable bears stress (e.g. *çırílçıplak*). Emphatically reduplicated words cannot occur with the modifiers in 15.4, such as *çok* 'many' or *en* 'most'.

9.2 *m*-Reduplication

The function of *m*-reduplication is to generalize the concept denoted by a particular word or phrase to include other similar objects, events or states of affairs. This is a colloquial usage. The reduplicated word or phrase is stressed on the stressable syllable, and this pattern is copied on to the reduplication.

(1) Doktor önce hastanın **gözüné mözüné** baktı, sonra sorunu anlamadığını söyledi.
'The doctor first checked the patient's *eyes, etc.*, then said that s/he didn't understand the problem.'

(2) Bu koltuk **çirkin mirkin** değil.
'This armchair isn't *ugly, or anything like that.*'

(3) Avukat belgeleri **okudu mokudu** ve sonra hepsini alıp götürdü.
'The lawyer *read* the documents, *etc.* and then took them all.'

m-reduplication involves the repetition of a word or phrase in a modified form. If this word or phrase begins with a vowel, the modifying consonant 'm' is prefixed to its second occurrence:

etek metek 'skirt(s) and the like'
içecek miçecek 'drinks and the like'

If the word or phrase begins with a consonant, this consonant is *replaced* by 'm' in its second occurrence:

kapı mapı 'door(s) and the like'
çay may 'tea and the like'

In most cases the reduplicative form immediately follows the word that it reduplicates. One exception is *-sI* compounds (10.2) where either the entire compound is repeated with only its first word undergoing *m*-reduplication or, occasionally, the first word is repeated on its own:

(4) a. Ben adam **tarih hocasıymış marih hocasıymış** anlamam. Fransız tarihini ondan daha iyi biliyorum.
b. Ben adam **tarih marih hocasıymış** anlamam. Fransız tarihini ondan daha iyi biliyorum.
'I don't care if he is *a history teacher or whatever*. I know more about French history than he does.'

9.3 Doubling

Doubling is the repetition of a word or similar sounding words, quite commonly used across various constructions in Turkish. Nouns, adverbs, adjectives, measure terms and verbs can be doubled.

(i) Doubled adverbs, doubled nouns, doubled adjectives and doubled distributive numerals (15.7.3) all occur with an adverbial function (16.1.3):

yavaş yavaş	'slowly'
çabuk çabuk	'quickly'
kapı kapı	'door to door'
damla damla	'in drops'
sabah sabah	'so early in the morning'
usul usul	'slowly and softly'
rahat rahat	'comfortably', 'easily'
birer birer	'one by one'

(ii) Doubled adjectives are also used as modifiers with plural nouns, both to draw attention to the quality denoted by the adjective and to indicate a large quantity of the item in question:

koca koca (ağaçlar)	'many huge (trees)'
sarı sarı (evler)	'many yellow (houses)'

(iii) When doubled measure terms are used adjectivally, they are usually used without plural marking on the noun that is modified. These forms indicate a large quantity or a great variety of the item in question:

çeşit çeşit yiyecek(ler)	'all kinds of (dishes)'
boy boy kutu(lar)	'boxes of all sizes'
kutu kutu kitap	'many boxes of books'

(iv) The clitic *mI* (see 11.1.1.5 for other uses) inserted between two occurrences of an adjective intensifies its meaning. These forms are colloquial and are usually used either as predicative adjectives or in indefinite noun phrases:

Adam kurnaz mı kurnaz.	'The man is extremely sly.'
güzel mi güzel bir kız	'a remarkably pretty girl'

Forms doubled with the aid of *mI* can occasionally be used as adverbs:

yavaş mı yavaş (okuyor)	'(s/he reads) very slowly'

9.3.1 Doubling in lexical formations

There are a number of idiomatic expressions that are created by the coupling of two items. These two items can be pairs of similar-sounding words or similar-sounding stems that do not exist independently:

konu komşu	'neighbours'
çoluk çocuk	'wife and children'
ufak tefek	'tiny'
eğri büğrü	'crooked'
paldır küldür	'with an enormous noise'
süklüm püklüm	'in a crestfallen manner'

9.3.2 Doubling with -(y)A₂

In this type of doubling, a nominal gets doubled and the second occurrence is affixed with *-(y)A₂* (7.2.2.2), creating adverbs. This is common with:

Space-denoting nominal:

> *üst üste* 'one on top of each other'
> *alt alta* 'underneath one another'
> *yan yana* 'next to each other'
> *karşı karşıya* 'across from each other'

Body-part-denoting nouns:

> *kolkola* 'arm in arm'
> *elele* 'hand in hand'
> *başbaşa* (of two people) 'alone together'
> *burun buruna* (of s.o/s.t. one is trying to keep away from) 'in too close proximity'

Human-denoting nouns:

> *kadın kadına* 'woman to woman'
> *erkek erkeğe* 'man to man'

For the counterpart of this construction based on verb roots, see 26.3.8 (i).

Chapter 10

Noun compounds

In this chapter we discuss noun compounds, word-like units functioning like a noun but made up of two words. There are two types of noun compound:

(i) Bare compounds (compounds which do not have the suffix *-(s)I*): *kız kardeş* 'sister', *naylon torba* 'plastic bag', *Yeşilbahar Sokak* 'Yeşilbahar Street', *büyükbaba* 'grandfather', *ağaçkakan* 'woodpecker', *yapboz* 'jigsaw' (10.1)
(ii) *-(s)I* compounds: *at arabası* 'horse-drawn vehicle', *gaz sobası* 'kerosene stove', *Atatürk Bulvarı* 'Atatürk Boulevard', *buzdolabı* 'refrigerator', *A harfi* 'the letter A' (10.2)

Whichever the type, some compounds are fully lexicalized and their meaning cannot generally be deduced from their parts:

tutkal 'adhesive' (*tut* 'hold' and *kal* 'remain')
karafatma 'cockroach' (from *kara* 'black' and *Fatma* 'a woman's name')
keçiboynuzu 'carob' (from *keçi* 'goat' and *boynuz* 'horn')

Others are transparent in their meaning:

altbölüm 'subsection'
karabiber 'black pepper'
sokak lambası 'street lamp'

Compounding is a productive process and, especially *-(s)I* compounds, but also some types of bare compound can be produced spontaneously. For example, based on *deniz tuzu* 'sea salt', a novel compound *nehir tuzu* 'river salt' might be uttered in a conversation. Similarly, there might be an occasion in which *pembe biber* 'pink pepper' is used, based on *karabiber* 'black pepper'. As seen in the above examples, some compounds are written as one word.

In the vast majority of compounds, the first word modifies or restricts the meaning of the second one which is called the **head**.

Phrasal compounds in which the modifier is a noun clause, e.g. *savaşın uzun bir süre devam edeceği korkusu* 'the fear that the war would go on for a long time', are discussed in 24.6. For stress in compounds, see 4.2.

10.1 Bare compounds

Compounds which do not have the compounding suffix *-(s)I* are of different types in terms of the word class of their components. Among the most common types are noun-noun compounds, adjective-noun compounds, noun compounds with derived nominals, and verb-verb compounds. For nominal-verb compounds, see 13.3.2.

10.1.1 Noun-noun compounds

These consist of two juxtaposed nouns with no suffixation to mark the relation between them. This type of compounding is of restricted occurrence. Its main areas of usage are listed below.

(i) Compounds in which the first noun specifies the sex of the person denoted by the second noun:

erkek kardeş	'brother'
kız arkadaş	'girlfriend'

(ii) Compounds in which the first noun is the (given) name of a person and the second noun indicates their profession, expresses their relationship to the speaker, or is one of the commonly used words of address (such as *bey* for men or *hanım* for women):

Ali Bey	
Nadire Hanım	
Ayşe hoca	'[the] professor Ayşe'
Nalan hemşire	'[the] nurse Nalan'
Selma teyze	'Aunt Selma'
Fuat amca	'Uncle Fuat'

(iii) The names of various sciences and disciplines:

dilbilim	'linguistics'
toplumbilim	'sociology'

(iv) The names of various cooked dishes:

şiş kebap	'shish kebab'
kuzu fırın	'oven-cooked lamb'

(v) Compounds where the first word is a spatial nominal:

altbölüm	'subdivision'
iç hatlar	'domestic lines'
önsöz	'preface'
karşı saldırı	'counter-attack'
dışbükey	'convex'
yantümce	'subordinate clause'

(vi) Compounds where the first noun is *öz* 'self':

özyönetim	'self-governance'
özgüven	'self-confidence'

(vii) Street names in which the second noun is *sokak* 'street':

Akgül Sokak	'Akgül Street'

The use of noun-noun compounds such as *Akgül Sokak* are used interchangeably with the corresponding *-(s)I* compound form (with *Sokağı* instead of *Sokak* (10.2)). Even official usage is not consistent and the abbreviation '*Sok.*', commonly used in postal addresses and on street signs, obscures this variation.

10.1.2 Adjective-noun compounds

These compounds are made up of an adjective and a noun. As in bare-noun compounds, there is no suffixation to mark the relation between the two components. The majority of these compounds are written as single words:

karabiber	'black pepper'
darboğaz	'(economic) bottleneck'
kabakulak	'mumps'
akciğer	'lung(s)'
sarı humma	'yellow fever'

10.1.3 Noun compounds with derived nominals

In these compounds, one of the components is a noun and the other one is a nominal derived from a verb by one of the suffixes *-(A/I)r*, *-mA*, *-mAz*, *-mIş*, *-(y)An* and *-(y)IcI* (7.2.1.1).

In some of these compounds, the derived nominal appears as the first word:

çal-ar saat	'alarm clock'
çık-maz sokak	'dead-end (street)'
dol-ma kalem	'ballpoint pen'
geç-miş zaman	'past tense'
kur-ucu üye	'founding member'

The derived nominal can also be the second word in a compound:

bilgisayar	'computer'
hacıyatmaz	'roly-poly'
oyunbozan	'spoilsport'
ağaçkakan	'woodpecker'
dalgakıran	'breakwater'

10.1.4 Verb-verb compounds

Quite limited in number, these are compounds composed of two verb roots:

gelgit	'tide'
çekyat	'sofa bed'
yapboz	'jigsaw'

10.2 -(s)I Compounds

This is by far the most common type of compounding in Turkish. *-(s)I* compounds consist minimally of two juxtaposed nouns, the first of which has no suffixes while the second is marked with the 3rd person possessive suffix *-(s)I* (8.1.2). Some examples are:

otobüs bilet-i	'bus ticket'
el çanta-sı	'handbag'
masa örtü-sü	'tablecloth'
çay bardağ-ı	'tea glass'
çocuk bahçe-si	'children's playground'
kavuniç-i	'(a pale tone of) orange'
kahvereng-i	'brown'

A much less common type of *-(s)I* compound is one where the second item is an adjective and the compound is itself used as an adjective:

samansarı-sı	'pale yellow'
tahtakuru-su	'bedbug'

The plural of a *-(s)I* compound is formed by attaching the 3rd person possessive suffix (in this case always *-I*) to the plural form of the second noun:

otobüs biletler-i	'bus tickets'
el çantalar-ı	'handbags'
çay bardaklar-ı	'tea glasses'

There are a few cases, however, where the possessive suffix is treated as an integral part of the word and the plural suffix follows it:

ayakkabı-lar 'shoes'
yüzbaşı-lar '(army) captains'

In a very small number of cases the plural can be formed either way:

kasımpatı-lar/kasımpat-lar-ı 'chrysanthemums'

10.2.1 The functions of -(s)I compounds

The function of the 3rd person possessive suffix (8.1.2) in *-(s)I* compounds is not to signify possession of one thing by another. Rather, it serves as a grammatical indicator of the relation between the nouns that form the compound. This relation can be of different types. For example, *barış antlaşması* 'peace treaty' is a treaty *for* securing peace between two or more countries, *İstanbul antlaşması* 'Istanbul treaty' is a treaty signed *in* Istanbul. *Elma çekirdeği* 'apple pip' is the pip *of* an apple but *elma reçeli* 'apple jam' is a jam *made of* apples.

The following are a few of the typical functions of *-(s)I* compounds.

(i) *-s(I)* compounds are productively used to designate institutions, official bodies and geopolitical entities:

Efes Lokanta-sı	'the Ephesus Restaurant'
Dışişleri Bakanlığ-ı	'the Ministry of Foreign Affairs'
Dünya Banka-sı	'the World Bank'
Beşiktaş Stadyum-u	'Beşiktaş Stadium'
Koç Hastane-si	'Koç Hospital'
Türkiye Cumhuriyet-i	'the Republic of Turkey'
Sovyetler Birliğ-i	'the Soviet Union'

(ii) *-s(I)* compounds can provide the name for particular topographical features or places:

Ağrı Dağ-ı	'Mount Ararat'
Van Göl-ü	'Lake Van'
İstanbul Boğaz-ı	(lit.'Istanbul strait') 'the Bosphorus'

(iii) The second noun in *-(s)I* compounds can further describe the type of the entity that the first word denotes. Thus, the first noun is interchangeable with the whole compound and can be used on its own without any loss of meaning, rendering the head optional. This is common in time expressions in which a date or the name of a day or month is compounded with the noun denoting the unit of time in question (16.4.1.1):

> *1912 (yıl-ı)* '(the year) 1912'
> *cuma (gün-ü)* 'Friday'
> *ocak (ay-ı)* '(the month of) January'

Other nouns are words such as *nota* 'note', *harf* 'letter' or *sayı* 'numeral', or indeed any noun that is available as a description of the first noun in the appropriate context:

> *Fa (nota-sı)* '(the note) F'
> *Q (harf-i)* '(the letter) Q'
> *üç (sayı-sı)* '(the numeral) three'
> ☺ *(emoji-si)* '(the emoji) ☺'
> *Art Nouveau (ekol-ü)* '(the) Art Nouveau (school)'

Where the second noun denotes a topographical or a geographical feature or a geopolitical entity, this group of compound looks deceptively similar to the one in (ii).

> *Erciyes (Dağ-ı)* '(Mount) Erciyes'
> *Ağrı (şehr-i)* '(the town of) Ağrı'
> *Nepal (ülke-si)* '(the country of) Nepal'

The difference between these and the compounds in (ii) is that, for example *Nepal ülkesi* 'the country of Nepal' above can also be referred to as *Nepal* but in the identical looking construction *Nepal müziği* 'Nepalese music', 'the music of Nepal', the head of the construction (*müzik*) is not optional.

In a similar type of construction, the name of a person can be compounded with a derogatory adjective as an insult:

> *Hilmi şapşal-ı* 'that fool Hilmi'
> *Firuze dangalağ-ı* 'that idiot Firuze'

10.2.2 *-(s)I compounds and words expressing nationality*

-(s)I compounding is obligatory in cases where something non-human is specified as peculiar to, or characteristic of, a specified nation. Words of nationality in these compounds are nouns:

> *Türk kahve-si* 'Turkish coffee'
> *Türk Lira-sı* 'Turkish Lira'
> *Alman ekmeğ-i* 'German bread'
> *Fransız edebiyat-ı* 'French literature'

Note that for some nationalities, the noun used as a modifier in *-(s)I* compounds is not necessarily identical with the word used to designate a person of that nationality:

Yunan müziğ-i	'Greek music'
Hint diller-i	'Indian languages'

When the head noun is one that denotes human beings, adjectival constructions with *-lI* are preferred (7.2.2.2, 15.2.1 (21)).

In the case of countries for which Turkish does not have a separate noun of nationality, the name of the country is used in place of it in *-(s)I* compounds:

Çin fener-i	'Chinese lantern'
Brezilya takım-ı	'the Brazilian team'

Names of other geographical or geopolitical entities (e.g. continents, regions, cities) are also used in *-(s)I* compounds in the same way (see also 10.2.1 (i) and (ii)):

bir Afrika ülke-si	'an African country'
Ortadoğu siyaset-i	'Middle East(ern) politics'
Akdeniz iklim-i	'Mediterranean climate'
Uşak halı-sı	'Uşak carpet' (carpet made in Uşak or in that style)

When nouns of nationality (*Türk*, *Alman*, etc.) occur in compounds denoting human beings, the second noun can be left without a suffix, forming a noun phrase with a noun modified by a term of nationality used as an adjective:

İngiliz çocuklar-ı/İngiliz çocuklar	'English children'
Japon askerler-i/Japon askerler	'Japanese soldiers'
Rus sporcu-su/Rus sporcu	'(the/a) Russian athlete'
Yunan başbakan-ı/Yunan başbakan	'the Greek prime minister'

For some speakers, there may be a subtle difference between the meanings of the *-(s)I* compound and the noun phrase containing the adjective. While the latter identifies one or more individuals who just happen to have a certain nationality, the *-(s)I* compound either (i) expresses a whole class or group generically (such as English children), or (ii) presents a person not primarily as an individual human being but as someone functioning in some capacity on behalf of his/her nation or country.

10.3 Embedding compounds within other compounds

Compounds can often be embedded within other compounds. For example, compounds such as *İngiliz edebiyatı* 'English literature' or *göz hastalıkları* 'diseases of the eye' can act as modifiers in other compounds:

İngiliz Edebiyat-ı Bölüm-ü 'Department of English Literature'
göz hastalıklar-ı hastane-si 'hospital for diseases of the eye'

Note that in these cases the marker *-(s)I* occurs on the head of each compound. Hence longer forms can contain several markers, one for each head:

Türkiye Cumhuriyeti Milli Eğitim Bakanlığı Kadıköy Kız Yüksek Meslek Okulu Müdürlüğü 'The Directorate of the Kadıköy Technical College for Girls under the Ministry of National Education of the Republic of Turkey'

The head of this multi-layered compound is *müdürlük* 'directorate', which is modified by the following construction, itself a *-(s)I* compound:

Türkiye Cumhuriyet-i Milli Eğitim Bakanlığ-ı Kadıköy Kız Yüksek Meslek Okul-u 'Kadıköy Technical College for Girls under the Ministry of National Education of the Republic of Turkey'

The head of this compound is *okul* 'school', which has two simple modifiers, *meslek*, here meaning 'technical' and the adjective *yüksek* 'high', which when combined with *okul* means 'college'. *Kız* 'girl' modifies *yüksek meslek okulu* 'technical college' and *Kadıköy* modifies *kız yüksek meslek okul-u* 'technical college for girls'. *Kadıköy Kız Yüksek Meslek Okulu* is modified by *Türkiye Cumhuriyeti Milli Eğitim Bakanlığı*, which is also a construction with embedded compounds. The head of this compound is *bakanlık* 'ministry', modified by the noun phrase *milli eğitim* 'national education'. The compound *Milli Eğitim Bakanlığı* 'Ministry of National Education' is modified by *Türkiye Cumhuriyeti* 'Republic of Turkey', itself a compound.

Note that when two or more compounds have identical heads and are components of a larger compound, only one occurrence of *-(s)I* on the head is possible. For example, if the compounds *kız okulu* 'girls' school' and *meslek okulu* 'technical college' appear in the same compound, there will only be one occurrence of *-(s)I* on the head:

Kadıköy Kız Yüksek Meslek Okul-u 'Kadıköy Technical College for Girls'
Polonya gölge tiyatro-su 'Polish shadow theatre'

10.4 Separability of the constituents of compounds

The constituents of bare noun compounds and *-(s)I* compounds usually form a single unit and are inseparable. However, both types, but especially *-(s)I* compounds where the meaning is deducible from the parts, can be separated when they are conjoined by *ve (de)* 'and' (28.3.1.1) or *veya/yahut/ya da* 'or' (28.3.3.1). When they have the same head the first occurrence of the head can be omitted. The head may or may not have plural marking:

kız ve erkek çocuklar	'female and male children', 'girls and boys'
Fransız veya Alman sineması/sinemaları	'(the) French or German cinema(s)'

In compounds with identical modifiers, the first modifier can be omitted.

ofis masa ve sandalyeleri	'office tables and chairs'
Fransız sineması veya tiyatrosu	'(the) French cinema or theatre'

Adjectives, determiners and numerals modifying the head noun are placed before the whole compound in the same order as they are placed before the head of a noun phrase (15.9):

güzel *bir masa örtüsü*	'*a beautiful* tablecloth'
birtakım ilginç *çocuk kitapları*	'*some interesting* children's books'

However, in compounds which refer to official bodies, an adjective (but not determiners or numerals) may be placed before the head noun:

eski *Dışişleri Bakanı/Dışişleri* **eski** *Bakanı*
'the former Foreign Secretary'

geçici *Nüfus Dairesi Müdürü/Nüfus Dairesi* **geçici** *Müdürü*
'the temporary Registry Office Director'

Chapter 11

Clitics

Clitics are particles that are attached to phrases. Most clitics can attach to any type of phrase and thus have freedom of movement, unlike suffixes, which are fully integrated with the word to which they are attached. Some clitics undergo vowel harmony (Chapter 3) but others are non-harmonic. An important aspect of clitics is that they are all unstressable and, in the majority of cases, cause stress to appear on the stressable syllable of the phrase they are attached to.

In section 11.1 we discuss the properties of individual clitics and in 11.2 their properties regarding stress when they are with unstressable suffixes of other clitics.

11.1 The clitics of Turkish

The clitics of Turkish are the following:

(i) The additive connective *bile* 'even' and the multifunctional marker *diye*, both of which are word-like clitics
(ii) The discourse connectives *dA, ya, -(y)sA/ise*, the discourse connective and subordinator *ki*
(iii) *mI*, the most typical function of which is to form yes/no questions
(iv) Various person markers
(v) The copular markers *-(y)DI, -(y)mIş, -(y)sA* (8.3.2), the (copular) converbial marker *-(y)ken* (8.5.2.2) and the generalizing modality marker *-DIr* (8.3.3)
(vi) The comitative/instrumental and conjunctive marker *-(y)lA/ile* (8.1.4)

Of these, the last two groups are discussed elsewhere in this book (except for their interaction with the clitics in this section). The clitics discussed in this chapter, with the exception of the discourse connective *-(y)sA* and person markers, are written separately from the preceding word.

Most of the bare postpositions (17.2) share properties with clitics. We discuss these in 4.4.3.

11.1.1 The properties of individual clitics

The list below is a summary of Turkish clitics. Each clitic is discussed in detail in the cross-referenced sections.

11.1.1.1 bile

This word-like clitic is an additive connective (27.4.2.1 (i), 28.3.1.1 (iv)):

(1) Araba **bile** almış.
    'S/he's *even* bought a car.'

11.1.1.2 dA

The first consonant of this marker is usually pronounced [d] (sometimes [tʰ] following voiceless stops (1.1.1.1). Its vowel harmonizes with the vowel in the preceding syllable (3.2.2):

(2) ánnem **de**
    'my mother *too*'

(3) Yapárım **da**.
    'I will do [it], *too*'

The clitic *dA* is a conjunction and discourse connective with focus-related additive, adversative, continuative/topic-shifting and enumerating functions. It occurs after stressed constituents, except when it is a continuative/topic-shifting connective. Its functions are as follows:

(i) Continuative/topic-shifting connective (23.3.3.1 (i), 28.3.1.1 (iii.a)):
    Where *dA* has this function, the topic phrase that it follows bears secondary stress (5.2.2):

   (4) Bu hediyeyı **de** Envér aldı.
       '*As for* this present, Envér bought it.'

(ii) Focus-related additive (28.3.1.1 (iii.b), 27.4.2)
     When *dA* functions as an additive connective, it is often the stressable syllable of the word preceding it that bears stress.

   (5) Seyrétmiyorum **da**.
       '*And moreover,* I don't watch [it]'

   (6) Çekmecedé **de** hiçbir şey yok.
       'There's nothing in the drawer, *either*.'

When it combines with a form containing the possibility suffix *-(y)Abil*, it can be inserted after *-(y)A* in colloquial speech:

(7) a. Bakabilírim **de**.
'I can *also* look'

b. Baká **da** bilirim.
'I can *also* look' (colloquial)

(iii) Adversative (28.3.4.5 (i)):
Conversely, when *dA* functions as an adversative connective, the preceding *syllable* bears stress, even if it belongs to an item that is not normally stressable:

(8) *Seyretmiyorúm* **da** *(anlattıklarındán biliyorum)*.
'I don't watch [it] *but* know about it (from [people] telling [me about it])'.

(iv) Enumerating (28.3.2):

(9) Ayşé **de** Semrá **da**
'*both* Ayşe *and* Semra'

In these constructions *dA* attaches to each item that is enumerated and each one receives stress.

(v) Converbial (26.1.7)
In this function, *dA* is a subordinator in temporal adverbial clauses and places stress on the preceding syllable:

(10) Otúr **da** konuşalım.
'Let's talk after you sit down.'

See also the usage of *dA* in combination with the conditional markers *-sA* and *-(y)sA* (27.4.2.1-2) and its doubled form *da...da* as an enumerator (28.3.2).

11.1.1.3 diye

The word-like clitic *diye* has several functions:

(i) Adjectival function (15.3.8)

(11) demirhindi **diye** bir baharat
'a spice called tamarind'

(ii) As a subordinator in noun clauses (24.3.1)

(12) Liseyi bitirdi **diye** biliyorum.
'I think s/he finished high school.'

(iii) As a subordinator in adverbial clauses (26.1.1)

(13) Yarışmaya katıldı **diye** eleştiriliyor.
'S/he is criticized for having taken part in the competition.'

11.1.1.4 ki

ki, (unlike the adjectival/pronominal *-ki(n)* (8.1.4)), cannot be stressed. It can assign stress to the stressable syllable of the preceding word or to the syllable preceding it, even if this syllable is otherwise unstressable (11.2.1). It has the following functions:

(i) Subordinator connecting a noun clause to a superordinate clause (24.3.2):

(14) İnanıyorúm [**ki** herşey düzelecek].
'I believe [*that* everything will come right].'

(ii) Subordinator connecting an adverbial clause to a superordinate clause (26.1.2):

(15) Sana bunu söylüyorúm [**ki** sonradan şaşırmayasın].
'I'm telling you this [so that you won't be surprised later].'

(iii) Repudiative discourse connective (28.3.4.7):

(16) Göstericilere katıl(ma)dím **ki**!
'But I did(n't) join the demonstrators!'

(iv) Exclamation (12.4):
In exclamations, *ki* comes at the end and is used with *o kadar* or *öyle(sine)* 'so':

(17) Londra sonbaharda o kadar güzel olúr **ki**!
'London is so beautiful in autumn!'

(v) Relative clause marker (25.6):
   a. In non-restrictive relative clauses (25.6.1):

   (18) Semra [**ki** partileri sevmez], o bile eğlendi.
   'Even Semra, [who doesn't like parties,] had fun.'

   b. In restrictive relative clauses (25.6.2):

   (19) Bir şöför [**ki** park etmeyi bilmesin,] ona güvenip arabasına binilmez.
   'A driver [who doesn't know how to park a car] isn't to be trusted to drive one around.'

   c. *ki* can also be used following the demonstrative pronoun *şu* and *o* (18.2) to present the content of a fact, belief, desire, etc., referred to by a pronominal relative clause (25.3):

   (20) Bildiğim **şu** [**ki,** herkesin tatile ihtiyacı var].
   'All I know is [*that* everyone needs a holiday].'

   (21) Anlaşılan **o** [**ki,** yakında seçim olacak].
   '[It seems (to be pretty obvious)] [*that* there will soon be an election].'

   d. Comment (25.6.3):
   In this function, *ki* introduces a clause that supplies a comment or additional information about the phrase that has just been uttered:

   (22) Bugün hava açarsa, [**ki** açacağını pek sanmıyorum,] bahçede mangal yakacaklarmış.
   'If the weather brightens up today, [*which* I don't really think it will,] they're going to have a barbecue in the garden apparently.'

11.1.1.5 *mI*

The clitic *mI* has the following functions:

(i) Question marker in yes/no questions (19.1.1) and alternative questions, both direct (19.1.2) and indirect (24.4.3.2):
   When *mI* is added to a main clause predicate, its position depends on what kind of suffixes or clitics (if any) appear at the end of the predicate. *mI* immediately *precedes* any of the items listed below:

   a. The copular markers *-(y)DI* and *-(y)mIş* (8.3.2):

   (23) Gitse **miydik**?
   'Should we have gone?'

(24) Burada **mıymış**?
'Was it here?'

Note that in 3rd person plural forms, the combinations -*mIydI* and -*mIymIş* can occur after or before -*lAr*:

(25) Koşuyor*lar* **mıydı**?/ Koşuyor **muydu***lar*?
'Were they running?'

b. The person markers in Group 2 (8.4.2), except for the 3rd person plural marker and the colloquial combinations with *-(y)AcAK* mentioned in (e) below):

(26) Gidiyor **musun**?
'Are you going?'

(27) Hazır **mıyız**?
'Are we ready?'

c. The generalizing modality marker -*DIr* (8.3.3) in 3rd person forms:

(28) Unutmuş **mudurlar**?
'[Do you think] they have forgotten?'

(29) Evde **midir**?
'[Do you think] s/he is at home?'/'Is s/he at home?'

Otherwise, that is, in forms with -*DIr* containing markers of the other persons, it immediately precedes the person marker:

(30) (Acaba) geçmiş **miyimdir**?
'I wonder if I have passed.'

On the other hand, *mI* immediately *follows* any of the items listed below:

a. The person markers in Group 1 (8.4.1):

(31) Gördün **mü**?
'Did you see?'

(32) Gitsek **mi**?
'Should we go?'

b. The person markers in Group 3 (8.4.3) (except for the 2nd person forms which do not combine with the question particle for semantic reasons):

   (33) Kalayım *mı*?
       'Shall/should I stay?'

   (34) Başlasın *mı*?
       'Should s/he/it start?'

c. The 3rd person plural forms -*lAr, sInlAr*:

   (35) Git**sinler** *mi*?
       'Should they leave?'

   (36) Okulda**lar** *mı*?
       'Are they at school?'

For an exception to this ordering rule, see (25) above.

d. A subject complement (12.1.1.2) that is not followed by any predicate markers:

   (37) Akıllı **mı**?
       'Is s/he intelligent?'

   (38) Benimki **mi**?
       'Is it mine?

e. The colloquial forms of the combination of future marker with 1st or 2nd person markers (8.2.3.3):

   (39) [arıjdʒán mı] 'Are you going to look for [it]?'
   (40) [jürijdʒǽz **mi**] 'Are we going to walk?'

(ii) Adverbial clause marker (26.1.6, 27.6.2):
When *mI* functions as an adverbial clause marker it follows verb forms which have the perfective suffix -*DI*:

   (41) git**tin mi**
       'as soon as you go'

   (42) evimizi sattık **mı**
       'once we've sold our house'

Clauses with *mI* functioning as an adverbial have a slight rise of intonation at the end, unlike questions, where the intonation falls at the end (5.1 (ii)).

(iii) Intensifier in doubled forms (9.3 (iv)):

(43) hızlı **mı** hızlı
'very fast'

(iv) Challenge to a reported assertion (19.6):

(44) Taksi **mi** bulamamış ne!
'Seems like s/he couldn't fine a cab!'

11.1.1.6 ya

The clitic *ya* is non-harmonic and typically places stress on the syllable that precedes it, even if this syllable is otherwise unstressable (11.2.1). It has the following functions:

(i) Contrastive adversative conjunction ('but') (28.3.4.5 (ii)):

(45) Gittim **ya** onu göremedim.
'I went there but couldn't see her/him.'

This usage is colloquial and occurs only where an affirmative sentence is followed by a negative one.

(ii) Repudiative discourse connective that occurs in sentence-final position (28.3.4.7):

(46) Görmedim dedim **ya**!
'I told you I didn't see him/her!'

(iv) Reminding discourse connective that occurs in sentence-final position (28.3.12):

(47) Hani sana göstermiştim **ya**, işte o elbise.
'Remember the dress I showed you? That one.'

For the stressable discourse connective *ya* that precedes a phrase and introduces alternatives or a speculative question, see 28.3.3.1 and 28.3.1.1(vii):

(48) **Ya** parası yoksa?
'What if s/he doesn't have any money?'

The clitic *ya*, which has a short vowel, should not be confused with the interjection *ya*, the contracted form of *yahu*, which has a long vowel.

11.1.1.7 -(y)sA/ise

This is a discourse connective with topic-shifting and contrastive functions (23.3.3.1 (ii), 28.3.4.5 (iii)). It assigns secondary stress to the syllable preceding it and there is an intonational phrase break after it. This clitic either occurs as -(y)sA, or less commonly as the separate form *ise*. It is added to all types of noun phrase and can follow case markers:

(49) ben**se**
'as for me'

(50) Ahmet'**se**/Ahmet **ise**
'as for Ahmet'

(51) Zehra'yı**ysa**/ Zehra'yı **ise** arayamadım.
'As for Zehra, I couldn't call her.'

(52) Onların**sa** çok parası var.
'As for them, they have a lot of money.'

It can also attach to any adverbial expressing location in time:

(53) Öğleden sonra**ysa** yürüyüşe çıktık.
'And in the afternoon, we went for a walk.'

When this clitic attaches to the 3rd person singular pronoun *o* 'he/she/it', only its free form can be used:

(54) o **ise**
'as for him/her/it'

Note that the form *oysa* (28.3.4.4) is a discourse connective with the quite different meaning of 'whereas'.

11.1.1.8 Person markers

There are a group of unstressable person markers which are clitics (8.4).

(i) The 1st and 2nd person markers belonging to Group 2 (8.4.2) (*-(y)Im, -sIn, -(y)Iz, -sInIz*):

(55) Hűrüz.
'We are free.'

(56) Anlamışsın.
'You have understood [it].'

(ii) The 2nd person markers of Group 3 (8.4.3) (*-sIn, -sInIz*) and Group 4 (8.4.4) (*-yIn, -yInIz*):

(57) anlayásınız (diye)
'(so that) you understand'

(58) Otúrun.
'Sit down.'

Note that the 3rd person markers in Group 3 and Group 4 (*-sIn, -sInlAr*) are stressable.

(iii) The 3rd person plural marker *-lAr* of Group 2 when it is attached to a non-case-marked subject complement:

(59) Tutsáklar.
'They are prisoners.' (See also Chapter 22 (39).)

11.2 Clitics, unstressable suffixes and stress

When there is more than one clitic or unstressable suffix present, only one of them retains its stress-generating force.

11.2.1 Unstressable suffixes and clitics in the same word or phrase

(i) When an unstressable suffix (4.3.2) or clitic is added to a regular word (4.1.1) stress remains on the syllable preceding it:

(60) a. bisiklét   b. bisiklét-**le**
        'bicycle'   'by bicycle'

(61) a. Oturacák.   b. Oturacák **mı**?
        'S/he will sit down.' 'Will s/he sit down?'

(62) a. okuldá   b. okuldá-**ysa**-lar '
        'at school'   'if they are at school'

(ii) With irregular words (4.1.2) the addition of an unstressable suffix or clitic may or may not change change the existing position of stress within that word.

(63) a. İstánbul
     b. İstánbulda-**ydım.**
        'I was in Istanbul.'

(64) a. Afríka
b. Afrikalilaş-**árak**/Afríkalılaş-**arak**
'by becoming Africanized'

Similar to (68b), with the addition of *bile* 'even', *mI* (interrogative), *-(y)sA/ise* 'as for', or *diye* in its adjectival function to an irregular word, the stress may either remain in its original position or it may be attracted to the position just before the clitic:

(65) a. İstánbul **bile**/İstanbúl **bile**
'even Istanbul'

b. İstánbul**sa**/İstanbúl**sa**
'as for Istanbul'

(iii) Where an unstressable suffix co-occurs with a clitic, stress falls on the syllable immediately before the first one (or immediately before its unstressable segment):

(66) Ailécek **mi**?
'As a family?'

(67) Oturúyormuşsun **bile**.
'(Apparently) you were already sitting.'

(iv) Where two or more clitics occur adjacently, the first one is stressed:

(68) Sokağa çıktín **da mı** havanın nasıl olduğunu biliyorsun?
'Is it because you have gone out that you know what the weather is like?'

11.2.2 Clitics in separate phrases

Clitics vary in the degree of prominence, particularly height of pitch, which they produce in the affected syllable. From this aspect, *ki*, *mI* and have a stronger effect (see also 11.2.3). When these occur with the other clitics, the phrase that they attach to predominates, irrespective of the order of the phrases:

(69) a. Kağıtları **da** okumúş **mu**?
b. Okumúş **mu** kağıtları **da**?
'Has s/he read the papers too?'

(70) a. Çerçeveleri **bile** temizlemişsín **ya**!
b. Temizlemişsín **ya** çerçeveleri **bile**!
'But you have even cleaned the frames!'

When *ki* and *mI* co-occur, it is *mI* that occurs earlier and predominates:

(71) Tohumları soğuktá **mı** bırakmıştın **ki**?
'Had you left the seeds in the cold, then?'

11.2.3 The combination of clitics with the negative marker -mA

The negative marker -*mA* usually generates stress, causing it to fall on the preceding syllable (8.2.2, 5.2.1 (i)). However, when it occurs in combination with one of the clitics *mI* (interrogative), *dA* (in its additive function) or *bile* 'even' stress falls before whichever one occurs first in the sentence:

(72) Bu gözlükle sahneyí **mi** göremiyormuş?
'Can't s/he see the STAGE with these glasses?'

(73) Yeni öğrencilerini daha gö́rmedin **mi**?
'Haven't you seen your new students yet?'

(74) Bén **de** íçmeyeceğim.
'I'm not going to have [any] either.'

(75) Semra ücretini alámamış **bile**.
'Semra couldn't even [succeed in] getting her wages.'

The pre-stressing effect of *ki, ya* or adversative *dA* in clause-final position is strong enough to neutralize the pre-stressing effect of a preceding -*mA*. When -*mA* occurs with any of these clitics stress falls on the syllable preceding *ki, ya* or *dA*:

(76) Kimseyle konuşmadím **ki**!
'But I didn't talk to anyone!'

(77) O filmi görmedím **de** aynı yönetmenin başka filmlerini gördüm.
'I didn't see that film, but I have seen other films by the same director.

This happens even if the syllable in question is otherwise unstressable:

(78) (Hani) eski gazeteleri atmamıştím **ya** ...
'Remember I hadn't thrown away the old newspapers...?'

Part 3

Syntax: The structure of sentences

Chapter 12

Simple and complex sentences

From the structural point of view, sentences are either **simple** (i.e. contain only a main clause, as in (1)) or **complex** (i.e. contain a main clause and one or more subordinate clauses, as in (2)):

(1) Dün okullar açıldı.
'The schools opened yesterday.'

(2) Dün [yolda giderken] [yıllardır görmediğim] bir arkadaşıma rastladım.
'Yesterday, [as I was walking along the street], I ran into a friend [whom I hadn't seen for years].'

In this book we indicate **subordinate clauses** using '[ ]' (square brackets).

In 12.1, we discuss the main constituents of simple sentences and in 12.2, we focus on the agreement between the subject and the predicate. The structure of complex sentences is summarized in 12.3 and discussed in detail in Chapters 24–27. Sentences can also be classified functionally, as **statements**, **questions**, **volitional utterances** and **exclamations**. These are discussed in 12.4.

12.1 Constituents of a sentence: Subject and predicate

12.1.1 Predicate

The **predicate** expresses an event, a process or a state in which the **subject** is involved:

(3) Necla bir hafta içinde projeyi **bitirecek**.
'Necla *will complete* the project within a week.'

(4) Bu çocuk hasta**ydı**.
'This child *was* ill.'

The predicate of a simple sentence or of the main clause in a complex sentence is described as **finite**. Some subordinate clauses also have finite predicates (12.3).

DOI: 10.4324/9780429435836-15

According to the type of predicate they have, sentences are divided into two types: verbal sentences and nominal sentences.

12.1.1.1 Verbal sentences

These are sentences whose predicates are **finite verbs** (8.2 (i)):

(5) Bu gün evde **kal-a-ma-m**.
   stay-PSB-NEG-1SG
   'I *can't stay* at home today.'

For a detailed discussion of the properties of verbal sentences, see Chapter 13.

12.1.1.2 Nominal sentences

These are sentences whose predicate either does not contain an overt verb at all or whose verb is one of the forms of the **copula** (*ol-* 'be', 'become', 'exist' or *-(y)-* 'be' (8.3.1)). This type of predicate is called a nominal predicate.

(6) Necla öğretmen.
   'Necla [*is*] a teacher.'

Non-modalized utterances with non-recurrent present time reference, such as (6), do not have an overt copula. Past tense (21.2.1) or evidential modality (21.4.3) can be indicated by **copular markers** (8.3.2):

(7) a. Necla öğretmen-**di**.
      teacher-P.COP'
      'Necla *was a teacher*.'

   b. Necla ev-de-**ymiş**.
      home-LOC-EV.COP
      '*Apparently* Necla *is/was* at home.'

For the expression of other types of tense, aspect and modality, it is necessary to use the suppletive form *ol-* of the copula (12.1.1.3):

(8) Necla öğretmen **ol-acak-tı**.
   teacher be-FUT-P.COP
   'Necla *was going to be* a teacher.'

Turkish nominal sentences are of two kinds: **linking** and **existential**.

Linking sentences

These correspond to the pattern *x is y* and contain the following constituents (listed in the unmarked order in which they occur, that is, unless they are focused, backgrounded or topicalized (23.3)):

(i) A subject (if overtly expressed (12.1.2, 18.1.5))
(ii) A subject complement as (part of) the predicate
(iii) A copular marker (suffixed to or immediately following the subject complement). In present tense sentences which are not aspectually or modally marked, the copula has no overt expression. Person/number marking of the predicate is attached to the copular marker, if there is one, otherwise to the subject complement. For the usage of the different forms of the copula, see 12.1.1.3.

Linking sentences optionally contain:

(iv) One or more adverbials.

(9) Ben   osırada   öğretmen-di-m.
SUBJECT   ADVERBIAL   SUBJECT.COMPLEMENT-COPULAR.
MARKER-PERSON.MARKER
(PREDICATE)
I   at.that.time   teacher-P.COP-1SG
'I was a teacher at the time.'

The function of the **subject complement** is to provide some kind of description of the subject, such as identification, characterization, location, state of belonging, etc. The subject complement may be an adjectival, a noun phrase or a postpositional phrase. If a noun phrase, it may be marked for any grammatical case except the accusative case:

(10) O saatte **biraz yorgun** olabilirim.   (Adjectival)
'At that hour I may be *a bit tired*.'

(11) Siz **çok iyi bir doktor**sunuz.   (Non-case-marked noun phrase)
'You are *a very good doctor*.'

(12) Sözüm **sana**ydı.   (Dative-marked noun phrase)
'My words were *for you*.'

(13) Herkes **ona karşı**ymış.   (Postpositional phrase)
'Apparently, everyone is/was *against him/her*.'

Linking sentences are negativized by means of *değil* 'not', which is placed between the subject complement and the copular marker:

(14) Dün ev-de **değil**-di-k.
    home-LOC not-P.COP-1PL
    'We were*n't* at home yesterday.'

For further examples, see 20.2.1.

Existential sentences

Whereas linking sentences present or assume knowledge of a subject and relate some attribute or identification to it, existential sentences merely assert the existence or presence of a subject. The statement is usually made in relation to either (i) a location in time or space or (ii) a possessor. There are thus two kinds of **existential sentences**: **locative** and **possessive**.

Locative existential sentences

These are of the type *there is an x (in y)* or *x has y*. The basic constituents of a locative existential sentence (listed in the unmarked order in which they occur, i.e. unless they are focused, backgrounded or topicalized (23.3)) are:

(i) At least one adverbial of place or time
(ii) The subject (shown in bold below)
(iii) One of the two existential expressions *var* 'present/existent' and *yok* 'absent/ non-existent' that function as subject complements. For the usage of the copula *ol-* instead of *var/yok*, see 12.1.1.3.
(iv) A copular marker (as in linking sentences. This marker is not present in the case of present tense sentences which are not marked for aspect or modality).
(v) 1st or 2nd person marking if required. *Yok* but not *var* may also take a 3rd person plural marker

(15) Buzdolab-ın-da iki şişe bira **var**.
    fridge-NCM-LOC two bottle beer existent
    '*There are* two bottles of beer in the fridge.'

(16) O gün ben **yok**-tu-m.
    that day I non.existent-P.COP-1SG
    'I *wasn't* [there] that day.'

(17) Evde **yoklar**.
    '*They are not* at home.'

When the expression indicating 'location' denotes persons or institutions, locative existential sentences express the concept *x has y*:

(18) Ben-de bir kitap var.
    I-LOC a book existent
    'I have a book.'

If the subject of such a sentence is **definite** or **specific** (Chapter 22), it may be topicalized (23.3.3) and thus placed at the beginning of the sentence:

(19) **Bu kitap** bende var.
'I have *this book*.'

Although close in meaning, locative existential sentences of the type *there is an x (in y)* cannot be used interchangeably with linking sentences (i.e. *x is y*) where the subject complement is a locative noun phrase:

(20) Banyoda Murat vardı.   (Locative existential sentence)
'Murat was in the bathroom.'

(21) Murat banyodaydı.   (Linking sentence)
'Murat was in the bathroom.'

The difference between these two is that (20) would be used in a situation where one wanted to indicate who the person in the bathroom was (hence 'Murat' is focused) whereas (21) would be used if one wanted to indicate Murat's whereabouts (hence 'bathroom' is focused) (23.3.1). Note that the negative form of (20) can be expressed only by *yok* whereas that of (21) can be expressed by either *değil* or *yok*. See 20.3 (37) for an example.

Possessive existential sentences

These express the concept *x has y*. Their basic constituents (listed in the unmarked order in which they occur, i.e. unless they are focused, backgrounded or topicalized (23.3)) are:

(i) A genitive-possessive construction (14.4) or a possessive-marked noun phrase, which is the subject
(ii) *var* 'present/existent' or *yok* 'absent/non-existent'
(iii) A copular marker (not overtly expressed in the case of present tense sentences which are not marked for aspect or modality)

Possessive existential sentences optionally contain:

(iv) One or more adverbials
  The adverbials, if there are any, are generally placed before the possessive-marked noun phrase. They may either precede or follow the genitive-marked possessor constituent (if there is one):

(22) a. Ayten-in **İstanbul'da** iki arkadaş-ı var.
  Ayten-GEN   two friend-3SG.POSS
  'Ayten has two friends *in Istanbul.*'

  b. **İstanbul'da** Ayten' in iki arkadaşı var.
  'Ayten has two friends *in Istanbul.*'

(23) **O gün** paramız yoktu.
'We had no money *that day*.'

Note that the concept *x has y* can be expressed by both possessive existential sentences and locative existential sentences:

(24) a. O gün bizde para yoktu.   (Locative existential; crs. (23))
    'We had no money that day.'

   b. Benim bir kitabım var.   (Possessive existential; crs. (18))
    'I have a book.'

Possessive existential sentences are used for expressing possession or relations between people and things which are either of a permanent nature or are considered as such. The possessed constituent in these constructions cannot have definite status (22.1) and cannot contain one of the definite determiners (15.6.2). Possessive existential sentences are mainly used for expressing the following:

(i) Familial and other personal relations, as in (22)
(ii) Part-whole relations:

(25) Masanın üç ayağı var.
    'The table has three legs.'

(iii) Authorship:

(26) Shakespeare'in birçok oyunu var.
    'Shakespeare has [written] many plays.'

(iv) Ownership:

(27) Murat'ın yatı var.
    'Murat has a yacht.'

Locative existential sentences, on the other hand, when they are used to express 'have', denote simply the location of an entity in the clothing worn, the bag or other container being carried, or the home occupied, by a human being or group at a particular time:

(28) Nejat'ta sadece 10 dolar varmış.
    'It seems Nejat only has 10 dollars [on him].'

(29) Acaba sizde limon var mı?
    'Have you by any chance got a lemon?'

The subject in these constructions can be definite or non-definite (i.e. indefinite (22.2) or categorial (22.3):

(30) Murat'ta **bu resim/bir resim/resim** var.
'Murat has *this/a picture/pictures*.'

The predicates *var* and *yok* can be replaced by the more formal verb *bulun-* 'be found' in locative existential sentences:

(31) Kurulda iki eski başbakan **var/bulun**uyor.
'*There are* two former prime ministers in the committee.'

(32) Bizim markette fazla sebze **yok/bulunma**z.
'*There aren't* many (types of) vegetables in our market.'

bulun- can also be used in relative clauses (Chapter 25 (8)) or as an auxiliary verb (13.3.1.2).

12.1.1.3 The complementarity of -(y)- and var/yok with ol-

The complementarity of -(y)- and ol-

When the concept *be* is expressed by the copula *-(y)-* (8.3.1, 8.3.2), this takes one of the following forms with the meanings shown:

(i) Past tense and stative aspect, in which case the copular form *-(y)DI* is used (21.2.1 and 21.3.4.1)
(ii) Evidential modality, in which case *-(y)mIş* is used (21.4.3)
(iii) Conditional modality, in which case *-(y)sA* is used (Chapter 27)

-(y)- also occurs in the non-finite form *-(y)ken* (26.2.3 (iv), 26.3.16 (iii)).

(33) Buranın adı Koyundere-**ymiş**.
Koyundere-EV.COP
'*I am told* that this place *is* called Koyundere.'

Note that *-(y)-* is omitted after a stem ending in a consonant:

(34) Bu bina eskiden okul**muş**.
'Apparently this building used to *be* a school.'

ol-, which is another form of the copula (8.3.1), is used in all other instances, e.g. when a nominal predicate expresses:

(i) Future tense (21.2.3):

(35) Bugün iş-te **ol-*acağ***ım.
today work-LOC be-FUT-1SG
'I *shall be* at work today.'

(ii) Habitual aspect (21.3.2):

    (36) Her gün iş-te **ol-*uyor*-**um.
           every day work-LOC be-IMPF-1SG
           'I *am* at work every day.'

(iii) Perfective aspect (21.3.4.1):

    (37) Bu ay işe gidişim sorunlu **oldu**.
           'Going to work this month *was* problematic for me.'

(iv) Necessitative modality (21.4.2.2):

    (38) Bugün iş-te **ol-*malı*-**ydı-m.
                work-LOC be-OBLG-P.COP-1SG
           'I *should* have *been* at work today.'

(v) Possibility (21.4.2.1):

    (39) Bugün iş-te **ol-*abil*-**ir-di-m.
                work-LOC be-PSB-AOR-P.COP-1SG
           'I *could* have *been* at work today.'

(vi) Commitment (21.4.4.6):

    (40) Bugün iş-te **ol-*ur*-**um.
                work-LOC be-AOR-1SG
           'I *will be* at work today.'

It is also used to express the nominal predicates of subordinate clauses:

    (41) [bugün iş-te **ol-*an***] kadın
           work-LOC be-PART woman
           'the woman who *is/was* at work today.'

The complementarity of *var/yok* and *ol-*

In a way closely parallel to its function as a suppletive form of the copula *-(y)-*, *ol-* is used (instead of *var/yok*) to produce future tense and aspectually or modally marked existential predicates, as in:

    (42) Eskiden bütün otobüslerde biletçi **ol-*ur*-**du.   (Habitual aspect)
                                           be-AOR-P.COP
           'There *used to be* a conductor on all the buses.'

(43) Daha büyük bir arabamız **ol**-*sa* keşke.   (Volitional modality)
     be-COND
     '*If only* we *had* a larger car.'

ol- is used instead of *var/yok* also in non-finite existential predicates:

(44) [ev-de su **ol**-ma-dığ-ı] zaman/için (crs. Evde su **yok**.)
     house-LOC water exist-NEG-CV-3SG.POSS time
     'when there [*isn*'t any water in the house]'

(45) [bahçe-si **ol**-an] ev (crs. Evin bahçesi **var**.)
     garden-3SG.POSS exist-PART house
     'the house [that *has* a garden]'

For further discussion of aspectual distinctions in nominal sentences, including the use of *ol-* to express *become*, see 21.3.4. *ol-* is also used as an auxiliary verb in compound verb forms (13.3.1.2).

12.1.2 Expression of the subject

In Turkish, the subject is not always overtly expressed within the sentence. Sentences without an overtly expressed subject and the conditions under which these occur are discussed in 18.1.5.

If the subject is expressed, this is always by some kind of **noun phrase** (Chapter 14), which can be simple such as a single pronoun as in (46) or a noun modified by determiners, numerals and/or adjectives as in (47):

(46) **Ben** o adamı sevmiyorum.
     '*I* don't like that man.'

(47) Her yıl bu kentte **iki bin beş yüz yeni bina** yapılıyor.
     'Every year, *two thousand five hundred new buildings* are constructed in this town.'

It can also be complex, i.e. a noun clause (Chapter 24):

(48) [**Jale'nin işten çıkartıldığı**] doğru değilmiş.
     'Apparently it's not true [*that Jale has been dismissed from her job*].'

The subject of a simple sentence or main clause is always in the non-case-marked form. Subjects of certain kinds of relative clauses and of most noun clauses, on the other hand, receive genitive case marking (Chapters 24–25).

For the factors determining the position of the subject in the sentence, see 23.1–2.

12.2 Agreement of subject and predicate

The predicate shows agreement with the subject in terms of person and number.

12.2.1 Person and number marking on the predicate

First and second persons

In all sentences which have a 1st or 2nd person subject, the addition of the appropriate person marker (8.4) to the predicate is obligatory whether or not the subject is separately represented in the sentence by a pronoun.

(49) (Biz) yorgun-**uz**.
(we) tired-1PL
'We are tired.'

(50) (Sen) yeni komşularımızla tanıştı**n** mı?
'Have you met our new neighbours?'

The only exception to this is sentences which have pronominalized determiners as subjects ((75), (78)–(79)).

Third person singular

Turkish does not have overt marking of the 3rd person singular on predicates:

(51) Annem yorgun.
'My mother's tired.'

(52) Ahmet hiçbir şey yapmadı.
'Ahmet hasn't done anything at all.'

The only exception is the 3rd person optative and imperative forms where the singular is marked by *-sIn*:

(53) Öğleden sonra bize gel**sin**.
'Let him/her come round to us this afternoon.'

In situations like the opening sentence of a work of fiction, where there is no preceding discourse that might identify a non-overt subject, it is the *absence* of any person markers on the predicate that indicates the 3rd person singular status of this subject:

(54) Çok yorgundu.
'S/he was very tired.'

Where the subject is overtly expressed by a noun phrase denoting a collectivity of human beings, such as *aile* 'family' or *halk* 'people', this predicate does not have plural person marking.

(55) **Yöre halkı** denizden çok dağları bilir.
'*The people in that region* are more familiar with mountains than with the sea.'

A sentence with an explicitly singular 3rd person human subject may be given a plural-marked predicate if the speaker wishes to express deference towards that individual.

(56) Selim Bey evde**ler** mi acaba?
'Is Selim Bey at home, I wonder?'

Third person plural
Where a 3rd person plural subject is not expressed by an overt noun phrase and the referents are animate, plural marking of the predicate is *obligatory*:

(57) Bodrum'a gitti**ler**.
'They've gone to Bodrum.'

(58) Dün çok yorgundu**lar**.
'Yesterday they were very tired.'

12.2.2 Agreement of a 3rd person predicate with different types of plural subject

12.2.2.1 Subject marked with the plural suffix

In a sentence where the subject is overtly expressed by a plural noun phrase, the 3rd person plural marker is often omitted from the predicate. The regularity with which this happens differs according to whether the noun phrase is modified by a numeral, whether the entities referred to by the subject are human or non-human, and whether they are specific or non-specific.

(i) Noun phrases with numeral modifiers:
If the subject is a noun phrase containing a numeral modifier, the predicate does not take plural marking:

(59) Bu sınıfta **elli iki öğrenci** var.
'There are *fifty-two pupils* in this class.'

(60) Dün **otuz üç mektup** geldi.
'Yesterday *thirty-three letters* came.'

However, where the subject noun phrase is the head of a partitive construction (14.5), refers to human beings, and is situated at some distance from the verb, plural marking of the verb may occur:

(61) {Yarışmacılar arasından **iki üç kişi**}, jürinin ısrarına rağmen yaşlarını söylememiş(ler).
'{**Two or three** of the competitors}, despite insistent requests from the judges, have apparently not stated their ages.'

The use of a non-case-marked noun phrase containing a numeral modifier in a sentence with a plural-marked verb is usually adverbial (equivalent to a phrase with *olarak* (16.1.9 (ii.b)), indicating that the action denoted by the verb is perceived as a group activity.

(62) **Üç kedi** birbirlerini bir daha kovalamadılar.
'*The three cats* didn't chase one another anymore.'

(63) **İki kız kardeş** seyahate gittiler.
'They went on holiday, *[just] the two sisters [together]*.'

(ii) Specific human subjects:
In the case of specific human subjects, plural marking of the predicate is optional but common. It draws attention to the distinctness of the individuals constituting the set which is referred to and may imply that the participation of each one in the action or state described by the predicate is not identical but in some way individuated. If the predicate in such a sentence is not given plural marking, the implication is that the speaker is more interested in the event or state as a whole than in the internal makeup of the group of individuals involved. (64) and (65) illustrate the optionality of plural marking of the predicate in sentences with an overtly expressed, specific and plural-marked human subject.

(64) **Bazı arkadaşlarımız** bu fikre katılmadı(**lar**).
'*Some of our colleagues* didn't agree with this idea.'

(65) **Senin çocuklar** burada değil(**ler**).
'*Your children* are not here.'

Where the idea of individuated action by the participants is inherent in the meaning of the predicate, plural marking of the predicate is more or less obligatory:

(66) **Öğrenciler** sürekli aralarında konuşuyorlardı.
'*The students* were talking among themselves all the time.'

(iii) Specific animal subjects:
In the case of specific animal subjects, use or non-use of plural marking on the predicate makes little difference. For some speakers, plural marking of

the predicate indicates the individual activity on the part of the members of the subject instead of as a group.

(67) **Köpekler** geceleri hep havlar(**lar**)dı.
'At night *the dogs* would always bark.'

(iv) Specific inanimate subjects:
As for sentences with specific inanimate subjects, plural marking of the predicate is common in the case of entities seen as moving or acting through a force that is in some way inherent to them:

(68) **Ağaçlar** artık yapraklarını döküyor(**lar**)dı.
'By now *the trees* were shedding their leaves.'

(69) **Arabalar** çok hızlı geçiyor(**lar**)dı.
'*The cars* were speeding past.'

Otherwise, where the sentence expresses a situation in which the role of the inanimate plural-marked subject is not an *active* one, plural marking is seldom encountered:

(70) **Buradaki odalar** banyoluymuş.
'Apparently *the rooms here* have en-suite facilities.'

(71) **Anahtarlar** buraya bırakılıyor.
'*The keys* are left here.'

(v) Indefinite subjects:
Even if human, animate or quasi-animate, a plural-marked subject which is indefinite, as in (72 (i)), does not trigger plural marking on the predicate:

(72) Bu resimleri **çocuklar** yapmış.
  (i) '*Children* painted these pictures.'
  (ii) '*The children* painted these pictures.'

Sentences with plural-marked subjects and no plural marking on the predicate can be ambiguous, as (72) illustrates. The addition of plural marking to the predicate, however, indicates unambiguously the *definite* status of the subject:

(73) Bu resimleri **çocuklar** yapmış**lar**.
'*The children* painted these pictures.'

12.2.2.2 Subjects containing determiners

Where the subject noun phrase contains one of the determiners that occur only in non-plural-marked noun phrases, such as *birkaç* 'a few', 'several', *birçok* 'many', *kaç* 'how many' and *her* 'every' (14.3.1.1 (ii)), the predicate is usually not plural-marked:

(74) **Birçok kişi** çocukluğunu pek düşünmez.
'*Many people* don't think much about their childhood.'

12.2.2.3 Pronominalized determiners as subjects

When the subject is a pronominalized determiner (18.4 (iv)), such as *hiçbirimiz* 'none of us', *bazılarınız* 'some of you', *hangileri* 'which of them', 'which (ones)', *(bir)çoğumuz* 'many/most of us' or one of the pronominalized forms derived from the adverb *hep* (18.4 (v)), such as *hepimiz* 'all of us', marking of the predicate with the appropriate person suffix may or may not be obligatory, depending on the quantified pronoun. In the case of 3rd person subjects, the pronominalized determiner may be the head of a partitive construction (14.5.2–3), as in (80) and (82) below.

(i) *hiçbirimiz/hiçbiriniz/hiçbiri* 'none of us/you/them':
Where the 1st or 2nd person form of this pronoun occurs as subject, 1st or 2nd person marking of a verbal predicate is optional:

(75) **Hiçbirimiz** bugün sokağa çıkmadı(**k**).
'*None of us* went out today.'

Most speakers, however, regularly add person marking to nominal predicates:

(76) Neden **hiçbiriniz** evde değil**siniz**?
'Why are *none of you* at home?'

With the 3rd person form *hiçbiri* 'none of them', the predicate may or may not be plural marked:

(77) **Hiçbiri** gelmeyecek(**ler**).
'None of them is going to come.'

(ii) *bazı(ları)mız/bazı(ları)nız/bazısı/bazıları/kimimiz/kiminiz/kimisi/kimileri* 'some of us/you/them':
With the 1st or 2nd person forms of these pronouns, person marking is optional on both verbal and nominal predicates:

(78) **Bazılarımız** bu konudan hoşlanmıyor(**uz**).
'*Some of us* don't like this topic.'

(79) **Kiminiz** burada değildi(**niz**).
'*Some of you* weren't here.'

With the 3rd person forms *bazısı, bazıları/kimisi/kimileri* 'some of them', the preferred form is for the predicate not to have plural marking:

(80) Komşulardan **bazıları** evde yoktu.
'Some of the neighbours weren't at home.'

(iii) *çoğumuz/çoğunuz/çoğu/çokları* 'most of us/you/them', *birçoğumuz/ birçoğunuz/birçoğu/birçokları* 'many of us/you/them':
With the 1st and 2nd person forms of these determiners, person marking is optional:

(81) **(Bir)çoğunuz** mesajlara cevap vermedi(**niz**).
'Many/most of you have not responded to the messages.'

With the 3rd person forms plural marking is optional:

(82) Misafirlerin **çoğu** şarap içti(**ler**).
'Most of the guests drank wine.'

(iv) *Hepimiz/hepiniz/hepsi* 'all of us/you/them':
With the 1st and 2nd person forms of these quantified pronouns referring to all-inclusive groups, person marking is obligatory in both nominal and verbal predicates:

(83) **Hepimiz** tatilde deniz kıyısına gidiyor**uz**.
'*All of us* go to the seaside in the vacation.'

The 3rd person form is most commonly used without a person marker, but it may also be used with a 3rd person plural marker:

(84) Oyuncuların **hepsi** yeni kostümler istiyor(**lar**).
'*All the actors* want new costumes.'

For *hangi*, see 19.2.1.4.

12.2.2.4 Conjoined subjects

Where a pair or series of conjoined subjects includes *ben* 'I' or *biz* 'we', the predicate is marked for 1st person plural:

(85) **Arkadaşlarımla ben** bu akşam dışarı çıkmıyor**uz**.
'*My friends and I* aren't going out tonight.'

Where a pair or series of conjoined subjects includes *sen/siz* 'you' and excludes *ben* 'I' or *biz* 'we', the predicate is marked for 2nd person plural:

(86) **Sen ve arkadaşların** Almanya'ya hangi yıl gitti**niz**?
'What year did *you and your friends* go to Germany?'

Where a group of conjoined subjects includes both a 1st person pronoun and a 2nd person pronoun, the tendency is for the 1st person pronoun to be the last in the series of conjoined subjects:

(87) **Ya Ahmet ya siz ya da ben** hazırlıklara gönüllü katılmalıyız.
'*Either Ahmet or you or I* must volunteer for the preparations.'

When both subjects are 3rd person, the predicate may or may not have plural marking, according to the principles explained in 12.2.2.1.

Subjects conjoined by the *ve* 'and' (28.3.1.1 (i)), *veya* 'or', *ya da* 'or', *ya...ya* 'either...or' (28.3.3.1), *hem...hem, gerek...gerek, dA...dA* 'both...and', (28.3.2), *ne...ne* 'neither...nor' (20.4) can be in any order between themselves and a pronoun can be the first or the second constituent:

(88) **Ne Ayşe ne ben** yalandan hoşlanmıyoruz.
'*Neither Ayşe nor I* like lying.'

(89) **Sen** *ya da* **Ahmet**, bugün oraya gidip bu işi bitirin.
'*You or Ahmet* should go there and finish it off today.'

Subjects conjoined by *-(y)lA/ile* (8.1.4, 28.3.1.1 (ii)) behave somewhat differently. If one of these is a personal pronoun, it usually occurs as the second item. Since the person marker on the predicate indicates this person, this pronoun may be omitted (see also 18.1.5):

(90) **Ahmet'le (ben)** dün deniz kenarında yürüyüş yaptık.
'Yesterday *Ahmet and I* went for a walk on the seashore.'

Note, however, that sentences where the pronoun of a conjoined subject is deleted may be ambiguous. Since the predicate of such a sentence has plural marking (this is obligatory in the 1st and 2nd persons and optional in the 3rd person), it may be unclear whether the 'hidden' pronoun is singular or plural:

(91) **Ahmet'le** dün deniz kenarında yürüyüş yaptı**k**.
  (i) 'Yesterday *Ahmet and I* went for a walk on the seashore.'
  (ii) 'Yesterday *we and Ahmet* went for a walk on the seashore.'

Note also that *-(y)lA/ile* functions as a conjunction only when it is between the two items it conjoins. Otherwise, it functions as a postposition:

(92) **Ben Ahmet'le** dün deniz kenarında yürüyüş yaptı**m**.
'Yesterday I went *with Ahmet* for a walk on the seashore.'

In such a case the constituent bearing *-(y)lA/ile* is not part of the subject, but forms with the comitative marker an adverbial of manner (16.4.3 (vii)); hence the predicate in (92) has 1st person singular marking because of its agreement with *ben* 'I'. For the postpositional function of *-(y)lA/ile*, see 17.2.1 (iii) and 13.2.3.2. For the inclusive nature of *-(y)lA/ile*, see 28.3.1.1 (ii).

12.2.3 Personal pronouns as subject complements

When the subject complement of a linking sentence is a personal pronoun, the person marker agrees with this pronoun rather than with the subject:

(93) Ayşe **ben-im**.
Ayşe I-1SG
'*I* am Ayşe.'

Note that (93) is a sentence where the subject complement and the subject of a regular linking sentence such as (94) are swapped:

(94) **Ben** Ayşe-yim.
I Ayşe-1SG
'*I* am Ayşe.'

This kind of reversal can occur only where the subject complement (*Ayşe* in (94)) is a non-case-marked noun phrase.

There is an important difference in the meaning of these sentences (rendered by the position of sentence stress in English) in that (93) corresponds to '*I* am Ayşe' (i.e. a response to the question *Who is Ayşe?*) whereas (94) corresponds to 'I am *Ayşe*' (i.e. a response to the question *Who are you?*).

12.3 Complex sentences and subordination

Complex sentences contain at least one subordinate clause in addition to a main clause. Structurally, the predicate of a subordinate clause can be **finite** (i.e. identical in form to a main clause predicate):

(95) [Maç birazdan **başla-yacak**] de-n-iyor.
match soon start-FUT say-PASS-IMPF
'It is said [that the match *will be starting* soon].'

(96) [Çocuğun babası **kim**] bilinmiyor.
'It's not known [*who* the father of the child *is*].'
(lit. '[Who is the father of the child] is not known.')

However, the majority of subordinate clauses are **non-finite** (i.e. contain a verbal predicate with one of the subordinating suffixes in 8.5):

(97) [Maç-ın birazdan **başla-yacağı**] söyleniyor.
match-GEN soon start-SUB-3SG.POSS
'It is said [*that* the match *will be starting* soon].'

(98) [Maç **başla-yınca**] herkes ayağa fırladı.
match start-SUB
'[*When* the match *started*] everyone jumped to their feet.'

(99) [Maç-ı **izle-yen**] kişiler yağmurdan sırılsıklam olmuşlar.
match-ACC watch-SUB
'The people [*who watched* the match] got soaked.'

A finite subordinate clause can be directly connected to the superordinate clause (as in (97)) or it can be linked to the superordinate clause by means of a subordinator (e.g. *diye*):

(100) [Maç birazdan **başlayacak**] *diye* biliyorduk.
'We thought [(*that*) the match *would be starting* soon].'

The subordinators that link finite clauses to superordinate clauses are the following: *diye* (24.3.1 and 26.1.1), *ki* (24.3.2 and 26.1.2), *madem (ki)* (26.1.3), *nasıl (ki)* (26.1.4), *-DI mI* (26.1.6 and 27.6.2), *dA* (26.1.7) and some other formal, less frequently used or obsolescent subordinators containing *ki*, such as *ola ki*, *meğer ki*, *kim ki*, *ne zaman ki*. The Persian-derived subordinator *ki* stands at the beginning of its clause in the manner of Indo-European subordinators such as its French and Italian cognates *que*, *che*.

Subordinate clauses have three different functions:

(i) **noun clauses** function as subjects or objects
(ii) **relative clauses** function as adjectival phrases (except for pronominal relative clauses (25.3) which function as subjects or objects)
(iii) **adverbial clauses** function as adverbials

These clauses are discussed in detail in Chapters 24–7.

The clause within which a subordinate clause occurs is called the **superordinate clause**. The superordinate clause may either be the main clause of the sentence or another subordinate clause. In the examples below the superordinate clauses are shown in bold italics. In (101), the superordinate clause is a main clause and the subordinate clause is an adverbial clause, and in (102), the superordinate clause is a noun clause and the subordinate clause is an adverbial clause:

(101) ***Füsun bu kitap-lar-ı*** [öğretmenlik yap-ar-**ken**] ***kullan-mış-tı***.
Füsun this book-PL-ACC teaching do-AOR-SUB use-PF-P.COP
'*Füsun used these books* [*when she was working as a teacher*].'

(102) ***Füsun-un*** [kullan-ıl-mı-yor **diye**] ***kitap-lar-ı***
Füsun-GEN use-PASS-NEG-IMPF SUB book-PL-ACC
sat-ma-sı
sell-SUB-3SG.POSS
'*Füsun's selling the books* [*on the grounds that they were not being used*]'

Note that a clause that contains *ki* can only be subordinate to a main clause.

12.4 Functional sentence types

Sentences can be classified functionally, that is according to the type of utterance that they express. The four major types of utterance are statements, questions, volitional utterances and exclamations, all of which can be expressed by both verbal and nominal sentences.

(i) Statements:

(103) Köyde Bayram'ın ailesi zengin sayılıyormuş.
'In the village, Bayram's family is apparently considered rich.'

(104) Bayram'ın ailesinin diğer köylülerden daha çok toprağı var.
'Bayram's family has more land than the other villagers.'

(ii) Questions:
What marks a sentence as a question is the presence either of the interrogative clitic *mI* or of a **wh-phrase** such as *ne zaman* 'when' or *kaç* 'how many'. For a full discussion of how questions are expressed in Turkish, see Chapter 19.

(iii) Volitional utterances:
These are utterances which express the speaker's attitude towards the possible performance of an action or the occurrence of an event. The most common types include commands, suggestions and wishes (21.4.4).

(105) Saat ikiden sonra beni telefonla ara. (Command)
'Ring me after two o'clock.'

(106) Bu akşam dışarda yiyelim. (Suggestion)
'Let's eat out this evening.'

(107) Çabuk bitirseler bari. (Wish)
'I hope at least they finish quickly.'

(iv) Exclamations:
Exclamations often contain a wh-phrase (19.2), such as *ne* 'what', *ne kadar* 'how (much)', *nasıl* 'how' or *ne biçim* 'what kind (of)'. Exclamations of this kind have the intonation pattern of statements (5.1 (i)) and are thus distinguishable from questions.

(108) Burası **ne (kadar)** *güzel* bir yer!
'*What* a *beautiful* place this is!'

(109) Ay **nasıl** güldük!
'Oh, *how* we laughed!'

(110) Bu **ne biçim** yapı!
'*What a* construction!'

Exclamations can also be expressed with *o kadar/öyle(sine)...ki* 'so' (26.1.2.3) or *pek* (20.5.4.2):

(111) Su **o kadar** soğuktu **ki**!
'The water was *so* cold!'

(112) Çocuğu **öylesine** seviyor **ki**!
'S/he loves the child *so much*!'

(113) **Pek (de)** tatlı bir oğlunuz varmış!
'*What a* sweet son you have!'

Chapter 13

The verb phrase

A **verb phrase** is the fundamental part of a verbal sentence (12.1.1.1) and consists of a **verb**, its **complements** and **adverbials** that modify the verb. At its simplest, a verb phrase consists of a verb:

(1) **Otur**.
'Sit (down)'.

In our examples below, we illustrate verb phrases as they appear in verbal sentences. If the verb is **transitive**, a verb phrase has a direct object:

(2) **Kapıyı kapat**ma.
'Don't *close the door*.'

A verb phrase can also contain adverbials that modify the verb. The example below shows a phrase consisting of a verb, its complement (the direct object *suyu* 'water') and three adverbials (*yavaşça* 'slowly', *sürahiden* 'from the jug', *masadaki bardağa* 'into the glass on the table'):

(3) **Suyu yavaşça sürahiden masadaki bardağa döktü**.
'S/he *slowly poured the water from the jug into the glass*.'

Both main clauses (4) and subordinate clauses (bracketed section in (5)) contain verb phrases.

(4) Ahmet çay-ı bardak-tan iç-ecek.
Ahmet tea-ACC glass-ABL drink-FUT
'Ahmet will drink the tea from a glass.'

(5) [Ahmet-in **çay-ı bardak-tan iç**-me]-si gerek-iyor-du.
Ahmet-GEN tea-ACC glass-ABL drink-VN-3SG.POSS be.necessary-IMPF-P.COP
'Ahmet was supposed to *drink the tea from a glass*.'

DOI: 10.4324/9780429435836-16

Verbs and the constituents of the verb phrase are discussed in 13.1. In 13.2, we describe the structure of verb phrases which have causative, passive, reflexive and reciprocal verbs and in 13.3, we discuss auxiliary verbs.

Other elements that are associated with verb phrases are discussed elsewhere, namely stress in 4.4.1, 23.1.1, negation in Chapter 20, and tense, aspect and modality in Chapter 21. The ordering of verbal inflectional suffixes is discussed in 8.2 (see also 6.3). The majority of examples used in this chapter have the unmarked word order *subject-(object)-verb*. For variations in word order, see Chapter 23.

13.1 Constituents of the verb phrase

13.1.1 The verb

The internal structure of a verb phrase depends primarily on the transitivity or intransitivity of the verb. This distinction relates to the ability of a verb to take a direct object (13.1.2.1). Verbs which cannot take direct objects such as *git-* 'go', *düş-* 'fall', *otur-* 'sit', *kork-* 'be afraid (of)' and *sevin-* 'be happy (about)' are **intransitive**:

(6) Londra'ya gidelim.
 'Let's go to London.'

(7) Ayşe çok hızlı koşuyordu.
 'Ayşe was running very fast.'

Verbs such as *ye-* 'eat', *gör-* 'see', *yaz-* 'write' and *boya-* 'paint', on the other hand, have direct objects (bold in the examples below) and are **transitive**:

(8) Erol **duvar-lar-ı** yanlışlıkla boyamış.
 wall-PL-ACC
 'Erol apparently painted *the walls* by mistake.'

(9) Bugün sınıfta **çok önemli konular** işledik.
 'Today in class we covered [some] *very important topics*.'

However, there is a group of intransitive verbs that can also be used transitively. These are verbs of motion such as *yüz-* 'swim', *koş-* 'run' and *yürü-* 'walk' and they may take direct objects expressing distances:

(10) Normal bir koşucu **100 metre-lik bir mesafe-yi**
 100 metre-ADJ a distance-ACC
 30 saniyenin altında koşabilir.
 'An ordinary athlete can run *a distance of 100 metres* in under thirty seconds.'

In the majority of cases, the direct object and the adverbials in a verb phrase can be omitted if they are recoverable from the context. For example, in (11) the verb *işle-* 'cover (a topic)' appears without its direct object because the information is recoverable from the context (see also 28.4.3):

(11) A. Bugün sınıfta **önemli konular** işlediniz mi?
'Did you cover *important topics* in class today?'

B. İşledik.
'[Yes,] we did.'

13.1.2 Complements of the verb

In a verb phrase, a **complement** is a constituent that 'completes' the meaning of the verb and that stands in a particular structural relationship to it. The complement of a verb is a noun phrase which can be simple or complex (Chapters 14 and 24). It represents the person(s) or thing(s) (other than the subject) affected by the action of the verb. Some verbs (e.g. *öksür-* 'cough' or *yüz-* 'swim') have meanings which are complete in themselves and do not have any kind of complement. Other verbs, such as *yık-* 'destroy', *anla-* 'understand' and *kork-* 'fear' denote actions or states which have complements. There are two types of complement: **direct objects** and **oblique objects**.

13.1.2.1 Direct object

A direct object denotes a person or thing which is brought into being or to which something is done by the action of the subject. In Turkish, the noun phrase which constitutes the direct object is usually non-case-marked if non-definite (i.e. indefinite (22.2) or categorial (22.3)) but if definite it has the accusative case marker *-(y)I*.

Indefinite direct object

(12) **Bir mektup** yaz-dı-m.
a letter write-PF-1SG
'I wrote *a letter*.'

Categorial direct object

(13) Her yaz açık hava sinema-sın-da **film**
every summer open air cinema-NCM-LOC film

seyr-ed-er-ler-di.
watch-AUX-AOR- 3PL-P.COP

'They used to watch *films* in outdoor cinemas every summer.'

Definite direct object

(14) **Bu parça-yı** ancak çok iyi bir piyanist çal-abil-ir.
 this piece-ACC only very good a pianist play-PSB-AOR
 'Only a very good pianist can play *this piece*.'

13.1.2.2 Oblique object

Oblique objects denote persons or things which are not directly affected by the action of the verb but which are an integral part of its meaning. They have one of the dative, locative, ablative or comitative/instrumental markers. They occur with intransitive verbs, especially with those which express emotion, such as *hoşlan-* 'like', 'fancy', *kork-* 'fear', *sevin-* 'be happy (about)', *üzül-* 'be sad (about)' and *kız-* 'be angry (about/with)'. Which particular case marker appears on the complement noun phrase is determined by the verb.

Dative-marked oblique object

Verbs such as *inan-* 'believe', *güven-* 'trust', *acı-* 'feel sorry (for)', *sevin-* 'be pleased (about)', *üzül-* 'be sad/sorry (about)', *kız-* 'be angry (about/with)', *kıy-* 'be merciless (towards)', *bayıl-* 'adore', *tap-* 'worship' and those that are nominal-verb compounds such as *razı ol-* 'agree (to)', *gıcık ol-/kıl ol-* 'be irritated (by)' (colloquial), *boyun eğ-* 'submit (to)', *sıkıl-* 'be upset (by)' and *uy-* 'match', 'comply (with)' take complements with dative case marking:

(15) Herkes **piyanist-*e*** bayıl-dı.
 pianist-DAT adore-PF
 'Everyone adored *the pianist*.'

(16) Bazı insanlar [**tatsızlık çıkar-may**]-*a* bayıl-ıyor.
 conflict create-VN-DAT love-IMPF
 'Some people love [*creating conflicts*].'

Locative-marked oblique object

Verbs such as *diret-* 'insist (on)', *ısrar et-* 'insist (on)' and those that are nominal-verb compounds such as *karar kıl-* 'decide (on)', *kusur et-* 'fail (in)' take complements in the locative case:

(17) Kocası **evin rengin*de*** ısrar ediyor.
 'Her husband is being insistent *about the colour of the house*.'

(18) Çocuk [**okul-a git-me-mek**]-*te* diret-iyor.
 school-DAT go-NEG-VN-LOC insist-IMPF
 'The child *refuses to go to school*.'
 (lit. '...insists on [*not going to school*].')

Ablative-marked oblique object

Verbs such as *hoşlan-* 'like', 'fancy', *iğren-* 'be disgusted (by)', *soğu-* 'lose one's love (for)', *bık-* 'get fed up (with)', *sıkıl-* 'get bored (with)', *faydalan-* 'take advantage (of)', 'benefit (from)', *kork-* 'be afraid (of)', *şüphelen-* 'suspect' and verbs that are nominal-verb compounds such as *nefret et-* 'hate', *memnun kal-* 'be happy (with)', *vazgeç-* 'give up' take complements in the ablative case:

(19) Nermin kazadan sonra **evin*den*** soğudu.
'After the accident, Nermin became apprehensive *about* [living in] her house.'

(20) Nermin bir gün geldi ki [**yemek yap-mak**]-*tan* bık-tı.
                                food-make-VN-ABL be.fed.up-PF
'The day came when Nermin got fed up *with* [*cooking*].'

Comitative/instrumental-marked oblique object

Verbs such as *ilgilen-* 'show an interest (in)' and verbs that are nominal-verb compounds such as *alay et-, dalga geç-* 'make fun (of)' (colloquial) take complements which have the comitative/instrumental marker:

(21) Serap **kız kardeşi*yle*** hep alay ediyor.
'Serap always makes fun *of her sister*.'

(22) Erol **sinema-*yla*** çok ilgilen-iyor-du.
                 cinema-COM/INS very show.interest.in-IMPF-P.COP
'Erol was very interested in films.'

The oblique objects of some verbs are not uniquely associated with a single case suffix. The complement of the verb *utan-* 'be ashamed', 'embarrassed' has ablative case marking if it is a simple noun phrase, but if it is a clause (24.4.1.3) it can have either ablative or dative marking:

(23) Erol o kadar utangaç ki **doktor*dan*** bile utanıyor.
'Erol is so shy that he is even embarrassed [to be seen] *by the doctor*.'

(24) Erol o kadar utangaç ki [**konuş-mak**]-*tan*/[**konuş-may**]-*a*
                             speak-VN-ABL   speak-VN-DAT
bile utanıyor.
'Erol is so shy that he is even embarrassed *to speak*.'

Some verbs which take oblique objects also have direct objects, such as *mahkum et-* 'sentence (to)', 'condemn (to)', *it-* 'lead (into)', *sürükle-* 'drag (into)', *zorla-* 'force (to/into)'. The oblique objects of these verbs are either abstract nouns or clauses formed with *-mAK* (24.4.1.3).

(25) Allahtan **kimse-yi ölüm-e** mahkum etmediler.
    no.one-ACC death-DAT
    'Luckily they didn't condemn anyone to death.'

For another example, see (46) in Chapter 23.

13.1.3 Adverbials

The adverbials in a verb phrase modify the verb by describing:

(i) Its destination or target (indicated by the dative case marker):

***araba-ya** git-*	'go *to the c*ar'
***ayna-ya** bak-*	'look *in the mirror*'
***oğlan-a** paket-i ver-*	'give the package *to the boy*'

(ii) Its location (indicated by the locative case marker):

***kanape-de** uyu-*	'sleep *on the sofa*'
***biz-de** kal-*	'stay *at our place*'
***durak-ta** otobüs bekle-*	'wait for a bus *at the bus stop*'

(iii) The source of the action or the space through which an action takes place (indicated by the ablative case marker):

***büro-dan** kağıtlar-ı al-*	'take the papers *from the office*'
***mutfak-tan** yemeğ-i getir-*	'bring the food *from the kitchen*'
***evlerin üstün-den** geç-*	'pass *over the houses*'

(iv) The beneficiary/recipient of an action (indicated by the dative case marker):

***misafir-e** yol-u göster-*	'show *the guest* the way'
***arkadaşın-a** hediye al-*	'buy a gift *for your friend*'
***köpekler-e** barınak yap*	'make a shelter *for (the) dogs*'

(v) The manner in which the action takes place, indicated by:
   a. The comitative/instrumental marker

   ***bıçak-la** ekmek kes-*   'cut bread *with a knife*'

   b. A simple adverb

   ***yavaş** yürü-*   'walk *slowly*'

c. A derived adverb

    korkak-ça *kaç-*   'run away *in a cowardly fashion*'

d. An adjective used adverbially

    güzel *oku-*   'study *well*'

For a full discussion of adverbials, see Chapter 16.

13.2 Transitivity and voice

In many instances where English has unrelated stems for transitive and intransitive pairs (e.g. *drop* and *fall*) or identical verbs with transitive and intransitive meaning (e.g. *change* (something) and *change* (in the sense of *go through a change*)), Turkish also has unrelated transitive and intransitive pairs (e.g. *sok-* 'insert', 'put in', *gir-* 'enter'). But in the vast majority of cases Turkish uses **voice suffix**es to alter the transitivity of a verb. There are four voice suffixes (8.2.1): **causative, passive, reflexive and reciprocal**. In the overwhelming majority of cases the final suffix of a verb derived in this fashion automatically indicates the transitivity or intransitivity of a stem. Almost all verb stems ending in the passive, reflexive or reciprocal suffixes *-Il*, *-(I)n*, *-(I)ş* or the composite suffixes *-lAn* or *-lAş* (7.2.2.1), are intransitive and almost all verb stems ending in the causative suffix (*-DIr*, *-t*, *-It*, *-Ir*, *-Ar*, *-Art*) or the composite suffix *-lAt* (7.2.2.1) are transitive. Some exceptions are *edin-* 'acquire', which is transitive, and *koşuştur-* 'run about' and *tuttur-* 'insist', which are intransitive. *örtün-* 'cover oneself' can be used intransitively or transitively (e.g. *örtündüler* 'they covered themselves' or *battaniyeleri örtündüler* 'they covered themselves with blankets').

Transitivizing intransitive verbs by attaching the causative suffix (8.2.1.1):

değiş- 'change'	*değiş-tir-* 'change (s.t.)'
yürü- 'walk'	*yürü-t-* 'make (s.o.) walk'
ürk- 'be scared (of)'	*ürk-üt-* 'scare', 'startle'
düş- 'fall'	*düş-ür-* 'drop'
çık- 'go/come out'	*çık-ar-* 'remove', 'get (s.t.) out'

Intransitivizing transitive verbs by attaching the passive (8.2.1.2) or reflexive suffix (8.2.1.3):

yık- 'destroy'	*yık-ıl-* 'be destroyed', 'collapse'
eğ- 'bend (s.t.)'	*eğ-il-* 'bend over'
sakla- 'hide (s.t.)'	*sakla-n-* 'hide'
yıka- 'wash'	*yıka-n-* 'be washed', 'get washed', 'have a bath/shower'

The addition of a voice suffix to a stem does not always result in a simple change in transitivity; it may produce a meaning unpredictable from that of the root (e.g. *koy-* 'put', *koyul-* 'set about (doing s.t.)', *sev-* 'love', *sevin-* 'be happy (about)', *uğraş-* 'be busy (with)', *uğraştır-* 'give (s.o.) hassle'.

13.2.1 Causative constructions

The attachment of the causative suffix (i.e. one of the forms *-DIr, -t, -It, -Ir, -Ar, -Art*, 8.2.1.1) to some stems, e.g. *ak-* 'flow', merely results in a change in transitivity:

(26) a. Bütün atık su-lar deniz-e ak-tı.
 all waste water-PL sea-DAT flow-PF
 'All the waste water flowed into the sea.'

b. Bütün atık su-lar-ı deniz-e **ak-*ıt*-tı-lar**.
 all waste water-PL-ACC sea-DAT flow-CAUS-PF-3PL
 'They *released* all the waste water into the sea.'

The causative suffix can attach to both intransitive and transitive verbs. It expresses one of the concepts 'cause', 'make', 'have', 'let' or 'allow'.

(i) Causitivizing intransitive verbs
 In the case of intransitive verbs, the person or thing that is made to perform or undergo the action denoted by the verb is in the accusative case:

(27) Çocukları iki saat yürü-t-tü-ler.
 walk-CAUS-PF-3PL
 'They *made* the children walk for two hours.'

(28) Bebek dün gece beni uyu-t-ma-dı.
 sleep-CAUS-NEG -PF
 'The baby didn't *let* me sleep last night.'

(ii) Causitivizing transitive verbs
 In a causative construction based on a transitive verb (e.g. *aç-* 'open'), the performer of the action denoted by this verb (the **causee**) can be expressed by a dative-marked noun phrase. The causee is usually human, but can also be an inanimate entity to which inherent power is attributed, such as a computer or mechanical device:

(29) Nuran **Deniz-*e*** kapı-yı aç-tır-dı.
 Deniz-DAT door-ACC open-CAUS-PF
 'Nuran *made Deniz* open the door.'

(30) **Annes*ine*** bulaşık yıkatmıyor.
'S/he doesn't *let his/her mother* wash the dishes.'

(31) Şule elini **makina*ya*** kaptırdı.
'Şule had her hand caught *in the machine*.'

Causative constructions with dative-marked noun phrases can sometimes be ambiguous because a dative-marked noun phrase can have an adverbial function (13.1.3):

(32) Bu ev-i **Ahmet-e** yap-tır-dı-m.
this house-ACC Ahmet-DAT make-CAUS-PF-1SG

This sentence can mean 'I got *Ahmet* to build this house' where the dative-marked noun phrase *Ahmet'e* denotes the person who has built the house, or it may mean 'I had this house built *for Ahmet*' where this same noun phrase marks the beneficiary. To resolve such ambiguities beneficiaries can be expressed by postpositional phrases:

(33) Bu evi **Ahmet için** yaptırdım.
Ahmet for
'I had this house built *for Ahmet*.'

Sentences in which the beneficiary is indicated by other means are preferred to sentences where both the causee and the beneficiary are indicated by a dative-marked noun phrase.

Causation can also be expressed by means of a complex sentence containing verbs like *zorla-* 'force' (24.4.1.3 (64)), *sağla-* 'ensure' or *yol aç-* 'cause' (24.4.2.2 (97)).

13.2.1.1 Multiple occurrences of the causative suffix

The causative suffix can attach to a stem already containing a causative suffix:

(34) Su-lar-ı durmadan (**temizlikçi-ye**) balkon-dan aşağı
water-PL-ACC continuously cleaner-DAT balcony-ABL down

ak-*ıt-tır*-ıyor.
flow-CAUS-CAUS-IMPF

'S/he is always *getting/making* the cleaner (to) *run* the water down off the balcony.'

Whether the verb is intransitive or transitive, causative sentences without a dative-marked noun phrase (indicated in brackets above) are more common than those that have one. In the event of the dative noun phrase being omitted from (34), the sentence would mean 'S/he is always getting the water run down off the balcony'.

If the verb is transitive (e.g. *kes-* 'cut'), an additional causative suffix is often used simply as a means of emphasizing causation, but it may also imply the addition of another intermediary. In most cases, a transitive stem with two causative suffixes is identical in meaning to its single causative counterpart:

(35) a. Saç-ım-ı kes-**tir**-di-m.
hair-1SG.POSS-ACC cut-CAUS-PF-1SG
'I *had* my hair cut.'

b. Saçımı kes-**tir**-**t**-ti-m.
cut-CAUS-CAUS-PF-1SG
'I *had* my hair cut.'

The double occurrence of the causative is even more clearly preferred when the causee and the beneficiary are both expressed in the sentence:

(36) **Karı-sın-a/karısı için** bir ev
BENEFICIARY
wife-3SG.POSS-DAT/wife-3SG.POSS for a house

yap-**tır**-**t**-mış **bir İngiliz mimar-a**.
CAUSEE
make-CAUS-CAUS-EV/PF a British architect-DAT

'He got *a British architect* to build a house *for his wife*.'

In colloquial speech, a third occurrence of the causative suffix only highlights the fact that the event was caused, rather than adding one more intermediary to the clause.

13.2.1.2 Causatives of verbs of emotion

Causative constructions based on certain verbs of emotion such as *kork-* 'fear', *ürk-* 'be scared/intimidated', *kız-* 'be angry (with)' and *sevin-* 'be happy (about)' have a special structure. Their oblique objects lose their case marker and function as subjects in their causativized counterparts (37b):

(37) a. Hayvan-lar **güneş tutulmasın-dan** ürk-üyor.
animal-PL solar eclipse-ABL be.frightened-IMPF
'Animals are frightened *by solar eclipses*.'

b. **Güneş tutulması** hayvan-lar-ı ürk-*üt*-üyor.
solar eclipse animal-PL-ACC be.frightened-CAUS-IMPF
'*Solar eclipses* scare animals.'

There are some verbs of emotion (such as *soğu-* 'lose one's love (for)', *nefret et-* 'hate') which do not follow this pattern. The complements of these verbs cannot become the subject of their causativized counterparts; they remain the oblique object and keep their case marking:

(38) a. Oğlum **yünlü kazaktan** nefret ediyor.
'My son hates [wearing] *woollen sweaters.*'

b. Sıcak havalar oğlumu **yünlü kazaktan** nefret et*tir*di.
'The warm weather *made* my son hate *woollen sweaters.*'

13.2.2 Passive constructions

In Turkish both transitive and intransitive verbs can combine with the passive suffix (8.2.1.2).

13.2.2.1 Passivizing a transitive verb

This is usually done for purposes of topicalizing (23.3.3) the direct object and de-emphasizing or suppressing the agent or perpetrator of the action denoted by the verb. The process of passivization has the effect of making the direct object of a transitive verb the subject of a passive one. In the examples below the corresponding active sentence is shown in brackets:

(39) **Ev** bu yıl artık sat-**ıl**-acak. (cf. Biz **evi** bu yıl artık satacağız.)
house this year finally sell-PASS-FUT
'*The house* will finally *be* sold this year.'

(40) **Fırın** şu anda tamir ed-**il**-iyor. (cf. Tamirci **fırını** tamir ediyor.)
Oven at.the.moment repair AUX-PASS-IMPF
'The oven is *being* repaired at the moment.'

13.2.2.2 Expressing the agent in a passive sentence

Although one of the reasons for passivization is to de-emphasize the agent of an action, it is still possible to express the agent in a passive clause. The agent in passive constructions is expressed either by using the postposition *tarafından* (17.3.2), a locative or ablative noun phrase or the adverbial suffix -CA_1 (16.1.6 (iii)).

In a *tarafından* phrase, the agent acts as the complement of the postposition *tarafından* 'by'. These phrases are equivalent to 'by' phrases in English but are used less frequently. Agentless passive sentences are much more common in Turkish than those containing a *tarafından* phrase.

(41) En iyi oyun **birinci sınıf öğrencileri tarafından** hazırlanmış.
'The best play was performed *by the first year students.*'

A *tarafından* phrase usually comes immediately before the verb in a passive sentence. Phrases with *tarafından* can normally only refer to animate entities, usually to human beings. Occasionally, they can be used with personifying effect to refer to machines (e.g. *makina tarafından* 'by the machine'). An inanimate agent can usually only be expressed by means of some other type of adverbial, particularly by an ablative- or locative-marked noun phrase (14.3.3.4–5):

(42) a. **Ayışığ-ı** keten-i parçala-r-mış.
moonlight-NCM linen-ACC destroy-AOR-EV.COP
'Apparently, *moonlight* fragments linen.'

b. Keten **ayışığ-ın-*dan/da*** parçala-n-ır-mış.
linen moonlight-NCM-ABL/LOC destroy-PASS-AOR-EV.COP
'Apparently, linen gets fragmented *by moonlight* / [as a result of being] *in the moonlight*.'

(43) a. **Fırtına** bütün evleri yıktı.
'*The storm* destroyed all the houses.'

b. **Fırtına-*dan/da*** bütün evler yıkıldı.
storm-ABL/LOC
'All the houses were destroyed *by the storm* / [as a result of being] *in the storm*.'

Another way of expressing the agent in a passive construction is by attaching the suffix -CA_1 (7.2.2.2, 16.1.6 (iii)) to the agentive noun phrase. This can be done only when the agent of an action is an official body, such as a ministry or an organization or group of people. This usage is typical of formal discourse and is mostly confined to official speeches and broad- casts.

(44) Bugün **Başbakanlık-*ça*** vergi-ler konusunda
today government-ADV tax-PL regarding

önemli bir açıklama yap-ıl-acak.
important an announcement make-PASS-FUT

'An important announcement regarding taxes is expected to be made today *by the prime minister's office*.'

(45) Bu toplantı **okulumuz*ca*** düzenlendi.
'This meeting was organized *by our school*.'

13.2.2.3 Impersonal passives

The addition of a passive suffix to an intransitive verb produces an impersonal passive construction:

(46) Adalara artık deniz otobüsüyle mi gid-**il**-ecek?
                                                                     go-PASS-FUT
'Will hovercraft be the way that [people] go to the islands now?'

In such constructions, there is no particular person or group of persons that is understood as performing the action denoted by the verb, therefore such sentences cannot have agent phrases. The closest English equivalents are active sentences with 'people', 'one' or the impersonal 'you' as subject.

Impersonal passives occur most often with aorist marking to express a general property of a particular entity (21.4.1.1). (47) below indicates a property of cobblestone streets:

(47) Arnavut kaldırım-ı üst-ün-de
     cobblestone.street-NCM top-3SG.POSS-LOC

     topuklu pabuç-la yürü-**n**-me-z.
     high.heeled shoe-COM walk-PASS-NEG-NEG.AOR

     '[You] can't walk on cobblestone streets wearing high-heeled shoes.'

In impersonal passive constructions, the action denoted by the verb is understood to be attributed to human beings, therefore sentences such as the following cannot refer to actions by inanimate entities (e.g., a flower pot).

(48) Parmaklık o kadar alçak ki balkondan aşağı düş-**ül**-ebil-ir.
                                                                                        fall-PASS-PSB-AOR
'The railing is so low that [one] could fall off the balcony.'

13.2.2.4 Double passive constructions

When a transitive verb combines with two passive suffixes, the result is again an impersonal passive which refers to a property of a particular entity. These constructions are quite marginal and are almost always used with the aorist suffix. In double passive constructions, the first occurrence of the passive suffix has an intransitivizing function.

(49) Böyle laf-a **kır-*ıl-ın*-**ır.
     such word-DAT hurt-PASS-PASS-AOR
     '[One] can *be hurt* by such words.'

(50) Bu duruma tabii ki **üz-ül-ün**-ebil-ir.
     sadden-PASS-PASS-PSB-AOR
    '[One] can of course *be upset* by this situation.'

For a sentence containing a passive *-mAk* clause, see 24.4.1.4.

Some irregular cases

(i) Some speakers tend to use a second passive suffix after *-(y)Abil* as in *yap-ıl-abil-in-ir* '[it] can be done'. This duplication does not serve any syntactic function, nor does it change the meaning of a form with a single passive suffix.

(ii) Some forms which have two passive suffixes (such as *söyle-n-il-* 'be said', *de-n-il-* 'be said' and *ye-n-il-* 'be eaten') are not 'double passive' constructions in the sense described above, but are identical in meaning to their counterparts with a single passive suffix (i.e. *söyle-n-* 'be said', etc.).

(iii) In the spoken language, the form *ko-n-ul-* 'be placed' is used alongside *koy-ul-* 'be placed' as the passive form of *koy-* 'place', 'put'.

(iv) The passive form of *kapa-* and *kapat-* 'close' is *kapat-ıl-*:

(51) Okul meğer belediye başkanı tarafından kapat-**ıl**-mış.
                                            close-PASS-EV/PF
    'The school was apparently closed down by the mayor.'

The stem *kapan-*, unless used in a reflexive sense (13.2.3.1), denotes the action of closing in an intransitive sense:

(52) Köşedeki dükkan yedide kapa-**n**-ıyor.
                            close-PASS-IMPF
    'The shop on the corner closes at seven.'

(v) *Anlaşıl-* 'be understood', 'be clear' is an irregular passive form whose root is *anla-* 'understand'.

(vi) For the different passive forms of the verbs *rica et-* 'request' and *tavsiye et-* 'advise' in indirect commands, see 24.4.2.2 (i.d).

13.2.3 Constructions with non-productive voice suffixes

The reflexive and reciprocal suffixes are intransitive. These combine with only a limited number of verbs.

13.2.3.1 Reflexive constructions

Reflexive constructions contain the reflexive suffix *-(I)n* (8.2.1.3) which combines only with transitive verbs. In the most common type of reflexive construction, the agent of an action performs the action on himself/herself:

(53) Bu kız daha sabahleyin yıka-**n**-mış-tı.
    wash-REF-PF-P.COP
    'This girl had taken a bath/shower only that morning.'

(54) Kedim durmadan yala-**n**-ıyor-du.
    lick-REF-IMPF-P.COP
    'My cat was licking herself incessantly.'

(55) O sıralarda bütün kadınlar eve kapa-**n**-mış-tı.
    close-REF-PF-P.COP
    'In those days all women used to stay indoors/kept themselves at home.'
    (lit. '...all women had shut themselves up at home.')

In another type of reflexive construction, the way in which the agent is affected by the action is somewhat indirect, as in *giyin-* 'get dressed' (from *giy-* 'put on' (a garment)):

(56) Aferin! Çabucak giy-**in**-di-n.
    put on-REF-PF-2SG
    'Good for you! You got dressed very quickly.'

The vast majority of reflexive verbs are intransitive. However, there are a few that can be used transitively:

(57) Hergün **kokular** sür**ün**üyor.
    'S/he puts on *perfume* every day.'

Although the reflexive suffix and the pronoun *kendi* 'self' are mutually exclusive when *kendi* functions as a reflexive pronoun, there are some instances when the reflexive suffix can co-occur with *kendi* in its other functions. This happens when *kendi* is:

(i) Used emphatically (18.1.2.2 (i)):

(58) Çocuklar **kendi**-leri yıka-**n**-abil-ir-ler.
    self-3PL.POSS wash-REF-PSB-AOR-3PL
    'The children can have a shower *themselves*.'

(ii) Used in its doubled form *kendi kendi-* (18.1.3) with dative case marking:

(59) Çocuklar **kendi kendi**-lerin-e yıka-**n**-abil-ir-ler.
    self self-3PL.POSS-DAT wash-REF-PSB-AOR-3PL
    'The children can have a shower *by themselves*.'

For the derivational usage of *-(I)n*, see 7.2.1.2.

13.2.3.2 Reciprocal constructions

Reciprocal constructions are intransitive constructions which describe an event in which at least two agents perform the same action upon each other. The verb is marked with the reciprocal suffix *-(I)ş* (8.2.1.4), as in *döviiş-*'fight each other':

(60) Kemal-le Zeki döv-**üş**-tü(-ler).
Kemal-CONJ Zeki beat.up-REC-PF(-3PL)
'Kemal and Zeki had a fight.'

In reciprocal constructions there is more than a single way of expressing the two (or more) agents of the action. One of these is by using a conjunction such as *ve* or *-(y)lA/ile* 'and' (28.3.1.1 (i–ii)) which forms a composite subject as in (60) above. In such cases, the verb can have plural person marking. Alternatively, one of the agents can be expressed as an adverbial of manner (16.4.3 (vii)), by means of the comitative suffix *-(y)lA/ile* 'with' used as a postposition (17.2.1 (iii)):

(61) Kemal Zeki-**yle** dövüştü.
Zeki-COM
'Kemal fought *with* Zeki.'

In these constructions, there is only one subject (here *Kemal*) and the verb therefore has singular person marking (see also 12.2.2.4). There is a slight difference between the meanings of the two constructions. While the two agents of the action, Kemal and Zeki, have equal standing as agents of the verb in (60), (61) is a statement about an action performed by Kemal, in which Zeki is also involved.

The reciprocal pronoun *birbir-* 'each other' (18.1.4) can be used in reciprocal constructions with *-(y)lA* as a manner adverb:

(62) Kemal-le Zeki **birbir-leri-yle** döv-üş-tü-ler.
Kemal-CONJ Zeki each.other-3PL.POSS-com beat.up-REC-PF-3PL
'Kemal and Zeki fought *(with) each other*.'

For other examples of verbs to which the reciprocal suffix can be added, see 8.2.1.4. The reciprocal suffix also appears in the verb-deriving composite derivational suffix *-lAş* (7.2.2.1).

13.2.4 Combinations of voice suffixes

More than one voice suffix can attach to a verb. Since these suffixes affect the transitivity of a clause, the order in which they are attached is very important.

Apart from the double occurrences of the passive and the causative which are explained above, other combinations are also possible. When the passive suffix attaches to a verb, the only other voice suffix that can follow it is a second passive (13.2.2.3–4).

Causative (+ causative) + passive

This is the most productive of combinations. In such constructions, the verbal complex as a whole (e.g. *dik-tir-il-* below) is passive and therefore the sentence does not contain a direct object:

(63) **Herkes-e** birer ağaç dik-**tir-il**-di.
    everyone-DAT a tree plant-CAUS-PASS-PF
    (i) 'It *was arranged* that a tree be planted *for everyone.*'
    (ii) '*Everyone was made* to plant a tree.'

Where, as in (63), there is just one causative suffix on the verb, a dative-marked noun phrase (such as *herkese*) is more often used to express a beneficiary as in (63 (i)), than to express the causee as in (63 (ii)). By contrast, when a passive suffix is attached to a double causative, the more likely interpretation is the one where the dative-marked noun phrase expresses the causee as in (64 (i)):

(64) **Bütün öğrenci-ler-e** resim-ler yap-**tır-t-ıl**-dı.
    all student-PL-DAT picture-PL paint-CAUS-CAUS-PASS-PF
    (i) '*All the students* were made to paint (pictures).'
    (ii) 'It was arranged for pictures to be painted *for every student.*'

The addition of a causative suffix followed by a passive suffix produces a stem different in meaning and structure from the corresponding root. For example, both the root *piş-* 'cook (intransitive)' and the stem *piş-ir-il-* (*piş-* CAUS-PASS) 'be cooked' are intransitive, but a sentence with *piş-ir-il-* can contain an agent, whereas this is not a possibility with simple verbs.

(65) Fasulye [kart ol-duğ-un-dan] üç saat-te **piş**-ti.
    bean stringy be-CV-3SG.POSS-ABL three hour-LOC cook-PF
    '[Because the beans were stringy] they took three hours to *cook.*'

(66) Keşke şu fasulye-ler **doğru dürüst bir ahçı tarafından**
    if.only this bean-PL proper a cook by

    piş-*ir-il*-se-ydi!
    cook-CAUS-PASS-COND- P.COP

    'If only these beans *had been cooked by a proper cook!*'

Reciprocal + causative

In these sequences, the last voice suffix is causative. The stem is therefore transitive, and the sentence contains a direct object:

(67) Baba-ları **kardeş-ler-i** öp-*üş-tür*-dü.
father-3PL.POSS sibling-PL-ACC kiss-REC-CAUS-PF
'The(ir) father *made* the sisters/brothers *kiss each other*.'

Note that *-(I)ştır* may also function as a derivational suffix (7.2.1.2).

Reciprocal + passive

Reciprocal + passive sequences produce impersonal constructions (13.2.2.3-4):

(68) Bu arena-da her zaman döv-**üş-ül**-müş-tür.
this arena-LOC always beat.up-REC-PASS-PF-GM
'People have always fought in this arena.'

Reciprocal + causative + passive

This sequence produces intransitive stems with a passive sense:

(69) Onlar bura-da döv-**üş-tür-ül**-dü.
they here-LOC beat-REC-CAUS-PASS-PF
'They *were made* to fight *each other* here.'

Reflexive + passive

These are impersonal passive constructions (13.2.2.3) because the stem to which the passive is added is intransitive:

(70) Sokak-ta soy-u**n-ul**-ma-z.
street-LOC undress-REF-PASS-NEG-NEG.AOR
'[*One*] *cannot get undressed* in the street.'

13.3 Auxiliary verbs

An auxiliary verb cannot stand on its own and occurs with another verb or nominal. The following are the auxiliary verbs in Turkish:

(i) Bound auxiliaries:
These are the suffixes *-(y)Abil, -(y)Iver, -(y)Agel, -(y)Ayaz, -(y)Adur, -(y)Akal, -mAyAgör*.

(ii) Free auxiliaries:
These are verbs such as *ol-, bulun-, et-, gel-, dur-, kal-, düş-, eyle-, buyur-*

The forms of the copula (*i-, -(y)-, ol-*) are also auxiliary verbs. For *i-* and *-(y)-*, see 8.3.1–2 and for *ol-* and *bulun-*, see 12.1.1.2–3.

13.3.1 Compound verb forms

Bound and free auxiliaries combine with other items to form compound verbs.

13.3.1.1 Compound verb forms containing bound auxiliaries

The verb roots *bil-* 'know', *ver-* 'give', *gel-* 'come', *yaz-* 'almost make a mistake' (obs.), *dur-* 'stay' and *kal-* 'remain', 'be left' combine with the converbial suffixes *-(y)A* and *-(y)I* (8.5.2.2 (ii)) to form the composite suffixes *-(y)Abil*, *-(y)Iver*, *-(y)Agel*, *-(y)Adur*, *-(y)Ayaz* and *-(y)Akal* (8.2.3.2 (ii)). They appear in Position 2 (8.2.3.2) on the verb stem.

The most common of these suffixes is the possibility suffix *-(y)Abil* (21.4.2.1).

(71) Her gün çikolata yi-**yebil**-ir-im.
    every day chocolate eat-PSB-AOR-1SG
    'I could eat chocolate every day.'

-(y)Iver mostly indicates swiftness and suddenness of an action, as in (72), or the ease with which an action is performed, as in (73):

(72) O anda odaya bir adam gir-**iver**-di.
                        enter-AUX-PF
    '*Suddenly,* a man entered the room.'

(73) Şu pencereyi kapa-**yıver**-sene.
    '[*Why don't* you] just close that window?'

Forms containing *-(y)Iver* can be doubled by the repetition of the stem containing the converbial suffix *-(y)I* (8.5.2.2 (ii)) for emphatic effect:

(74) Çocukluğum rüyalarımda **canlanı canlanıveriyor**.
    'In my dreams my childhood comes alive.'

The remaining bound auxiliaries, some semi-lexicalized or obsolescent, are infrequent in everyday speech. *-(y)Agel* indicates that the action denoted by the verb is habitual and customary:

(75) Onlar [Hristiyan olmamalarına rağmen] yıllardır Noel'i
    kutla**yagel**mişlerdir.
    'They have been celebrating Christmas for years, [even though they aren't Christians].'

The compounds containing *-(y)Adur* and *-(y)Akal* are semi-lexicalized. *-(y)Adur* is mostly used with motion verbs such as *git-* 'go' or *yürü-* 'walk', *koş-* 'run' to indicate the continuous nature of the action. Verbs with *-(y)Adur* are usually imperative:

(76) Sen yürü**yedur**, ben sana yetişirim.
    'You *keep on* walking, [and] I'll catch you up.'

-(y)Akal is almost exclusively used with the verbs *bak-* 'look', *don-* 'freeze' (in the metaphorical sense) and *şaş-* 'be surprised', producing the forms *bakakal-* 'be amazed', *donakal-* 'be stunned' and *şaşakal-* 'be dumbfounded':

(77) [Söylediklerini duyunca] don**akal**dık.
    'We were stunned [when we heard what you said].'

The verb roots *dur-* 'stay' and *kal-* 'remain', 'be left' can also be used as free forms. These separate verb forms are more productive than their suffixed counterparts *-(y)Adur* and *-(y)Akal* and are used following the conjunctive suffix *-(y)Ip* (28.2):

(78) Şan derslerine **gid-ip *dur*-uyor** ama şarkı söylediği yok.
    go-CONJ AUX-IMPF
    'S/he *keeps going* to singing lessons, but s/he doesn't sing.'

(79) Burada böylece **otur-up *kal*-dı-k**.
    sit-CONJ AUX-PF-1PL
    'We were just *left sitting* here.'

The verb *gör-* 'see', together with the negative marker *-mA*, creates the compound verb marker *-mAyAgör* 'whenever', 'as soon as'. With the addition of Group 3 person markers (8.4.3), this functions as the head of a finite adverbial clause of time (20.8 (90)), which also expresses the speaker's frustration or discomfort regarding the event expressed by the main clause. The whole sentence containing this time adverbial usually expresses a habitual event.

(80) (Bir) uyu**mayagör**eyim, bebek hemen ağlamaya başlıyor.
    '*Whenever/As soon as* I fall asleep, the baby starts crying.'

13.3.1.2 Compound verb forms containing free auxiliaries

The free auxiliaries *ol-* and *bulun-* can form compounds with other verbs. *Ol-* is fully productive while *bulun-* is limited in usage. These auxiliaries function as buffer stems which, acting as carriers for tense/aspect/modality suffixes, supplement the tense/aspect marking that is already present on the **lexical verb** in a finite clause (*bitir-* in (81)):

(81) Bu arada da ders-imiz-i **bitir-miş** *ol-acağ-ız*.
meanwhile and lesson-1PL.POSS-ACC finish-PF AUX-FUT-1PL
'And in the meantime, *we will have finished* our homework.'

For a survey of the wide range of compound verb forms in common use in finite clauses, see 21.5. For those occurring in conditional clauses, see 27.2.1.3 and 27.2.6.

In non-finite compound verb forms, the free auxiliaries act as bearers of the subordinating suffix, freeing the lexical stem to carry a tense/aspect marker (24.4.7, 25.4.1, 26.2.3 (i)):

(82) [Semra'yla **konuş-uyor** *ol-duğ-un* sıralarda] bütün
                      speak-IMPF AUX-CV-2SG.POSS
sırlarını anlatmıştın.
'[At the time when you *were on speaking terms* with Semra], you told [her] all your secrets.'

In compound verbs with *bulun-*, the lexical verb has to be inflected with *-mIş*. As an auxiliary verb *bulun-* is generally confined to formal or pedantic discourse:

(83) Kayıtları bugün saat 17 itibariyle **kapat-mış** *bulun-uyor-uz*.
                                        finish-PF AUX-IMPF-1PL
'*We* [officially] *finished* registration at 5 p.m. today.'

However, it can have a different function, that of attributing an element of involuntariness to the action denoted by the verb, suggesting that it was carried out either by mistake or as an unintended result of some other action:

(84) [Ankara'ya bir kere **gel-miş** *bulun-duğ-umuz-a* göre]
                           come-PF AUX-CV-1PL.POSS-DAT seeing.that

bari Kale'yi gezelim.

'[Since we *have landed up* in Ankara *anyway*], why not visit the castle?'

For *bulun-* as a main verb, see Chapter 12 (31)–(32).

In compound verbs with free auxiliaries, only the lexical verb can carry voice suffixes. *-(y)Abil* (and to a lesser extent *-(y)Iver*) can occur on the auxiliary verb or the main verb:

(85) **Gör-*ül*-müş ol-*abil*-ir** mi-yiz?
see-PASS-PF AUX-PSB-AOR INT-1PL
'*Could* we have *been* seen?'

(86) Anne-sin-i **gör-*ebil*-miş ol-du**.
mother-3SG.POSS-ACC see-PSB-PF AUX-PF
'S/he *has managed to see* his/her mother.'

For the combination of compound verb forms with the negative marker, see 20.1.2.

A rather less productive compound verb form contains -*mAzlIktAn gel* -'pretend to'. This construction is restricted to verbs of perception and cognition, such as *duy*- 'hear', *anla*- understand', etc., and is identical in meaning to the form which contains an additional negative marker, -*mAmAzlIktAn gel*-. Another alternative form is -*mAzdAn gel*-:

(87) Beni **duymazlıktan/duymamazlıktan/duymazdan** *geldi*.
'S/he *pretended* not to hear me.'

The parts of a compound verb can be separated by clitics (Chapter 11), most commonly by *bile*, *dA* and *mI*:

(88) Çok geç oldu. Bu saatte kapılar kapan**mış bile/da ol**abilir.
'It's become quite late. At this hour, the gates may *already have been closed*.'

13.3.2 Nominal-verb compounds

Nominal-verb compounds are made up of a bare nominal (noun or adjective) followed by a verb used as a free auxiliary. *ol-*, *et-*, *yap- gel-*, *dur-*, *geç- kal-*, *çık-*, *düş-* and the formal and pedantic forms *buyur-* and *eyle-* form nominal-verb compounds such as *sebep ol-* 'cause', *yardım et-* 'help', *inat et-* 'be obstinate', *takdir et-* 'appreciate', *işbaşı yap-* 'start work', *karşı gel-* 'oppose', *karşı dur-* 'resist', *mecbur kal-* 'be obliged', *karşı çık-* 'oppose', *zayıf düş-* 'become weak', *af buyur-* 'forgive' (only used in requests), the obsolescent *istirham eyle-* 'ask for mercy'. In some cases, the nominal and the auxiliary verb are joined up as in *affet-* 'forgive', *hallet-* 'solve' and *hallol-* 'be solved'. For the phonological properties of words combining with *et-*, see 2.1. These compounds are inflected like ordinary verbs:

(89) Ahmet arkadaş-lar-ın-a hep **yardım ed**-er.
Ahmet friend-PL-3SG.POSS-DAT always help AUX-AOR
'Ahmet always *helps* his friends.'

(90) [Beni anlamamak]-ta **inat ed**iyor.
'S/he *obstinately refuses* to understand me.'

Another type of nominal-verb compound is expressions where a bare noun stands in a direct object relation to a verb and the whole expression has been lexicalized:

şarkı söyle 'sing', *ders çalış-* 'study', 'do one's homework', *yemek ye-* 'eat', 'have a meal', *sigara iç-* 'smoke'. For the referential status of the nominal in these compounds, see (22.3 (iv)).

The nominal and the verb can be separated in both types of nominal verb-compound by clitics (Chapter 11), most commonly by *bile*, *dA* and *mI*:

(91) Evlerini satmaya **mecbur *bile* ka**labilirler.
'They may *even be obliged* to sell their house.'

(92) Hastalıktan sonra annem **zayıf *da* düştü.**
'After her illness, my mother *became weak as well.*'

(93) Sevgi hafta sonları hep **ders *mi* çalışır?**
'*Does* Sevgi always *study* during the weekend?'

Chapter 14

The noun phrase

A noun phrase is any sequence of words that can function as the subject of a sentence:

(1) Bunu **sen** al.
 '*You* take this one.'

(2) [**Her gün oraya gidip gelmek**] zor.
 'It's difficult [*to go there and back every day*].'

A noun phrase can also function as some kind of complement, such as:

An object:

(3) **Yeni komşuları** tanımıyordum.
 'I didn't know *the new neighbours*.'

A subject complement:

(4) O sırada **lise öğrencisi**ydik.
 'We were *high school students* at the time.'

The complement of a postposition:

(5) Bunları [**Amerika'nın dış politikasını daha iyi anlamak isteyenler**] *için* yazıyorum.
 'I'm writing all this for *people who want to understand American foreign policy better*.'

The most complex kinds of noun phrases are subordinate clauses, which are discussed elsewhere in this book: noun clauses, as in (2), form the subject of Chapter 24 and pronominal relative clauses, as in (5), are explained in 25.3.

In this chapter we look first at the structure of the noun phrase (14.1), then consider the extent to which distinctions of countability are grammaticalized (14.2).

DOI: 10.4324/9780429435836-17

The next sections explain how noun phrases are inflected for number (14.3.1), person (possessive) (14.3.2) and case (14.3.3). The last two sections examine composite structures involving a combination of two noun phrases: the genitive-possessive construction (14.4) and partitive constructions (14.5). For stress in noun phrases, see 4.4.2. In this chapter and elsewhere, we use curved brackets to indicate noun phrases where necessary.

14.1 Structure of the noun phrase

The Turkish noun phrase consists of an obligatory constituent called the **head** and one or more optional constituents known as **modifiers**. (6)–(8) are noun phrases of varying degrees of complexity. In each case the head is shown in bold:

(6) {**oda**}
'the *room*'

(7) {büyük bir **oda**}
'a large *room*'

(8) {[Mustafa'nın çalışma odası olarak kullandığı] **oda**}
'the *room* that Mustafa uses as a study'

All modifiers in the Turkish noun phrase, however complex, precede the head. The head is the location for any inflectional suffixes that pertain to the noun phrase as a whole:

(9) {Bu kattaki en güzel oda-**lar-ımız**}-**ı** size ayırdık.
    room-PL-1PL.POSS-ACC
'We've given you {our best rooms on this floor}.'

14.1.1 Items which can function as the head of a noun phrase

There are three word classes that can function as the head of a noun phrase: nouns, compounds and pronouns. Some examples of each are given below:

(i) Nouns:

a. Common nouns
adam 'man', *para* 'money', *tarih* 'history'

b. Proper nouns
Mustafa, İstanbul, Avrupa

(ii) Compounds (Chapter 10):
kız öğrenci 'female student', *taş duvar* 'stone wall', *gelgit* 'tide', *otobüs bileti* 'bus ticket', *Türk kahvesi* 'Turkish coffee'

(iii) Pronouns (Chapter 18):
sen 'you', *bu* 'this (one)', *orası* 'that (place)', *hangisi* 'which (one)', *öteki* 'the other (one)'

Of these three classes, pronouns differ from the other two in that they very rarely occur with any modifiers.

14.1.2 Modifiers in the noun phrase

Modifiers that may be present in a noun phrase fall into two classes: **determiners** and **adjectival constructions**.

Determiners (15.6) constitute a small class of items whose function is to specify the limitation (or lack of limitation) of the potential referent of a noun phrase, such as *bu* 'this/these', *aynı* 'the same', *her* 'every', etc.

Adjectival constructions (15.1–5) attribute some kind of quality to the head of a noun phrase. Turkish adjectivals range from simple adjectives, such as *iyi* 'good', *yeni* 'new', *zengin* 'rich', *yüksek* 'high', through various kinds of more complex forms and phrases to relative clauses (Chapter 25), which have a sentence-like internal structure.

(10) {**küçük bir kız**}
    little   a   girl
    ADJ   DET N
'a *little* girl'

(11) {**şu raf-ta-ki bütün eski kitap-lar**}
    that   shelf-LOC-ADJ   all   old   book-PL
    DET   ADJ   DET   ADJ   N
'all the *old* books *on that shelf*'

(12) {[**Deniz-in sev-diğ-i**] **bazı Türk yemek-ler-i**}
    Deniz-GEN   like-PART-3SG.POSS   some   Turk   dish-PL-NCM
    ADJ   DET   NC
'*some* Turkish dishes *that Deniz likes*'

14.2 Countability

There is no clear grammatical distinction in Turkish between countable and uncountable nouns. As shown in 14.2.1 and 14.3.1.2, both the indefinite article and the plural suffix can be used with almost any noun. However, nouns denoting non-discrete, continuous entities such as *su* 'water', *toprak* 'earth', *müzik* 'music' are not normally combinable with numerals or with the quantifying determiners *kaç* 'how many', *birkaç* 'a few,' 'several' or *birçok* 'many', unless the context makes clear that the counting is based upon either a conventional *measure* of the substance in question, as in (13) or distinct *types* of the substance, as in (14):

(13) Bakkaldan **birkaç bira** al.
a. few beer
'Get *a few* [*bottles of*] *beer* from the corner shop.'

(14) Bu memleketin en az **beş altı müziğ**-i var
five six music-3SG.POSS
'There are at least *five or six* [*kinds of*] *music* in this country.'

Conversely, the quantifier *biraz* 'a little', 'some' cannot normally be used as a determiner with nouns that denote discrete, countable entities, such as *çocuk* 'child', *şehir* 'city', *resim* 'picture'. However, in very informal registers this combination can occur where a speaker envisages a group of items in a vague, undefined way, without giving any importance to their individuality, sometimes accompanied by the terms *falan* and/or *filan* to highlight their arbitrariness:

(15) Masada **biraz kalem, kitap** falan vardı galiba.
'I think there were *some pens, books* and suchlike on the table.'

All words denoting fruits and vegetables are used interchangeably to refer either to an individual item (16) or to the type (17):

(16) Dün **üç şeftali** yedim.
'I ate *three peaches* yesterday.'

(17) Şuradan **biraz şeftali** alalım.
'Let's get *some peaches* from here.'

14.2.1 Uses of the indefinite article bir with noun phrases that do not denote discrete entities

(i) As in the case of numerals in general, *bir* 'one', 'a(n)' can designate a conventional measure of the substance in question:

(18) Bana **bir su** ver.
'Give me *a* [*glass of*] *water.*'

(ii) It can also refer to one instance of a quality or state:

(19) İçime **bir rahatlık** girdi.
'*A* [*sense of*] *relief* came over me.'

(iii) In combination with an adjectival, it attributes a quality to a particular instance or type of the class denoted by the noun:

(20) **Güzel bir pirinç** buldum.
'I've found *a nice [kind of] rice*.'

14.3 Nominal inflection

The inflectional suffixes that can be added to the head of a noun phrase are those set out in 8.1. In this section we look at how three of these sets of suffixes, namely the plural suffix (8.1.1), person (possessive) suffixes (8.1.2) and case suffixes (8.1.3), affect the meaning of a noun phrase.

14.3.1 Number

14.3.1.1 Plural marking with -lAr

The only suffix marking number in Turkish nominals is the plural suffix *-lAr*. The basic meaning of this suffix is to denote more than one item from the class indicated:

boş odalar 'vacant rooms'
kimler 'who' (referring to more than one person)

A noun phrase containing one of the quantifying determiners *bazı, kimi, bir kısım* 'some', 'certain', *birtakım* 'some', 'a number of' normally has to be plural-marked:

(21) **Bazı insan-*lar*** çocuklarına tuhaf adlar koyarlar.
some person-PL
'*Some people* give their children strange names.'

However, there are some fixed expressions in which singular nouns do occur with these determiners, e.g. *kimi/bazı zaman* 'sometimes', *bazı kimse* 'some people'. In the case of the quantifiers *bütün/tüm* 'the whole', 'all', the meaning of the noun phrase is crucially affected by whether the head is plural-marked or not:

(22) **Bütün sınıf** ayağa kalktı.
'*The whole class* rose to its feet.'

(23) Bu yıl **bütün sınıf*lar*** daha kalabalık olacak.
'This year *all the classes* are going to be larger.'

Restrictions on the use of plural marking:

(i) *-lAr* is not used where plurality is already indicated by the presence of a numeral as a modifier in the noun phrase:

üç çocuk   'three children'
yirmi beş dakika   'twenty-five minutes'

The only exceptions to this rule are the proper names of well-known groups:

Üç Silahşörler   'the Three Musketeers'
Yedi Cüceler   'the Seven Dwarfs'

(ii) Where certain quantifying determiners (15.6.1 (ii)), that is, *çok* 'a lot of', '(too) many', '(too) much', *fazla* 'too much', 'too many', *az* 'not much', 'not many', *biraz* 'a little', *birkaç* 'a few', 'several', *bir miktar* 'some', *bu/şu/o/ne kadar* 'this much', 'that much', 'so much', 'how much', *kaç* 'how many' and *her* 'every' are used in a noun phrase, the head noun is always left in the singular form:

her Türk vatandaşı   'every Turkish citizen'
kaç kişi   'how many people'
birkaç boş oda   'a few empty rooms'
çok kitap   'a lot of books'

The determiner *birçok* 'many' sometimes occurs with a plural-marked head noun although the non-marked form is generally preferred and is obligatory in the case of *kişi* 'person':

birçok kadın(lar)   'many women'
birçok kişi   'many people'

(iii) The combination of *bir* and *-lAr*:
The head of a noun phrase which includes the indefinite determiner *bir* 'a(n)' (15.6.1 (i)) normally has to be in the singular form. However, in the case of the pluralized forms of the pronouns *bir şey* 'something', 'anything' (18.6.1) and *bir yer* 'somewhere', 'anywhere', the sequence *bir . . . lAr* regularly occurs in colloquial contexts:

(24) Harun o gün bana **bir şeyler** söyledi.
'Harun told me *some things* that day.'

(25) Bu yaz **bir yer(ler)e** gidiyor musunuz?
'Are you going *anywhere* this summer?'

The combination *bir...lAr* is occasionally encountered (again in colloquial usage) with other nouns. It conveys that the referent is conceived as being plural, but that its identity is unknown or unknowable.

(26) **Bir sesler** duydum galiba.
'I think I heard *something*.'
(lit. '... some sounds.')

14.3.1.2 Further uses of the plural suffix -lAr

There are several other uses of *-lAr* which are observed particularly (although not exclusively) in nouns whose primary denotation is an uncountable substance.

(i) A plurality of conventional measures or portions of the thing concerned:

(27) **Çay-lar**-ı koyayım mı?
tea-PL-ACC
'Shall I pour out *the tea*?'

This particular use of *-lAr* can occur even with nouns whose primary denotation is a countable entity:

(28) **Balıklar** yendikten sonra **tavuklar** geldi.
'After *the fish* had been eaten *chicken* arrived.'

(ii) A plurality of separate quantities of the thing concerned:

(29) **Kir(ler)** bir türlü çıkmıyordu.
'*The dirt* just wouldn't come out.'

(30) Bu işte **büyük para(lar)** var.
'There's *big money* involved in this business.'

(iii) In the case of substances with a granular composition, the addition of the plural suffix shifts attention from the substance en masse to its constituent elements:

(31) **Kum-lar**-ı parmaklarının arasından geçiriyordu.
sand-PL-ACC
'S/he was sifting *the (grains of) sand* through her fingers.'

(iv) The plural suffix can be used to designate a plurality of types of a substance:

(32) Bizim Migros'ta güzel **şaraplar** var.
'There are nice *wines* at our Migros.'

(v) Certain expressions can be intensified by the addition of *-lAr* to the noun, for example:

(33) **Kan(lar)a** bulanmıştı.
'S/he was covered *(all over) in blood*.'

(vi) The addition of *-lAr* can also highlight the spatial extent of the substance referred to, whether in area or volume terms:

(34) **Kum(lar)a** uzandım.
'I lay down on *the sand*.'

(vii) In the case of nouns expressing abstract states, the addition of the plural suffix usually expresses a plurality of occurrences of this state:

(35) Böyle **tembellikler**im çok oluyor.
'I'm often lazy like this.' ('Such *acts of laziness* on my part occur often.')

(viii) *-lAr* can be added to certain expressions of time and place, giving a sense of approximation or giving the expression a wider meaning. The list below gives some common examples. Although the locative case-marked form is shown for several items, other case markings also occur according to context.

buralarda	'around here'
bir yerler	'anywhere', 'somewhere'
oralar (güzel)	'(It's nice) round there.'
Erzurum taraflarında	'around Erzurum', 'in the Erzurum area'
uzaklarda	'in the distance'
1995 ortalarında	'about the middle of 1995'
mayıs başlarında	'at about the beginning of May'
bu haftanın sonlarına doğru	'towards the end of this week'
o sıralarda	'at about that time'
o tarihlerde	'around that date', 'at that period'
şimdilerde	'these days'
sonraları	'later on'
bir zamanlar	'once' (= at some time in the past)

Approximations about people's age fit into the same pattern:

kırkbeş yaşlarında bir adam	'a man of about forty-five'
o yaşlarda	'at about that age'

(ix) For the use of *-lArI* to express recurrent time (*sabahları* 'in the morning(s)', *cumartesileri* 'on Saturdays', etc.), see 16.4.1.1 (72).

(x) When attached to the name of a famous person, *-lAr* means 'and people like that':

   (36) Dünyadan **Atatürkler, Nehrular** geçmeseydi şimdiye kadar ne hale gelirdik?
   'If *people like Atatürk and Nehru* had not passed through the world, what state would we be in by now?'

(xi) Another function of *-lAr* attached to the name of a person is to produce an expression referring to the group normally associated with that person. This group could consist just of the named person and his/her spouse/partner or it could be their family, group of friends, etc. The precise meaning varies with the context and this usage is confined to informal situations.

   (37) **Ahmetler** gelmedi.
   '*Ahmet and his wife/girlfriend/family/gang* didn't come.'

The same usage can occur with expressions of relationship (with first or second person singular possessive marking only). Note that in such expressions the possessive suffix *precedes* the plural suffix.

   (38) **Abla-m-lar** nerede?
   elder.sister-1SG.POSS-PL
   'Where are *my elder sister and her boyfriend/husband (etc.)*?'
   (cf. abla-lar-ım (elder.sister-PL-1SG.POSS) 'my elder sisters')

14.3.1.3 Transnumeral uses of the unmarked form

A noun phrase that is unmarked for number, that is, whose head does not carry the plural suffix and which does not have a numeral or other quantifying determiner among its modifiers, may be either singular or **transnumeral** (number-neutral) in meaning. If it has definite status, it will have singular meaning, but if it has generic or categorial status, it will have transnumeral meaning. These various referential statuses are discussed in detail in Chapter 22.

   (39) **İlaç** bana çok iyi geldi.
   '*The medicine* did me a lot of good.'

   (40) **İlaç** hastaya göre seçilmelidir.
   '*The medicine/Medicines* must be chosen according to the patient.'

   (41) Doktor bana **ilaç** yazmadı.
   'The doctor didn't prescribe me *any medicine(s).*'

The noun phrase *ilaç* 'medicine' is definite and therefore singular in (39), generic and therefore transnumeral in (40) and categorial, therefore again transnumeral, in (41).

14.3.2 Person (possessive suffixes)

The possessive suffixes (8.1.2) correspond to the six grammatical persons. A noun phrase marked with a possessive suffix (except where this is a 3rd person suffix functioning as a compound marker (10.2) or pronominalizer (18.4)) is understood as denoting a person or thing that is possessed. The possessive suffix indicates only whether the possessor is 1st, 2nd or 3rd person, singular or plural. Note that a 2nd person plural suffix does not always indicate plurality of the possessor. It may denote the formality of the speaker's relationship with a singular addressee or possessor (8.1.2, 18.1.1).

(42) Arkadaş-lar-**ınız** ne kadar kalacaklar?
friend-PL-**2PL.POSS**
'How long are *your* friends going to stay?'

(43) Ahmet oda-**sın**-ı arıyordu.
room-**3SG.POSS**-ACC

Numara-**sı** akl-**ın**-da kalmamıştı.
number-**3SG.POSS** mind-**3SG.POSS**-LOC

'Ahmet was looking for *his* room. *Its* number was no longer in *his* head.'

If there is a need to be more explicit about or to emphasize, the identity of the possessor, this can be done by a genitive-possessive construction, that is, by modifying the possessed constituent with a genitive-marked noun phrase (14.4).

Certain combinations of the possessive suffixes with plural and/or case suffixes give rise to potential ambiguity:

(i) Following a consonant-final stem, the sequences [2SG.POSS + case] and [3SG. POSS + case] are indistinguishable, because of the 'n' that is included in the 3rd person possessive suffix before a case suffix or -CA_1 (6.2, 8.1.2). (44) can therefore be read in two ways:

(44) Ev-**in**-i daha gör-me-di-m.

    a. house-**2SG.POSS**-ACC
       'I haven't seen *your* house yet.'

b. house-3SG.POSS-ACC
      'I haven't seen *his/her* house yet.'

(ii) A single *-lAr* can sometimes express two different notions of plurality simultaneously: plurality of the thing possessed and plurality of the (3rd person) possessor. The form *-lArI* on a noun phrase is capable of three interpretations:

   a. Plural + 3rd person singular possessive
   b. 3rd person plural possessive
   c. Plural + 3rd person plural possessive

   This ambiguity is illustrated in (45):

   (45) a. Bilet-**ler-i** burada.
           ticket-PL-3SG.POSS
           '*His/her* tickets are here.'

        b. Bilet-**leri** burada.
           ticket-3PL.POSS
           '*Their* ticket is here.'

        c. Bilet-**leri** burada.
           ticket-PL.3PL.POSS
           '*Their* tickets are here.'

   In (a), *-lAr* indicates the plurality of the tickets. In (b), it is part of the suffix *-lArI*, indicating a 3rd person plural possessor ('their'). In (c), it is performing both functions simultaneously.

(iii) The 2nd/3rd person ambiguity identified in (i) is sometimes compounded with the 3rd person singular/plural ambiguity identified in (ii):

   (46) a. Arkadaş-**lar-ın**-a soralım.
           friend-PL-2SG.POSS-DAT
           'Let's ask *your* friends.'

        b. Arkadaş-**lar-ın**-a soralım.
           friend-PL-3SG.POSS-DAT
           'Let's ask *his/her* friends.'

        c. Arkadaş-**ların**-a soralım.
           friend-3PL.POSS-DAT
           'Let's ask *their* friend.'

        d. Arkadaş-**ların**-a soralım.
           friend-PL.3PL.POSS-DAT
           'Let's ask *their* friends.'

In (d), the element *-lAr* is again expressing plurality both of the possessor and of what is possessed (here 'friends'). Such potential ambiguities are resolved by using modifiers forming genitive-possessive constructions, as explained in 14.4 below.

14.3.2.1 Marking possession in -(s)I compounds

Because only one possessive suffix can be attached to a noun at any one time, if a suffix indicating possession is added to a *-(s)I* compound (10.2) the compound marker *-(s)I(n)* has to be dropped. As a result, the non-possessed forms and the 3rd person possessed forms of any particular *-(s)I* compound are indistinguishable:

yatak oda-sı
  (i) bed room-NCM   'bedroom'
  (ii) bed room-3SG.POSS 'his/her bedroom'

yatak oda-m
bed room-1SG.POSS   'my bedroom'

In the case of noun compounds that end in a consonant, where case marking is present the 2nd/3rd person ambiguity discussed in 14.3.2 (i) also arises:

(47) Ders kitab-**ın**-ı beğenmedim.
    (i) lesson book-NCM-ACC
        'I didn't like *the* textbook.'

    (ii) lesson book-**2SG.POSS**-ACC
        'I didn't like *your* textbook.'

    (iii) lesson book-**3SG.POSS**-ACC
        'I didn't like *his/her* textbook.'

Where a plural suffix is present, the kinds of ambiguity discussed in 14.3.2 (ii) and (iii), regarding whether the plurality affects the possessed item, the possessor or both, also arise:

(48) a. Telefon numara-**lar-ın**-ı yazdım.
    (i) telephone number-PL-NCM-ACC
        'I've written down *the* telephone number*s*.'
    (ii) telephone number-**PL-2SG.POSS**-ACC
        'I've written down *your* telephone number*s*.'
    (iii) telephone number-**PL-3SG.POSS**-ACC
        'I've written down *his/her* telephone number*s*.'

b. Telefon numara-**ların**-ı yazdım.
   (i) telephone number-**3PL.POSS**-ACC
       'I've written down *their* telephone number.'
   (ii) telephone number-**PL.3PL.POSS**-ACC
       'I've written down *their* telephone number*s*.'

In all of these cases, except for the non-possessive (47 (i)) and (48 (a.i)), the use of a genitive-marked noun phrase can eliminate the ambiguity (14.4).

14.3.3 Case

Turkish has five case suffixes (8.1.3), which mark respectively the **accusative**, **dative**, **locative**, **ablative** and **genitive** cases. The comitative/ instrumental marker *-(y)lA/ile*, which shares some properties with case suffixes, is discussed in 8.1.4 and 17.2.1 (iii). The function of case marking (or its absence) is to indicate the relationship between the noun phrase to which it is attached and other sentence constituents.

14.3.3.1 The non-case-marked noun phrase

A noun phrase is left without case marking when it functions as one of the items listed below:

(i) The subject of one of the following types of clause:
   a. A main clause:

       (49) Bunu belki **siz** bilebilirsiniz.
            'Perhaps *you* may know this.'

   b. A finite subordinate clause:

       (50) [**Herkes** görsün diye] kartı masanın üstünde bırakıyorum.
            'I'm leaving the card on the table [so that *everyone* will see it].'

   c. A non-finite adverbial clause (for exceptions see 26.2.1):

       (51) [**Ahmet** gelince] ona sorabiliriz.
            '[When *Ahmet* comes] we can ask him.'

   d. A conditional clause:

       (52) [**Ahmet** gelirse] ona sorabiliriz.
            '[If *Ahmet* comes] we can ask him.'

   e. A relative clause of the type where the verb in the relative clause is marked with *-(y)An* and contains a subject (25.1.1.1 (ii.b)):

       (53) [**su** akma***yan***] musluklar
            'taps from which no *water* flows/flowed'

(ii) A subject complement:
   a. In nominal sentences (12.1.1.2):

   (54) Hakan'ın karısı **mimar**mış.
   'Hakan's wife is *an architect*, apparently.',

   b. In small clauses (24.5):

   (55) [Tanju'yu **arkadaş**] sayıyorduk o zamanlar.
   'In those days we regarded [Tanju as *a friend.*']

(iii) A non-definite (i.e. indefinite (22.2) or categorial (22.3)) direct object:

   (56) Bu konuda **kitap(lar)** okumuş.
   'It seems s/he has read *books* on this subject.'

   (57) Bana da ver **bir çay**.
   'Give me *a [glass of] tea*, too.'

Note that indefinite direct objects sometimes have to or may take accusative case marking (14.3.3.2).

(iv) The complement of certain postpositions:
   a. The bare postpositions *gibi* 'like', *için* 'for', *-(y)lA/ile* 'with', *kadar* 'as ... as' (17.2.1):

   (58) O adam **para için** her şeyi yapar.
   'That man would do anything *for money.*'

   b. Possessive-marked postpositions denoting spatial relations, such as *iç-in-de* 'in(side)', *alt-ın-da* 'under', *arka-sın-da* 'behind': The non case-marked form (as opposed to the genitive-marked form) occurs where the complement is non-specific or the postposition is used in a metaphorical or non-spatial sense (17.3.1.2):

   (59) Ellerim **çamur içinde** kalmıştı.
   'My hands were *covered in mud.*'

   c. Other possessive-marked postpositions, such as *boyunca* 'all along', 'throughout', *yüzünden* 'on account of' (for list, see 17.3.2):

   (60) **Yol *boyunca*** konuştu.
   'He talked *all the way.*'

(v) An adverbial, especially of time or distance (16.1.4):

(61) **O gün** siz yoktunuz.
'You were not there *that day*.'

14.3.3.2 The accusative case marker

The main function of the accusative case marker is to indicate the direct object of a transitive verb. However, as seen in the previous section, some direct objects are left in the non-case-marked form. The rules for the use and omission of accusative case marking are as follows:

(i) The use of the accusative suffix is obligatory where the direct object is definite (22.1):

(62) **Bütün arkadaşlarımızı** çağıralım.
'Let's invite *all our friends*.'

(ii) Accusative case marking is usually necessary where a non-definite direct object precedes the verb but does not occupy the immediately pre-verbal position (22.2–3):

(63) **Birçok şey*i*** şu raflara koyabiliriz. (Indefinite)
'*A lot of things* we can put on these shelves.'

(64) **Patlıcan*ı*** her gün yiyebilirim. (Categorial)
'I could eat *aubergines* every day.'

(iii) An indefinite direct object which is in the immediately preverbal position must still take the accusative suffix in the following circumstances:

a. If the direct object is marked with a possessive suffix or is a pronominalized adjectival, numeral or determiner (18.4):

(65) **Bir arkadaş-*ım-ı*** getireceğim.
a friend-1SG.POSS-ACC
'I'm going to bring *a friend of mine*.'

(66) **Komşulardan bazı-*sın-ı*** çağırmışlar.
some-3SG.POSS-ACC
'They've apparently invited *some of the neighbours*.'

(67) **Şurada*kini*** beğendim.
'I like *the one over here*.'

The only exception to this rule is where a 3rd person possessive suffix is functioning as the marker of a *-(s)I* compound (10.2). Thus, the indefinite direct object below is non-case-marked:

(68) Her yemekten sonra **bir Türk kahve-*si*** içer.
   a Turk coffee-NCM
   'After every meal, s/he has *a (cup of) Turkish coffee.*'

b. If the direct object is a noun phrase modified by the interrogative determiner *hangi* 'which' (19.2.1.4)
c. If the direct object is an indefinite or plural **generic** (22.4.3)
d. If the direct object refers to a member or members of a previously mentioned or implied group:

   (69) Paketin içindekiler eksik çıktı. **İki kitab*ı*** göndermemişler galiba.
       'The contents of the parcel are incomplete. I think they've failed to send *two [of the] books.*'

   (70) Salon kalabalıktı. **Kapıya yakın duran bir adam*ı*** tanıdım.
       'The room was crowded. I recognized *a man standing near the door.*'

The accusative maker is also used for marking the *subject* of small clauses (24.5.1):

(71) [**Tanju'yu** iyileşti] sanıyordum.
    'I thought [Tanju had recovered].'

For an explanation of other factors that can trigger accusative marking of indefinite direct objects, see 22.2.1.

14.3.3.3 The dative case marker

The functions that may be performed by a noun phrase marked with the dative case suffix are listed below.

(i) An adverbial indicating one of the following:

   a. The recipient or beneficiary of an action:

      (72) **Çocuğ*a*** doğru dürüst bakamıyor.
          'S/he can't look after *the child* properly.'

      (73) **Aysel'*e*** anahtar verdim.
          'I've given *Aysel* a key/keys.'

   b. The destination or target of an action:

      (74) Beni **Paris'*e*** gönderdiler.
          'They sent me *to Paris.*'

(75) Bu koltuk **oturma odasına** konacak.
'This armchair is to be put *in the sitting-room*.'

c. The price at which something is sold or offered for sale:

(76) Bu bisikleti **üç bin liraya** almıştım.
'I bought this bicycle *for three thousand liras.*'

(77) Evin tamiratı **bir servete** mal oldu.
'The renovation of the house cost *a fortune*.'

d. Expressing (relative) future time reference (16.4.1.1).

e. Purpose:
This kind of dative-marked noun phrase is almost always a *-mAK* clause (26.3.12):

(78) [**Seni gör*mey***]*-e* geldim.
'I've come [*to see you*].'

(ii) The oblique object (13.1.2.2) of many verbs of emotion, e.g. *sevin-* 'be pleased (about)', *üzül-* 'be sorry (about)', *kız-* 'be angry (with/about)', *can-ı sıkıl-* 'be annoyed (about)' and certain other verbs, e.g. *benze-* 'resemble', *uy-* 'conform (to)', 'comply (with)', *inan-* 'believe', *güven-* 'trust':

(79) [**Ayşe'nin geleceğin**]*-e* sevindik.
'We're glad [*Ayşe's going to come*].'

(80) **Annemin isteğin*e*** uymadım.
'I didn't comply *with my mother's wish*.'

(iii) The complement of:

a. Certain bare postpositions, e.g. *doğru* 'towards', *göre* 'according to', 'since', *kadar* 'until' (17.2.2):

(81) **Saat iki*ye* kadar** çalıştık.
'We worked *until two o'clock*.'

b. Certain adjectives, e.g. *yakın* 'near', *uygun* 'suitable (for)' (15.5):

(82) **Okul*a* yakın** bir ev arıyorlar.
'They're looking for a house *near the school*.'

c. Certain nouns expressing attitude, derived from transitive verbs:

(83) **Hukuğ*a* saygı** esastır.
'Respect *for the law* is fundamental.'

(84) Çocuklarımıza *sevgi*miz bize yalan söyletebiliyor.
'Our *love for our children* can make us tell lies.'

(iv) The causee of a causative construction based on a transitive verb, that is, the person who is made or allowed to perform the action (13.2.1 (ii)):

(85) Filiz bütün ev işlerini **kocasına** yaptırıyor.
'Filiz makes *her husband* do all the housework.'

14.3.3.4 The locative case marker

The locative suffix expresses physical or abstract location. A noun phrase in the locative case can function as one of the following:

(i) A time or place adverbial:

(86) **O günler***de* Selim çok sigara içiyordu.
'*At that time* Selim was smoking a lot.'

(87) İnsanlar artık komşularını bile tanımıyorlar **büyük kentler***de*.
'People don't even know their neighbours nowadays *in big cities*.'

For clock time and dates, see 16.4.1.1.

(ii) The oblique object (13.1.2.2) of a small number of verbs, such as *karar kıl-* 'decide (on)', *ısrar et-* 'insist (on)':

(88) [**Hepsini denemek**]-*te* ısrar etti.
'She insisted *on [trying them all]*.'

(iii) **A subject complement:**
   a. In linking sentences (12.1.1.2):

   (89) Anahtar **yerin***de* değil.
   'The key is not *in its place*.'

   b. In small clauses (24.5):

   (90) [Onu **İstanbul'***da*] sanıyordum.
   'I thought [s/he was *in Istanbul*].'

(iv) The locational constituent of an existential sentence:

(91) **Köy***de* elektrik var mıydı?
'Was there electricity *in the village*?'

(v) Within a larger noun phrase, a compound adjectival modifier expressing metaphorical 'location' in some kind of attribute (size, shape, colour, name, age, etc. (15.3.2)):

(92) **otuz metre derin-liğ-in-*de*** bir kuyu
thirty metre deep-N.DER-NCM-LOC a well
'a well *thirty metres deep*'

14.3.3.5 The ablative case marker

The ablative case marker indicates that a noun phrase is functioning as one of the following:

(i) An adverbial associated with concepts such as departure, separation, source or cause:

(93) Ali **oda*dan*** çıktı.
'Ali left *the room*.'

(94) Zavallı bunu **yorgunluk*tan*** yapmıştır.
'The poor thing must have done this *out of tiredness*.'

In association with the verb *geç-* 'pass', an ablative noun phrase indicates a place or space through which someone/something travels:

(95) Gelirken **şehir merkezin*den* geç**tiniz mi?
'Did you *come through* the city centre on your way here?'

This usage is very frequent with the possessive-marked spatial postpositions (17.3.1.1 (iii)).

(ii) The oblique object (13.1.2.2) of certain verbs of emotion, especially those which reflect the concepts of aversion, e.g. *kork-* 'be afraid (of)', *iğren-* 'be disgusted (by)', *nefret et-* 'hate', *bık-* 'get fed up (with)', *hoşlan-*'like':

(96) **O adam*dan*** nefret ediyorum.
'I hate *that man*.'

(97) Gürcan **yağmurlu havalar*dan*** hoşlanır.
'Gürcan likes *wet weather*.'

Certain other verbs, notably *vazgeç-* 'give up', *faydalan-/yararlan-* 'benefit (from)' and *oluş-* 'consist (of)' also take ablative-marked objects:

(98) Zerrin [**tenis oynamak**]-*tan* vazgeçti.
'Zerrin gave up [*playing tennis*].'

(iii) The complement of:
   a. Certain bare postpositions, e.g. *önce* 'before', *sonra* 'after', *başka* 'apart from', *dolayı* 'because of' (17.2.3):

   (99) **Oku***ldan sonra* genellikle futbol oynuyor.
         '*After school* he usually plays football.'

   b. Certain adjectives, e.g. *hoşnut* 'content (with)' (15.5 (iii)):

   (100) **İş***inden hoşnut* görünüyor.
         'S/he seems *content with her job*.'

(iv) Within a larger noun phrase, a modifier expressing:
   a. The material from which something is made:

   (101) Padişahın {**som altı***ndan* bir taht} vardı.
         'The king had a throne *of solid gold*.'

   b. An entity, set or category of which the head constituent expresses a part or member (14.5):

   (102) {**Çikolatalı pasta-dan** iki dilim} yedi.
         chocolate cake-ABL two slice
         'S/he ate two slices *of the chocolate cake*.'

   (103) {**Yakın arkadaşlarımdan** biri} evleniyordu.
         'One *of my close friends* was getting married.'

   Unless the partitive construction is the subject of a verbal or linking sentence, it is possible for its head to be deleted:

   (104) {**Memleketin en iyi ressamlarından** (biri)} sayılır.
         'S/he is regarded as *among*/(one of) *the best painters in the country*.'

   See also examples (129) and (130) below.

(v) In adjectival or adverbial structures expressing comparison (15.4.2, 16.8), the **modifier** that expresses the object of comparison:

   (105) Mustafa'nın evi **bundan** (daha) büyük.
         'Mustafa's house is bigger *than this*.'

For the use of the ablative case-marker in time adverbials, see 16.4.1.1 (70)–(71).

14.3.3.6 The genitive case marker

The basic function of the genitive case marker is to mark a noun phrase as denoting the possessor of some item expressed by another constituent. An important secondary function is to mark the subject of certain kinds of non-finite subordinate clause.

(i) As the expression of a possessor, a genitive-marked noun phrase can function as:
  a. The **modifier** in a **genitive-possessive construction** (a composite noun phrase whose head is marked by a possessive suffix (14.4)):

  (106) {**Bu çocuğun** annesi} nerede?
  'Where is *this child's* mother?'

  (107) {**Ayten'in** iki kız kardeşi} var.
  '*Ayten* has two sisters.'

  b. A subject complement in nominal sentences (12.1.1.2):

  (108) Fotoğraf makinesi **benim** değil, **babamın**.
  'The camera's not *mine*, it's *my father's*.'

  c. A subject complement in small clauses (24.5):

  (109) [Bu odayı artık **Fatma'nın**] sayıyorum.
  'I now regard [this room as *Fatma's*].'

(ii) The types of non-finite subordinate clause in which an overt subject is genitive-marked are:
  a. Most non-finite noun clauses marked with *-mA*, *-DIK* or *-(y)AcAK* (see Chapter 24, especially 24.4.6):

  (110) [**Turgut-un** gel-me-sin]-i istiyorum.
  Turgut-GEN come-VN-3SG.POSS-ACC
  'I want [*Turgut* to come].'

  (111) [**Bunun** bir roman olduğun]-u söylemişti.
  'S/he said [*this* was a novel].'

  b. Those types of relative clause whose verb is suffixed with *-DIK* or *-(y)AcAK* plus a possessive suffix (25.1.1.2):

  (112) [**Siz-in** söyle-dik-ler-iniz]-i beğendim.
  you-GEN say-PART-PL-2PL.POSS-ACC
  'I liked [what *you* said].'

  (113) [**Anne-n-in** getir-eceğ-i] pasta yetecek mi?
  mother-2SG.POSS-GEN bring-PART-3SG.POSS cake
  'Will the cake [*your mother*'s going to bring] be enough?'

14.4 The genitive-possessive construction

The genitive-possessive construction is a composite noun phrase constructed of two noun phrases marked as follows:

(noun phrase + genitive) + (noun phrase + possessive)

The first noun phrase, which carries genitive case marking, is the modifier and indicates the possessor. The second noun phrase, which carries possessive marking, is the head of the composite noun phrase and indicates the entity which is possessed:

Ali-**nin** oğl-**u**   'Ali's son'
Ali-GEN son-3SG.POSS

oda-**nın** kapı-**sı**   'the door of the room'
room-GEN door-3SG.POSS

The possessive suffix on the head has to agree in terms of grammatical person with the possessor-modifier, as illustrated below:

ben-im ev-**im**   'my house'
I-GEN house-1SG.POSS

Fatma-nın ev-**i**   'Fatma's house'
Fatma-GEN house-3SG.POSS

It is the possessive-marked head of the genitive-possessive construction that is the bearer of any case marking needed to indicate the relation of this composite noun phrase to other sentence constituents:

(114)   Bu haber-i {Ali-nin **oğl-un**}-***dan*** al-dı-m.
          this news-ACC Ali-GEN son-3SG.POSS-ABL get-PF-1SG
          'I heard this news *from* {Ali's *son*}.'

If the genitive-possessive construction is the direct object of its clause, its head must be accusative-marked, whether definite or not (14.3.3.2 (iii.a)):

(115)   {Taslağ-ın **birçok yer-in**}-*i* değiştirmişler.
          draft-GEN many place-3SG.POSS-ACC
          'They seem to have changed *a lot of places in the draft*.'

In informal styles the genitive-marked modifier may be backgrounded, that is, placed after the predicate (23.3.2):

(116)   Kız arkadaşını gördün mü **Mehmet'in**?
          'Did you see Mehmet's girlfriend?'

A genitive-possessive construction can itself function as the possessor constituent in a larger genitive-possessive construction:

(117)   {{**Ayten-in anne-sin**}-**in ism-in**}-i biliyor musun?
          Ayten-GEN mother-3SG.POSS-GEN name-3SG.POSS-ACC
          'Do you know *Ayten's mother's name*?'

Where the possessed entity (*öğretmen* below) is singular and the possessor is plural, the 3rd person *singular* suffix is often used on the head, in order to avoid ambiguity with the parallel construction in which the entity possessed is plural:

(118) {Çocuk-lar-ın öğretmen-**i**} İngiliz.
child-PL-GEN teacher-3SG.POSS
'*The children's teacher* is English.'

(119) {Çocukların öğretmen-**leri**} İngiliz.

(i) teacher-PL.3PL.POSS
'The children's teachers are English.'

(ii) teacher-3PL.POSS
'The children's teacher is English.'

Whereas sentences on the pattern of (118) clearly express the singularity of the possessed entity, the ambiguity of (119) shows that the plurality of an entity possessed by a plural possessor cannot be unambiguously articulated. However, (119 (i)) represents the more typical sense in which this pattern is used.

One function of the genitive-possessive construction is to resolve ambiguities of the kind noted above in 14.3.2, where *Arkadaşlarına soralım* (46) was shown to be capable of four different readings. (120) demonstrates how the addition of a genitive-marked pronoun modifier, combined in (c) with the use of singular possessive marking, eliminates these ambiguities:

(120) a. {**Sen-in** arkadaş-lar-ın}-a soralım.
you-GEN friend-PL-2SG.POSS-DAT
'Let's ask *your* friends.'

b. {**O-nun** arkadaş-lar-ın}-a soralım.
s/he-GEN friend-PL-3SG.POSS-DAT
'Let's ask *his/her* friends.'

c. {**Onlar-ın** arkadaş-ın}-a soralım.
they-GEN friend-3SG.POSS-DAT
'Let's ask *their* friend.'

d. {**Onlar-ın** arkadaş-ların}-a soralım.
they-GEN friend-PL.3PL.POSS-DAT
'Let's ask *their* friends.'

In informal styles, the head of a genitive-possessive construction is often left without possessive marking, particularly when the genitive-marked modifier is a 1st or 2nd person pronoun:

(121) Burası {**biz-im ev**}-den daha sıcak. (cf. Chapter 18 (87))
here we-GEN house-ABL more warm
'It's warmer here than [in] *our house.*'

(122) Nerede {**senin çocuklar**}?
'Where are *your children*?'

Such constructions occur only in contexts which fulfil the conditions governing the use of genitive-marked pronouns (18.1.5 (iii), 18.1.5.1 (iii)). Note also that the omission of possessive marking on the head is not permissible in possessive existential sentences (12.1.1.2). Thus, the possessive suffix on *araba* below is obligatory:

(123) {**Siz-in araba-*nız***} var mı?
you-GEN car-2PL.POSS existent INT
'Do you have a car?'

Apart from expressing possession, the genitive-possessive construction also articulates the relationship between different specimens of the same type. In this kind of genitive-possessive construction, the genitive-marked noun phrase expresses either a particular specimen or specimens of the type, as in (124) or the type itself, as in (125). The nominal in the head position is usually a pronominalized determiner or adjectival (18.4):

(124) Bu araba {**benimkinin tam *aynısı***} değil.
'This car is not *quite the same as mine.*'

(125) {**Bisikletin *motorlu*sun**}-a motosiklet denir.
'*The motorized version of a bicycle* is called a motorcycle.'

A further use of the genitive-possessive construction is to express a partitive relation (14.5.3).

14.5 Partitive constructions

There are three composite noun phrase constructions that are used to express part of a whole or to select one or more items from a type or set.

	Modifier	+	Head
(i)	(noun phrase + ablative) *şu elma-dan* 'a few kilos of these apples'	+	(bare noun phrase) *birkaç kilo*
(ii)	(noun phrase + ablative) *erkek öğrenciler-den* 'one of the male students'	+	(noun phrase + 3SG.POSS) *bir tane-si*

(iii) (noun phrase + genitive)   +   (noun phrase + 3SG.POSS)
hesabımdaki para-nın   *büyük kısm-ı*
'most of the money in my account'

(iv) (noun phrase + locative)   +   (noun phrase with numeral)
araların-da   +   *üç kişi*
'three people among them'

In each construction it is the genitive-, ablative- or locative-marked modifier constituent which expresses the whole or set, and the head constituent which expresses the part or the selected item(s). The head noun phrase is always indefinite (except in the case of one subtype of the bare-headed partitive, 14.5.1 (i)), whereas the modifier noun phrase is definite or some-times generic.

14.5.1 The bare-headed partitive construction with ablative-marked modifier

Structurally, the distinguishing characteristic of this construction is that the bare noun phrase functioning as the head must itself be headed by one of the following: (i) a proper name, (ii) a common noun or (iii) an item with an enumerating or measuring function:

(i) Bare-headed partitives in which the head noun phrase is a proper name:

These differ from all other kinds of partitive constructions in that the head noun phrase is definite. The function of the ablative-marked modifier noun phrase here is to provide additional, descriptive information about the person or place identified by the proper name:

(126) Bugünkü konuğumuz, {ünlü şair-ler-imiz-**den** ***Lâle Müldür***}.
                              famous poet-PL-1PL.POSS-ABL
'Our guest today is *Lâle Müldür*, [*one*] *of* our well known poets.'

(127) {Batı Afrika ülkelerin**den** ***Sierra Leone***}de iç savaş yıllarca sürdü.
'In *Sierra Leone, a country in West Africa*, the civil war went on for years.'

This type of partitive construction occurs also in the question used to ask the day of the week (the interrogative pronoun *ne* 'what' taking the place of the name of the day):

(128) Bugün {günler**den** *ne*}?
      '*What day* is it today?'

(ii) Bare-headed partitives in which the head noun phrase is itself headed by a common noun and in which the meaning of the head noun phrase is relatively independent of the modifier noun phrase.

The modifier noun phrase here may, as in type (i), have a descriptive rather than a truly partitive function:

(129) Rehberimiz, {Abdülhamit dönemi mimari eserlerin**den** *bir mescid*}e dikkat çekti.
'Our guide drew attention to *a small mosque, [one] of* the architectural works of Abdülhamit's reign.'

However, it may also identify the individual(s) expressed by the head as belonging to a specific set:

(130) {Bu yılki misafirlerimiz**den** *yirmi otuz aile*} şimdiden gelecek yıl için rezervasyon yaptılar.
'*Twenty or thirty families from among* our guests this year have already made reservations for next year.'

Where the noun phrase defining the set has been mentioned in the immediately preceding context, the ablative-marked modifier is usually one of the possessive-marked postpositions *iç-* or *ara-* 'among' (17.3.1.3 (i)):

(131) Bu yıl **bol misafirimiz** oldu. {*İçlerinden* yirmi otuz aile} de şimdiden gelecek yıl için rezervasyon yaptılar.
'This year we had *a lot of guests. From among them*, twenty or thirty families have already made reservations for next year.'

The forms with *iç-/ara-* are also preferred where the set is referred to from a 1st or 2nd person perspective:

(132) {**İçimizden/Aramızdan** birkaç kişi} geziden memnun kalmadı.
'Several *of our number* were not satisfied with the tour.'

(iii) Bare-headed partitive constructions in which the noun heading the head noun phrase is either the enumerator *tane* (15.8) or a word expressing a concept such as measure (e.g. *metre* 'metre', *dilim* 'slice', *şişe* 'bottle'), membership of a category (e.g. *örnek* 'example') or identity (e.g. *kopya* 'copy'):

(133) {Küçükler**den on *tane***} yeter mi?
'Will *ten of* the little ones be enough?'

(134) {Şu kırmızı çiçekli kumaş**tan on *metre***} alalım.
'Let's buy *ten metres of* that material with red flowers on it.'

Alternatively, the head noun phrase can be one of the quantifiers *bu/şu/o/ne kadar* (18.6.1):

(135) Şaraptan **şu kadar-ı (-nı)** bile içmedi.
           this much-ACC
'S/he didn't drink even this much of the wine.'

In this third subtype of bare-headed partitives, the meaning of the head noun phrase is highly dependent on that of the modifier, just as it is in the *-sI*-marked constructions described in the next section. The item(s) expressed by the head noun phrase in examples such as (133) and (134) are not individuated; the emphasis is purely on quantification and the referents are almost invariably non-human.

In this type of partitive construction, it is even possible for the head noun phrase to be omitted altogether. The ablative-marked noun phrase then simply indicates some or any undefined quantity of the substance or set of entities referred to:

(136) {Şu kırmızı çiçekli kuma**ştan**} alalım.
'Let's buy [*some*] *of* that material with red flowers on it.'

(137) {Bunlar**dan**} bizde de var.
'We've got [*some*] *of* these, too.'

14.5.2 The *-(s)i-marked partitive construction with ablative-marked modifier*

In this type of partitive construction, there is a close semantic dependency of the head upon the modifier, indicated not only by the possessive suffix but also by the fact that the head noun phrase does not contain a semantically autonomous noun. The head noun phrase usually consists of one of the following items:

(i) A numeral (suffixed with *-(s)I*)
(ii) *kaç-ı* 'how many of' or *birkaç-ı* 'a few of', 'several of'
(iii) A numeral, *kaç* or *birkaç* followed by *tane-si*
(iv) *bazı-sı/kimi-si/bir kısm-ı/bir bölüm-ü* 'some of'
(v) *birçoğ-u* 'many of'
(vi) *hangi-si* (or *hangiler-i* if a plural referent is intended) 'which of'
(vii) *hiçbir-i* 'none of'
(viii) *bu/şu/o/ne kadar-ı*
(ix) A pronominalized adjectival (18.4 (i)), such as *en akıllılar-ı* 'the most intelligent (ones)'.

The function of this construction is to pick out one or more items from a distinct set:

(138) {Komşularımız**dan bazısı**} televizyonlarını çok açıyorlar.
'*Some of* our neighbours turn their televisions on very loud.'

As in the case of the bare-headed partitive construction, the modifier may be expressed by the ablative-marked form of a postposition based on *iç-* or *ara-*. For examples, see Chapter 19 (67)-(68), (72).

In the case of heads based upon *tane*, the choice between this construction and the bare-headed version described in (iii) of the previous section offers a distinction of meaning:

(139) a. Bana {küçüklerden iki tane} lazım.
'I need *two of* the small ones.'

b. {Küçüklerden iki tanesi} bana lazım.
'I need *two of* the small ones.'

In (139a) the ablative-marked modifier noun phrase is understood *generically*, i.e as referring to a type of thing rather than to a discrete set. The head noun phrase denotes simply a certain number of items of the type specified ('small ones'). In (139b), on the other hand, the presence of *-(s)I* on the head noun phrase imparts a *definite* meaning to the modifier noun phrase, making it refer to a particular set of 'small ones' that is part of the shared knowledge of speaker and addressee.

When they are in the direct object role, *-(s)I*-marked partitives obligatorily take accusative case marking (14.3.3.2 (iii.a)):

(140) {Bu ilaç-lar-**dan hangi-ler-in**}-*i* alıyorsun?
these medicine-PL-ABL which-PL-3SG.POSS-ACC
'*Which (ones)* of these medicines are you taking?'

(141) {Pilav**dan şu kadarın**}-*ı* yarına saklayalım.
'Let's save *this much* of the rice for tomorrow.'

14.5.3 The -(s)i-marked partitive construction with genitive-marked modifier

The third way of expressing a partitive relation is by means of the genitive-possessive construction (14.4). In many cases this is interchangeable with the *-(s)I*-marked partitive construction with ablative-marked modifier (14.5.2):

(142) {Komşularımız**ın bazısı**} televizyonlarını çok açıyorlar.
'(*Some of* our neighbours) turn their televisions up very loud.'

(143) {Bu ilaçlar**ın hangilerin**}-i alıyorsun?
'*Which (ones)* of these medicines are you taking?'

The partitive uses of the genitive-possessive construction include, however, another type of relation which cannot be expressed using an ablative-marked modifier. These are relations of *proportion* or *totality*, often involving one of the following items as the head:

(i) *yarı-sı* 'half (of)'
(ii) *büyük kısm-ı/büyük bölüm-ü* 'the majority of', 'most of'
(iii) *çoğ-u* 'most of'
(iv) *hep-si* 'all of'
(v) *tüm-ü/bütün-ü* 'the whole of', 'all of'
(vi) *her bir-i* 'every one of'
(vii) *her* followed by a numeral suffixed with *-(s)I*

(144) {Dergiler**in hepsin**}-i Aysel'e geri verdim.
'I've given *all (of)* the magazines back to Aysel.'

(145) {Öğrenciler**in her birin**}-in ayrı bir mazereti vardı.
'*Every one of* the students had a different excuse.'

Fractions, being a precise kind of proportional relation, are expressed by an extended genitive-possessive construction (15.7.1).

Although not expressing a proportional relation, the pronominal quantifiers *bu/şu/o/ne kadar* (18.6.1) can also occur as the head of the genitive-possessive type of partitive construction:

(146) {Paranın ne kadarı}-nı ayıralım?
'{*How much of* the money} should we put aside?'

Finally, there is an idiomatic usage of the genitive-possessive partitive construction in which the head is *bir-i* or *tek-i* (lit. 'one (of)', the latter colloquial) and the modifier is a noun phrase headed by a singular noun with generic reference. The structure as a whole is used to introduce a human subject of whose identity the speaker claims no knowledge:

(147) Birkaç yıl önce {delikanlı**nın biri**} burada vurularak ölmüş.
'It's said that a few years ago *some* young man was shot dead here'.

14.5.4 Other features of partitive constructions

It is possible for an adverbial to intervene between the two constituents of any type of partitive construction:

(148) {Güney Amerika ülkelerinden **en çok** Arjantin}'le ticaret yapıyoruz.
'Among the South American countries, we do business *mostly* with Argentina.'

(149) {O kitaplardan **bugün** pek azı} kaldı.
'Very few of those books are left *today*.'

It is also possible for two separate heads to share a single partitive modifier (28.4.2.1 (iii)):

(150) Hafta sonlarında {çocuklarından **bazen biri, bazen iki tanesi**} geliyor.
'At the weekends *sometimes one, sometimes two* of his/her children come.'

Chapter 15

Adjectival constructions, determiners and numerals

Adjectival constructions are words, phrases or clauses that modify noun phrases. Simple adjectivals consist of a single word, that is, an **adjective** (7.1.1 (iii)):

(1) **küçük** evler
     '*small* houses'

(2) **beyaz** elbisem
     'my *white* dress'

Complex adjectivals vary in their degree of complexity. They range from structures consisting of a noun phrase marked with a suffix such as *-lI* or *-ki* to **relative clauses**, as in (4), which have a sentence-like structure:

(3) **bahçede*ki*** ağaç
     'the tree *in the garden*'

(4) [**manzarası olan**] bir ev
     'a house *which has a view*'

After a brief survey of the functions of adjectivals (15.1) and an overview of the ways in which adjectives can be formed in Turkish (15.2), section 15.3 examines the structure of complex adjectivals (except for relative clauses (Chapter 25)). The next two sections look at how adjectivals can be modified (e.g. *çok güzel* 'very nice', *daha küçük* 'smaller') or complemented (e.g. *buraya uygun* 'suitable for here').

In 15.6–15.8, we present other classes functionally related to adjectivals, namely **determiners** (e.g. *bir* 'a(n)', *bu* 'this'), numerals, the enumerator *tane* and measure terms. 15.9 explains how these items interact with adjectivals within the noun phrase.

DOI: 10.4324/9780429435836-18

15.1 Functions of adjectivals

Adjectivals express qualities that are ascribed to entities. In Turkish, as in other languages, they can be used **attributively**, that is, as a modifier of a noun phrase or **predicatively**, as the subject complement in a linking sentence (12.1.1.2) or small clause (24.5).

(i) Attributive function:
In Turkish, attributive adjectivals, whether simple or complex, always precede the noun they qualify:

yüksek ağaç   'tall tree'
şekerli kahve   'coffee with sugar'
beş yatak odalı ev   'five-bedroomed house'
yedi yaşında bir çocuk 'a seven-year-old child'
evin önündeki arabalar 'the cars in front of the house'

(ii) Predicative function:
Predicative adjectivals, on the other hand, function as subject complements and therefore normally follow the noun phrase expressing the entity that they describe:

As subject complement in linking sentences (12.1.1.2)

(5) Ağaç **yüksek**.
    tree tall
    'The tree is *tall*.'

(6) Çocuk **yedi yaş-ın-da**.
    child seven age-NCM-LOC
    'The child is *seven years old*.'

As subject complement in small clauses (24.5)

(7) [Ev **beş yatak oda-lı**] say-ıl-ır.
    house five bed room-ADJ consider-PASS-AOR
    '[The house] can be considered [*five-bedroomed*].'

(8) [Selim-i **zengin**] say-mı-yor-um.
    Selim-ACC rich regard-NEG-IMPF-1SG
    'I don't regard [Selim as *rich*].'

However, in accordance with the general principles affecting word order in the sentence, it is possible for a predicative adjective to precede the subject noun phrase (Chapter 23 (74)).

15.2 Adjectives

From the point of view of form, we can divide adjectives into two main groups, according to whether or not they contain a **productive** derivational suffix (7.2). Adjectives such as *düşmanca* 'hostile', *başarılı* 'successful' or *bilimsel* 'scientific' are **derived** by means of a productive suffix (in this case -*CA$_1$*, -*lI* or -*sAl*, 7.2.2.2) and therefore have a predictable semantic relationship with an item from another word class (in this case the nouns *düşman* 'enemy', *başarı* 'success' and *bilim* 'science').

15.2.1 Forming adjectives by means of derivational suffixes and compounding

There are many suffixes which productively derive adjectives from nominal stems (principally from nouns) or from verb stems. The most commonly occurring suffixes that derive adjectives from nominal stems are -*CA$_1$*, *CI*, -*lI*, -*lIk*, -*sAl* and -*sIz* (7.2.2.2):

(9) **yaz-*lık*** ev
summer-ADJ house
'holiday home'

-*(y)IcI* and -*(s)Al* are the most commonly occurring suffixes deriving adjectives from verb stems (7.2.1.1):

(10) **gör-*sel*** sanat-lar
see-ADJ art-PL
'*visual* arts'

Adjectives may also be formed by compounding (10.2):

(11) **çimen yeşili** bir yatak örtüsü
'a *leaf green* bed cover'

15.2.2 Intensive forms

Some adjectives have intensive forms produced by reduplication of the initial syllable:

yeni 'new'   →   ***yep**yeni*   'brand new'
başka 'different' →   ***bam**başka*   'completely different'

A full explanation of this process is given in 9.1 and a list of the adjectives (and adverbs) thus formed is provided in Appendix 1.

15.3 Complex adjectivals

15.3.1 Adjective + noun

Adjectivals on this pattern are formed from a limited range of adjective-noun combinations. The nouns include *boy* 'size', *beden* 'size' (of clothing), *biçim* 'form', 'kind', *tarz* 'style':

(12) **küçük boy** kitaplar
'*small-format* books'

(13) **eski tarz** mobilya
'*old-style* furniture'

The noun *marka* 'make', 'brand' can be preceded in this type of structure by a brand name instead of an adjective:

(14) **Opel marka** bir araba
'an *Opel* car'

15.3.2 Locative-marked noun phrase

This type of adjectival phrase expresses qualities such as age, size, shape, colour or style. The noun phrase to which locative case marking is attached is either a *-(s)I* compound or has the form Adjective + Noun. Where used attributively, this type of adjectival occurs only in indefinite noun phrases (22.2):

(15) **dört yaş-ın-*da*** bir çocuk
four age-NCM-LOC
'a *four-year-old* child'

(16) **geniş çap*ta*** bir arama
'a *wide-ranging* search'

15.3.3 Ablative-marked noun phrase

Adjectivals on this pattern express the material from which something is made:

(17) **som altın*dan*** bir taht
'a throne *of solid gold*'

(18) **gazete kağıdın*dan*** torbalar
'bags *made from newspaper*'

15.3.4 Noun phrase marked with -lI

In addition to its function of forming derived adjectives from nouns, *-lI* is highly productive in forming adjectivals from noun phrases. This suffix means 'possessing', 'characterized by' or 'provided with' whatever is expressed by the noun phrase (7.2.2.2).

(19) **sarı saç-lı** kız yellow
hair-ADJ
'*blonde-haired* girl'

(20) **uzun boy-lu** adamlar
long stature-ADJ
'*tall* men'

(21) **Batı Afrika'lı** şairler
'*West African* poets'. (See also 10.2.2)

If the noun phrase to which *-lI* is suffixed is a *-(s)I* compound (10.2), the compound marker has to be deleted. Thus, from *yatak oda-sı* 'bedroom' adjectival phrases such as *beş yatak oda-lı* 'five-bedroomed' are derived.

15.3.5 Noun phrase marked with -lIk

Adjectivals of this type are formed from quantitative expressions of the form numeral + noun and according to the meaning of this noun can express weight, length, capacity, duration, price, etc.:

(22) **beş metre*lik*** bir kablo
'a *five-metre* cable'

(23) **iki litre*lik*** bir kova
'a *two-litre* bucket'

When the noun to which *-lIk* is attached is *kişi* 'person', the adjectival usually has the meaning 'sufficient/suitable for…people':

(24) Otobüste sadece **iki kişi*lik*** yer kalmış.
'It seems there are only two seats left on the bus.'
(lit. '…space *for two people*…')

Where *-lIk* is attached directly to a numerical expression, it denotes value or price (in Turkish lira, if not otherwise specified):

(25) Demet **üç milyon*luk*** bir daire almış.
'Apparently, Demet has bought a *three-million (-lira)* flat.'

15.3.6 Locative-marked noun phrase + -ki

The attachment of *-ki* (8.1.4) to a locative-marked noun phrase is an extremely productive construction, creating an attributive adjectival phrase from a locational expression. Adjectival phrases formed on this pattern are used predominantly in noun phrases that have definite status (22.1), sometimes also in those that are indefinite but specific (22.2.1):

(26) {**Bahçe-de-ki** (bazı) ağaç-lar} yapraklarını dökmeye başladı.
garden-LOC-ADJ (some) tree-PL
'The/Some trees *in the garden* have begun to shed their leaves.'

This construction occurs also with possessive-marked postpositions (17.3) that include the locative case marker:

(27) **Arka-mız-da-*ki*** (bir) araba bizi geçmek istiyor.
back-1PL.POSS-LOC-ADJ (a) car
'The/A car *behind us* wants to overtake us.'

(28) **Benim hakkımda*ki*** fikriniz yanlış.
'Your opinion *of me* is wrong.'

15.3.7 Temporal adverbial + -ki

Any adverbial expressing location (as opposed to duration) in time (16.4.1.1) that either has no case marking or is locative-marked can similarly be converted into an adjectival phrase by the addition of *-ki* (8.1.4):

(29) Mehmet'in **o gün*kü*** halini çok iyi hatırlıyorum.
'I well remember the state Mehmet was in *that day*.'

(30) **(Saat) ikide*ki*** ders iptal olmuş.
'The *two o'clock* class has apparently been cancelled.'

15.3.8 Noun phrase + diye

Aside from its wide range of functions (11.1.1.3), *diye* has an adjectival function (not found in more formal registers) of indicating what something is called. Adjectivals constructed with *diye* are used exclusively in indefinite noun phrases (22.2):

(31) Bizim mahallede Güneş Gıda **diye** bir market var.
'In our neighbourhood there's a self-service shop *called* Güneş Gıda.'

(32) Mehmet **diye** bir oğlu daha var.
'S/he's got another son, *called* Mehmet.'

15.3.9 Relative clause

Relative clauses are the most complex form of adjectival, having a sentence-like structure with a participle as their verb. These are fully discussed in Chapter 25.

(33) [Arka-mız-dan gel-**en**] araba bizi geçmek istiyor.
back-1PL.POSS-ABL come-PART car
'The car [*that's following* us] wants to overtake us.'

15.3.10 Possessive-marked noun phrase + adjective (truncated relative clause)

This type of adjectival construction tends to occur with non-specific noun phrases (Chapter 25 (97)–(99)):

(34) [**sap-ları kopuk**] birkaç çanta
handle-PL.3PL.POSS broken a.few bag
'a few bags *with broken handles*'

15.4 Modification of adjectives

Adjectives can be modified by a preceding adverbial of degree (16.5) in order to indicate the intensity of the attribute denoted by the adjective. Most adverbials of degree, such as *çok* 'very', 'too' or *biraz* 'a little', 'a bit', relate to abstract notions of quantity, but two of them (*daha* 'more' and *en* 'most'), express respectively a comparative or superlative degree. These modifiers are almost always stressed in a sentence (4.4.2).

15.4.1 General modification

15.4.1.1 By simple adverbials of degree

Simple adverbials of quantity and degree (listed in 16.5), such as *çok* 'very', 'too' and *biraz* 'a little', 'a bit', 'rather', occur as modifiers of adjectives:

(35) **çok** temiz
'*very* clean'

(36) **biraz** aptal
'*a bit* stupid'

15.4.1.2 By complex adverbials

The other means of general modification of adjectives is a phrase or clause headed by the postpositions *gibi* 'like' and *kadar* 'as...as' (17.2.1 (i), (iv)). This may be a postpositional phrase:

(37) **Filiz'in evi gibi** temiz
'clean *like Filiz's house*'

Alternatively, it may be an adverbial clause (26.3.13):

(38) [**inan-ıl-a-ma-yacak kadar**] temiz
believe-PASS-PSB-NEG-CV
'*unbelievably* clean'

(39) [**bekle-diğ-imiz kadar**] temiz
expect-CV-1PL.POSS
'as clean [*as we expect(ed)*]'

15.4.2 Comparatives

The comparative form of an adjective is formed by the adverb *daha* 'more'. *daha* precedes the adjectival constituent and can itself be modified by the degree adverbs *çok* 'much' and *biraz* 'a little':

(40) (çok) **daha** rahat
'(much) *more* comfortable'

(41) (biraz) **daha** güzel
'(a little) prett*er*'

daha usually takes an ablative-marked complement:

(42) bu araba-***dan* daha *geniş*** bir araba
this car-ABL more spacious a car
'a *more spacious* car *than* this one'

(43) hepimiz***den* daha *hevesli*** bir üye
'a member *more enthusiastic than* any of us'

Alternatively, it can be used with a phrase of comparison containing *kıyasla oranla* or *nazaran* 'compared with':

(44) Semra'*ya kıyasla* daha *becerikli*
'*more competent than* Semra'

The complement of *daha* can be a non-finite noun clause (24.4):

(45) [**Beni son gördüğünüz**]**-den** daha iyiyim.
'I'm better *than* [*when you last saw me*].'

The complement of *daha* can be omitted when the person or object to which someone or something is compared is obvious from the context:

(46) Size (bu evden) **daha uygun bir ev** düşünemiyorum.
'I cannot think of *a more suitable house* for you (than this house).'

Alternatively, *daha* can be omitted if an ablative complement is present:

(47) Bu makine öbürün**den** ucuz.
'This machine is cheap*er than* the other one.'

The concept 'even more …', 'even …er' in comparisons is expressed using one of the clitics *bile* or *dA* (11.1.1.1–2, 28.3.1.1 (iii.b–iv)). If *daha* is not present, the clitic is inserted between the ablative complement and the adjective:

(48) Bu makine öbürün**den** *de* ucuz /öbürün**den bile** ucuz.
'This machine is *even* cheap*er than* the other one.'

If *daha* is present, the clitics *dA* or *bile* can alternatively be placed immediately after it. This is the only strategy available where there is no ablative complement:

(49) Mustafa yakışıklı bir delikanlıydı. Ama kardeşi **daha da / daha bile** yakışıklıydı.
'Mustafa was a handsome young man. But his brother was *even more* handsome.'

daha can modify an adjective which is the head of a genitive-possessive construction (14.4) or is otherwise being used pronominally (18.4):

(50) bu resm-*in* **daha** güzel-*i*
this picture-GEN more nice-3SG.POSS
'a nic*er* [version] of this picture'

(51) bu resim-den **daha** güzel-i
this picture-ABL more nice-3SG.POSS

'a picture nic*er* than this one'
(lit. 'a nic*er* one than this picture')

To express the notion *less*, Turkish uses the phrase *daha az:*

(52) bizimkinden ***daha az* gürültülü** bir sokak
'a street *less noisy* than ours'

Note that *az* used without a preceding *daha* in a comparative construction is a colloquial and shortened form of *biraz* 'a little', and expresses 'a little more' (*not* 'less'). The same meaning is conveyed by *az daha*:

(53) bundan *az* (*daha*) **büyük** bir araba
'a car *slightly bigger* than this one'

15.4.3 Superlatives

The superlative form of an adjective defines the entity or set expressed by the following noun as the one which possesses (within a larger set of such entities) the highest degree of the attribute denoted by the adjective. The superlative form of an adjective is formed in Turkish by placing the adverbial *en* 'most' before it:

(54) **en** ilginç düşünce
'the *most* interesting idea'

(55) **en** küçük bardaklar
'the *smallest* glasses'

Superlative adjectival constructions can be modified by one of the following:

(i) A locative expression with or without *-ki*:

(56) **listedeki *en*** başarılı çocuk
'*the most* successful child *on the list*'

(57) [**yarışmaya katılanlar**] **arasında/içinde *en*** başarılı çocuk
'*the most* successful child *among the ones* [*who entered the competition*]'

(ii) A genitive-marked noun phrase (forming a genitive-possessive construction (14.4) with the noun phrase that is qualified by the superlative adjective):

(58) **bu ilac-ın *en*** iyi taraf-ı
this medicine-GEN most good side-3SG.POSS
'*the best* thing *about this medicine*'

In the case of a few verbs of emotion such as *sev-* 'like', *beğen-* 'admire' and *kork-* 'fear', *en* can modify the verb in a relative clause directly (rather than modifying an adverb of degree such as *çok* 'much' which in turn modifies a verb (16.8):

(59) [(**benim**) *en* **sevdiğim**] tiyatro oyuncusu
       'the actor [*I like the most*]'

en can modify an adjective which is the head of a genitive-possessive construction (14.4):

(60) bu resim-ler-**in** *en* güzel-**i**
       these picture-PL-GEN most beautiful-3SG.POSS
       'the *most* beautiful *of* these pictures'

15.5 Complementation of adjectives

Certain adjectives, in at least some of their senses, require a noun phrase complement to complete their meaning. The case marking required on the complement is fixed for any given adjective. Some common examples of complement-taking adjectives are given below.

(i) Non-case-marked complement:

   (61) su **dolu** kova-lar
         water full bucket-PL
         'buckets *full of* water'

(ii) Dative-marked complement:

   (62) ödü**le layık** bir öğrenci
         'a student *worthy of* a prize'

   (62) bu oda**ya uygun** bir tablo
         'a picture *suitable for* this room'

(iii) Ablative-marked complement:

   (64) öğrencilerin**den memnun** bir öğretmen
         'a teacher *pleased with* his/her students'

(iv) Instrumental-marked complement:

   (65) kar**la kaplı** sokaklar
         'streets *covered in* snow'

   (66) güvenlik**le ilgili** bir konu
         'a matter *relating* to security'

15.6 Determiners

The class of determiners in Turkish (14.1.2) consists of the items listed below. Many of these items also occur, either in the same form or with the addition of the 3rd person possessive suffix, as pronouns (18.4).

Determiners fall into two classes, indefinite and definite, according to the referential status they impart to the noun phrase in which they occur (Chapter 22).

15.6.1 Indefinite determiners

(i) Indefinite article:

bir	'a(n)'

Note that in *bir* and the items in the following list which contain *bir* (except *biraz*), the final 'r' is colloquially omitted before a consonant (e.g. *bi kadın* 'a woman'). See also 1.1.1.1 (section on /r/).

(ii) Quantifiers:

birkaç (tane)	'a few', 'several'
birtakım	'some', 'a number of'
birçok	'many', 'a lot of'
biraz	'a little', 'some'
bir miktar	'some', 'a certain amount of'
bazı/kimi/bir kısım	'some', 'certain'
bu/şu/o/kadar	'this much', 'that much', 'so much'
çok	'a lot of', '(too) many', '(too) much'
çoğu	'most'
az	'not much', 'not enough'
fazla	'too much', 'too many'
hiçbir	'no', 'any' (20.5.2)
herhangi bir	'any' (20.5.2)

For the combinability of quantifying determiners with noun phrases denoting discrete or non-discrete entities, see 14.2. Several of the quantifiers cannot be used in a plural-marked noun phrase (14.3.1.1). *Bazı* and *kimi*, by contrast, are almost always used with plural marking on the head noun.

The quantifiers *bu/şu/o kadar* share the same differentiation in meaning as demonstrative pronouns (see 18.2). For the usage of *bu/şu/o* as determiners, see (15.6.2 (i)).

(iii) Interrogatives:

hangi	'which'	(19.2.1.4)
kaç (tane)	'how many'	(19.2.1.5)
ne kadar	'how much'	(19.2.1.6)

nasıl (bir) /
ne gibi (bir)   'what kind of (a)'   (Chapter 19 (94)–(95))

(iv) Markers of similarity and otherness:

böyle/şöyle/öyle (bir)   'such (a)'
başka (bir)   '(an)other'
bu/şu/o gibi bir   'a ... like this/that'

The forms *böyle/şöyle/öyle* are derived from the demonstratives (15.6.2 (i)) and share the same differentiation in meaning (explained in 18.2).

(v) Markers of arbitrariness (colloquial):

falanca/filanca   'such and such'
falanca and filanca should be in italics.

If this emendation changes the pagination of Numerals and Cardinal numerals, then the entry Cardinal numerals in the index should be amended accordingly.

15.6.2 Definite determiners

(i) Demonstratives:
bu   'this', 'these'
şu   'this', 'that', 'these', 'those'
o   'that', 'those'

For the pronominal use of the demonstratives, see 18.2, where the semantic differences between the three forms are also explained.

(ii) Universal quantifiers:
her   'every'
bütün/tüm   'the whole (of)', 'all'

(iii) Markers of identity or (exclusive) otherness:
aynı   'the same'
öteki/öbür/diğer   'the other'

For the pronominal use of these determiners, see 18.4-5.

(iv) Ordinal numerals (15.7.2) and the related items *ilk* 'first' and *son* 'last'
Noun phrases with definite determiners obligatorily have accusative case marking when functioning as direct objects (22.1 (iii)).

15.7 Numerals

15.7.1 Cardinal numerals

The cardinal numerals of Turkish are the following:

sıfır	'zero'	*yirmi*	'twenty'	*milyar*	'billion'
bir	'one'	*otuz*	'thirty'	*trilyon*	'trillion'
iki	'two'	*kırk*	'forty'	*katrilyon*	'quadrillion'
üç	'three'	*elli*	'fifty'		(= billion billion)
dört	'four'	*altmış*	'sixty'		
beş	'five'	*yetmiş*	'seventy'		
altı	'six'	*seksen*	'eighty'		
yedi	'seven'	*doksan*	'ninety'		
sekiz	'eight'	*yüz*	'(one) hundred'		
dokuz	'nine'	*bin*	'(one) thousand'		
on	'ten'	*milyon*	'million'		

The numerals from one to nine follow higher numerals to form the numerals from 11 to 99 and these follow any other higher numerals:

on iki	'twelve'
yetmiş üç	'seventy-three'
yüz kırk beş	'one hundred and forty-five'
bin yüz doksan dokuz	'one thousand one hundred and ninety-nine'

When the numerals from *yüz* '(one) hundred' to *katrilyon* 'quadrillion' are in their multiple forms, they are preceded by lower numerals:

üç yüz	'three hundred'
kırk iki bin	'forty-two thousand'
dokuz milyon altı yüz altmış bin	'nine million six hundred and sixty thousand'

yüz 'hundred' and *bin* 'thousand' are not preceded by *bir* when they indicate 'one hundred' and 'one thousand' (thus *yüz* 'one hundred', *bin* 'one thousand'), but *milyon, milyar, trilyon* and *katrilyon* are (i.e. *bir milyon* 'one million', etc.).

Turkish has three different words for *half*. The word *yarım* behaves just like a cardinal numeral and is used only when referring to one half of an entity on its own, e.g. *yarım bardak* 'half a glass', *yarım portakal* 'half an orange'. The concept *and a half* is expressed by the word *buçuk*, e.g. *iki buçuk* 'two and a half'. The expression, *yarı* 'half' is (i) a noun used as the head of a partitive construction (14.5.3), e.g. *paranın yarısı* 'half (of) the money' and (ii) an adverb of degree (16.5), e.g. *yarı ölü* 'half-dead'. The word *çeyrek* 'a quarter' is the only numeral which needs a conjunction: *üç ve bir çeyrek* 'three and a quarter'. Note that a construction without the conjunction (and *bir*) indicates a totally different numeral, e.g. *üç çeyrek* 'three-quarters'. 'Quarter' can also be expressed as *dörtte bir* ('one in four'). This structure, which contains the locative suffix *-DA*, is one of the means for expressing fractions, e.g. (2/3) '*üçte iki* 'two-thirds', (3/4) *dörtte üç* 'three-quarters'. The other way of expressing fractions is by using the expression *bölü* 'divided by', e.g.

(2/5) *iki bölü beş* 'two-fifths/two over five'. Decimals are expressed by the whole number followed by *virgül* 'comma' or by a fraction, e.g. (3,32) *üç virgül otuz iki*, 'three point three two', (5,6) *beş onda altı* 'five [and] six-tenths'. The word *yüzde* expresses *per cent*, e.g. *yüzde beş* (%5) 'five per cent'. These structures are used as the heads of genitive-possessive constructions (14.4) when expressing either the full number or the entity or set of which the fraction is a part:

    (67)   yirmi-***nin*** sekiz-**de** yedi-***si***
              twenty-GEN eight-LOC seven-3SG.POSS
              'seven-eighths of twenty'

    (68)   para-mız-***ın*** yüz-**de** doksan beş-***i***/%95'***i***
              money-1PL.POSS-GEN hundred-LOC ninety five-3SG.POSS
              '95% of our money'

When fractions follow whole numbers, they are expressed without conjunctions, e.g. *üç onda dokuz* 'three [and] nine-tenths'. Conjunctions are also not used when two numerals are juxtaposed to give an approximation, e.g. *bir iki dükkan*'one or two shops' (28.1).

It should be noted that, unlike determiners, numerals can occur in noun phrases that have either indefinite or definite status. They can be combined with some determiners (15.9.1). In general, a noun phrase containing a numeral cannot have plural marking (14.3.1.1). Numerals can also be pronominalized (18.4 (ii)).

15.7.2 Ordinal numerals

Ordinal numerals are formed by the suffix *-(I)ncI* (7.2.2.2), e.g. *altıncı* 'sixth', *yüzbeşinci* 'one hundred and fifth':

    (69)   **iki*nci*** öneri
              'the *second* proposal'

When ordinal numerals are used in titles, they are written with a full stop following the numeral, e.g. *7. (yedinci* 'seventh'):

    (70)   **18.** Uluslararası Tıp Kongresi
              'The *18th* International Medical Conference'

Streets which are named numerically are expressed in ordinal numerals: *10. Sokak* (*Onuncu Sokak*) '10th Street', *4. Cadde* (*Dördüncü Cadde*) '4th Avenue'. The word *ilk* (15.6.2 (iv)) is another term for *birinci* 'first':

    (71)   soldan **ilk/birinci** ev
              'the *first* house on the left'

15.7.3 Distributive numerals

Distributive numerals are formed by the suffix *-(ş)Ar* (7.2.2.2), e.g. *altışar* 'six each', *onar* 'ten each', *seksen ikişer* 'eighty-two each'. When added to numbers exceeding a thousand and denoting round numbers (such as two thousand, five million, seven billion, etc.), the suffix is attached to the first numeral, e.g. *sekizer bin* 'eight thousand each', *onar milyon* 'ten million each'. For multiples of a hundred *-(ş)Ar* can be attached either to the first numeral or to *yüz*:

(72) **üçer** yüz/üç **yüzer**
'three hundred each'

The presence of a distributive numeral requires at least one plural noun phrase in the clause:

(73) Ahmet **çocuklara ikişer** hediye verdi.
'Ahmet gave *the children two* gifts *each.*'

(74) *Ahmet'le Mehmet* Semra'ya **ikişer** hediye verdiler.
'*Ahmet and Mehmet each* gave Semra *two* gifts.'

Distributive numerals are also used in pairs (9.3) to form manner adverbials (16.4.3), e.g. *beşer onar* 'in fives and tens', *üçer üçer* 'in threes'.

15.8 The enumerator tane and measure/type terms

Cardinal numerals are often used with the enumerator *tane* (or *adet*), usually when modifying nouns denoting discrete, non-human entities:

(75) **on *tane*** tabak
'*ten* plates'

Measure terms such as *şişe* 'bottle', *bardak* 'glass', *avuç* 'handful', *metre* 'metre', etc., and type terms such as *çeşit/tür* 'kind', *tip* 'type' are used in the same way:

(76) **sekiz *bardak*** su
'*eight glasses* [*of*] water'

tane and measure terms can also be used with distributive numerals:

(77) **ikişer *tane*** araba
'*two* cars *each*'

Most of these terms can combine with the 3rd person possessive suffix *-(s)I* (8.1.2) and function as heads of genitive-possessive constructions (14.4):

(78) **Limon-un *tane*-si** 20 peni.
Lemon-GEN ENUM-3SG.POSS
'*The lemons* are 20p *each*.'

(79) **İpeğin *metre*si** ne kadar?
'How much is *the silk per metre*?'

The possessive-suffixed forms also occur as pronominals (18.4 (ii–iii)):

(80) Çok pahalı bir ilaç. ***Şişesi*** 100 sterlin.
'It's a very expensive medicine. [It's] £100 *per bottle*.'

dolusu '...ful' can also be used as a measure term when compounded with a preceding noun:

(81) **iki *oda dolusu*** eski gazete
'*two roomfuls* of old newspapers'

The adverbials *yaklaşık (olarak)*, *aşağı yukarı* 'approximately', *hemen hemen* 'almost' can occur before any numerical expression:

(82) **Aşağı yukarı** 100 sayfa okudum.
'I've read *about* 100 pages.'

15.9 The position of determiners and numerals within the noun phrase

The position of a determiner within the noun phrase depends both on the type of determiner involved and the type of adjectival construction(s) that are also present.

15.9.1 Numerals with determiners

The cardinal numerals follow most determiners:

(83) ***aynı* üç** konuşmacı
'*the same three* speakers'

(84) ***bu* yedi (tane)** iskemle
'*these seven* chairs'

The combination *her* + numeral, with or without the addition of the clitic *dA* (11.1.1.2) to the noun phrase head, is equivalent to 'all' + numeral in English:

(85) ***Her* dört** daireyi (***de***) beğendik.
'We liked *all four flats.*'

Even if *her* is not present, placing *dA* after a noun phrase containing a numeral modifer has the effect of giving the phrase definite reference (18.4 (ii), 22.1):

(86) (*Her*) **iki** çocuk *da* uyumuş.
'*Both* children had gone to sleep.'

15.9.2 Determiners or numerals with adjectives

Definite determiners and numerals normally precede adjectives:

(87) **o** küçük dolap
'*that* small cupboard'

(88) **aynı** tatsız yemekler
'*the same* tasteless food'

(89) **üç** tarihi şehir
'(the) *three* historic cities'

However, if the superlative marker *en* is present (15.4.3), the position of a numeral is after the adjective:

(90) a. **dört** başarılı öğrenci
'*(the) four* successful students'

b. *en* başarılı **dört** öğrenci
'*the four most* successful students'

The indefinite article *bir* usually follows the adjective, but can precede it:

(91) genç **bir** adam/**bir** genç adam
'*a* young man'

(92) açık **bir** pencere/**bir** açık pencere
'*an* open window'

There is a subtle difference in meaning between the two word orders with the indefinite article. Because modification within nominal phrases in Turkish operates from left to right, placing the adjectival to the left of *bir* has the effect of making the sequence {adjectival + head} be perceived as a semantic unit. Thus, in (91), the form *bir genç adam* denotes a member of the class 'young man', whereas the form *genç bir adam* denotes a young member of the class 'man'. This latter order, which is much the more common, gives more prominence to the adjective.

Where *bir* means 'one', usually in relation to an already mentioned set, it always precedes an adjective and receives stress:

(93) Burada ekonomik ve toplumsal sorunlarımızı konuşuyoruz. **BİR** önemli toplumsal sorunumuz da ailenin dağılmasıdır.
'We're talking about our economic and social problems here. *One* major social problem that we've got is the dispersal of the family.'

An adjective that is itself modified (15.4.1) has to precede *bir*, whether *bir* is being used in the article or the numeral function:

(94) *çok* önemli **bir/BİR** sorun
'*a/one very* important problem'

Indefinite determiners normally precede an adjective, but *birkaç, birçok, bazı* and *kimi* (15.6.1 (ii)) can sometimes follow it:

(95) **birkaç** kırık iskemle/kırık **birkaç** iskemle
'*a few* broken chairs'

15.9.3 Determiners or numerals with complex adjectivals formed with -DAn, -lI or -lIk

The situation with these adjectivals (15.3.3, 15.3.4, 15.3.5) is similar to that with simple adjectives, but here the post-adjectival position is more freely available, not only to all indefinite determiners but also to cardinal and ordinal numerals plus *ilk* and *son*:

(96) **birtakım** ceviz ağac-ın-***dan*** sehpa-lar /
some walnut wood-NCM-ABL small.table-PL

ceviz ağacın***dan*** **birtakım** sehpalar
walnut wood-NCM-ABL some small.table-PL

'*some* small tables *made of* walnut wood'

(97) **ilk** yüzme havuz***lu*** villa/yüzme havuz***lu*** **ilk** villa
'*the first* house *with* a swimming pool'

(98) **on tane** üçer dörder metre***lik*** heykel /
üçer dörder metre***lik*** **on tane** heykel
'*ten* statues, each three or four metres [high]'

As with adjectives (15.9.2), if a -*li* adjectival is modified by the superlative marker *en*, a numeral can only follow, not precede:

(99) *en* yüksek tirajlı **beş** gazete
      '*the five* newspapers with the high*est* circulation'

15.9.4 Determiners or numerals with locative-marked complex adjectivals

Locative-marked complex adjectivals (15.3.2) can occur with definite determiners only if *-ki* is added (15.9.5). Other determiners or numerals are usually placed after the adjectival:

(100) Turhan Kural adın*da* **bir** yazar
       '*a* writer *by* the name of Turhan Kural'

(101) orta büyüklük*te* **dört** patates
       '*four* medium-size*d* potatoes'

15.9.5 Determiners or numerals with adjectivals formed with -ki

In general, determiners and numerals have to follow *-ki* adjectivals (15.3.6, 15.3.7):

(102) gazetede*ki* **öbür** resim
       '*the other* picture in the paper'

(103) romanda*ki* **her** önemli kişi
       '*every* important character in the novel'

If a determiner or numeral is placed before a locative + *-ki* construction, it is usually understood as modifying the immediately following locative-marked noun phrase rather than the larger one, of which the *-ki* adjectival is a part:

(104) **öbür** gazedeki resim
       'the picture in *the other* paper'

(105) **her** romandaki önemli kişi
       'the important character in *every* novel'

However, *bütün/tüm* 'all' and the demonstratives form exceptions to this general pattern. In the case of *bütün/tüm*, the determiner is understood as modifying the larger noun phrase, regardless of its position:

(106) **bütün** çekmecedeki para/çekmecedeki **bütün** para
'*all* the money in the drawer'

(107) **bütün** yedi yaşındaki çocuklar/yedi yaşındaki **bütün** çocuklar
'*all* (the) seven-year-old children'

Placing a demonstrative before a locative + -*ki* adjectival creates a potential ambiguity as to whether the determiner forms part of the smaller or the larger noun phrase:

(108) **bu** masadaki kitaplar

   (i) **bu** masadaki kitaplar
   'the books on *this* table'

   (ii) **bu** masadaki kitaplar (= masadaki **bu** kitaplar)
   '*these* books on the table'

In (i) *bu* is understood to modify *masa* 'table' and in (ii) to modify *kitaplar* 'books'.
   In practice, any potential ambiguity is usually eliminated by the way in which the words are uttered. If the demonstrative is intended as a modifier of the noun closest to it, as in (108 (i)), it is slightly stressed. If, on the other hand, it is intended as a modifier of the larger noun phrase, as in (108 (ii)), it is unstressed and sometimes followed by a very slight pause.

15.9.6 Determiners or numerals with relative clauses

Relative clauses (Chapter 25) behave rather similarly to -*ki* adjectivals in the way they interact with determiners and numerals. The position following the relative clause is the standard one for all these items:

(109) [Jale'nin sevdiği] **iki** yer
'(the) *two* places [Jale likes]'

(110) [Korkut'u o halde görmüş olan] **bütün** arkadaşlarımız
'*all* our friends [who have/had seen Korkut in that state]'

However, under certain conditions the determiner or numeral can optionally precede the relative clause:

(i) If the relative clause consists only of a verb (participle):

(111) **birkaç** (tane) [oynayan] çocuk/[oynayan] **birkaç** (tane) çocuk
' *a few* children [playing]'

(112) **şu** [gördüğünüz] kalabalık/[gördüğünüz] **şu** kalabalık
'*this* crowd [that you see]'

(ii) If the relative clause is of the type marked by *-(y)An* (25.1.1.1) and does not contain, apart from its verb, any constituent other than a one-word, non-case-marked adverbial, as in (113) or a categorial direct object (13.1.2.1, 22.3), as in (114):

(113) **her** [*hızlı* akan] nehir/[*hızlı* akan] **her** nehir
'*every* [*swiftly*-flowing] river'

(114) **kimi** [*ün* yap-an] oyuncular/[*ün* yap-an] **kimi** oyuncular
some fame make-PART actor-PL
'*some* actors [who become famous]'

(iii) Demonstratives can be placed before any kind of relative clause, but if this contains a noun phrase (other than a categorial direct object) there is potential ambiguity of the kind noted for demonstratives preceding *-ki* adjectivals (15.9.5 (108)):

(115) **o** çocuğun yaptığı resim

(i) [o çocuğ-un yap-tığ-ı] resim
that child-GEN make-PART-3SG.POSS picture
'the picture [(which) *that* child painted]'

(ii) **o** [çocuğun yaptığı] resim (= [çocuğun yaptığı] **o** resim)
'*that* picture [(which) the child painted]'

As explained in the case of *-ki* constructions, the ambiguity is, in practice, usually eliminated by the manner of utterance.

Chapter 16

Adverbial constructions

Adverbs (7.1.1 (iv)) are words that modify verbs, nominal predicates, adjec-tivals, other adverbials or whole sentences. '**Adverbial**' is a broader term used to cover all types of sentence constituent that perform the function of an adverb. Adverbials vary widely in structure (16.1) from single words (e.g. *herhalde* 'probably', *bugün* 'today') through noun phrases with or without suffixes (e.g. *bu sabah* 'this morning', *beş buçukta* 'at half-past five') and postpositional phrases (e.g. *havaya rağmen* 'in spite of the weather') to adverbial clauses (e.g. *yanlışımı anlayınca* 'upon realizing my mistake').

The syntactic functions of adverbials are reviewed in 16.2. The subsequent sections focus in turn on the various semantic roles that adverbial constructions play in the sentence and are organized as follows: modal adverbials (16.3), adverbials of time, place, manner (16.4), quantity or degree (16.5) and respect (16.6), and focus-sensitive adverbials (16.7). Section 16.8 describes the modification of adverbs.

Postpositional phrases, which form a major type of relatively complex adverbials, are treated separately in Chapter 17. **Adverbial clauses** form the subject of Chapter 26, except for **conditional clauses**, which are discussed in Chapter 27.

16.1 Types of adverbial construction

16.1.1 Simple adverbs

These are words whose sole or primary grammatical function is adverbial. Examples are *şimdi* 'now', *ancak* 'only', *çabuk* 'quickly', *maalesef* 'unfortunately'.

16.1.2 Adjectives used as adverbs

Many lexical items whose primary function is adjectival (e.g. *güzel* 'beautiful', *kolay* 'easy', *yeni* 'new') can be made to function adverbially (e.g. 'well', 'easily', '(only) just') simply by placing them in the immediately preverbal position (for further examples, see 23.2.1 (iii)).

(1) Özdemir o şarkıyı **güzel** söyledi.
  'Özdemir sang that song *well*.'

DOI: 10.4324/9780429435836-19

If there is a **categorial** direct object (22.3), the adverbial has to precede it:

(2) Özdemir **güzel *şarkı*** söyler.
'Özdemir sings *(songs) well*.'

(3) Ben **zor *dikiş*** dikiyorum.
'I sew [only] *with difficulty*.'

Not all adjectives can be used adverbially, even if their meaning is appropriate to the description of actions. With the exception of formations with *-lI* and *-sIz* (7.2.2.2), most derived adjectives (15.2.1) can modify verbs only indirectly, either by modifying a locative-marked noun phrase such as *bir biçimde/bir şekilde* 'in a ...manner' or by standing as complement to *olarak* (16.1.9):

(4) **Erkeksi *bir biçimde*** konuşur.
'S/he talks *in a masculine way*.'

(5) Bu sorunu **bilimsel *olarak*** araştırmalıyız.
'We must investigate this problem *scientifically*.'

The same restriction applies to adjectives of foreign origin:

(6) Başkan **demokratik *bir şekilde*** seçilmemişti.
'The chairman had not been *democratically* elected.'

16.1.3 Doubled forms

Certain adverbials are formed by the reduplicated use of a noun, adjective or adverb (9.3). This is not a fully productive process and the usage and/or meaning of such forms may be more restricted than the simple form. Thus, *yavaş yavaş* always means 'slowly' or 'gradually', whereas the adjective *yavaş* can mean 'quiet' or 'gentle' in addition to 'slow'. Many of these doubled forms that modify verbs are either used only in affirmative sentences or only in negative sentences e.g. *rahat rahat* 'readily', 'easily' is confined to affirmative sentences whereas its negative counterpart *kolay kolay* 'readily', 'easily' is used only in negative sentences:

(7) Kimse buradan **kolay kolay** kaçamaz.
'No one could *easily* escape from here.'

The temporal adverbials *sabah sabah* and *akşam akşam*, meaning approximately 'so early in the morning' and 'so late at night' respectively, are used with the implication that the performance of the action at the time in question is socially unacceptable.

(8) **Sabah sabah** ne diye bu kadar gürültü yapıyorsunuz?
'Why are you making such a noise *at this unearthly hour*?'

16.1.4 Noun phrases without case marking

Non-case-marked noun phrases are used for certain types of time location (16.4.1.1), duration of time (16.4.1.2) and expressions of distance:

(9) **Beş kilometre** yürümüşüz.
    'We seem to have walked *five kilometres*.'

16.1.5 Noun phrases with oblique case marking

Noun phrases with dative, locative or ablative marking occur in a wide range of adverbial functions, discussed in 13.1.3, 14.3.3.3–5.

(10) Berna **koca-sın-*dan*** ayrıl-mış-tı.
     Berna husband-3SG.POSS-ABL separate-PF-P.COP
     'Berna had separated *from her husband*.'

16.1.6 Noun or adjective suffixed with -CA$_1$

For an overview of the functions of the unstressable suffix -CA_1 (and its colloquial alternative -CAK_2 (iii-iv) in some contexts), see 7.2.2.2. Here we illustrate the various adverbial meanings which -CA_1 formations can express.

(i) Manner:

(11) **Yavaş-*ça*** Jale'nin koluna dokundu.
     gentle-ADV
     'S/he *gently* touched Jale's arm.'

(12) Osman **çocukça** davranıyor.
     'Osman is behaving *childishly*.'

(13) Şarkıyı **Fransızca** söyledi.
     'She sang the song *in French*.'

(ii) Long duration:

(14) Bu mektubu **haftalarca** beklemiştik.
     'We had waited *weeks* for this letter.'

(iii) The collective or institutional agent of a passive verb (13.2.2.2):

(15) Yunus Emre [**Türk halkınca** sevilen] bir şairdir.
     'Yunus Emre is a poet [loved *by the Turkish people*].'

(iv) Collective involvement in an action or state:

(16) Onlar herşeyi **ailece** yaparlar.
     'They do everything *as a family*.'

(v) The respect in which a description is applicable:

(17) Babası **dünyaca** meşhur bir ressamdı.
'His/Her father was a *world*-famous painter.'

(vi) The viewpoint of a person:

(18) **Bence** endişelenecek bir şey yok.
'*In my view,* there's nothing to worry about.'

16.1.7 Constructions with -DIr

This type of adverbial structure occurs with two types of constituent:

(i) A low cardinal numeral, expressing the number of times an event has been repeated up to the moment of speech:

(19) **Üçtür** kalkıp geliyoruz, evde yoksun.
'Three times we've made the effort to come, [but] you're never at home.'

(ii) A noun phrase denoting a period of time, expressing duration up to the time of utterance (16.4.1.2 (iii.b)).

16.1.8 Postpositional phrases

Postpositional phrases form the subject of Chapter 17. Their most characteristic function is adverbial (17.4.1):

(20) **Evdeki durumdan *dolayı*** Filiz gelemeyebilir.
'*Because of the situation at home,* Filiz may not be able to come.'

16.1.9 Constructions with olarak

olarak, the converbial form of *ol-* 'be' formed with *-(y)ArAk* (26.3.8), has been lexicalized as a marker of certain types of adverbial phrase:

(i) It produces adverbials from adjectives, generally from derived adjectives (16.1.2).

(21) Raporu **yazılı *olarak*** sunmuşlardı.
'They had submitted the report *in writing.*'

For the omission of *olarak* from such sentences, see 24.5.1 (ii).

(ii) Following a noun phrase, it forms an adverbial indicating:

(a) Status or classification:

(22) Bunu sana **avukat *olarak*** değil, **arkadaş *olarak*** söylüyorum.
'I'm saying this to you not *as a lawyer* but *as a friend.*'

(23) Şimdilik bu sandığı **masa *olarak*** kullanıyoruz.
'For the moment, we're using this chest *as a table.*'

(24) **Meyva *olarak*** ne var?
'What is there *in the way of fruit*?'

(b) Collective involvement in an action or state (see *-CA₁*, 16.1.6 (iv)):

(25) **Aile *olarak*** müziğe meraklılar.
'*As a family*, they're interested in music.'

Where the group involved is expressed by a noun phrase containing a numeral modifier, *olarak* may be omitted:

(26) Biz **üç arkadaş** (***olarak***) konuşuyoruz.
'We are chatting *as a group of three friends.*'

For further examples, see Chapter 12 (62)–(63).

16.1.10 Constructions with olmak üzere

olmak üzere, another converbial form of *ol-* 'be' (26.3.2, 26.3.12) is used to produce two kinds of adverbial:

(i) A construction indicating the internal composition of a set or group, in quantitative or proportional terms. The quantitative or proportional expression is marked with a 3rd person possessive suffix. This usage is rather formal.

(27) Biz-im koğuş-ta bazı-sı ağır **ol-mak üzere** on beş kadar hasta
we-GEN ward-LOC some-3SG.POSS serious be-CV 15 about patient

yat-ıyor-du.
lie-IMPF-P.COP

'In our ward there were about fifteen patients, some of them in a serious condition.'

(ii) A construction introduced by *başta* 'at the head', indicating the entity/entities to which a statement principally applies. In terms of meaning, this construction has affinities with the 'particularizing adverbials' discussed at 16.7.2. However, here the identification of the particularized individual or group *precedes* the mention of the larger set of which it forms a part and the particularized constituent is not focused:

(28) **Başta** kamu işçi-ler-i **olmak üzere**
head.LOC public.sector worker-PL-NCM be-CV

bütün işçi-ler sıkıntı-da.
all worker-PL hardship-LOC

'All manual workers, *particularly* the public sector workers, are suffering.'

16.1.11 Truncated relative clauses as adverbials

For the main discussion of truncated relative clauses, see 25.4.1.1. In addition to its adjectival function (15.3.10), this structure can occur adverbially, with the optional addition of *olarak*:

(28) Annem [**arka-sı biz-e dönük** (olarak)] oturuyordu.
back-3SG.POSS we-DAT turned
'My mother was sitting *with her back turned towards us.*'

Where the truncated relative clause is a lexicalized phrase, the possessive suffix on its subject may remain in the 3rd person singular or may agree with the subject of the sentence:

(29) O toplantıdan [**el-i/-imiz boş**] dön-dü-k.
hand-3SG.POSS/1PL.POSS empty come.back-PF-1PL
'We came back from that meeting *empty-handed*.'

16.1.12 Adverbial clauses

Adverbial clauses are the most complex kinds of adverbial construction. Some types of adverbial meaning, such as reason, purpose, condition and concession, are expressed predominantly by means of adverbial clauses. For detailed discussion, see Chapters 26 and 27.

16.2 Syntactic functions of adverbials

Adverbials play a modifying role within a sentence or clause. In broad terms what is modified is either (i) the sentence or clause as a whole, (ii) a verb, (iii) an adjective or (iv) another adverb. Each of these patterns is illustrated below:

(i) Adverbial modifying the sentence or a clause as a whole:

(30) Telefon numaram sizde vardır **herhalde**.
'*I expect* you've got my telephone number.'

(ii) Adverbial modifying a verb (in the main clause or a subordinate clause, 13.1.3):

(31) [**Hızlı** yürüseydik] 19.10'daki trene yetişebilirdik.
'[If we had walked *fast*], we could have caught the 19.10 train.'

(iii) Adverbial modifying an adjective (15.4):

(32) Bu oda bana **oldukça** karanlık geldi.
'This room seems to me *quite* dark.'

(iv) Adverbial modifying another adverb (16.8):

(33) Çocuğa **fazla** sert davranıyor.
'S/he treats the child *too* harshly.'

16.3 Modal adverbials

Modal adverbials express the speaker's stance towards the statement that is being made. Some of them, such as *yanılmıyorsam* 'if I'm not mistaken', *doğrusunu isterseniz* 'to tell you the truth', have the structure of a conditional clause (Chapter 27). Most modal adverbials are used as discourse connectives. For further discussion, see 28.3.

Modal adverbials fall into a number of functional groups:

(i) Adverbials indicating the speaker's degree of commitment to the truth of a statement:

gerçekten/hakikaten	'really'
sahiden	'really'
muhakkak/mutlaka	'definitely'
kesinlikle/kesin (olarak)	'definitely'
belli ki	'clearly', 'it's clear that…'
anlaşılan	'evidently'
dikkat edilirse	'it will be noted that…'
aslına bakılırsa	'the truth of the matter is that…'
herhalde	'probably', 'presumably', 'I expect'
bakarsın	'it might just happen that'
büyük bir ihtimalle/ büyük bir olasılıkla	'in all probability'
yanılmıyorsam	'if I'm not mistaken'

benim bildiğim	'as far as I know'
biliyorum	'I know'
biliyorsun(uz)	'as you know'
galiba/sanırım	'I think'
zannedersem	'I think'
zannediyorum	'I think'
belki	'perhaps'
sözde/güya	'allegedly', 'supposedly'
bence	'I think', 'in my opinion'
bana kalırsa	'my own view would be that...'
açıkçası	'frankly'
sanki	'it seems that...'

(34) [Herkesin para katkısında bulunması] isteniyor **anlaşılan**.
 '*Evidently* everyone is expected [to make a financial contribution].'

(35) **Sanırım** Necla'nın sınavı bugün olacaktı.
 '*I think* Necla's exam was going to be today.'

For the affinity of certain of this group of modal adverbials, such as *muhakkak, herhalde, belki*, with the aorist form of the verb and the generalizing modality marker *-Dlr* see the discussion of assumptions (modalized statements) in 21.4.1.4 (ii). For modal adverbs used in questions see 19.5.

(ii) Adverbials indicating the speaker's attitude towards the situation described by a statement:

inşallah	'God willing', 'hopefully', 'I hope'
umarım	'I hope'
Allahtan/bereket versin	'fortunately'
çok şükür	'thank goodness', 'fortunately'
iyi ki	'it's good (that ...)', 'thank goodness'
en azından/hiç olmazsa/	
hiç değilse	'at least'
bari	'at least', 'may as well' (see (v) below)
maalesef/ne yazık ki	'unfortunately'
tabii (ki)/doğal olarak	'of course', 'naturally'
sözde	'supposedly'

(36) Ambülans çabuk geldi **çok şükür**.
 '*Fortunately,* the ambulance came quickly.'

(iii) Politeness strategies:
 This type of modal adverbial is used in order to mitigate the chance of a remark causing offence.

doğrusu/doğrusunu isterseniz   'to be honest', 'to tell you the truth'
affedersiniz   'if you'll pardon the expression'
deyim yerindeyse   'if the expression is acceptable',
                                   'if I can put it this way'

(37) **Doğrusunu isterseniz** ben hiçbir zaman Osman'ı o mevkiye layık görmemiştim.
'*To be honest*, I had never regarded Osman as worthy of that office.'

(iv) The modal adverb *meğer(se)*:

meğer (or *meğerse*) can be added to a sentence evidentially marked by *-mIş* or *-(y)mIş* in order to indicate that the statement expresses a revision of the speaker's earlier belief about a situation in the light of new information, new observation or new experience. The nearest English equivalent is usually 'it turns/turned out that...'.

(38) Anahtar palto-m-un ceb-in-de-*ymiş*
key coat-1SG.POSS-GEN pocket-3SG.POSS-LOC-EV.COP

meğerse.
it.turns.out

'It turns/turned out that the key was in the pocket of my coat.'

(v) The modal adverbs *bari, oldu olacak, en azından, hiç olmazsa, hiç değilse* (at least), and *keşke* (if only):

hiç olmazsa, hiç değilse, en azından, oldu olacak and, to an extent, *bari*, all mean 'at least'. *hiç olmazsa, hiç değilse* and *en azından* are used interchangeably, and can introduce statements of all modalities. *bari* is used exclusively in volitional utterances (21.4.4.1 (i.c)). There is something of the notion of 'at least' in its meaning, but the nearest equivalent in English often involves 'might as well' in the sense of 'no reason why not'. *Oldu olacak* has a stronger sense of bowing to circumstances and is used, sometimes mockingly, to express the excessive nature of an event or activity.

bari can present a suggestion or command as justified or facilitated by current circumstances. In this function it is replaceable with *oldu olacak* when the verb has optative marking (8.2.3.3), as in (39–40):

(39) Ancak birkaç tane kalmış. Onları da bitir*eyim* **bari/oldu olacak**.
'There are only a few left. I *may as well* finish them too.'

(40) İstediğimiz evi kaçırdık, **bari/oldu olacak** öbürüne bak*alım*.
'We've missed the house we wanted, [but] we *might as well* have a look at the other one.'

(41) **Bari** bu akşam o kadar geç kalma. Dün çok merak etmiştim.
'*At least* don't be so late back tonight. Yesterday I got really worried.'

In counterfactual wishes (21.4.4.1 (i.c)), *bari* expresses a comment on something that has happened. If this is a regretful comment, *bari* can be replaced by *en azından, hiç olmazsa, hiç değilse*, and by *keşke*:

(42) **Bari/Hiç olmazsa/keşke** birimiz bileti kullanabil*seydik*.
'*I wish* one of us could *at least* have used the ticket.'

If, however, the comment is sarcastic, *bari* is interchangeable with *oldu olacak*. (43) could be uttered as a mocking comment on someone's excessive actions:

(43) **Bari/Oldu olacak** bütün dükkanı satın al*saydı*n.
'You *might as well* have bought the whole shop'.

For another example, see Chapter 21 (157).

In non-volitional utterances pointing to a positive aspect of an otherwise regrettable situation, 'at least' is expressed by *en azından, hiç olmazsa* or *hiç değilse*:

(44) **Hiç olmazsa** birimiz bileti kullanabildik.
'One of us was *at least* able to use the ticket.'

For modal adverbs that occur only in questions, see 19.5. For the modal adverb *sakın*, which occurs only in certain kinds of negative-marked sentences see 20.7.

16.4 Circumstantial adverbials

In contrast to the class of modal adverbials, which consists of a limited range of expressions, the class of circumstantial adverbials is wide open. In addition to an inventory of fixed items, such as *şimdi* 'now', *ileri* 'forward', *çabuk* 'quickly', it includes a large range of grammatical strategies which can be freely used in the formation of more complex constructions.

In terms of their semantic functions, circumstantial adverbials express concepts such as time, place, manner, reason, purpose, condition and concession. Detailed discussion is here confined to the expression of time, place and manner. For the other categories reference is generally provided to other chapters in which more complex adverbial structures are discussed.

16.4.1 Time adverbials

In the following sections, we look at the means by which various kinds of temporal relations are expressed: location in time (16.4.1.1), duration (16.4.1.2) and frequency (16.4.1.3). For the wide range of adverbial *clauses* which perform temporal functions, see 26.1.2.1, 26.1.6 and 26.3.16.

16.4.1.1 Location in time

Temporal location is the time at which or within which an event happens or a state holds. In Turkish this is often, but by no means always, expressed by locative case marking. We first describe how clock time and dates are expressed in Turkish and then proceed to consider more general aspects of the subject.

Clock time

The use of the word *saat* 'hour' is optional in all expressions of clock time and if used must precede the numeral indicating the hour. Locations on the hour are expressed with the locative suffix on the numeral:

*(saat) altı-**da***   'at six (o'clock)'
(hour) six-LOC

For the half-hours, *buçuk* 'and a half' follows the numeral and it is to this word that the locative suffix is attached:

*(saat) on buçuk**ta***   'at half-past ten'

An exception is that for 'half-past twelve' the word *yarım* 'half' is used:

*(saat) yarım**da***   'at half-past twelve'

For time locations less than thirty minutes after the hour, the word *geçe* (the *-(y)A* converb (26.3.8) of *geç-* 'pass') follows the number of minutes, which in turn follows the accusative-marked form of the hour numeral:

*(saat) iki**yi** beş **geçe***   'at five past two'

For time locations less than thirty minutes before the hour, the word *kala* (the *-(y)A* converb (26.3.8) of *kal-* 'be left') follows the number of minutes, which in this case follows the dative-marked form of the hour numeral:

*(saat) dörd-**e** yirmi **kala***   'at twenty to four'
(hour) four-DAT twenty to

The word *çeyrek* 'quarter' is used for 'quarter past' and 'quarter to':

*(saat) yedi**yi** **çeyrek** geçe*   'at quarter past seven'
*(saat) on iki**ye** **çeyrek** kala* 'at quarter to twelve'

As an alternative to all of the above, the conventions of the twenty-four hour clock may be used, with the locative suffix attached to the minute figure:

*(saat) yirmi otuz**da***   'at 20.30'

Days of the week

The name of the day may either be used on its own or made into a -*(s)I* compound (10.2) with *gün* 'day'. Case marking is generally not used when expressing time location with respect to a certain day of the week:

(45) Çarşamba (gün-ü) Konya'ya gidiyorum.
      Wednesday (day-NCM)
      'I'm going to Konya *on Wednesday*.'

For alternative forms, see (ii) 'Dative case' in the section on case marking below.

Dates

Time location involving dates always requires the locative suffix. In the expression of time location in a certain year, the number expressing the year may be compounded with *yıl* (or *sene*) 'year'. Years are expressed just like simple numerals:

(46) a. bin dokuz yüz doksan beş**te** (written *1995'te*)
      b. bin dokuz yüz doksan beş yılın**da** (written *1995 yılında*) 'in 1995'

Similarly, in the expression of location in a certain month, the name of the month may be compounded with *ay* 'month':

(47) şubat-**ta**/şubat ay-ın-**da**
      February-LOC/February month-NCM-LOC
      '**in** February'

In oral exchanges, the months are sometimes referred to by the numerical position they have within a calendar year, eg. *üçüncü ay* 'third month', for March.

Time location on an exact date is expressed by placing the cardinal number before the name of the month and adding the locative suffix to the latter. Note that, in the case of an exact date, the name of the month is written with an initial capital.

(48) on yedi haziran**da** (written *17 Haziran'da*)
      'on the 17th of June'

If the year is expressed as well, this follows the name of the month, and the locative suffix appears on the year.

(49) sekiz kasım bin dokuz yüz seksen dört**te** (written *8 Kasım 1984'te*)
      'on the 8th of November 1984'

Another way of expressing the date of an event is to use a genitive-possessive construction (14.4):

(50) haziran-**ın**/haziran ay-ın-**ın** on yedi-**sin**-de
      June-GEN/June month-NCM-GEN seventeen-3SG.POSS-LOC
      'on the 17th of June'

The year can be incorporated with the name of a month in one of two ways:

(i) As a -(s)I compound:

(51) bin dokuz yüz seksen dört kasımında
'in November 1984'

(ii) In a genitive-possessive construction:

(52) a. bin dokuz yüz seksen dörd**ün** kasımında
b. bin dokuz yüz seksen dörd**ün** kasım ayında
c. bin dokuz yüz seksen dört yılının kasım ayında
'in November 1984'

If the exact date is specified in an expression of the type exemplified in (52), this is usually done by combining a genitive-possessive construction with the pattern exemplified in (48) above:

(53) a. bin dokuz yüz seksen dörd**ün** sekiz kasımında
b. bin dokuz yüz seksen dört yılının sekiz kasımında
'on the 8th of November 1984'

Other less precise expressions of calendar time are illustrated below:

eylül/eylülün başında	'at the beginning of September'
nisanın ortasında	'in the middle of April'
ekim/ekimin sonunda	'at the end of October'
ay başında/sonunda	'at the beginning/end of the month'
ayın ortasında	'in the middle of the month'
ayın birinde	'on the first (day) of the month'
bin sekiz yüz otuzlarda (written *1830'larda*)	'in the 1830s'
bin sekiz yüz otuzlu yıllarda (written *1830'lu yıllarda*)	'in the 1830s'

Seasons of the year

yaz 'summer' and *kış* 'winter' have special forms for expressing location: *yazın* 'in summer', *kışın* 'in winter' (7.2.2.2). *ilkbahar* (or *bahar*) 'spring' and *sonbahar* 'autumn', on the other hand, take the locative case marker:

(54) **Kışın** başlayan yağmurlar **ilkbaharda** da sürdü.
'The rain that began *in the winter* continued *in the spring*, too.'

Other phrases expressing location in time:

(i) The following adverbials express time locations in terms of their relation to the moment of speech (present, past, future):

a. Present:

şimdi	'now'
şu anda/an itibariyle	'at the moment', 'at this moment'
şu sıra(lar)(da)	'at the moment'
bu günlerde	'at the moment'
şimdilerde	'at the moment', 'these days'
bugün	'today'

b. Past:

dün	'yesterday'
dün sabah	'yesterday morning'
dün akşam	'yesterday evening/night'
dün gece	'last night'
evvelsi gün	'the day before yesterday'
evvelki (hafta/ay/yıl)	'the (week/month/year) before last'
önceki (hafta/ay/yıl)	'last (week/month/year)', 'the (week/month/year) before last'
geçen gün	'the other day'
geçenlerde	'a few days ago', 'recently'
geçen/geçtiğimiz (hafta/ay/yıl)	'last (week/month/year)'
...önce/evvel	'...(amount of time) ago'
demin	'a few moments ago', 'just now'
son zamanlarda	'recently'
yakında	'recently' (with negative verbs)
(bu) yakınlarda	'recently'
eskiden	'in the past', 'formerly'
bir zaman(lar)/ bir vakitler/ zamanında/vaktiyle	'in the past', 'formerly'

c. Future:

akşam	'this evening', 'in the evening'
yarın	'tomorrow'
yarın sabah	'tomorrow morning'
yarın akşam	'tomorrow evening'
öbürsü gün	'the day after tomorrow'
gelecek/önümüzdeki (hafta/ay/yıl)	'next (week/month/year)'
haftaya	'next week'
seneye	'next year'
... sonra	'in ...(amount of time from now)'
yakında/biraz sonra	'soon'
yakınlarda	'in the near future' (only with negative verbs)

(ii) The following adverbials express time locations without reference to how they relate to the moment of speech:

a. Parts of the day:

sabah/sabahleyin	'in the morning', 'this morning'
öğlen/öğleyin/öğle zamanı	'at midday'
öğleden sonra	'in the afternoon' 'this afternoon'
akşam üstü/üzeri	'in the early evening'
akşam/akşamleyin	'in the evening'
gece/geceleyin	'at night', 'in/during the night'

b. More general expressions:

önce/evvela	'first', 'at first'
ilkönce	'first of all'
... önce/evvel '	'...(amount of time) before/ago'
(bir) önceki(gün/hafta/ay/yıl)	'the previous (day/week/month/year)'
sonra	'then', 'later'
daha sonra	'later (on)'
...sonra	'...(amount of time) later'
sonraki/ertesi (gün/hafta/ay/yıl)	'the next (day/week/month/year)'
çok geçmeden	'before long'
o zaman	'then'
o zamanlar	'at that time'
o sırada	'at that point'
bu arada	'meanwhile'
bir ara	'at one point'

Expressions referring to present time

As shown in list (i.a) above, there are several expressions that refer to a time location which includes the moment of speech and can be translated by 'at the moment'. However, they differ in the range of time they express. *Şu anda* is the only one that can be focused on the actual moment of speech:

(55) **Şu anda** bir şey duyamıyorum, ama demin bir cızırtı vardı.
 '*At the moment* I can't hear anything, but just now there was a crackling sound.'

The other three expressions refer to a much broader period of days or even weeks, extending both backwards and forwards from the moment of speech:

(56) Korkut **bu günlerde/şu sırada** tezini bitirmeye çalışıyor.
 'Korkut is trying to finish his thesis *at the moment*.'

As for the adverb *şimdi* 'now', this does not always refer to present time. It can refer to the very near future:

(57) **Şimdi** gelirim.
'I'll be back *in a moment.*'

It can also refer to the immediate past, in which usage it is placed in the immediately preverbal position and receives stress (23.1.1.1):

(58) Ahmet Bey **ŞİMdi** çıktı.
'Ahmet Bey has *just* left.'

Synonymous with *şimdi* in this usage are *henüz* and *yeni,* both of which can refer also to a *relative* immediate past, as in (59) below. All three of these adverbs are commonly reinforced by the modifier *daha* 'only' (16.4.1.4 (v.c)):

(59) O sırada buraya **daha yeNİ** taşınmıştık.
'At that time, we had *only just* moved here.'

önce 'before' and *sonra* 'after'

As shown in the above lists, *önce* and *sonra* as adverbials have a number of different usages. For their functions as postpositions, see 17.2.3 (vi)–(vii).

(i) Used without modifiers, *önce* means 'first' or 'at first' and *sonra* 'then' or 'later':

(60) **Önce** bütün kitabı gözden geçir, **sonra** [önemli gördüğün] bölümlere geri dön.
'*First* look over the whole book, *then* go back to the sections [you consider important].'

(ii) Both *önce* and *sonra* can be preceded by a noun phrase indicating an *amount of time.* The adverbial phrases thus formed can have as their reference points either the moment of speech or any other time location established in the preceding discourse:

(61) a. ***Yirmi yıl*** **önce** burası tarlaydı.
'*Twenty years ago,* this was a field.'

b. Filiz Hanım yalnız yaşıyordu. Kocası ***yirmi yıl*** **önce** ölmüştü.
'Filiz Hanım lived alone. Her husband had died *twenty years before.*'

(62) a. ***Beş gün*** **sonra** sınavım var.
'I've got an exam *in five days' time/five days from now.*'

b. ***Beş gün*** **sonra** sınava girdim.
'*Five days later* I took the/an exam.'

(iii) When placed in the immediately preverbal position (23.1.1.1), *sonra* can mean '(only) later', 'not until afterwards'. In this usage, it often takes ablative case marking and is stressed:

(63) [Coşkun'un evli olduğun]-u **sonra(dan)** öğrendim.
'*It was (only) later that* I found out [that Coşkun was married].'

Case marking (8.1.3) and its absence in expressing location in time

(i) No case marking:
The following nouns denoting parts of the day usually remain non-case-marked when they are used in the singular form to express location in time: *sabah* 'morning', *akşam* 'evening', *gece* 'night'. If used without a determiner (15.6), these words are understood as referring either to the day of the speech situation or the previous night or to another day on which attention is already focused.

(64) **Gece** yağmur yağmıştı, yerler ıslaktı.
'It had rained *during the night*, [so] the ground was wet.'

This applies also to noun phrases in which the singular form of *sabah* 'morning', *akşam* 'evening', *gece* 'night', *gün* 'day', *hafta* 'week', *ay* 'month', *yıl/ sene* 'year' is preceded by one of the following determiners, adjectives or by an ordinal numeral: *bir* 'a(n)', *bu* 'this', *o* 'that', *geçen* 'last', *gelecek* 'next', *önceki* 'the previous', 'last', *sonraki* 'the next', *ertesi* 'the next', *ilk* 'the first', *son* 'the last':

(65) **(Bu) sabah** bir öğrencim telefon etti.
'A student of mine rang *this morning*.'

(66) **Gelecek hafta** boş vaktin var mı?
'Do you have any free time *next week*?'

(ii) Dative case:
Where location in time is concerned, dative case marking always produces (relative) future reference. This is a colloquial usage; the standard equivalents are also shown below. In this function, dative case can be used for words indicating the parts of a day, the days of the week, weeks, months and seasons.

(67) [**Akşam*a*/Akşam/O akşam** misafirlerimiz olacağı için] yemek yapmakla meşguldük.
'[As we were expecting guests *that evening*] we were busy cooking.'

(68) Tesisatı **geçen perşembe*ye*/ geçen perşembe** bitireceklerdi.
'They were going to finish the plumbing [job] *by last Thursday*.'

(iii) Locative case:
Apart from dates and clock time (hours and half-hours), locative case marking (-*DA*) occurs in noun phrases of which the head is the plural-marked form of any of the time nouns listed in (i) above, e.g. *son ay**larda*** 'in the last (few) months', *o yıl**larda*** 'in those years'. It also occurs in noun phrases of

which the head is any other noun or noun compound denoting a period of time, e.g. *Osmanlı döneminde* 'in the Ottoman period', *çocukluğumda* 'in my childhood'.

When locative case marking occurs in a quantified time expression, it indicates the time *within which* a task is (to be) performed or within which a certain number of occurrences of an event are observed. The postposition *içinde* (17.3.1.2) is often used instead of simple locative case marking in such expressions:

(69) **Üç hafta*da*/Üç hafta *içinde*** bu kavşakta iki defa kaza oldu.
'*In the space of three weeks* there have twice been accidents at this junction.'

(iv) Ablative case:
Expressions of time location that include ablative case marking (*-DAn*) without any following postposition usually emphasize the earliness of the time referred to. Fixed expressions of this kind include *erkenden* 'early', *önceden* 'beforehand', *şimdiden* 'already', *sabahtan* '(already) in the morning', *akşamdan* '(already) the evening before', *çoktan* 'long ago', 'long since':

(70) Ben **şimdi-*den*** üşüyorum.
now-ABL
'I'm *already* feeling cold.'

(71) Nermin'ler **sabah*tan*** gelmişler.
'Nermin and her friends have apparently been here *since this morning*.'

In the adverbial *sonradan* 'after the event', '(only) afterwards', the ablative case marking has the opposite effect of drawing attention to the *lateness* of the occurrence of an event (see (63) above).

Recurrent time locations

To express the regular occurrence of an event on a certain day of the week or at a certain time of the day or year, *-lArI(n)* (7.2.2.2) is added to the name of the day or to any of the following expressions: *sabah* 'morning', *öğleden sonra* 'in the afternoon', *akşam* 'evening', *gece* 'night', *yaz* 'summer', *kış* 'winter':

(72) **Pazartesi*leri*/Pazartesi gün*leri*** Taksim'deki büromuzda çalışıyorum.
'*On Mondays* I work at our office in Taksim.'

16.4.1.2 Duration

(i) The duration of an activity may be expressed by a non-case-marked noun phrase:

(73) **Birkaç dakika** bekledik.
 'We waited *for a few minutes.*'

(ii) Alternatively, an adverbial of quantity (16.5) may be used:

(74) Misafirler **az** oturdular.
 'The guests did*n't* stay *long.*'

(iii) To present a situation as having started some time ago/before and still continuing (at the moment of speech or at some reference point in the past), one of the following is used:

 a. The postposition *beri* (17.2.3 (ii))
 b. The suffix *-DIr* (8.3.3) attached to the noun phrase denoting the period:

(75) **Üç yıldır/üç yıldan beri** burada çalışıyorum.
 'I've been working here *for three years.*'

(iv) Expressions of intended duration of stay, modifying a verb of motion, are constructed in one of two ways:

 a. With the postposition *için* 'for' (17.2.1 (ii))
 b. By attaching the composite suffix *-lIğInA* to the expression of duration:

(76) Birkaç gün **için**/Birkaç gün**lüğüne** Fransa'ya gidiyorum.
 'I'm going to France *for a few days.*'

16.4.1.3 Frequency

The principal adverbials expressing general notions of frequency are:

hep/her zaman	'always', 'all the time'
sık sık	'often', 'frequently'
çok defa	'many times', 'often'
genellikle	'usually', 'generally'
bazen	'sometimes'
kimi zaman	'sometimes'
kâh ... kâh	'sometimes ... sometimes'
arada bir/arasıra	'occasionally'
arada sırada	'occasionally'

zaman zaman	'from time to time'
seyrek	'seldom'
hiç	'never', 'ever'
hiçbir zaman	'never', 'ever'
asla/katiyen	'never'
pek	'very often' (only with negative verb)

Of these expressions, *hiç*, *hiçbir zaman*, *asla*, *katiyen* and *pek* are discussed in 20.5.

Quantified frequency is expressed with locative marking of the noun expressing the relevant time unit (day, week, etc.), followed usually by *bir* 'once', otherwise by a numeral or quantifier followed by *kez*, *defa* or *kere*, all meaning 'time' in the sense of 'instance of repetition':

(77) Şükran'la [**ay***da* **bir** görüşmey]-e çalışıyoruz.
'Şükran and I try [to get together *once a month*].'

(78) Artık makine **yı***l***da dört beş kez/defa/kere** arızalanıyor.
'The machine is now breaking down *four or five times a year*.'

16.4.1.4 Other time adverbials

(i) *ancak*

As a temporal adverb, *ancak* (see also 16.7) means 'only just [in time for something]' and is placed immediately before the predicate:

(79) Uçağa **ancak** yetiştik.
'We *only just* caught the plane.'

For *ancak* as an adversative connective, see 28.3.4.1.

(ii) *artık*
This indicates that a turning point has been reached.

a. In affirmative sentences it is usually equivalent to 'now', but it is a 'now' that expresses the climax of some development in the past:

(80) **Artık** Türkçe'yi güzel konuşuyorsun.
'You *now* speak Turkish very well.'

b. With a negative predicate it means 'no longer', 'any more':

(81) İstanbul'da evimiz yok **artık**.
'We *no longer* have a house in İstanbul.'

(iii) *bir an önce*
   This is an expression meaning 'as soon as possible':

   (82) Evi **bir an önce** satmak istiyoruz.
   'We want to sell the house *as soon as possible*.'

   A synonym not restricted to colloquial styles is *en kısa zamanda* 'in the shortest [possible] time'.

(iv) *bir daha*
   Literally 'once more', this expression is used in the sense of 'again'. It is used mostly in negative sentences and is indeed the only means of expressing 'again' with a negative predicate:

   (83) O adamı **bir daha** görmek istemem.
   'I do*n't ever* want to see that man *again*.'

   In affirmative sentences 'again' is usually expressed by *gene*, *yine*, *tekrar* or *yeniden*, this last having sometimes the meaning of 'all over again':

   (84) Binayı yıkıp **yeniden** yapacaklarmış.
   'They're going to pull the building down and *re*build it, apparently.'

(v) *daha*:
   This is an adverb with several meanings/functions. For its comparative function see 15.4.2, 16.8.

   a. With an affirmative predicate *daha* means 'still':

   (85) Süleyman **daha** uyuyor.
   'Süleyman is *still* asleep.'

   b. With a negative predicate it means 'yet' and in this function is synonymous with *henüz*, which is slightly more formal:

   (86) **Daha/Henüz** hazır değilim.
   'I'm not ready *yet*.'

   c. Placed before an adverbial expressing a time location prior to the moment of speech, *daha* emphasizes either the closeness or the distance of that time:

   (87) Bu sorun **daha** *iki yıl önce* vardı.
   'This problem *already* existed *two years ago*.'

(vi) *hâlâ*:
This conveys the notion 'still' more emphatically than *daha*:

(88) Yılmaz **hâlâ** aynı yerde çalışıyor.
'Yılmaz is *still* working in the same place.'

(vii) *hazır*:
As an adverb, *hazır* (primarily an adjective meaning 'ready', 'present') is used almost exclusively in converbial clauses marked by *-(y)ken* (26.2.3 (ii), 26.3.16 (iii)). It expresses the idea that the state of affairs described by the subordinate clause provides an opportunity for the performance of the action specified in the superordinate clause:

(89) [**Hazır** Ali buradayken] bilgisayar sorunumuzu ona soralım.
'[*Now that* Ali is here], let's ask him about our computer problem.'

(viii) *hemen, derhal:*
These mean 'immediately', 'at once':

(90) Bardakları **hemen** yıka.
'Wash the glasses *immediately*.'

(ix) *neredeyse*:
This conveys that an event is/was expected imminently:

(91) Misafirler **neredeyse** gelir.
'The guests will be arriving *at any moment*.'

See Chapter 21 (18) for a related example.

16.4.2 Place adverbials

In general terms, location in, on or at a place is expressed by locative case marking of a noun phrase (14.3.3.4 (i), 13.1.3):

(92) Selim'in **Berlin-*de*** kızkardeşi varmış.
    Berlin-LOC
'Apparently, Selim has a sister *in Berlin*.'

Movement to, into or on to a place is expressed by dative case marking of a noun phrase (14.3.3.3 (i), 13.1.3 (i)):

(93) Artık **ev-*e*** gidiyorum.
    house-DAT
'I'm going *home* now.'

Movement away from or out of a place is expressed by ablative case marking of a noun phrase (14.3.3.5 (i), 13.1.3 (iii)):

(94) Arkadaşımı **havaalanın-*dan*** alacağım.
                 airport-ABL
     'I'm going to collect my friend *from the airport*.'

Other spatial relationships are expressed by the set of possessive-marked postpositions designated as Group 1 (17.3.1). *iç*-POSS-OBL and *üst*-POSS-OBL are often used in preference to simple case marking of the noun phrase where the difference between the concepts of *on* and *in* is felt to be important.

The attachment of the above case markers to the locative pronouns *bura-* 'here', *şura-* 'here', 'over there' and *ora-* 'there' (18.3.1) produces adverbials meaning 'here', over there' and 'there':

(95) Bak, **şura*da*** yeni bir leke var.
     'Look, there's a new mark *here*.'

(96) **Ora*ya*** ne zaman gidiyorsunuz?
     'When are you going *there*?'

Directional adverbials

The following adverbs, whether in their bare form or with dative case marking, express directional movement:

içeri	'in', 'inside'
dışarı	'out', 'outside'
yukarı	'up'
aşağı	'down'
ileri	'forward'
geri	'back'

(97) **İçeri(ye)** girelim mi?
     'Shall we go *in*?'

(98) **Yukarı(ya)** çıktılar.
     'They went *up(stairs)*.'

Locative and ablative case marking also occurs. The final vowel of *içeri*, *dışarı*, *yukarı* and *ileri* is usually dropped when the locative or ablative suffix is added:

(99) Annem **aşağı*da*** oturuyor.
     'My mother lives *downstairs*.'

(100) **İçer(i)*den*** güzel yemek kokuları geliyordu.
'Nice smells of food were coming *from inside*.'

The word *öte* 'far side' is used adverbially only with locative, dative or ablative case marking:

(101) Makinalar çalışırken **öte*de*** durmak lazım.
'When the machines are working, one has to stand *away*.'

The locative, dative and ablative forms of *her yer* 'everywhere' function as universal place adverbials:

(102) Artık **her yerde** McDonalds var.
'There are McDonald's *everywhere* now.'

16.4.3 Manner adverbials

The following are some of the most common means of expressing the manner in which an action is performed:

(i) The words *çabuk* 'quickly' and *yavaş* 'slowly', 'softly' These are the only commonly occurring simple adverbs expressing manner:

(103) **Çabuk** gel!
'Come *quickly*!'

(ii) An adjective placed in the immediately preverbal position (16.1.2, 23.1.1.1):

(104) Sevgi bunu **iyi** yapar.
'Sevgi would this *well*.'

(iii) A doubled form (16.1.3):

(105) Bunu yarın **rahat rahat** bitiririz.
'We'll finish this *comfortably* tomorrow.'

(iv) A noun or adjective suffixed with -CA_1 (16.1.6 (i))
(v) An adjective (usually derived or of foreign origin) followed by *bir biçimde*, *bir şekilde* or *olarak* (see 16.1.2)
(vi) One of the demonstrative adverbials *böyle* 'like this', *şöyle* 'like this/that', *öyle* 'like that'. These are derived from the demonstrative determiners *bu/şu/o* and are differentiated from each other in similar ways (18.2). They also function as adverbials of degree (16.5) and as determiners (15.6.1 (iv)):

(106) Kalemi **şöyle** tut.
'Hold the pen *like this*.'

(107) [Mustafa'nın **öyle** konuşması] hoş olmadı.
'It was unpleasant [that Mustafa talked *like that*].'

(vii) A noun phrase marked with the comitative/instrumental marker *-(y)lA/ile* (8.1.4), the uses of which are explained in 17.2.1 (iii) (unless it is used as a conjunction (28.3.1.1 (ii)):

(108) Ömer okula **ablasıyla** gidiyor.
'Ömer goes to school *with his elder sister.*'

(viii) A postpositional phrase headed by *gibi* 'like':

(109) **Öğretmen *gibi*** konuşuyorsun.
'You're talking *like a teacher.*'

(ix) A possessive noun phrase followed by an adjective:

(110) '**Elimiz boş** gitmeyelim'
'We shouldn't go *without a gift.*'

(x) Several types of adverbial clause (26.1.5, 26.3.8)

16.4.4 Other types of circumstantial adverbial

The range of adverbial relationships that can be expressed by postpositional phrases and adverbial clauses is extremely wide. Here we present an overview of the principal means for expressing four more circumstantial categories that are expressed mainly by postpositional phrases (Chapter 17) or adverbial clauses (Chapters 26 and 27).

Reason (or cause)
(i) Ablative case marking:
Although this case has associations with the concept of cause (14.3.3.5 (i)), there are not many contexts in which ablative case marking alone (without a postposition) is sufficient to express it. For examples, see Chapter 13 (42b–43b) and Chapter 14 (94).
(ii) A number of postpositions, all meaning approximately 'because of', 'as a result of'. These are the bare postpositions *dolayı, ötürü*, taking ablative-marked complements (17.2.3) and the possessive-marked postpositions *sayesinde, nedeniyle, yüzünden* (17.3.2, 17.3.2.1 (viii)).
(iii) A finite adverbial clause marked with the subordinator *diye* (26.1.1.1) or a non-finite adverbial clause marked with *-DIğI için, -DIğIndAn*, etc., meaning 'because' (26.3.14)

(iv) A number of discourse connectives, all meaning 'because of this' or 'as a result', such as *onun için, dolayısıyla, bu nedenle, bu yüzden* (28.3.6)

All the strategies described in (i)–(iii) above present two situations/events in a cause-result sequence.

(v) The discourse connective *çünkü* 'because' (28.3.6) presents an explanation for a situation already stated, that is, in a result-cause sequence.

Purpose
(i) The bare postposition *için* 'for' (17.2.1 (ii))
(ii) The possessive-marked postposition *uğruna* 'for the sake of' (17.3.2 (vi), 17.3.2.1 (ix))
(iii) A finite adverbial clause containing the subordinator *diye* (26.1.1.2) or *ki* (26.1.2.2) and having optative marking on the verb
(iv) A non-finite adverbial clause marked with *-mAk için, -mAsI için, -mAyA, -mAk üzere* (26.3.12)

Condition
(i) A conditional clause marked with *-sA* or *-(y)sA* (Chapter 27)
(ii) A finite adverbial clause marked with *-DI mI* (27.6.2)
(iii) A non-finite adverbial clause marked with *-DIğI takdirde, -mAsI durumunda/ halinde* (27.6.1)
(iv) The discourse connectives *o halde/öyleyse* 'in that case' (28.3.9 (ii))

Concession
(i) The bare postpositions *rağmen/karşın* 'in spite of', taking ablative-marked complements (17.2.2 (v))
(ii) Non-finite adverbial clauses marked with *-DIğI halde, -mAsInA rağmen/ karşın, -mAklA birlikte/beraber* (26.3.3)
(iii) The discourse connectives *bununla birlikte/beraber, buna rağmen/ karşın*, all meaning 'in spite of this', 'nevertheless' (28.3.4.2)

16.5 Adverbials of quantity or degree

The adverbials in this category differ from circumstantial adverbials in that they can modify adjectives and other adverbials as well as verbs. Some of them (*en, gayet, son derece, oldukça*), in fact, either cannot modify verbs at all or are very restricted in the extent to which they can do this.

çok	'much', 'very', 'too (much)'
daha	'more'
en	'most'

pek	'very', 'much'
(bir) hayli	'very'
fazla(sıyla)	'too (much)', 'excessively'
aşırı (derecede)	'excessively'
gayet	'extremely'
son derece	'extremely'
yarı	'half'
epey(i), epeyce	'quite'
oldukça	'quite', 'fairly'
az	'not much'
biraz	'a little', 'a bit', 'rather'
böyle(sine)/şöyle(sine)/öyle(sine)	'such', 'so'
bu/şu/o kadar/derece/denli	'such', 'so', 'so much'
ne kadar	'how much', 'how'
neredeyse/az daha/az kalsın	'nearly'

The following examples illustrate the different kinds of modification performed by this type of adverbial:

(111) Bu dersi **biraz *zor*** buldum.   (*biraz* modifies adjective)
'I found this lesson *rather difficult*.'

(112) Bu dersi **biraz *zor*** yaptım.   (*biraz* modifies adverbial)
'I did this lesson *with some difficulty*.'

(113) [Bu dersi yaparken] **biraz *zorlandım*.**   (*biraz* modifies verb)
'*I struggled a bit* while [doing this lesson].'

With verbs expressing a process that extends over time, adverbials of quantity express *temporal duration* (16.4.1.2).

(114) **Çok** beklediniz mi?
'Have you been waiting *long*?'

Pek and *o kadar* have a particular affinity with negative sentences. For details, see 20.5.4.2–3.

Other types of adverbials of quantity/degree are:

(i) Postpositional phrases with *kadar* following a non-case-marked (or genitive) complement (17.2.1 (iv))
(ii) Non-finite clauses marked by *-(y)AcAk kadar/derecede* or *-DIğI/-(y)AcAğI kadar* (26.3.13)

16.6 Adverbials of respect

A number of strategies are available for indicating the respect in which, or point of view from which, a statement is regarded as applicable:

(i) The suffix -CA_1 (16.1.6 (v)) is in restricted use for this purpose:

(115) Kağan **yaşça** küçük ama **vücutça** büyüktü.
'Kağan was small *in terms of age*, but big *in terms of physical size*.'

(ii) A variety of expressions and constructions incorporating the nouns *bakım* 'view', *açı* 'angle' or *yön* 'direction' are in much more common use:

(116) **Bir bakıma** [Ali'nin geç gelmesi] iyi oldu.
'*In a way* it was good [that Ali was late].'

(117) **O yönden/O açıdan** en büyük başarılarımızdan biriydi.
'*From that point of view*, it was one of our greatest achievements.'

The forms *açısından* and *bakımından* are possessive-marked postpositions (17.3.2 (94)).

(iii) The bare postposition *yana* (with ablative-marked complement, 17.2.3 (viii)) can be used in the same sense as *açısından* and *bakımından*, but is far less common.

16.7 Focus-sensitive adverbials

Turkish has a small category of adverbials that occur with focused phrases. Some of these occur only before the focused constituent of a sentence (23.3.1) and serve to highlight it in a particular way. The adverbial is placed immediately before the focused constituent, which is typically either a noun phrase or a circumstantial adverbial, but may also be a verb. The clitics *bile* (28.3.1.1 (iv)), *dA* (28.3.1.1 (iii.b)) and *ya* (11.1.1.6) interact with focus as well.

16.7.1 Exclusive adverbials

The following are all used in the sense of 'only': *yalnız, ancak, sade(ce), sırf, salt, bir (tek)*. They restrict the applicability of what is being said to the focused constituent:

(118) Mektubu **yalnız/bir tek** Mustafa'YA/göstermiştim.
'I had shown the letter *only to Mustafa*.'

(119) **Ancak/Yalnız/Sadece** iKİ defa geldiler.
'They came *only twice*.'

(120) **Sırf** [üstünlüğünü kanıtlaMAK] amacıyla yapıyor bunları.
'He's doing all this [*merely in an effort to prove his superiority*].'

bir, *tek* and *bir tek* are used mainly with pronouns or proper nouns, where no possibility of ambiguity with the determiner or numeral senses of *bir* ('a(n)', 'one') or the adjectival sense of *tek* 'single' arises:

(121) Bunun sırrını **bir/tek/bir tek** SEN biliyorsun.
'*Only* you know the secret of this.'

16.7.2 Particularizing adverbials

This small class of adverbials has a function somewhat similar to that of exclusive adverbials, but they are less absolute in their restrictive effect. The main items are *daha çok* 'mainly', *en çok* 'mostly', *asıl*/*esas* 'really' and *özellikle*/*bilhassa* 'especially', 'particularly':

(122) Buraya **daha çok** üniVERsite öğrencileri geliyor.
'It's *mainly* university students who come here.'

(123) **En çok**/**Özellikle** AKdeniz ülkelerinde yetişir zeytin ağacı.
'The olive tree grows *mostly/particularly* in Mediterranean countries'.

For *özellikle*/*bilhassa* as conjunctions/discourse connectives (where they are not focus-sensitive) see 28.3.5 (iii).

asıl and *esas* as particularizing adverbials are quite colloquial;

(124) Bunu **asıl** senin AMcan iyi yapar.
'It's your uncle who would *really* make a good job of this.'

16.7.3 The adverb *tam*

The effect that *tam* has on the focused constituent is to emphasize that it is to be understood in the precise or full sense of the words used. In affirmative contexts it is usually equivalent to 'precisely', 'exactly', 'just' or 'right' in English.

(125) Ben de **tam** oNU söyleyecektim.
'I was about to say *precisely* that.'

(126) **Tam** iKİ buçukta geldiler.
'They came at *exactly* half-past two.'

(127) Mehmet tam arkamDAN geliyordu.
Mehmet was following *right* behind me.'

(128) [Biz **tam** kapıdan çıkaCAKken] Selma aradı.
'*Just* as we were about to go out of the door, Selma rang.'

Where the focused constituent is a subject complement or a verb, *tam* is mainly confined to negative contexts. In the affirmative versions of (129) and (130) it would usually be replaced by one of its cognates *tamamen/tamamıyla* 'completely':

(129) [Söylediğiniz] **tam** doğru deĞİL.
'What you say is not *quite* correct.'

(130) [Ne istediklerin]-i **tam** anlaYAmadık.
'We can't *quite* understand [what they want].'

In some of the above sentences, *tam* can alternatively occur at the end of the clause.

There is just one kind of affirmative linking sentence in which the subject complement can be highlighted by *tam*. Here the subject complement takes the form {*bir*+noun} and the addition of *tam* makes the sentence categorise the subject as an absolute example of the entity denoted by this noun:

(131) **Tam** bir fiYASkoydu.
'It was *a complete fiasco.*'

(132) [Çocuğun yaşaması] **tam** bir muciZE oldu.
'The child's survival was *an absolute miracle.*'

16.8 Modification of adverbs

The only kinds of adverbials that can be modified are adjectives functioning as adverbs (16.1.2) and the quantitative adverbs *çok* 'much', *fazla* '(too) much', *az* 'little' and *daha* 'more' (16.5). Note that while *fazla* on its own (at least in affirmative sentences) means, 'too much' *daha çok* and *daha fazla* are synonymous, meaning 'more'.

Modification of adverbs occurs in exactly the same way as modification of adjectives (15.4). Some examples are:

(133) Sen bu konu üzerinde (benden) ***daha* çok/*daha* fazla** çalıştın.
'You have worked *more* (than me) on this topic.'

(134) [Bu sorunu ***en iyi*** anlayan] kişi sizsiniz.
'You are the person [who understands this problem *best*].'

(135) Nazlı [***şaşılacak kadar***] **hızlı** yürür.
'Nazlı walks *amazingly fast.*'

(136) **Bir bebek kadar** sessiz uyuyor.
'S/he is sleeping *as quitly as a baby*.'

The forms *en az* 'at least' and *en çok/fazla* 'at most' are used to modify numerical expressions:

(137) Kadının **en az** on iki kedisi var.
'The woman has *at least twelve* cats.'

Chapter 17

Postpositional phrases

Turkish has a large number of postpositions which follow their complements. These make up postpositional phrases (17.1). Turkish postpositions fall into two main categories: **bare postpositions** (17.2), which carry no suffixes, and **possessive-marked postpositions** (17.3), which are marked by a possessive suffix agreeing with the complement. After discussing all these types of postposition and the principal members of each class, in 17.4 we consider the syntactic functions that postpositional phrases can perform. Stress in postpositional phrases is discussed in 4.4.3.

17.1 Structure of the postpositional phrase

A **postpositional phrase** consists of a noun phrase followed by a postposition. The postposition is the head of the phrase and the noun phrase is its **complement**. In each of the examples below, the postposition is shown in bold:

(1) sen-in **için**
you-GEN for
'*for* you'

(2) çıkış kapı-sın-a **doğru**
exit gate-NCM-DAT
towards '*towards* the exit'

(3) ev-imiz-in **arka-sın-da**
house-1PL.POSS-GEN back-3SG.POSS-LOC
'*behind* our house'

(4) ben-im **yer-im-e**
I-GEN place-1SG.POSS-DAT
'*instead of* me'

Turkish postpositions may be classified according to the way in which they relate syntactically to their complements. There are two major subdivisions: bare postpositions, exemplified in (1) and (2) above and discussed in 17.2, and possessive-marked postpositions, exemplified in (3) and (4) above and discussed in 17.3.

17.2 Bare postpositions

Bare postpositions are invariable in form. They fall into distinct groups according to what case marking they require on their complements.

17.2.1 Postpositions taking non-case-marked or genitive complements

There are four items in this group:

gibi	'like'
için	'for'
-(y)lA/ile	'with', 'by'
kadar	'as . . . as'

In general, the complements of these postpositions are left in the non-case-marked form:

(5) bizler **gibi**
'*like* us'

(6) başka bir kalem**le**
'*with* another pen'

(7) Atatürk **kadar** ünlü
'*as* famous *as* Atatürk'

The only exception to this rule is that if the complement is one of the pronouns *ben* 'I', *sen* 'you', *biz* 'we', *siz* 'you', *bu* 'this (one)', *şu* 'this'/'that (one)', *o* 'that (one)', *kim* 'who' it normally takes genitive case marking:

(8) sizi**n** için
'for you'

This does not, however, apply to the plural-marked forms of these pronouns, *bizler, sizler, bunlar, şunlar, onlar, kimler*, which remain in the non-case-marked form, see (5) above.

The eight pronominal forms which require genitive case marking with *için, gibi, kadar* and *-(y)lA/ile* display the same property in respect of the possessive-marked postpositions discussed in 17.3. We refer to them as **genitive-attracting pronouns**, a term which should be understood as excluding their plural-marked forms. The usage of these four postpositions is presented individually below.

(i) *gibi* 'like':

    (9) Fatma **senin gibi** çok çalışıyor.
        'Fatma works very hard, *like you*.'

    (10) [**Seninki gibi** bir çanta almay]-ı düşünüyordum.
        'I was thinking of [buying a bag *like yours*].'

The complement of *gibi* can be modified by *tıpkı* 'just like' (e.g. *tıpkı senin gibi* 'just like you').

Note that the demonstrative pronouns *bu/şu/o* (18.2) can combine with *gibi* with or without genitive marking. These combinations are roughly synonymous with the determiners *böyle/şöyle/öyle* 'such (a)' (15.6.1 (iv)):

    (11) **O gibi/Onun gibi/Öyle** adamlar insanı kolaylıkla aldatabiliyorlar.
        'Men *like that* can easily fool people.'

Combinations of *gibi* with the demonstratives can also be pronominalized by means of 3rd person possessive marking (18.4). In this case the demonstrative is genitive-marked:

    (12) **Bu-nun gibi-ler-i** bence daha güzel.
        this-GEN like-PL-3SG.POSS
        'I think *the ones like this* are nicer.'

For *ne gibi (bir)* 'what kind of (a)', see 19.2.1.9 (94)–(95).

(ii) *için* 'for':

    (13) Selim **benim için** bir şey bıraktı mı?
        'Did Selim leave anything *for me*?'

bunun/onun için often have the causal meaning 'because of this/that', 'so' (28.3.6 (ii)):

    (14) Dün sürekli yağmur yağdı, **onun için** hiç sokağa çıkmadık.
        'Yesterday it rained continually, *so* we didn't go out at all.'

With certain complements, such as *iş* 'work' and *para* 'money', a phrase headed by *için* can express purpose:

    (15) Ferit **iş için** Arjantin'e gitmişti.
        'Ferit had gone to Argentina *on business*.'

(iii) *-(y)lA/ile* 'with', 'by':

This postposition is also known as the comitative/instrumental marker (8.1.4). As a postposition *-(y)lA/ile* has six main meanings, the first four comitative and the other two instrumental:

a. In the company of a person or persons:

(16) Ercan baloya **kimin*le*** gitmiş?
'*Who* did Ercan go to the ball *with*?'

b. In association with a person or persons in some reciprocal activity (13.2.3.2):

(17) Meryem yarın **arkadaş(lar)ı*yla*** buluşacakmış.
'Meryem is apparently going to meet up *with her friend(s)* tomorrow.'

c. Carrying an object with oneself:

(18) Tapu dairesine **kimlik kartın*la*** gitmeyi unutma.
'Don't forget to take *your identity card with you* to the land registry office.'

d. In a manner characterized by some quality:

(19) Size **memnuniyet*le*** yardım ederim.
'I'll help you *with pleasure*.'

e. Using an instrument:

(20) Mehmet ekmeği **keskin bir bıçak*la*** kesti.
'Mehmet cut the bread *with a sharp knife*.'

f. Using a means of transport or communication:

(21) Jale işe **araba*yla*** gidiyor.
'Jale goes to work *by car*.'

(22) Sonucu size **mektup*la*** bildiririz.
'We will inform you of the result *by letter*.'

For the use of *-(y)lA/ile* as a complement marker, see 13.1.2.2 and for its use as a conjunction ('and'), see 28.3.1.1 (ii). For subjects conjoined by *-(y)lA/ile*, see 12.2.2.4, 13.2.3.2.

(iv) *kadar* 'as...as':

This postposition has a comparative function, with two meanings:

a. The same degree of a certain quality:
In this meaning the phrase that *kadar* forms with its complement modifies an adjective or adverb (15.4.1.2, 16.8):

(23) **Senin kadar *akıllı*** bir insan tanımıyorum.
'I don't know anyone *as clever as you.*'

(24) Bugün Demet **kadar *hızlı*** koşabildim.
'Today I was able to run *as fast as* Demet.'

b. The same quantity of occurrence or performance. In this meaning, the postpositional phrase modifies a verb:

(25) Hülya, Yücel **kadar *öksür***müyordu.
'Hülya was not *coughing as much as* Yücel.'

Note that the demonstrative pronouns *bu/şu/o* (18.2) and *ne* can combine with *kadar* without genitive marking to form determiners (15.6.1 (iv)) and adverbials of quantity or degree (16.5).

17.2.2 Postpositions taking dative complements

(i) *doğru* 'towards':
This postposition can have either temporal or spatial meaning:

(26) **Akşam-a doğru** kar yağmaya başladı.
evening-DAT towards
'*Towards evening* it began to snow.'

(27) Kızlar **denize doğru** koşuyordu.
'The girls were running *towards the sea.*'

(ii) *göre* 'according to', 'since':
This postposition expresses the following types of relation:

a. Conformity:

(28) **Hava raporuna göre** öğleden sonra yağmur yağacakmış.
'*According to the weather forecast,* it's going to rain this afternoon.'

b. Comparison:

(29) **Ötekine göre** bu otelin pek bir konforu yok.
'This hotel has few comforts *compared with the other.*'

c. Appropriateness:

(30) Bu oda tam **sana göre**.
'This room is just *right for you.*'

For examples with *göre* in adverbial clauses, see 26.3.7.

(iii) *kadar* 'until', 'by', 'as far as':
When used with a dative-marked complement, *kadar* (and its much less used synonym *dek*) has either temporal or spatial meaning, in both cases involving a terminal point:

a. Temporal:

(31) **Saat bire kadar** beklerim.
'I'll wait *until one o'clock.*'

(32) **Cumaya kadar** biter.
'It will be finished *by Friday.*'

(33) **Beş dakikaya kadar** gelirim.
'I'll be back *within five minutes.*'

b. Spatial:

(34) **Van'a kadar** gidemedik.
'We weren't able to get *as far as Van.*'

Optionally, to emphasize the length of the period or distance referred to, *ta* [tʰaː], [tʰa] can be placed before the complement in colloquial usages.

(35) [Kocasının her gün *ta* **Polatlı'ya kadar** gidip gelmesi] gerekiyor.
'Her husband has to go *all the way to Polatlı* and back every day.'

For *kadar* with a non-case-marked or genitive complement, see 17.2.1 (iv).

(iv) *karşı* 'against', 'towards'. This postposition expresses the following types of relation:

a. Opposition:

(36) **Sana karşı** değiller.
'They're not *against you.*'

b. Attitude:

(37) **Tarık Bey'e karşı** büyük saygım var.
'I have great respect *for Tarık Bey.*'

c. Proximity (in certain more or less fixed temporal expressions):

(38) **Sabaha karşı** fırtına dindi.
'*Towards morning* the storm died down.'

(v) *rağmen/karşın* 'in spite of':

(39) Şebnem **hastalığına rağmen** çalışmaya devam ediyor.
'Şebnem is carrying on working *in spite of her illness*.'

For *gelince* 'as for', see 23.3.3.1.

17.2.3 Postpositions taking ablative complements

(i) *başka/gayrı* 'apart from', 'other than':

(40) **Bundan başka** bir şey var mı?
'Is there anything *other than this*?'

(ii) *beri* 'since', 'for':
Postpositional phrases headed by *beri* always have temporal meaning. They express the duration, prior to a given reference point, of a state of affairs or a process which, at the point of time referred to, *is/was still continuing*. The reference point is understood to be the moment of utterance, unless the predicate is marked by *-(y)DI*, in which case a past reference point will have been established in the preceding discourse. When *beri* has the sense of 'since', the complement noun phrase expresses the time at which the state or process began:

(41) **Pazartesiden beri** hasta-yım.
Monday-ABL since ill-1SG
'I've been ill *since Monday*.'

(42) Mehmet **ekim baş-ın-dan beri** yurtdışın-da-ydı.
Mehmet October beginning-NCM-ABL since abroad-LOC-P.COP
'Mehmet had been abroad *since the beginning of October*.'

(43) Koray **1995'ten beri** Kanada'da yaşıyor.
'Koray has been living in Canada *since 1995*.'

When *beri* has the sense of 'for', the complement noun phrase expresses the amount of time that has/had elapsed since the start of the process or the onset of the state:

(44) **Üç günden beri** hastayım.
'I've been ill *for three days*.'

(45) Koray **birkaç yıldan beri** Kanada'da yaşamaktaydı.
'Koray had been living in Canada *for several years*.'

If (as in the above examples) the postpositional phrase headed by *beri* modifies the main predicate of the sentence, this predicate is usually presented in the form which expresses the state or process as ongoing at the reference point (see the discussion of imperfective aspect in 21.3.1–2). It can therefore be a nominal predicate, as in (41), (42), (44) or a verbal predicate with progressive aspect (*-(I)yor, -mAktA*), as in (43), (45). However, when the complement of *beri* is a point in time (rather than an amount of time) a quantified predicate is often expressed with perfective aspect (*-DI, -mIş*):

(46) **O zamandan beri** *üç defa* araba değiştir*di*m.
'I've changed my car *three times since then.*'

Perfective marking of a predicate modified by any kind of *beri* phrase is also common where the negative marker *-mA* is present:

(47) **Yıllardan beri** kendine yeni ayakkabı al***ma****mış*tı/almıyordu.
'S/he hadn't bought herself/himself any new shoes *for years.*'

In the case of a negative predicate, there can be a clear difference in meaning between the perfective and imperfective versions of the same sentence:

(48) a. Toplantı-dan beri konuş-**ma-mış**-lar.
meeting-ABL since speak-NEG-EV/PF-3PL
'Apparently, they *haven't* spoken since the meeting.'

b. Toplantı-dan beri konuş-**mu-yor**-lar-mış.
meeting-ABL since speak-NEG-IMPF-3PL-EV.COP
'Apparently, they *haven't been* speak*ing* since the meeting.'

(iii) *bu yana* 'since':
This item is synonymous with *beri* in its 'since' meaning, except that the temporal reference point is usually the present moment, not a point of time in the past. Thus, *bu yana* could be substituted for *beri* in (41) but not normally in (42).

(iv) *dolayı* 'because of':
This postposition has a synonym *ötürü*, which is less frequently used.

(49) **Üzüntüsünden dolayı** Ayşe o akşamki toplantımıza katılamadı.
'*Because of her distressed state,* Ayşe wasn't able to join our gathering that evening.'

(v) *itibaren* 'from', 'with effect from':
This is a temporal postposition indicating the time at which some planned or anticipated state of affairs or process is or was due or expected to begin.

(50) Bu tarife, **1.07.2023 tarihinden itibaren** geçerlidir.
'This timetable is effective *from 1.07.2023.*'

(vi) *önce/evvel* 'before':

 (51) Onlar **benden önce** gelmişler.
   'They arrived *before me*.'

(vii) *sonra* 'after':

 (52) **Her yemekten sonra** mutlaka bir fincan Türk kahvesi içer.
   'S/he invariably drinks a cup of Turkish coffee *after every meal*.'

önce and *sonra* differ from other postpositions in that they can be modified by an immediately preceding adverbial, either an adverbial of quantity such as *çok* 'much' or *biraz* 'a little' (16.5), or an expression denoting a period of time, such as *beş dakika* 'five minutes' or *bir yıl* 'a year':

 (53) **Yemekten *biraz* sonra** Ahmet işine döndü.
   '*A little while after lunch* Ahmet returned to his work.'

 (54) Onlar **benden *beş dakika* önce** gelmişler.
   'They apparently arrived *five minutes before me*.'

For the (non-postpositional) adverbial functions of *önce* and *sonra*, see 16.4.1.1. For adverbial clauses formed with the subordinators *-mAdAn once* and *-DIktAn sonra*, see 26.3.16 (vi).

(viii) *yana* 'as regards', 'in favour of':

 (55) Berna **akrabadan yana** şanslı sayılır.
   'Berna can be reckoned fortunate *in terms of relatives*.'

 (56) **İdam cezasından yana** değilim.
   'I'm not *in favour of capital punishment*.'

17.3 Possessive-marked postpositions

Possessive-marked postpositions are derived from nouns and have the form noun + POSS + OBL. To the nominal stem (e.g. *arka* 'back', *yer* 'place') is added (i) a possessive suffix which shows person agreement with the complement noun phrase, and (ii) one of the dative, locative or ablative case markers, or in a few cases, the adverbial suffix $-CA_1$ or the instrumental marker $-(y)lA$. In this chapter, we use the abbreviation OBL to cover all of these suffixes.

A striking difference between postpositional phrases with bare and possessive-marked postpositions is that the complement of a possessive-marked postposition is often not overtly expressed (18.1.5). This happens (mainly in Group 1, as explained below) in cases where the possessive suffix itself, and/or mention of its referent in the immediately preceding context, is sufficient to identify the complement:

(57) (Biz-im) **ön-*ümüz*-de** beş kişi vardı.
we-GEN front-1PL.POSS-LOC
'There were five people in front of *us*.'

(58) Turgut sıraya girdi. **Ön-ün-de** beş kişi vardı.
front-3PL.POSS-LOC
'Turgut entered the queue. There were five people in front of *him*.'

Another important way in which possessive-marked postpositions differ from bare postpositions is that their complements can be dislocated and occur *after* them. This is in situations where the complement is the head of a relative clause in which the postposition is the 'possessor' of the head (25.1.1.2 (iii)):

(59) [**içine** öteberi atılan] bir ***dolap***
'a *cupboard in which* all sorts of things were dumped'

(60) [hepimizin **uğruna** çalıştığımız] ***dava***
'the *cause for which* we are all working'

For another example, see Chapter 25 (16).

Possessive-marked postpositions can be divided into two groups, which differ in respect of (i) whether or under what circumstances, their complements take genitive case marking, (ii) whether their own case marking is variable or fixed, and (iii) whether or not their complements can be omitted.

17.3.1 Group 1: spatial relations

The postpositions in this group express spatial relations. In all cases, their complements can be omitted if readily understood from the context. Dative, locative or ablative case marking is selected according to the type of spatial meaning to be expressed. The nouns upon which this group is based are shown below, together with the postpositional meaning that they generate. Note that in their postpositional usages these nouns denote not only a particular part of a physical object but also a space situated in relation to that object. Thus, *ön* can mean 'the space in front', *üst* 'the space above', *yan* 'the space beside', etc.

ön	'front'	→ 'in front of'
arka	'back'	→ 'behind'
iç	'interior'	→ 'inside', 'in'
dış	'exterior'	→ 'outside'
üst	'top'	→ 'on top of', 'above', 'on'
alt	'bottom'	→ 'under', 'underneath', 'below'
yan	'side'	→ 'beside', 'next to'
karşı	'opposite side'	→ 'opposite'
ara	'space'	→ 'between', 'among'
etraf/çevre	'surroundings'	→ 'around'
öte	'far side'	→ 'beyond'

17.3.1.1 Group 1 possessive-marked postpositions with genitive complements

The postpositions in this group usually form a genitive-possessive construction (14.4) with their complement noun phrase.

(i) As in the case of noun phrases in general (14.3.3.3 (i)), dative case marking is required where the postpositional phrase expresses the destination or target of an action:

(61) Küçük kız (ben-**im**) **yan-ım**-*a* geldi.
 I-GEN side-1SG.POSS-DAT
 'The little girl came *over to* me.'

(62) Bu tabloyu kanepe**nin üstüne** asalım.
 'Let's hang this picture *above* the sofa.'

(ii) Location requires locative case marking (14.3.3.4):

(63) Dolab-**ın arka-sın**-*da* bir şey var mı?
 cupboard-GEN back-3SG.POSS-LOC
 'Is there anything *behind* the cupboard?'

(iii) Motion from, out of or through a space requires ablative case marking (14.3.3.5 (i)):

(64) Kanepe-**nin alt-ın**-*dan* bir fare çıktı.
 sofa-GEN bottom-3SG.POSS-ABL
 'A mouse ran out *from under* the sofa.'

(65) Arabayla park**ın içinden** geçilmez.
 'One can't go *through* the park by car.'

17.3.1.2 Group 1 possessive-marked postpositions with non-case-marked complements

There are various contexts which require the complement of a Group 1 possessive-marked postposition to be left in the non-case-marked form rather than being given genitive case marking. These are all contexts in which the complement is 3rd person, and even if it is plural (as in (73)–(74)), the possessive marking on the postposition is always 3rd person singular.

(i) Contexts where the postposition is used in a non-physical sense or with a metaphorical meaning. (66)–(68) show various such uses of *içinde* 'in':

   (66) Bütün bunları **iki saat *içinde*** mi yaptınız? (cf. Chapter 16 (69))
   'Did you do all these *in two hours*?'

   (67) **Ter *içinde*** kalmıştım.
   'I was *(covered) in sweat*.'

   (68) Seyhan **korku *içinde*** kapıya hafifçe vurdu.
   '*In [a state of] fear*, Seyhan gently knocked on the door.'

Metaphorical uses of *altın(d)a* 'under' are also common:

   (69) Bütün okullar **Bakanlığın denetimi *altına*** alındı.
   'All schools were brought *under the control of the Ministry*.'

   (70) Hep **babasının etkisi *altında*** yaşadı.
   'He lived constantly *under the influence of his father*.'

(ii) Contexts where the complement is non-specific:

   a. Non-specific indefinite complement (22.2.1):

   (71) Bu hesapları **bir kağıt *üstünde*** yapmak daha kolay olacak.
   'It will be easier to do these calculations *on a piece of paper*.'

   b. Categorial complement (22.3):

   (72) Sanık ne zaman **yargıç *önüne*** çıkar acaba?
   'I wonder when the accused will appear *before a judge*?'

   c. Generic complement (22.4.2):

   (73) Genellikle **kardeşler *arasında*** kuvvetli bir dayanışma olur.
   'There is usually a strong solidarity *between siblings*.'

The two conditions described in (i) and (ii) above often occur together. For example, the complements of *içinde* in (67) and (68) are categorial and the use of *arasında* in (73) is non-spatial.

17.3.1.3 Particular features of individual postpositions in Group 1

(i) *iç* + POSS + OBL can also be used in the non-physical sense of 'among', that is, expressing inclusion in a set or group. In this particular sense, it is interchangeable with *ara* + POSS + OBL:

(74) Ali'nin giysileri **içinde/arasında** işine yarayacak bir şey bulabilirsin.
'You may find something *among* Ali's clothes to fit your needs.'

For the partitive use of *iç/ara* + POSS + ABL, see 14.5.1 (ii), 25.3, 19.2.1.4–5.

(ii) Some speakers use the form *içeri* + POSS + OBL (e.g. *içerisinde*) in preference to *iç* + POSS + OBL (e.g. *içinde*). (For *içeri* in adverbial uses without possessive affixation, see 16.4.2.)

(iii) *Üst* has a synonym *üzer-*, which does not occur as a bare noun. It is interchangeable with *üst* in the postpositional function, but nowadays its usage is mainly confined to non-physical senses, as exemplified in (76)–(77).

(75) Masanın **üstünde/üzerinde** bir şey yok.
'There's nothing *on* the table.'

The dative forms *üstüne/üzerine*, with a non-case-marked complement, can mean 'on' in the metaphorical sense of 'on the subject of':

(76) Gençlerde uyuşturucu kullanımı **üstüne/üzerine** araştırma yapıyor.
'S/he's doing research *on* the use of drugs among young people.'

Üzerine also means 'on', 'upon' in a temporal sense, expressing a sequential and causal relation between two events. In this usage also, the complement is left in the non-case-marked form (unless it is one of the genitive-attracting pronouns):

(77) Kocasının ölümü **üzerine** kendi memleketine döndü.
'*On* her husband's death she went back to her own country.'

For *bunun üzerine* as a temporal discourse connective, see 28.3.8.

(iv) In addition to its literal meaning of 'beside', *yan* + POSS + OBL has a number of metaphorical senses. Most of these still belong to the realm of physical space and require any definite or specific complements to be genitive-marked:

(78) Babalarının yanında sigara içmezler.
'They don't smoke *in* their father*'s presence.*'

(79) Çocuk daha çok anneannesi**nin yanında** kalıyor.
'The child lives mainly *with* his grandmother.'

(80) **Yanımda** beş kişi çalışıyor.
'I've got five people working *for me.*'

In the abstract sense of 'in comparison with', *yan* + POSS + LOC may or may not have a genitive-marked complement:

(81) [Ali'nin yaptıkları](**-nın**) **yanında** bunlar pek parlak değil.
'*Compared with* [the ones Ali made/makes], these are not very wonderful.'

(v) In its sense of 'between', *ara* + POSS + OBL can take two or more conjoined complements. In the case of two complements, they are generally conjoined by *-(y)lA/ile* but also by *ve* (28.3.1.1 (ii)) and the second is usually left without case marking, even in contexts referring to physical space:

(82) Benim odam*la* onunki **arasında** kalın bir duvar vardı.
'There was a thick wall *between* my room *and* his/hers.'

The second of the conjoined complements may be given genitive marking:

(83) Ahmet'*le* çocuklar(**ın**) **arasında** bir sorun mu var?
'Is there some problem *between* Ahmet *and* the children?'

If one of the complements conjoined by *ara* + POSS + OBL is a personal pronoun, it usually occurs as the second item and if it is one of the genitive-attracting pronouns, it must be genitive-marked:

(84) baba-sı-*yla* (biz-**im**) ara-**mız**-da
   father-3SG.POSS-CONJ we-GEN between-1PL.POSS-LOC
   '*between* his/her father *and* us/me'

Some speakers may use a pronoun as the first of the two conjoined complements:

(85) **bizim***le* babası arasında
   '*between us* and his/her father'

As the examples above illustrate, *ara-* is marked with the same person as the *second* of the two complements (unlike the person marking of predicates with subjects conjoined by *-(y)lA/ile* (12.2.2.4 (ii)).

Where the pronoun is singular, the person marking on *ara-* is also singular:

(86) Ayşe-yle **sen-in** ara-**n**-da
Ayşe-CONJ you-GEN between-2SG.POSS-LOC
'between Ayşe and *you*'

Where the pronoun is 3rd person plural, the person marking on *ara-* may be (3rd person) singular or plural:

(87) Ayşe'yle **onlar(ın)** arasında/**aralarında
'between Ayşe and *them*'

If there are more than two complements, the last two have to be conjoined by *ve* (not by *-(y)lA/ile* (28.3.1.1 (ii))):

(88) Babası, amcası **ve bizim** aramızda eski bir dostluk vardı.
'There was a longstanding friendship *between* his father, his uncle *and us*.'

In the case of conjoined complements which are proper names of places, the use of an overt conjunction is optional, whether there are two or more complements:

(89) Diyarbakır **ile** Urfa arasında/Diyarbakır-Urfa arasında otobüs işletiyordu.
'He ran a bus service between Diyarbakır *and* Urfa.'

(90) Diyarbakır, Urfa, Gaziantep arasında otobüs işletiyordu.
'He ran a bus service between Diyarbakır, Urfa [*and*] Gaziantep.'

17.3.2 Group 2: abstract relations

Group 2 of the possessive-marked postpositions differ from those in Group 1 in several ways:

(i) Whereas the Group 1 postpositions, at least in their literal senses, denote relations of physical space, the items in Group 2 are mostly concerned with abstract relations.
(ii) There is not always a clear connection between the meaning of the noun upon which the postposition is based and the meaning of the postposition, which may have evolved over time.
(iii) The case marking of these postpositions is fixed, not variable as in group 1. In some instances, the adverbial suffix $-CA_1$ or the instrumental marker *-(y)lA/ile* replaces case marking.
(iv) With the exception of the genitive-attracting pronouns (17.2.1), the complements of these postpositions are almost always left in the non-case-marked form. For further exceptions, see 17.3.2.1.

(v) Where a 3rd person plural complement is overtly expressed, the possessive marker on the postposition is always 3rd person singular:

(91) **Çocuk-lar saye-*sin*-de** alışveriş işleri pek sorun olmuyor.
child-PL *saye*-3SG.POSS-LOC
'*Thanks to the children*, shopping is not really a problem.'

(vi) The only postpositions in this group whose complements can be deleted are *adına* (in its meaning as defined below), *hakkında, sayesinde* and *uğruna*.
(vii) The postpositions listed in (vi) are also the only ones in this group that can have relativized complements (as in (60) above).

A list of the most common Group 2 possessive-marked postpositions is given below. Because they are used mainly with 3rd person complements, they are shown here for convenience with the 3rd person singular possessive suffix.

açı	'angle'	*açı-sın-dan*	'from the point of view of', 'in terms of'
ad	'name'	*ad-ın-a*	'in the name of', 'on behalf of'
aracılık	'mediation'	*aracılığ-ı-yla*	'through (the mediation of)'
bakım	'aspect'	*bakım-ın-dan*	'from the point of view of', 'in terms of'
boy	'length'	*boy-un-ca*	'all along', 'throughout'
gerek	'requirement'	*gereğ-in-ce*	'in accordance with'
hak	'right'	*hakk-ın-da*	'about'
itibar	'respect'	*itibar-ı-yla*	'in respect of', 'in terms of'
konu	'subject'	*konu-sun-da*	'on the subject of', 'about'
neden	'reason'	*neden-i-yle*	'because of'
saye (obs.)	'shadow'	*saye-sin-de*	'thanks to'
sıra	'time'	*sıra-sın-da*	'at the time of'
süre	'period'	*süre-sin-ce*	'during the period of'
taraf	'side'	*taraf-ın-dan*	'by' (an agent)
uğ(u)r	'good luck'	*uğr-un-a*	'for the sake of'
vasıta	'mediation'	*vasıta-sı-yla*	'through (the mediation of)'
yer	'place'	*yer-in-e*	'instead of'
yol	'way'	*yol-u-yla*	'by','by means of'
yüz	'reason'	*yüz-ün-den*	'because of'

Examples with genitive complements (genitive-attracting pronouns):

(92) Ömer ben-*im* **hakk-ım-da** neler söyledi?
I-GEN *hakk*-1SG.POSS-LOC
'What did Ömer say *about* me?'

(93) Bütün bunları (siz-*in*) **saye-niz-de** yapabildik.
                   you-GEN *saye*-2PL.POSS-LOC
     'It is *thanks to* you that we have been able to do all this.'

Examples with non-case-marked complements:

(94) Sağlık **açısından/bakımından** bu kadar çikolata yemek doğru değil.
     '*From the* health *point of view*, it's not good to eat so much chocolate.'

(95) Türkiye'deki depremler **konusunda** bir kitap yazmış.
     'S/he's written a book *about* the earthquakes in Turkey.'

17.3.2.1 Particular features of individual postpositions in Group 2

(i) *aracılığıyla* and the synonymous *vasıtasıyla* are unusual among the Group 2 postpositions in that their complements are often genitive-marked. This is a matter of speakers' personal preference:

(96) Onlar Timur('un) **aracılığıyla**/Timur('un) **vasıtasıyla** tanışmışlar.
     'Apparently they first met *through* Timur.'

(ii) Unlike the other Group 2 postpositions, *boyunca* can refer to a spatial dimension:

(97) Sahil **boyunca** küçük köyler vardı.
     '*All along* the coast there were small villages.'

Alternatively, it can have temporal reference:

(98) Konferans **boyunca** fısıldaşmaya devam ettiler.
     'They continued to whisper to each other *throughout* the lecture.'

(iii) While in the sense of 'in respect of', 'in terms of', *itibarıyla* has largely been replaced by *açısından* and *bakımından*, it also occurs in some formal registers as a synonym of *itibaren* (17.2.3).

(iv) *gereğince* is used only in legalistic language:

(99) Kanunun ilgili maddesi **gereğince** bir sözleşme hazırlanır.
     'A contract is drawn up *in accordance with* the relevant article of the law.'

(v) *konusunda* is not generally used with complements referring to human beings, except in the context of an organized exposition such as a book, an article or a lecture. Thus, for example, *yabancı öğrenciler* 'foreign students' could be substituted for *depremler* 'earthquakes' in (95) above. See also 20.1.3.

(vi) *süresince* (and its synonym *müddetince*) differ from the temporal usage of *boyunca* (see (ii)) in that they do not emphasize the long duration of an activity or state:

(100) Yokluğum **süresince** komşum her gün uğrayıp kediye yiyecek verdi.
'*During* my absence my neighbour came in every day and fed the cat.'

(vii) *tarafından* is used to express the agent of a passive verb (13.2.2).

(viii) In the expression of causality, *yüzünden* is used only when speaking of causes that have undesirable results:

(101) Sıcak havalar **yüzünden** son zamanlarda işler yavaş gidiyor.
'*Because of* the hot weather there has been slow progress recently.'

Causes that have desirable results can be expressed by *sayesinde*:

(102) Sıcak havalar **sayesinde** denize bol bol girebildik.
'*Because of* (*thanks to*) the hot weather we've been able to swim in the sea a lot.'

Nedeniyle is neutral in terms of the desirability of the outcome, but it is restricted to relatively formal registers:

(103) Yazların sıcaklığı **nedeniyle** bu bölgede muz ve hurma yetişmektedir.
'*On account of* the hot summers, bananas and dates grow in this region.'

(ix) *uğruna* 'for the sake of' is used only with inanimate complements:

(104) Güzellik **uğruna** bu kadar sıkıntıya katlanmaya değer mi?
'Is it worth suffering so much *for the sake of* beauty?'

17.4 Syntactic functions of the postpositional phrase

The range of syntactic functions that can be performed by a postpositional phrase depends upon the postposition that heads it. There are three possible functions: (i) adverbial, (ii) adjectival, and (iii) predicative.

17.4.1 Adverbial function

The most characteristic function of a Turkish postpositional phrase is adverbial, either at the level of the sentence or within the verb phrase and the great majority of examples already given in this chapter fall into this category. There are no postpositions that *cannot* head a postpositional phrase with adverbial function. Postpositional phrases headed by *kadar* (with non-case-marked or genitive complement), can also modify adjectives and adverbs (see (23) and (24) above, also 15.4.1.2).

17.4.2 Adjectival function

Among the bare postpositions, the following can head postpositional phrases that function adjectivally within a noun phrase: *gibi*, *kadar* (with non-case-marked or genitive complement), *göre*, *başka*:

(105) **senin kadar** bir çocuk
'a child *of the same size/age as you*'

(106) tam **anneme göre** bir şapka
'a hat just *right for my mother*'

For other examples, see (10)–(11) and (40) above. Note that *başka* also occurs as an adjective meaning 'other', different'.

Postpositional phrases headed by *önce* and *sonra*, in common with other temporal adverbial phrases, can be converted from adverbial to adjectival function by the addition of *-ki* (15.3.7):

(107) bahçe-nin **yağmur-dan önce-*ki*** hal-i
garden-GEN rain-ABL before-ADJ state-3SG.POSS
'the state of the garden *before the rain*'

Postpositional phrases headed by possessive-marked postpositions can be used adjectivally only if the postposition has locative case marking, and again the addition of *-ki* is necessary to effect the conversion from adverbial to adjectival function (15.3.6):

(108) **Harun-la ara-mız-da-*ki*** gerginlik
Harun-CONJ between-1PL.POSS-LOC-ADJ tension
'the tension *between Harun and me/us*'

(109) **sendikacılık tarihi konusunda*ki*** araştırmalarınız
'your research *on* (*the subject of*) *the history of trade unionism*'

17.4.3 Predicative function

Some types of postpositional phrase can be the subject complement in a linking sentence (12.1.1.2). All the bare postpositions whose phrases can be used adjectivally also occur in predicates. So also do *için*, *karşı*, *yana* and the locative-marked forms of the possessive-marked postpositions:

(110) Bu çiçekler **sizin için**miş.
 'Apparently these flowers are *for you*.'

For further examples, see (30), (36) and (56) above.

In the case of the possessive-marked postpositions, it is only those that are locative-marked that can function predicatively:

(111) Can'ın arabası **evin önünde**.
 'Can's car is *in front of the house*.'

The addition of *-ki* is not required unless pronominalization is intended (18.5):

(112) Can'ın arabası **evin önünde***ki*.
 'Can's car is *the one in front of the house*.'

Chapter 18

Pronouns and pronominal constructions

Pronouns are expressions that are used when referring to persons, things or states of affairs that have previously been mentioned, whose referents are obvious from the context or whose content is only partially specified, such as:

(1) **Onlar** eşyalarını daha toplamamış.
'*They* haven't packed their luggage yet.'

(2) **Şuradaki**nden de bir tane istiyorum.
'I also want one of *the kind over there*.'

(3) Kapıda **birisi** var.
'There's *someone* at the door.'

This chapter describes personal pronouns such as *ben* 'I', *kendim* 'myself', *birbir-* 'each other' (18.1) and the conditions under which they are used (18.1.5), demonstrative pronouns such as *bu* 'this (one)' (18.2), locative pronouns such as *şurada* 'here', 'over there' (18.3), pronouns formed by the suffix *-(s)I*, such as *iyisi* 'a nice(r) one', *bazısı* 'some (of them)' (18.4), pronouns formed by the suffix *-ki*, such as *benimki* 'mine', *öteki* 'the other (one)' (18.5), pronominal quantifiers such as *herkes* 'everyone', *bir şey* 'something', and other pronominal expressions (18.6).

Interrogative pronouns (e.g. *kim* 'who', *nerede* 'where') are discussed in 19.2 and pronominal quantifiers which interact with negation (e.g. *kimse* 'no one', 'anyone') are discussed in 20.5. Pronominal relative clauses are discussed in 25.3.

18.1 Personal pronouns

18.1.1 Simple personal pronouns

The simple personal pronouns of Turkish are:

ben	'I'	*biz*	'we'
sen	'you' (familiar)	*siz*	'you' (plural), (formal singular)
o	'he', 'she', 'it'	*onlar*	'they'

biz

biz 'we', which is the 1st person plural form, may also refer to the 1st person singular, either in very formal contexts where the speaker wishes to express his/her humble status as compared to the addressee(s) or ironically in imitation of such a stance:

(4) Efendim, **biz** sizin kadar bilemeyiz bu konuları tabii ki.
'Naturally, *I* cannot know these subjects as well as you [do].'

siz and *sen*

The 2nd person form *siz* is used in the following circumstances:

(i) To indicate the plurality of the 2nd person (i.e. 'you both/all')
(ii) When addressing a person with whom one is on formal terms (in which case both parties normally address each other as *siz*)
(iii) When one is addressing a person who is taken to be of higher rank or status

(5) **Siz** şu sıralarda sinemaya gittiniz mi?
  (i) 'Have *you (both/all)* been to the cinema lately?'
  (ii) 'Have *you* (= formal singular) been to the cinema lately?'

Children are almost always addressed as *sen*, older people are generally addressed as *siz*, and new acquaintances most commonly address each other as *siz*. Speakers who normally address each other as *sen* may, in a formal situation (such as a committee meeting), adopt the conventional formality of *siz*. However, the choice between *siz* and *sen* varies among speakers since the notion of formality depends largely on the social background of the persons involved and, to some degree, on the speakers' attitude towards the norms of social hierarchy.

bizler and *sizler*

biz 'we' and *siz* 'you' can combine with the plural suffix. Using *bizler* and *sizler* instead of *biz* and *siz* has only a marginally different effect and is confined to the following circumstances:

(i) Where the speaker wishes to individuate the members of a group, especially in cases where the speaker wants to indicate that the action was carried out, or the event experienced, individually, not as a group:

(6) **Bizler** kırık not alınca çok üzülürdük.
'*We* (each of us) would be sad when *we* (each of us) got a bad mark.'

(ii) For referring to multiple groups of persons:

(7) ***Sizler*, Ankaralı ve İstanbullular**, Türkiye'nin geri kalanını tanımıyorsunuz.
'*You, people from Ankara and Istanbul*, don't know the rest of Turkey.'

(iii) When talking to a person with whom one uses the formal *siz*, to indicate that one is referring to a group that that person belongs to (e.g. his/her family or friends, etc.):

(8) **Sizler** nasılsınız?
'How are *you (both/all)*?'

(iv) When addressing a customer or client as a replacement for *siz*:

(9) **Sizlere** nasıl yardımcı olabilirim?
'How can I help *you*?'

o and *onlar*

For the use of these forms as resumptive pronouns in relative clauses introduced by *ki*, see 25.6 (ii). For the use of other pronominal expressions used resumptively, see Chapter 27 (90)–(92).

The inflection of simple personal pronouns

Pronouns, like other noun phrases, can be inflected for case, e.g. *beni* 'me' (as direct object), *onları* 'them' (as direct object), *size* 'to you', *sende* 'on you'. The dative form of the 1st and 2nd persons singular is irregular, the stem vowel becoming 'a': *bana* 'to me', *sana* 'to you'. Another irregularity concerns the 3rd person singular pronoun *o*. The case markers and the plural suffix do not attach directly to *o*, but do so only through the mediation of the consonant 'n': *ondan* 'from him/her/it', *onlar* 'they', etc. (6.2). The genitive case marker of the 1st person forms is *-Im*: *benim* 'my', *bizim* 'our'. For the combination of simple personal pronouns with the comitative/instrumental marker *-(y)lA,* see 8.1.4.

18.1.2 kendi

The word *kendi* has five functions, one adjectival and the rest pronominal. It usually refers to human beings, but in its adjectival function (18.1.2.1) and its emphatic function (18.1.2.2 (i)) it may refer to inanimate (usually abstract) concepts.

Kendi (in its bare or inflected forms) can be *followed* by the noun phrase which is its **antecedent** (i.e. the expression the pronoun refers to):

(10) Mobilyaları değiştirmek **kendi** fikriydi ***Ahmet'in***.
'It was *Ahmet's own* idea to change the furniture.'

(11) **Kendinizi** anlatmadınız *siz* hiç.
'*You* haven't talked about *yourself* at all.'

18.1.2.1 Bare form kendi

In its bare form, *kendi* functions as an adjectival modifier of a possessive-marked noun phrase and means 'own' (as in 'his own', 'our own'). In this usage, *kendi* is not inflected for person or case. The possessive-marked noun phrase modified by *kendi* may form part of a genitive-possessive construction (14.4) in which the genitive-marked constituent is the antecedent:

(12) Hırsızlığı **Erol-un** *kendi* **şirket-in**-den biri yapmış.
       Erol-GEN own company-3SG.POSS-ABL
       'It was apparently someone from *Erol's own company* who committed the burglary.'

(13) Erken emeklilik (**ben-im**) *kendi* **isteğ-im**-di.
       I-GEN own wish-1SG.POSS-P.COP
       'It was *my own wish* [to take] early retirement.'

When the possessive-marked noun phrase is in the 3rd person (e.g. *anahtarlarını* 'his/her own keys' below) and does not have a genitive-marked modifier, *kendi* can refer to any 3rd person in the same clause, but it is most commonly understood as referring to the subject:

(14) Semra, Elif'e *kendi* anahtar-lar-ın-ı vermiş.
       own key-PL-3SG.POSS-ACC
       'It seems Semra gave Elif her own keys.'

The more likely intended meaning of (14) is that Semra gave Elif Semra's own keys. However, another possible meaning would be that she gave Elif Elif's own keys.

The antecedent of adjectival *kendi* can denote an inanimate entity:

(15) Bu karışıklık, **sorun-un** *kendi* **özellik-ler-in**-den kaynaklanıyor.
       problem-GEN own property-PL-3SG.POSS-ABL
       'This confusion is a result of *the very properties of the problem*.'

(16) Bu, **evin** *kendi* rengi.
       'This is *the original colour* of the house.'

18.1.2.2 Inflected kendi-: emphatic, reflexive, simple pronominal and resumptive usages

The pronoun *kendi-* can be inflected for person, in which case it combines with the possessive suffixes described in 8.1.2:

kendim	1st person singular	*kendimiz*	1st person plural
kendin	2nd person singular (familiar)	*kendiniz*	2nd person plural or formal singular
kendi(si)	3rd person singular	*kendileri*	3rd person plural

Note that in the case of the 3rd person, the person marker *-(s)I* is sometimes omitted.

The forms above can be further inflected for case, e.g. *kendi-m-den* 'from myself', *kendi-niz-i* '(you) yourself/yourselves' (formal singular or plural accusative), etc. Note that 'n' has to be attached to the 3rd person forms *kendi*, *kendisi* and *kendileri* when these are inflected for case, e.g. *kendine/kendi-sine* 'to him/her(self)', *kendilerinde* 'on them(selves)' (6.2, 8.1.2).

(i) Emphatic usage of inflected *kendi-*:
kendi- inflected for person can be used for purposes of emphasizing the subject of a main clause, as in *I myself*, *they themselves*, etc. In such emphatic constructions *kendi-* can be used with or without a pronoun matching it in person, but in all cases a matching person marker on the predicate is obligatory:

(17) Evde (**ben**) **kendim** oturacağım için bu renkleri seçtim.
(I) self-1SG.POSS
'I chose these colours because I will be living in the house *myself*.'

(18) (**Ayşe**) **kendi(si)** istemiş sınava girmeyi.
'*Ayşe herself* wanted to take an exam.'

If the antecedent is an inanimate entity, it generally has genitive marking (see also (15)):

(19) **Bu kuralın kendisi** yönetmeliğe aykırı.
'*This rule* is *itself* contrary to the general regulations.'

(20) **Plan-ın *kendi*-sin-de** bir sorun var.
plan-GEN self-3SG.POSS-LOC
'There is a problem with *the plan itself*.'

Genitive marking is also very common with 3rd person animate entities:

(21) Arabayı **Erol'un kendi-si** yıkayacak.
Erol-GEN/self-3SG.POSS
'*Erol* is going to wash the car *himself*.'

On the other hand, the 1st and 2nd person pronouns as antecedents of emphatic *kendi-* can be genitive-marked only in noun clauses and relative clauses (see (26)–(27)).

The form *kendisi* can be replaced by *kendi*. Where the antecedent is non-case-marked, this produces no difference of formality:

(22) Arabayı **Erol/o kendi** yıkayacak.
'*Erol* is going to wash the car *himself.*'

However, where the antecedent is genitive-marked, the use of *kendi* is confined mostly to colloquial speech:

(23) Arabayı **Erol-un kendi** yıkayacak.
Erol-GEN self
'*Erol* is going to wash the car *himself.*'

Unlike the 1st and 2nd person emphatic forms, which, in main clauses, occur only as subjects, the 3rd person emphatic forms *kendisi* and *kendileri* can function as objects and adverbials. In these cases, the antecedent (*o*, *onlar* or any appropriate noun phrase) appears in the genitive form:

(24) Meclis'e belli bir saatte gidersen

Başbakan-ın kendi-sin-i bile görebilirsin.
prime minister-GEN self-3SG.POSS-ACC

'If you go to parliament at a certain time, you will even be able to see the *Prime Minister himself/herself.*'

(25) Sonuçları **onlar-ın kendi-lerin-den** öğrenebilirsin.
they-GEN self-3PL.POSS-ABL
'You can find out the results from *them in person.*'

An emphatic construction with *kendi-* can be the subject of a noun clause (Chapter 24) or relative clause (Chapter 25). When it is the subject of a relative clause, speakers' preferences vary. The verb can agree with it (as in (26a)) or 3rd person singular possessive marking on the verb can be used (as in (26b)):

(26) a. [(***ben-im***) **kendi-m-in** bile
I-GEN self-1SG.POSS-GEN even

anla-ya-ma-dığ-*ım*] bir makale
understand-PSB-NEG-PART-1SG.POSS an article

b. [(**ben-im**) ***kend-im-in*** bile
I-GEN self-1SG.POSS-GEN even

anla-ya-ma-dığ-*ı*] bir makale
understand-PSB-NEG-PART-3SG.POSS an article

'an article that even *I* couldn't understand *myself*'

When an emphatic construction with *kendi-* functions as the subject of a noun clause, the verb agrees with it. The antecedent (*siz* 'you' below) usually has genitive marking, but it may also be non-case-marked (27a). *Kendiniz* can also be used on its own in its non-case-marked form (27b):

(27) a. [(*Siz-(in)*) **kendi-niz** oraya git-me-*niz*] gerekiyor.
you(-GEN) self-2PL.POSS there go-VN-2PL.POSS
'*You* should go there *yourself.*'

b. [Oraya **kendi-niz** git-me-*niz*] gerekiyor.
'*You* should go there *yourself.*'

(ii) Reflexive usage of inflected *kendi-*:
kendi- is the standard means for expressing reflexivity (8.2.1.3, 13.2.3.1). In its usage as a reflexive pronoun, *kendi-* is inflected for person and case and has as its antecedent an item that plays a different grammatical role in the sentence from itself. In its usage as a reflexive pronoun, *kendi-* is inflected for person and case.

(28) **Kendi-n-den** başkasına güvenemiyor musun?
self-2SG.POSS-ABL
'Can't you trust anyone but *yourself*?'

The antecedent of reflexive *kendi-* is usually the subject of its own clause:

(29) *Semra* aday olarak **kendisini/kendini** öne sürecekmiş.
'Apparently *Semra* is going put *herself* forward as a candidate.'

(30) [**Siz-in kendi-niz-i** eleştir-me-*niz*]
you-GEN self-2PL.POSS-ACC criticize-VN-2PL.POSS

ne kadar kolay-mış!
how easy-EV.COP

'How easy *you* seem to find it to criticize *yourself*!'

This can be indicated simply by placing the appropriate person marker on the predicate:

(31) **Kendi-m-**e bakamıyor-**um**.
self-1SG.POSS-DAT-1SG
'*I* can't take care of *myself.*'

A 3rd person antecedent whose identity is clear from previous mention similarly does not have to be expressed within the clause by an overt noun phrase:

(32) *Ninem* çok yaşlı. Artık **kendine** bakamıyor.
 '*My granny's* very old. *She* can't take care of *herself* any longer.'

The antecedent can also be a constituent other than the subject:

(33) Sanki ***bana* kendi-m-i** anlatıyorlardı.
 I.DAT self-1SG.POSS-ACC
 '[It was] as if they were talking to *me* about *myself*.'

In the absence of an antecedent within the same clause, reflexive *kendi-* may refer to a person indicated in the superordinate clause:

(34) [**Kendimize** araba almak] istiyor**uz**.
 '*We* want [to buy a car for *ourselves*].'

There are also cases where there is no antecedent in the sentence, yet a reflexive can still be used because the person to whom it refers is understood to be the subject of a non-person-marked verb, such as *almak* below:

(35) Bu durum-da [**kendi-niz-e** araba al-mak]
 this situation-LOC self-2PL.POSS-DAT car buy-VN

 çok zor olacak.
 very difficult be-FUT

 'Under these circumstances, it is going to be very difficult [[for you] to buy a car for *yourself*].'

There is a slight difference in the reflexive usage of the two 3rd person forms *kendi* and *kendisi*. The antecedent of *kendi* is more likely to be within the same clause, indicated either by a noun phrase or by person marking on the verb:

(36) a. Erol [***Ziya'nın* kendin-e** bir araba al-dığ-ın]-ı
 Erol Ziya-GEN self-DAT a car buy-VN-3SG.POSS-ACC

 san-ıyor
 think-IMPF

 'Erol thinks *Ziya* has bought a car for *himself*.'

 b. Erol [**kendine** bir araba aldığın]-ı sanıyor.
 'Erol thinks *he* has bought a car for *himself*.'

In (36a) *Ziya* is by far the most probable antecedent for *kendi*. In (36b), where the subject of the subordinate clause is not expressed by an overt noun phrase (hence the antecedent is the possessive marker), the most likely referent is *Erol*.

The 3rd person form *kendisi*, on the other hand, can refer either to an antecedent in its own clause, in which case it is being used as a reflexive, or (much more freely than *kendi*) to an antecedent in the superordinate clause, in which case it is being used as a simple personal pronoun (see (iii)).

(37) **Erol [Ziya'nın kendi-sin-e** bir araba
Erol Ziya-GEN self/s/he-3SG.POSS-DAT a car

al-ma-**sın**]-ı söyle-di.
buy-VN-3SG.POSS-ACC tell-PF

(i) 'Erol told *Ziya* to buy *himself* a car.'
(ii) 'Erol told Ziya to buy *him* a car.' (Most likely intended referent of 'him' is *Erol*. It may possibly refer to someone else.)

(iii) Third person simple pronominal usage of inflected *kendi-*:
The 3rd person form *kendisi* can be used as a simple personal pronoun corresponding to *he* or *she*. In the contexts below, where the antecedent is a person mentioned in the preceding sentence, conversation or text, *kendisi* is interchangeable with, but slightly more formal than, *o*.

(38) Ahmet hâlâ uyuyor. **Kendisi/o** bu günlerde çok yorgun.
'Ahmet is still asleep. *He*'s very tired these days.'

(39) A. Kulüpteki arkadaşların nasıl?
'How are your friends at the club?'

B. Bilmem, **kendi-lerin-i/onlar-ı** çoktandır görmedim.
s/he-3PL.POSS-ACC/they-ACC

'I don't know. I haven't seen *them* for a long time.'

kendisi and *o* are also interchangeable where the pronoun occurs in a subordinate clause and refers to a person mentioned in the main clause:

(40) **Ahmet [kendisine/ona** saygısızlık edenler]-i sevmiyor.
'Ahmet doesn't like people who are disrespectful towards him.'
(Most likely intended referent of 'him' is *Ahmet*. It may possibly refer to someone else.)

Such sentences are therefore always potentially ambiguous where more than one possible antecedent is available.

kendileri can also be used with 3rd person singular reference as a deferential substitute for *kendisi*. In sentences with this usage of *kendileri*, all references to the person in question are made in the plural form. Note that in this usage *kendileri* cannot be replaced by *onlar*.

(41) Sayın Cumhurbaşkanı bugün yurda dönüyor**lar**.

Kendi-leri gezi-**lerin**-den çok verimli sonuçlarla
s/he-3PL.POSS visit-3PL.POSS-ABL

dön-dük-**lerin**-i ifade et-ti-**ler**.
return-VN-3PL.POSS-ACC say-PF-3PL

'The president is returning home today. S/he stated that s/he was returning from his/her visit with very beneficial results.'

(iv) Usage of 3rd person *kendi-* as a resumptive pronoun:
The 3rd person form of *kendi-* (but not *o*) can optionally be used as a **resumptive pronoun** in relative clauses with *-DIK/-(y)AcAK* where it refers to the head of the relative clause (25.1.1.2 (ii)):

(42) [(***Kendi-lerin-i***) defalarca aradığımız] **yetkili-ler**
s/he-3PL.POSS-ACC   person.in.charge-PL
telefonlarımıza cevap vermediler.
'*The people in charge*, [whom we have rung many times], have not responded to our calls.'

In relative clauses formed by *ki*, both *kendi* and *o* can be used as resumptive pronouns:

(43) **Hocalarımız**, [ki *onlar/kendileri* matematikçi]...
'*Our professors*, [*who* are mathematicians]...'

For other examples, see 25.6.1.

18.1.3 kendi kendi-

Kendi kendi-, the second element of which is obligatorily inflected for person and case, is an emphatic version of *kendi-* in its reflexive usage and occurs in the same contexts:

(44) (**Kendi**) **kendimden** nefret ediyorum.
'I hate *myself*.'

When *kendi kendi-* is in the dative case, it expresses the performance of some action alone or unaided:

(45) Ahmet **kendi kendi-sin-e/kendin-e** yurt dışına çıkamaz.
       own self-3SG.POSS-DAT
'Ahmet cannot go abroad *on his own*.'

(46) Bu ütüler bir süre sonra **kendi kendi(leri)ne** kapanıyor.
'These irons switch *themselves* off after a while.'

As a result, there is a clear difference between a dative-marked *kendi-* and a dative-marked *kendi kendi-*:

(47) a. Biz **kendimize** yemek pişiriyoruz.
       'We are cooking a meal *for ourselves*.'

   b. Biz **kendi kendimize** yemek pişiriyoruz.
       'We are cooking a meal *by ourselves*.'

18.1.4 The reciprocal pronoun birbir- 'each other', 'one another'

The pronoun *birbir-* is used in contexts where two or more parties act mutually (as is the case with the reciprocal suffix, 8.2.1.4, 13.2.3.2). *Birbir-* is obligatorily inflected for person by combining with the plural possessive suffixes (8.1.2):

birbirimiz   (1st person plural)
birbiriniz   (2nd person plural)
birbiri/birbirleri (3rd person plural)

These forms can be further inflected for case, e.g. *birbirinizi* (2nd person plural accusative), *birbirimizden* (1st person plural ablative), etc. As in the case of *kendi-*, an 'n' appears before case suffixes in the 3rd person forms, as in *birbirinden, birbirlerine*, etc. (6.2).

birbiri and *birbirleri* are interchangeable when referring to two or more persons who are involved in a mutual activity:

(48) Ayşe'yle Semra **birbir-in-den/birbir-lerin-den** hiç hoşlanmıyor(**lar**).
                    each.other-3SG.POSS-ABL/each.other-3PL.POSS-ABL
'Ayşe and Semra don't like *each other* at all.'

When referring to interacting groups, again both forms can be used, but here *birbirleri* is the neutral form while *birbiri* is colloquial.

(49) Almanya ve Brezilya takımları **birbirlerinden** haklı olarak korkuyorlar.
'The German and Brazilian teams are justifiably scared *of each other*.'

When the antecedent of a reciprocal pronoun is the subject of that clause, it does not necessarily have to be expressed by an overt noun phrase. It may be omitted in accordance with the principles explained in 18.1.5:

(50) (*Siz*) **birbirinizle** çok iyi anlaşıyor**sunuz**.
'*You* get along very well with *each other*.'

(51) (**Onlar**) **birbir-lerin-i** artık gör-mü-yor-*lar*.
each.other-3PL.POSS-ACC any.more see-NEG-IMPF-3PL
'*They* don't see *each other* any more.'

Where there is an antecedent, it does not have to precede *birbir-*. It can come after it in the sentence as long as the general constraints on word order are not violated (Chapter 23):

(52) **Birbirlerine** çok düşkün **Ayşe'yle Semra**.
'*Ayşe and Semra* are very attached to *each other*.'

The antecedent of a reciprocal pronoun can also be a constituent other than the subject:

(53) *Biz-i* **birbir-imiz-e** şikayet et-ti-n.
we-ACC each.other-1PL.POSS-DAT complain-PF-2SG
'You complained *to us* about *each other*.'

(54) *Size* **birbirinizden** hiç söz etmedim.
'I never talked to *you* about *each other*.'

The only contexts in which a reciprocal pronoun can function as the subject of a clause are a non-finite noun clause (24.4), a relative clause formed with *-DIK/-(y)AcAK* (25.1.1.2), or one of the types of non-finite adverbial clause that has genitive case marking of an overt subject (26.2.1). In these cases, the reciprocal pronoun is inflected for genitive case and its antecedent is in the superordinate clause:

(55) (**Siz**) [birbir**inizin** yarışmayı kazanmasın]-ı mı istiyorsun**uz**?
'Do *you* want *each other* to win the competition?'

(56) (**Biz**) [birbir-**imiz-in** sev-diğ-i] renk-ler-i sev-mi-yor-**uz**.
we each.other-1PL.POSS-GEN like-PART-3SG.POSS colour-PL-ACC
like-NEG-IMPF-1PL
'*We each* don't like the colours that *the other(s)* like(s).'

(57) **İnsanlar** her zaman [birbir(**ler**)**inin** istediği gibi] davranmıyor**lar**.
'*People* don't always behave as *each other* want.'

Note that the verb of a subordinate clause with *birbir-* as its subject is always marked for 3rd person.

18.1.5 The omission and usage of personal pronouns

In this section, we discuss the omission and usage of subject pronouns and of genitive-marked modifiers of possessive constructions, both of which occur in association with person markers (on the predicate or possessed constituent). For the omission and usage of object pronouns, see 28.4.2.1 (ii).

Note that the 3rd person pronouns *o(nun)* and *onlar(ın)* do not occur nearly as frequently as *ben(im)*, *sen(in)*, *biz(im)* and *siz(in)* to express a grammatical subject or a genitive-marked modifier. This is because a 1st or 2nd person pronoun is the only noun phrase that can be used to refer to the speaker (and his/her associates) and the addressee(s) (and any associated people) in any particular speech situation.

(i) Omission of subject pronouns in finite clauses:
In Turkish, main clause predicates are obligatorily marked for person, (12.2.1) and subject pronouns are not syntactically necessary. In the 3rd person singular, person marking is effected by the *absence* of a person suffix (except for the optative/imperative -*sIn*, see 8.4.3–4,).

(58) O zaman öğrenci-ydi-**k**.
then student-P.COP-1PL
'We were students then.'

(59) Paris-e gid-ecek-miş.
Paris-DAT go-FUT-EV.COP
'S/he's apparently going to go to Paris.'

(60) Öğleden sonra biz-e gel-**sin**.
afternoon we-DAT come-OPT.3SG
'Let him/her come round to us this afternoon.'

(ii) Omission of subject pronouns in non-finite clauses:
Subjects of noun clauses, relative clauses formed with -*DIK/-(y)AcAK,* and some types of adverbial clause are indicated by the appropriate possessive

marker (8.1.2) on the predicate. The use of personal pronouns referring to the subject is therefore not normally required in these clauses either:

(61) [Ev-e dön-me-**m**] zor olmadı.
  home-DAT return-VN-1SG.POSS
  'It wasn't difficult [for *me* to return home].'

(62) [Ev-e git-tiğ-**im**]-de kapılar açıktı.
  home-DAT go-CV-1SG.POSS-LOC
  '[When *I* arrived home] the doors were open.'

(iii) Omission of genitive-marked pronouns as modifiers of possessive noun phrases:
Like personal pronouns expressing subjects, genitive-marked personal pronouns expressing possessors, such as *benim* 'my', *sizin* 'your', are also normally omitted where matching possessive markers are present:

(63) Yeni palto-**m**-u gördün mü?
  new coat-1SG.POSS-ACC
  'Have you seen *my* new coat?'

A 1st or 2nd person genitive-marked pronoun is even less acceptable as the modifier of a possessive-marked noun phrase where the person to whom the pronoun refers is also the subject of the clause. Thus, in (65) it would not be appropriate to use the pronoun *benim* to modify *anahtarlarım*:

(64) Anahtar-lar-**ım**-ı kaybet-ti-**m**.
  key-PL-**1SG.POSS**-ACC lose-PF-**1SG**
  '*I*'ve lost *my* keys.'

18.1.5.1 Conditions under which personal pronouns are used

(i) Usage of subject pronouns in finite clauses:
A subject pronoun is used in the following circumstances:

a. Where a subject contrasts with that of the preceding or following sentence or conjoined clause:

(65) Zeki bugün sokağa çıkmayacakmış. **Sen** bir yere gitmeyi düşünüyor muydun?
  'It seems Zeki won't be going out today. Were *you* thinking of going anywhere?'

(66) A. Yeni komşularımızı nasıl buldunuz?
     How did you find our new neighbours?

B. **Ben** o kadar beğenmedim, ama Selim çok hoşlanmış
göründü.
I didn't particularly like [them], but Selim
looked as if he was very taken [with them].

b. Where the subject is focused (23.3, 23.3.1):

(67) Bu sabah çocukları **BEN** giydirdim.
'It was *I* who got the children dressed this morning.'

(68) **SEN** de çok güzel şarkı söylersin
'*You* sing very nicely, too.'

c. Where a 1st or 2nd person subject is identified as one of a set of people actually or potentially involved in some action or situation:

(69) A. Bu filmi seyretmek isteyen var mı?
'Does anyone want to watch this film?'

B. **Ben** isterim.
'*I* do.'

(70) O gün **sen**, Ayten ve Yavuz sınava girmiştiniz.
'That day *you*, Ayten and Yavuz had had an exam.'

See also 12.2.2.4.

d. Where a 3rd person subject is an entity that was introduced in a non-subject role in the previous sentence:

(71) Kitabı Zerrin'e verdim. **O** ne zamandır onu okumak istiyordu.
'I gave the book to Zerrin. *She* had been wanting to read it for ages.'

e. Where, despite the continuance of the same subject, there is a shift from a statement about a specific event to a generalization (21.4.1.1) about the person involved:

(72) **Zeki** anahtarlarını kaybetmiş. **O** zaten oldum olası dağınıktır.
'*Zeki* has lost his keys. *He* has always been [so] disorganized.'

(73) Bilet almayı unuttum. **Ben** böyle şeyleri unuturum hep …
'*I*'ve forgotten to buy a ticket. *I* always seem to forget such things.'

f. In the opening sentence of a conversation or a sentence in which the speaker introduces a new topic of discussion:

(74) Ayşe, **ben** şimdi çıkıyorum.
'Ayşe, *I*'m going out now.'

(75) **Siz** herkesin konuştuğu şu İran filmini gördünüz mü?
'Have *you* seen this Iranian film that everyone's talking about?'

(ii) Usage of subject pronouns in non-finite clauses:
A subject pronoun is used in a noun clause or relative clause in the following circumstances:

a. Where it contrasts with the subject of the superordinate clause, the previous clause or a clause with an identical function:

(76) *Annem* [**senin** gelmen]-i istiyor.
Mum wants [*you* to come].

(77) [***Zeki'nin*** uçağa yetişmesi] [**benim** yetişmem]-den daha kolay.
'It is easier for *Zeki* to catch the flight than [for *me* (to catch it)].'

(78) [**Benim** yazdığım] mektubu almışlar. [**Senin** yazdığın] mektup daha ellerine geçmemiş.
'They've received the letter [that *I* wrote]. The letter [that *you* wrote] evidently hasn't reached them yet.'

b. Where the subject is focused (23.3, 23.3.1):

(79) Yemeğin hazırlığına katılmamış olduğum için [bulaşıkları **beNİM** yıkamam] kararlaştırıldı.
'As I had taken no part in the preparation of the meal, it was decided [that *I* should do the washing-up].'

c. Where there is a shift of sentence topic (23.3.3) from the entity performing or undergoing an action (e.g. *Zeki* in (80) below) to the action itself:

(80) [*Zeki'nin* kaza geçirdiğin]-i duydum. [**Onun** kaza geçirmesi] bütün planları altüst edecek.
'I've heard [that Zeki has had an accident]. [*His* having an accident] will upset all the plans.'

d. In the opening sentence of a conversation or a sentence in which the speaker introduces a new topic of discussion:

(81) Ayşe, [**benim** şimdi çıkmam] gerekiyor.
'Ayşe, *I*'ve got to go out now.'

(82) [**Sizlerin** yazın Amerika'ya gideceğiniz] doğru mu?
'Is it true [that *you* will be going to America in the summer]?'

(iii) Usage of genitive-marked pronouns as modifiers of possessive noun phrases: The referent of a 3rd person genitive-marked pronoun is always someone/something *other* than the subject of the clause. For example, in both of the following examples *onun* 'his/her' indicates a person other than *Semra*:

(83) Semra **on-un** anahtar-lar-ın-ı kaybet-miş.
Semra s/he-GEN key-PL-3SG.POSS-ACC lose-PF/EV
'Apparently, Semra lost *his/her* keys.'

(84) Semra, **Elif**'e **onun** anahtarlarını vermiş. (cf. (14))
'Semra gave *Elif her/his* keys.' (Most likely intended referent of 'her/his' is *Elif* or any person other than *Semra*.)

If it is intended that the possessive-marked noun phrase refer to the subject within the same clause (*Semra* in (84)), then *onun* is omitted. In such cases the possessive suffix can refer to any 3rd person in the clause or to some previously mentioned person:

(85) **Semra** anahtarlarını kaybetmiş.
'Apparently, *Semra* lost *her* keys.' (Most likely intended referent of 'her' is *Semra*.)

(86) **Semra, Elif**'e anahtarlarını vermiş. (cf. (14))
'Apparently, *Semra* gave *Elif her/his* keys.' (Most likely intended referents of 'her' are either *Semra* or *Elif*.)

A genitive-marked pronoun is used in the following circumstances:

a. When the possessed entity is compared with something else:

(87) *Burası* **bizim evimiz**den daha sıcak.
'It's warmer *here* than [in] *our house*.'

(88) Zeki'nin arabası evin önündeymiş. **Senin** arabanı garaja soktum.
'Zeki's car is in front of the house. I put *your* car in the garage.'

b. When the possessor is focused:

(89) Ahmet bugün çok sevinçli. Öğretmen en çok **oNUN** yazısını beğenmiş.
'Ahmet is very happy today. It seems the teacher liked *his* essay best.'

c. In the opening sentence of a conversation or a sentence in which the speaker introduces a new topic of discussion:

(90) Ayşe, **benim** anahtarım nerede?
'Ayşe, where's *my* key?'

(91) **Bizim** başka bir haberimiz daha var.
'*We*'ve got another piece of news, too.'

18.2 Demonstrative pronouns: *bu*, 'this (one)' *şu* 'this/that (one)', *o* 'that (one)'

The demonstrative pronouns are derived from the demonstrative determiners (15.6.2 (i)):

bu	'this (one)'	*bunlar*	'these'
şu	'this (one)', 'that (one)'	*şunlar*	'these', 'those'
o	'that (one)'	*onlar*	'those'

Note that the plural forms contain 'n' before the plural suffix. Similarly, when singular demonstrative pronouns are inflected for case, the case markers are preceded by 'n', as in *bunda* 'on/in this one', *şunu* 'that one (ACC)', *ona* 'to that one' (6.2, 8.1.3).

The difference between *bu*, *şu* and *o* is, from one point of view, a gradation in proximity. *Bu* refers to closer objects and *o* refers to ones that are furthest away. However, a major difference between *şu* and the others is that while *bu* and *o* usually refer to objects mentioned before, the referent of *şu* is almost always something to which the speaker is drawing attention for the first time. *şu* is therefore sometimes accompanied by an ostensive gesture, either looking in the direction of the item in question or pointing to it. In the following examples, the usage of *şu* implies that the referent, e.g. a particular bowl, has not been under discussion before this point, whereas in the case of *bu* there is no such implication.

(92) Meyvaları **şuna** koyalım.
'Let's put the fruit in *this one*.'

(93) Meyvaları **buna** koyalım.
'Let's put the fruit in *this one*.'

Similarly, the referent of *şu* can be a statement that the speaker is about to make. In the following examples, *bu* and *şu* are not interchangeable; *bu* stands for a statement that has just been made, whereas the referent of *şu* is to follow.

(94) On dakika sonra dükkanlar kapanıyor ve evde kahve yok. En önemli sorun **bu**.
'The shops close in ten minutes and there's no coffee in the house. *This* is the most urgent problem.'

(95) En önemli sorun **şu**: on dakika sonra dükkanlar kapanıyor ve evde kahve yok.
'The most urgent problem is *this*: the shops close in ten minutes and there's no coffee in the house.'

o is used when a concrete item referred to is not within the visual field of the speaker or the addressee(s), but it has been previously mentioned. Both *o* and *bu* can be used when an object which is in the shared context of the discourse participants is topicalized (23.3.3):

(96) Adamın şapkasının rengini hatırlıyor musun? İşte **o/bu**, filmde çok önemli bir ayrıntıydı.
'Do you remember the colour of the man's hat? Now *that* was a very significant detail in the film.'

şu ki and *o ki* can occur following a pronominal relative clause (25.3):

(97) Dediğim **şu ki**, bu tip boyalar ancak dış yüzeylerde kullanılabiliyor.
'What I'm saying is, these types of paint can only be used on exterior surfaces.'
(lit. 'What I'm saying is *this*, *that* these types...')

(98) Görünen **o ki**, dünyanın iklimi değişiyor.
'It seems that the world's climate is changing.'

For the demonstrative adverbials, adverbs of degree and determiners derived from *bu/şu/o* (i.e. *böyle/şöyle/öyle*), see 16.4.3 (vi), 16.5, and (15.6.1 (iv), respectively.

18.3 Locative and directional pronouns

18.3.1 Locative pronouns: bura- 'here', şura- 'here', 'over there' and ora- 'there'

Locative pronouns are derived from *bu/şu/o* and display similar differentiating characteristics in terms of their reference (18.2).

Like the question word *nere-* 'where' (19.2.1.3), *bura-* 'here', *şura-* 'here', 'over there' and *ora-* 'there' are used in their bare form in colloquial contexts or in regional dialects. Otherwise, they must have either a case suffix or a possessive suffix (or both) and either of these may be preceded by the plural suffix: *buraya* '(to) here' or *adan* 'from there', *şuran* 'this part of you', *şuramın* 'of this part of me', *buralarda* 'around here' (14.3.1.2 (viii)). The oblique-case-marked forms without possessive suffixes function adverbially (16.4.2 (95)–(96)).

The forms *burası* 'this place', *şurası* 'this place', 'that place over there' and *orası* 'that place (already mentioned)' are formed with the 3rd person possessive suffix *-(s)I* (8.1.2). Like their interrogative counterpart *neresi* 'what place' (19.2.1.3), they function as subjects:

(99) **Burası** çok kalabalık.
  '[It] is very crowded *here*.'

(100) **Şurası** dinlenmek için ideal bir yer.
  '*That (place over there)* is an ideal place to rest.'

The accusative and genitive forms *burasını(n)/şurasını(n)/orasını(n)* can be used instead of *burayı/buranın, şurayı/şuranın* and *orayı/oranın*:

(101) **Bura-sın-ı** çok sevdim, **bura-da** kalalım.
  here-3SG.POSS-ACC   here-LOC
  'I like [it] *here*, let's stay *here*.'

bura-/şura-/ora- can also occur with the 1st and 2nd person possessive markers:

(102) **Şuranız**a bir düğme daha lazım.
  'You need another button *here* (= on this part of you).'

Additionally, they can be modified by a genitive-marked noun phrase:

(103) *Filmin* **orası** çok önemliydi.
  '*That part of the film* was very important.'

18.3.2 Directional pronouns

Directional pronouns are formed by the attachment of the 3rd person possessive marker *-(s)I* (8.1.2) to directional adverbials of place, such as *dışarı* 'out', 'outside' and *aşağı* 'down', 'downstairs' (16.4.2):

(104) **Aşağısı** çok dağınık.
  '*It*'s very untidy *downstairs*.'

When these forms are used as direct objects, accusative case marking is obligatory, but the possessive marker may be omitted:

(105) Alıcılar **içeri-yi/içeri-sin-i** görmedi.
      inside-ACC/inside-3SG.POSS-ACC
  'The buyers haven't seen *inside* yet.'

The form *ötesi* 'the far side' is usually used with a modifier:

(106) **Köyün ötesinde** bir dere var.
'There is a stream *beyond the village*.'

The usage of *beri* (and forms derived from it, e.g. *beriki* 'the other (one) (nearby)') is confined to provincial dialects. For *öteki* 'the other (one)', see 18.5.

18.4 Pronominalized adjectives, numerals and determiners

The possessive markers (8.1.2) are the main device used for creating pronouns from a range of other grammatical categories. The pronouns are listed here in the 3rd person singular possessive form, which is by far the most common form they are used in, although forms containing 1st, 2nd and 3rd person plural possessive markers are also possible. Note that an accusative case marker is obligatory when they are used as direct objects (see 14.3.3.2).

The possessive suffixes create pronominals from various categories:

(i) Pronominalized adjectives:
Adjectives ((7.1.1 (iii), 15.2), Chapter 14 (124)) can be used as stems creating pronominalized forms, e.g. *eskisi* 'the old one', *çirkini* 'an uglier version':

(107) Çamaşır makinası bozulmuş. **Yeni-sin-i** almamız lazım.
　　　　　　　　　　　　　　　new-3SG.POSS-ACC
'The washing machine has broken down. We have to get *a new one*.'

Simple adjectives can be used with any of the possessive suffixes, including the 1st and 2nd person singular forms (see also Chapter 14 (125)):

(108) Kızkardeşin senin şişman**ın**.
'Your sister is a plumper version *of you*.'

The pronominalized adjective can itself be modified (15.4.2–3), by the comparative *daha* or superlative *en*:

(109) Bunun (daha) büyü**ğü** yok mu?
'Isn't there *a larger one than this*?'

(110) En küçü**ğümüz** Teoman'dı.
'*The youngest of us* was Teoman.'

(ii) Pronominalized numerals:
Numerals (15.7) (with or without the enumerator *tane* or measure/type terms (15.8); see also 14.5.2–3) can also create pronominalized forms, e.g. *ikisi*

'two (of them)', *beş tanesi* 'five (of them)', *üç bardağı* 'three glasses (of it)'. Numerals cannot be used with the 3rd person plural possessive suffix.

(111) Bütün kalemler kayboldu sanmıştım ama **ikisi/iki tanesi** burada.
'I thought all the pencils were lost, but *two (of them)* are here.'

Note that the addition of *her* 'every' and/or the clitic *dA* (11.1.1.2) to pronominalized numerical expressions makes them definite. Thus, for example, *her ikisi* and *(her) ikisi de* mean 'both (of them)' (15.9.1).

(iii) Pronominalization involving the enumerator *tane* and measure/type terms:
The enumerator *tane* and measure/type terms (15.8) can be the base for pronominalized forms on the above pattern, but only with the 3rd person singular possessive suffix: *tanesi* 'each one (of...)', *şişesi* 'a bottle (of...)'.

(112) **Kilosunu** bin liradan satacaklar.
'They're going to sell it for a thousand liras *a kilogram*.'

Expressions consisting of a numeral followed by the enumerator *tane* or a measure term can be used pronominally without the addition of a possessive suffix. This usage is generally confined to inanimate referents:

(113) Çamaşır makinası bozulmuş. **Yeni bir tane** almamız lazım. (cf. (107))
'The washing machine has broken down. We must get *a new one*.'

(114) **İki kilo** versene.
'Give me *two kilograms*.'

(iv) Pronominalized determiners:
Most of the indefinite and definite determiners listed at 15.6.1–2 (see also 14.5.2–3) can be pronominalized by the addition of possessive suffixes. In their 3rd person singular forms these pronouns are *aynısı* 'the same (one)', *başkası* 'another (one)', *bazısı* 'some (of them)', *birçoğu* 'many (of them)', *bir bölümü/bir kısmı* 'some (of it/them)', *biri(si)* 'one (of them)' (for *biri(si)*, 'someone', see 18.6.1), 'one (of them)', *birkaçı* 'a few (of them)', *bu/şu/o/ne kadarı* 'this/that/how much (of it)', *bütünü* 'all of it', *çoğu* 'most (of them)', 'most people', *diğeri* 'the other (one)', *hangisi* 'which (one)', *herhangi biri(si)* 'any (one)', *hiçbiri(si)* 'none (of them)' (20.5.2), *ilki* 'the first (one)', *kaçı* 'how many (of them)', *kimisi* 'some (of them)', *ne kadarı* 'how much (of it)', *öteki(si)/öbürü/diğeri* 'the other (one)', *sonuncusu* 'the last (one)', *böylesi* 'this kind', 'this way'. Of these determiners, *birkaç, çok, hiçbir, kaç* and *ne kadar* (except when this latter is used with adjectives) cannot be used with the 3rd person plural possessive suffix.

(115) **Aynısını** istiyorum.
'I want *the same one*/[one of] *the same*.'

(116) **Bazılarımız** senin gibi düşünmüyor.
'*Some of us* wouldn't agree with you.'

(v) Pronominalization of the adverbial *hep* 'always':
This creates *hepsi* 'all (of it/them)'. (*hep* cannot be used with the 3rd person plural possessive suffix.)

(117) **Hepsini** katılımcılara mı vereceksiniz?
'Are you going to give *all of it/them* to the participants?'

(118) **Hepimiz** galaya davet edildik.
'*All of us* have been invited to the premier.'

For pronominalized relative clauses, see 25.3.

18.5 Pronominal expressions with *-ki*

The suffix *-ki* (8.1.4), which is used for forming attributive adjectives (15.3.6–7), has a pronominal function when used without a following noun phrase. This usage is possible only where the type of entity that is being talked about is obvious from the context:

(119) **Bahçe-de-ki-ler** yapraklarını dökmeye başladı. (cf. Chapter 15 (26))
garden-LOC-PRON-PL
'*The ones in the garden* have begun to shed their leaves.'

(120) **Bu sabahkinde** okudum.
'I read it *in this morning's (one)*.'

öteki(si)/öbürki(si) (the latter colloquial) are pronominal usages based on *öteki/öbür* 'the other' (15.6.2):

(121) **Öteki** size daha çok uydu galiba.
'*The other one* seemed to suit you better.'

In addition, *-ki* can attach to any genitive-marked noun phrase to form a possessive pronominal expression. Note that genitive-based *-ki* forms cannot be used adjectivally.

(122) Yeni bir bilgisayar almam gerek. **Benimki** iyi çalışmıyor.
'I have to buy a new computer. *Mine* isn't working properly.'

(123) Ayşe'nin arabası **Ahmet'inkiyle** karşılaştırılınca çok yeni duruyor.
'Ayşe's car looks very new when compared *to Ahmet's*.'

When such possessive pronominal expressions are used as predicates, they identify the subject as an entity among similar entities that are in a possessed relation to the subject complement:

(124) Bu palto **Ahmet'in**.
'This coat is *Ahmet's*.'

(125) Bu palto **Ahmet'inki**.
'This coat is *the one that is Ahmet's*.'

The first sentence simply indicates who the coat belongs to. The second one indicates that among the possible coats that are in question, this particular one is Ahmet's.

18.6 Other pronominal expressions

18.6.1 Pronominal quantifiers

The pronominal quantifiers of Turkish are *herkes* 'everyone', *her şey* 'everything', *biri(si)* 'someone' and *bir şey* 'something', 'anything', *bu/şu/o/ne kadar* 'this much', 'that much', 'so much', 'how much'. These can be inflected for case and, with the exception of *herkes*, for person as well.

(126) Artık otobüslerde **herkesten** para alıyorlar, genç olsun, yaşlı olsun.
'Nowadays they charge *everyone* on buses, whether they are young or old.'

(127) Yanına **bu kadarını** mı aldın?
'Have you taken only this much (of it) with you?'

biri is a colloquial version of *birisi*:

(128) **Biri(si)ni** mi arıyorsun?
'Are you looking for *someone*?'

bir şey 'something', 'anything' can be used in the singular or in the plural form (14.3.1.1 (iii)) with both affirmative and negative predicates:

(129) Şu sıralar ilginç **bir şey/bir şeyler** okumuyor musun?
'Aren't you reading *anything* interesting these days?'

(130) Söyleyecek **bir şeyim** yok
'I have *nothing* to say.'

(131) Sabahtan beri **bir şey-ler-im-i** arıyorum ama bulamıyorum.
        something-PL-1SG.POSS-ACC
'I've been looking for *some things of mine* all day.'

The expressions *kimse* 'no one', 'anyone', *hiç kimse* 'no one', *hiçbiri(si)* 'none (of them)', *hiçbir şey* 'nothing' are discussed in 20.5.1–3.

For other examples, see Chapter 14 (141), (146).

18.6.2 insan 'one'

insan 'person, human being' is used pronominally like the English generic pronoun 'one':

(132) **İnsan** bazen [hiçbir şey bilmediğin]-i sanıyor.
      'Sometimes *one* thinks [one doesn't know anything].'

(133) Bazı günler her şey zor geliyor **insana**.
      'Some days everything seems to be difficult (*for one*).'

18.6.3 şey

şey, literally 'thing', is probably one of the most commonly used expressions in colloquial Turkish, replacing anything from a word to a whole clause. It is used where the speaker cannot immediately call to mind the appropriate expression for what s/he intends to say. What it replaces may or may not follow in the conversation, depending on whether its referent is clear enough from the context.

(134) Ay arabanın **şeyini** kırmışlar!
      'Oh God, they've broken the car's *thingumajig!*'

(135) **Şey** gibi olmasın ama, sana bir şey sormak istiyorum.
      'I would like to ask you something, without sounding as if...you know...'

(136) Ziya'nın lafları biraz **şeysiz** kaçtı.
      'Ziya's words lacked a bit of, how shall I put it...'

It can also be used as a filler between sentences or as a gradual start to a conversation, sometimes as a means of introducing a topic that the speaker finds difficult or embarrassing to broach.

(137) **Şey**...Biraz konuşmamız lazım.
      'Uhmmm...we have to talk a bit.'

Chapter 19
Questions

Questions in Turkish are formed either by the insertion of the question clitic *mI* which forms **yes/no questions** (19.1.1) and **alternative questions** (19.1.2), or by using a **wh-phrase** such as *ne zaman* 'when', *kim* 'who' or *hangi* 'which' (19.2).

(1) Bahçeye ağaç dikecekler **mi**?
    'Will they plant trees in the garden?'

(2) Otobüs durağı **nerede**?
    '*Where* is the bus stop?'

Echo questions, questions which seek clarification or express surprise, are discussed in 19.3. 19.4 focuses on how phrases in subordinate clauses may be questioned, 19.5 discusses **modal adverbs** that are used in questions, and 19.6 explains **rhetorical questions**. **Indirect questions** (questions in the form of noun clauses) are discussed in 24.4.3.2 and speculative conditional questions introduced by *ya* in 28.3.1.1 (vii).

19.1 Questions with *mI*

The clitic *mI* is unstressable and forms yes/no questions and alternative questions. The phonological properties of *mI* and its location within a predicate are described in 11.1.1.5. Sentence stress usually occurs immediately before *mI* unless there are other factors affecting stress in the sentence (19.1.5). The exact position of stress generated by *mI* in combination with unstressable suffixes and clitics is discussed in 11.2.

19.1.1 Yes/no questions

Yes/no questions are formed by inserting *mI* after a sentence or a phrase, or in some cases, within a phrase. There are two types of yes/no question: direct questions and tag questions.

19.1.1.1 Direct yes/no questions

In direct yes/no questions where the entirety of a proposition (i.e. the content of a sentence) is questioned, the clitic *mI* attaches to the predicate. Its exact position at the end of or within the predicate depends on the specific form of the predicate (11.1.1.5):

(3) Kedi-ler iki konserve-yi de **bitir-miş-ler *mi*?**
cat-PL two can-ACC both finish-EV/PF-3PL INT
'*Have* the cats *finished* both tins?'

(4) Bugün **evde *misin*?**
'*Are you at home* today?'

(5) Pervin o sırada **çalışıyor *muydu*?**
'*Was* Pervin *working* at that point?'

(6) Ay sonunda projeyi **tamamlamış olacaklar *mı*?**
'*Will they have completed* the project by the end of the month?'

(7) Nuri sana **yardım etti *mi*?**
'*Did* Nuri *help* you?'

mI can also attach to a phrase within the sentence, with effects that are described in 19.1.4. A phrase to which *mI* is attached generally occurs just before the predicate. However, like other focused phrases (23.3.1), a *mI*- phrase can also occur in other positions, as long as it is not placed after the predicate:

(8) Zehra Londra-ya **eylül-de mi** gid-ecek?
Zehra London-DAT September-LOC INT go-FUT
'Is Zehra going to London in *SEPTEMBER*?'

(9) Zehra **eylülde mi** Londra'ya gidecek?
'Is Zehra going to London in *SEPTEMBER*?'

The intonation of questions with *mI* usually has a high rise just before *mI*, followed by falling intonation (5.1 (ii)), whether *mI* is placed at the end of the sentence or not:

(10) Saatini ileri alDIN **mı**?
'Have you put your watch forward?'

(11) BabasıNI **mı** özlemiş Hasan?
'Is Hasan missing his father?'

In questions where *mI* is placed at the end, there is an alternative intonation pattern used by some speakers. The intonation pattern of these sentences, namely a fall after the stressed phrase, followed by another fall and then rising intonation at the end (5.1 (iii)), is somewhat similar to that of wh-questions (19.2) and *mI* questions expressing disbelief (19.1.4 (iii)):

(12) Sorularını   HOcana sor-du-n **mu**?
'Well then, have you asked your professor your questions?'

There are other cases where questions with *mI* do not end with falling intonation:

(i) Questions where *mI* is used for expressing surprise or disbelief (19.1.4 (iii))
(ii) Questions where *mI* occurs with another stressed phrase (19.1.5)
(iii) Questions where *mI* occurs with a wh-phrase (echo questions, 19.3)

19.1.1.2 Tag questions

A tag question is a question that is annexed to a statement and is used to seek confirmation of that statement. There are two forms of tag question:

(i) *değil mi*, which is a combination of the negative word *değil* 'not' (20.2) and *mI*
(ii) *öyle mi*, which is a combination of the demonstrative adverbial *öyle* 'like that' (16.4.3) and *mI*

Both forms can be tagged to affirmative or negative predicates which are verbal or nominal.

(13) Tiyatroya gitmeden önce

yer ayır-t-ma-mış-tı-n, *değil mi*?
reserve-CAUS-NEG-EV/PF-P.COP-2SG not INT

'You hadn't reserved seats before going to the theatre, *had you*?'

(14) Esra, **Handan-ın abla-sı-ymış**, *öyle mi*?
  Handan-GEN elder.sister-3SG.POSS-EV.COP thus INT
  'So Esra is Handan's elder sister, *is that right*?'

Questions with *değil mi* are unmarked tag questions, corresponding to 'isn't it', 'can you', etc. in English. This question type is used when the speaker seeks corroboration of a statement that s/he believes to be true.

(15) Cemal bugün okul-a git-me-di, **değil mi**?
  Cemal today school-DAT go-NEG-PF not INT
  'Cemal didn't go to school today, *did he*?'

Tag questions with *öyle mi* follow a much more tentative assertion, embodying information newly acquired by the speaker or information that contradicts the speaker's previous assumption. *öyle mi* can also be used with the discourse connective *demek (ki)* 'so' which expresses an inference (28.3.7).

(16) Demek (ki) Cemal bugün okula gitmedi, **öyle mi**?
  '*So,* Cemal didn't go to school today then?'

In (15) the speaker assumes that Cemal hasn't gone to school. In (16), on the other hand, the speaker voices surprise at the possibility of Cemal not having gone to school, implying an expectation that he would have done so. *öyle mi* can be used on its own as a response to new information, especially where this has come as a surprise:

(17) A. Bu yaz çok yağmur yağacakmış.
  'Apparently, there is going to be a lot of rain this summer.'

  B. **Öyle mi**?
  '*Really*?'

Since *değil* is the standard form for negating the linking type of nominal sentence (20.2 and 12.1.1.2), sentences with the sequence *değil + mi* are potentially ambiguous between a direct yes/no question with a negative nominal predicate (18) and a tag question following an affirmative nominal predicate (19). In the written language, only the latter has a comma before *değil mi*. In the spoken language, these two sentences have different intonation patterns. A direct yes/no question has one intonational phrase: a high rise followed by a fall (5.1 (ii)):

                                                                  ↗ ↘
(18) Tiyatroya gitmeden önce yer ayırtmak lazım **deĞİL mi**?
                  necessary not INT
  '*Isn't it* necessary to reserve seats before going to the theatre?'

A sentence containing a tag question has two intonational phrases, sometimes separated by a pause before *değil*. The first intonational phrase has a slight rise followed by a fall (the pattern for statements (5.1 (i))) and the second one, consisting just of the tag question, has a high rise followed by a fall:

(19) Tiyatroya gitmeden önce yer ayırtMAK lazım, **deĞİL mi**?
                 necessary not INT
   'It's necessary to reserve seats before going to the theatre, *isn't it*?'

öyle and *değil mi* can be used together as a reinforced form of *değil mi* (i.e. *öyle değil mi*):

(20) Ağaçlara baharda aşı yapılmadı, **öyle değil mi**?
   'The trees weren't injected in spring, *were they*?'

19.1.2 Alternative questions

These are questions which present two or more alternatives, equivalent to questions with 'or' in English. The clitic *mI* is placed after each of the alternatives presented, which can optionally be connected by *yoksa* 'or' (28.3.3.1). The phrases *mI* can attach to are described in 19.1.3.

Where they are predicates, the second may simply be the negation of the first, as in (21)–(22):

(21) Cemal okula **git-ti *mi***, (yoksa) **git-me-di *mi***?
       go-PF INT (or) go-NEG-PF INT
   'Did Cemal go to school or not?'

(22) Bu hastanede ameliyathane **var *mı***, (yoksa) **yok *mu***?
              existent INT (or) non-existent INT
   'Is there an operating theatre in this hospital or not?'

In alternative questions, each alternative has a rise followed by a fall, the second one usually with a higher rise, and sometimes with a rise-fall in the juncture point between the two alternatives:

(23) Tosca-yı VERdi mi yazmışTI (yoksa) PucCİni mi?
   Tosca-ACC Verdi INT compose-EV/PF-P.COP (or) Puccini INT
   'Did Verdi or Puccini compose Tosca?'

19.1.3 Positions for mI other than the end of the sentence

In addition to attaching to predicates, *mI* can attach to subjects, objects and adverbials:

(24) Yalnız başına burada ***kitap* mı** okuyordun?
                           book INT
     'Were you reading a book here all alone?'

(25) ***Kedi-den* mi** korkuyorsun yoksa?
     cat-ABL INT
     'Are you afraid of cats, then?'

The position of the clitic *mI* in a noun phrase is fixed. It attaches to the head of the phrase even when what is being questioned is one of the modifying constituents of that phrase:

(26) a. {**İki orta yaşlı adAM**} *mı* çal-mış araba-yı?
        two middle aged man INT steal-EV/PF car-ACC
        'Did *two middle-aged MEN* steal the car?'

     b. {**İKİ orta yaşlı adam**} *mı* çalmış arabayı?
        'Did *TWO middle-aged men* steal the car?'

It is the location of stress that indicates whether it is the entire noun phrase, as in (25a), or some particular part of it, as in (25b), that is questioned.

The unmarked position for *mI* in other types of phrase and construction is at the end of those particular phrases or constructions. This applies to postpositional phrases, genitive-possessive constructions, and partitive constructions, as well as to compound verbs with free auxiliaries (13.3.1.2) and nominal-verb compounds (13.3.2):

(27) {***Murat-ın ev-i***} mi satılmış?
     Murat-GEN house-3SG.POSS INT
     'Has *Murat's house* been sold?'

However, *mI* can also attach to the constituents in these phrases other than the head:

(28) {***Murat' ın*** **mı**} evi} satılmış?
     'Is it *Murat's* house that has been sold?'

(29) Sen şimdi o filmi **gör-müş** *mü* **ol-du-n**?
                                   see-EV/PF INT BE-PF-2SG
     'Do you consider yourself as having seen that film now?'

(30) Sana **yardım** *mı* **et-ti** o adam?
         help INT make-PF
     'Did that man *help* you?'

It can also attach to the modifier in an adjectival or adverbial construction:

(31) **Çok *mu* güzel** bir adam, bu sözünü ettiğin?
very INT beautiful a man
'Is he a *really* beautiful man, this one you're talking about?'

(32) Umduğundan **daha da *mı* hızlı** yüzdün?
'Did you swim *even* fast*er* than you expected?'

In addition, *mI* can attach to subordinate clauses (12.3) or to the constituents inside them:

(33) a. Aynur [**Zehra-yla buluş-tuk-tan sonra**] *mı* çocuk-lar-ı
Aynur Zehra-COM meet-CV.ABL after INT child-PL-ACC

okul-dan al-dı?
school-ABL pick.up-PF

'Was it [*after meeting Zehra*] that Aynur picked up the children?'

b. Aynur [**Zehra'yla *mı*** buluşmadan önce] çocukları okuldan aldı?
'Was it [before meeting *Zehra*] that Aynur picked up the children?'

19.1.4 The effect of placing mI after a particular phrase

The placement of *mI* after a particular phrase serves three different purposes. One of these is to narrow down the questioned part of a proposition and thus to question only a particular phrase within a sentence. Alternatively, *mI* can be placed after a particular phrase to question the whole proposition. Finally, it can be used as an expression of surprise at a situation that has just come to the attention of the speaker.

(i) Using *mI* for questioning a specific part of a proposition:
One of the reasons why *mI* is inserted after a phrase is to focus a particular part of a proposition, thereby making it the specific target of the question. This generally implies that the information in the remainder of the sentence is assumed by the speaker to be already in the knowledge base shared between him/her and the addressee(s).

(34) ***Ahmet* mi** para-lar-ı ev-de unut-muş?
Ahmet INT money-PL-ACC house-LOC forget-EV/PF
'Was it *Ahmet* who left the money at home?'

(35) Banka-ya *sabah-leyin* **mi** gid-ecek-sin?
bank-DAT morning-ADV INT go-FUT-2SG
'Will you be going to the bank *in the morning*?'

The intonation of these sentences is a high rise followed by a fall (5.1 (ii)), which is typical of direct yes/no questions (19.1.1.1):

(36) Kitabı AhmeT'E **mi** verdin?
'Is it Ahmet that you've given the book to?'

(ii) Using *mI* immediately before the predicate to question the whole proposition: Placing *mI* after a particular phrase (and immediately before the predicate) can also serve the purpose of questioning the whole proposition:

(37) Nermin pazar-a **mı** git-miş?
Nermin market-DAT INT go-EV/PF
'Has Nermin gone to the market?'

As noted in 19.1.1.1, questioning the whole proposition is also done by means of placing *mI* after the predicate:

(38) Nermin pazara gitmiş **mi**?
'Has Nermin gone to the market?'

However, although both of these questions involve the whole proposition, they cannot be used in the same context. Questions that have the structure of (37) are used when the speaker has an assumption about the situation s/he is asking about, usually because there are non-linguistic clues (visual or perceptible by other senses) available to him/her. Those like (38), on the other hand, are out-of-the-blue questions, where the speaker has no assumptions about the situation. In the examples above, a speaker can use (37) upon seeing Nermin in a coat or with a market bag, a context which is unsuitable for (38). (37) is used in contexts where a speaker simply wants to know if Nermin has been to the market, a context in which (38) cannot be used.

The same phenomenon occurs in nominal sentences as well:

(39) a. Bir sıkıntın **mı** var?
'Are you worried about something?'

b. Bir sıkıntın var **mı**?
'Do you have any troubles?'

(iii) Using *mI* as an expression of surprise or disbelief:
mI can be placed after a particular constituent within a clause to highlight surprise or disbelief to form an echo question (19.3 (ii)). In this case, the constituent just before *mI* is not the target of the question. Instead, the validity of the whole proposition is questioned. Such sentences have an intonation pattern similar to wh-questions (19.2), which is a slight rise followed by a fall-rise (5.1 (iii)), but they usually start with a higher pitch than wh-questions. The phrase that *mI* is attached to usually occurs just before the predicate:

(40) Kitabı AhmeT'E **mi** verdin?
'You GAVE the BOOK to AHMET?'

19.1.5 Yes/no questions in contrastive contexts

In such questions, *mI* attaches to the predicate and the whole proposition is questioned:

(41) Peki, sen hiç oPEra-ya git-ti-n **mi**?
well.then you ever opera-DAT go-PF-2SG INT
'Well then, have you ever been to the OPERA?'

Although these sentences have one of the intonation patterns used by some speakers in yes/no questions (19.1.1.1), highlighting a particular constituent by stressing it in such sentences can serve to contrast it with another (previously mentioned) constituent. For example, (41) could be uttered after someone has mentioned that they have never been to the theatre.

19.2 Wh-questions

Wh-questions are formed by using a question phrase (a wh-phrase) such as *kim* 'who', *nerede* 'where', etc. The wh-phrases in Turkish are the following:

kim	'who'
ne	'what'
hangi	'which'
nere-	'where'
hani	'where' (colloquial)
ne zaman	'when'

kaç	'how many', 'what time'
ne kadar	'how much'
nasıl	'how'
niye	'why'
neden	'why'
niçin	'why'

Wh-phrases are normally stressed, whether they are in the main clause or a subordinate clause. The only exception to this is when they occur with another stressed constituent (19.2.3). The intonation pattern of wh-questions is a slight rise followed by a fall-rise (5.1 (iii)).

(42) **HAN**gi tablo-yu müze-ye bağışla-mak ist-iyor-sun?
which painting-ACC museum-DAT donate-VN want-IMPF-2SG
'*Which* painting do you want to donate to the museum?'

(43) Ev-e **NE zaman** gid-ecek-sin?
home-DAT when go-FUT-2SG
'*When* will you be going home?'

19.2.1 Wh-phrases

19.2.1.1 kim 'who'

kim is used in questions where the target of the question is a person. It can combine with all the inflectional suffixes that attach to nouns (8.1, 14.3):

(44) Resimleri **kim** değerlendirecek?
'*Who* will evaluate the paintings?'

(45) Bu hediyeyi **kim-den** aldın?
who-ABL
'*Who* did you get this gift *from*?'

kim obligatorily has accusative case marking when it functions as a direct object (22.1):

(46) Nuri **kim-i** görmüş?
who-ACC
'*Who(m)* did Nuri see?'

kim can have plural marking when the speaker knows or assumes that more than one person (or a type of person) is involved:

(47) En çok **kim-ler-in çocuk-lar-ı** okulda başarılı oluyormuş?
       who-PL-GEN child-PL-3SG.POSS
       '*Whose children* (the children of what type of people) are the most successful at school?'

When *kim* combines with the comitative/instrumental marker *-(y)lA/ile*, the result is *kiminle* 'with whom' (8.1.4). However, *kimle* is also used in colloquial speech:

(48) En çok **kim-(in)-le** şakalaşmayı seviyorsun?
       who-(GEN)-COM
       '*Who* do you most like to fool around *with*?'

kim can also combine with the copula, the copular markers and *-DIr* (8.3.3), (19.2.2.1).

19.2.1.2 ne 'what'

ne is used in questions where the target is an inanimate object, a substance or an abstract concept. It can combine with all the inflectional suffixes that attach to nominals (8.1, 14.3):

(49) Bu kutunun içinde **ne-ler** var?
       what-PL
       '*What's* in this box?'
       (lit. 'What things are…')

(50) Serap Almanya'ya **ne-yle** gidiyor?
       what-INS
       '*How* (= by what means) is Serap going to Germany?'

ne is also used when the modifier in a *-sI* compound is the target of a question:

(51) O adam *ne* **doktor-u**?
       that man what doctor-NCM
       'What is the specialization of that doctor?'
       (lit. '*What sort of doctor* is that man?')

When used as a direct object, the non-case-marked *ne* indicates that the speaker has no preconceptions about the answer, whereas the accusative-case-marked *neyi* implies that the speaker has a number of items in mind and expects the answer to refer to one of those items:

(52) **Ne** istiyorsun?
 '*What* do you want?'

(53) **Neyi** istiyorsun?
 '*What* do you want?'

neli, nesiz
ne can combine with the suffixes *-lI* 'with' and *-sIz* 'without' (7.2.2.2) to form adjectives:

(54) **Ne-li** dondurma sev-er-sin?
 what-ADJ ice.cream like-AOR-2SG
 '*What kind* of ice cream do you like?'

It can also combine with the suffix *-CI* (7.2.2.2), most typically in its occupational sense and much less commonly (in specific contexts) denoting an ideology:

(55) Baba-sı **ne-ci**?
 father-3SG.POSS what-DER
 '*What* is the *occupation/ideology* of his/her father?'

nesi, neyi
nesi is the more commonly used 3rd person possessive form of *ne*. *neyi* (6.2 (iii)) is slightly dated:

(56) Akdeniz-in **ne-si/ney-i** insanları çekiyor?
 Mediterranean-GEN what-3SG.POSS
 '*What* is it *about* the Mediterranean that attracts people?'

ne and the idiom *ne biçim* 'what kind of...' can also be use in exclamations (12.4 (iv)).

ne can also combine with the copula, the copular markers and *-DIr* (8.3.3), (19.2.2.1).

19.2.1.3 nere- 'where'

The word *nere-* is used in its bare form only in non-standard dialects of Turkish. In standard Turkish, it is always inflected and it can combine with all the inflectional suffixes that attach to nouns (8.1, 14.3):

(57) Elbise-ler-in-i **nere-den** al-dı-n?
 clothes-PL-2SG.POSS-ACC where-ABL buy-PF-2SG
 '*Where* did you buy your clothes *from*?'

(58) En çok **nere-ler-i** görmek istiyorsun?
 where-PL-ACC
 '*What places* do you most want to see most?'

(59) İğne-yi **nere-n-den** yap-acak-lar?
 injection-ACC where-2SG.POSS-ABL make-FUT-3PL
 'On what part of you are they going to do the injection?'
 (lit. '*Where on you*...?').

nerede, neresi

nerede (often pronounced [næɹdɛ]) is used when inquiring about the location of a person or object:

(60) Patagonya **nere-de**?
 where-LOC
 '*Where is* Patagonia?'

neresi is the form used when inquiring about a place itself, as opposed to the location of a particular person or object:

(61) Bura-sı **nere-si**?
 here-3SG.POSS where-3SG.POSS
 '*Where* are we?'
 (lit. '*What place* is this?')

neresi seeks as an answer a property or a characteristic that describes a location rather than the whereabouts of a place. For example, the response to a question like (62) would be a remark which contains a characteristic of Patagonia, such as *Arjantin'in güneyinde yarı kurak bir plato* '[It is] a semi-arid plateau in southern Argentina':

(62) Patagonya **nere-si**?
 where-3SG.POSS
 '*What and where* is Patagonia?'

The response to (60), on the other hand, is *Arjantin'de* 'In Argentina'.
 The inflected forms *nere-* can combine with with the copula, the copular markers and *-DIr* (8.3.3), (19.2.2.1).

19.2.1.4 *hangi* 'which'

hangi 'which' (15.6.1 (iii)) modifies a noun phrase:

(63) Ahmet **hangi doktora** güveniyor?
'*Which* doctor does Ahmet trust?'

A noun phrase containing *hangi* is always marked with the accusative case when it is the direct object:

(64) **Hangi *kitab-ı*** satın alacaksın?
which book-ACC
'*Which* book will you buy?'

Like most determiners, *hangi* can be pronominalized (18.4) by the addition of a possessive suffix:

(65) Kazanan **hangisi**ydi?
'*Which of them* (was the one who) won?'

(66) **Hangi-ler-iniz-den** para istediler?
which-PL-2PL.POSS-ABL
'*From which (ones) of you* did they ask for money?'

hangi can be used with an ablative- or genitive-marked modifier (14.5.2–3), including the ablative-marked forms of *iç-* or *ara-* 'among' (17.3.1.3 (i)). It follows the same rules as other subjects containing a pronominalized determiner (12.2.2.2):

(67) (***Asistanlardan***) **hangisi** bugün görevli?
'*Which one (of the assistants)* is on duty today?'

(68) ***İçinizden/aranızdan*** **hangisi** bu işte gönüllü olarak çalışmak istiyor(sunuz)?
'*Which one among you* would like to work as a volunteer?'

The pronominalized form of *hangi* can combine with the copula, the copular markers and *-DIr* (8.3.3), (19.2.2.1).

19.2.1.5 *kaç* 'how many'

kaç (15.6.1) is used for inquiring about the number of entities denoted by a noun phrase. It occupies the position of a numeral in a noun phrase (15.9.2) and can be used with the enumerator *tane* and measure terms such as *avuç* '(a) handful (of)' (15.8). The noun that follows never has plural marking (14.3.1.1 (ii)).

(69) Günde **kaç (tane) çay** içiyorsun?
'*How many [cups of] tea* do you drink a day?'

(70) Okula bu yıl **kaç kişi** alacaksınız?
'*How many people* will you admit to the school this year?'

As a pronoun (suffixed with a possessive marker (18.4 (iv)) it can occur with modifiers, which are usually ablative-marked, but can also be genitive-marked (14.5.2–3):

(71) **Öğrencilerden kaçı** derse girmemiş?
'*How many of the students* appear to have been absent?'

As in the case of *hangi* above, the modifier in the partitive construction can be an ablative-marked phrase based on *iç-* or *ara-* 'among' (17.3.1.3):

(72) **İçinizden kaçı** araba kullanmayı biliyor?
'*How many of you* know how to drive?'

kaç is also used when asking about clock time (16.4.1.1):

(73) Saat **kaç**?
'What time is it?'

(74) Oyun **kaçta** başlıyor?
'What time does the play start?'

(75) **Kaçla kaç** arasında arayayım seni?
'Between what [times] should I call you?'

In questions about a person's age, *kaç* is the modifier in a *-sI* compound (10.2, 15.3.2):

(76) O çocuk **kaç** yaşında?
'How old is that child?'

kaç can combine with the copula, the copular markers and *-DIr* (8.3.3), (19.2.2.1).

19.2.1.6 ne kadar 'how much'

ne kadar 'how much' is used for asking about the following:

(i) The quantity of a particular (usually uncountable) inanimate entity:

(77) Muhallebiye **ne kadar şeker** koyulur?
'*How much sugar* is used in milk pudding?'

(78) Bundan **ne kadar** istiyorsun?
'*How much* of this do you want?'

(ii) The degree to which a particular adjective or adverb is applicable:

(79) Yeni bürosu acaba **ne kadar** *büyük*?
'*How big*, I wonder, is his/her new office?'

(80) Bu araba **ne kadar** *hızlı* gider?
'*How fast* does this car go?'

(iii) The price of an item:

(81) Bu elbise **ne kadar**?
'*How much* is this dress?'

(iv) The quantity of time or space involved in a particular action, in which case it is used adverbially:

(82) Bu sabah **ne kadar** koştun?
'*How long/how far* did you run this morning?'

(83) Ameliyat **ne kadar** sürecek?
'*How long* will the operation last?'

As the complement of temporal postpositions such as *içinde/zarfında* 'within', *önce* 'before' and *sonra* 'after' (16.4.1.1), *ne kadar* is usually used with *zaman* 'time' to inquire about the amount of time associated with a particular event:

(84) Yemeğin altını, kaynadıktan **ne kadar (zaman) sonra** kapatıyorsunuz?
'*How long after* the food comes to the boil do you turn off the heat?'

(85) *Ne kadar* **(zaman)dır** Londra'da oturuyorsunuz?
'*How long* have you been living in London?'

With the addition of a 3rd person possessive suffix, the pronominalized form *ne kadarı* (18.4 (iv)) can be used with a genitive-marked modifier (14.5.3):

(86) **İş-in** *ne kadar-ın-ı* Zeynep'e bırakacaksın?
job-GEN how.much-3SG.POSS-ACC
'*How much of the job* will you leave to Zeynep?'

ne kadar can also combine with the copula, the copular markers and *-DIr* (8.3.3), (19.2.2.1), and sentences with *ne kadar* can be used as exclamations (12.4 (iv)).

19.2.1.7 ne zaman 'when'

ne zaman is used for questioning the time of an event.

(87) **Ne zaman** eve gidiyorsun?
'*When* are you going home?'

It also occurs in postpositional phrases where the complement is a time expression:

(88) *Ne zamandan* **beri** sigara içiyorsun?
'*Since when* have you been smoking?'

(89) *Ne zamana* **kadar** bekleyeyim?
'*When* shall I wait *till*?'

19.2.1.8 neden, niye, niçin 'why'

neden, *niye* and *niçin* occur in questions which seek the reason or motive for an action or state of affairs:

(90) Kedilere **neden/niye/niçin** doğru dürüst yemek vermiyorsun?
'*Why* aren't you feeding the cats properly?'

19.2.1.9 nasıl 'how'

nasıl 'how' is used in questions which inquire about the manner in which an action is performed:

(91) Semra'nın evine **nasıl** gidiliyor?
'*How* does one go to Semra's house?'

(92) Bunu bana **nasıl** yapabildin?
'*How* could you do this to me?'

It can occur as a subject complement in linking sentences (12.1.1.2):

(93) **Nasıl**sın?
'*How* are you?'

It can also occur as a determiner (15.6.1 (iii)), usually with a following *bir*, but also with a plural noun phrase. In this usage, it can be replaced by *ne gibi* 'what kind of':

(94) **Nasıl/ne gibi bir ev**e taşınmak istiyorsunuz?
'*What kind of house* do you want to move to?'

(95) Kerime Nadir'in romanları **nasıl/ne gibi romanlar**, romantik mi mesela?
'What kind of novels are Kerime Nadir's novels? For example, [are they] romantic?'

nasıl appears with *ol-* 'be' and *dA* in a number of phrases such as *nasıl oldu da/ nasıl olmuş da* 'how come', 'how was it that', *nasıl oluyor da* 'how is it that':

(96) **Nasıl oldu da** bu kadar az çalışarak üniversiteyi bitirebildi?
'*How come* s/he worked so little and still managed to graduate from university?'

nasıl can occur in exclamations (12.4 (iv)) and it can combine with the copula, the copular markers and *-DIr* (8.3.3), (19.2.2.1).

19.2.2 The position of wh-phrases in a sentence

The most common position for a wh-phrase is immediately before the predicate:

(97) Semra'lar artık **nere-de** otur-uyor?
                      where-LOC live-IMPF
'*Where* do Semra and her family live now?'

(98) Parti-de **kim-ler** var-dı?
    party-LOC who-PL existent-P.COP
'*Who* was there at the party?'

Another frequently used position for wh-phrases is the position that their answers would occupy in the corresponding affirmative sentences:

(99) **Kim** onlar-ı okul-dan kaç-ar-ken gör-müş?
    who they-ACC school-ABL run.away-AOR-CV see-EV/PF
'*Who* saw them running away from school?'

(100) Bu boya-lar-dan **hangi-sin-i**
     this paint-PL-ABL which-3SG.POSS-ACC

     yan-da-ki dükkan-dan al-dı-n?
     next.door-LOC-ADJ shop-ABL buy-PF-2SG

     '*Which* of these paints did you buy from the shop next door?'

In colloquial speech, a wh-phrase can be placed in other positions as long as it is before the predicate:

(101) Erol'un **kim** doktor olduğunu söyledi?
'*Who* said Erol was a doctor?'

Unlike other wh-phrases, those corresponding to non-case-marked direct objects and oblique objects have a fixed position. These occur immediately before the predicate (23.2.1):

(102) Bugün hastalara öğle yemeğinde **ne** ver-di-ler?
what give-PF-3PL
'*What* did they give the patients today for lunch?'

(103) Necla **ne-den** korkuyor?
what-ABL fear-IMPF
'*What* is Necla scared *of*?'

Note that where *neden* means 'why' it can be in any position before the predicate.

19.2.2.1 Position of wh-phrases in linking sentences

Wh-phrases can occupy the position of subject complements in linking sentences and can combine with the copula, the copular markers and -*DIr* (8.3.3).

(104) Fransa'nın cumhurbaşkanı **kim**dir?
'*Who is* the president of France?'

(105) Kızının adı **ne**ydi?
'*What was* your daughter's name?'

(106) Tiyatroya vardıklarında **saat kaçmış**?
'*What time was [it]* when they arrived at the theatre?'

(107) Domates **ne kadar**dı?
'*How much* are/were the tomatoes?'

(108) Yeni alışveriş merkezindeki dükkanlar **nasıl**dı?
What were the shops in the new shopping centre like?

nere- 'where' requires one of the nominal inflectional markers before combining with the copular markers or -*DIr*:

(109) Genel seçimde **nere-de-ymiş-ler?**
where-LOC-EV.COP-3PL
'*Where were they* during the general election?'

hangi 'which' requires a possessive suffix before combining with the copular markers or *-DIr*.

(110) Yarışı kazanan yüzücü **hangi-si-ydi?**
which-3SG.POSS-P.COP
'*Which one was* the swimmer who won the race?'

The most common place for a wh-phrase that is a subject complement is at the end of the sentence, which is the unmarked position for predicates of linking sentences (23.1.2.1):

(111) Soru-lar-ı dağıt-acak ol-an kişi **kim**-di?
question-PL-ACC distribute-FUT be-PART person who-P.COP
'*Who* was the person that was supposed to distribute the questions?'

However, it can also occur at the beginning of a sentence:

(112) **Ne**-dir bana sormak istediğin soru?
what-GM
'*What* is the question you wanted to ask me?'

kim 'who', *nere-* 'where' and *hangisi* 'which one' can occur as subjects where the subject complement is a noun, an adjective or a pronominal:

(113) Depremde **kim** oradaydı?
'*Who* was there at the earthquake?'

(114) Şu anda **neresi** sıcaktır?
Where is [it] hot at the moment?

(115) İki kadından **hangisi** senin öğretmenindi?
'*Which one* of the two women was your teacher?'

19.2.3 Wh-phrases and stressed phrases

In a wh-question, it is possible for a phrase other than the wh-phrase to be stressed. This happens when the speaker wants the addressee to focus on a particular phrase in the question. In such cases, the stressed phrase *precedes* the wh-phrase.

(116) Çocuk-lar ev-de değil-se *süt-Ü* **kim** iç-ti?
child-PL home-LOC not-COND.COP milk-ACC who drink-PF
'If the children aren't at home, then *who* drank the MILK?'

(117) *DuvarlaRI* **ne zaman** boyayacaklar?
   '*When* will they paint the WALLS?'

19.2.4 Multiple wh-phrases

In the event of two wh-phrases occurring in the same sentence, they appear in the order in which their corresponding responses would appear in an unmarked sentence (23.1). In such cases, the first question phrase has stress and the sentence can have either the same intonation pattern as wh-questions (i.e. rising intonation at the end, 5.1 (iii)) or it may have falling intonation at the end:

(118) **KİM** **kime neyi** verdi?
   '*WHO* gave *what to whom*?'

19.3 Echo questions

An echo question follows a question or statement which has just been uttered, either because the initial question or statement is unexpected and has come as a surprise or because part of it has not been heard or understood properly. Echo questions may also be used for inquiring about the validity of a question or statement that has been uttered.

19.3.1 Echo questions following a question

Depending on the form of the initial question, these may contain a wh-phrase *and* the interrogative clitic *mI*. The interrogative clitic immediately follows a stressed wh-phrase, and the intonation is that of wh-questions, a slight rise followed by a fall-rise (5.1 (iii)):

(119) **NEreye mi** gidiyorum?
   a. 'Are you asking me *where* I'm going?'
   b. '*Where* am I GOING?'

The echo question in (119) would be a response to *Nereye gidiyorsun?* 'Where are you going?'

If the wh-phrase is the subject complement, it occurs at the end and is not stressed. In these questions, stress falls on the phrase that *mI* is attached to.

(120) *HülYA* **mı kim**?
   'Are you asking *who* Hülya is?/*Who* is HÜLYA?'

19.3.2 Echo questions following a statement

These have the same structure as ordinary wh-questions but are higher in pitch and do not contain a fall in intonation:

(121) **Nereye** gidiyorsun?
    (i) '*Where* did you say you were going?'
    (ii) 'You're going *WHERE*?'

See 19.1.4 (iii) for details.

19.3.3 derken constructions

The word *derken* (lit. 'while saying') is used as a means for requesting clarification of part of a statement. It follows the phrase for which clarification is requested:

(122) A. Rektör, kendisiyle görüşmek isteyen bir profesörü terslemiş.
    'It seems the rector scolded a professor who wanted to talk to him/her.'

    B. Terslemiş **derken**?
    '*What do you exactly mean by* 'scolded?'

(123) A. Bu kafede ara sıcak var mı?
    'Do they serve warm starters in this café?'

    B. Ara sıcak **derken**?
    '*What do you mean by* 'warm starters'?

19.4 Questioning parts of subordinate clauses

The constituents of subordinate clauses can be questioned, just like those of main clauses:

(124) Zehra [sen-in ***kim-i*** ara-dığ-ın]-ı sanıyormuş?
    you-GEN who-ACC look.for-VN-2SG.POSS-ACC
    '*Who* did Zehra think you were looking for?'

In (124), a constituent of a noun clause (Chapter 24) has been questioned. (125) illustrates the questioning of a constituent of a relative clause (Chapter 25):

(125) [***Nere-ye*** gid-en göçmen-ler] kolay kolay geri dönmüyorlar?
    where-DAT go-PART migrant-PL
    '(The) migrants going *where* don't easily return to their homeland?'

Finally, (126) exemplifies the questioning of a constituent of an adverbial clause (Chapter 26):

(126) [**Para-n-ı** *nere-de* **bul-a-ma-yınca**] telaşa kapıldın?
money-2SG.POSS-ACC where-LOC find-PSB-NEG-CV
'*Where* was it that when you couldn't find your money [there] you got worried?'

19.5 Modal adverbs used in questions

19.5.1 hani

hani is a modal adverb which means 'show me' or 'present me with':

(127) **Hani** çocukların kırdıkları vazo?
'*So where is* the vase that the children broke?'

Questions with *hani* do not necessarily target the location of a particular object or person but demand or seek confirmation of the presence of an entity of which both speech participants are aware. *hani* resembles the rhetorical usage of questions with 'where', in which the speaker does not actually ask for the whereabouts of a particular object but asks to be presented with it.

(128) **Hani** benim payım?
'*So where's* my share, *then*?'

(129) Semra'ya aldığın hediye **hani**?
'*So where's* the present you bought for Semra?'

hani can be used in combination with the inflected forms of *nere-* (19.2.1.3). *hani* and *nere-* are usually adjacent but sentences with *hani* at the beginning and *nere-* at the end are also used:

(130) Semra'ya aldığın hediye **hani nerede**?
'*So where's* the present you bought for Semra?'

(131) **Han**i bana vereceğin para **nerede**?
'*So where* is the money you were going to give me?'

hani can also be used with other wh-phrases in order to question the validity of a statement or to show disbelief:

(132) **Hani *ne zaman*** yaptın dersini?
'*When* did you do your homework, *then*?'

(133) **Hani *kim*** görmüş çocukların camlara taş attığını?
'*So who* saw the children throw stones at the windows, *then*?'

For the discourse-connective function of *hani,* see 28.3.12.

19.5.2 acaba

acaba indicates doubt or curiosity and is roughly equivalent to 'I wonder (if)' in English. It can be used in wh-questions and yes/no questions, both verbal and nominal. It is generally placed either at the beginning or the end of a sentence, but it can also occur in other positions (23.2.1).

(134) **Acaba** misafirler ***saat kaçta*** gelecek?
'*I wonder what time* the guests will arrive.'

(135) Semra'ya hediye alsam **mı acaba**?
'*I wonder if* I should buy a present for Semra.'

acaba, together with *ki* (28.3.4.7), can be used with wh-phrases, most commonly with *kim* 'who', in shortened versions of questions. These questions follow a comment which contains an indefinite noun phrase denoting a human or *biri(si)* 'someone':

(136) A. Bir hayranı Semra'ya aşk mektubu yazmış!
'An admirer has written a love letter to Semra!'

B. ***Acaba* kim ki**?
'Who can it be?'/ 'I wonder who?'

Alternatively, *acaba* can be dropped altogether in these constructions:

(137) A. Kapıda biri var.
'There's someone at the door.'

B. Bu saatte **kim ki**?
'Who can it be at this hour?'

For the usage of *acaba* with deliberative *-sA,* see 21.4.4.4.

19.5.3 yoksa

yoksa can be used in yes/no questions to indicate a sudden realization on the speaker's part that the situation might be different from what s/he expected:

(138) **Yoksa** çocuklara daha yemek vermedin ***mi***?
'Haven't you fed the children yet, *then*?'

(139) Eski halılarını satıyor **mu**sun **yoksa**?
'Are you selling your old carpets, *then*?'

In this usage, in contrast to its use in connecting alternative questions (19.1.2), *yoksa* generally occurs at the beginning or the end of a sentence. For its conditional sense, see 28.3.9.

19.5.4 bakalım

bakalım 'let's see' is an expression of anticipation, usually indicating the speaker's curiosity about a prospective event. Except where it is used in commands, it occurs in sentences that contain either a wh-phrase or the question clitic *mI*, but these sentences are not real questions, as they do not seek a response.

(140) **Bakalım** doktorlardan **hangisi** o hastayı ameliyat edecek.
'*Let's see which (one)* of the doctors will operate on that patient.'

(141) Dersini zamanında bitirebilecek **mi**sin **bakalım**.
'*Let's see if* you can finish your homework on time.

19.6 Rhetorical questions

Rhetorical questions have the form of questions, but they are not real questions as they do not seek answers. They are a stylistic means for expressing the content of a statement in more emphatic terms. In an colloquial spoken narrative, yes/no questions containing an optative negative form (-*mAyA*-, -*mAsIn*), or *(-yA...-(y)A* (9.3.3)) are used to present an event or action as almost unbelievably perverse or outrageous:

(142) Yepyeni şemsiyemi takside unut-**ma-ya-yım mı**?
         forget-NEG-OPT-1SG INT
'*Would you believe it*, I left my brand new umbrella in the taxi!'

(143) Bunun üzerine Turgut elindeki bardağı duvara doğru

fırlat-**ma-sın mı**?
hurl-NEG-OPT.3SG INT

'Then, *would you believe it*, Turgut hurled the glass in his hand against the wall.'

Rhetorical questions can sometimes be used to convey exasperation. These constructions can be in the form of either yes/no questions or wh-questions, and they are usually followed by *ki* (28.3.4.7):

(144) Semra dürüstçe konuşmayı biliyor **mu ki**?
'Can anyone imagine Semra speaking honestly!'
(lit. 'Does Semra know how to speak honestly?')

(145) A. Evde değilsin sanıyordum.
'I thought you weren't at home.'

B. **Nerey**e gideceğim **ki**?
'*Where* do you expect me to go?'
(lit. 'Where am I going to go?')

In another type of rhetorical question, *ne* is used following a question containing *mI*. Such combinations express the speaker's uncertainty about a situation or their challenge to a reported assertion, and they sometimes have a dismissive tone.

(146) Artık okula gitmeyecek **miymiş, ne**?
'Apparently, s/he won't be going to school any more!'

(147) Diyet **mi** yaptı, **ne**?
'S/he's supposed to have been on a diet or something.'

Another construction type involving *ne* is used when the speaker wishes to express his/her resentment or exasperation with a situation. These constructions have *ne* as the modifier in a *-(s)I* compound whose head is either a noun, or a verb inflected with *-mA* (8.5.1.2) and the impersonal *-sI* (Chapter 24 (60)):

(148) **Ne** hazırlanması! Bir sayfa bile okuyamadım!
'Getting prepared? I didn't even manage to read a page!'

These constructions usually have a somewhat belligerent tone when they are the response to a remark the speaker finds inappropriate or ill-informed:

(149) A. Senin araban spor araba mı?
'Is your car a sports car?'

B. **Ne** spor arabası! Benim arabam 120 kilometreyi bile ancak yapıyor!
'A sports car? My car can barely go up to 120 kilometers!

Chapter 20

Negation

This chapter discusses the means of negating clauses in Turkish, and expressions interacting with negation. Sections 20.1–20.3 describe the conditions in which the markers of negation *-mA*, *değil* and *yok* are used. In 20.4, we discuss the negative connective *ne... ne...* 'neither... nor... ', and in 20.5-7 expressions which occur mainly in negative sentences, such as *hiç* 'never', 'ever', 'at all', *kimse* 'no one', 'anyone', *asla* 'never', etc. Section 20.8 focuses on the usage of *-mA* without negative meaning.

20.1 *-mA*

The negative marker *-mA* (8.2.2) is unstressable. Its interaction with stress and intonation is discussed in 5.2.1 (i) and 11.2.3. For the irregular combination of *-mA* with other suffixes, see 8.2.3 and for converbial suffixes containing *-mA*, see 8.5.2.2 (i).

20.1.1 Negating clauses with simple verbs

-mA is the primary means used for negating verbal sentences and subordinate clauses.

(1) Ağaçları kes-**me**-yecek-ler.
            cut.down-NEG-FUT-3PL
    'They *won't* cut down the trees.'

(2) Ahmet [Zeki'yi gör-**me**-yeceğ-in]-i iddia ediyordu.
                  see-NEG-VN-3SG.POSS-ACC
    'Ahmet was claiming that he *wouldn't* see Zeki.'

(3) [Ayşe-nin durumu bil-**me**-diğ-in]-i hiç bir zaman düşün-**me**-di-m.
                 know-NEG-VN-3SG.POSS-ACC think-NEG-PF-1SG
    'I never thought that Ayşe *didn't* know about the situation.'

DOI: 10.4324/9780429435836-23

In sentences with **small clauses** (24.5), the negation marker can occur on either the main clause verb or the verb of the subordinate clause (but usually not both).

(4) [Zeki'yi Fransızca konuşuyor] addet-**mi**-yor-lar.
      consider-NEG-IMPF-3PL
   'They *don't* consider [Zeki a speaker of French].'

(5) [Zeki'yi Fransızca konuş-**mu**-yor] addediyorlar.
      speak- NEG-IMPF
   'They consider [Zeki *unable* to speak French].'

Where the main clause verb is *bil-* 'think' or *san-* 'think' and the sentence contains a small clause, the negation marker can only occur on the verb of the subordinate (small) clause:

(6) [Nuran'ı daha ehliyetini al**ma**dı] biliyordum.
   'I was under the impression [that Nuran *hadn't* got her driving licence yet].'

20.1.2 Negating clauses with compound verb forms

In compound verbs formed with free auxiliaries (13.3.1.2), the negative marker can be on either the **lexical verb** or the **auxiliary verb**. When it is on the lexical verb, it negates the predicate. This position of *-mA* indicates the non-performance of the action.

(7) İyi ki bakkal yiyecekleri eve yollayabiliyor. Bu yağmurda sokağa

   çık-ma-mış ol-du-k.
   go.out-NEG-PF be-PF-1PL

   'Fortunately, the grocer can do home deliveries of food. We *avoided having to go out* in this rain.'
   (lit. 'We ended up not having gone out...')

(8) Yakında bu kıyıdan denize **girile*mez* olacak**.
   'Soon it *will be impossible* to bathe in the sea along this shore.'
   (lit. '...going into the sea will be not be able to be done.')

The occurrence of the negative marker with a compound verb containing *bulun-* is rare but possible.

(9) O telaş içinde hastanın ateşine **bak*ma*mış bulundum**.
   'In the confusion I *neglected to take* the patient's temperature.'

The negative marker can also occur on the auxiliary verb *ol-* (but not *bulun-*). Placing the negative marker on the auxiliary verb expresses the denial of an expectation that the speaker assumes to exist:

(10) Bir yıl Çin'de kalmakla Çince **öğren-miş ol-*maz*-sın**.
                                           learn-PF be-NEG.AOR-2SG
      'You *won't have learnt* Chinese by staying in China for one year.'

The frequently used form *-mIş olmadı* indicates that the action has only been partially realized, usually because some component of the meaning of the verb phrase is considered by the speaker unfulfilled:

(11) Sokağa çıkalım diye tutturdun ama bir blok yürümekle sokağa

      çık-mış ol-ma-dı-k.
      go.out-PF be-NEG-PF-1PL

      'You kept saying we should go out, but walking one block *doesn't count as having gone out.*'
      (lit. '…but by walking one block we didn't end up having gone out.')

Putting the negative marker on both verbs (as in the second of the two compound verbs below) is a means for denying the non-performance of an action:

(12) Böylesi daha iyi. Hem onları fazla **meşgul et-*me*-miş ol-ur-uz**
                                                        occupy AUX-NEG-PF be-AOR-1PL

      hem de ziyaretlerine **git-*me*-miş ol-*ma*-yız**.
                                    go-NEG-PF be-NEG-1PL

      'It's better this way. We *won't have taken up* too much of their time, and at the same time we *won't have neglected* to visit them.'
      (lit. '…we will not have not paid them a visit.').

For the position of *-mA* in combination with compound verbs containing bound auxiliaries, see 8.2.3 (in particular *-(y)Iver* and *-(y)Abil*; see also *-yA*). There are significant differences in meaning when the negative marker appears with the possibility suffixes *-(y)Abil* and *-yA* (21.4.2.1).

(13) a. Arabanın lastiklerini değiştir-**e-me**-m.
                                                        PSB-NEG
        'I *cannot* change the tires of the car.'
        (I am unable to change them.)

      b. Arabanın lastiklerini değiştir-**me-yebilir**-im.
                                                     NEG-PSB
        'I *may not* change the tires of the car.'
        (I may keep them.)

      c. Arabanın lastiklerini değiştir-**e-me-yebilir**-im.
                                                   PSB-NEG-PSB

          I *may not be able to* change the tires of the car.
          (I may, for some reason or another, be unable to change them.)

20.1.3 -(y)Ip...-mA 'whether/if...(or not)'

-(y)Ip...-mA constructions correspond to 'whether/if... (or not)' in English. They are non-finite noun clauses (24.4) which contain two identical verbs, the first one affixed with the conjunctive suffix *-(y)Ip* (8.5.2.2, 28.2) and the second one affixed with the negative marker and one of the subordinating suffixes *-DIK, -(y)AcAK, -mA, -mAK* or *-(y)Iş* (8.5). These constructions express affirmative and negative alternatives for the same situation. *-(y)Ip...-mA* constructions occur particularly commonly as objects of verbs of cognition such as *bil-* 'know', *anla-* 'understand' and *fark et-* 'notice' or of the verbs *söyle-* 'say', *sor-* 'ask' (24.4.3.2):

(14) [Çocukları tatile **götür-üp götür-me-mey**]-e henüz
take-CONJ take-NEG-VN-DAT

karar ver-**me**-di-ler.
decide-NEG-PF-3PL

'They haven't yet decided [*whether or not to take* the children on holiday].'

(15) Ahmet [Nuran'a Noel hediyesi **alıp almayacağın**]-ı bilmiyor.
'Ahmet doesn't know [*whether or not he will buy* Nuran a Christmas present].'

(16) a. Elif [**kalıp kalmayacağın**]-ı söyledi mi?
'Has Elif said [*whether or not she'll be staying*]?'

b. Herşey [**kadının suçlu olup olmamasın**]-a bağlı.
'Everything depends on [*whether or not the woman is guilty*].'

When used in sentences with nominal predicates, *-(y)Ip...-mA* constructions usually occur as the complement of the postposition *konusunda* 'about' (17.3.2.1):

(17) Osman [bu yaz tatile **çıkıp çıkmama**] *konusunda* tereddütlüymüş.
'Osman is apparently hesitating about [*whether to go on holiday this summer*].'

20.2 değil

20.2.1 Negating nominal sentences

değil 'not' is primarily the means of negating the linking sentences (12.1.1.2). It can combine with the suffixes that occur in nominal predicates, namely the copular markers (8.3.2), *-DIr* (8.3.3), the person markers belonging to Group 2 (8.4) and the converbial marker *-(y)ken* (8.5.2.2):

(18) Nejat gençliğinde bu kadar **inatçı değil-di**.
　　　　　　　　　　　　　　　stubborn not-P.COP
　　　'Nejat *wasn't* so *stubborn* when he was young.'

(19) Bu yaptığın **çocukluk değil**(**-dir**) de nedir?
　　　　　　　　　childishness not(-GM)
　　　'This behaviour of yours is *nothing but childish*.'
　　　(lit. 'If this behaviour of yours is not childishness what is it?')

(20) [*Evde* **değil-sin**] sandık.
　　　　　　　not-2SG
　　　'We thought [*you weren't at home*].'

(21) [Anneleri *ev-de* **değil-ken**] çok daha derli toplu oluyorlar.
　　　　　　　　home-LOC not-CV
　　　'They are much tidier [*when* their mother *isn't at home*].'

20.2.2 Negating verbal sentences

değil can also be used for negating verbal sentences. In this case, the verb is typically conjugated with the imperfective marker *-Iyor*, less commonly with the future marker *-(y)AcAK* or the perfective marker *-mIş* (see 8.2.3 (iii)):

(22) Her yere taksiyle **gid-iyor değil-im**.
　　　　　　　　　　　go-IMPF not-1SG
　　　'It's not the case that I go everywhere by taxi.'

However, negating a verbal sentence with *değil* is different from negating it with *-mA* as in (22):

(23) Her yere taksiyle **git-*mi*-yor-um**.
　　　　　　　　　　　go-NEG-IMPF-1SG
　　　'I don't go everywhere by taxi.'

While negating a sentence with *-mA* simply asserts a state of affairs, negating a verbal sentence with *değil* repudiates an assumption which has either been overtly expressed or which the speaker attributes to others who he or she believes to hold such an opinion. In the case of (22), the assumption is that the speaker regularly takes a taxi.

değil can also occur with negated verb forms. Such sentences are affirmative as a result of being doubly negated:

(24) Bu sınavlarda neden bu kadar güçlük çekildiğini
anla-mı-yor değil-im.
understand-NEG-IMPF not-1SG

'I DO understand why [people] have so much difficulty with these exams.'
(lit. 'It's *not* the case that I *don't* understand...')

(25) Herhalde böyle önemli bir konuda ona akıl **danış*ma*yacak değil-iz.**
'We will naturally ask for his/her opinion on a matter as important as this.'
(lit. 'It's *not* the case that we *won't* ask...')

A verb inflected with the perfective marker -*DI* can be followed by *değil* only if it also has a negative marker. In this case, any person marking has to attach to the verb instead of to *değil*:

(26) Olanları **gör-*me*-di-m değil**, ama tam hatırlayamıyorum.
see-NEG-PF-1SG not
'It's *not* that I *didn't* see what went on; it's just that I can't quite remember.'

20.2.3 *değil* in elliptical sentences

değil can be used as a means of **ellipsis** (28.4.2), by replacing a particular part of a sentence. It replaces a (verbal) negative predicate in sentences which contain an identical but affirmative predicate. For example, a sentence such as (27) can be paraphrased as (28):

(27) Elma yemiyorum, armut yiyorum.
'I'm not eating an apple, I'm eating a pear'

(28) Elma **değil**, armut yi-yor-um.
apple not pear eat-IMPF-1SG
'I'm eating pears, *not* apples.'

The part that contains *değil* can also follow the main assertion:

(29) Armut yiyorum, elma **değil**.
'I'm eating pears, *not* apples.'

In addition to replacing a predicate, *değil* can also replace a noun and its determiner (together with the predicate):

(30) Büyük **değil**, küçük bir elma iste-miş-ti-m.
big not small a(n) apple want-PF-P.COP-1SG
'I had asked for a small apple, *not* [a] big [one].'

Alternatively, *değil* can be used in a function semantically equivalent to *şöyle dursun* and *bir yana* (28.3.1.4), for contrasting or comparing two events or entities in terms of the scale of their improbability, in a similar way to 'let alone' in English. In these sentences, *değil* precedes the constituent whose actualization is regarded as less probable, and this constituent usually precedes that to which it is contrasted. The intonation peak of such sentences is the contrasted constituent, which is almost always followed by *bile* 'even' (28.3.1.1 (iv)). The constituent to which something is contrasted is also stressed. Usually *değil* receives secondary stress (5.2):

(31) **Değil** *sinema-ya gitmek*, televizYON bile seyred-ecek
not cinema-DAT GO-INF television even watch-PART

zaman-ım yok.
time-1SG.POSS non-existent

'I don't even have time to watch TV, *let alone go to the cinema.*'

(32) Ahmet **değil** *saksafon*, ısLIK bile çalamaz.
'Ahmet can't even whistle, *let alone play the saxophone.*'

For the use of *şöyle dursun/bir yana/bırak(ın)* 'let alone' in a similar function, see 28.3.1.4.

20.3 *yok*

The negative existential expression *yok* 'non-existent' is the negated form of *var* 'existent' (12.1.1.2):

(33) Evde bir tane bile fazla ampul **yok**.
'*There isn't* even one spare light bulb in the house.'

(34) Çorbanın tuzu **yok**.
'The soup *doesn't have* any salt [in it].'

yok can also be used in a double negative construction with *değil*:

(35) Maaşımdan şikayetim **yok değil** ama idare ediyorum işte.
'I'm *not without* complaints about my salary, but well, I get by.'

In colloquial speech, *yok* is commonly used as the negative response to a question, instead of *hayır* 'no':

(36) A. Bugün sinemaya gidecek misin?
'Will you be going to the cinema today?'

B. **Yok** (gitmeyeceğim).
'*No* (I won't).'

For the usages of *yok* as a connective, see 28.3.4.9 and 28.3.5 (ii).

Where a negative linking sentence includes a locative-marked expression, *yok* and *değil* are interchangeable (12.1.1.2 (20)-(21)):

(37) Semra **parti-de değil-di/yok-tu**.
party-LOC not-P.COP/absent-P.COP
'Semra wasn't at the party.'

Note that when *yok* is used, the position of the locative noun phrase (*partide* 'at the party') is not fixed in the sentence, whereas when *değil* is used the locative-marked noun phrase has to immediately precede it. *Yok* is also a less formal version of *hayır* 'no'.

20.4 The negative connective *ne . . . ne* 'neither . . . nor'

ne...ne is a negative connective where each *ne* attaches to a phrase (either simple or complex). The last *ne* conjunct can be emphasized by using *de*:

(38) **Ne** yabancılar **ne** (**de**) mahalle halkı otobüs turlarından memnunlar.
'*Neither* the foreigners *nor* the locals are happy with the coach tours.'

(39) Görüşmeler hakkında **ne** hükümetten, **ne** iş adamlarından, **ne**
(**de**) işçi sendikalarından bir bilgi alamadık.
'We weren't able to get any information about the negotiations from either the government, the businessmen *or* the trade unions.'

Sentences containing *ne...ne* can have either affirmative or negative predicates but negative predicates are more common in everyday speech. Sentences with affirmative or negative predicates have separate intonation contours and stress patterns. When the predicate is affirmative the first *ne* receives secondary stress, there is a rise in intonation after the first conjunct, and primary stress falls on the constituent before the predicate:

(40) Bu filmden **ne** kadınlar **ne** erkekLER hoşlandılar.
'*Neither* the women *nor* the men liked this film.'

If the predicate is negative, all of the *ne* conjuncts have an identical intonation contour, where both *ne* and the stressable syllable within the conjunct receive secondary stress, and primary stress falls on the predicate (on the syllable before the negative marker):

(41) Bu filmden **ne** kadınlar **ne** erkekler hoşLANmadılar.
'*Neither* the women *nor* the men liked this film.'

The second conjunct can be placed after the predicate, but only when the predicate is affirmative:

(42) Bu sandviççide **ne** çay var, **ne de** kahve.
'There is *neither* tea *nor* coffee in this sandwich shop.'

(43) **Ne** yiyecek bulabildim **ne (de)** içecek.
'I couldn't find *either* food *or* drink.'

The *ne...ne* connective can conjoin pairs of any type of phrase, such as adverbial phrases, adjectival phrases, verb phrases, etc. It can also conjoin clauses:

(44) **Ne** tamir işleriyle uğraşır, **ne** yemek pişirmesini bilir, **ne (de)** çocuklarla ilgilenir.
'S/he *neither* does any repair jobs, *nor* knows how to cook, nor takes care of the children.'

(45) O kitaba sadece şöyle bir göz gezdirdim, yani **ne** okudum **ne (de)** okumadım.
'I just glanced at that book, I mean I *neither* read [it], *nor* didn't read [it].'

(46) Oğlum **ne** bisiklete binmeyi, **ne (de)** araba kullanmayı öğrendi.
'My son *neither* learned how to ride a bicycle, *nor* how to drive a car.'

Where the conjuncts are verb phrases the preferred form of the verbs is affirmative:

(47) **Ne** dersini yapıyorsun, **ne (de)** sınavlara giriyorsun.
'You are *neither* doing your homework, *nor* are you taking your exams.'

20.5 Expressions interacting with negation

There are a number of expressions which are very restricted in their ability to occur with affirmative predicates. They can occur in all types of negative sentence, and some can also occur in affirmative or negative questions. These expressions are:

hiç	'never', 'ever', 'at all'
hiçbir (+ noun phrase)	'no/any ...'

hiçbiri(si)	'none/any (of) . . .'
hiçbir şey	'nothing', 'anything'
hiçbir yer	'nowhere', 'anywhere'
hiçbir zaman	'never', 'ever'
hiçbir koşulda, hiçbir koşul/ şart altında, hiçbir durumda	'under no/any circumstances'
kimse/hiç kimse/hiçbir kimse	'no one', 'anyone'

Note that the negative meanings shown in the list above, such as 'never' and 'no one', are produced only by a combination of one of the expressions shown above with one of the markers of negation (*-mA, değil, yok*). This is illustrated in the following pair of examples:

(48) Evde **kimse** var mı?
     no.one/anyone existent INT
     'Is there *anyone* in the house?'

(49) Evde **kimse** *yok* mu?
     no.one/anyone not.existent INT
     'Is*n't* there *anyone*/Is there **no one** in the house?'

There are also certain other expressions which interact with negation. These are *artık* 'any more', *bir daha* 'once more', 'again', *daha/henüz* 'yet' (16.4.1.4), *kolay kolay* 'readily', 'easily' (16.1.3 (7)) and the ones in 20.5.4 below.

20.5.1 *hiç* 'never', 'ever', 'at all'

hiç is an adverb that is subject to different conditions depending on whether the sentence in which it occurs is a question or not. A sentence which is not a question and which contains *hiç* must also contain one of the markers of negation (*-mA, değil, yok*), and *hiç* intensifies this negative element:

(50) Bu adam **hiç** uyanık **değil**.
     at.all clever not
     'This man *isn't* clever *at all*.'

(51) Trende yer **yok**-muş **hiç**.
     place non-existent-EV.COP at.all
     'It seems there *aren't* any seats [left] *at all* on the train.'

hiç also occurs in yes/no questions with or without negative marking:

(52) **Hiç** sabah güneşin doğuşunu seyret-ti-n *mi*?
     ever   watch-PF-2SG
     'Have you *ever* watched the sun rise?'

(53) **Hiç** bin-**me**-di-n *mi* uçağa?
ever board-NEG-PF-2SG
'*Haven't* you *ever*/Have you *never* been on a plane?'

20.5.2 hiçbir 'no', 'any', and expressions containing hiçbir and herhangi bir 'no', 'any'

Hiçbir functions as a determiner in noun phrases (15.6.1):

(54) **Hiçbir** çocuk arkadaşından ayrılmak istemez.
'*No child* would want to be separated from his/her friend(s).'

It also occurs in the following:

(i) The pronominalized form *hiçbiri(si)* 'none [of]', 'any [of]' (14.5.2–3, 18.4)
(ii) The composite expressions *hiçbir şey* 'nothing', 'anything', *hiçbir yer* 'nowhere', 'anywhere', *hiçbir zaman* 'never', 'ever', which incorporate the noun phrases *şey* 'thing', *yer* 'place' and *zaman* 'time'
(iii) The adverbials *hiçbir koşulda*, *hiçbir koşul/şart altında*, *hiçbir durumda* 'under no/any circumstances'

All the forms that *hiçbir* appears in are found mainly in sentences containing one of the markers of negation (*-mA*, *değil*, *yok*):

(55) **Hiçbir yere** git*me*yin.
'*Don't* go *anywhere*.'

(56) **Yolculardan hiçbiri(si)** yerini vermek iste*me*di.
'*None of the passengers* wanted to surrender their seat.'

(57) **Hiçbir zaman** mutlu *değil* miydi?
'*Wasn't* s/he *ever* happy?'

(58) Dolapta **hiçbir şey** *yok*.
'*There's nothing* in the fridge.'

Some speakers use expressions containing *hiçbir* in affirmative questions as well. But the more common alternative, which is also the only way of expressing *any* in affirmative sentences that are not questions, such as (60), is *herhangi bir* 'any' (15.6.1, 18.4 (iv)):

(59) **Herhangi bir** yerde su *var* mı?/**Hiçbir** yerde su *var* mı?
'*Is there [any]* water anywhere?'

(60) Artık bunlardan **herhangi birini** alıp gidelim.
'Let's just take *any one* of these and go.'

20.5.3 (hiç) kimse 'no one', 'anyone'

Like *hiç*, *kimse* and its reinforced form *hiç kimse* are subject to different conditions depending on whether the sentence in which they occur is a question or not. A sentence which is not a question and which contains *(hiç) kimse* must also contain one of the markers of negation (*-mA*, *değil*, *yok*):

(61) (**Hiç**) **kimseyi** içeri al**mı**yorlarmış.
'Apparently, they are*n't* letting *anyone* in.'

(62) Bugün (**hiç**) **kimse** evinde **değil**.
'*No one* is at home today.'

In affirmative questions the simple form *kimse* is preferred:

(63) İçeride **kimse** var **mı**?
'Is there *anyone* inside?'

hiçbir kimse can be used as a further reinforcement of *hiç kimse*:

(64) Partiye **hiç(bir) kimse** gelmedi.
'*(Absolutely) No one* came to the party.'

The plural suffix is sometimes added to *(hiç) kimse* in colloquial speech, producing a slightly intensified meaning (14.3.1.2 (33)):

(65) Beni artık (**hiç**) **kimseler** sevmiyor.
'*No one* loves me any more.'

An even more informal alternative is *(hiç) kimsecik(ler)* (for *-CIK*, see 7.2.2.2).
When *(hiç) kimse* is the subject, the predicate has 3rd person singular marking. Similarly, when *kimseler* or *kimsecikler* expresses the subject, the non-specific reference of these pronouns precludes plural marking of the predicate (12.2.2.1 (iv)).

(66) Bu günlerde dükkanına **kimse(ler)** uğramıyor.
'*No one* has been going to his/her shop recently.'

Note that *kimse* and the forms containing it have accusative case marking when functioning as the direct object:

(67) Bu günlerde **kimseyi/kimseleri** görmüyorum.
'I *haven't* been seeing *anyone* recently.'

20.5.4 Modifiers of negation markers

Apart from *hiç* (20.5.1), which intensifies the meaning of a negation marker, other adverbials can also modify the markers *-mA*, *değil* and *yok*, given in the sections below. For *kolay kolay* 'readily', 'easily', see 16.1.3 (7) and for *artık* 'no longer', 'any more', see 16.4.1.4 (ii.b).

20.5.4.1 asla 'never', katiyen 'never'

Both of these adverbs reinforce the meaning of a negative marker. However, unlike *hiç*, if negating an event, they either express a determination on the part of the subject that the event described shall never occur, or that there was no possibility of the recurrence of the event. They can also be used for denying a state of affairs. *asla* and *katiyen* are found only in sentences that contain one of the markers of negation (*-mA*, *değil*, *yok*):

(68) Karısından **asla** özür dile*mez*.
'He *never* apologizes/will *never* apologize to his wife.'

(69) Bizde **katiyen** yalan *yok*!
'We *never* lie!'

(70) Senaryo bu şekliyle **asla** bitmiş *değil*.
'The script is *nowhere near* finished in its current form.'

20.5.4.2 pek 'much', 'very', (pek) fazla 'much', 'too much'

When *pek* or *fazla* which are adverbials of degree (16.5) modify one of the markers of negation (*-mA*, *değil*, *yok*), their function is not to intensify, but rather to reduce the absoluteness of the negative meaning. Where the predicate is verbal, they are often used with *bir şey* 'something' (18.6.1):

(71) Odam **pek** büyük *değil*.
'My room's *not very* big.'

(72) O konuşmadan **pek/fazla** bir şey hatırla*mı*yorum.
'I *don't* remember *much* about that lecture.'

They can also be used together, with *fazla* following *pek*.

(73) Yeni buluşlarla ilgili **pek fazla** bir şey oku*ma*dım.
'I *haven't* read *much* about new inventions'

Both *pek* and *fazla* can also occur in affirmative sentences. In the case of *pek*, this happens only where either (i) it modifies an adjective or one of the determiners *çok* 'much', *az* 'little', or (ii) the sentence expresses an exclamation (12.4).

(74) Salonunuz **pek** genişmiş!
'Your living room is really large!'

(75) Yurt dışına **pek** az çıktık.
'We haven't been abroad very often.'

When *fazla* is used in an affirmative sentence, it is synonymous with *fazlasıyla* 'excessively' (16.5). See also 16.8.

20.5.4.3 o kadar 'so', 'such', 'all that'

Another adverbial of degree, *o kadar* (16.5), has a particular function in negative sentences, where the quantity or degree it refers to may not have been explicitly specified in the preceding discourse, but is simply implied to be considerable:

(76) Aslında dondurmayı **o kadar** sev*m*iyorum.
'Actually, I'm *not all that* keen on ice cream.'

o kadar can also be modified by *pek* or *hiç*:

(77) a. Arkadaşım fala **pek o kadar** meraklı ***değil***.
'My friend *is not that* interested in fortune telling.'

b. Bu filmin **hiç o kadar** korkulacak bir yanı ***yok***.
'This film *isn't that* scary.'

(78) Onlar (**pek**) **o kadar** varlıklı ***değil***lermiş.
'It seems they're *not so very* wealthy.'

20.6 Expressions interacting with negation in subordinate clauses

20.6.1 Expressions interacting with negation in noun clauses

When one of the expressions listed in 20.5 occurs in a noun clause (Chapter 24), the verb of the clause can be either affirmative or negative. The verb of a noun clause containing one of these expressions can be affirmative only if the main clause predicate has negative marking (i.e. *-mA, değil, yok*):

(79) [**Kimse**-nin bu kitab-ı oku-duğ-un]-u
no.one-GEN this book-ACC read-VN-3SG.POSS-ACC

san-*m*-ıyor-um.
think-NEG-IMPF-1SG

'I *don't* think *anyone* has read this book.'

(80) [**Hiçbir şey**in denize atılması] doğru *değil*.
    'It *isn't* right for *anything at all* to be thrown into the sea.'

(81) [Hasan'ın sana yardım için **hiçbir şey** yaptığı] *yok*.
    'Hasan does *absolutely nothing* to help you.'

The verb of a noun clause containing *hiç* 'never', 'ever', 'at all' (20.5.1) and *(hiç) kimse* 'no one', 'anyone' (20.5.3) can be affirmative also in questions:

(82) [**Kimse**nin kapıyı çaldığın]-ı duydun mu?
    'Did you hear [anyone ring the door bell]?

20.6.2 Expressions interacting with negation in relative clauses and adverbial clauses

Where a relative clause (Chapter 25) or an adverbial clause (Chapter 26) contains one of the expressions listed in 20.5, the verb of that clause is obligatorily negative:

(83) [Ortalıkta **hiç** iz bırak*ma*yan] hırsız, yandaki evi de soymuş.
    'It seems that the burglars, [who *hasn't* left *any* traces], has also burgled the house next door.'

(84) Necla [kocasından **hiçbir** haber ala*ma*yınca] tutuklandığını sanmış.
    '[When Necla *didn't* hear from her husband *at all*], she thought he had been arrested.'

One exception is clauses with *-(y)Ip* (28.2) which have to be left without negative marking if the verb in the superordinate clause is negative:

(85) Onunla **hiçbir zaman** görüşüp konuşa*ma*dık.
    'We *never* managed to see each other and talk.'

20.7 Sakın 'be sure', 'mind (you don't)', 'I wonder if ...', 'I do hope...'

sakın is a modal adverb that has to co-occur with the negative marker *-mA*. It occurs in two different kinds of structure:

(i) A negative suggestion, prohibition or warning is strongly reinforced by the presence of *sakın*. The verb form may be 1st person plural optative, as in (86), or may contain any one of the imperative person markers from Group 4 (8.4.4) other than *-sAnA* and *-sAnIzA*.

(86) **Sakın** saat 6'dan önce git-**me-ye-lim**!
    go-NEG-OPT-1PL
    '*We must be sure* not to go before six o'clock!'

(87) **Sakın** [gece geç saatte sokağa çık-a-yım] de-**me-yin**!
    go- OPT-1SG say-NEG-2PL
    '*Don't you ever think* of going out late at night!'

(ii) *sakın* also occurs with *ol-* 'be' (imperative or optative). These sentences have an intonation pattern similar to yes/no questions (5.1 (ii)), and they present to the addressee a conjectural possibility for consideration, corroboration or denial. (88) is close in meaning to, but presents a rather stronger assertion than, (186) in 21.5.1:

(88) **Sakın** Ayşe bu fotoğrafı Hatice'ye göstermiş olmasın?
    (i) 'I wonder if Ayşe has shown this photograph to Hatice?'
    (ii) 'I do hope Ayşe hasn't shown this photograph to Hatice.'

20.8 Usage of -*mA* without negative meaning

In some constructions containing -*mA,* the expected negative meaning is not present. One such construction is rhetorical questions (19.6):

(89) Benden habersiz randevumu iptal et**mesin mi**?
    '*Would you believe it*, s/he cancelled my appointment without letting me know.'

Other forms in which -*mA* does not have a negative meaning are -*mAyAgörsün* and -*mAsIn* both of which form adverbial clauses (Chapter 26) indicating time. They both contain the 3rd person optative marker -*sIn*. 1st person singular forms with -*(y)AyIm* are also encountered.

(90) Kadın ekmek kırıntılarını pencereye koy**mayagörsün**, kuşlar bir anda ortaya çıkıyorlar.
    '*Whenever/as soon as* the woman puts the bread crumbs in the window sill, the birds appear.'

(91) Amcam biraz telaşlan**masın**, hemen tansiyonu yükseliyor.
    '*Whenever/as soon a*s my uncle becomes anxious, his blood pressure goes up.'

Both suffixes are used in complex sentences where the action in the subordinate clause containing the suffix is immediately followed by the action expressed in the main clause.

Chapter 21

Tense, aspect and modality

Tense, aspect and modality are grammatical categories mainly affecting the verbal constituent of a clause, although adverbials may also contribute to their expression. **Tense** (21.2) expresses the temporal location of the situation being talked about, indicating whether this is before, at, or after a particular reference point (usually, but not always, the moment of speech).

(1) a. Okul-lar pazartesi açıl-**dı**.
    school-PL Monday open-PF
    'The schools *started* on Monday.'

   b. Okullar pazartesi açıl-**acak**.
                         -FUT
    'The schools *will start* on Monday.'

Aspect (21.3) indicates whether the situation is presented as completed, ongoing, or part of a recurring pattern.

(2) a. Ahmet bir elma ye-**di**.
       an apple eat-PF
    'Ahmet *ate* an apple.'

   b. Ahmet bir elma yi-**yor**-du.
                    -IMPF-P.COP
    'Ahmet *was eating* an apple.'

   c. Ahmet sabahları bir elma ye-**r**-di.
                              -AOR-P.COP
    '*Ahmet used to eat* an apple in the morning.'

Modality (21.4) is a complex category, being concerned with possibility and necessity, with the speaker's degree of commitment to the factuality of a statement, and with the speaker's desire for something to happen or not happen.

(3) a. Sevil bu konu-yu araştır-**abil-ir**.
 this matter-ACC investigate-PSB-AOR
 'Sevil *can/could/may* look into this matter.'

b. Sevil bu konuyu araştır-**mış-tır**.
 PF-GM
 '*Presumably* Sevil has looked into this matter.'

c. Sevil bu konuyu araştır-**sın**.
 3SG
 '*I want* Sevil to look into this matter.'

In Appendix 2, we present an inventory of all the suffixes that contribute to the expression of tense, aspect and modality (with the exception of the 3rd person optative/imperative which does not have overt marking). As in most languages, there is considerable overlap between the articulation of the three categories.

21.1 The expression of tense, aspect and modality

In Turkish tense, aspect and modality are marked by a combination of suffixes from the following categories:

(i) Verbal tense, aspect and modality suffixes (8.2.3)
(ii) Copular markers and *-DIr* (8.3)

The copular markers are restricted in the range of tense, aspect and modality meanings they cover. In order to make available in nominal sentences (12.1.1.2), the full range of tense, aspect and modality specification, the copular auxiliary verb *ol-* is used as the carrier of suffixes of Position 3 (12.1.1.3). In verbal sentences, the use of compound verb forms containing free auxiliaries (13.3.1.2) makes possible combinations of tense, aspect and modality marking that cannot be achieved on a single verb stem and thus constitutes an integral part of the overall system for the expression of these categories. The role of compound verb forms is discussed in 21.5.

Tense, aspect and modality are only fully articulated in finite verb forms. For discussion of the extent to which tense, aspect and modality can be marked in the non-finite verb forms used in subordinate clauses, see 21.4.2.1–2, 24.4.7, 25.4.1 and 26.2.3.

21.2 Tense

In this book, we use the term 'tense' in the strict sense of the grammatical marking of *location in time*.

In Turkish, the primary tense differentiation is between past and non-past. The suffixes involved in the expression of present and future tense (*-(I)yor*, *-mAktA* and *-(y)AcAK*) are markers of **relative tense**. This means that the expression of absolute present and future tense is dependent on the *absence* of any other tense marker, such as the past copula *-(y)DI*, which would indicate a reference point other than the moment of speech.

21.2.1 Past tense

The markers of past tense are the verbal suffixes *-DI* and *-mIş* and the copular marker *-(y)DI* (with its relatively uncommon alternant *idi*).

(i) *-DI* and *-mIş*:
These suffixes express both past tense and perfective aspect (21.3), that is, they express past events that are viewed as a completed whole.

    (4)   Ev-i sat-**tı**-nız mı?
            house-ACC SELL-PF-2PL INT
            '*Did you sell/Have you sold* the house?'

    (5)   Kerem'in babası ona biraz para ver-**miş**.
                                      give-EV/PF
            'Apparently, Kerem's father *gave/has given* him some money.'

(ii) *-(y)DI*:
The past copula expresses past tense and imperfective aspect (21.3), that is, it presents a situation as it was at some time in the past. This can be a state of affairs, as in the nominal sentences (6) and (7), or it can be an event which was ongoing (8) or anticipated (9) at the time referred to:

    (6)   Bodrum-da-**ydı**-k.
                -LOC-P.COP-1PL
            'We *were* in Bodrum.'

    (7)   Evde hiç para yok-**tu**.
                      non-existent-P.COP
            'There *was* absolutely no money in the house.'

    (8)   Ayten bir bankada çalış-***ıyor*-du**.
                            work-IMPF-P.COP
            'Ayten *was* work*ing* in a bank.'

    (9)   Yeni bir öğretmenimiz ol-***acak*-tı**.
                                be-FUT-P.COP
            'We *were going to* have a new teacher.'

The suffixes *-DI* and *-mIş* and the copular marker *-(y)DI* differ not only in terms of aspect but also in terms of their precise tense values. Except for contexts in which it is not a tense marker at all but a marker of counterfactual modality (21.4.1.3, 27.2.3.2), the past copula *-(y)DI* expresses past tense in absolute terms, that is, it locates a situation in a time prior to the moment of speech. *-mIş*, by contrast, is a marker of relative past tense. When followed by *-(y)DI* or by the auxiliary verb *ol-*, it can refer to a time that is prior to *any* reference point established by the context:

(10) [Dön-düğ-üm-de] herkes yat-**mış**-*tı*.
return-CV-1SG.POSS-LOC everyone go.to.bed-PF-P.COP
'[When I came back] everyone *had* gone to bed.'

It is quite possible for this reference point to be after the moment of speech, that is, in the future:

(11) İnşallah [ben dön-ünce-ye kadar] uyu-**muş** *ol-acak*-sın.
I. hope I return-CV-DAT until sleep-PF AUX-FUT-2SG
'I hope you *will have* gone to sleep [by the time I get back].'

As for *-DI*, its primary function in terms of tense is the same as that of *-(y)DI*, but in colloquial usage it can combine with *-(y)DI* in the sequence *-DIydI*, in which context (only) it acquires the relative tense value typical of *-mIş*. For the position of a person marker in *-DIydI* forms see 8.4.1.

(12) Ben sana bu sabah söyle-**di-ydi**-m/söyle-**di**-m-**di**.
I you-DAT this morning say-PF-P.COP-1SG/say-PF-1SG-P.COP
'I *(had) told* you this morning.'

It should be noted that forms in *-mIştI* and *-DIydI* do not always locate an event prior to a specific reference point in the past. Sometimes, as in (12), the combination of two past tense markers simply serves to indicate that the situation being talked about is located in a past time that is quite separate from the speech context.

21.2.2 Present tense

Turkish has no marker of present tense as such. In verbal sentences, present tense is indicated by a combination of the following:

(i) A marker of progressive aspect (21.3.2), usually *-(I)yor*, less commonly *-mAktA*, and
(ii) The absence of the past copular marker *-(y)DI*

Progressive aspect, which presents a situation as ongoing at a particular point in time, is equivalent in tense terms to 'relative present'. (13) is the non-past version of (8) above:

(13) Ayten bir bankada çalış-**ıyor**.
'Ayten *works/is working* in a bank.'

In nominal sentences without *ol-* (12.1.1.2), present tense is indicated simply by the absence of the past copula. (14) and (15) are the non-past versions of (6) and (7) above.

(14) Bodrum-da-yız.
 -LOC-1PL
'We*'re* in Bodrum.'

(15) Evde hiç para yok.
'There*'s* absolutely no money in the house.'

For the use of past tense perfective forms to express (entry into) a state ongoing at the moment of utterance, see 21.3.3.

21.2.3 Future tense

(i) Among the verbal suffixes, the only explicit marker of future tense is *-(y)AcAK*:

(16) Herkes bu roman-a bayıl-**acak**.
everyone this novel-DAT love-FUT
'Everyone will love this novel.'

In nominal sentences, the auxiliary *ol-* (12.1.1.3) serves as the bearer of *-(y)AcAK*:

(17) [Geldiğiniz zaman] anahtar kapıcıda **olacak**.
'The key *will be* with the caretaker when you arrive.'

Like *-mIş*, *-(y)AcAK* expresses tense in relative rather than absolute terms. When combined with the past copula, it locates an event or state at a time subsequent to some past reference point established by the discourse context. The future time to which the *-(y)AcAK* component of *-(y)AcAktI* refers may or may not be future in relation to the moment of speech:

(18) ***Geçen/Önümüzdeki yıl*** yeni bir öğretmen-imiz ol-**acak-tı**.
last/next year new a teacher-1PL.POSS BE-FUT-P.COP
'*Last year/Next year* we *were going to* have a new teacher.'

(ii) The imperfective aspect marker *-(I)yor* is regularly used with future reference when talking about events that are scheduled or fixed:

(19) Yarın Londra'ya gid**iyor**uz.
'We*'re going* to London tomorrow.'

(20) Konser kaçta baş**lıyor**?
'What time *does* the concert start?'

The use of *-(I)yor* for the expression of planned future events indicates a strong confidence on the speaker's part that events will indeed run according to the schedule. The use of *-(y)AcAK* in such contexts would suggest a more independent prediction, or would be used in the case of a schedule's breaking down. For example, (21) is more likely than (20) in the case of a concert that had not started at the scheduled time:

(21) Konser kaçta başla**yacak**?
'What time *is* the concert *going to* start?'

As in its other functions, *-(I)yor* in its future tense function is actually a marker of relative tense and, in the context of a narrative, the combination *-(I)yordu* can express a scheduled event anticipated at some reference point in the past:

(22) Füsun telaşlıydı. Birkaç gün sonra annesi gel**iyordu**.
'Füsun was agitated. Her mother *was coming* in a few days' time.'

(iii) The aorist form of the verb often has future time reference, but any tense component of its meaning is conditioned by its primary function as a marker of various kinds of modality (21.4.1.4, 21.4.4.5–6).

(iv) The construction *-mAk üzere* 'on the point of ...-ing', 'about to' can be used to express action that is or was imminent:

(23) [Sen telefon et-tiğ-in sıra-da]
you telephone-AUX-CV-2SG.POSS time-LOC

sokağ -a çık-**mak üzere**-ydi-m.
street-DAT go.out-VN on-P.COP-1SG

'I was *on the point of* going out [when you rang].'

For the converbial uses of *-mAk üzere,* see 26.3.2, 26.3.12.

(v) Another construction that expresses the expected imminent occurrence of an event is the juxtaposition of the *-DI* and *-(y)AcAK* forms of the same verb. This is used only in the 3rd person and usually of events that are not within the control of a human agent:

(24) Bu çantanın sapı kop**tu** kop**acak**.
'This bag's strap is about to break.'

21.3 Aspect

Aspect is that part of the grammar of a language which expresses the temporal viewpoint from which a situation is presented. It may be viewed 'from the outside', as a completed whole, with both its starting point and its endpoint visible. This is called **perfective** aspect. Alternatively, it may be viewed 'from the inside', as being incomplete and ongoing at the time in question. This internal perspective, known as **imperfective** aspect, is also the typical viewpoint for the presentation of static situations (states).

At another level, imperfective forms are used for presenting any kind of situation (event or state) as occurring habitually, or as a general rule or pattern. In habitual statements it is the recurring pattern of events, rather than any individual event or state, that is presented as ongoing at the time in question.

21.3.1 Perfective and imperfective

The distinction between perfective and imperfective applies mainly to sentences in the past tense. Perfective aspect is expressed by the verbal suffixes *-DI* and *-mIş*, and imperfective aspect is expressed by the verbal suffixes *-(I)yor*, *-mAktA* and *-(A/I)r/-z* and by the past copular marker *-(y)DI*.

Perfective

    (25) a. Geçen hafta her gün iki saat çalış-**tı**-m.
                                  work-PF-1SG
        'Last week I *worked* for two hours every day.'

        b. İki saat çalış-**mış**-ım.
           work-EV/PF-1SG
        'I *seem to have worked* for two hours.'

Imperfective

    (26) a. Saat ikide çalış-**ıyor-du**-m.
                work-IMPF-P.COP-1SG
        'At two o'clock I *was working*.'

        b. Saat ikide ofis-te-**ydi**-m.
           office-LOC-P.COP-1SG 'At two o'clock I *was* at the office.'

        c. Genellikle iki saat çalış-**ır-dı**-m.
                    work-AOR-P.COP-1SG
        'I *would* usually *work* for two hours.'

The forms *-mIştI* and *-DIydI* (21.2.1) combine elements of perfectivity and imperfectivity. They express the state ensuing upon the completion of an action or event.

21.3.2 Subdivisions of imperfective: progressive and habitual

Within imperfective aspect there is a further distinction between **progressive** and **habitual**, which applies in both past and non-past contexts. Progressive aspect views a *specific situation* as incomplete. This situation may be dynamic (an event) or static (a state). In either case it is presented as being ongoing or continuing at the temporal reference point. Habitual aspect, on the other hand, indicates that a situation is incomplete in a different way: not at the level of any specific occurrence but in the sense that it is part of a *recurrent pattern*, which is shown as ongoing at the temporal reference point.

Of the imperfective markers noted above, *-(I)yor* occurs with both progressive and habitual meaning while *-mAktA* generally expresses progressive aspect but can occur with habitual meaning in relatively formal contexts. The difference between *-(I)yor* and *-mAktA* is largely stylistic, with *-(I)yor* being less formal and therefore much the more common in conversation. *-mAktA* may occur where a speaker wishes to emphasize the intensity of the ongoing event.

The range of aspectual meanings of *-(I)yor* and *-mAktA* in present tense sentences is illustrated below:

Progressive (event)

(27) A. Şu an-da ne yap-**ıyor**-sunuz?
 this moment-LOC what do-IMPF-2PL
 'What *are* you *doing* at the moment?'

 B. Yemek yi-**yor**-uz.
 meal eat-IMPF-1PL
 'We*'re having* dinner.'

(28) Bugün aile yapı-sı hız-la değ iş-**mekte**-dir.
 today family structure-NCM speed-COM change-IMPF-GM
 'Today the structure of the family *is changing* rapidly.'

Progressive (state)

(29) Sen Ömer-i ben-den daha iyi tanı-**yor**-sun.
 you Ömer-ACC I-ABL more well know-IMPF-2SG
 'You *know* Ömer better than me.'

(30) Çizgi-nin üst taraf-ın-da birkaç beyaz nokta
 line-GEN upper side-3SG.POSS-LOC several white spot

 gör-ül-**mekte**-dir.
 see-PASS-IMPF-GM

 'Several white spots *are seen* above the line.'

Habitual

   (31) Fatma genellikle Ankara-ya otobüs-le gid-**iyor**.
        Fatma usually Ankara-DAT bus-INS go-IMPF
        'Fatma usually *goes* to Ankara by bus.'

   (32) Türkiye artık televizyon ihraç et-**mekte**-dir.
        Turkey now television export AUX-IMPF-GM
        'Now Turkey *exports/is exporting* televisions.'

A precisely similar range of meanings is seen in past tense sentences with *-(I)yordu* and *-mAktAydI*:

   (33) Saat ikide çalış-**ıyor-du**-m.   (Progressive: event)
                            IMPF-P.COP-1SG
        'At two o'clock I *was working*.'

   (34) Sen Ömer'i benden daha iyi tanı-**yor-du**-n.   (Progressive: state)
                                      IMPF-P.COP-2SG
        'You *knew* Ömer better than me.'

   (35) Genellikle yazın bu rakam art-**makta-ydı**.   (Habitual)
                                     IMPF-P.COP
        'This figure *would* usually *increase* in the summer.'

The aorist forms *-(A/I)r/-z* never express progressive aspect. In past habituals, *-(A/I)rdI/-zdI* are often interchangeable with *-(I)yordu* or *-mAktAydI* (or their negative forms):

   (36) a. O zamanlarda Mehmet çok sigara iç-**er-di**.
                                          AOR-P.COP
           'At that time Mehmet smoked/used to smoke a lot/Mehmet was a heavy smoker.'

        b. O zamanlarda Mehmet çok sigara iç-**iyor-du**.
                                          IMPF-P.COP
           'At that time Mehmet was smoking a lot.'

The difference in meaning between the two past habitual forms *-(A/I)rdI* and *-(I)yordu* reflects the 'general rule'/'observed facts' dichotomy between the aorist and other finite forms discussed in 21.4.1.1. *-(A/I)rdI* usually refers to a long-term pattern of behaviour, which in the case of a human subject is viewed as an inherent characteristic of that person.

-(A/I)rdI is potentially ambiguous between the past habitual meaning seen in (36a) and the counterfactual meaning 'would have...' (21.4.1.3) which occurs most typically in the main clause of certain types of conditional sentence.

21.3.3 Events and states

There is a close interaction between aspect marking and the event/state distinction. Although both events and states can be presented from an imperfective viewpoint, perfective aspect occurs typically in the expression of events. A number of verbs, particularly those expressing a bodily posture or a psychological state (perception, cognition or emotion), have a dynamic (event) meaning when used in a perfective form, and a stative (state) meaning when used in a progressive form. Some examples are given below.

	Event	State
dur-	'stop'	'stand'
otur-	'sit down'	'be sitting'
yat-	'lie down', 'go to bed'	'lie', 'be in bed'
uyu-	'fall asleep'	'be asleep'
tanı-	'recognize'	'know'

The effect of aspect marking on the meaning of these verbs is illustrated below:

(37) a. Tülay yan-ım-a ***otur-du***. (Event)
Tülay side-1SG.POSS-DAT sit-PF
'Tülay *sat down* beside me.'

b. Yemek-te Tülay yan-ım-da ***otur-uyor-du***. (State)
dinner-LOC Tülay side-1SG.POSS-LOC sit-IMPF-P.COP
'Tülay *was sitting* beside me at dinner.'

In the case of psychological verbs such as *sevin-* 'be glad' (and some others, such as *üşü-* '(begin to) feel cold'), there is often a high degree of interchangeability between a perfective *-DI* or *-mIş* (expressing entry into a state) and a progressive *-(I)yor* (expressing the state itself):

(38) a. [Mehmet-in gel-eceğ-in]-e ***sevin-di***-m. (Entry into state)
Mehmet-GEN come-VN-3SG.POSS-DAT be.glad-PF-1SG
'I *was*/I *'m glad* [to hear] that Mehmet's coming.'

b. [Mehmet'in geleceğ in]-e ***sevin-iyor***-um. (State)
IMPF-1SG
'I *'m glad* Mehmet's coming.'

(39) a. ***Anla*-dı-**n mı? (Entry into state)
PF-2SG INT
'*Have* you understood?/*Do* you understand?'

b. ***Anlı*-yor** mu-sun? (State)
IMPF INT-2SG
'*Do* you understand?'

In the case of some of the verbs that have this dual event/state quality, in particular those involving physical states, it is possible for perfective forms to indicate not just entry into the state (of sleep, sitting, etc.) but the maintenance of that state over a period of time:

(40) Sekiz saat ***uyu*muş**um.
'I *seem to have slept* for eight hours.'

(41) Bütün gün evde ***otur*d**uk.
'We *sat* at home all day.'

Turkish also has a small class of verbs which can directly express only the *entry into a state*. The existence of the state at some particular time is expressed by a perfective form. The most important verbs in this class are *acık-* 'get hungry', *susa-* 'get thirsty', *yorul-* 'get tired', *bık-* 'get tired (of)/bored (with)', *kız-* 'get angry', *kal-* 'be left':

(42) **Susa-dı-**m.
get.thirsty-PF-1SG
'I'm thirsty.'

21.3.4 Aspect in nominal sentences

Aspectual marking in nominal sentences requires the presence of the copular verb *ol-* (12.1.1.3) to act as the bearer of one of the aspectual suffixes discussed in 21.3.1. Two particular forms are aspectually significant: *oldu* (contrasting with *-(y)DI/idi* and *vardı*) and *oluyor*.

21.3.4.1 The distinction between oldu and -(y)DI/idi or vardı

In its copular functions the verb *ol-* can have either dynamic or stative meaning, a distinction that generally corresponds to the distinction between 'become' and 'be' in English. The past copular marker *-(y)DI/idi*, on the other hand, being a marker of imperfectivity, can only express states ('be'). This means that the distinction between *oldu* and *-(y)DI/idi* often corresponds to that between 'became' and 'was':

(43) 1994'te Ahmet derneğin başkanı **oldu**.
'In 1994 Ahmet *became* president of the society.'

(44) 1994'te Ahmet derneğin başkanı**ydı**.
'In 1994 Ahmet *was* president of the society.'

However, there are certain kinds of nominal sentence in which *oldu* does not express a change of state (as 'become' does), but rather the outcome of a process of evaluation or ranking.

(45) Geçen hafta-ki toplantı çok sıkıcı **ol-du**.
last week-ADJ meeting very boring be-PF
'Last week's meeting *was* very boring.'

In the case of ranking, a sequential ordering item such as *ilk* 'first', *son(uncu)* 'last', *ondan sonraki* 'the next' or an ordinal numeral (15.7.2) will be involved:

(46) Gürkan [bana bu olay-dan bahsed-en] ***üçüncü*** kişi **ol-du**.
Gürkan I.DAT this incident-ABL mention-PART third person be-PF
'Gürkan *was* the *third* person [to mention this incident to me].'

The superlative marker *en* 'most' (15.4.3) is another typical element of these evaluative sentences:

(47) [***En*** beğenilen] tablo bu **oldu**.
'The picture [that was *most* admired] *was* this one.'

In existential sentences, *oldu* expresses the event of coming into existence rather than the (past) state of existing. In (48), the choice of *oldu* rather than *vardı* would reflect the fact that each act of asking was a completed event.

(48) Partide [seni soran]lar **oldu/vardı**.
'There *were* people [asking after you] at the party.'

(49) Fatma'nın bir kızı **oldu**.
'Fatma *(has) had* a daughter.'

The same aspectual distinction applies to *olmuş* and *-(y)mIş/imiş*.

21.3.4.2 Habitual aspect in nominal sentences

Habitual aspect in nominal sentences is marked by *oluyor* in non-past contexts and by *oluyordu* or *olurdu* in past contexts. The pairs of sentences below illustrate the difference between a single state that obtains/obtained at some particular moment, and a habitually recurring state:

(50) a. Şu anda **ev-de-yim**.
　　　　　　home-LOC-1SG
　　　'At the moment *I'm at home*.'

b. Bu saatte **ev-de ol-uyor-um**.
　　　　　　home-LOC be-IMPF-1SG
　'*I'm [usually] at home* at this time [of day].'

(51) a. Ögrenciler o gün neşeli-**ydi**-ler.
　　　　　　　　　　　　cheerful-P.COP-3PL
　　　'The students *were* cheerful that day.'

b. Öğ renciler neşeli **ol-uyor**-lar-**dı**/**ol-ur**-lar-**dı**.
　　　　　　　cheerful be-IMPF-3PL-P.COP/BE-AOR-3PL-P.COP
　'The students *were (usually/always)* cheerful.'

(52) a. Bu akşam film var.
　　　'There's a film this evening.'

b. Bazı akşamlar film **oluyor**.
　　'Some evenings there's a film.'

21.3.4.3 Other meanings of oluyor

The copular form *oluyor* is sometimes used in sentences expressing an identification or classification and has the effect of making a statement sound less abrupt or less categorical. This is a stylistic refinement which is in decreasing use:

(53) Halil benim dayızadem (**oluyor**).
　　'Halil is my cousin.' (son of my maternal uncle)

(54) En ucuzu bu (**oluyor**) galiba.
　　'This one seems to be the cheapest.'

In some instances of this optional usage of *oluyor*, an element of habituality can be detected.

(55) Ortak dilimiz Fransızcaydı/Fransızca **oluyordu**.
　　'Our common language was French.'

Another optional usage of *oluyor* occurs where a speaker wants to emphasize the ongoing, subjective experience of a situation, process or activity.

(56) Anne babaları arasındaki bu gerginlik, çocuklar için zor (**oluyor**) tabii.
　　'This tension between their parents is, of course, hard for the children.'

21.4 Modality

Unlike tense and aspect, modality is not related to the concept of time. It is concerned with whether a situation is presented as a directly known fact, or in some other way. A main clause that is marked by one of the following tense, aspect and modality suffixes is *modally neutral*, that is to say it is presented as reflecting a fact directly known to the speaker:

(i) In verbal sentences: *-DI, -(I)yor, -mAktA*
(ii) In nominal sentences: no marker or *-(y)DI*

Modalized utterances are of various kinds. They may present:

(i) A generalization, general rule, or statement of principle: *-(A/I)r/-z, -DIr* (21.4.1.1)
(ii) An assumption or hypothesis: *-(A/I)r/-z, -DIr, olacak, olmalı* (21.4.1.3–4)
(iii) A statement concerning the possibility or necessity of the occurrence of an event or state: *-(y)Abil/-(y)AmA, -mAlI* (21.4.2)
(iv) A statement based upon knowledge acquired indirectly: *-mIş, -(y)mIş* (21.4.3)
(v) An expression of desire or willingness for an event or state to occur: imperative, optative, conditional and aorist forms (21.4.4)

The suffixes *-mIş* and *-(y)AcAK* have modal force in some contexts but not in others. In the case of *-mIş* this is grammatically determined: *-mIş* becomes purely a tense/aspect marker when followed by *-(y)DI, -DIr* or *ol-*. By contrast, whether *-(y)AcAK* is to be understood as (unmodally) marking future tense or (modally) expressing an assumption or an instruction depends on the speech context in a more general way.

21.4.1 Generalizations and hypotheses

The Turkish system of modality marking allows for a distinction to be made between (neutral) statements that reflect the direct experience, knowledge or observation of the speaker and (modal) statements that make assertions of a more general, theoretical nature or express assumptions or hypotheses. The grammatical markers that express these types of modality are predominantly the aorist forms *-(A/I)r/-z* in verbal sentences and the generalizing modality marker *-DIr* in nominal sentences.

21.4.1.1 Statements of permanent or generalized validity

Verbal sentences with aorist

In reviewing the types of generalization that are expressed by the aorist, we shall compare statements expressed in this form with the corresponding statements marked with the imperfective marker *-(I)yor*. In its habitual aspect sense (21.3.2),

-(I)yor expresses a different kind of generalization from the aorist, one that refers to a state of affairs which has been directly observed or experienced by the speaker without implying that it has the status of a rule or principle.

There are four main types of generalization expressed by the aorist:

(i) Scientific and moral axioms:

(57) İki iki daha dört ed-**er**.
two two more four make-AOR
'Two and two make four.'

(58) Para mutluluk getir-**me-z**.
money happiness bring- NEG-NEG.AOR
'Money doesn't bring happiness.'

In contrast with (58), which claims to be a universal truth, (59) reflects the speaker's own experience or observation from life:

(59) Para mutluluk getir-mi-**yor**.
NEG-IMPF
'Money doesn't bring happiness.'

(ii) Normative or prescriptive statements:
The use of the aorist is standard in text types, ranging from constitutions to recipes that lay down a procedure that is to be followed. However, such statements are usually capable of either a descriptive or a prescriptive reading:

(60) Başbakan, Cumhurbaşkanı tarafından görevlendiri**lir**.
'The Prime Minister *is* appointed by the President.'

(61) Burada musluk suyu içil**mez**.
'One *doesn't* drink the tap water here.'
(lit. 'The tap water is not drunk...')

The corresponding form with *-(I)yor*, on the other hand, is more descriptive:

(62) Burada musluk suyu içil**miyor**.
'Here people *don't* drink the tap water.'
(lit. 'The tap water is not drunk...')

The passive of the negative aorist form is regularly used in public notices expressing prohibitions:

(63) *Giril**mez***   'No entry'
*Park yapıl**maz***   'No parking'

(iii) Generic statements about the characteristic qualities or behaviour of a class:

(64) Kaplumbağa yavaş yürür.
'A tortoise walks slowly.'

(65) Bebekler çok süt içer.
'(The) Babies drink a lot of milk.'

The substitution of *-(I)yor* for the aorist in sentences like (64), where the subject is bare, changes the reference of this noun phrase from generic to specific (22.7). Thus, in (66) *kaplumbağa* most likely refers to a specific tortoise:

(66) kaplumbağa yavaş yürüyor.
'The tortoise *walks/is walking* slowly.'

In (67) the plural-marked *bebekler* could retain its generic reading (22.7), but could also refer to a specific group of *bebekler*:

(67) Bebekler çok süt içiyor(lar).
'The babies *are drinking/drink* a lot of milk.'

(vii) Statements about the characteristic qualities or behaviour of an individual:

(68) Ali sigara iç-**me-z**.
     NEG-NEG.AOR
'Ali doesn't smoke.'

(69) Ali sigara iç-**mi-yor**.
     NEG-IMPF
'Ali doesn't smoke.'

The sentence in (68) could be paraphrased as 'Ali is a non-smoker'. Its counterpart (69) merely describes Ali's observed habitual behaviour. This difference in meaning is underlined by the fact that an adverbial restricting the time span to which the statement applies, such as *bu günlerde* 'at the moment' (16.4.1.1), would be possible only with *içmiyor*:

(70) Ali **bu günlerde** sigara içmiyor.
'Ali's not smoking *at the moment*.'

Nominal sentences with -DIr

One of the functions of the generalizing modality marker *-DIr* in a nominal sentence is to define or classify a subject, or to ascribe certain permanent qualities or inherent characteristics to it. However, this usage of *-DIr* is nowadays largely confined to formal language.

(71) Antropoloji [insan topluluklarını inceleyen] bir bilim(**dir**).
'Anthropology *is* a science which studies human communities.'

Where a generalization ascribes a certain quality to an entire class, and the subject complement is adjectival, the less formal counterpart of *-DIr* is not the absence of a marker, as above, but *olur* or *oluyor*. These forms give the statement a less absolute, more modest tone than *-DIr*. Like other *-(I)yor* forms, *oluyor* conveys the idea that the utterance reflects the speaker's own experience:

(72) Çocuklar bencil **ol-ur/ol-uyor**.
    be-AOR/be-IMPF
   'Children *tend to be/are usually* selfish.'

For *oluyor* as a marker of habitual aspect, see 21.3.4.2.

21.4.1.2 The use of -DIr in formal communication

In academic or official communications or other formal contexts, the use of *-DIr* is by no means confined to nominal sentences. *-DIr* is also regularly affixed to the following finite verbal forms: *-mIş, -(y)AcAK, -mAlI, -mAktA*.

(73) Osmanlı Türkleri de bu kültüre katkıda bulun*muş*lar**dır**.
    'And the Ottoman Turks contributed to this culture.'

(74) Bu teknik, [[yüzeysel yapıları farklı olan] eserlerin karşılaştırılmasını]ı kolaylaştır**acaktır**.
    'This technique *will* facilitate the comparison of works [which have different surface structures].'

The modal function of *-DIr* in these verbal sentences is to indicate that a claim of some significance is being made and that this is based on some well-founded authority which gives it a kind of permanence that transcends the explicit tense marking of its content.

21.4.1.3 Hypothetical and counterfactual situations

Hypothetical and counterfactual situations imply the fulfilment of some condition (27.2.3–6):

(75) Koşma, düş**er**sin.
    'Don't run; you*'ll* fall over.'

(76) Senden iyi mühendis ol**ur**.
    'You *would* make a good engineer.'
    (lit. 'From you [a] good engineer would come into existence.')

Counterfactual situations differ from hypotheticals in that the condition upon which they depend is known to be unrealizable. They are expressed by *-(A/I)rdI/-mAzdI* or *-(y)AcAktI*:

> (77) Ben bu reng-i seç-**me-z-di**-m.
> I this colour-ACC choose-NEG-NEG.AOR -P.COP-1SG
> 'I *wouldn't have* chosen this colour.'

-(y)AcAktI is an option only where reference is to a pre-planned or scheduled event:

> (78) [O konser-e git-mek] hoş ol-**ur-du**/ol-**acak-tı**.
> that concert-DAT go-VN nice be-AOR-P.COP/be-FUT-P.COP
> 'It *would have* been nice [to go to that concert].'

In counterfactual utterances, the past copula *-(y)DI* is as much a marker of modality as of tense, and the reference is not always to past time (27.2.3.2).

21.4.1.4 Assumptions, conjectures and hopes

The principal grammatical markers of non-factual probability judgements (asumptions, conjectures, hopes) are the aorist and *-DIr*. Such utterances are usually also marked by a modal adverbial (16.3) such as *kesinlikle* 'definitely', *herhalde* 'probably', 'presumably', 'I expect', *belki* 'perhaps', *umarım* 'I hope' or *inşallah* 'God willing', 'hopefully'. Where no modal adverbial is used the utterance will usually be understood as having the medium strength of an assumption marked by *herhalde* as in (82) below.

(i) Verbal sentences with *-(A/I)r/-z*:
Assumptions expressed with the aorist always have future time reference, and denote events that are not envisaged as planned or predetermined:

> (79) Mehmet geç gel-**ir**.
> late come-AOR
> 'Mehmet *will (probably)* be late.'

> (80) **Umarım** Semra vazonun yokluğ unu farket-**me-z**.
> notice- NEG-NEG.AOR
> '*I hope* Semra won't notice the absence of the vase.'

(ii) Nominal and verbal sentences with *-DIr*:
In this type of utterance, *-DIr* is attached not only to 3rd person but also to 1st and 2nd person predicates (see 8.3.3).

> (81) *İnşallah* hasta değ il-im-**dir**.
> hopefully ill not-1SG-GM
> '*I hope* I'm not ill.'

(82) *Herhalde* bir yerlerde karşılaş-**mış**-ız-**dır**.
                                                 PF-1PL-GM
     'We *have probably* met somewhere or other.'

(83) *Mutlaka* bugün telefon ed-**ecek**-ler-**dir**.
                                         FUT-3PL-GM
     'They *will definitely* ring today.'

-(y)AcAktIr expresses the assumption that the predicted action is planned or otherwise predetermined. Example (83), therefore, expresses greater confidence in the realization of the prediction than if the aorist had been used.

(iii) Informal conjectures without grammatical marking of modality:
In colloquial speech, the conjectural status of a statement relating to past or present time can be indicated without *-DIr*, simply through the inclusion of an appropriate modal adverb:

(84) Unuttu **herhalde**.
     'S/he's *probably* forgotten.'/'*I expect* s/he forgot.'

(iv) Probability statements with *olsa gerek*:
This construction (the conditional form of the copular/auxiliary verb *ol-* followed by *gerek* 'necessary') is used mostly in the 3rd person:

(85) En iyisi bu **olsa gerek**.
     'This one is *probably* the best.'

olsa gerek occurs also in compound verb forms (21.5).

(v) Non-future predictions with *olacak*:
The future form of *ol-* can be used with present tense reference to make a confident statement about an entity that is not within sight at the moment of speech, but is near enough for the prediction to be immediately verified:

(86) A. Zarflar nerede?
         'Where are the envelopes?'

     B. İkinci çekmecede **olacak**lar.
        'They'*ll be* in the second drawer.'

For the occurrence of this usage of *olacak* in compound verb forms, see 21.5.1.

(vi) Assumptive use of *olması gerek/lazım*:
The construction *-mA-*POSS *gerek/lazım* is one of the means of expressing objective necessity, as explained in 21.4.2.2. The 3rd person form with the copular/auxiliary *ol-* as the verb can have the secondary function of expressing a strong assumption based upon knowledge of other relevant facts. The time reference is either present or, where there is a preceding verb form with *-mIş*, past:

(87) Bu saatte [Ali'nin işte **olması**] **lazım**.
'Ali *must be* at work at this hour.' (I know his hours of work.)

(88) [Herkesin afişi gör**müş olması**] **gerek**.
'Everyone *must have* seen the notice.' (It was in an obvious place.)

(vii) Deductions with *olmalı*:
The obligative form (21.4.2.2) of the copular/auxiliary verb *ol-* expresses an inference drawn about a past or present event or state from strong circumstantial evidence. In nominal sentences, the time reference is present tense:

(89) Kapı açık, evde **olmalı**lar.
'The door's open; they *must be* at home.'

For the use of *olmalı* following the *-mIş* or *-(I)yor* form of other verbs, see 21.5.1–2 and (90) below.
In the context of a narrative, *olmalı* can be used with the addition of the past copular marker to express a deduction made at a certain juncture in the story:

(90) Ali ceplerini aradı, telefon yoktu: lokantada unut**muş olmalıydı**.
'Ali searched his pockets, the phone wasn't there; he *must have* left it in the restaurant.'

21.4.2 Possibility and necessity

The concepts of possibility and necessity differ from other types of modality in having objective components that are independent of the speaker's perception or attitude. *Ahmet can swim two kilometres* and *The card has to be inserted slowly* are examples respectively of **objective possibility** and **objective necessity**.

21.4.2.1 The expression of possibility

The suffixes which mark possibility and impossibility (8.2.3.1–2) are the verbal suffixes *-(y)Abil* and *-(y)AmA* (the latter, a composite suffix incorporating the negative marker *-mA*). The markers of possibility and impossibility enter into a wide range of combinations with the markers of tense, aspect, and other types of modality. Non-finite verb forms can also be marked for (im)possibility:

(91) konuş-**abil**-mek
talk-PSB-VN
'to *be able to* talk'

(92) gör-**e**-**me**-yen-ler
see-PSB-NEG-PART-PL
'those *unable to* see'

Where *-(y)Abil* is added to the negative stem of a verb, it denotes the possibility of the action *not* occurring, or the freedom of the subject not to perform it:

(93) söyle-***me*-yebil**-mek
say-NEG-PSB-VN
'to *be able not to* say'

Objective possibility and the question of actualization

Objective possibility denotes either the ability of a person to perform a certain action or the absence of any impediment to the occurrence of an event. In statements of objective possibility, the choice of tense/aspect/modality marking (following *-(y)Abil/-(y)AmA*) determines whether the possibility or impossibility is understood as **actualized** (taking effect) or not.

(i) Statements marked with *-DI*, *-mIş*, *-(I)yor* or *-mAktA* (with or without a following *-(y)DI*) always imply the actualization of the possibility or impossibility:

(94) Geçen yıl Bodrum'a dört defa gid-**ebil**-***di***-k.
go-PSB-PF-1PL
'Last year we *were able to* go to Bodrum four times.'
(Implies that we did this.)

(95) Filiz o gün oğluyla konuş-**a**-**ma**-***mış-tı***.
talk-PSB-NEG-PF-P.COP
'Filiz *hadn't been able to* talk to her son that day.'
(Implies that she had not talked to him.)

The combination of (im)possibility marking with the future marker *-(y)AcAK* signifies that the speaker confidently predicts the occurrence of a possibility (or the absence of it) at some future time. It also strongly implies actualization, particularly in the case of impossibility:

(96) Yeni evimizden işime bisikletle gid**emeyeceğ**im.
'From our new house I *shan't be able to* go to work by bicycle.'
(Implies that I shall not go by bike.)

The form *-(y)Abiliyor* can additionally be used to express the fact that a situation tends to occur from time to time:

(97) Plastik parçalar zamanla aşın**abili***yor*.
'The parts made of plastic *can/tend to* erode with time.'

(ii) Statements with aorist marking simply assert that the possibility of something happening exists or does not exist, leaving the question of actualization open. Aorist-marked (im)possibility statements fall into one or other of the categories of modalized statement typically expressed by the aorist:

a. Statements of generalized validity (21.4.1.1):

(98) Kaplumbağa hızlı yürü-**ya-me-z**. (cf. (64))
walk-PSB- NEG-NEG.AOR
'A tortoise *can't* walk fast.'

b. Hypothetical statements (21.4.1.3):

(99) Masayı şuraya koy**abilir**iz.
'We *can/could* put the table here.' (If we so decide(d).)

c. Assumptions, conjectures and hopes with future time reference (21.4.1.4 (i)):

(100) Belki bunca zamandan sonra birbirimizi
tanı-**ya-ma**-yız.
recognize-PSB-NEG-1PL

'Maybe we *won't be able to* recognize each other after all this time.'

(iii) The combination of aorist *-(y)Abilir* or *-(y)AmA(z)* with the past copular marker *-(y)DI* produces counterfactual meaning. Affirmative predicates signal that a possibility perceived as having been in existence at some time in the past was not actualized:

(101) Daha uygun bir saat seç**ebilird**iniz.
'You *could have* chosen a more convenient time.' (Implies that you didn't.)

In the case of negative predicates, the counterfactuality is more complicated. Instead of asserting what could have happened (but did not) in a given situation in the past, the speaker envisages a situation *different from* what actually did happen and asserts the impossibility of that imaginary scenario being actualized. For example, in (102) the speaker is understood to have achieved success with the help of others, *not* on his/her own.

(102) Ben bunu tek başıma yap**amazdı**m.
'I *couldn't have* done this on my own.'

(iv) The combination of *-(y)AcAK* or *-(I)yor* with the past copular marker *-(y)DI* express a hypothetical event. These constructions can contain one of the adverbials neredeyse/az daha/az kalsın 'nearly':

(103) Neredeyse düş**ecektim**/düş**üyordum**.
'I nearly fell'.

Speaker-generated possibility

Speaker-generated possibility (as distinct from objective possibility) is of two types: **permissive** and **speculative**.

(i) Permissive possibility:
The granting of permission by the speaker to the addressee(s) or to a third party is expressed by *-(y)Abilir*:

(104) Bilgisayarımı [ne zaman istersen] kullan-**abil-ir**-sin.
                              use-PSB-AOR-2SG
'You *can* use my computer [whenever you like]. (I give you permission to do so.)

Prohibition is expressed by *-(y)AmAz*:

(105) Burada otur-**a-ma-z**-sınız.
        sit-PSB- NEG-NEG.AOR-2PL
'You *can't* sit here.' (I/We don't allow it. / It is not allowed.)

Requests for permission are expressed with the 1st person interrogative of the above forms:

(106) Bir şey sor**abilir** miyim?
'*Can/May* I ask something?'

(ii) Speculative possibility:
A statement of speculative possibility expresses a judgement about the possibility of some event occurring. It is usually expressed with *-(y)Abilir*:

(107) Bugün yağmur yağ**abilir**.
'It *may/could* rain today.'

Occasionally, speculative possibility is expressed with *-(y)AbileceK*. The use of this form effectively neutralizes the distinction between objective and speculative possibility, and gives a greater sense of authority to a statement about the possible occurrence of a future event:

(108) Bu evler birkaç yıl sonra yıkıl**abilecek**.
 'These houses *may* be demolished in a few years' time.'

Speculations with *-(y)Abilir* can be expressed about negative or (objectively) impossible situations as well as positive ones:

(109) Yağmur yağ -*ma*-**yabil**-**ir**.
  NEG-PSB-AOR
 'It *may not* rain.'/'It'*s possible (that)* it wo*n't* rain.'

(110) Coşkun'u ikna ed-*e*-*me*-**yebil**-**ir**-im.
  AUX-PSB-NEG-PSB-AOR-1SG
 'I *may not* be able to persuade Coşkun.'

With verbs in general the negative possibility aorist form *-(y)AmA(z)* does not occur with speculative meaning. However, in the case of the copular/auxiliary *ol-* 'be', this form can be used to negate a speculative possibility on the basis of other known facts:

(111) Osman Ankara'da ol**amaz**.
 'Osman *can't* be in Ankara.' (e.g. Because I saw him in London an hour ago.)

(112) Sen bu ceketimi daha önce gör-*müş* ol-**a-ma-z**-sın.
  see-PF AUX-PSB- NEG-NEG.AOR-2SG
 'You *can't have* seen this jacket of mine before.' (e.g. Because I have only just bought it.)

Ambiguity of *-(y)Abilir*

In sentences expressing events in which human agency is involved, the sequence *-(y)Abilir* is potentially ambiguous between objective, speculative and permissive readings:

(113) Ahmet tez-in-i bu oda-da yaz-**abil**-**ir**.
  thesis-3SG.POSS-ACC this room-LOC write-PSB-AOR

  (i) 'Ahmet *can/could* write his thesis in this room.'
   (There is nothing to prevent him from doing this.) (Objective)

  (ii) 'Ahmet *can* write his thesis in this room.'
   (I permit him to use the room for this purpose.) (Permissive)

(iii) 'Ahmet *may* write his thesis in this room.'
(I consider it possible that he will decide to do so. / Perhaps he will do so.) (Speculative)

The expression of possibility in subordinate clauses formed with *-DIK/-(y)AcAK*

As explained elsewhere in this book, certain types of subordinate clause involve a choice between *-DIK* and *-(y)AcAK* as the verbal marker:

(i) Noun clauses expressing indirect statements and questions (24.4.3)
(ii) Certain types of relative clause (25.1.1.2)
(iii) Certain types of adverbial clause (26.2, 26.3)

The distinction in meaning between these two forms is generally one of tense, with *-DIK* expressing relative present or relative past, and *-(y)AcAK* relative future. However, where one of these suffixes is combined with a possibility marker, the *-DIK/-(y)AcAK* distinction often involves modality as much as tense. The combinations *-(y)AbildiK* and *-(y)AmAdIK* always express actualized possibility/impossibility:

(114) [Selim-in neden bun-u yap-**a-ma-dığ**-ın]-ı anlıyordum.
Selim-GEN why this-ACC do-PSB-NEG-VN-3SG.POSS-ACC
'I understood [why Selim *couldn't/wasn't able to/hadn't been able to* do this].'
(Implies that Selim was not doing/had not done it.)

By contrast, the combinations *-(y)AbileceK* and *-(y)AmAyAcAK* have a number of different modal values in subordinate clauses:

(i) An objective possibility (or impossibility) that is expected to be actualized at some (relative) future time. This usage is equivalent to *-(y)AbileceK* in finite clauses:

(115) [Toplantıya katıl-**a-ma-yacağ**-ım]-ı söyledim.
attend-PSB-NEG-VN-1SG.POSS-ACC
'I said [I *wouldn't be able to* attend the meeting].'

(116) Kartı [herkesin gör-**ebil-eceğ**-i] bir yere koymuştu.
see-PSB-PART-3SG.POSS
'S/he had put the card in a place where everyone *would be able to* see it.'

(ii) Two of the kinds of objective possibility that are articulated by the aorist combinations *-(y)Abilir* and *-(y)AmA(z)* in finite clauses, in which the question of actualization is unresolved:

Generalizations

(117) [Yaşlıların gençleri kıskan**abilecek**lerin]i herkes bilir.
'Everyone knows [that the old *can* be jealous of the young].'

Hypothetical situations

(118) [O çocuğun yap**amayacağ**ı] hiçbir şey yok.
'There is nothing [that boy *couldn't* do].' (If he set his mind to it)

(iii) Counterfactual situations (expressed in finite clauses by *-(y)Abilirdi* and *-(y)AmAzdI*)

(119) Osman [Ali'ye yardım ed**ebileceğ**i halde] hiçbir şey yapmadı.
['Although Osman *could have* helped Ali], he did nothing.'

(iv) Permissive possibility and its denial:

(120) Özdemir'e [bilgisayarımı kullan**abileceğ**in]-i söyledim. (cf. 104))
'I told Özdemir [that he *could* use my computer].'

(v) The affirmative form *-(y)AbileceK* (attached to a positive or negative stem) can express speculative possibility:

(121) [Başkanlık konusunda Coşkun'u ikna ed*eme*yebileceğim için] başka kişiler üzerinde de durmamız gerekiyor. (cf. (110))
'[As I *may not be able to* persuade Coşkun about the chairmanship,] we have to consider other people too.'

As in the case of aorist impossibility forms in finite clauses, the subordinate impossibility combination *-(y)AmAyAcAK* can be used in a speculative context only when attached to the copula/auxiliary *ol-*:

(122) [Osman'ın Ankara'da ol**amayacağ**ın]-ı biliyordum. (cf. (111))
'I knew [that Osman *couldn't* be in Ankara].'

21.4.2.2 The expression of necessity/obligation

The grammatical marker of necessity (or obligation) is the suffix *-mAlI* (8.2.3.2).

(123) Ankara-ya git-**meli**-yim.
Ankara-DAT go-OBLG-1SG
'I *must* go to Ankara.'

Necessity is also regularly expressed by lexical means. This involves articulating the action that is considered necessary as a non-finite noun clause (24.4.1–2), which is then treated in one of the following ways:

(i) As the subject of a nominal sentence which has *gerek/lazım* 'necessary' or *şart* 'essential' as the subject complement:

    (124) [Ankara-ya git-me-m] **lazım/gerek/şart**.
              Ankara-DAT go-VN-1SG.POSS necessary/essential
              'I have to go to Ankara.'/'It's essential for me to go to Ankara.'
              (lit. '[My going to Ankara] is *necessary/essential*.')

(ii) As the subject of a verbal sentence with *gerek-* 'be necessary' as the predicate:

    (125) [Ankara'ya git-me-m] **gerek**-iyor.
                       go-VN-1SG.POSS be.necessary-IMPF
              'I have to go to Ankara.'
              (lit. '[My going to Ankara] is *necessary*.')

(iii) As the modifier in a *-(s)I* compound of which the head is *zor/ mecburiyet* 'compulsion' or *durum* 'situation':

    (126) [Ankara'ya git-mek] **zor**-un-da-yım/
                       go-VN compulsion-NCM-LOC-1SG/

                  durum-un-da-yım.
                  situation-NCM-LOC-1SG.

              'I have to/am obliged to go to Ankara.'
              (lit. 'I am in the *compulsion/situation* of [going to Ankara].')

Note that *zorunda* also has a synonym *mecburiyetinde* (from *mecburiyet* 'obligation'). The use of *durumunda* in this construction is slightly more formal than *zorunda* and is not favoured by all speakers.

All four versions of the statement in (123)–(126) refer to an obligation that is presented as existing at the moment of speech but not (yet) fulfilled. In many contexts they could be used interchangeably. However, apart from the fact that the constructions with *şart* and *zorunda* express a stronger, more unavoidable obligation than those with *gerek*, *lazım* or *gerek-*, there is a more fundamental difference between *-mAlI* (123), on the one hand, and all the lexicalized constructions (124)–(126) on the other. *-mAlI* expresses an obligation perceived or imposed by the speaker (**speaker-generated**), while the lexicalized constructions present an **objective** obligation, that is, one arising from external factors operating independently of the speaker. The difference corresponds roughly to that between (speaker-generated) 'must'/'should'/'ought' and (objective) 'have to' in English.

In addition to the personalized forms illustrated in (123)–(126), objective necessity can also be expressed impersonally, with a *-mAk* clause (24.4.1.1) as the subject of *lazım* or *gerek-*:

(127) [Burasını da doldurmak] **gerek**iyor mu?
'*Is it necessary to/Does one have to* fill in this part as well?'

Speaker-generated obligation *-mAll*

A sentence marked with *-mAll* that has a 1st person subject expresses an action which the speaker feels obliged (often morally obliged) to perform (but has not yet done so):

(128) Mustafa'ya yardım et**meli**yiz.
'We *must* help Mustafa.'

Where the subject is 2nd or 3rd person the utterance is tantamount to the speaker's imposing an obligation on the addressee(s) or someone else:

(129) Önce annene sor**malı**sın.
'You *must* first ask your mother.'

3rd person expressions of obligation can be given a more authoritative or didactic tone by the addition of *-DIR* (21.4.1.2):

(130) Herkes [çevresindekilerle iyi geçinmey]-e çalış**malı*dır*.
'Everyone *should* try to [get on well with those around them].'

Sometimes the 3rd person singular form (with or without *-DIr*) is used with impersonal meaning:

(131) Bu sorun bir an önce halledil**meli(dir)**.
'This problem *must* be solved as soon as possible.'
(lit. '[One] must solve…')

The affixation of *-mAll* to a negative stem expresses an obligation *not* to behave in a certain way:

(132) [Beni gördüğün]-ü hiç kimseye söyle-*me*-**meli**-sin.
                                                tell-NEG-OBLG-2SG
'You *mustn't* tell anyone [that you've seen me].'

Deductions expressed with *olmalı* (21.4.1.4 (vi)) constitute a quite different kind of speaker-generated necessity.

The question of whether an obligation is actualized

As in the case of possibility, the issue of whether an obligation is to be presented as actualized or not determines the choice of grammatical marking. All the examples that we have given so far express an obligation (objective or speaker-generated) that is perceived to exist at the moment of speech or as a general principle. Such statements are inherently indeterminate with regard to actualization.

Actualized obligation

The suffixes *-DI*, *-mIş* and *-(y)AcAK* imply the actualization of an obligation. The suffix *-(I)yor*, on the other hand, is ambiguous with regard to actuality. The constructions that can be marked for actualization are:

(i)   *-mA*-POSS *gerek-*
(ii) *-mA*-POSS *lazım gel-*
(iii) *-mAk zorunda kal-/durumunda kal-*

Examples of actualized obligation are given below:

(i) A specific event in the past:

   (133) a. [Zeki-ye yüz dolar ver-***me-m***] ***gerek***-ti.
              Zeki-DAT hundred dollar give-VN-1SG.POSS be.necessary-PF

          b. [Zeki-ye yüz dolar ver-***mek***] ***zor-un-da kal***-dı-m.
                                    give-VN compulsion-NCM-LOC be.left-PF-1SG
             'I *had to* give Zeki a hundred dollars.' (And therefore I did.)

(ii) Recurrent obligation:
     The only forms which unambiguously imply the actualization of a recurring obligation are *-mAk zorunda kalıyor(du)*:

   (134) **Her ay** Zeki'ye yüz dolar ver-***mek zor***-un-da

          kal-ıyor-um/kal-ıyor-du-m.
          IMPF-1SG/IMPF-P.COP-1SG

          'I *have/had to* give Zeki a hundred dollars *a month*.' (And therefore I do/did.)

The use of *vermem gerekiyor(du)* would be equally grammatical in (134), but would make the sentence ambiguous as to whether the obligation was fulfilled or avoided. See (125), (137) and (139) for sentences where *gerekiyor(du)* has a non-actualized or even (in the case of (137)) a counterfactual interpretation.

(iii) Firmly expected future (or relative future) obligation:
The marking of an obligational expression with *-(y)AcAK* indicates that the obligation is or was regarded as certain to occur at some time in the future and that its actualization will/would be unavoidable:

(135) Yakında yeni bir televizyon
al-***ma-mız* gerek-ecek**(-ti).
buy-VN-1PL.POSS be.necessary-FUT-P.COP

'We *shall (would)* soon *have to* buy a new television.'

Non-actualized obligation

Obligation expressed by *-mAlI* (without the addition of the past copula) is inherently unresolved in respect of actualization. The addition of *-(y)DI* to *-mAlI* produces one of two possible meanings:

(i) In the great majority of cases, it gives a counterfactual reading (21.4.1.3). In other words, it indicates that an obligation perceived by the speaker was not fulfilled at the time that it obtained:

(136) O para-yı geri ver-**meli-ydi**-n.
that money-ACC back give-OBLG-P.COP-2SG
'You *ought to have* given that money back.' (But you didn't.)

The forms *lazımdı, gerekiyordu* and *gerekirdi* can also be used counterfactually, like *-mAIIydI*:

(137) Dünkü toplantıda bu konuyu konuşmamız
gerekiyordu/gerekirdi.
'We *were supposed to* discuss/*should have* discussed this at yesterday's meeting.' (But we didn't.)

(ii) In the context of a narrative, *-mAIIydI* sometimes projects an obligation on to a subject at a particular juncture in the story. The outcome of the obligation is unknown at this point, that is, the question of actualization remains open:

(138) Hüseyin artık karar ver**meliydi**. [Herkesi bu kadar oyalaması] ayıptı.
'Hüseyin *must* now take a decision. It was shameful [for him to keep everyone waiting so long].'

This same indeterminacy with regard to whether an obligation that occurred in the past was actualized or not can also be expressed by adding the past copular marker to any of the lexical strategies exemplified in (124)–(126). This is illustrated in (139), which does not inform the addressee whether the speaker actually went on to say anything:

(139) Herkes bana bakıyordu. Artık bir şey söylemem **gerekiyordu**/**söylemek zorundaydım.**
'Everyone was looking at me. Now I *had to* say something.'

The expression of necessity in subordinate clauses

In subordinate clauses necessity and obligation can be expressed only by using one of the constructions with *gerek-* (or *lazım gel-*), *zorunda kal-* or (for obligations that are still in existence at the time on which attention is focused) *zorunda ol-*. The distinctions between objective and speaker-generated, and between actualized and non-actualized, necessity are neutralized in these non-finite constructions.

(140) a. Adam [gitmesi **gerek**-tiğ-in]-i söyledi.
be.necessary-VN-3SG.POSS-ACC
b. Adam [gitmek **zor-un-da ol**-duğ-un]-u söyledi.
compulsion-NCM-LOC be-VN-3SG.POSS-ACC
'The man said [he *had to* go]'.

21.4.3 Evidentially marked statements with -mIş or -(y)mIş

Another major category of speaker-generated modality consists of statements based upon knowledge acquired indirectly. This is called **evidential** modality and is marked by the verbal suffix *-mIş*, which (as explained in 21.2.1 and 21.3.1) also marks relative past tense and perfective aspect, and the copular suffix *-(y)mIş*, which is purely a marker of evidential modality. The source of the indirect knowledge upon which these statements are based is usually either a statement made by someone else or a resultant state (e.g. a flat tire as an indicator of the tire having burst). In the case of *-(y)mIş,* the modality marker sometimes simply indicates that the statement expresses a new discovery on the part of the speaker, which has not yet been fully assimilated to his/her existing stock of knowledge.

For the use of the modal adverbial *meğer(se)* in evidentially marked statements, see 16.3 (iv).

21.4.3.1 Information-based evidential statements

When speakers are transmitting information that they have received verbally from any other source, they give their statement evidential marking. Use of evidential marking is not a matter of choice. Failure to use it when making a statement about a situation of which one has no direct knowledge is a breach of conversational conventions, because it suggests that a different kind of knowledge (personal experience or observation) is involved. The English equivalents of *-mIş/-(y)mIş* in this usage are expressions like 'apparently', 'it seems', 'I gather'. The way in which the verbal suffix -*mIş* replaces -*DI* in the verbal transmission of information is illustrated in (141), which represents three separate, consecutive encounters between the individuals involved:

(141) a. (Ali, to Gül):

  Bahçe-ye bir meşe ağac-ı dik-**ti**-m.
  garden-DAT an oak tree-NCM plant-PF-1SG
  'I've planted an oak tree in the garden.'

  b. (Gül, to Orhan):

  Ali bahçe-sin-e bir meşe ağacı dik-**miş**.
  garden-3SG.POSS-DAT   EV/PF
  'Ali has *apparently* planted an oak tree in his garden.'

  c. (Orhan, to Ali):

  Sen bir meşe ağacı dik-**miş**-sin, bana göstersene.
                EV/PF-2SG
  '*I've heard* you've planted an oak tree; why don't you show it to me?'

(142a) could be from a newspaper report:

(142) a. İki tarafın temsilcileri Hilton Otelinde bir araya gel**di**ler.
  'Representatives of the two sides met at the Hilton Hotel.'

  b. (Ahmet, having read this news, relaying it to Gürkan:)
  İki tarafın temsilcileri Hilton Otelinde bir araya gel**miş**ler.
  '[*I've read that*] representatives of the two sides met at the Hilton Hotel.'

If the information received and transmitted by a speaker is anything other than a completed, past tense event, the evidential copular marker -*(y)mIş* is used. Unlike the verbal suffix -*mIş*, the copular -*(y)mIş* has no tense or aspect content. The aspectual meaning of a sentence with -*(y)mIş* is identical with that of the same sentence without evidential marking. However, the fact that not more than one copular marker may appear together on one verb gives rise to an ambiguity of tense reference (non-past/past) in -*(y)mIş* sentences, which can be resolved only by a time adverbial or by the discourse context:

(143) a. (Ayşe, to Çiğdem):
  Annem biraz rahatsız.
  'My mother's not very well.'

b. (Çiğdem, to Nesrin):
Ayşe'nin annesi biraz rahatsız-**mış**.
unwell-EV.COP
'*It seems* Ayşe's mother is not very well.'

(144) a. (Ayşe, to Çiğdem):

O gün annem biraz rahatsız**dı**.
'My mother *was* not very well *that day*.'

b. (Çiğdem, to Nesrin):

O gün Ayşe'nin annesi biraz rahatsız**mış**.
'*Apparently*, Ayşe's mother *was* not very well *that day*.'

The information-based evidential is relatively uncommon in the 1st and 2nd persons. In 1st person utterances, it may express information that the speaker has acquired from others about what s/he did when too young to remember, or while asleep or unconscious:

(145) [Bir yaş-ın-da-yken] kalp ameliyat-ı ol-**muş**-um.
one age-NCM-LOC-CV heart operation-NCM AUX-EV.COP-1SG
'I had a heart operation [when I was a year old].'

Alternatively, it may express what the speaker presents as a view of him/her held by other people, sometimes with the modal adverb *sözde* 'supposedly' (16.3 (ii)):

(146) Sözde inatçı-**ymış**-ım.
supposedly obstinate-EV.COP-1SG
'I am supposedly obstinate.'

An information-based 2nd person evidential utterance presents to the addressee some information about himself/herself that the speaker has acquired from another source.

(147) Siz babamla tanışıyor**muş**sunuz galiba.
'*I believe* you know/knew my father.'

21.4.3.2 Result-based evidential statements

Another use of the verbal suffix *-mIş* is to express the occurrence of an event that the speaker did not witness but is able to infer from its result, to which s/he has direct access. For example, any comment on a manufactured item which refers to something that was evidently done or not done during the course of its production requires to be expressed in this form. The same applies to the reporting of an accidental event such as a burst or breakage, which the speaker did not witness but whose result s/he has encountered.

>(148) (Commenting on a painting)
>Ressam iki figürün arasını boş bırak**mış**.
>'The painter has left the space between the two figures empty.'

>(149) (On finding one's glasses are not in one's pocket)
>Gözlüğümü yanıma almamışım.
>'I *seem* not to have brought my glasses with me.'

21.4.3.3 Use of the evidential copula to express a newly discovered state of affairs

Another use of the evidential copula *-(y)mIş* is to indicate that the state of affairs described is a new discovery as far as the speaker is concerned. There is often an element of surprise.

>(150) (On opening the fridge)
>Aaa, yiyecek hiçbir şey yok**muş**.
>'Oh, there's absolutely nothing to eat.'

>(151) (First comment to a friend after meeting his daughter)
>Kızın pek tatlı**mış**.
>'Your daughter is lovely.'

21.4.3.4 Evidentiality in questions

The function of an evidential marker in a question differs from its function in a statement in one fundamental respect. Here it is not the speaker's own knowledge but the addressee's that is being marked as indirect. If the speaker anticipates that, in answering his/her question, the addressee will be passing on information gained indirectly, or presenting a new discovery, s/he will recognize this by marking the question evidentially:

>(152) (Addressed to someone surfing the internet)
>Bugün dolar ne kadar**mış**?
>'How much *does it say* the dollar is today?'

>(153) (Addressed to someone who has gone into the kitchen)
>Fasulye ol**muş** mu?
>'Do the beans *seem* to be done?'

21.4.4 Volitional utterances

Volitional utterances are not statements, but expressions of the speaker's (or in interrogative forms the addressee's) will or desire in relation to the situation expressed.

21.4.4.1 Wishes

Turkish distinguishes two types of wishes: personal ones expressed with *-sA(ydI)* and formulaic ones expressed with 2nd or 3rd person imperative forms.

(i) Apart from being used in the construction of conditional clauses (Chapter 27), the verb forms *-sA/-sAydI* (8.2.3.3) express **personal wishes**.

    a. 1st person forms of *-sA* can express a fully realizable wish to perform some action:

        (154) Bu akşam güzel bir film seyret-**se**-k.
                                      watch-COND-1PL
             '*It would be nice* to watch a good film this evening.'

    b. *-sA* can also express wishes whose fulfilment is beyond the speaker's control and may be actually impossible. These correspond to constructions with 'if only' in English and are optionally marked by the modal adverb *keşke* 'if only' or by the adverbial *bir* 'once':

        (155) ***Keşke*** daha çok param ol**sa**.
              '*If only* I had more money.'

        (156) Bu soğuklar (***bir***) bit**se** artık...
              '*If only* this cold weather would come to an end...'

    c. *-sAydI* (or its colloquial alternative *-(y)AydI* (8.2.3.3)), again often combined with *keşke* or *bari* (16.3 (v)), expresses a counterfactual wish or regret, usually but not always relating to past time:

        (157) ***Keşke/bari*** Hülya'ya söyleme**seydi**n.
              '*I wish/ If only* you hadn't told Hülya.'

Wishes expressed by *-sAydI/(-(y)AydI* can have a reproachful, quasi-obligative tone:

        (158) [Madem uykun vardı], misafir çağırma**saydın**/çağırma**yaydın**.
              '[Since you were sleepy], you *would have done better* not *to* invite guests.'

(ii) Turkish has a large number of formulaic wishes (of which we give only a few examples here) that are used in particular social situations. Some are expressed with the basic 2nd person imperative forms (verb stem with no suffix or *-(y)In* (Group 4, 8.4.4, 21.4.4.2 (i)):

güle güle otur(un)	'enjoy living [here]' *(said to people who have moved into a new home)*
güle güle kullan(ın)	'enjoy using [it]' *(said to people who have acquired a new possession or to whom one has given a gift)*

Others (some of them religious in content) are expressed with the 3rd person singular Group 3 person marker *-sIn* (8.4.3):

*kolay gel****sin***	'may it go easily' *(said to people who are working)*
*afiyet ol****sun***	'may there be good health' *(said to people who are eating, especially by a host/cook in response to a compliment about the food s/he has provided, or after a meal is finished)*
Allah rahmet eylesin	'may God have mercy [on him/her]' *(said on someone's death)*

21.4.4.2 Commands

(i) Basic 2nd person commands are expressed by adding either no marker (familiar singular) or *-(y)In(Iz)* to the verb stem (Group 4, 8.4.4).

(159) Bu para-yı baba-n(ız)-a ver(**-in**).
this money-ACC father-2SG/PL.POSS-DAT give(-2PL)
'Give this money to your father.'

The longer 2nd person plural form *-(y)InIz* is used mainly for formal public directives:

(160) Lütfen kemerlerinizi bağla**yınız**.
'Please fasten your seatbelts.'

In ordinary social situations, *-(y)In* is the standard plural/polite imperative.

(ii) 3rd person instructions: *-sIn(lAr)*:
The 3rd person imperative forms (Group 4, 8.4.4) express instructions for something to be done by someone other than the addressee.

(161) Çocuklar burada kal**sın(lar)**.
'*Let* the children stay here.'/'*I want* the children to stay here.'/'*See to it that* the children stay here.'

If the speaker is only interested in getting an action done (or preventing its being done) a passive form may be used:

(162)   Artık bura-ya afiş as-ıl-ma-sın.
        from.now.on here-DAT notice hang-PASS-NEG-3SG
        '*Let* no notices be put up here from now on.'/'*I* don't *want* any notices put up from now on.'/'*See to it that* no notices are put up here from now on.'

When a 3rd person imperative form is used in a question, the speaker is consulting the addressee as to whether s/he wishes a certain action to be performed or a situation to occur:

(163)   Çocuklar burada *mı* kalsın(lar)?
        '*Should* the children stay here?'/'*Do you want* the children to stay here?'/'*Do you think it would be best* for the children to stay here?'

(iii) Persuasive commands: -sAnA, -sAnIzA (Group 4, 8.4.4):
Utterances with -*sAn(Iz)A* are not so much commands but pointers to, or reminders of, something that needs to be done. They often express a certain impatience on the part of the speaker that the action indicated, the desirability of which is obvious to him/her, has not been performed by the addressee(s) of their own accord.

(164)   Artık yat**san**(ız)a, uyukluyorsun(uz).
        '*Why don't you go to bed* now? You're nodding off.'

(iv) Imperative use of the future marker -*(y)AcAK*:
Aside from its main function of expressing an expectation about future events on the factual plane, -*(y)AcAK* can also express the other kind of expectation, that is, an action that someone in a position of authority or power expects others to perform:

(165)   Oraya bir daha gitmeyeceksin, anladın mı?
        'You're not *to* go there again, do you understand?'

This type of volitional modality can be projected into the past:

(166)   Bütün bunlar at-ıl-**acak**-*tı*.
        all these throw.away-PASS-FUT-P.COP
        'All these *were supposed to* be thrown away.'

21.4.4.3 Suggestions: 1st person optative forms -(y)Aylm, -(y)Allm

The 1st person singular optative *-(y)AyIm* (8.2.3.3, Group 3, 8.4.3) expresses an action that the speaker proposes to perform. It often accompanies the actual performance of the action.

(167) Sana yardım ed**eyim**.
'*Let me* help you.'

The 1st person plural form *-(y)AlIm* expresses action that the speaker proposes for performance jointly with the hearer(s) and/or other people.

(168) Biraz konuş**alım**.
'*Let's* have a bit of a chat.'

(169) Hediyeleri Mehmet'e göster-me-**ye-lim**.
                              show-NEG-OPT-1PL
'*Let's* not show Mehmet the presents.'

In questions, both of the above forms become consultative, asking the addresse(s) whether or how they would like the proposed action to be performed:

(170) Sana yardım ed**eyim** *mi*?
'*Shall I* help you?'

(171) Şu tabakları *nere*ye koy**alım**?
'*Where shall/should we* put these plates?'

(172) Hediyeleri Mehmet'e gösterme**yelim** *mi*?
'*Should we* not show the presents to Mehmet?'/'*Don't you want us* to show the presents to Mehmet?'

21.4.4.4 Deliberation about possible action: questions with -sAm, -sAk

When a finite verb with the conditional suffix *-sA*, marked for 1st person, is used in a question, it has consultative force. The difference between questions with the conditional suffix and questions with the optative forms discussed in 21.4.4.3 is that in the case of the conditional forms, the speaker regards the decision to be taken as more problematical. S/he is not clear in his/her own mind about the desirability of the proposed action, or the form that it should take, and s/he does not expect the hearer to be able to provide a simple answer. Because of this uncertainty, questions with *-sAm/-sAk* are usually marked with the modal adverbial *acaba* 'I wonder' (19.5.2):

(173) Bu konuda **kim**e danışsam *acaba*?
'*I wonder who I should* consult about this?'

(174) *Acaba* başka bir yere **mi** gitsek?
'*I wonder if* we *should* go somewhere else?'

21.4.4.5 Requests and offers: 2nd person aorist interrogative

Requests and offers are identical in form.

Requests

(175) Ben-im-le hastane-ye gel-**ir mi-sin**?
I-GEN-COM hospital-DAT come-AOR INT-2SG
'*Would you* [*please*] come with me to the hospital?'

The addition of the possibility suffix *-(y)Abil* makes the request more tentative:

(176) Bana biraz yardım e**debil**ir misiniz?
'*Could* you [please] give me a bit of help?'

Offers

(177) Çay iç**er misiniz**?
'*Will you* have/*Would you* like some tea?'

Offers cast as a negative question are more persuasive in tone:

(178) Otur-**ma-z mı-sınız**?
sit.down- NEG-NEG.AOR INT-2PL
'*Won't you* sit down?'

21.4.4.6 Expression of commitment: first person aorist

The 1st person (usually singular) of the aorist is used to express a commitment or promise entered into at the moment of, and by the act of, the utterance itself. This may well be a response to a request (also expressed in the aorist, 21.4.4.5):

(179) A. Benimle evlen**ir** misin?
'*Will* you marry me?'

B. Evlen**ir**im
'Yes, I *will*.'

In some contexts, ambiguity between the modality of commitment and the modality of probability (21.4.1.4) may undermine the degree of confidence inspired by a 1st person aorist utterance. The modally neutral *-(y)AcAK* form in (180b), presenting the promised action as a matter of future fact, may carry more conviction, because it indicates a pre-existing plan on the part of the speaker, and also suggests that s/he has checked its practicability.

(180) (a) Akşama kadar dönerim. (Promise)
'I*'ll* be back by this evening.'

(b) Akşama kadar döneceğ im. (Statement of plan/
'I'm *going to* be back by this evening.' firm prediction)

(181) Hiç kimseye söyle-**me**-m. (Promise)
tell-[AOR].NEG-1SG
'I *won't* tell anyone at all.'

21.5 Tense, aspect and modality in compound verb forms

Compound verb forms consisting of a lexical verb followed by the auxiliary *ol-* (or *bulun-*, 13.3.1.2) provide within a single verbal complex two verb stems which are separately (and nearly always differently) marked for tense, aspect and/or modality. The lexical verb is marked for relative tense or for aspect, as follows:

PERFECTIVE/RELATIVE PAST *-mIş*
RELATIVE FUTURE *-(y)AcAK*
PROGRESSIVE *-(I)yor*
HABITUAL *-(A/I)r/-z*

The auxiliary form that follows adds a further dimension of tense or aspect, or some kind of modality:

oldu	past tense, perfective aspect
olmuş	(relative) past tense, perfective aspect, evidential modality
oluyor	habitual aspect
olacak	(i) (relative) future tense
	(ii) non-factual modality (assumption)
	(iii) volitional modality (command)
olur	non-factual modality (assumption or hypothesis)
olsa gerek	non-factual modality (probability)
olmalı	non-factual modality (deduction)
olabilir	non-factual modality (speculative possibility)
olsa	volitional modality (wish)
olayım/olalım	volitional modality (1st person)
olsun	volitional modality (3rd person)

The number of possible combinations that can occur in compound verb forms is extremely large, and we do not attempt to offer an exhaustive list. The table below shows, for each finite form of *ol-*, which suffixes commonly occur on the lexical verb preceding it.

-mIş, -(y)AcAk, -(A/I)r/-z	*oldu*
-(A/I)r/-z	*olmuş*
-mIş, -(y)AcAk	*oluyor*
-mIş, -(I)yor	*olacak*
-mIş	*olur*
-mIş, -(I)yor	*olsa gerek*
-mIş, -(I)yor	*olmalı*
-mIş, -(I)yor	*olabilir*
-(I)yor	*olsa*
-mIş	*olsun*
-mIş	*olsun*

21.5.1 Compound forms in which the lexical verb is marked with *-mIş*

-mIş is the most frequently occurring marker of the lexical verb in compound verb forms. In general terms, it presents an event as being completed prior to some reference point.

The auxiliary form *oluyor* signals a habitually recurring reference point:

(182) Genellikle **saat yediye kadar** dükkanı kapat**mış oluyor**uz.
'We *have usually* shut the shop *by seven o'clock*.'

olacak indicates that the reference point is in the future:

(183) **O zamana kadar** herkes git**miş olacak**.
'Everyone *will have* gone *by then*.'

In the case of modal forms expressing assumptions, such as *olsa gerek* (21.4.1.4 (iii)), *olmalı* (21.4.1.4 (vii)) and *olabilir* (21.4.2.1), the reference point is usually the moment of speech:

-mIş olsa gerek

(184) [Bahçeyi bu hale getirmek için] aylarca uğraş**mış olsa**n gerek.
'You *must have* worked for months [to get the garden looking like this].'

-mIş olmalı

(185) Kayseri'yi gör**müş olmalı**yım ama hiç hatırlamıyorum.
'I *must have* seen Kayseri, but I don't remember [it] at all.'

mIş olabilir

(186) Ayşe bu fotoğrafı Hatice'ye göster**miş olabilir**.
'Ayşe *may have* shown this photograph to Hatice.'

In some occurrences of the *-mIş olacak* combination, *olacak* can have one of the modal values noted elsewhere in this chapter:

(i) Non-future prediction (21.4.1.4 (v))
This usage is rather rare.

(187) A. Turgut bana selam vermedi.
'Turgut didn't say hello to me.'

B. Seni o kıyafette tanıma**mış olacak**.
'He *won't have* recognized you in that outfit.'

(ii) Volitional modality (command) (21.4.4.2 (iv))

(188) Akşama kadar bütün bu gazeteler paketlen**miş olacak**, tamam mı?
'All these newspapers *are to* be parcelled up by this evening, is that understood?'
(lit. '...*are to have been*...')

Compound forms with *-mIş olur* present a hypothetical situation, such as one dependent upon the fulfillment of a condition:

(189) [Daha geç bir saatte gitsek] sokaklar boşal**mış olur**.
'[If we went later in the day] the streets *would* be less crowded.'
(lit. '...*would have* emptied...')

With *olmalı* an obligative reading is possible in addition to the assumptive one noted above:

(190) 6.30'a kadar yola çık**mış olmalıyız**.
'We *must be* on the road by 6.30.'
(lit. '...*must have* set out...')

The optative forms *olayım/olalım* and the 3rd person imperative forms *olsun(lar)* can combine with *-mIş* to express the suggestion or (in a noun clause, 24.2, 24.3) the wish that an action be completed by a certain time:

(191) [Bu akşama kadar bu odayı bitir**miş olalım**] istiyoruz.
'We want [*to have* finished this room by this evening].'

21.5.1.1 The resultative usage of compound verb forms with -mIş

A further element of meaning that is present in some instances of compound forms with -*mIş* is that the event is presented as happening as the *result* (intentional or not) of the performance of some other act. This meaning is always present in the combination -*mIş oldu*, which expresses, as a completed event, *entry into the state* of having done something (a concept difficult to express in English, 21.3.3):

(192) Dördüncü bölümün bitmesiyle kitabın yarısı yazıl**mış oldu**.
'With the completion of the fourth chapter, half of the book
has been written.'

The resultative function of -*mIş* can occur also with *oluyor*, *olacak* and *olur*:

(193) Bu tür davranışlarla onu küçük düşür**müş oluyor**sun.
'You humiliate him/her by this kind of behaviour.'
(You *are habitually* in the state of *having* humiliated him/her.)

(194) [Beni bu yükten kurtarmakla] bana büyük bir iyilik yap**mış olacak**sınız.
'You *will have* done me a great favour [by ridding me of this burden].'

With resultative -*mIş oluyor* does not always express habitual aspect. It can simply mark (relative) present tense, imparting a sense that the impact of the completion of the event is/was very much current at the reference point. Thus, -*mIş oluyor* is virtually synonymous with -*mIş oldu* in all instances where the reference point is the moment of speech, as in (192) above:

(195) Bu bölümün bitmesiyle kitabın yarısı yazıl**mış oluyor**.
'With the completion of this chapter, half of the book
has been written.'

Finally, resultative -*mIş* can occur with the optative/imperative forms of *ol-*. (196) could be an explanation given retrospectively for the purchase of a large number of different perfumes:

(196) [Bu kokuların her birini birer defa dene**miş olayım**] demiştim.
'I thought [*I would like to have* tried each of these perfumes once].'

21.5.2 Compound forms in which the lexical verb is marked with -(I)yor

These forms indicate that an event is/was/will be ongoing at some reference point.

-(I)yor olacak marks the reference point as being in the future:

> (197) Saat altıda çalış**ıyor olacağ** ım.
> 'I *shall be* work*ing* at six o'clock.'

Combinations of *-(I)yor* with *olsa gerek*, *olmalı*, and *olabilir* express assumptions or conjectures about a situation current at the moment of speech:

> (198) Çok gürültü var, yukarıda birisi matkap kullan**ıyor olmalı/olsa gerek**.
> 'There's such a noise; someone upstairs *must be* us*ing* a drill.'

> (199) Ali'nin patronu onu sev**miyor olabilir**.
> '*It's possible* Ali's boss doesn't like him.'

-(I)yor olsa articulates a counterfactual wish about the present state of affairs:

> (200) Keşke sıcak bir ülkede yaş**ıyor olsam**.
> 'If only I *were* liv*ing* in a hot country.'

21.5.3 Compound forms in which the lexical verb is marked with -(y)AcAk

This pattern is in very restricted use in main clauses, although it is highly productive in conditional clauses (27.2.1.3, 27.2.6) and in relative clauses (25.4.1). The combination *-(y)AcAk oldu* expresses an action that a person decided (somewhat hesitantly) to perform. It is nearly always followed by a statement expressing or implying the reversal of that decision:

> (201) Bir şey söyle**yecek oldu**m, ama tam o anda kapı çaldı.
> 'I *was about to* say something, but just at that moment the door (bell) rang.'

A much less common usage is the replacement of *-(y)AsI* with *-(y)AcAK* in the example above.

Compounds with *-(y)AcAk oluyor* give the same kind of situation a habitual context:

> (202) Bazen bir şey söyle**yecek oluyor**um ama bir türlü çıkmıyor.
> 'Sometimes I *get almost to the point of* saying something, but it just doesn't come out.'

21.5.4 Compound forms in which the lexical verb is marked with -(A/I)r or -mAz

Aorist marking of the lexical verb is restricted to compounds in which the auxiliary has perfective marking (the modally neutral *-DI* or evidential *-mIş*).

(i) *-(A/I)r oldu/olmuş*:
   The affirmative aorist form followed by *oldu/olmuş* expresses the fact that an event began or has begun to happen recurrently, or as a matter of habit:

   (203) Son zamanlarda sık sık tiyatroya gid**er olduk**.
   'Recently we *have started* going to the theatre a lot.'

(ii) *-mAz oldu/olmuş*:
   The negative aorist form with *oldu/olmuş* expresses the fact that a formerly recurrent event (has) ceased to happen:

   (204) O olaydan sonra Hakan bir süre bize uğra**maz oldu**.
   'After that incident, Hakan *stopped* call*ing* on us for a while.'

21.5.5 The addition of the past copula *-(y)DI* to compound verb forms

The past copula *-(y)DI* (21.2.1 (ii)) can be added to the auxiliary component of any compound verb form. It has one of two functions:

(i) In most cases, it indicates a reference time prior to the moment of speech for the relative tense or aspect marked on the lexical verb:

   (205) Genellikle saat yediye kadar dükkanı kapat**mış oluyordu**k.
   'We *had* usually shut the shop by seven o'clock.'

   (206) Nilgün annesinin rahatı için her şeyi yapardı. Onu çok sev**iyor olmalıydı**.
   'Nilgün would do everything to keep her mother comfortable. She *must have* loved her very much.'

(ii) The other function of *-(y)DI* is to indicate counterfactuality. This occurs only with the modal forms *olur* (21.4.1.3), *olabilir* (21.4.2.1), *olmalı* (21.4.2.2) and *olsa* (21.4.4.1). In its counterfactual function, *olmalıydı* expresses an unfulfilled obligation (21.4.2.2). The reference is not necessarily to a past time:

   (207) Bu saatte çalış**ıyor olmalıyd**ım.
   'I *should/ought to be* work*ing* at this time of day.'

In the case of the aorist, there can be ambiguity between past and counterfactual meaning. For example, (208) could be understood as expressing either a habitual state of affairs in the past or a state of affairs that did not occur but would have if some condition had been fulfilled:

(208) Saat dörde kadar mektuplar postalan**mış olurdu**.
'By four o'clock the letters *would have* been posted.'

Chapter 22

Definiteness, specificity and generic reference

This chapter deals with the referential function of noun phrases. Speakers can use noun phrases with specific or non-specific reference, and if they are referring to specific entities, they can use various means to indicate whether or not they expect their hearers to be able to identify the person(s) or thing(s) they are talking about. In Turkish, the **referential status** of a noun phrase depends on one or more of the following factors:

 (i) What kind of determiners, if any, are present (15.6)
 (ii) The use or non-use of accusative marking on direct objects (14.3.3.2)
 (iii) Word order (22.5)
 (iv) Sentence stress (22.6)
 (v) The tense, aspect and modality of the predicate (22.7)

Four referential statuses can be identified in Turkish, and these are explained in the successive sections of this chapter.

Both **definite** (22.1) and **indefinite** (22.2) noun phrases are always marked for number:

  (1) {Çocuk-lar} {araba}-yı yıkadılar.
      child-PL   car-ACC
      DEF.PL   DEF.SG
      '{The children} washed {the car}.'

  (2) {Başka bir oda}-da {birtakım kutu-lar} vardı.
      other a room-LOC   some box-PL
      INDEF.SG   INDEF.PL
      'There were {some boxes} in {another room}.'

This is in contrast to the second non-definite status that exists in Turkish, namely **categorial** (22.3), in which the distinction between singular and plural is neutralized (14.3.1.3) and the noun phrase indicates merely the 'kind' to which reference is being made:

(3) Sen daha {**çocuk**}sun.
 'You're still {*a child*}.'

The fourth referential status, **generic** reference (22.4), involves the use of a noun phrase in a generalizing function, to refer to an entire class of entities, or to a(ny) typical member of that class:

(4) Eskiden {**çocuk**}, büyüklerine saygı gösterirdi.
 'In the past {*a child*} showed respect to his/her elders.'

Specificity is a category that overlaps the boundary between definite and indefinite. All definites are specific, but as explained in 22.2, indefinites may be either specific or non-specific. All categorial noun phrases are non-specific, as (in a somewhat different sense) are all noun phrases used generically.

22.1 Definite status

A noun phrase marked as definite refers to a specific entity or entities that the speaker assumes to be unambiguously identifiable by the hearer. In Turkish, the minimal requirements for a noun phrase to be interpreted as definite are:

(i) The absence of an indefinite determiner (15.6.1).
(ii) Accusative case marking where the noun phrase is functioning as direct object

In (5) all three of the noun phrases are definite:

(5) {**Garson**} {**temiz tabak-lar**}-ı {**masa**}-ya koydu.
 waiter clean plate-PL-ACC table-DAT
 '*The waiter* put *the clean plates* down on *the table*.'

The following classes of noun phrase are inherently definite:

(i) The proper names of people, places and institutions:

(6) **Osman'ı** dün gördük.
 'We saw *Osman* yesterday.'

(7) **Ankara'yı** severim.
 'I like *Ankara*.'

(8) **Anıtlar Yüksek Kurul-un-*u*** bundan sorumlu tutuyorum.
  NCM-ACC
 'I hold *the High Commission on Monuments* responsible for this.'

(ii) Certain pronouns, namely:
   a. The simple personal pronouns (18.1.1):

   (9) Murat **sen-*i*** seviyor.
        you-ACC
        'Murat loves *you*.'

   b. The demonstrative pronouns (18.2):

   (10) **Şunlar*ı*** da yıkamamız lâzım.
        'We've got to wash *these*, too.'

   c. The pronominal quantifiers *herkes* 'everyone' and *her şey* 'everything' (18.6.1):

   (11) Ömer **herkes*i*** sinirlendirdi.
        'Ömer got on *everyone*'s nerves.'

   d. *öbürü/öteki(si)/diğeri* 'the other (one)' (and their plural forms *öbürleri/ötekiler(i)/diğerleri*) (18.4–5):

   (12) Bir anahtar burada, **öbür-ün-*ü*** gördün mü?
                            NCM-ACC
        'One key is here; have you seen *the other(one)*?'

(iii) A noun phrase that includes one of the definite determiners (15.6.2):

   (13) Bana {**bu** oda}-*yı* ver-di-ler.
        I.DAT this room-ACC give-PF-3PL
        'They have given me {*this* room}.'

   (14) İkiniz {**aynı** kitab}-*ı* mı okuyorsunuz?
        'Are you both reading{*the same* book}?'

22.2 Indefinite status

A noun phrase has indefinite status if it includes *bir* 'a(n)', any of the other indefinite determiners (15.6.1) or a distributive numeral (15.7.3):

   (15) Aslında{daha büyük **bir** ev}istemiştik.
        'Actually, we had wanted {*a* larger house/flat}.'

   (16) {**Bazı** arkadaşlar} bugün gelmedi.
        '{*Some* colleagues} didn't/haven't come today.'

   (17) Şimdi {**biraz** su} katacaksın.
        'Now you have to add {*a little* water}.'

A noun phrase that includes a cardinal numeral is also interpreted as indefinite unless (i) a definite determiner (15.6.2) is also present, or (ii) the noun phrase is an accusative-marked direct object:

(18) {**Yetmiş üç** bilet} satılmıştı. (Indefinite)
 '{*Seventy-three* tickets} had been sold.'

(19) {*O* **iki** bilim insanı}, sonraki yıllarda önemli (Definite)
 keşiflerde bulunacaklardı.
 '{*Those two* scientists} were to make important
 discoveries in the following years.'

(20) {Bizden aldıkları **on iki** tabağ}-*ı* hiçbir zaman geri vermediler.
                             ACC (Definite)
 'They never gave back {*the twelve* plates they had borrowed from
 us}.'

Noun phrases that include neither a determiner nor a numeral but are marked with the plural suffix *-lAr* have indefinite status in some contexts but not in others. They are unambiguously indefinite where they occur as non-case-marked direct objects:

(21) Çocuklarına sık sık {pahalı hediye-**ler**} alıyor.
                          present-PL
 'S/he frequently buys expensive presents for his/her children.

Otherwise, their referential status (definite, indefinite or generic) is determined by the word order (22.5), stress pattern (22.6) or tense, aspect and modality (22.7) of the sentence.

Note that *şey* 'thing' and *yer* 'place' do not occur in the plural-marked form as indefinites unless preceded by either an adjective or a determiner (14.3.1.1).

As indefinite noun phrases always express new information, they occupy the pre-predicate position (23.3.1) and most often the immediately preverbal position. If they are non-case-marked direct objects, as in (21), they are placed in this position. For examples and exceptions, see 23.1.1.1 and 23.2.2.

22.2.1 Specific and non-specific indefinites

A noun phrase marked as indefinite can perform one of two referential functions:

(i) It can refer to a **specific** entity (or set of entities) known to the speaker, which is being introduced into the discourse as a new item, and which is assumed not to be familiar to, or not to be identifiable by, the hearer:

(22) Dün sokakta {çok eski **bir** arkadaşım}-la karşılaştım.
 'Yesterday I bumped into {*a* very old friend of mine} in the street.'

(23) Yarınki toplantıya {**birkaç** kişi} gelemeyecekmiş.
'{*Several* people} [have said they] are not going to be able to get to the meeting tomorrow.'

(ii) It can denote a **non-specific** entity or set of entities whose identity is unknown or unknowable to the speaker and whose very existence may be only imaginary. Non-specific indefinites occur mainly in clauses expressing a future or hypothetical event or in negative statements or questions.

(24) [{Daha büyük **bir** araba} almay]-ı düşünüyoruz.
'We're thinking of [buying {*a* larger car}].'

(25) {Yeni **bir** şey} söyle-me-di.
new a thing say-NEG-PF
'He didn't say {*any*thing new}.'

The distinction between specific and non-specific indefinites is reflected (although generally more in terms of tendencies than strict differentiation) in certain features of Turkish grammar:

(i) In direct objects, the use of plural marking without a determiner is largely confined to specific indefinites. Thus, the plural-marked indefinite form in (26) refers to specific shirts that have been purchased:

(26) Dün Korkut-a **yeni gömlek-*ler*** al-dı-k.
yesterday Korkut-DAT new shirt-PL buy-PF-1PL
'Yesterday we bought *(some) new shirts* for Korkut.'

If the predicate were changed in such a way that the shirts lost their specificity, the categorial form (22.3) would be preferred to the indefinite form:

(27) a. Korkut'a **yeni gömlek** almamız lazım.
'We need to get *a new shirt/(some) new shirts* for Korkut.'

b. Korkut'a **yeni gömlek** almadık.
'We didn't buy Korkut [*any*] *new shirts*.'

c. Korkut'a **yeni gömlek** aldın mı?
'Did you buy Korkut [*a*] *new shirt*/[*any*] *new shirts*?'

(ii) Where an indefinite noun phrase incorporates a relative clause whose verb is of the form *-mIş (olan)* or *-(y)AcAk (olan)*, the likelihood of *olan* being omitted is much higher in non-specific indefinites than in specific ones (25.4.1.1):

(28) a. {[Masaya **bırakılmış**] bir not} yeterli olurdu.
'{A note [*left* on the table]} would have been enough.'

b. {[Masaya **bırakılmış** *olan*] bir not}-ta kaloriferler, çöplerin toplanması, pencerelerin kilitlenmesi gibi konularda bilgiler vardı.

'In {a note [*that had been left* on the table]} there was information about the central heating, rubbish collection, locking of windows, etc.'

In (28a) no note has been left. The subject noun phrase therefore represents a purely hypothetical entity. This noun phrase is thus non-specific and *olan* is omitted from the relative clause modifying it. In (28b), on the other hand, the factual and affirmative past tense predicate *vardı* indicates that a specific note is being described.

(iii) The optional use of accusative marking on an indefinite direct object in the immediately preverbal position favours a specific reading:

(29) a. {Gürcistan folkloruyla ilgili bir kitap} arıyorum.
'I'm looking for {a book about Georgian folklore}.'

b. {Gürcistan folkloruyla ilgili bir kitab}-ı arıyorum.
'I'm looking for {a book about Georgian folklore}.'

(29a) implies that the speaker would be interested in *any* book about Georgian folklore that might be available. (29b), on the other hand, where the object is given accusative marking, implies that the speaker has a specific title in mind.

(30) a. Bazen masaya {bir örtü} yayardık.
'Sometimes we would spread {a cloth} on the table.'

b. Bazen masaya {[sarı çiçeklerle işlenmiş] bir örtü}
-(yü) yayardık.
'Sometimes we would spread on the table
{a cloth [embroidered with yellow flowers]}.'

c. Bazen masaya {[Ayşe-nin biz-e Meksika-dan getir-diğ-i]
Ayşe-GEN we-DAT Mexico-ABL bring-PART-3SG.POSS

bir örtü}-(yü) yayardık.
a cloth-ACC.

'Sometimes we would spread on the table {a cloth [that Ayşe had brought us from Mexico]}.'

The three sentences in (30) show a gradation from total ambiguity with regard to specificity in (a) to unambiguous specificity in (c). In (a) the speaker has not provided the cloth with any descriptors at all. The likelihood of accusative marking being used here is extremely small. In (b) the cloth is given quite a detailed description, and it seems likely that one specific tablecloth is intended. In (c) the specificity of the cloth is virtually assured through its linkage to the action of a specific individual. However, although accusative marking is much more acceptable in (b) and (c) than in (a), it is important to note that the non-case-marked version of these sentences is also perfectly acceptable, and if used it would not force a non-specific reading. In other words, accusative marking is not a requirement for giving the direct object in such sentences a specific reading, but if used it does lend weight to that interpretation.

(31) a. Program-da {bazı değişiklik-ler} yap-ma-mız
programme-LOC some change-PL make-VN-1PL.POSS

gerek-ebil-ir.
be.necessary-PSB-AOR

'It may be necessary for us to make {some changes} to the programme.'

b. Programda {[şu anda akılda olmayan] bazı değişiklik-ler}(-i)

some change-PL(-ACC)
yapmamız gerekebilir.

'It may be necessary for us to make {some changes} to the programme [that are currently unpredictable].'

c. Programda {[yetkililerin istediği] bazı değişiklikler}(-i)
yapmamız gerekebilir.
'It may be necessary for us to make {some changes} to the programme [that are required by the authorities].'

(31a–c) are modalized statements about a hypothetical possibility (21.4.2.1) and in such a context it would be very difficult to understand the indefinite direct object in anything but a non-specific sense. (31b-c) show, then, that grammatically non-obligatory accusative marking of an indefinite direct object is not necessarily motivated by specificity but can simply be a function of the complexity of the noun phrase itself. The kind of complex modification provided by a relative clause considerably increases the tendency towards the use of accusative marking.

As explained in 14.3.3.2, certain types of indefinite direct object (notably those occurring in the pre-predicate area but not in the immediately preverbal position, and those marked for possession) obligatorily take accusative marking. It should be noted that this grammatically conditioned accusative marking is also quite independent of the specific/non-specific distinction. Thus, the obligatorily accusative-marked direct objects in (32) and (33) both have a non-specific interpretation owing to the hypothetical modality of the sentence:

(32) {Birçok şey}-i şu raflara koyabiliriz.
'{A lot of things} we can put on these shelves.'

(33) İsterse Ahmet {bir arkadaşın}-ı getirebilir.
'Ahmet can bring {a friend (of his)} if he wants.'

22.3 Categorial status

A categorial noun phrase is not marked for number. It denotes an unspecified quantity or number of items of a certain kind, or an unspecified quantity of a certain substance. Note that, unlike generic noun phrases (22.4), categorial noun phrases do not refer to a class of entities *as a whole*, or to a *typical* member of a class. Categorial noun phrases are used in contexts where distinctions of number or quantity are irrelevant:

(34) Şu anda konuşamayacağım, **müşteri** var.
 'I can't talk now; I've got *customers/a customer*.'

(35) O gün **kar** yağmıştı.
 '*Snow* had fallen on that day.'

The formal characteristics of noun phrases used with categorial status are that:

(i) They cannot be modified by any determiners.
(ii) They cannot be plural-marked.
(iii) When functioning as subject they mostly occupy the immediately pre-predicate position (23.2.1).
(iv) When functioning as direct object they do not receive accusative case marking unless topicalized (23.3.3).

There are certain contexts in which the use of the categorial form is regularly preferred to a number-marked form:

(i) A subject complement that serves simply to categorize the entity or entities expressed by the subject noun phrase rather than attributing any individual properties to them:

(36) Bence bu kitap **roman** değil, **otobiyografi**.
 'In my view this book is not *a novel*, [it's] *an autobiography*.'

(37) Oğlumun bütün öğretmenleri **kadın**.
 'All of my son's teachers are *women*.'

(38) Biz [onları **İtalyan**] sanıyorduk.
 'We thought [they were *Italian*].'

Note that if the subject complement is a plural-marked noun phrase, as in (39b), it acquires definite status:

(39) a. Onlar **dokTOR**-muş(-lar).
     doctor-EV.COP(-3PL)
     'Apparently they're *doctors*.'

b. Onlar **doktor-LAR**-mış.
   doctor-PL-EV.COP
   'Apparently they're *the doctors*.'

In (39a) the suffix *-lar* is the Group 2 person marker (3rd person plural) (8.4.2) affixed to the evidential copular suffix *-(y)mIş* (8.3.2). It gives the predicate agreement in number as well as in person with the plural subject *onlar*. In (39b), on the other hand, *-lar* is the nominal plural marker (8.1.1) affixed to the noun phrase *doktor*.

(ii) The subject of an interrogative or negative existential sentence (12.1.1.2):

(40) **Kardeş**iniz var mı?
      'Have you any *brothers or sisters*?'

(41) Bizim apartmanımızda hiç **çocuk** yok.
      'There are no *children* at all in our block of flats.'

(iii) The non-specific subject or direct object of an interrogative or negative verbal sentence:

(42) **Misafir** mi gelecek?
      'Are you expecting *guests*?'
      (lit. 'Are *guest(s)* going to come?')

(43) Amerikalılar oraya **asker** göndermemişti.
      'The Americans had not sent *(any) troops* there.'

(iv) The direct object in sentences where attention is focused on an action or activity rather than on the entity/entities affected or produced by it:

(44) Ne güzel **şarkı söylü**-yor-sun!
      how beautiful song sing-IMPF-2SG
      'How beautifully you *sing*!'

(45) Ayşe bütün gün **kitap oku**yor.
      'Ayşe *reads books* all day.'

Many bare noun + verb combinations (such as *şarkı söyle* 'sing') are nominal-verb compounds (13.3.2), lexicalized as expressions that will be found in dictionaries. The fact that these lexicalized expressions exist does not in any way prevent the same noun being used with the same verb but with a different referential status. For example, the direct object noun phrase *o şarkıyı* below is definite, referring to a specific song that the speaker assumes the addressee can identify:

(46) **O şarkı-yı** ne güzel söyledin!
      that song-ACC
      'How beautifully you sang *that song*!'

In (47), on the other hand, *iki sigara* is indefinite. The quantification is crucial, but identification of the particular cigarettes smoked is not sought:

(47) Bugün yalnız **iki sigara** içtim.
 'I have smoked only *two cigarettes* today.'

(v) The subject of a sentence in which attention is focused on an action, or the impact of that action, rather than on the identity of the person or thing doing it:

(48) Geçen kış evimize **hırsız** girdi.
 'Last winter our house was burgled.'
 (lit. '…[a] burglar/burglar[s] got into our house.')

(49) Tatildeyken beni **arı** soktu.
 'While on holiday I was stung by a bee.'
 (lit. '…[a] bee/bee[s] stung me.')

Outside the types of context identified in (i)–(v) above, the choice between categorial and indefinite reference depends on how much importance the speaker attaches to the number aspect of the entity s/he is talking about.

(50) a. Dayım bize **hediye** getirmişti.
 'My uncle had brought us *a present/presents*.'

 b. Dayım bize **bir hediye** getirmişti.
 'My uncle had brought us *a present*.'

 c. Dayım bize **hediyeler** getirmişti.
 'My uncle had brought us *presents*.'

In (a) attention is focused on the uncle's action rather than on the present(s) brought. (b) and (c), on the other hand, suggest that the speaker is going to go on to say something more about the actual present(s).

22.4 Generic reference

A noun phrase is said to have generic reference when it refers not to any specific entity or entities but to *an entire class*, or to *a typical member* of that class. In Turkish, generic reference can be affected by both singular and plural noun phrases.

22.4.1 Generic reference by singular noun phrases

22.4.1.1 The bare generic

The bare generic is a noun phrase without either *bir* or plural marking, which is used with generic reference. Among the different forms of generic reference, the bare generic evokes most strongly the idea of the 'class' as a single whole, as opposed to the class viewed as a collection of separate individuals. It is the form used in the subject noun phrase of laws of nature (51), definitions and classifications (52) and proverbs (53), and are mostly used with the aorist suffix or with *-DIr*. In general, it produces a more absolute, unqualified axiom than the other forms.

(51) **Kuş** uçar.
'*Birds* fly/*A bird* flies.'

(52) **Balina** memeli bir hayvan-dır.
whale mammal an animal-GM
'*The whale* is a mammal.'

(53) **Dert** gitmez, değişir.
'*Problems* don't go away, they change.'

(54) **Hırsız** pencereden girer.
'*Burglars*/*a burglar* come(s) in through windows/a window'.

The use of *insan* 'human being' in the sense of the English generic pronoun 'one' (18.6.2) is a special instance of the bare generic:

(55) **Para sıkıntısı *insan-a*** üzüntü ver-ir.
money problem person-DAT distress give-AOR
'*Money problems* cause *one* distress.'

22.4.1.2 The indefinite generic

The indefinite generic is a noun phrase marked with *bir* that has generic reference. It expresses a typical member of a class. It occurs mainly in the following contexts:

(i) A noun phrase that includes adjectival modifiers (Chapter 15):

(56) {*Akıllı* **bir insan**} borçlanmaktan kaçınır.
'{*A wise person*} avoids getting into debt.'

(57) {[*Yurtdışında okumak isteyen*] **bir öğrenci**} iyi İngilizce öğrenmeli.
'{*A student* [*who wants to study abroad*]} must learn English well.'

(58) {[*Elli yaşını geçmiş (olan)*] **bir insan**}-ın bu memlekette iş bulması kolay değil.
'It's not easy for {*a person over fifty*} to find work in this country.'

(ii) A noun phrase that includes one of the indefinite determiners *herhangi bir* 'any', *böyle/şöyle/öyle* 'such a' or *bu/şu/o gibi bir* 'a ... like this/that' (15.6.1):

(59) {**Herhangi bir anne**} bu sorunu tanır.
'{*Any mother*} would recognize this problem.'

(60) {**Öyle bir okul**}-da okumak zor.
'It's hard to study in {*such a school*}.'

(iii) A noun phrase followed by *bile* 'even' (28.3.1.1 (iv)):

(61) Bunu {**bir çocuk**} *bile* anlayabilir.
'*Even {a child}* could understand this.'

22.4.2 Generic reference by plural noun phrases

The plural generic, consisting of a plural-marked noun phrase, is closer in meaning to the indefinite generic than to the bare generic, in that it also generalizes from individual to class rather than vice versa. It makes reference to the collectivity of individuals that are seen as constituting a class. In comparison with the bare generic, the plural generic makes a less absolute kind of generalization, hinting at the possibility that it will not apply equally to all members of the class.

The plural generic could be substituted for the indefinite generic in all the examples given in 22.4.1, with the exception of (59) (because *herhangi* has to be followed by *bir* and a singular noun phrase). The plural equivalents of (56) and (60) are given below:

(62) {**Akıllı insan*lar***} borçlanmaktan kaçınır.
'{*Wise people*} avoid getting into debt.'

(63) {**Öyle okul*lar***}-da okumak zor.
'It's hard to study in {*such schools*}.'

The plural generic is the form preferred for making generalizations about classes of human beings:

(64) **Norveçli*ler*** soğuğa alışıktır.
'*(The) Norwegians* are used to the cold.'

(65) Kimse **politikacı*lar***a güvenmez.
'No one trusts *politicians*.'

The 'individuation' conveyed by the plural generic makes it appropriate for the expression of quite modest or homely generalizations based upon the speaker's personal observation or experience:

(66) {**Kalorifersiz evler**} nispeten ucuz oluyor.
'{*Flats without central heating*} are relatively cheap.'

(67) a. Bugün **gençler** [yemek yapmasın]-ı bilmiyorlar.
'*Young people* today don't know [how to cook].'

b. {**Bugünkü gençler**} [yemek yapmasın]-ı bilmiyorlar.
'{*Today's young people*} don't know [how to cook].'

22.4.3 Generic noun phrases as direct objects

Bare generics are usually non-case-marked in the direct object function:

(68) Sen **çocuk** sevmezsin.
'You don't like *children*.'

(69) Ayten **şapka** seviyor.
'Ayten loves *hats*.'

In sentences where a direct object with no determiner has accusative marking, the referential status of the noun phrase is usually definite:

(70) Ayten **şapkayı** seviyor.
'Ayten loves *the hat*.'

However, such noun phrases can also be open to a generic interpretation:

(71) Ayten **şapkayı** başkalarında seviyor, ama [saçları güzel olduğu için] kendisi pek giymiyor.
'Ayten likes *hats* on other people, but [because she has beautiful hair] she herself doesn't wear [them] much.'

A bare generic direct object is particularly likely to be accusative-marked where (i) it denotes animate beings, and (ii) the subject of the sentence is itself a bare generic:

(72) **Kedi köpeği** kovar.
'*A cat* drives away/can drive away *a dog*.'

(73) **Mühendis mimarı** kıskanır.
'*The/An engineer* is usually jealous of *the/an architect*.'

Two other types of bare generic are obligatorily accusative-marked when they are direct objects:

(i) *-sI* compounds (10.2.2) whose modifier constituent is a noun of nationality:

(74) Arkadaşım **Türk kahvesini** sevmiyor.
'My friend doesn't like *Turkish coffee*.'

(ii) Noun phrases expressing entities regarded as social 'institutions':

(75) Kızın ailesi [**okulu** önemsemiyor] görünüyor.
'The girl's family appears [not to regard *school* as important].'

Indefinite and plural generics occurring as direct objects also have to be accusative-marked:

(76) Ahmet o anda [**koşuya hazırlanan**] **bir atlet***i* andırıyordu.
'At that moment Ahmet looked like {*an athlete* [*preparing for a race*]}.'

(77) Ali **doktorları** sevmez.
'Ali doesn't like *doctors*.'

22.5 The effect of word order on referential status

In the case of a subject noun phrase, its position in the sentence can have a determining effect on its referential status. In (78), where the noun phrase is not plural-marked, the difference in word order gives a categorial reading in (a) and a definite reading in (b). This is because a categorial subject occupies the immediately preverbal position (23.1.1.1 (v)), whereas the usual unmarked position for a definite subject is at the beginning of the sentence (23.1). While it is possible for a definite subject to be placed in the immediately preverbal position for purposes of emphasis or contrast (23.3) the likelihood of (a) below being uttered with the meaning of 'It was *the burglar* (not anyone else) who got in through here' is small.

(78) a. Buradan **hırsız** girmiş. (cf. (48))
'*A burglar/Burglars* got in through here.'

b. **Hırsız** buradan girmiş.
'*The burglar* got in through here.'

In (79) the subject noun phrase has plural marking, which gives the possibility of an indefinite or (contrastive) definite reading in (a), but exclusively a definite reading in (b). As explained in 23.1.1.1 (vi), a plural-marked indefinite subject without determiner occupies the immediately preverbal position.

(79) a. Arka sıra-lar-da **öğrenci-ler** otur-acak.
 back row-PL-LOC student-PL sit-FUT
 (i) '*Students* will sit in the back rows.'
 (ii) 'It's *the students* who will sit in the back rows.'

b. **Öğrenciler** arka sıralarda oturacak.
'*The students* will sit in the back rows.'

22.6 The effect of stress on referential status

In a sentence that consists only of a plural-marked subject noun phrase and a verb, differential stress patterns determine the referential status of the noun phrase. It is understood as indefinite if it bears sentence stress itself, as in (80a) below, and as definite if the stress is on the verb, as in (80b).

(80) a. Rapor**LAR** yazıldı.
       '*Reports* were written.'

     b. Raporlar yazıl**DI**.
       '*The reports* were written.'

22.7 The effect of tense, aspect and modality on referential status

The tense, aspect or modality of the predicate is the most important indicator of whether a subject noun phrase has definite or generic reference. A bare generic subject noun phrase almost always occurs with one of the predicate types identified in 21.4.1.1 as expressing permanent or generalized validity, namely verbal predicates containing the aorist suffix -*(A/I)r/-z* and nominal predicates optionally marked by -*DIr*. A generic interpretation is often not possible with finite verb forms that express perfective aspect (21.3.1) or (definite) future tense, that is, -*DI*, -*mIş* and -*(y)AcAK*. The contrast between the pair below shows that only in the case of predicates that can be applied holistically to an entire class of entities is the use of one of these forms compatible with a generic interpretation:

(81) a. **Bilgisayar** hepimizin işini kolaylaştırdı.
       '*The computer* has made things easier for all of us.'

     b. **Bilgisayar** Kenan'ın odasına kon**du**.
       '*The computer* was put in Kenan's room.'

(81a) is capable of either a generic or a definite reading (computers in general, or a particular computer), while (81b) must refer to a specific computer because 'putting' is an action that can only be performed on individual entities, not on an entire class.

(82) below has the aorist marking characteristic of sentences which make generalized statements about behaviour or qualities regarded as typical of a class of entities, and translation (i) expresses this generic interpretation. However, since the aorist is used equally to express the characteristic behaviour or qualities of an individual (21.4.1.1), (82) can also be understood as a statement about a particular cat as expressed in translation (ii):

(82) **Kedi** süt iç*er*.
    (i) '*Cats* drink milk.'/'*A cat* drinks milk.'
    (ii) '*The cat* drinks milk.'

The substitution of *-(I)yor* for the aorist in (82) eliminates altogether the possibility of a generic reading. *Kedi* here has to have definite reference to a specific cat.

(83) **Kedi** süt iç*iyor*.
    (i) '*The cat* is drinking (some) milk.'
    (ii) '*The cat* drinks milk.'

However, there are contexts in which *-(I)yor* is readily compatible with a generic subject (cf. (66)–(67)). This usage is particularly common in statements with plural generic subjects for which only a limited degree of generality is claimed and which reflect the speaker's own experience rather than a universal law.

(84) a. {**Bu makineler**} iyi kesmiyor.
    '{*These machines*} don't cut well.'

    b. {**Bu tür makineler**} iyi kesmiyor.
    '{*This kind of machine*} doesn't cut well.'

(84a) is ambiguous between a generic interpretation ('machines of this kind') and a definite one (referring to a specific set of machines known to both speaker and addressee). The replacement of the simple demonstrative by the explicitly generic modifier *bu tür* 'this kind (of)' eliminates the ambiguity. Other explicitly generic modifiers derived from the demonstratives are *bu/o gibi (bir)* '(a)...like this/that' and *böyle/şöyle/öyle (bir)* 'such (a)' (22.4.1.2 (ii)).

(85) illustrates the effect of the generalizing modality marker *-DIr* on the referential status of a noun phrase in a nominal sentence. The noun phrase *hanımelinin* is in a possessor/modifier role in this sentence, but the same effect would be observable in a subject.

(85) a. **Hanımeli**-nin koku-su çok güzel.
    honeysuckle-GEN smell-3SG.POSS very beautiful
    'The smell of *(the) honeysuckle* is lovely.'

    b. **Hanımeli**nin kokusu çok güzel-*dir*.
                                         GM
    'The smell of *honeysuckle* is lovely.'

    c. **Hanımeli**nin kokusu çok güzel-*di*.
                                         P.COP
    'The smell of *the honeysuckle* was lovely.'

(a) is ambiguous between a generic reading (honeysuckle plants in general) and a definite one (referring to a particular honeysuckle plant). The addition of -*DIr* in (b) forces the generalized reading. (c), on the other hand, shows that, just as in verbal sentences perfective aspect is usually incompatible with generic reference, so in nominal sentences past tense marking usually excludes the generic interpretation. The latter would be possible only in the case of a change in the situation of an entire class of entities over time:

(86) 1920'lerde **otomobil** yaygın değil*di*.
 '*Cars* were not common in the 1920s.'

Chapter 23

Word order

In Turkish, word order is variable. Changing the order of the constituents in a sentence is used as a means of distinguishing new information from background information and of making a certain constituent prominent in the discourse. Shifting the position of sentence stress also serves a similar purpose. Hence variations in word order, together with the position of sentence stress, affect the meaning of a sentence. Although there are many possible arrangements for the stressed and unstressed constituents in a sentence, here we discuss only the most common patterns of word order variation.

Which particular syllable receives stress within a constituent that requires to be stressed is determined by the rules of word stress explained in Chapter 4.

23.1 gives an overview of the unmarked order of sentence constituents in simple sentences with a single prominent stress and 23.2 explores this topic in more detail. Variations in word order are discussed in 23.3. Section 23.4 is about constituents that are dislocated from phrases and from subordinate clauses.

23.1 Unmarked sentences: word order and stress

The term **unmarked order** refers to the ordering of constituents in the opening sentence of a dialogue or discourse, where no information is presupposed. The position of almost any constituent can change under focusing, backgrounding, or topicalization (23.3).

The unmarked order of major constituents in affirmative sentences is as follows:

Verbal sentence with intransitive verb

(1) Ben   artık   sabahları   koşuyorum.
    SUBJECT   ADVERB   ADVERB   PREDICATE
    'I have started running in the mornings.'

Verbal sentence with transitive verb

(2) Terzi   elbisemi   yeni   bitirmiş.
    SUBJECT   OBJECT   ADVERB   PREDICATE
    'Apparently, the dressmaker has just finished my dress.'

DOI: 10.4324/9780429435836-26

Linking sentence (12.1.1.2)

> (3) Hava   çok   soğukmuş.
>   SUBJECT ADVERB   PREDICATE
>   'The weather (turns out to be) very cold.'

Locative existential sentence (12.1.1.2)

> (4) Evde   süt   yoktu.
>   ADVERB SUBJECT PREDICATE
>   'There was no milk in the house'.

Possessive existential sentence (12.1.1.2)

> (5) Benim   iki kedim   var.
>   SUBJECT   PREDICATE
>   'I have two cats.'

Utterances in the unmarked order have a specific position for primary stress although they have no particular part which is conceptually more prominent than the others. In this chapter, (and occasionally elsewhere in this book) a stressed syllable or word is indicated by capital letters. Bold type and/or italics do *not* indicate stress.

For the word order in questions and in negative statements, see Chapter 19 and Chapter 20.

23.1.1 Verbal sentences

The unmarked order in verbal sentences is as follows:

(i) The subject is at the beginning.
(ii) The predicate is at the end.
(iii) A non-case-marked direct object or any indefinite constituent with the occasional exception of an animate subject, occurs immediately before the verb.
(iv) An oblique object is placed immediately before the verb.
(v) Modal adverbials occur either at the very beginning of the sentence, or after the subject.
(vi) Sentence stress falls on the predicate or on the constituent before it.

Stress pattern of verbal sentences with intransitive verbs

> (6) Ali öğle.yemeğin-den sonra **dinlen-İR.**
>   Ali lunch-ABL   after rest-AOR
>   'Ali *rests* after lunch.'

(7) Meral gençliğ-in-de **BANka-da** çalış-tı.
Meral youth-2SG.POSS-LOC bank-LOC work-P
'Meral worked at *a/the bank*.'

Stress pattern of verbal sentences with transitive verbs

(8) Biz bugün iş-i **bitir-eCEğ-iz**.
we today job-ACC finish-FUT-1PL
'We are going to *finish* the job today.'

(9) Ben hergün **gaZEte** oku-r-um.
I every.day newspaper read-AOR-1SG
'I go through the *newspapers* every day.'

23.1.1.1 The immediately preverbal position

There are certain constituents that occupy the position immediately before the verb. These are:

(i) Subject complements (12.1.1.2):

(10) Meral çabucak **hasta** oldu.
'Meral quickly became *ill*.'

(ii) Small clauses (24.5):

(11) Ben [**Meral-i hasta**] sanıyordum.
'I thought [*Meral [was] ill*].'

(iii) Adjectives used adverbially (16.1.2):

(12) Bu yemek odası takımı mutfakta **iğreti** duruyor.
'This dining room set looks *out of place* in the kitchen.'

(13) Nilgün problemleri **yavaş** çözer.
'Nilgün solves (the) problems *slowly*.'

(iv) Non-case-marked direct objects (which may be indefinite (22.2) or categorial (22.3) noun phrases):

(14) Dün bana **başka bir telefon numarası** vermiştin.
'Yesterday you gave me *a different telephone number*.'

The next two conditions apply to the existential expressions *var* 'present/existent' and *yok* 'absent/non-existent' as well.

(v) Categorial and indefinite subjects:

(15) a. Elimi **cam** kesti.
'*Some glass* cut my hand.'

b. Bu tarafta **cam** yok.
'There isn't *any glass* on this side.'

(vi) Plural-marked indefinite subjects without a determiner:

(16) a. Yukarıya **yeni kiracılar** taşınmış.
'*New tenants* have apparently moved in upstairs.'

b. Yukarıda **yeni kiracılar** var.
'There are *new tenants* upstairs.'

Clitics (Chapter 11) can come between such phrases and the predicate.

There are certain other phrases that also tend to occur in the immediately preverbal position:

(i) Oblique objects, unless there is also an adverb (13.1.1.2):

(17) İsanların çoğu **ölümden** korkar.
'Most people fear *death*.'

(18) Sen **babama** *hep* kızardın.
'You *always* got angry with *my father*.'

(ii) Adverbial clauses of manner (26.3.8):

(19) Neslihan elbiselerini [**üstüne denemeden**] alır.
'Neslihan buys her clothes [*without trying them on*].'

(iii) Case-marked indefinite noun phrases (22.2):

(20) Dün sokakta **bir hırsız-ı** kovala-mış-lar.
                      a thief-ACC chase-EV/PF-3PL
'Apparently, they chased *a thief* in the street yesterday.'

(21) Müdür resmi evrakları **bir sekreter-e** verdi.
                      a secretary-DAT give-PF
'The director gave the official documents *to a secretary*.'

(iv) Indefinite animate and inanimate subjects (22.2):

(22) Sabah eve **bir adam** geldi.
'*A man* came to the house this morning.'

(23) Dolabın arkasına **bir şey** düşmüş.
'*Something* seems to have fallen down behind the cupboard.'

However, if a sentence contains an indefinite subject and a definite direct object, the tendency is to place the indefinite subject before the definite object:

(24) **Bir kadın çiçekleri** suluyor.
'*A woman* is watering *the flowers*.'

For the position of adverbs in verbal sentences, see 23.1.3.1.

23.1.2 Nominal sentences

23.1.2.1 Linking sentences

In linking sentences (12.1.1.2), the predicate is placed at the end and the subject at the beginning. Sentence stress falls on the subject complement which is before the copular marker if there is one (*müdür* 'director' in (25), and the possessive suffix *-ü* in (26)):

(25) Rezan bu banka-da **müDÜR**-dü.
    this bank-LOC director-P.COP
    'Rezan was *a director* at this bank.'

(26) Rezan bu banka-nın **müdüR-Ü**-ydü.
    this bank-GEN director-3SG.POSS-P.COP
    'Rezan was *the director of* this bank.'

Stress falls on the subject complement irrespective of whether there is an overt copular marker or not:

(27) Rezan on yıldır **piLOT**.
    'Rezan has been *a pilot* for 10 years.'

When there is an adjective modifying the nominal predicate, stress falls on the adjective:

(28) Rezan **iYİ** bir pilot.
    'Rezan is a *good* pilot.'

Stress falls on *değil* 'not' if the sentence is negative (20.2.1):

(29) Havanın sıcak olacağı kesin **deĞİL**.
    'It is not certain that the weather will be hot.'.

23.1.2.2 Existential sentences

In locative existential sentences (12.1.1.2), the initial position is occupied by a locative noun phrase. The subject occupies the position immediately before the predicate, which comes at the end. Stress falls on the subject if the sentence is affirmative and on *yok* 'non-existent' if it is negative.

(30) Bu köy-de **genetik bir hastaLIK** var-mış.
    this village-LOC genetic a disease existent-EV.COP
    'Apparently, there is a *genetic disease* in this village.'

(31) Bizim okulda müzik bölümü **YOK**.
'*There isn't* a music department in our school.'

In possessive existential sentences, the subject which is a genitive-possessive construction (14.4) occupies the initial position and the predicate comes at the end. Stress falls on the subject if the sentence is affirmative.

(32) **Aliye'nin hasta-SI** var.
Aliye-GEN patient-3SG.POSS.existent
'*Aliye* has a *patient*.'
(lit. 'Aliye's patient exists.')

(33) **Kitabımızın ÜÇ bölümü** var.
'*Our book* has *three sections*.'

As in locative existential sentences, *yok* 'non-existent' attracts the stress in negative sentences:

(34) Hasan-ın imza yetki-si **YOK**.
Hasan-GEN signature authorization-3SG.POSS non-existent
'Hasan *does not have* authorization to sign.'

(35) Bu kutunun anahtarı **YOK**.
'This box doesn't have a key.'

For the position of adverbs in nominal sentences, see 23.2.1, 23.2.3.

23.2 The unmarked order of major constituents

23.2.1 Subjects and modal adverbs

In most cases, the position of modal adverbs and subjects is interchangeable:

(36) *Meğer* **Hasan** çoktan tıbbı bitirmişmiş.
as.it.turns.out Hasan
'*It turns out that Hasan* completed his medical studies a long time ago.'

(37) **Necla** *galiba* artık bankada değil.
Necla I.think
'*I* don't *think Necla* is with the bank any more.'

In locative existential sentences, modal adverbs tend to precede the subject, but they can also occur at the very beginning of a sentence:

(38) Kadıköy'de ***bildiğim karadıyla* güzel bir kütüphane** varmış.
as.far.as.I.know nice a library
'*As far as I know*, there is *a nice library* in Kadıköy.'

(39) ***Demek ki*** o lokantada **dondurucu** yok.
    evidently   freezer
    '*Evidently*, there is no *freezer* in that restaurant.'

In possessive existential sentences, the modal adverb usually precedes the subject or the possessive-marked noun phrase within the subject:

(40) (Biz-im) ***gerçekten* video-muz** yok.
    we-GEN really video.player-1PL.POSS
    'We really don't have a video player.'

23.2.2 Objects

Non-case-marked direct objects and oblique objects occur in the immediately pre-verbal position.

(41) Her sabah kahvaltıdan önce **kahve** içerim.
    'Every morning, I drink *coffee* before breakfast.'

An exception to this is when they are followed by certain clitics (Chapter 11) or adverbials (23.1.1.1 (13)):

(42) **Bir çay *da*** bana ver.
    'Give me *a (glass of) tea, too.*'

(43) Ahmet'ten **mektup *mu*** aldın?
    'Have you had *a letter* from Ahmet?'

Definite and other accusative-marked direct objects usually occur near the beginning of the sentence, following the subject noun phrase and/or modal adverbial, if present:

(44) Ahmet herhalde **bütün parayı** bir haftada bitirir.
    '(Ahmet) would (probably) get through *all the money* in a week.'

(45) (Öğretmen) {[**dersi baltalayan**] **öğrencilerden birkaç tanesin**}-**i** idareye bildirdi.
    '(The teacher) reported *several of the students* [*who had disrupted the class*] to the authorities.'

In sentences which contain both an accusative-marked direct object and an oblique object, the former precedes the latter:

(46) Hasta anne-sin-**i** ye-mey-**e** zorla-dı.
    sick mother-3SG.POSS-ACC eat-VN-DAT force-PF
    'S/he forced his/her sick mother to eat.'

Otherwise, there are generally no clear-cut rules determining the ordering of two or more case-marked noun phrases (objects or adverbials) in relation to one another, *where all or both are definite*. The general principle is that the more predictable a constituent is (e.g. from previous mention or from presence in the conversational context) the earlier in the sentence it is likely to appear.

(47) Ahmet öğrenci-ler-**e** sınav kağıt-ların-**ı** verdi.
student-PL-DAT exam paper-3PL.POSS-ACC
'Ahmet gave the students their exam papers.'

(48) Şu masa-**yı** yandaki oda-**ya** götür.
table-ACC   room-DAT
'Take this table into the room next door.'

If a sentence has two accusative-marked or two dative-marked noun phrases because there are two clauses in the sentence, then each noun phrase occupies its unmarked position within its own clause:

(49) Ahmet **sen-i** [**ben-i** tanı-mı-yor] san-dı.
you-ACC I-ACC know-NEG-IMPF think-PF
'Ahmet thought *you* [didn't know *me*].'

(50) **Doktor-a** [**hasta-ya** bak-ma-sın]-ı söyle-di.
doctor-DAT patient-DAT check-VN-3SG.POSS-ACC tell-PF
'S/he told *the doctor* [to check *the patient*].'

For an example with two dative noun phrases in causative constructions, see Chapter 13 (36).

23.2.3 Adverbial constructions

Adverbial constructions of time generally precede those expressing location, which in turn precede those expressing manner:

(51) Ben **şimdi** derslerimi **aşağıda bilgisayar-la** veriyorum.
now   downstairs computer-INS
'*Now* I'm giving my lectures *downstairs with a computer*.'

Adverbials expressing reason or purpose often occur at the beginning of the sentence and can precede the subject:

(52) [**Mehmet ona borcunu ödemediği için**] Ali **bu yıl** kendi borçlarını **zor** ödeyecek.
'[*Because Mehmet hasn't paid his debt to him*] Ali will pay his own debts *with great difficulty this year.*'

(53) [**Bozulmasın diye**] annem köfteleri buzdolabına koymuştu.
'My mother had put the meatballs in the fridge [*so that they wouldn't go off*].'

Most adverbials of time may also precede the subject:

(54) **Dün** annem doktordaydı.
'*Yesterday* my mother was at the doctor's.'

(55) **Hafta sonları** çocuklar buradalar.
'The children are here *at the weekends.*'

Where two adverbials of time or place occur together, the one with the broader meaning precedes the other:

(56) **Her gün 14.30-da** uçak varmış.
every day 14.30-LOC
'It seems there is a plane *at 14.30 every day.*'

23.3 Word order variations

The major constituents of a sentence can appear in almost any order (with some restrictions on indefinite noun phrases). For example, a verbal sentence containing a subject, a direct object (with an accusative case marker) and a verb has six possible orders (with the further possibility of inserting adverbials at the beginning, the end or between constituents):

(57) a. Ali ev-i sat-tı.
Ali house-ACC sell-PF
'Ali sold the house.'

b. Evi Ali sattı.
c. Ali sattı evi.
d. Evi sattı Ali.
e. Sattı Ali evi.
f. Sattı evi Ali.

Although these sentences are equally grammatical, they are used in different contexts. For example, (b) and (c) are interchangeable if *Ali* is stressed, a strategy which guides the addressee to focus his/her attention on Ali, and indicates that it was Ali who sold the house. (e) and (f) emphasize the selling of the house, as a verb which is at the beginning of a sentence obligatorily carries stress. On the other hand, (b) and (d) are more or less interchangeable if *evi* 'the house (ACC)' bears stress. These sentences are used in circumstances when the emphasis is placed on this constituent, e.g. to draw attention to the fact that it is the house and not some other building that Ali sold. This interpretation applies to (a) as well if *evi* 'the house' bears stress. These are a few of the possible interpretations of (a)–(f).

The word order in nominal sentences is also changeable. In linking sentences, the subject can follow the predicate if the subject complement is to be emphasized, as in (b):

(58) a. Emine yaratıcı bir şarkıcı.
Emine creative a singer.
'Emine is a creative singer.'

b. Yaratıcı bir şarkıcı Emine.

A locative existential sentence consisting of three constituents can have six orders:

(59) a. Bende bu uygulama yok.
I(LOC) this app not.existent
'I don' have this app.'

b. Bende yok bu uygulama.
c. Bu uygulama yok bende.
d. Bu uygulama bende yok.
e. Yok bende bu uygulama.
f. Yok bu uygulama bende.

The differences in meaning in the locative existential sentences above are slight as 'yok' usually attracts stress. However, the position of stress can vary, thereby yielding differences similar to those for verbal sentences. For example, (e) and (f) are more likely to be used in a context where the possession of a particular application is emphatically denied.

In possessive existential sentences, word order permutations are slightly more restricted than locative existential sentences:

(60) a. Didem-in iki köpeğ-i var.
Didem-GEN two dog-3POSS.SG existent
'Didem has two dogs.'

b. Didem'in var iki köpeği.
c. İki köpeği var Didem'in.

d. Var Didem'in iki köğeği.
e. Var iki köpeği Didem'in.

(d), and (e) can be used interchangeably in contexts where the speaker intends to emphasize the fact that Didem has two dogs, possibly following a comment that questions or refutes the existence of Didem's two dogs. The various meanings that the remaining sentences convey depend on the position of stress. For example, if in (c) *var* 'existent' is stressed, the sentence will have the same meaning as (d) and (e), whereas if *iki köpeği* 'two dogs (3POSS.SG)' is stressed, it may be used in a context where the number of dogs is relevant.

Changing the order in which constituents appear in unmarked sentences, that is, **scrambling** them, has three general purposes:

(i) Emphasizing a particular constituent:
This strategy which is called **focusing** is used to highlight the information provided by the constituent in question. This may be because it is new information, that is, it refers to something that has not previously been mentioned, or because the speaker wishes to contrast this item of information with another one (perhaps previously mentioned).

(ii) De-emphasizing a particular constituent or constituents:
Some of the constituents in a sentence may have relatively less informative value than others, generally as a result of having been mentioned earlier, or simply because they are uttered as afterthoughts. Such pieces of information are described as **backgrounded**.

(iii) Making a particular constituent the pivot of the information in a sentence:
A particular constituent may act as the information centre in terms of signalling what the sentence is about. This is called a **topic**.

Placing (or not placing) sentence stress on a constituent plays as important a role in determining its information value as scrambling does. Focused constituents are almost always stressed, while back-grounded constituents rarely are. Those signalling topics usually take secondary stress (5.2.2).

In many cases the acoustic quality of stress in sentences with scrambled order is different from the quality of stress of unmarked sentences. In particular, a focused constituent usually gets heavy stress, with an accent higher in pitch than the stressed constituent of an unmarked sentence. However, we do not attempt to indicate such differences in this book.

The following conditions apply to scrambled constituents:

(i) Focused phrases bear stress.
(ii) Focused phrases appear in the area preceding the predicate, either immediately before the predicate or in their unmarked position as long as they carry stress.

(iii) Backgrounded information follows the predicate and is not stressed.
(iv) Topics (sometimes followed by topic shifters) usually occur at the beginning of a sentence.
(v) The predicate is obligatorily stressed (and focused) if it is at the beginning of a sentence.
(vi) Certain semantic properties of noun phrases, such as definiteness, specificity and animacy also affect word order (22.5, 23.1.1.1 (22)-(23)).

23.3.1 The position of focused constituents: the pre-predicate area

The term 'pre-predicate area' is a cover term for the preverbal position(s) in a verbal sentence and the position(s) before the predicate in nominal sentences. This is the area for focused constituents which generally present new information. Generally speaking, all types of constituent can be focused and can occur in any position before the predicate as long as they bear stress.

The most typical position for focused phrases in verbal sentences is immediately before the verb:

(61) Fatma çiçek-ler-i **BUgün** sula-yacak.
Fatma flower-PL-ACC today water-FUT
'Fatma will water the plants TODAY.'

(62) Bazı günler ön bahçe-de **çocuk-LAR** oynu-yor.
some day-PL front garden-LOC child-PL play-IMPF
'Some days CHILDREN play in the front garden.'

A less common strategy for focusing a constituent is to place stress on it in its unmarked position:

(63) **BUgün** çiçekleri sulayacaksın.
'You will water the plants TODAY.'

The most typical strategy for focusing a constituent in linking sentences is to place stress on it in its unmarked position or to place it before the predicate:

(64) a. **HülYA** 2005'ten beri profesyonel tenis oyuncusu.
b. 2005'ten beri **HülYA** profesyonel tenis oyuncusu.
'HÜLYA has been a professional tennis player since 2005.'

In locative existential sentences, focused constituents can be stressed in their unmarked position or they can be placed before the predicate:

(65) **BeşİKtaş'ta** satılık bina yok./Satılık bina **BeşİKtaş'ta** yok.
'There are no buildings for sale IN BEŞİKTAŞ.'

In possessive existential sentences, a focused phrase is generally stressed in its unmarked position:

(66) **Ahmet'İN** iki arabası var.
 'AHMET has two cars.'

(67) Kraliyet ailesinin **LONdra'da** 150 kadar gayrimenkulu var.
 'The royal family has about 150 properties in LONDON'.

Focused constituents can be used with focus-sensitive adverbials and connectives such as *ancak* 'only' (16.7), *dA* 'also' and *bile* 'even' (28.3.1.1).

(68) *Ancak* **öZEL izin-le** gir-il-ebil-iyor-muş
 only special permit-INS enter-PASS-PSB-IMPF-EV.COP

 kulis-e
 back.stage-DAT

 'One can only go backstage *by special permit*.'

(69) **KomşuLAR** *da* bazı günler ön bahçede oturuyor.
 'Some days *the neighbours* too sit in the front garden.'

Like any other constituent, a predicate can be focused by placing stress on it. When stressed, predicates can occupy any position, including their unmarked sentence-final position:

(70) Ama ben bütün mektupları dün **yırtTIM**.
 'But I TORE UP all the letters yesterday.'

In linking sentences and existential sentences, the subject complement is stressed.

(71) Onların hepsi **öğretMEN**. (Cevapları tabii ki bilecekler.)
 'They are all TEACHERS. (Of course they'll know the answers.)'

(72) Evde peynir **VARdı**!
 'THERE IS/WAS cheese in the house.'

23.3.2 The position of background information: the post-predicate area

The area following the predicate is the site for information which is backgrounded, information which is assumed to be shared by the speaker and the addressee, or which has only just been mentioned in the discourse. Placing constituents here also has the effect of rendering another constituent more prominent, sometimes leaving this latter as the only phrase before the predicate. Note that the strategy of backgrounding is restricted to spoken and informal written Turkish. In formal written styles, constituents are not normally placed after the predicate.

(73) Hiç seyahat-e GİT-me-miş **yalnız başına daha önce**.
never trip-DAT GO-NEG-EV/PF alone before
'S/he's apparently never been on holiday *alone before*.'

(74) GüZEL-miş **bu ev**.
nice-EV.COP this house
'It's nice, *this house*.'

(75) Tatil-DE **biz-im bütün komşu-lar**.
holiday-LOC we-GEN all neighbour-PL
'*Our neighbours* are on holiday.'

The relative positioning of the constituents in the post-predicate area is insignificant. More than one constituent can follow the predicate and they can occur in any order. If all the constituents in a sentence follow the predicate, then the predicate is obligatorily stressed. The sentences below are informationally identical:

(76) a. Bitir-Dİ **Fatma üniversite-yi bu yıl**.
finish-PF Fatma university-ACC this year
'Fatma FINISHED university this year.'

b. Bitir-Dİ **üniversite-yi bu yıl Fatma**.
c. Bitir-Dİ **bu yıl Fatma üniversite-yi**.

No constituent occurring in the post-predicate area can bear stress; as a result, the post-predicate area cannot host stress-requiring elements such as wh-phrases (19.2.1) or *mI*-phrases (19.1). (Note that *mI*-phrases can appear after the predicate in alternative questions in cases where the second mention of a shared verb is omitted (Chapter 19 (23)).

The constituents that are most commonly backgrounded are definite noun phrases and adverbials. However, it is possible for a non-definite noun phrase to be placed in the post-predicate area if it refers to an entity or category that has been mentioned (or implied) in the immediately preceding discourse:

(77) Ayşe senin arkadaşlarınla ne kadar rahat konuşuyordu.
Üniversiteye girdiği yıl BİLmiyordu hiç **İngilizce**.
'How fluently Ayşe was talking to your friends. She didn't know any *English* the year she entered university.'

(78) BaNA da getir **bir kahve**. (cf. (42))
'Bring me *a (cup of) coffee*, too.'

(79) VAR-mış **siz-in bakkal-da kopya kağıd-ı**!
existent-EV.COP you-GEN grocer-LOC carbon paper-NCM
'Your grocer DOES sell carbon paper!'

(80) YOK **burada doktor**.
'There ARE no doctors here.'

Backgrounding can also take place within a noun clause. '(…)' refers to where a constituent would normally occur in an unmarked sentence:

(81) [(…) Piyano çal-dığ-ın-ı **Ayşe-nin**] BİL-mi-yor-du-m.
piano play-VN-3SG.POSS-ACC Ayşe-GEN know-NEG-IMPF-P.COP-1SG
'I didn't know [*Ayşe* played the piano].'

23.3.3 The topic position

The initial position in a sentence is often used to indicate what the sentence is 'about', in other words, its topic. As explained in 23.1, in unmarked sentences it is usually the subject (if overtly expressed) that occupies the topic position. However, through scrambling it is possible to topicalize any constituent except those that obligatorily occur in the position immediately before the predicate. In some of the translations in this section passivization has been used in order to reflect the informational effect of topicalizing a non-subject constituent. In the sentences below, an adverb, a subject, and a possessor have been topicalized.

(82) **Hergün akşam saat 6'da** akŞAM haberleri var.
'Every evening at 6 p.m. there is the evening news.'

(83) **Huri** benim EN iyi arkadaşım.
'*Huri* is my best friend.'

(84) **Bu arabanın** cam sileckleRİ yok.
'*This car* doesn't have windshield wipers.'

Where a non-definite direct object is topicalized, it has to be given accusative marking if it is no longer in the immediately preverbal position (14.3.3.2 (ii)).

(85) **Suluboya-yı** ancak usTA bir ressam böyle kullan-abil-ir.
watercolour-ACC
'*Watercolours* can only be used like this by a highly skilled painter.'

An indefinite noun phrase can be topicalized only if it refers to a member or members of a group or category that has been mentioned or implied in the preceding discourse:

(86) Partiye gelenlerin çoğu bahçeye çıkmıştı. **Birkaç çocuk** orada babamlaydı.
'Most of the ones who had come to the party had gone out into the garden. *Several children* were with my father out there.'

Such a noun phrase may be left without case-marking in the direct object function:

(87) **Bir tane** de bana ver.
'Give me *one*, too.'

Noun phrases with categorial status (22.3) cannot be topicalized as *subjects*. This means that subject noun phrases that occur in the topic position without plural marking and without a determiner are interpreted as definite (22.1) or generic (22.4).

It should be noted that not all sentences in Turkish have overtly expressed topics. The continuation of a subject-topic from one sentence to another is signalled by the *absence* of a noun phrase referring to the subject in the second and subsequent sentences in the sequence (18.1.5).

Topicalization can also take place within a noun clause.

(88) Ayşe [**yaprağ -ı** annesi (. . .) sar-ıyor] san-dı.
Ayşe vine.leaf-ACC mother-3SG.POSS stuff-IMPF think-PF
'Ayşe thought *the vine leaves* were being stuffed by her mother.'

23.3.3.1 Topic shifters

There are a number of markers in Turkish which signal a change of topic: the clitics *dA* and *-(y)sA/ise* and the expressions *gelince* 'as for...' (the *-(y)IncA* converbial form of *gel-* 'come', i.e. 'when one comes to...') and *desen(iz)* 'as for...' (the 2nd person singular or plural conditional form of *de-* 'say' i.e. 'if one were to mention...'). *-(y)sA/ise*, *gelince* and *desen(iz)* are placed immediately after the new topic at the beginning of a sentence. The position of a *dA* marked topic is somewhat less rigid and although as a topic shifter *dA* most commonly appears after the first constituent in a sentence, it can also occur in other positions.

(i) The clitic *dA* (11.1.1.2) is the least emphatic marker of topic shift. It signals a continuity or connection between two events or situations and is usually equivalent to 'and' or 'so' in English (28.3.1.1 (iii.a)).

(89) Kimse Semra'ya gel dememiş, o **da** evDE oturacakmış.
'No one asked Semra to come, *so* she'll be staying at home.'

A non-focused *subject* combined with *dA* may occur in the post-verbal position:

(90) Derslerini yapmamışlar. Onları UYARDIM ben **de**.
'It seems they haven't done their homework. *So*, I've warned them'.

For other functions of *dA*, see 28.3.1.1 (iii.b) and 28.3.2.

(ii) The clitic *-(y)sA/ise* (11.1.1.7) sends a stronger signal, indicating that a significantly different point is going to be made about the new topic. This may be a direct contrast with what has been said about the previous topic:

(91) Kardeşim hep kolayına kaçıyor, ben**se** her işi en iyi şekilde yapmaya çalışıyorum.
'My sister/brother always takes the easy way out, *whereas* I try to do everything in the best way possible.'

Alternatively, it may be a rather striking, perhaps even surprising, further development of the same theme:

(92) Kağıtları ancak toparlayabildim. Kitaplar**sa** hâlâ kutularda duruyor.
'I have only managed to tidy up the papers. *As for* the books, they are still in their boxes.'

(93) Ahmet Semra'yı hiç aramıyormuş. Semra'nın**sa** buna hiç aldırdığı yok.
'Apparently, Ahmet doesn't call Semra any more. Semra, *for her part*, couldn't care less.'

(iii) *gelince* and the more informal *desen(iz)* phrases correspond to 'as for…' constructions in English. *gelince* has a dative-marked complement and *desen(iz)* has a bare complement, both of which act as antecedents to obligatory pronouns later in the sentence. In *desen(iz)*, the person marker depends on the level of familiarity with the addressee. Both *gelince* and *desen(iz)* signal that the speaker wishes to draw particular attention to the statement that is about to be made.

(94) Hayri ve Faruk bugün babalarına hediye alacaklarını söylediler.

Ahmet'e *gelince* / Ahmet *desen(iz)* o nasıl olsa çok düşünceli-dir.
Ahmet-DAT as.for / Ahmet as.for he anyway very thoughtful-GM

Al-mış-tır bile.
buy-PF-GM already

'Hayri and Faruk said they would be buying their father a present/presents today. *As for Ahmet*, well, *he's* very considerate in any case. He will have bought [one] already.'

All topic-shift markers, with the topics that they mark, form intonational phrases ending in a slight rise (5.1 (iii)). There is usually a short pause after *gelince/deseniz*; this may also occur after *-(y)sA*, but is not normally heard after *dA*.

23.4 Dislocated constituents

In addition to the possibility of placing any major constituent after the predicate, some constituents can cross the boundaries of the phrase or the clause of which they are part and occur at the end of the sentence.

23.4.1 Dislocated adjectival constructions

Adjectival constructions can be displaced from their position before a noun, and they can appear in the position following the predicate. This usually occurs where the modifying phrase is added as an afterthought:

(95) Burada (…) bir elbise-m var-dı **eteğ-i sökük**.
 here a dress-1SG.POSS existent-P.COP hemline-3SG.POSS unstitched
 'I had a dress here, *with its hemline unstitched*.'

(96) Bütün zeytinyağlı-lar-da (…) şeker var-dır **bir iki kaşık**.
 all cold.vegetable.dish-PL-LOC sugar existent-GM one two spoonful
 'All cold vegetable dishes have sugar in them, [just] *one or two spoonfuls*.'

(97) Bana bir (…) su ver, **soğuk**.
 'Give me a glass of *cold* water.'

23.4.2 Dislocated constituents of genitive-possessive constructions

The modifier of a genitive-possessive constructions, that is, the genitive-marked noun phrase (14.4), can be displaced:

(98) Tartışma bölümünde (…) son filminden söz etmediniz **Handan İpekçi'nin**.
 In the discussion session you didn't mention the latest film of *Handan İpekçi*.

If the genitive-possessive construction is in a subordinate clause, the preferred position of the dislocated modifier is in the post-predicate position of the main clause, rather than that of the subordinate clause:

(99) [(...) Araba-sı ol-ma-dığ-ın]-ı mı söyle-di-n **Ahmet-in**?
car-3SG.POSS be-NEG-VN-3SG.POSS-ACC INT say-PF-2SG
'Did you say Ahmet didn't have a car?

23.4.3 Dislocated constituents of noun clauses

Mostly subjects, but also other constituents of a noun clause, can be dislocated and placed at the end of the sentence:

(100) [(...) Piyano çal-dığ-ın]-ı bil-mi-yor-du-m **Ayşe'nin**.
piano play-VN-3SG.POSS-ACC know-NEG-IMPF-P.COP-1SG Ayşe-GEN
'I didn't know [*Ayşe* played the piano].'

(101) [Zerrin'in (...) (...) gör-me-sin]-i iste-mi-yor-du-m
Zerrin-GEN see-VN-3SG.POSS-ACC want-NEG-IMPF-P.COP-1SG

hediye-sin-i şimdiden.
present-3SG.POSS-ACC yet

'I didn't want [Zerrin to see *her present yet*].'

Alternatively, constituents of a noun clause can be placed at the beginning of a sentence for topicalization:

(102) **Yaprağ-ı** aşçı [herhangi biri-nin (..) sar-abil-eceğ-in-e]
vine.leaf-ACC cook anyone-GEN stuff-PSB-VN-3SG.POSS-DAT

inan-mı-yor-du.
believe-NEG-IMPF-P.COP

'The cook didn't believe [that (just) anyone could stuff *vine leaves*].'

Chapter 24

Noun clauses

Noun clauses are noun phrases (Chapter 14) that have a clausal structure. They are subordinate clauses that perform within the larger sentence the same functions as noun phrases, that is, those of subject, object, etc. Structurally, they may be one of two types:

(i) **Finite** (i.e. identical in structure to a full sentence, 12.3):

    (1) [Üniversite-ye gid-e-yim] isti-yor.
        university-DAT go-OPT-1SG want-IMPF
        'S/he wants [me to go to university].'

(ii) **Non-finite** (i.e. with their verbal constituent marked by one of the subordinating suffixes -*mAK*, -*mA*, -*DIK*, -*(y)AcAK* or -*(y)Iş*, 8.5, 12.3):

    (2) [Konu-yu iyice anla-**mak**] gerek.
        topic-ACC thoroughly understand-VN necessary
        'One has to understand the topic thoroughly.'

Within the finite category a further division exists: **bare finite noun clauses** (24.2) are juxtaposed to, or inserted within, the **superordinate** clause, as in (1) above, while **finite noun clauses** with a **subordinator** (24.3, 12.3) are linked to their superordinate clause by a preceding *ki* or a following *diye* or *gibi*:

    (3) [Sen Londra-da-sın **diye**] bil-iyor-du-m.
        you London-LOC-2SG SUB think-IMPF-P.COP-1SG
        'I thought [*that* you were in London].'

In 24.4 we present a detailed account of the wide range of non-finite noun clause patterns and functions. 24.5 is devoted to the special kind of noun clause known as a **small clause**, the subject of which is also a constituent of the superordinate clause. The chapter concludes with a brief discussion of noun clauses as modifiers in noun compounds (24.6).

DOI: 10.4324/9780429435836-27

In the interests of clarity, we have confined both the discussion and the examples in this chapter to sentences in which the noun clause is embedded directly in the main clause. However, it should be borne in mind that all types of noun clause, with the exception of those formed with *ki* (24.3.2), regularly occur embedded in other clauses which are themselves subordinate to the main clause (12.3).

24.1 Finite and non-finite noun clauses

The subordinating suffix that is attached to the predicate of non-finite noun clauses gives them a much more recognizably *nominal* structure than a finite noun clause can have. In all noun clauses marked with *-DIK* or *-(y)AcAK* and in most that are marked with *-mA* or *-(y)Iş* (8.5), the subject is indicated by a possessive suffix attached to the verbal noun. The subject may also be referred to more explicitly by a genitive-marked noun phrase, which gives the noun clause the overall structure of a genitive-possessive construction. For omission of genitive marking on the subject, see 24.4.6.

(4) [(Sen-**in**) piyano çal-***dığın***]-ı bilmiyordum.
    you-GEN piano play-VN-2SG.POSS-ACC
    'I didn't know [you played the piano].'

(5) [(Sen-**in**) piyano çal-***ma*-n**]-ı beklediler.
    you-GEN piano play-VN-2SG.POSS-ACC
    'They expected [you to play the piano].'

Non-finite noun clauses have the same kind of mobility within the sentence as noun phrases (23.3). Some types of finite noun clause, on the other hand (especially the bare type and those formed with *ki*), are considerably more restricted in the positions that they can occupy in relation to the main predicate.

In general terms the non-finite types of noun clause are more universally acceptable than their finite equivalents (where these indeed exist). Except for the presentation of direct speech (24.2.1 (i)) and the use of *ki* clauses with cognitive verbs (24.3.2.2), the use of finite noun clauses is largely confined to informal styles of speech and writing.

24.2 Bare finite noun clauses (finite noun clauses without a subordinator)

These occur as subjects or objects of the verbs *de-* 'say', *iste-* 'want' and verbs of cognition.

24.2.1 Subject or object of the verb de-

de- 'say' occurs only with finite noun clauses. It can be used not only to express a spoken utterance but also for the expression of unspoken thoughts. Here we shall discuss three different uses of *de-*.

(i) The most straightforward use of *de-* is in representations of direct speech, where the speaker claims to present the exact words spoken in another context by himself/herself or someone else. It should be noted that *de-*, whether in a finite form or a non-finite one such as *diye* (24.3.1), is the *only* verb that can be used for this purpose. The quotation itself occupies the immediately preverbal position (23.1.1.1).

(6) O gün Suzan "Artık dayan-a-m-ıyor-um"
that day Suzan now bear-PSB-NEG-IMPF-1SG

de-miş-ti bana.
say-PF-P.COP I.DAT

'That day Suzan had *said* to me "I can't bear [it] any longer".'

(7) Bana genellikle "Sen küçüksün, gelemezsin" **de**-n-iyor-du.
say-PASS-IMPF-P.COP
'I was usually *told* "You're too young; you can't come".'

(ii) The second use of *de-* differs only slightly from the first. Here the subordinate clause is not claimed to present the exact words uttered by a specific person on a specific occasion, but rather to encapsulate the gist of a more generalized utterance, attributed to unspecified people. Quotation marks are not found with this usage of *de-*.

(8) [New York ağustosta çekilmez] **di**-yor-lar.
say-IMPF-3PL
'People *say* [New York is unbearable in August].'

(iii) The use of *de-* to express thoughts rather than utterances is very common in colloquial speech. Although the context may imply that the thought is articulated in speech, quotation marks are not used, because the emphasis is on the substance of the thought rather than on a particular utterance of it.

(9) [Tören bir saat sürer] **di**yelim.
'Let's *suppose* [the ceremony will last an hour].'

Where the verb in the subordinate clause is in one of the optative forms (i.e. contains one of the suffixes *-sIn*, *-(y)AyIm* or *-(y)AlIm*) or the conditional *-sA*, the thought is also a desire for something to happen (21.4.4).

(10) [Herkes yiyeceklerini kendi getir***sin***] **di**yorum ben.
'I *think* [everyone *should* bring their own food].'

(11) [Bu belirsizlik bit-*se* artık] **di**-yor-du-k.
this uncertainty end-OPT now say-IMPF-P.COP-1PL
'[*If only* this uncertainty *would* end], we *thought*.'

Note that the verb *söyle-*, the other verb which means 'say', contrasts with *de-* in terms of the type of noun clause that can be used with it. *Söyle-* can only be used with non-finite clauses (24.4.2.2, 24.4.3.1); moreover, it always denotes a *spoken* utterance.

24.2.2 Subject or object of a verb of perception or cognition

(i) A finite *question* clause can be the subject or object of a verb of cognition such as *bil-* 'know', *anla-* 'understand'. The main verb is usually negative or interrogative:

(12) [Çocuğ-un baba-sı kim] **bil**-in-iyor mu?
child-GEN father-3SG.POSS who know-PASS-IMPF INT
'Is it *known* [who the child's father is]?'

(13) [Ertan'ı neden bu kadar beğeniyorsun] **anla**yamıyorum.
'I can't *understand* [why you admire Ertan so much].'

(ii) A false perception can be expressed by a finite noun clause subordinated to the verb *san-/zannet-* 'think' or *bil-* 'assume' (i.e. a small clause, 24.5):

(14) Biz [sen git-ti-n] **san**-dı-k.
we you go-PF-2SG think-PF-1PL
'We *thought* [you had left].'

(15) Genellikle [Elif öğretmen] **bil**inirdi.
'Usually it was *assumed* that [Elif was a teacher].'

(iii) A number of forms such as *sanırım* 'I think', *biliyorum* 'I know', *biliyorsun(uz)* 'you know', *bakarsın* 'you'll see' have been lexicalized as modal adverbials (16.3).

24.2.3 Subject or object of the verb *iste-*

A sentence whose main verb is *iste-* 'want' can also have a finite noun clause as its subject or object, although here the verb in the subordinate clause is always in the optative form (i.e. is marked with *-sIn*, *-(y)AyIm* or *-(y)AlIm*) (21.4.4.2–3).

(16) [Birer birer gir-**e-lim**] **iste**-n-iyor-muş.
one.by.one go.in-OPT-1PL want-PASS-IMPF-EV.COP
'Apparently, they *want* [us to go in one by one].'

(17) [Her taraf mermerle kaplan**sın**] **iste**yor.
'He *wants* [everywhere to be covered in marble].'

24.3 Finite noun clauses with a subordinator

The subordinators that mark certain types of finite noun clause are *diye, gibi* and *ki*.

24.3.1 Clauses formed with diye

The subordinator *diye* (11.1.1.3) is the *-(y)A* converbial form of the verb *de-* 'say' (26.3.8) and its functions are quite clearly derived from the various meanings of *de-* discussed in 24.2.1. *diye* is of very common occurrence in the formation of both noun and adverbial clauses (26.1.1). It always stands at the end of its clause. Noun clauses with *diye* function as subject or object of the following classes of verbs:

(i) Verbs of communication other than *de-*
(ii) Verbs of perception and cognition
(iii) Verbs of emotion

(i) Verbs of communication other than *de-*:
Where a piece of direct speech is presented as the subject or object of a main verb other than *de-*, such as *sor-* 'ask' or *bağır-* 'shout', *diye* has to intervene between the quotation and this main verb:

(18) "Akşam-a gel-ecek mi-sin?" **diye *sor*-**du
evening-DAT come-FUT INT-2SG SUB ask-PF

anne-m bana.
mother-1SG.POSS I.DAT

'"Will you be coming back tonight?" my mother *asked* me.'

As the object of *konuş-* 'talk', a *diye* clause expresses action that has been agreed upon by two or more people as in (19a); this need not be treated as a quotation. Alternatively, in formal speech or writing, the verb *konuş-* can be used with another word that acts as a subordinator, *şeklinde* '(lit.) in the shape of' which introduces a quotation, as in (19b). Again, with the verb *konuş-* (or *tartış-* 'discuss') some speakers exceptionally place a case-marker on the complement, *despite* it being finite, as in (19c). This usage is colloquial and not very widespread.

(19) a. [Herkes bir yemek yapıp getirsin **diye**] ***konuş***muştuk.
'We had *agreed* [*that* everyone should make and bring one dish].'

b. [Herkes bir yemek yapıp getirsin **şeklinde**] ***konuş***tu.
'S/he said ["Everyone should make and bring one dish."].'

c. [Herkes bir yemek yapıp getirsin]-**i** ***konuş***tuk.
'*We* talked about [[the proposition] "Everyone should make and bring one dish."].

(ii) Verbs of perception and cognition:
The principal verbs of perception and cognition that occur with *diye-* marked objects are: *bil-* (in this context meaning not 'know' but 'think' (= suppose)), *düşün-* 'think' (= speculate, be of the opinion that), *bekle-* 'expect', *duy-* 'hear', *işit-* 'hear', *oku-* 'read'.

(20) [Bir torununuz olmuş **diye**] ***duy***dum.
'I *heard* [*that* you have had a grandchild].'

See also example (3) above.

(iii) Verbs of emotion:
All verbs of emotion that take an oblique object (13.1.2.2) can alternatively have a clausal object which is marked by *diye*:

(21) Teoman [memur onu azarladı **diye**] çok ***sinirlen***mişti.
'Teoman *was very annoyed* [*that* the official had reprimanded him].'

In the case of *kork-* 'be afraid', the verb in the subordinate clause receives the conditional suffix *-(y)sA*:

(22) Meral, [Turgut onu Selim'le gör-ür-*se* **diye**]
                             see-AOR-COND.COP SUB
kork-uyor-du.
be.afraid-IMPF-P.COP

'Meral *was afraid* [*that* Turgut would see her with Selim].'

24.3.2 Clauses formed with ki

Unlike other noun clauses in Turkish, which can be placed either before or after the main predicate, clauses with *ki* (11.1.1.4) obligatorily follow the main predicate:

(23) Sanıyorum [**ki** iş-in-i bırak-mak isti-yor].
I.think that job-3SG.POSS-ACC leave-VN want-IMPF
'I think [(*that*) s/he wants to leave his/her job].'

The use of a *ki* clause rather than either of the other types of finite noun clause has the effect of highlighting the main predicate, thus drawing attention to the status of what is about to be uttered: an obvious fact, a surmise on the part of the speaker, a desire, etc. Note that the main predicate preceding a *ki* clause is rarely cast in an interrogative form. For the stress-related properties of *ki* see 11.2.

Speakers also use *ki* structures as an organizational device to gain time for articulating the substantive content of their communication. Although of common occurrence, *ki* clauses are perceived as marked structures and therefore do not normally occur repeatedly within a single utterance or paragraph.

24.3.2.1 Subject or object of the verb de-

The use of *de-* 'say' followed by a *ki* clause is an alternative to the type of structure discussed in 24.2.1, where *de-* immediately follows the clause expressing the utterance or thought. *ki* clauses occur in all the three functions of *de-* identified in 24.2.1:

(i) Representations of direct speech (cf. (6)):

(24) O gün Suzan bana **de**-miş-ti **ki**:
that day Suzan I.DAT say-PF-P.COP SUB

"Artık dayan-a-m-ıyor-um".
now bear-PSB-NEG-IMPF-1SG

'That day Suzan had *said* to me "I can't bear [it] any longer".'

(25) Bana genellikle **de**niyordu **ki**: "Sen küçüksün, gelemezsin". (cf. (7))
'I was usually *told* "You're too young; you can't come".'

(ii) Generalized sayings (cf. (8)):

(26) **Di**yorlar [**ki** New York ağustosta çekilmez].
'People *say* [(*that*) New York is unbearable in August].'

(iii) Thoughts and wishes (cf. (10)):

(27) Ben **di**yorum [**ki** herkes kendi yiyeceklerini kendi getir**sin**].
'I *think* [(*that*) everyone *should* bring their own food].'

There is no difference in formality between the two alternative structures with *de-*. Sentences in which *de-* is used to express thoughts rather than utterances are less likely to be structured with a *ki* clause, unless, as in (27), they can be construed as containing both speech and thought elements simultaneously.

24.3.2.2 Subject or object of a verb of perception or cognition

ki clauses can occur with verbs of cognition and also with verbs that express an attitude (belief, supposition, claim, etc.) towards the truth of a proposition:

(28) Artık **bil**iyoruz [**ki** onların uzlaşmaya hiç niyetleri yok].
'Now we know [that they have no intention of coming to an agreement]'.

(29) *Anlaşıl*ıyor [**ki** Fransızca'ya olan talep iyice azalmış].
'*It's clear* [*that* the demand for French has considerably declined].'

(30) Bir gün *duy*duk [**ki** adam taşınıp gitmiş].
'One day we *heard* [*that* the man had moved away].'

(31) İddia ediyorlar [**ki** o para şirkete aitmiş].
'They claim [that that money belonged to the company].'

Although in general the main clause introducing this type of *ki* clause is affirmative, there are two quite frequent patterns in which a negative form of *san-* 'think' occurs.

(i) The sentence is introduced by 1st person singular aorist *sanmam* and the verb in the subordinate clause (usually 3rd person) has optative marking (8.4.3) indicating the 'unreality' of the imagined situation:

(32) **Sanmam** [**ki** bu kadar şanssızlık başkalarının başına gelebil*sin*].
'*I don't think* [anyone else could have so much bad luck].'

(ii) The sentence is introduced by the 2nd person imperative form *sanma(yın)* and the verb in the subordinate clause has any marking:

(33) **Sanmayın** [**ki** ben bu kadına yaptıklarınızı unutacağım].
'*Don't imagine* [*that* I shall forget what you have done to this woman].'

Where the main clause verb is an affirmative form of *anlaşıl-* or *san-* the demonstrative adverbial *öyle* 'like that' (16.4.3 (iii)) is sometimes inserted before it:

(34) (*Öyle*) **san**ıyorum [**ki** arkadaşlarımızın çoğu ağustosta gelemeyecekler].
'I *imagine* [*that* most of our friends won't be able to come in August].'

This *öyle* is also seen in the lexicalized expression *öyle gel-* 'seem (to someone)', which is always used in combination with the dative-marked form of a personal pronoun:

(35) ***Bana öyle gel-*iyor** [**ki** Ömer'le ablasının araları pek iyi değil].
I.DAT seem-IMPF SUB
'It *seems to me* [*that* Ömer and his sister don't get on very well].'

This construction is identical in meaning to *gibi gel-* constructions (24.3.3).

Where a *ki* clause expresses a discovery made on performing a certain action, the verb of perception itself may be omitted:

(36) Kapıyı açtım [**ki** içerisi insan dolu].
'I opened the door [*and saw*] [*that* the place was full of people].'

24.3.2.3 Subject or object of the verb iste-

As in the case of bare finite noun clauses with *iste-* (24.2.3), the verb in a *ki* clause which is dependent on the verb *iste-* 'want' is always suffixed with one of the optative forms *-sIn*, *-(y)AyIm* or *-(y)AlIm* (21.4.4.2–3):

(37) İsteniyormuş [**ki** birer birer gir*elim*]. (cf. (16))
'Apparently, what they want is [for us to go in one by one].'

(38) Aslında istiyor [**ki** her taraf mermerle kaplan*sın*]. (cf. (17))
'Actually what he wants is [for everywhere to be covered in marble].'

24.3.2.4 The combination of adjectival predicates with ki

The combinations of adjectives such as *tabii* 'natural' and *belli* 'clear, 'obvious' with *ki* have become frozen forms (*tabii ki*, *belli ki*) which function as modal adverbials (16.3):

(39) Tabii [**ki** ben hiç öyle bir şey kastetmemiştim].
'Of course [I had meant nothing of the sort.]'

(40) Belli [**ki** birbirini çekemiyorlar].
'It's obvious [*that* they can't stand each other].'

24.3.3 Clauses formed with gibi

The role of *gibi* as a subordinator is derived from its primary function as a postposition meaning 'like' (17.2.1). As a subordinator it occurs mainly in adverbial clauses (26.1.5), but when it stands between a finite subordinate clause and a main verb which is *gel-* it marks a noun clause.

The idiom *gibi gel-*, optionally combined with the dative-marked form of a personal pronoun or of any noun phrase referring to human beings means 'seem (to someone)' (just like *öyle gel-* with a *ki* clause, 24.3.2.2). The finite noun clause immediately preceding *gibi* is the subject of the sentence.

(41) [Meryem yeni işine pek ısınamadı] **gibi gel**-iyor **bana**.
　　　　　　　　　　　　　　　　　seem-IMPF I.DAT
'*It seems to me* [*that* Meryem is not very happy in her new job].'

(42) **Sana** [bu işi büyütüyorum] **gibi ge**lebilir.
 '*It* may *seem to you* [*that* I'm making too much fuss about this].'

A more informal variant of this construction, occurring only in the first person and giving a rather more tentative meaning, is *gibime gel-* (used in lieu of *bana ... gibi gel-*):

(43) [O çocukta bir tuhaflık var] **gibi-m-e gel**-iyor.
 gibi-1SG.POSS-DAT gel-IMPF
 '*I have a feeling* [there's something odd about that child].'

Note that other verbs meaning 'seem', such as *gibi dur-/gibi görün-/gibi gözük-* and the verb *gibi yap-* 'pretend' behave differently from *gibi gel-* (24.5.3 (160)–(161)).

24.4 Non-finite noun clauses

In the following sections we describe in turn the functions of noun clauses formed with each of the following subordinating suffixes: *-mAK, -mA, -DIK, -(y)AcAK, -(y)Iş*.

24.4.1 Clauses formed with -mAK

The verb form suffixed with the subordinator *-mAK* (8.5.2), often called the **infinitive**, is the 'citation' form of the verb, used when talking about a verb as a lexical item:

(44) Öyle bir hareket için 'sıyrıl**mak**' fiilini kullanırız.
 'We use the verb *sıyrılmak* for such an action.'

Noun clauses formed with *-mAK* are used primarily (i) for talking about an activity, action or state in general terms, or (ii) with main verbs that express a subject's behaviour or attitude towards an action or activity that they perform or may perform.

The crucial difference between *-mAK* clauses and those with *-mA* is that *-mA* clauses in the majority of cases contain their own subject (24.4.2), whereas *-mAK* clauses do not. A *-mAK* clause usually has an *understood subject* which is indicated by a noun phrase or person marker occurring in the superordinate clause (24.4.1.1). For example, in (45) the subject of the *-mAK* clause is indicated by the 1st person marking on the main verb:

(45) [Sokağa çık-**mak**] isti-yor-**um**.
 go.out-*mAK* want-IMPF-1SG
 'I want [to go out].'

The subject of a *-mA* clause, on the other hand, cannot be the same as the subject of the superordinate clause:

(46) [Sokağa çık-**ma-*n***]-ı isti-yor-**um**
    go.out-*mA*-2SG.POSS-ACC want-IMPF-1SG
    'I want [*you* to go out].'

In the following sections, we review the functions of *-mAK* constructions with and without case marking.

24.4.1.1 The non-case-marked form *-mAk*

Like all non-case-marked noun phrases (14.3.3.1), a noun clause containing *-mAk* without the addition of any case suffixes can function as subject (47), subject complement (48) or direct object (49) within the clause in which it is embedded. The only verb which regularly takes a *-mAk* clause as its direct object is *iste-* 'want' (49). Other transitive verbs require the accusative-marked form *-mAyI* (24.4.1.2).

(47) [Türkçe öğren**mek**] zor.
    '[Learn*ing* Turkish] is difficult.'/'It's difficult [*to* learn Turkish].'

(48) Hayattaki en büyük nimetlerden biri [sevil**mek**]-tir.
    'One of the greatest blessings in life is [*to* be loved].'

The question of what is understood to be the subject of the *-mAk* clause depends on whether the main clause (or another clause in which the *-mAk* clause is embedded) is verbal or nominal.

(i) Where the superordinate clause is **verbal**, the understood subject of the *-mAk* clause (the 'doer' of the verb in the *-mAk* clause) can be one of the following constituents of this superordinate clause:

a. The subject:

(49) ***Sen*** [nereye git**mek**] istiyor***sun***?
    'Where do *you* want [*to* go]?'

For another example, see (45) above and for passive *-mAk* clauses which are the subject of their superordinate clause, see 24.4.1.4.

b. The direct object:

(50) [Bütün gün müze gez**mek**] ***biz***i çok yormuştu.
    '[Go*ing* round museums all day] had worn *us* out.'

c. The oblique object:

    (51) [Ev taşı**mak**] *Nevin*'e çok kolay geldi.
         '[Mov*ing* house] came very easily to *Nevin*.'

(ii) Where a *-mAk* clause forms part of a **nominal sentence**, the understood subject of the *-mAk* clause may or may not be identifiable:

  a. If the *-mAk* clause is the subject of the sentence, the doer of the noun clause may be made explicit by the use of a postpositional phrase with *için* 'for' (and sometimes a dative noun phrase) in the main clause:

    (52) [Kimseye bir şey söyleme**mek**] kolay değil **ben**im için.
         '[Not tell*ing* anyone anything] is not easy for *me*.'

In the absence of such a phrase, the subject of the noun clause may be inferable from the context. In (53) it is the speaker:

    (53) [Sizinle konuş**mak**] hoş oldu.
         'It's been nice [talk*ing* to you].'

In (54), on the other hand, it is either the addressee or some third party:

    (54) [Bütün gece otur**mak**] çok zor olmuştur.
         'It must have been very hard [sitt*ing* up all night].'

A *-mak* clause that is the subject of a sentence can also denote an activity, action or state in the abstract, without relation to any particular subject:

    (55) [Bir çocuğa öyle bir şey söyleme**mek**] lazım.
         'One shouldn't say such a thing to a child.'

For the use of *-mAk* clauses in impersonal obligative expressions such as that in (55), see Chapter 21 (127).

  b. If the *-mAk* clause is the subject complement and the subject of the sentence is marked with a possessive suffix, the subject of the noun clause will be understood to be the person referred to by that suffix:

    (56) Amac-*ım*, [beş yıl içinde zengin ol-**mak**]-tı.
         aim-1SG.POSS five years within rich be-VN-P.COP
         '*My* aim was [*to* get rich in five years].'

Where, in a sentence of this type, the main clause subject has no possessive marking, the subject of the noun clause may be inferable from the context:

(57) Amaç, [beş yıl içinde zengin ol**mak**]-tı.
'The aim was [*to* get rich in five years].'

In some cases, as in (57) above, the noun clause has no identifiable subject and is understood to be applicable to human beings in general.

24.4.1.2 The accusative-marked form -mAyI

This form (sometimes spelt -*mAğI*, 8.5.1.2) occurs where the noun clause is the direct object of any transitive verb (although with *iste-* 'want' it is formal and much less common than -*mAk*).

(58) Şükrü [yemek yap-**may**]-*ı* bil-iyor mu?
Şükrü food make-VN-ACC know-IMPF INT
'Does Şükrü know [how to cook]?'

(59) [Bu yaz İtalya'ya git**mey**]-*i* düşünüyoruz.
'We're thinking of [going to Italy this summer].'

With a small number of main verbs, notably *bil-* 'know (how)', *öğren-* 'learn' and *sev-* 'like', the noun clause is sometimes marked with -*mAsInI* rather than -*mAyI*, with no change in meaning. The 3rd person possessive suffix has no obvious referent in such sentences.

(60) Şükrü [yemek yap-**ma-sın**]-*ı* bil-iyor mu?
Şükrü food make-VN-3SG.POSS-ACC know-IMPF INT
'Does Şükrü know [how to cook]?'

(61) Ahmet [araba kullan**masın**]-*ı* sever.
'Ahmet likes [driving].'

24.4.1.3 The oblique case-marked forms -mAyA, -mAktA (-mAdA), -mAktAn

(i) These forms occur where the verb in the main clause is one that requires an oblique object (13.1.2.2). The dative-marked form -*mAyA* is sometimes spelt -*mAğA* (8.5.1.2). Verbs such as *başla-* 'begin', *karar ver-* 'decide', *devam et-* 'continue', *çalış-* 'try' require the dative case:

(62) [Her gün beş sayfa yaz-**may**]-*a çalış*-ıyor-um.
every day five page write-VN-DAT try-IMPF-1SG
'I *try* [to write five pages every day].'

Some verbs such as *zorla-* 'force', *ikna et-* 'persuade' require a human direct object in addition to the oblique object:

(63) **Beni [konuşmay]-*a zorla*ma!**
 '*Don't force me* [to talk]!'

Verbs such as *diren-/diret-/ısrar et-* 'insist (on)' and *yarar gör-* 'see benefit/point (in)' require the locative case:

(64) Demet [otobüs-le git-**mek**]-*te diret*-iyor.
 Demet bus-INS go-VN-LOC insist.on-IMPF
 'Demet is *insist*ing *on* [going by bus].'

Some speakers use the form *-mAdA* in the same function as *-mAktA*.

Verbs such as *vazgeç-* 'stop', 'decide not (to)', *kork-* 'be afraid (of/to)', *çekin-* 'be reluctant (to)', *kaçın-* 'avoid', *nefret et-* 'hate' take an ablative-marked object:

(65) [Sigara iç-**mek**]-*ten vazgeç*-meli-siniz.
 cigarette smoke-ABL give.up-OBLG-2PL
 'You must *give up* [smoking].'

A few verbs take as their oblique object a *-mAk* clause marked with the comitative/instrumental marker *-(y)lA*, such as *övün-* 'boast (of)', *suçla-* 'accuse [s.o.] (of)':

(66) Ayten'i [eski bilgisayarını bana ver**mek**]-*le* suçluyorlar.
 'They are *accus*ing Ayten *of* [giving her old computer to me].'

(ii) Locative marking occurs also in existential sentences with *fayda/ yarar* 'benefit', 'use' as the subject. As with non-case-marked *-mAk* (24.4.1.1), the subject of the noun clause in these constructions may be entirely unspecified, as in (67), or may be implied in the context, as in (68).

(67) [Yaşlıları dinle**mek**]-*te fayda var*.
 '*There is benefit in* [listening to old people].'

(68) [Babana bir kere daha sor**mak**]-*ta yarar var*.
 '*It's worth* [asking your father once more].'

However, the negative versions of such sentences are more often cast as a possessive existential with the genitive-marked form of *-mA* (24.4.2.1 (ii)).

(iii) Ablative case marking also occurs where the noun clause expresses an object of comparison (14.3.3.5 (v)):

(69) [Evi kendim temizle**mek**], [başkasına temizlet**mek**]-*ten* daha kolay geliyor.
'I find it easier [to clean the house myself] *than* [to get someone else to clean [*it*]].'
(lit. 'It comes more easily to...')

24.4.1.4 Passive *-mAK* clauses subordinated to main verb *iste-*, *çalış-*, *başla-*

A sentence containing a *-mAK* clause with passive marking also obligatorily has passive marking on its main verb if that main verb is *iste-* 'want', 'try' or *çalış-* 'try':

(70) [Özellikle keman konçerto-su çal-**ın**-mak] iste-**n**-di.
particularly violin concerto-NCM play-PASS-VN want-PASS-PF
'It was particularly the violin concerto that the orchestra wanted played.'

(71) [Sınır-lar geç-**il**-me]-ye çalış-**ıl**-dı.
border-PL cross-PASS-VN-DAT try-PASS-PF
'Attempts were made to cross the borders.'

Although not common, it is possible for such a sentence to have a subject that is not 3rd person:

(72) [Yürüyüş sırasında önce polis, sonra düzenleyiciler tarafından durdu-**rul**mak] iste**ndik**.
'During the march attempts were made to stop *us*, first by the police, then by the organizers.'

More frequently, the verb in the *-mAK* clause may be intransitive, that is, an impersonal passive (13.2.2.3):

(73) [Deprem bölge-sin-e ulaş-**ıl**-ma]-ya çalış-**ıl**-ıyor.
earthquake area-NCM-DAT reach-PASS-VN-DAT try-PASS-IMPF
'Efforts are being made [to reach the earthquake area].'

If the passive *-mAK* clause is subordinated under the main verb *başla-* 'start', the main verb may or may not have passive marking:

(74) [Kitaplar satılma]-ya başladı/başlandı.
'[The books] started [to be sold].'

24.4.2 Clauses formed with -mA

In general terms, noun clauses formed with *-mA* are less abstract in meaning than those formed with *-mAK*. One result of this is that many *-mA* verbal nouns have become lexicalized as ordinary nouns with concrete meanings (7.2.1.1). When *-mA* is used as a productive inflectional suffix, by far the most common pattern is for it to be followed by a possessive suffix referring to the subject of the noun clause (24.4.2.2). However, there are two types of *-mA* clause in which possessive suffixes do not occur and we deal with these first.

24.4.2.1 -mA without possessive suffixes

(i) The plural form *-mAlAr*
   This is not a very common pattern. It is used to form the subject of a sentence describing repeated instances of an action or activity performed or undergone by unspecified subjects:

   (75) O sıralarda [sabahın erken saatlerinde polis tarafından

   uyan-dır-ıl-**ma-lar**],
   wake.up-CAUS-PASS-VN-PL

   [karakol-a götür-ül-**me-ler**],
   police.station-DAT take-PASS-VN-PL

   [gözaltına al-ın-**ma-lar**] günlük olaylardandı.
   detain-PASS-VN-PL

   'At that time [being woken up by the police in the early hours of the morning, being taken to the police station and being detained in custody] were daily occurrences.'

(ii) The genitive-marked form *-mAnIn*
   This form behaves exactly as if it were the genitive-marked form of *-mAK*. Like *-mAK* it is either used to denote an activity, action or state in general terms or it can have an implied subject inferable from the speech context. These genitive-marked noun clauses occur as modifiers in genitive-possessive constructions where the possessive-marked noun phrase is an abstract noun such as *anlam* 'meaning', 'sense', *fayda/yarar* 'benefit', 'use', *zarar* 'harm', *neden/sebep* 'reason' or *amaç* 'purpose':

   (76) Ben-ce {[Ali-yi çağır-**ma**]-***nın anlam-ı***} yok.
   I-ADV Ali-ACC summon-VN-GEN sense-3SG.POSS non-existent '
   I don't think *there's any point in* [asking Ali to come].'

(77) {[Sigarayı bırak**ma**]-*nın faydasın*}-ı ilk günlerde görmeyebilirsin.
'You may not experience *the benefit of* [*giving up smoking*] in the first few days.'

For similar constructions with possessive-marked -*mA* clauses, see 24.4.2.2.

24.4.2.2 -mA with possessive suffixes

A noun clause with possessive-marked -*mA* as its verbal constituent denotes an action, activity or state that is predicated of a certain subject. This subject may be more explicitly referred to by a genitive-marked noun phrase which, if present, usually stands at the beginning of the clause:

*(siz**in**) bu evi beğen**meniz***	'your liking this house'
*Can'**ın** erken gelmesi*	'Can's coming early'
*kapı**nın** güzel kapatılmaması*	'the door not being shut properly'

For contexts in which the subject is not (necessarily) genitive-marked, see 24.4.6. Also note that where the verbal component of the -*mA* clause is an impersonal passive (13.2.2.3), as in example (79) below, the verbal noun receives 3rd person singular marking that has no obvious referent.

In contrast to sentences containing noun clauses marked with -*DIK/-(y)AcAK* (24.4.3), which are to do with factual perception, knowledge, or communication, sentences constructed with -*mA* clauses deal with states and events in terms of description or evaluation, of causation processes in which they are involved, or of people's attitudes towards them or attempts to bring them about.

Below we describe the typical functions that -*mA* clauses can have in different grammatical roles within the sentence.

(i) As subject:
a. Description/evaluation:

(78) [Fatma Hanım-**ın** üç kat merdiven çık-**ma-sı**]
　　　　　　　GEN three storey stairs go.up-VN-3SG.POSS
çok zor.
very difficult

'It's *very difficult* [for Fatma Hanım to go up three flights of stairs].'

(79) Otobüslerde sigara iç-il-**me-si** yasak.
　　　　　　　cigarette smoke-PASS-VN-3SG.POSS prohibited
'Smoking is prohibited on buses.'

Subject *-mA* clauses are one of the major means of expressing necessity or obligation (21.4.2.2):

(80) [8.30'da havalimanında ol**mamız**] ***gerek***iyor.
  'We have to be at the airport at 8.30.'

The sequence *olması gerek/lazım* can also express an assumption (21.4.1.4).

b. Causation:

(81) [Ayla'**nın** işten hep geç ve yorgun gel**mesi**] evde gerginlik yaratıyordu.
  '[The fact that Ayla always got back from work late and tired] was creating tension in the house.'

c. Desired action or state:
A fuller treatment of this type is given in (iii.a) below, dealing with *-mA* clauses as direct objects. Where the *-mA* clause is the subject, the main predicate is usually the passivized form of *iste-* 'want':

(82) [Herkes-**in** birer hikaye anlat-**ma-sı**]
  everyone-GEN one.each story tell-VN-3SG.POSS

  iste-***n***-iyor-muş.
  want-PASS-IMPF-EV.COP

  'It seems they want [everyone to tell a story].'

d. Indirect commands, requests and recommendations:
These are the passivized versions of the type of sentence discussed in (iii.b) below:

(83) [Bu sıcaklarda yaşlıların sokağa çıkmaması] tavsiye ed*il*iyor.
  'Elderly people *are being* advised not to go out in this heat.'

In formal public requests, the noun clause as well as the main clause is sometimes cast in the passive form and the main clause verb has aorist marking:

(84) Yüksek sesle konuş-***ul***-ma-ma-***sı*** rica ol-**un**-ur.
          talk-PASS-NEG-VN-3SGPOSS request-pass-aor
  '[You] are requested not to talk loudly.'

(ii) As subject complement:
All of the functions performed by *-mA* clauses as subjects can also be performed when they are in the subject complement role (12.1.1.2):

(85) Önemli olan [sizin bu evi beğen**meniz**].
'The important thing is [that you (should) like this house].'

(86) Bizim ricamız [toplantı**nın** haftaya ertelen**mesi**] olacak.
'Our request is [that the meeting be postponed to next week].'
(lit. 'Our request will be...')

(iii) With accusative case marking as direct object:
Like all noun phrases marked for possession, possessive-marked -*mA* clauses always take accusative case marking when they are in the direct object role (14.3.3.2).

a. Desired actions or states:
In sentences expressing a desire for something to happen, the -*mA* clause is usually the object of the verb *iste-* 'want':

(87) [Bu tablo-**nun** şura-ya as-ıl-ma-**sın**]-*ı*
this picture-GEN here-DAT hang-PASS-VN-3SG.POSS-ACC

isti-yor-uz.
want-IMPF-1PL

'We want [this picture to be hung here].'

For the distinction between this construction and -*mAk iste-*, see (49).
Other verbs that can take a -*mA* clause as their direct object are *bekle-* 'expect' and *dile-* '(express the) wish (that)':

(88) [Kaçta orada olma-**nız**]-*ı* bekliyorlar?
'What time do they expect *you* to be there?'

b. Indirect commands, requests and recommendations:
These are sentences in which the -*mA* clause is the direct object of a verb that expresses an attempt to secure the performance of an action by others. The principal main verbs involved are *söyle-* 'tell', *emret-* 'order', *iste-* 'ask', *rica et-* 'request' and *tavsiye et-* 'recommend', 'advise'.

(89) Otel müdürü [oda-yı hemen boşalt-**ma-ların**]-*ı*
                room-ACC immediately vacate-VN-3PL.POSS-ACC
söyle-di.
say-PF

'The hotel manager told [*them* to vacate the room immediately].'

(90) Ceyda ***anne-m-e*** [herkes-**in** kalın giysiler-le
Ceyda mother-1SG.POSS-DAT everyone-GEN thick clothes-COM

gel-**me-sin**]-*i* söyle-miş.
come-VN-3SG.POSS-ACC say-EV/PF

'Ceyda told *my mother* [that *everyone* was to come in warm clothes].'

(91) [Turgut ***biz-den*** [taşınacağı gün kendisine
            we-ABL

yardım et-**me-miz**]-*i* istedi.
help AUX-VN-1PL.POSS-ACC

'Turgut has asked *us* [to help him on the day he moves].'

c. Causation:
A process that facilitates or obstructs the occurrence of the situation expressed by the noun clause has as its main predicate a verb such as *sağla-* 'ensure', *kolaylaştır-* 'make (it) easy (for)', *zorlaştır-* 'make (it) difficult (for)', *engelle-* 'hinder', *önle-* 'prevent':

(92) İlkbahardaki yağmurlar [mahsul**ün** bol ol**masın**]-*ı* sağladı.
'The spring rains ensured [that the harvest was plentiful].'

d. Object of verbs expressing attitude:
Some of the most commonly occurring verbs in this category are *beğen-* 'like', 'approve of', *kına-* 'deplore', *affet-/bağışla-* 'forgive', *hoş gör-* 'condone':

(93) [Kocası**nın** kendisine yalan söyle**mesin**]-*i* affedemiyordu.
'She couldn't forgive [her husband's lying to her].'

For *-mA* clauses as objects of verbs of perception and cognition see 24.4.5.1.

(iv) As oblique object:
a. Emotional attitude:
A *-mA* clause marked for dative or ablative case or with the instrumental marker can function as the oblique object of a verb of emotion (13.1.2.2, 24.4.5.2).

(94) Mehmet, [Ali-**nin** kendisini çağır-ma-**ma-sın**]-*a* gücendi.
            Ali-GEN   invite-NEG-VN-3SG.POSS-DAT
'Mehmet was offended *by* [Ali's not inviting him].'

(95) [Tülay'ın sürekli kendisinden söz **etmesin**]-*den* sıkılıyorum.
'I get bored *by* [Tülay talking about herself all the time].'

b. Causation:
Dative-marked *-mA* clauses occur as oblique objects of verbs such as *neden/sebep ol-* 'cause', *yol aç-* 'cause', *yardım et-* 'help', *müsaade et-/izin ver-* 'allow':

(96) Sıcak havalar, [meyvalar**ın** erken olgunlaş**masın**]-*a* yol açtı bu yıl.
'The hot weather has caused [the fruit to ripen early] this year.'

(97) Çocuklar [burayı topla**manız**]-*a* yardım etsinler.
'Get the children to help [you clear up in here].'

(98) Ev sahibimiz [kedi ya da köpek besle**memiz**]-*e* izin vermiyordu.
'Our landlady/landlord didn't allow [us to have a cat or dog].'

(v) With genitive marking:
Possessive-marked *-mA* clauses with genitive case marking on the verbal noun occur in the same kinds of structures as clauses with *-mAnIn* (24.4.2.1). If a possessive suffix is added to the verbal noun in a sentence such as (76) above, the noun clause acquires a specific subject:

(99) Ben-ce {[Ali-yi çağır-ma-**mız**]-*ın anlam*}-*ı* yok
I-ADV Ali-ACC summon-VN-1PL.POSS -GEN sense-3SG.POSS
non-existent
'I don't think there's any point in [*us* asking Ali to come].'

24.4.3 Clauses formed with -DIK/-(y)AcAK

The subordinating suffixes *-DIK* and *-(y)AcAK* are obligatorily followed by a possessive suffix referring to the subject of the noun clause. As in the case of possessive-marked *-mA* clauses, the subject of the noun clause, if overtly expressed within the clause rather than understood from the context, receives genitive marking (see 24.4.6 for exceptions). Again, as in the case of *-mA* clauses, an impersonal passive construction in the noun clause is given 3rd person singular possessive marking (as in example (103) below) without any obvious referent.

The forms *-DIK* and *-(y)AcAK* alternate with each other on the basis of the *tense* component of their meanings: *-DIK* refers to a time simultaneous with or earlier than that referred to by the superordinate predicate, while *-(y)AcAK* refers to a time later than the one in the superordinate clause. In other words, *-DIK* expresses relative present or relative past tense and *-(y)AcAK* relative future tense (21.2):

(100) a. [Orhan-**ın** bir şey yap-ma-**dığ**-ı] belliydi.
Orhan-GEN anything do-NEG-VN-3SG.POSS
'It was obvious [that Orhan *wasn't doing/hadn't done* anything].'

b. [Orhan-**ın** bir şey yap-ma-**yacağ**-ı] belliydi.
Orhan-GEN anything do-NEG-VN-3SG.POSS
'It was obvious [that Orhan *wouldn't do/wasn't going to do anything*].'

The fact that noun clauses with *-DIK* and *-(y)AcAK* are marked for tense points to the crucial difference between them and (possessive-marked) *-mA* clauses. *-DIK/-(y)AcAK* clauses are used almost exclusively in sentences that have to do with the *factual status* of an event or state (the truth or otherwise of its occurrence or of some aspect of its occurrence (who, what, where, etc.)).

The superordinate predicate in such sentences, if nominal, as in (100), expresses concepts such as truth or falsehood, certainty or uncertainty. If verbal, it is typically a verb expressing some cognitive process (knowledge, understanding, belief, opinion, etc.) or communication (saying, asking, etc.). The sentences in which *-DIK/-(y)AcAK* clauses occur are thus principally those known as **indirect statements** and **indirect questions**. In both types, the noun clause can occur either as subject, as direct object (with obligatory accusative case marking) or as oblique object.

24.4.3.1 Indirect statements

In an indirect statement, the content of the noun clause would, if formulated as an independent sentence, constitute a statement. The sentence as a whole may, however, take the form of either a statement or a question:

(i) With the noun clause as subject:
The superordinate predicate may be either nominal, as in (101a), or verbal, as in (101b):

(101) a. [Ayşe-**nin** ameliyat ol-**duğ-u**] doğru mu?
Ayşe-GEN operation AUX-VN-3SG.POSS true INT
'Is it true [*that* Ayşe has had an operation]?'

b. [Ayşe-**nin** ameliyat ol-**duğ-u**] söyle-n-iyor.
say-PASS-IMPF
'It is (being) said [*that* Ayşe has had an operation].'

The verbal predicate of a sentence with a *-DIK/-(y)AcAK* clause as its subject is the passivized form of a verb such as those listed in (ii) below.

(ii) With the noun clause as direct object:
This occurs with main verbs such as *bil-* 'know', 'think', *anla-* 'understand', 'realize', *san-* 'think', *düşün-* 'think', *tahmin et-* 'guess', *söyle-* 'say', *yaz-* 'write', *duy-/işit-* 'hear', *öğren-* 'learn':

(102) O gün Suzan bana [artık dayan-a-ma-**yacağ-ın**]-ı söylemişti.
       bear-PSB-NEG-VN-3SG.POSS-ACC
'That day Suzan had told me [*that* she couldn't bear [it] any longer].'
(cf. (6) and (24))

(103) [Bu hafta hiç çalış-ıl-ma-**yacağ-ın**]-ı tahmin ediyorum.
       work-PASS-NEG-VN-3SG.POSS-ACC
'I guess there's not going to be any work done this week.'

Where the noun clause is the object of *bil-* 'know', 'think', the factual status of its content depends on the position of stress within the sentence.

When stress is placed on the main verb *bil-*, it means 'know' and the content of the noun clause expresses an established fact:

(104) [Sen-in abla-n-ın yanında ol-duğ-un]-u bi**L-İ**yor-du-m.
       you-GEN sister-2SG.POSS-GEN with be-VN-2SG.POSS-ACC know-
       IMPF-P.COP-1SG
'I knew [you were with your sister].'

When, on the other hand, stress is placed within the noun clause, *bil-* is interchangeable with *san-* 'think' and the noun clause expresses a supposition that may turn out (or have turned out) to be false:

(105) [Senin **AB**lanın yanında olduğun]-u biliyordum/sanıyordum.
'I thought [you were with your sister].'

(iii) With the noun clause as oblique object:
This occurs with *inan-* 'believe' (dative marking) and *emin ol-* 'be sure' (ablative marking):

(106) [Bize o kadar büyük bir para ver-**ecek-lerin**]-*e* inanmamıştım.
                                  give-VN-3PL.POSS-DAT
'I never believed [*that* they would give us such a large amount of money].'

A -*DIK*/-(*y*)*AcAK* clause also occurs with ablative marking as the oblique object of possessive existential expressions (12.1.1.2) with *haber* 'knowledge (of)', 'awareness (of)' as subject:

(107) [Ahmet-in evlen-**diğ-in**]-*den* haber-**im** yok-tu.
       Ahmet-GEN marry-VN-3SG.POSS-ABL knowledge-1SG.POSS non-existent
       -P.COP
'I had no idea [*that* Ahmet had got married].'

(iv) With genitive marking on the noun clause:
This occurs with the expressions *farkında/ayırdında/bilincinde ol-* 'be aware that', where the noun clause becomes the possessor constituent in a genitive-possessive construction (14.4):

(108) [Bu iş-in iki günde bit-me-yebil-eceğ-i]-**nin**
finish-NEG-PSB-VN-3SG.POSS-GEN

fark-**ın**-da-yım.
aware-3SG.POSS-LOC-1SG

'I am aware [*that* this job may not be finished in two days].'

24.4.3.2 Indirect questions

Indirect questions are distinguished from indirect statements by the fact that the content of the noun clause would, if converted into an independent sentence, express a question.

The structures by which the various types of questions are expressed in Turkish are explained in Chapter 19. The corresponding structures for questions expressed indirectly in *-DIK/-(y)AcAK* clauses are as follows:

(i) Questions containing the *-(y)Ip...-mA* 'whether (or not)' construction (20.1.3):

(109) Annem bana [akşama **gel*ip* gel*me*yeceğim**]-i sordu. (cf. (18))
'My mother asked me [*if* I would be coming back that night (*or not*)].'

In terms of simple-sentence equivalents, these correspond both to yes/no questions (as in (18)) and to the kind of alternative questions in which the alternative presented is simply the negation of the predicate (= 'or not') (19.1.2).

(ii) Alternative questions involving an alternative which is not simply the negation of the predicate are expressed in a manner exactly parallel to that in simple sentences with the interrogative clitic *mI* placed after each of the alternative items (19.1.2). (110) contains the non-finite equivalent of example (23) in Chapter 19:

(110) [Tosca'yı Verdi'**nin** mi, (yoksa) Puccini'**nin** mi yaz**dığın**]-ı
bilmiyorum.
'I don't know [*whether* it was Verdi or Puccini who composed Tosca].'

(iii) Wh-questions are expressed simply by including the appropriate wh-phrase (19.2) in the noun clause:

(111) [Çocuğ-un baba-sı-**nın** *kim* ol-**duğ-u**]
child-GEN father-3SG.POSS-GEN WHO BE-VN-3SG.POSS

bil-in-iyor mu? (cf. (12))
know-PASS-IMPF INT

'Is it known [*who* the child's father is]?'

(112) [Ertan'ı *neden* bu kadar beğen**diğin**]-i anlayamıyorum. (cf. (13))
'I can't understand [*why* you admire Ertan so much].'

24.4.3.3 Other functions of -DIK/-(y)AcAK clauses

(i) Clauses with *-DIK* (not *-(y)AcAK*) also occur as the subject of sentences which comment on the frequency of a certain event or situation. The main verb here is usually *ol-* 'occur', *görül-* 'be seen', or *duyul-* 'be heard':

(113) O günlerde [akşamları birlikte çay iç**tiği**miz] çok *ol*urdu.
'In those days it was common [*for* us *to* have tea together in the evenings].'

(114) [Gökhan'ın içkiyi fazla kaçır**dığı**] hiç *görül*memişti.
'Gökhan had never been known [*to* have had too much to drink].'

Colloquially, this type of utterance can also be cast in the form of an interrogative or negative existential sentence:

(115) [Ahmet-i gör-**düğ**-ün] *var mı* bu günlerde?
Ahmet-ACC see-VN-2SG.POSS existent INT recently
'Have you seen anything of Ahmet recently?'

For another example, see Chapter 23 (93).

(ii) Although *-DIK/-(y)AcAK* clauses cannot, in general, be used to express evaluations or descriptions of events (24.4.2.2 (i.a)), the specific combination of *-DIK* with *iyi ol-* 'be good' does occur:

(116) [Bunu konuş**mamız**/konuş**tuğ**umuz] *iyi ol*du.
'It's good [*that* we have talked about this].'

(iii) Another use of genitive-marked *-DIK* clauses is in genitive-possessive constructions of which the head is a unit of time:

(117) [Adana-ya gel-**diğ-im**]-*in ikinci gün-ü* Turhan'la görüştük.
Adana-DAT arrive-VN-1SG.POSS-GEN second day-3SG.POSS
'Turhan and I met *on the second day after* [*my arrival* in Adana].'

24.4.4 Clauses formed with -(y)Iş

While productive as a derivational suffix forming abstract or semi-abstract nouns (7.2.1.1), as a subordinator *-(y)Iş* is more restricted in its functions than any of the other suffixes discussed in this chapter. It is almost always used to refer to an action or state predicated of a particular subject indicated, as usual, by the affixation of a possessive suffix. It therefore cannot be used in any of the functions of *-mAK*. It also cannot be used in sentences that bear upon the factual status of a proposition, nor in those that express a volitional stance (desire, command, request, permission, etc.) towards a situation. It is therefore excluded from most of the contexts in which *-DIK/-(y)AcAK* or *-mA* are used.

The verbal noun formed with *-(y)Iş* has two functions that are not shared by any of the other forms discussed in this chapter. It can express (i) the *manner* in which an action is performed, or (ii) a *single instance* of an event or action. In both of these functions *-(y)Iş* forms can have a status that is more noun-like than the other verbal nouns. This is illustrated in (118), where *sokuluş* 'manner of snuggling up', while remaining sufficiently verb-like to retain its oblique object *insana* 'to one', is preceded by the sequence *hoş bir* (ADJ *bir*) 'a nice', which occurs only in noun phrases.

(118) [O kedinin insana **hoş bir sokuluşu**] vardı.
'That cat had *a nice way of snuggling up* to one.'

Similarly, in the *single instance* reading, *-(y)Iş* clauses, unlike those formed with *-mA* or *-DIK/-(y)AcAK*, are countable:

(119) [Zehra'yı **her** gör-**üş**-ün]-ü ayrı bir zevkle hatırlıyordu.
      every see-VN-3SG.POSS-ACC
'S/he remembered with a separate pleasure *each occasion on which* s/he had seen Zehra.'

(120) [Türkiye'ye ikinci ve üçüncü gid**işler**imiz] 1982'de oldu.
'Our second and third *visits* to Turkey took place in 1982.'

24.4.5 Overlapping uses of -mA, -DIK/-(y)AcAK, -(y)Iş

24.4.5.1 As direct object of verbs of perception or cognition

All noun clause types capable of taking possessive suffixes can occur as objects of verbs of perception or cognition such as *gör-* 'see', *duy-* 'hear', *anla-* 'understand', *hatırla-* 'remember' and *unut-* 'forget'. However, the choice of subordinator in these cases has a clear effect on the meaning. While the use of *-DIK/-(y)AcAK* expresses the perception of a situation merely as a *fact*, the use of *-mA* or *-(y)Iş* expresses rather the perception of an inherent quality of the event or state. We illustrate this with two contrasting examples:

(121) a. [Çocuğ-un ağaç-tan düş-**tüğ**-ün]-ü gördüm.
b. [Çocuğ-un ağaç-tan düş-**me**-sin]-i gördüm.
c. [Çocuğ-un ağaç-tan düş-**üş**-ün]-ü gördüm.
child-GEN tree-ABL fall-VN-3SG.POSS-ACC see(PF.1SG)

All of the sentences in (121) could be translated 'I saw the child fall from the tree'. However, (a) is also open to the interpretation 'I saw that the child had fallen from the tree', where the fact is perceived only after the event has taken place. (b) and (c), on the other hand, tell us that the speaker witnessed the process of the child's fall. In a sense, therefore, both *-mA* and *-(y)Iş* in such contexts evoke more the idea of *how* something happens than the fact *that* it happens. Indeed, neither (b) nor (c) could be used in a context in which the fact of the child's fall had not already been established.

(122) a. Hakan [anne-sin-i sev-me-**diğ**-imiz]-i anlıyordu.
b. Hakan [annesini sev-me-**me**-miz]-i anlıyordu.
c. Hakan [annesini sev-me-**yiş**-imiz]-i anlıyordu.
Hakan mother-3SG.POSS-ACC love-NEG-VN-1PL.POSS-ACC understand(IMPF.P.COP)

In (a) the sentence means 'Hakan was aware *that* we didn't like his mother' and states Hakan's understanding of a situation at the factual level, whereas (b) and (c) mean 'Hakan understood our not liking his mother' and relate his understanding to the situation itself, implying that he understood *why* the speaker and others felt this way.

24.4.5.2 As oblique object of verbs of emotion

The semantic contrasts noted in 24.4.5.1 are neutralized where the noun clause is the object of a verb of emotion, such as *sevin-* 'be glad' or *üzül-* 'be sorry'. The *-DIK/-(y)AcAK* forms are fully interchangeable with *-mA* in such contexts, as shown below:

(123) Hepimiz [kadın-ın öyle bir suç işle-**me**-sin]-e üzüldük.
Hepimiz [kadın-ın öyle bir suç işle-**diğ**-in]-e üzüldük.
woman-GEN such a crime commit-VN-3SG.POSS-DAT
'We were all distressed [*that* the woman had committed such a crime].'

(124) [Hediyelerini beğen-me-**me**-miz]-den korkuyorlardı galiba.
[Hediyelerini beğen-me-**yeceğ**-imiz]-den korkuyorlardı galiba.
like-NEG-VN-1PL.POSS-ABL
'I think they were afraid [(*that*) we wouldn't like their present].'

-(y)Iş clauses also can express the object of a verb of emotion, provided (as always in the case of this suffix) that the situation is one that is *actualized*, that is, has happened or is ongoing at the moment of speech. The use of *-(y)Iş* also tends to be avoided with affirmative transitive verbs (such as *işle-*in (123)), unless the sense of manner is intended. (125) is an example with a negativized transitive verb, where all three forms would be acceptable (cf. (94) for the *-mA* version):

(125) Mehmet, [Ali-**nin** kendisini çağır-ma-*yış*-**ın**]-a gücendi.
            Ali-GEN   invite-NEG-VN-3SG.POSS-DAT
       'Mehmet was offended by [Ali's not inviting him].'

24.4.6 Omission of genitive marking on the subject of clauses formed with possessive-marked -mA, -DIK/-(y)AcAK

There are certain exceptions to the rule (24.1) that a noun phrase expressing the subject of a non-finite noun clause receives genitive case marking. In this section, we discuss four types of subject that do *not* normally receive case marking.

(i) A noun phrase with **categorial** status (22.3):
This is the only type of noun clause subject where the addition of the genitive suffix affects the meaning of the sentence, by changing the referential status of the subject from categorial to definite:

(126) a. [Buraya **araba** çarptığın]-ı tahmin ediyorum.
       'I guess [*a car* bumped here].'

b. [Buraya **araba-*nın*** çarptığın]-ı tahmin ediyorum
      car-GEN
   'I guess [*the car* bumped here].'

(127) a. [Çocuğa **para** verilmesi] yanlış olur.
       'It would be wrong [for the child to be given *money*].'

b. [**Para*nın*** çocuğa verilmesi] yanlış olur.
       'It would be wrong [for the child to be given *the money*].'

In types (ii)–(iv) below, on the other hand, genitive case marking, while unusual in (ii) and (iii), could be added without any effect on the meaning.

(ii) The subject of an existential clause (12.1.1.2):

(128) [Filiz'in odasında **yeşil perdeler** olduğun]-u hatırlıyorum.
      'I remember [that there were *green curtains* in Filiz's room].'

(iii) A possessive-marked *-mA* clause which is the subject of a *-DIK/ -(y)AcAK* clause expressing necessity:

(129) [Ahmet'in gel**mesi** [gerek**tiğin**]]-i düşünüyorum.
'I think [Ahmet *ought to* come].'

(iv) The indefinite subject of an intransitive or passive verb:

(130) [Bu odaya {**elli iskemle**}(**-nin**) *sığ*acağın]-a inanmıyorum.
                    fifty chair(-GEN)
'I don't believe [that *fifty chairs* will *fit* in this room].'

(131) [Bu sefer {**daha güzel sonuçlar**}(**-ın**) *çık*masın]-ı bekliyoruz.
'We are expecting [*better results to emerge* this time].'

(132) Mustafa, [yerine {**bir kadın**}(**-ın**) *ata-n*-ma-sın]-a içerliyor.
                     a woman(-GEN) appoint-PASS-VN-3SG.POSS
'Mustafa resents [the fact that *a woman* has *been appointed* in his place].'

24.4.7 The use of auxiliary ol- in non-finite noun clauses

As in the case of other types of non-finite subordinate clause (relative clauses 25.4.1 and adverbial clauses 26.2.3 (iii)), the auxiliary verb *ol-* is widely used in all types of non-finite noun clauses to add components of tense and aspect to the meaning of the clause. Where the auxiliary *ol-* is used, the lexical verb in the noun clause receives one of the tense/ aspect suffixes shown below and the subordinating suffix is attached to the auxiliary.

PERFECTIVE/PAST	*-mIş*
FUTURE	*-(y)AcAK*
PROGRESSIVE/HABITUAL	*-mAktA* and *-(I)yor*
HABITUAL	*-(A/I)r/-z*

For a full discussion of tense and aspect, see 21.2–3. For compound verb forms with *ol-* in finite clauses see 21.5.

By far the most common tense/aspect suffix to be used in non-finite noun clauses is *-mIş*. The inclusion of *-mIş* in a noun clause conveys that the event in question is envisaged as having been completed prior to a reference point specified or implied elsewhere in the sentence:

(133) [Çocukluğunda Atatürk'ü gör-**müş ol-mak**] kendisi için bir gurur
                                  see-PF AUX-VN
kaynağı idi.
'[*To have* seen Atatürk in his/her childhood] was a source of pride for him/her.'

(134) [Yarın akşama kadar kitapların yarısını gözden geçir**miş ol**ac**ağ**ımız]-ı tahmin ediyoruz.
'We reckon [that we *shall have* gone through half of the books by tomorrow evening].'

The use of *-(I)yor* or *-mAktA* in the noun clause can have one of two meanings:

(i) The situation in question is presented or envisaged as ongoing at the given reference point:

(135) [Filiz'in bu saatte çalış-**ıyor ol-ma**-sı] lazım.
                work-IMPF AUX-VN-3SG.POSS
(i) 'Filiz should/ought to *be* work*ing* at this hour.' (Obligation, 21.4.2.2)
(ii) 'Filiz must *be* work*ing* at this hour.' (Assumption, 21.4.1.4)

(136) [Toplantının devam et**mekte olduğ**un]-u söylediler.
'They said [the meeting *was* [still] go*ing* on].'

(137) [Tam o sırada Dekan'la görüş**üyor olacağ**ımız]-ı tahmin ediyordum.
'I reckoned [that we *would be* talk*ing* to the Dean at exactly that time].'

(ii) The situation is presented as occurring recurrently in a time span that includes the reference point:

(138) [Tülay'ın hafta sonları Ankara'ya gid**iyor olduğ**un]-u sanıyorum.
'I think [Tülay goes to Ankara at the weekends].'

It should be noted that the combination *-(I)yor olduK-* is in declining use. Many speakers would use the simple form *gittiğini* in (138).
    The use of *-mAktA olduK-* in a context of habituality is formal (cf. 21.3.2):

(139) [Bazı denetim işlerinin düzenli yapılma**makta olduğu**] belliydi.
'It was clear [that some checks *were* not be*ing* carried out regularly].'

Compound verb forms with *ol-* can be used to resolve the temporal ambiguity inherent in the subordinator *-DIK* (24.4.3):

(140) a. [Ali'nin bu kitabı oku**duğ**un]-u sanıyorum.
    'I think [Ali *has read/is reading* this book].'

b. [Ali'nin bu kitabı oku**yor**/oku**makta olduğ**un]-u sanıyorum.
    'I think [Ali *is reading* this book].'

c. [Ali'nin bu kitabı oku**muş olduğ**un]-u sanıyorum.
    'I think Ali [*has read* this book].'

-(y)AcAk ol- is rare in noun clauses, but *-(A/I)r/-z olduK-* is the equivalent of *-(A/I)r/-z oldu* in finite clauses (21.5.4):

(141) [Koray'la Hakan'ın görüş**mez olduk**ların]-ı işittim.
'I've heard that Koray and Hakan *have stopped* seeing each other.'

This construction is also declining in use, and many speakers would use *artık görüşmediklerini* instead.

24.5 Small clauses

Small clauses are a group of a variant kind of finite noun clause. They are unusual in that one of their constituents, the subject, is also a constituent (subject or object) of the main clause. The contexts in which small clauses occur are sentences where the main predicate is one of the types of transitive verb described below, or an intransitive verb meaning 'seem', 'appear'.

24.5.1 Small clauses occurring with main clause transitive verbs

The types of transitive verb which take small clauses are the following:

(i) Verbs of perception or cognition (24.2.2-3):
  a. *san-/zannet-* 'think', *bil-* 'think'
  b. *say-/addet-/farzet-* 'consider'
  c. *bul-* 'find', *gör-*, 'find', *iste-* 'want'

These verbs can occur with small clauses that have nominal predicates. The verbs in (i.a) and (i.b) can occur with small clauses containing verbal predicates as well. The occurrence of the verbs in (i.c) with small clauses that have verbal predicates is somewhat limited.

Small clause containing nominal predicate

(142) [Çocuğ-u **yakışıklı**] ***bul***-du-m.
       guy-ACC handsome find- PF-1SG
       'I *found* [the guy *handsome*].'

(143) [Ali'yi **iyi**] ***gör***medim.
       'Ali doesn't *seem well*.'

Small clause containing verbal predicate

(144) Biz [sen-i okul-u **bitir-di-n**] ***san***-ıyor-du-k.
       we you-ACC school-ACC finish-PF(-2SG) think-IMPF-P.COP-1PL
       'We *thought* [you *had completed* your studies].'

(145) Biz [kontratları **imzalandı**] *added*iyoruz.
'We *consider* [the contracts *signed*]'.

For the placement of negation in the type of constructions above, see Chapter 20 (4)–(6), (20).

(ii) Verbs expressing an act performed on an object which is or may be subject to a process of change, e.g. *ye-* 'eat', *iç-* 'drink', *kaldır-* 'put [s.t.] away', *as-* 'hang', *bırak-* 'leave [s.t.]'. In this case the predicate of the small clause is an adjective expressing the state of the object at the time when the action is performed on the very same entity (also known as secondary predication):

(146) Tülin [çayını **soğuk**] *iç*iyor.
'Tülin *drinks* [her tea *cold*].'

(147) [Gömlekleri **ütülü**] *kaldır*ırım hep.
'I always *put away* [the shirts *ironed*].'

In some of these constructions, *olarak* can be inserted after the predicate of the small clause (16.1.9 (i)).

(iii) Verbs expressing an action which gives someone or something status or quality, expressed by a noun, e.g. *yap-*, 'make', *seç-* 'elect', *ad(ını) koy-* 'name':

(148) [Ayşe'yi **müdür**] *yap*tık.
'We *made* [Ayşe *the director*].'

(149) [Kızın adını **Meryem**] *koy*dular.
'They *named* [the girl *Meryem*]'.

The verbs in (ii) and (iii) can only be used with small clauses containing nominal predicates (i.e. *soğuk, ütülü, müdür, Meryem* in (146)–(149)).

Where the main clause verb is transitive, the *subject* of a small clause (in boldface below) functions as the direct object of the main clause and is marked with the accusative case:

(150) Hepimiz [**bu konu-yu** kapan-dı] *added*-iyor-uz.
          all.of.us this issue-ACC close- consider-IMPF-P.COP-1PL
'All of us consider [*this issue* closed].'

(151) [**Mutfak bezini** ıslak] *bırak*mışsın.
'You left [*the tea towel* wet].'

Note that the verbs in (i.a) (in the case of *bil-* 'think', only for some speakers) can also have finite complements (24.2.2 (ii)), which means that the subject of the small clause remains non-case-marked.

(152) Biz [**sen** okul-u bitir-di-n] san-ıyor-du-k.
we you school-ACC finish-PF-2SG consider-IMPF-P.COP-1PL
'We thought [*you* had completed your studies].'

The subordinator *diye* (24.3.1) can be used after a small clause when the main clause verb is *bil-* 'think':

(153) Biz [Selim('i) Almanya'da] **diye bil**iyorduk.
'We *thought* [*that* Selim was in Germany.]'

24.5.2 Small clauses occurring with main clause intransitive verbs

When the main clause verb is intransitive (either in its root form or through passivization), the subject of the small clause (in boldface below) also functions as the *subject* of the main predicate.

(154) [**Mehmet** iyi] *(gibi) görün*-üyor-du.
Mehmet fine seem-IMPF-P.COP
'*Mehmet* was looking *fine*.'

(155) [**Biz** kurs-u tamamla-dı-**(k)**] added-il-iyor-**uz**.
we course-ACC complete-PF(-1PL) consider-PASS-IMPF-1PL
'*We* are considered [to have completed the course].'

Small clauses occurring with *benze-* 'look as if' as the main clause verb are idiosyncratic in that their own verb cannot be inflected for person. A further characteristic of *benze-* is that it requires dative marking of the small clause predicate:

(156) [**Sen** güneş-te fazla kal-mış]-*a benzi*-yor-**sun**.
(you) sun-LOC too.much stay-PF-DAT look-IMPF-2SG
'You look [as if *you* stayed too long in the sun].'

24.5.3 Tense/aspect and person marking

The verbal predicate of a small clause is usually marked with one of the suffixes *-mIş, -(I)yor, -(y)AcAK, -(A/I)r/-z* and *-DI*. When the main clause predicate is *san-/zannet-* 'think', the small clause can have a predicate marked with the past copula:

(157) [Sen o yıllarda öğretmen**din**] **san**ıyordum.
'I *thought* [you *were* a teacher during those years].'

The occurrence of person marking on the predicate of a small clause depends both on the predicate of the main clause and whether the small clause has a verbal or nominal predicate. The main clause predicates which allow person marking in the small clause when this latter has a verbal predicate are the ones in (i.a) and (i.b):

(158) Biz [sen-i git-ti-(**n**)] san-dı-k.
we you-ACC go-PF(-2SG) think-PF-1PL
'We thought [*you had left*].'

The optionality of person marking applies to the passive forms of these verbs as well see (155).

When the small clause has a nominal predicate, it can have person marking only if the main clause predicate is *san-/zannet-* 'think' and, for some speakers, *bil-* 'think':

(159) Onlar [bizi farkında değil(**iz**)] sanıyorlar.
'They think [we aren't aware of the situation].'

The verbs *gibi dur-/gibi görün-/gibi gözük-* 'seem', 'appear', are interchangeable and with these verbs, person marking may be attached either to the main verb or to the small clause predicate:

(160) a. [*Siz* hayat-ınız-dan memnun] **gibi dur**-uyor-*sunuz*.
you life-2PL.POSS-ABL happy like seem-IMPF-2PL
'*You* seem [to be *happy with your life*].'

b. [*Siz* hayatınızdan memnun-*sunuz*] **gibi dur**-uyor.
happy-2PL like seem-IMPF
'It seems [that *you are happy with your life*].'

Note that *gibi gel-* 'seem' (24.3.3) cannot be used with person marking on the main verb, that is, cannot be used in a sentence like (160a), but patterns with (160b) (cf. (41)-(42)). In contrast, *gibi yap-* 'pretend' can only be used with person marking on the main verb and patterns with (160a):

(161) [*Siz* hayatınızdan memnunmuş] **gibi yapıyor***sunuz*.
'You pretend [to be *happy with your life*].'

24.6 Noun clauses as modifiers in -(s)I compounds: phrasal compounds

Finite and non-finite noun clauses can function as modifiers in *-(s)I* compounds (10.2). In these 'phrasal' compounds not only does the modifier, in this case the noun clause, make more particular the meaning of the head noun, it also provides the content of the head noun. The nouns that occur most commonly as the heads of these complex *-(s)I* compounds generally denote one of the following:

(i) An utterance, e.g. *soru* 'question', *komut* 'order', *iddia* 'claim'
(ii) A belief or perception, e.g. *düşünce* 'thought', *inanç* 'belief', *beklenti* 'expectation', *duygu* 'feeling', *kaygı* 'anxiety', *umut/ümit* 'hope'
(iii) A state of affairs, e.g. *sorun/mesele* 'problem', *konu* 'issue'
(iv) A desire, e.g. *istek/arzu* 'wish', 'desire', *özlem/hasret* 'longing'
(v) Possibility or necessity, e.g. *olasılık/ihtimal* 'possibility', *gereksinim/ ihtiyaç* 'need', *zorunluk/mecburiyet* 'obligation'
(vi) A pattern of behaviour, e.g. *alışkanlık* 'habit', *eğilim* 'tendency', *gelenek* 'tradition'
(vii) Time, e.g. *zaman/vakit* 'time (general)', *saat* 'time (by the clock)'

Head nouns in categories (i)–(iii) above can be modified by either a finite or a non-finite noun clause. (162)–(164) contain *-(s)I* compounds with finite clause modifiers. These are generally more informal than their non-finite counterparts:

(162) Nuri Bey emekli olduktan sonra
[**ben artık hiçbir işe yaramıyorum**] *kaygı-sın*-a kapıldı.
                                                                          anxiety-NCM-DAT
'After he retired, Nuri Bey began to feel that he lacked purpose.'
(lit. '...started feeling [*an*] "*I'm of no use any more*" anxiety.')

(163) Herkesin kafasında
[**seçim-ler ne zaman yap-ıl-acak**] *soru-su* var.
election-PL when make-PASS-FUT question-NCM existent

'The question on everybody's mind is: [*when are the elections going to be held*]?'
(lit. 'On everybody's mind is *the question "When will the elections be held?"*')

(164) ["**Saat altıda hazır ol-un**"] *komut-un*-u aldık.
              ready be-IMP.2PL order-NCM-ACC
'We received *the order "Be ready at six o'clock"*.'

The finite noun clauses in the above three examples are a statement (162), a question (163) and a command (164). Their non-finite counterparts will therefore be respectively an indirect statement (24.4.3.1), an indirect question (24.4.3.2) and an indirect command (24.4.2.2 (iii.b)):

(165) Nuri Bey, emekli olduktan sonra [**artık hiç bir işe yaramadığı**] **kaygısına kapıldı.**
'After he retired, Nuri Bey began to feel [*that he lacked purpose*].'
(lit. '...started feeling [*an*] *anxiety* [*that he was no use any more*]')

(166) Herkesin kafasında [**seçimler*in* ne zaman yapıl*acağı*] sorusu** var.
'The question on everybody's mind is when the elections are going to be held.'
(lit. 'On everybody's mind is *the question of [when the elections will be held]*.')

(167) [**Saat altıda hazır ol*ma*] komutun**-u aldık.
'We received *the order [to be ready at six o'clock]*.'

Where the head noun of the *-(s)I* compound falls into one of the categories listed in (iv)–(vii) above, a finite clause modifier is usually not possible, although with category (iv) a finite clause with optative or conditional marking may occur colloquially:

(168) İçimde [**Ahmet-i gör-ebil-se-m**] *özlem-i* deprești.
Ahmet-ACC see-PSB-COND-1SG longing-NCM
'*The longing [about being able to see Ahmet]* overwhelmed me again.'

Otherwise, the form that a clausal modifier takes with one of these heads is a non-finite clause with *-mA* or *-mAk*. *-mA* is generally preferred to *-mAk* in noun clauses that function as modifiers of compounds.

(169) Aysel [**oğlunu Amerika'da okut*ma*(k)] isteğ**ini yenemiyordu.
'Aysel couldn't overcome *the/her desire [to get her son educated in America]*.'

(170) Öğleden sonra [**kardeşimin gel*me*(k)/gel*mesi*] ihtimali** var.
'In the afternoon there's *a possibility [that my brother/sister will come]*.'

(171) [**Başkalarından saygı bekle*me*(k)] alışkanlığı** insanı düş kırıklığına uğratır.
'*The habit of [expecting respect from others]* leads to disappointment.'

In this type of compound, person marking of the *-mA* verbal noun is possible only with highly impersonal heads such as *olasılık/ihtimal* 'possibility' (170). In other cases, person marking can attach only to the head:

(172) [Başkalarından saygı bekleme(k)] alışkanlığ**ımız** bizi düş kırıklığına uğratıyor.
'*Our* habit of [expecting respect from others] causes us disappointment.'

Chapter 25

Relative clauses

Relative clauses are subordinate clauses that perform an adjectival function (Chapter 15), that is, they are complex adjectival constructions that modify noun phrases. The most typical type of relative clause is non-finite (12.3), and contains one of the participle suffixes *-(y)An*, *-DIK*, or *-(y)AcAK* (8.5), corresponding to the relative pronouns 'who', 'which', 'that', 'whom', 'whose', 'where', etc. in English. Finite relative clauses, incorporating the subordinator *ki* (11.1.1.4), also occur, but the range of this type is quite limited (25.6). With the exception of *ki* clauses, all relative clauses *precede* the noun phrase they modify, in the same way that adjectives precede the noun they modify:

(1) küçük kız
    'the little girl'

(2) **oyuncak-lar-ın-ı kır-*an* kız**
    toy-PL-3SG.POSS-ACC break-PART girl
    'the girl *who* breaks/has broken her toys'

(3) **her gün okul-da gör-*düğ-üm* kız**
    every day school-LOC see-PART-1SG.POSS girl
    'the girl *who(m)* I see at school every day'

(4) **anne-si-yle tanış-*acağ-ım* kız**
    mother-3SG.POSS-COM meet-PART-1SG.POSS girl
    'the girl *whose* mother I'm going to meet'

(5) **baş-ın-da şapka ol-*an* kız**
    head-3SG.POSS-LOC hat be-PART girl
    'the girl *who* has a hat on her head'

Section 25.1 describes the principles of relativization and the function of the participle suffixes. Section 25.2 discusses the distinction between restrictive and non-restrictive relative clauses and 25.3 is about pronominal relative clauses.

DOI: 10.4324/9780429435836-28

25.4 examines the expression of tense and aspect in relative clauses and the conditions under which *olan* (where this is the relevant participial form) may be omitted. For the ordering of a non-finite relative clause with respect to other adjectivals and determiners in the noun phrase, see 15.9.6.

25.1 Principles of relativization

The noun that a relative clause modifies, that is, the **head noun**, can have one of several different relationships with the relative clause. For example, in (2) the relationship of the target of relativization (the head noun *kız* 'girl') to the relative clause is that of subject of the verb *kır-* 'break', in the same way *kız* is the subject of *kır-* in *kız oyuncaklarını kırdı* '*the girl* broke her toys'. In (3) it is the direct object of the verb *gör-* 'see', as it is in *her gün kızı okulda görüyorum* 'I see *the girl* at school every day'. In (4), on the other hand, *kız* is the possessor of *anne-si* 'her mother' in the same way the two noun phrases in the genitive-possessive construction *kız-ın anne-si* '*the girl*'s mother' are related. These processes are referred to as 'relativizing the subject', 'relativizing the direct object', 'relativizing the possessor', etc. The participle suffix used in non-finite relative clauses is selected on the basis of the nature of the relationship of the head noun to the relative clause in any particular instance. In many of the examples, we give a corresponding simple sentence showing the same relationships as in the relative clause in order to make the grammatical relationship between a constituent and its relative clause clearer. We use the abbreviation 'crs.' for the simple sentences that show the relationship.

When relativizing a constituent of a nominal sentence (12.1.1.2), the form *ol-* of the copula (12.1.1.3) is used as the bearer of the participle suffixes:

(6) [ağır yaralı ***ol*-an**] hastalar
seriously injured be-PART patients
'the patients [*who are* seriously injured]'

(7) [çocukların evde ***ol*acağı**] özel bir gün
'a special day [*when* the children *will be* at home]'

The construction in (6) corresponds to the nominal sentence *Hastalar ağır yaralı* 'The patients are seriously injured', and (7) to *Çocuklar özel bir günde evde olacak* 'The children will be at home on a special day'.

The verb *bulun-* 'be (found)' (12.1.1.2) can also be used when relativizing one of the constituents of a nominal sentence, especially where location is involved:

(8) [iç-in-de üç top ***bulun*-an/*ol*-an**] kutu
(crs. Kutunun içinde üç top var.)
inside-3SG.POSS-LOC three ball be-PART box
'the box [*which has/had* three balls inside it]'

25.1.1 Markers of non-finite relative clauses: the participle suffixes

25.1.1.1 -(y)An

A non-finite verb form which contains *-(y)An* does not get inflected for case or person, except in pronominal relative clauses (25.3). This participle occurs in the following circumstances:

(i) Where the relativized constituent is the subject of the verb in the relative clause:

(9) [sokak-ta düş-**en**] *çocuk*
 (crs. *Çocuk* sokakta düştü.)
 street-LOC fall-PART child
 '*the child* [who fell on the street]'

(10) [burada sat-ıl-**an**] *kitap-lar*
 (crs. *Kitaplar* burada satılıyor.)
 here sell-PASS-PART book-PL
 '*the books* [which are sold here]'

(11) [öğretmen ol-**an**] *Haydar*
 (crs. *Haydar* öğretmen.)
 teacher be-PART Haydar
 '*Haydar*, [who is a teacher]'

(ii) Where the relativized constituent is the possessor (14.4) of some constituent of the relative clause, and:
 a. Where this possessor is part of the subject of the verb in the relative clause, the relative clause begins with a non-case-marked noun phrase marked with a 3rd person possessive suffix. For example, in (12) below *komşumuz* 'our neighbour', which is the relativized constituent, is the possessor of *araba-sı* 'his/her car', and would thus be the modifier in the corresponding genitive-possessive construction *komşumuz-un araba-sı* 'our neighbour's car', which is understood to be the subject of *çalın-* 'be stolen' (crs. *Komşumuzun arabası çalındı* 'Our neighbour's car was stolen'). Curved brackets indicate the noun phrases under discussion.

(12) [araba-sı çal-ın-**an**] *komşu-muz*
 (crs. {*Komşumuzun* arabası} çalındı.)
 car-3SG.POSS steal-PASS-PART neighbour-1PL.POSS
 '*our neighbour* [whose car was stolen]'

(13) a. [rolü büyük olma**yan**] *oyuncu*
 (crs. {*Oyuncunun* rolü} büyük değil.)
 '*the actor* [whose part isn't big]'

b. [büyük (bir) rolü olma**yan**] *oyuncu*
(crs. {*Oyuncunun* büyük (bir) rolü} yok.)
'*the actor* [*who* does not have a big part]'

The different positions of the adjective in (13) point to a difference in the grammatical role it has and the associated corresponding statements. In the pattern represented in (13a), the adjectival descriptor (*büyük*) associated with the possessive-marked constituent (*rolü*) is predicative in function and thus corresponds to a linking sentence. In (13b), the adjective modifies the possessive-marked constituent and corresponds to an existential sentence (12.1.1.2).

b. Where this possessor is part of some constituent of the relative clause other than its subject, the relative clause must have a non-definite (i.e. categorial or indefinite) subject (indicated by bold italics in (14)–(16)).

The possessor can be part of any non-subject constituent (indicated by curved brackets in (14)–(18)), such as:

A direct object

(14) [koyun-ların-ı ***kurt*** kap-**an**] köylü-ler
(crs. {Köylülerin koyunlarını} kurt kaptı.)
sheep-PL.3PL.POSS-ACC wolf catch-PART villager-PL
'the villagers [*whose* sheep were caught by *wolves*]'
(lit. '...whose sheep wolves caught.')

An adverbial

(15) [çatı-sın-dan birkaç küçük ***kiremit*** düş-**en**] ev
(crs. {Evin çatısından} birkaç küçük kiremit düştü.)
roof-3SG.POSS-ABL a.few small tile fall-PART house
'the house [from the roof *of which* a few small *tiles* fell]'

A possessive-marked postpositional phrase

(16) [arka-sın-da ***adam*** ol-**an**] çocuk
(crs. {Çocuğun arkasında} adam var.)
back-3POSS.SG-LOC man be-PART child
'*the child* [behind *whom* there is a man]'

In (14) the relativized constituent, *köylüler* 'villagers' is the possessor of *koyun* 'sheep', and would thus be the modifier in the corresponding genitive-possessive construction *köylülerin koyunları*, which itself functions as the direct object of *kap-* 'devour' (crs. *Köylülerin koyunlarını kurt kaptı* 'Wolves devoured the villagers' sheep'). The non-definite subject may be modified (e.g. by a determiner and/or adjective, such as *birkaç* 'a few' and *küçük* 'small' in (15)).

In these constructions, the subject of the relative clause (i.e. *kurt* 'wolves', *kiremit* 'tiles', *adam* 'man' in the examples above) is non-definite and is placed immediately before the verb (23.1.1.1, 23.1.2.1). The constituent towards which the relativized constituent stands in a possessor relation (*koyunlarını* 'whose sheep' (ACC), *çatısından* 'from the roof of which', *arkasında* 'behind whom') is positioned at the beginning of the relative clause and is marked by a 3rd person possessive suffix.

If the subject is definite, a *-DIK/-(y)AcAK* construction is used (25.1.1.2 (iii)).

(iii) Where the relativized constituent is a possessed item (a noun phrase with possessive marking): *-(y)An* is used only in cases where the possessed item is part of the subject of the verb in the relative clause. Otherwise a *-DIK/-(y)AcAK* construction is used (25.1.1.2 (iv)). For example, in (17) below, the relativized constituent *arabası* 'car-3SG.POSS' is the possessed item in the genitive-possessive construction *komşumuz-un araba-sı* 'our neighbour's car', which is itself the subject of *çalın-* 'be stolen' (crs. *Komşumuzun arabası çalındı* 'Our neighbour's car was stolen').

(17) [komşumuzun çalın**an**] **arabası** (cf. (12))
(crs. {Komşumuzun *arabası*} çalındı.)
'our neighbour's *car*, [*which* was stolen]'

(18) [oyuncunun büyük olma**yan**] **rolü** (cf. (13b))
(crs. {Oyuncunun *rolü*} büyük değil.)
'the actor's *part*, [*which* isn't/wasn't big]'

(iv) Where the relativized constituent is a noun phrase expressing the location of the activity expressed by the relative clause: In these constructions, the constituent expressing the locational adverb stands in a modifier relation to the verb in the relative clause. The verb can be an intransitive verb (19) a passivized transitive verb (20–21) or a passivized intransitive verb (22). In (19–21) the subject of the relative clause (*uçurtma* 'kite', *kitap* 'book', *içki* 'alcoholic beverage') has categorial status (22.3).

(19) [uçurtma uçma**yan**] *bir çocuk bahçesi*
(crs. O çocuk bahçesinde uçurtma uçmuyor.)
kite fly-NEG-PART a playground
'*a playground* [*where* kites don't fly]'

(20) [kitap imzala**nan**] *yer*
(crs. O yerde kitap imzalanıyor.)
book sign-PASS-PART place
'*the place* [*where* books are signed]'

(21) [içki içilebilecek (ol**an**)] *lokantalar*
(crs. O lokantalarda içki içilebiliyor.)
alcoholic.beverage drink-PASS-PSB-FUT AUX-PART restaurants
'*restaurants* [*where* alcohol can be drunk]'

(22) [kolay gid-**il**-me-**yen**] *bir yer*
 (crs. O yere kolay gidilmiyor.)
 easily go-PASS-NEG-PART place
 '*a place* [*which* one cannot go to easily'

(v) Where the relativized constituent is the object or the adverbial modifier of a passivized intransitive verb: These constructions are impersonal and are usually expressed with 'one' in English (13.2.2.3).

Relativized oblique object of a passivized intransitive verb

(23) [hemen hemen hiç uy-**ul**-ma-**yan**] *bir kural*
 (crs. O kurala hemen hemen hiç uyulmuyor.)
           observe-PASS-NEG-PART a rule
 '*a rule which* is almost never observed'

Relativized modifier of a passivized intransitive verb

(24) [yaz kış otur**ulan**] *bir yer*
 (crs. O yerde yaz kış oturuluyor.)
 summer winter live-PASS-PART a place
 '*a place where* one can live all year round'

25.1.1.2 -DIK/-(y)AcAK with possessive suffixes

These participles have identical structural properties in terms of their role in relative clauses, but they differ in terms of tense. In very general terms, *-(y)AcAK* refers to future situations:

(25) [Fatma'nın yarın gör-**eceğ**-i] film
 Fatma-GEN tomorrow see-PART-3SG.POSS film
 'the film [*that* Fatma is *going to see/will* be seeing tomorrow]'

-DIK, on the other hand, mainly refers to past or ongoing situations:

(26) [Fatma-nın doku-**duğ**-u] halı
 Fatma-GEN weave-PART-3SG.POSS rug
 'the rug [*that* Fatma *is/was* weaving/wove/has woven]'

Temporal adverbs (such as *dün* 'yesterday', *şu anda* 'at the moment') are used in contexts where an explicit differentiation between past and present is necessary. For a more detailed description of the tense and aspectual properties of relative clauses, see 25.4.

Clauses with *-DIK/-(y)AcAK* have the structure of genitive-possessive constructions (14.4), that is, the participle has possessive marking agreeing with the subject, and the subject, if separately expressed by a noun phrase as in (25) and (26) above, is in the genitive case.

-DIK/-(y)AcAK are used in the following circumstances:

(i) Where the relativized constituent is the direct object of the verb in the relative clause:

    (27) [bil-**diğ**-im] ***bir turizm şirketi***
          (crs. {Bir turizm şirketi} biliyorum.)
          know-PART-1SG.POSS a tourism agency
          '*a tourist agency* [*that* I *know*]'

    (28) [gönder**ecek**leri] ***temsilci***
          (crs. {Bir temsilci} gönderecekler.)
          '*the representative* [*who*(*m*) they *will* send]'

(ii) Where the relativized constituent is the oblique object or the adverbial modifier of the verb in the relative clause (13.1.2.2, 13.1.3):

    (29) [benim kork**tuğ**um] ***bazı hayvanlar***
          (crs. Ben {bazı hayvanlardan} korkuyorum.)
          '*some animals* [*of which* I am/was afraid]'

    (30) [Turhan-ın et-i kes-**eceğ**-i] ***bıçak***
          (crs. Turhan eti {bıçakla} kesecek.)
          Turhan-GEN meat-ACC cut-PART-3SG.POSS knife
          '*the knife* [*with which* Turhan *will/would* cut the meat]'

In this construction type, where the relativized constituent refers to a human being and is in the 3rd person (as in the case of *birisi* 'someone' and *kişiler* 'people' in the examples below), a resumptive pronoun (18.1.2.2 (iv)) referring to the relativized constituent (*kendisi* in the case of 3rd person singular and *kendileri* in the case of 3rd person plural, 18.1.2.2 (iv)) can appear in the relative clause. *Kendisi* and *kendileri* carry the case marker or the postposition that the relativized constituent would be associated with in a corresponding finite clause:

    (31) [Erol-un (**kendi-si-yle**) konuş-abil-**eceğ**-i] ***birisi***
          (crs. Erol öyle birisiyle konuşabilir.)
          Erol-GEN *kendi*-3SG.POSS-COM talk-PSB-PART-3SG.POSS someone
          '*someone* [*with whom* Erol can/could/would be able to talk]'

    (32) [(bizim) (kendilerin**den**) nefret ettiğimiz] ***kişiler***
          (crs. Biz öyle kişiler**den** nefret ediyoruz.)
          '*the people* [*who*(*m*) we hate/hated]'

(iii) Where the relativized constituent is the possessor (14.4) of some constituent of the relative clause other than its subject, and:

  a. Where the relativized constituent is the possessor within the direct object:

   (33) [usta-nın kapı-sın-ı değiştir-**eceğ**-i] *çamaşır makinası*
   (crs. Usta {*çamaşır makinasının kapısını*} değiştirecek.)

   engineer-GEN door-3SG.POSS-ACC change-PART-3SG.POSS washing machine

   'the washing machine [*of which* the engineer is/was going to change *the door*]'

  b. Where the relativized constituent is the possessor within an adverbial:

   (34) [kız-ın-a piyano ders-i ver-**diğ**-im] *hanım*
   (crs. {*Bir hanımın kızına*} piyano dersi veriyorum.)
   daughter-3SG.POSS piano lesson-NCM give-PART-1SG.POSS lady
   '*the lady* [*to whose* daughter I give/gave piano lessons]'

  c. Where the relativized constituent is the possessor within a possessive-marked postposition:

   (35) [ön-ün-den köprü-nün geç-**tiğ**-i] *ev-ler*
   (crs. Köprü {*evlerin önünden*} geçiyor.)
   front-3SG.POSS-ABL bridge-GEN pass-PART-3SG.POSS house-PL
   '*the houses* [*in front of which* the bridge passes]'

The crucial difference between this strategy for relativizing a non-subject possessor and the one with *-(y)An* described above in 25.1.1.1 (ii.b) is that while the latter permits only non-definite subjects, the use of *-DIK/-(y)AcAK* allows definite subjects, such as *usta* 'the engineer' in (33), 'I' (expressed by the possessive marker) in (34), and *köprü* 'the bridge' in (35). In (36), the *-(y)An* construction parallel to (35), the subject *köprü* has the non-definite meaning 'a bridge/bridges':

(36) [ön-ün-den köprü geç-**en**] *ev-ler*
front-3SG.POSS-ABL bridge pass-PART house-PL
'(the) houses [*in front of which* a bridge passes]'

As a result of this difference, a relative clause of this type which has a proper noun as its subject (e.g. *Semra* below) is only grammatical with the *-DIK-/(y)AcAK* strategy:

(37) [arkasında ***Semra*-nın** otur**duğu**] çocuk
'the child [*behind whom Semra* is/was sitting]'

While a relative clause with a categorial subject has to be expressed with *-(y)An*, as in (36)), in the case of an indefinite subject (i.e. one in which a numeral or indefinite determiner is present), either kind of participle is possible:

(38) a. [*içine* birkaç çiçek konmuş ol**an**] bir vazo
 b. [*içine* birkaç çiçeği**n** konmuş ol**duğu**] bir vazo
 'a vase [*into which* a few flowers have/had been put]'

The tendency for the *-DIK-/(y)AcAK* strategy to be preferred with an indefinite subject increases with the degree of particularization given to the subject. Below, for example, it would be almost obligatory:

(39) [*içine* [Handan'ın bahçesinden toplanmış] birkaç çiçeğin konmuş ol**duğu**] bir vazo
 'a vase [*into which* a few flowers [*picked from Handan's garden*] had been put]'

(iv) Where the relativized constituent is a possessed item (a noun phrase with possessive marking):
-DIK/-(y)AcAK are used only in cases where the possessed item is *not* part of the subject of the verb in the relative clause. Otherwise, *-(y)An* is used (25.1.1.1 (iii)). (40) and (41) are examples of this type of *-DIK/ -(y)AcAK* clause in which the possessed constituent is respectively part of a direct object (*arabanın sol aynası* 'the left mirror of the car') and an oblique object (*ev sahibinin köpeği* 'the landlord's dog'):

(40) [araba-nın kır-**dığ**-ın] *sol ayna-sı*
 (crs. {*Arabanın sol aynasın*}-*ı kırdın.*)
 car-GEN break-PART-2SG.POSS left mirror-3SG.POSS
 'the left mirror of the car, [*which* you broke]'

(41) [ev sahib-in-in kork-**tuğ**-um] *köpeğ-i*
 (crs. {*Ev sahibinin köpeğin*}-**den** *korkuyorum.*)
 landlord-NCM-GEN fear-PART-1SG.POSS dog-3SG.POSS
 'the landlord's dog, [*which* I'm afraid of]'

25.1.1.3 *-DIK/-(y)ACAK without possessive suffixes*

There is a further type of relative clause in which the verb is marked with *-(y)AcAK* (or very rarely with *-DIK*) but without any person marking, and the relativized constituent stands in one of the following relationships to the relative clause:

(i) Non-definite direct object:

(42) [çayla yi**yecek**] bir şeyler
 (crs. Çayla insan bir şeyler yer/yiyebilir.)
 'things [*to* eat with tea]'

Although it is not overtly marked, the verbs in these constructions express possibility, a value normally associated with the modality suffix -*(y)Abil*. The lack of person marking on the verb indicates that the clause lacks an agent and has an impersonal flavour. As a result, these constructions can generally be interchanged with clauses where the verb is in the passive voice:

(43) a. [Hasan'a yönelt-**ecek**] soru
 (crs. Hasan'a birisi soru yönelt(ebil)ir.)
 direct-PART
 'a question/questions [to direct to Hasan]'

 b. [Hasan'a yönelt-**il-ecek**] soru
 direct-PASS-PART
 'a question/questions [to be directed to Hasan]'

Examples with passive are likely (as in (43b) to express obligation rather than possibility.

(ii) Adverbial:
This occurs particularly with one of the following nouns as the relativised constituent: *yaş* 'age', *durum* 'condition', 'situation', *hal* 'condition', *zaman* 'time', *yer* 'place':

(44) [Seni anla**yacak**] *yaş*(ta değil).
 (crs. Bu yaşta seni anlayamaz.)
 '(s/he is not) *old enough* [to understand you]'
 (lit. '...at an age to...')

(45) [Sokağa çık**acak**] *durum*(da mı)?
 (crs. Bu durumda sokağa çıkabilir mi?)
 'Is s/he in a *condition* [to go out]?'

(46) (Şimdi) [ağla**yacak**] *zaman* (değil).
 (crs. Böyle bir zamanda ağlanmaz.)
 '(This is not a *time* [for crying]'

(47) [Gid**ecek**] *hiçbir yer*(imiz yoktu).
 (crs. Hiçbir yere gidemezdik.)
 'We had absolutely *nowhere* [to go].'

Some -*(y)AcAK* participles have been lexicalized as nouns or adjectives (e.g. from *yak-* 'burn' *yakacak* 'fuel'). -*DIK* has a similar lexical usage. When it is used with no other suffix, it is highly unproductive, and forms nouns or adjectives (e.g.

tanıdık bir yüz 'a familiar face'). Its negativized form *-mAdIk* is more productive (e.g. *bakmadık* 'unsearched'). For both suffixes, see 7.2.1.1.

25.1.1.4 Summary of strategies of relativization

(i)	Relativizing subjects	*-(y)An*	25.1.1.1 (i)
(ii)	Relativizing direct objects	*-DIK/-(y)AcAK*	25.1.1.2 (i)
(iii)	Relativizing oblique objects	*-(y)An*	25.1.1.1 (v)
		-DIK/-(y)AcAK	25.1.1.2 (ii)
(iv)	Relativizing adverbials	*-(y)An*	25.1.1.1 (iv)
			25.1.1.1 (v)
		-DIK/-(y)AcAK	25.1.1.2 (ii)
(v)	Relativizing possessors		
	a. which are part of subjects	*-(y)An*	(25.1.1.1 (ii.a))
	b. which are not part of subjects	*-(y)An*	(25.1.1.1 (ii.b))
		-DIK/-(y)AcAK	(25.1.1.2 (iii))
(vi)	Relativizing possessed constituents		
	a. which are part of subjects	*-(y)An*	(25.1.1.1 (iii))
	b. which are not part of subjects	*-DIK/-(y)AcAK*	(25.1.1.2 (iv))

25.1.2 Relative clauses with embedded noun clauses

These are constructions where the relativized constituent (e.g. *kız* 'girl' in (48)) is a constituent of a noun clause (Chapter 24). The choice between *-(y)An* and *-DIK/-(y)AcAK* on the verb of this complex type of relative clause depends on whether the particular embedded noun clause is the subject of the relative clause or not. If it is, *-(y)An* is used; otherwise *-DIK/ -(y)AcAK* are used. The pattern here thus follows the general pattern described above (25.1.1):

(48) [[İstanbul-da otur-duğ-u] san-ıl-**an**] kız
Istanbul-LOC live-VN-3.SG.POSS think-PASS-PART girl
'the girl [*who* is/was thought [to be living in Istanbul]]'

In this example, the relativized constituent *kız* belongs to the noun clause *(kızın) İstanbul'da oturduğu* 'that (the girl) lives/lived in Istanbul'. The noun clause itself is the subject of the passive verb *sanıl-* 'be thought'. Therefore, *-(y)An* is selected.

Similarly, in the examples below the noun clauses *herkesin (bir konu) bilmesi* 'everyone's knowing a subject' and *(misafirlerin) gelmeleri* 'the guests' arrival' are each the subject of the relative clause within which they are embedded:

(49) [[herkesin bilmesi] gerek**en**] bir konu
'a subject [*which* everyone should know about]'

(50) [[gelmeleri] beklen**en**] misafirler
'the guests [*who* are expected [to arrive]]'

In the following examples, on the other hand, the noun clauses *(kızın) İstanbul'da oturduğun-u* 'that she lives/lived in Istanbul-ACC' and *(misafirlerin) gelmelerin-i* '*the guests' arrival*-ACC are not the subjects of the verb *san-* 'think' and *bekle-* 'expect', but their *direct objects*. Therefore, *-DIK/-(y)AcAK* are selected:

(51) [(ben-im) [Bolu-da otur-duğ-un]-u san-**dığ**-ım] kız
I-GEN Bolu-LOC live-VN-3SG.POSS-ACC think-PART-1SG.POSS girl
'the girl [*who* [I think/thought lives/lived in Bolu]]'

(52) [(biz-im [gel-me-lerin]-i bekle-**diğ**-imiz] misafirler
'the guests [(*whom*) we are/were expecting [to arrive]]'

The embedded verb in the noun clause takes whatever subordinator may be required by the verb of which it is a complement, that is, *-mA*, *-mAK*, *-(y)Iş*, *-DIK/-(y)AcAK*. Thus *-DIK* in *otur-duğ-un-u* (51) and *-(y)AcAK* in *evlen-eceğ-in-i* (53), are *not* participle suffixes but verbal noun markers:

(53) [Erol-un [evlen-**eceğ**-in]-i san-**dığ**-ı] kız
Erol-GEN marry-VN-3SG.POSS-ACC think-PART-3SG.POSS girl
(i)'the girl [*that* Erol thinks/thought [he (= Erol) will/would marry]]'
(ii) 'the girl [*that* Erol thinks/thought [will/would get married]]'

In the interpretation (53 (i)), the subject of the noun clause [(*Erol'un*) *evleneceği*] 'that he (= Erol) will marry' is the same as the subject of the relative clause [*Erol'un...sandığı*] '(that) Erol thought…'. The two can also be distinct, as in the second interpretation (53 (ii)), where the relativized constituent (*kız* 'girl') is understood to be the subject of the noun clause, or in (54), where the relative clause has a 1st person singular subject:

(54) [[Erol'un evleneceğin]-i düşündüğ**üm**] kız
'the girl [(*that*) I thought [Erol would marry]]'

In constructions where the noun clause subordinator is *-mA*, the two clauses always have separate subjects (24.4.2.2):

(55) [[al-***ma***-nız]-ı tavsiye et-tiğ-**im**] ilaç
take-VN-2PL.POSS-ACC suggest-PART-1SG.POSS medication
'the medication [that *I* suggested [*you* take]]'

25.2 Restrictive and non-restrictive relative clauses

Restrictive relative clauses express a limitation on the reference of the noun they modify and thus have an identifying function. For example, the relative clause in *yaprakları dökülen ağaçlar* 'trees that lose their leaves' (lit. 'trees whose leaves are shed') limits the reference of 'trees' to those that lose their leaves. Non-restrictive relative clauses, on the other hand, add new information about referents that are in no need of identification, and thus have a merely descriptive function. For example, the relative clause in *damadıyla hiçbir zaman iyi geçinmemiş olan Hayriye Hanım* 'Hayriye Hanım, who had never got on well with her son-in-law', provides additional information about Hayriye Hanım, a person whom the addressee is assumed to be able to identify.

In Turkish, the typical usage of a relative clause with a participle suffix is restrictive. Thus (56) is more likely to be interpreted as 'the trees (that) I like' rather than 'the trees, which I like so much'.

(56) sev-**diğ**-im ağaç-lar
like-PART-1SG.POSS tree-PL

As a result, in the spoken language proper nouns do not often occur as the relativized constituent of a relative clause, since their referents are not usually in need of identification. If a proper noun does occur in conversation as the head of a relative clause, this is again usually with a restrictive meaning. In (57) the usage of *bu* 'this' in the subsequent mention of the name makes the identifying function explicit:

(57) [Kenan'ın evleneceği] **Ayşe**, işte **bu Ayşe**.
'This is *the Ayşe* [that Kenan is going to marry].'

However, the non-restrictive usage of relative clauses is quite common in the written language:

(58) Bir ara koridorlarda konuşmak yasak edilimişti. Fakat [hemen hemen hiç uyulma**yan**] *bu kural* az sonra kaldırıldı.
'At one point a ban on talking in the corridors had been introduced. But *this rule*, [which was hardly observed at all,] was soon abandoned'.

Especially with proper names and titles, this can be used as a stylistic device to avoid a monotonous succession of finite clauses:

(59) [Bugün yurda dön**en**] *Cumhurbaşkanı*, saat 16'da bir basın toplantısı düzenleyecek.
'The *president*, [who is returning to the country today], will hold a press conference at 4 p.m.'

The omission of *olan* from a relative clause containing a compound verb form makes a non-restrictive interpretation unlikely (25.4.1.1). On the other hand, finite relative clauses with *ki* occur mainly in the non-restrictive function (25.6).

25.3 Pronominal relative clauses

These are constructions where the head noun that a relative clause modifies is omitted from the sentence because the referent of the relative clause is either clear from previous mention or is essentially self-identifying. Such clauses correspond to expressions such as 'the one(s) that', 'the person who', 'those who', 'what', 'anything that', etc. In these clauses, the number and case markers that would otherwise be attached to the noun appear on the participle itself, as illustrated in the pairs of examples below:

(60) a. [Opera sev-me-yen]-**ler-e** şaşıyorum.
 opera like-NEG-PART-PL-DAT
 'I am surprised at *those* [*who* don't like opera].'

 b. [Opera sevmeyen] kişi-**ler-e** şaşıyorum.
 person-PL-DAT
 'I am surprised at *people* [*who* don't like opera]'

(61) a. [Biz-im dik-ecek-**ler**-imiz]-**de** hata var.
 we-GEN sew-PART-PL-1PL.POSS-LOC
 'There is a fault with *the ones* [*that* we shall be making].'

 b. [Biz-im dik-eceğ-imiz] elbise-**ler-de** hata var.
 'There is a fault with *the dresses* [*that* we shall be making]'

Note that, in the case of -*DIK*/-*(y)AcAK*, the marker for plural associated with the omitted head noun (e.g. *elbise-ler* 'dresses' in (61b)) occurs *before* the person marker -*imiz* in the relative clause in (61a), following the order of nominal inflectional suffixes (8.1).

There is also a highly productive use of pronominal relative clauses as the subject of an existential sentence.

(62) [Öğleden sonra ara-**yan**] ol-ma-dı.
 (crs. '....ara**yan kimse** olmadı')
 call-PART be-NEG-PF
 '*No one* called in the afternoon.'
 (lit. 'There was *no one* [*who*...]'.)

(63) [Bu konuda bil-**diğ-im**] yok.
 (crs. '....bildi**ğim bir şey** yok')
 know-PART-1SG.POSS non-existent
 'I don't know anything about this matter.'
 (lit. 'There is *nothing* [*that* I know....]')

The addition of a possessive marker (8.1.2) to a pronominal relative clause imparts a partitive meaning. Like other pronominalized adjectivals, pronominalized relative clauses with a possessive suffix draw attention to a subgroup or a specimen within another group (14.4–5).

(64) [Opera **sev-me-yen-ler-imiz**] Verona'da konaklamayacaklar.
like-NEG-PART-PL-1PL.POSS
'Those [*among* us] *who don't like* opera won't be staying (overnight) in Verona.'

(65) [Rusça **bil-en-iniz**] var mı?
know-PART-2PL.POSS
'Is there *anyone* [*among you*] *who knows* Russian?'

The addition of a possessive marker is possible only when the relative clause contains *-(y)An* or one of its compound verb forms (25.4.1) *-mAz olan, -mIş (olan)* or *-(y)AcAk (olan)*: *okunamayanı* 'the illegible one', *anlaşılmaz olanları* 'the ones which are incomprehensible', *kullanılmışı* 'a used one':

(66) [**Boya-n-mış ol-an-ların**]-da hatalar gözükmüyor.
dye-PASS-PF AUX-3PL.POSS-LOC
'The mistakes are not visible on *the ones* [*which have been dyed*].'

Pronominalized relative clauses with possessive suffixes can be used in constructions with ablative modifiers (14.5.2), particularly those formed from *iç-* and *ara-* (17.3.1.3). The possessive suffix in these constructions is optional:

(67) [*İç-lerin-den* en zor oku-n-an(-ı)] bana düşmüş.
inside-3PL.POSS-ABL most difficult read-PASS-PART-3SG.POSS
'I seem to have got *the least legible* [*one*] *of all*.'

(68) [*Aralarında(n)* opera sevmeyenler(i)] Verona'da konaklamayacaklar.
'Those among them [who don't like opera] won't be staying (overnight) in Verona.'

They can also sometimes be used with genitive modifiers:

(69) [*onlar-ın çalış-ma-yan-lar-ı*]
they-GEN work-NEG-PART-PL-3SG.POSS
'*the ones among them who/that don't work*'

A rather unproductive type of relative clause with a possessive suffix is one where the possessive marker does not refer to a subtype within another type but is used in its standard function of marking the *possessed* constituent. The unusual aspect of these constructions is that the genitive noun phrase in such a construction is construed as the *direct object* of the verb inside the relative clause. These adjectival constructions are semi-lexicalized since they usually contain the verb *sev-* 'like', 'love' (hence, *seven* 'lover', 'admirer') or other verbs of emotion such as *iste-* 'want', *beğen-* 'admire', *nefret et-* 'hate':

(70) [**Opera-nın *sev-en-i***] çok.
 (crs. Operayı seven çok.)
 opera-GEN like-PART-3SG.POSS many
 '[There] are many *lovers of opera*.' ('[There] are many [people] who like opera.')

25.4 The expression of tense and aspect in relative clauses

None of the participle suffixes *-(y)An*, *-DIK* or *-(y)AcAK* have a unique time reference. They attach directly to a verb stem which is uninflected for tense and aspect and therefore using any of them on their own may result in ambiguity. For example, *yüzen kadın* can mean 'the woman who is/was swimming', or 'the woman who swims/ swam/has swum', and *çizdiğim eskiz* can mean 'the sketch I am/was making/make/made/have made'.

In order to indicate the time location of the situation in a relative clause, time adverbials may be used. Alternatively, a compound verb form is constructed by means of the auxiliary *ol-* (13.3.1.2) in order to enable the addition of certain tense and aspect markers (25.4.1).

-(y)An typically refers to non-future situations:

(71) [*dün* başla-**yan**] fırtına
 yesterday start-PART storm
 'the storm [that started *yesterday*]'

(72) [*iki yıldır* süren] kuraklık
 'the drought [that has been going on *for two years*]'

(73) [*şu anda* çalan] parça
 'the piece [that is playing *at the moment*]'

In colloquial speech, it can also refer to the future:

(74) [*Yarın* çık-**an**] gazete-de önemli bir yazı bulun-acak.
 tomorrow appear-PART paper-LOC important an article be-FUT
 'There will be an important article in the paper [that comes out *tomorrow*].'

-DIK also typically refers to non-future situations:

(75) [*geçen hafta* bitir-**diğ**-im] roman
last week finish-PART-1SG.POSS novel
'the novel [I finished *last week*]'

(76) [*şu sırada* oku**duğ**um] roman
'the novel [I am reading *at the moment*]'

It can also refer to situations which precede or are simultaneous with a future situation referred to in the superordinate clause:

(77) Sonunda [git-**tiğ**-in] okul nasıl olsa
in.the.end go-PART-2SG.POSS school in any case

bir spor akademi-si ol-acak.
a sports academy-NCM be-FUT

'In the end, whatever school [you go to], it will be a sports academy.'

-(y)AcAK refers to future situations. The futurity may be in relation to the time of utterance:

(78) [yarın oku-**yacağ**-ım] makale
tomorrow read-PART-1SG.POSS article
'the article [(that) I'm *going to* read tomorrow]'

Or it may be futurity with respect to any other point in time, which may itself be in the past:

(79) [Dün oku-**yacağ**-ım] makale-ye ancak bugün
yesterday read-PART-1SG.POSS article-ACC only today

bak-abil-di-m.
look.at-PSB-PF-1SG

'The article [that I *was going to* read yesterday], I managed to look at only today.'

(80) [Geçen hafta gö**receğ**im] film *Mavi Kadife*'ydi.
'The film [that I *was going to* see last week] was *Blue Velvet*.'

25.4.1 The use of auxiliary ol- in relative clauses

The strategy used for indicating finer specifications of tense and aspect in relative clauses is to attach the participle suffixes to the auxiliary verb *ol-* (8.2.3.3, 13.3.1.2) as in noun clauses (24.4.7) and adverbial clauses (26.2.3 (iii)). This strategy allows the verb of the relative clause to combine freely with some of the tense and aspect markers, producing compound verb forms such as *bak-mış ol-an* 'who has/had looked', *bak-maz ol-duğ-um* 'that I have/had stopped looking at', etc. However, it should be noted that even this strategy is, at times, insufficient, and verbs in relative clauses may not express tense and aspect as precisely as their finite counterparts do.

The attachment of the participle suffixes to the auxiliary *ol-* makes it possible to express the following tenses and aspects in a relative clause by adding the suffixes shown below to the lexical verb:

PERFECTIVE/PAST:	*-mIş*
FUTURE:	*-(y)AcAK*
PROGRESSIVE/HABITUAL:	*-mAktA* and *-(I)yor*
HABITUAL:	*-(A/I)r/-mAz*

For a full discussion of tense and aspect, see 21.2–3. For compound verb forms with *ol-* in finite clauses, see 21.5.

(i) *-mIş olan, -mIş olduK-, -mIş olacaK-*:

-mIş, which in some finite clauses marks perfective aspect, relative past tense and evidential modality (21.4.3), loses its modality value when followed by *ol-* (21.5). In relative clauses, as in other subordinate clauses (24.4.7, 26.2.3 (i)), it locates a situation unambiguously in a time period prior to that of another time referred to in the sentence. For example, one of the readings associated with (81a) below, namely the imperfective 's/he lost the book (that) s/he was reading', is not a possible interpretation of (81b), which contains *-mIş olduK-*.

(81) a. [Oku-**duğ**-u] kitabı kaybetti.
 read-PART-3SG.POSS
 'S/he lost the book [(that) s/he was reading/read/had read].'

 b. [Oku-***muş*** *ol*-**duğ**-u] kitabı kaybetti.
 read-PF AUX-PART-3SG.POSS
 'S/he lost the book [(that) s/he *had* read].'

The non-finite form *-mIş olacaK-* is equivalent to the finite compound form *-mIş olacak* (21.5.1). Thus, a relative clause which contains *-mIş olacaK-* is aspectually different from one that just contains a *-(y)AcAK* participle. For example, while (82a) identifies a certain book in terms of the occurrence of a future event, (82b) identifies it in terms of a future situation in which that event will already have been completed:

(82) a. [yarın bitire**ceğ**im] kitap
 'the book [that I'm *going to* finish tomorrow]'

b. [yarın bitir***miş* ol*acağ**ım] kitap
the book [that I *will have* finish*ed* tomorrow]'

However, a relative clause with *-mIş olan* or *-mIş olduK-* is sometimes just a slightly more formal variant of a relative clause marked simply by *-(y)An* or *-DIK*:

(83) [kızı dün gel**en**] kadın / [kızı dün gel***miş* ol*an*] kadın
'the woman [whose daughter came yesterday]'

(84) [Sizin dün gör**düğ**ünüz / gör***müş* ol*duğ***unuz] filmi ben yarın göreceğim.
'The film [(that) you saw yesterday], I'm going to see tomorrow.'

(ii) *-(y)AcAk olan, -(y)AcAk olduK-*:
The suffix *-(y)AcAK* indicates relative future tense (21.5.3). The combination of the tense suffix *-(y)AcAK* with *olan* is the standard means of expressing relative future tense in relative clauses that require *-(y)An* marking. (Compare the colloquial alternative strategy exemplified in example (74) above.)

(85) [Yarın çık-***acak ol*-an**] gazete-de önemli bir yazı bulun-acak. tomorrow come.out-FUT AUX-PART paper-LOC important an article be-FUT
'There will be an important article in the paper [that's *going to come out tomorrow*].'

(86) [Dün gösteril***ecek ol*an**] filmde sakıncalı sahneler bulunmuş.
'It seems that improper scenes were found in the film [that *was going to* be shown yesterday].'

Relative clauses with *-(y)AcAk olduK-* occur rather infrequently. They are identical in meaning to their counterparts with the participle suffix *-(y)AcAK*:

(87) a. [arkadaş-lar-ın al-**acak**-ları] televizyon
friend-PL-GEN buy-PART-3PL.POSS television

b. [arkadaş-lar-ın al-***acak ol*-duk**-ları] televizyon
friend-PL-GEN buy-FUT AUX-PART-3PL.POSS television
'the television [that [our] friends *are/were going to* buy]'

(iii) *-mAktA olan, -mAktA olduK-,* and *-(I)yor olacaK-*:
Both *-mAktA* and *-(I)yor* mark imperfective (progressive or habitual) aspect (21.3.2). In relative clauses *-mAkta* is more typically used with *olan* and *olduK-*, while *-(I)yor* is used with *olacaK*. Although verb forms with *-mAktA ol-* resolve ambiguities as described below, they are not favoured in everyday speech.

In the absence of an adverbial expressing frequency (such as *her gün* 'every day'), these forms are understood to have progressive meaning:

(88) [Oku-***makta ol*-duğ**-u] kitabı kaybetti. (cf. (81a))
read-IMPF AUX-PART-3SG.POSS
'S/he lost the book [(that) s/he *was* read*ing*].'

The use of a *-mAktA ol-* form of participle resolves the ambiguity of *-(y)An* and *-DIK* with regard to perfectivity in favour of the imperfective (progressive) meaning.

Where the relative clause contains a time adverbial that denotes an ongoing situation, such as *şu anda* 'at the/this moment' or *o sırada* 'at that time', the verb will be understood as progressive, whether *-mAktA olan/olduK-* are used or the simple *-(y)An* or *-DIK* participles. The use of *-mAktA ol-* in such cases is more formal:

(89) a. [*şu anda* Erol-a mektup yaz-***makta ol*-an**] kız
at this moment Erol-DAT letter write-IMPF AUX-PART girl
b. [şu anda Erol-a mektup yaz-**an**] kız
'the girl [who *at this moment* is writing a letter to Erol]'

(90) a. [*o sırada* seyret-***mekte ol*-duğ**-um] videolar
at that time watch-IMPF AUX-PART-1SG.POSS videos
b. [o sırada seyret-**tiğ**-im] videolar
watch-PART-1SG.POSS
'the videos [I was watching *at the time*]'

-(I)yor olacaK- marks progressive or habitual aspect in the (relative) future. These are formal usages which are in decline. The interpretation depends on contextual clues, in particular the type of time adverbial used:

(91) [[***Erol geldiği sırada***] seyred***iyor ol*acağ**ım] film eskilerden biri olacak(tı).   (Progressive)
'The film [that I *will (would) be* watch*ing at the time of Erol's arrival*] will (would) be one of the old ones.'

(92) [Yakında ***her gün*** gör***üyor ol*acağ**ım] terapist acaba bana dayanabilecek mi?   (Habitual)
'I wonder if the therapist [that I *will* soon *be* see*ing every day*] will be able to put up with me.'

(iv) *-(A/I)r olduK-, -mAz olan, -mAz olduK, -mAz olacaK:*
The aorist marker *-(A/I)r*, which in finite clauses can have aspectual or modal meaning (21.3.2, 21.4.1), is an aspectual marker with habitual meaning in relative clauses. It occurs only with *olduK-*:

(93) [Artık sık sık görüş**ür** *ol***duğ**umuz] komşularımızı başta hiç sevmemiştik.
'At first, we didn't like our neighbours, [whom we see quite often now].'

-mAz, the combination of the negative marker and the negative aorist, is used with all three forms of the participle, to express a habitually non-occurring action or state:

(94) Semra [yakında giy-e-me-z *ol*-**acağ**-ı] giysilerini
soon wear-PSB-Neg-NEG.AOR AUX-PART-3SG.POSS

bu günlerde özellikle giymek istiyor.

'Semra particularly wants to wear now the clothes [that she *will* soon *not* be able to *wear*].'

25.4.1.1 The omission of olan: truncated relative clauses

olan can be omitted from the forms *-mIş olan* (25.4.1 (i)) and *-(y)AcAk olan* (25.4.1 (ii)), in a way somewhat similar to the omission of 'who is', 'which was', etc. in some types of relative clause in English:

(95) [kömür-de piş-**miş**] patlıcan
(crs. kömürde piş**miş** *olan* patlıcan)
coal-LOC cook-PF aubergine
'aubergine [cooked on coal]'

(96) [iki kilometre yüz-**ecek**] birisi
(crs. iki kilometre yüz**ecek** *olan* birisi)
two kilometre swim-FUT someone
'someone [attempting/able to swim two kilometres]'

Note that *olan* cannot be omitted from relative clauses in which the verb is suffixed with *-mAktA*, *-(I)yor* or *-mAz*. However, it can be omitted from clauses which have nominal predicates and relativized possessors:

(97) [kapağ-ı boyalı] bir kutu
(crs. kapağı boyalı **olan** bir kutu)

lid-3SG.POSS painted a box
'a box with a painted lid'
(lit. '...whose lid is painted')

There are semantic differences between a relative clause which contains *olan* and a 'truncated' one where it is omitted. Truncated relative clauses are nearly always of the restrictive type (25.2). Moreover, there is a tendency for the head of a truncated relative clause to have non-specific reference. It may be a non-specific indefinite noun phrase (22.2.1), such as *bir öğrenci* ' a student' in (98), or *bir kadın* 'a woman' in (99), denoting any member of the class *öğrenci* or *kadın* that fits the description provided by the relative clause:

(98) [Notu düşük] **bir öğrenci** bu sınavı alamaz.
'*A student* [who has a low grade] cannot take this exam.'

(99) [Çocuğuma bakabilecek] **bir kadın** arıyorum.
'I'm looking for a woman [to look after] my child.'
(lit. '...who could look after...')

Or it can be a noun phrase with categorial status (22.3):

(100) Buralarda [önü bahçeli] **ev** yok mu?
'Is there no house [with a front garden] around here?'
(lit. '...the front of which has a garden?')

Or again, it can be a generic noun phrase (22.4), such as *bebek* 'baby' below, in which the truncated relative clause narrows down the class 'baby' in such a way as to designate only those that have eaten their food.

(101) [Yemeğ-in-i ye-miş] **bebek** ağlamaz.
food-3SG.POSS-ACC eat-PF
'*A baby* [that has eaten its food] doesn't cry.'

However, truncated relative clauses are sometimes used with *specific* noun phrases as their head. This occurs mainly where the relative clause contains *-(y)AcAk* and the head noun is plural-marked:

(102) [Sınava girecek] **öğrenciler** burada.
'*The students* [who will be taking the exam] are here.'

Relative clauses that contain *olan*, on the other hand, may be either restrictive as in (103) or non-restrictive as in (104):

(103) [Yemeğini ye**miş olan**] bebek ağlamaz.
'*A* baby [*that has* eaten its food] doesn't cry.'

(104) [Yemeğini ye**miş olan**] bebek hemen uykuya daldı.
'*The* baby, [*which had* eaten its food,] immediately fell asleep.'

25.5 Other complex adjectival constructions

The suffixes *-(y)IcI* and *-(A/I)r/-z* can also be used in complex adjectival constructions. Clausal formations with these suffixes are very rare in comparison with participial relative clauses and they are semi-lexicalized (see 7.2.1.1 *(-A/I)r, -mAz, -(y)IcI)* for examples; in all three cases (iii) under the relevant suffix).

25.6 Finite relative clauses with *ki*

Relativization with *ki* is a quite different strategy for forming relative clauses. In a reversal of the order in non-finite relative clauses, the relativized constituent precedes *ki* and the finite clause (12.3) it introduces. The subordinator *ki*, here functioning somewhat like a relative pronoun, is used mostly to form non-restrictive relative clauses, that is, simply to add new information about the referent of the head noun (25.2). It may also be used in restrictive relative clauses and parenthetical expressions.

25.6.1 *ki* in non-restrictive relative clauses

The head noun in these constructions almost always functions as the subject of the main clause. It is also usually 3rd person singular or plural:

(105) *Ayşe*, [**ki** şu anda mutfakta yemek pişiriyor,] birazdan ortaya çıkacak.
'*Ayşe*, [*who* is cooking in the kitchen at the moment,] will appear soon.'

(106) ***Komşu-muz***, [**ki** oldukça tanınmış bir piyanist-miş,]
neighbour-1PL.POSS SUB quite well.known a pianist-EV.COP

evinde sık sık oda müziği konserleri düzenliyor.

'*Our neighbour*, [*who* is apparently quite a well-known pianist,] often organizes chamber music concerts at his home.'

Finite relative clauses with *ki* are also used for emphatic purposes. In these constructions, the main clause can contain a reiterated subject, identical to the head and followed by *bile* 'even'. These constructions may also have 1st or 2nd person pronouns as their head:

(107) ***Sen*** [**ki** herkesin doğum gününü hatırlarsın], ***sen bile*** Semra'nınkini unuttun.
'*Even you*, [*who* remember everyone's birthday], forgot about Semra's.'

In certain circumstances, a 3rd person head either may or must be reiterated within the *ki* clause by a resumptive pronoun (18.1.2.2 (iii–iv)).

(i) If the head is the subject of the relative clause, and refers to someone whom the speaker holds in respect, one of the pronouns *kendisi* or *kendileri* may be added:

(108) **Komşumuz,** [**ki** *kendisi* oldukça tanınmış bir piyanistmiş] ... (cf. (106))
'*Our neighbour,* [*who* is apparently quite a well-known pianist] . . .'

The personal pronoun *o* can also be used instead of *kendisi* in such cases, but this usage is less common and it lacks the respectful tone. Where the head refers to more than one person, *onlar* or *kendileri* can be used:

(109) **Bodrum'da tanıştığımız bir çift,** [**ki** *onlar* öğretmenmiş] ...
'*A couple that we met in Bodrum,* [*who* apparently are teachers]...'

(ii) If the head is not the subject of the relative clause but instead functions within it as an object or adverbial, this function is made explicit by an appropriately case-marked 3rd person pronoun, *o/onlar* or *kendisi/ kendileri*, within the *ki* clause:

(110) Sınıflarında Gülten diye çok şımarık bir kız vardı, [**ki** Hülya *ondan/kendisinden* nefret ederdi].
'There was a very self-indulgent girl in their class called Gülten, [*whom* Hülya hated].'

(111) Dayımın çocukları, [**ki** biz *onlarla/kendileriyle* her yaz buluşurduk], çok güzel tenis oynuyorlardı.
'My cousins, [*whom* we used to meet every summer], were very good at tennis.'

25.6.2 *ki in restrictive relative clauses*

ki also has a certain limited usage in forming restrictive relative clauses. In such constructions (which have a rather literary flavour), the head is usually the subject of the relative clause, and the verb of this clause is negative and has optative marking. The main clause is also usually negative:

(112) Bizim okulda hiçbir öğrenci *yok* [**ki** Bilge Hanım'dan azar işit**memiş** ol**sun**].
'There is no student in our school [*who* has not been reprimanded by Bilge Hanım].'

If the head is not the subject of the main clause, a resumptive pronoun has to be used, such as *ona* in:

(113) Bir ahçı [**ki** baklava yap-may-ı bil-me-**sin**,]
a cook RP baklava make-VN-ACC know-NEG-3SG.OPT

ben ***on-a*** ahçı de-me-m.
I s/he-DAT cook call-[AOR.]NEG-1SG

'A cook [*who* can't make baklava]! I don't call *that* a cook.'

25.6.3 Comment usage of ki

ki clauses can also be used, in a way somewhat similar to a certain use of 'which' in English, to introduce a comment on, or expansion of, something that has just been said. The clause introduced by *ki* usually contains some kind of demonstrative, such as the pronoun *bu* 'this (one)' or *o* 'that (one)' (18.2), or the adverbial *öyle* 'like that' (16.4.3 (vi)), which refers to the entire situation expressed in the previous clause:

(114) Ziya beni görmek istemiyormuş, [**ki *bunu*** daha önce söylemişti].
'Apparently, Ziya doesn't want to see me, which he said before.'

This kind of *ki* clause often occurs parenthetically within a sentence, following an adverbial clause, on the content of which it provides a comment. For example, in (115) *ki* follows a conditional clause and in (116) it follows a temporal clause.

(115) [Parası yoksa,] [**ki *öyle*** olduğunu tahmin ediyorum,] şirketi kurtaramaz.
'[If s/he doesn't have any money,] [*which* I think is the case,] s/he won't be able to save the company.'

These *ki* clauses often do not correspond to relative clauses in English, and they do not always contain a demonstrative:

(116) [Ahmet'ler gelinceye kadar,] [**ki** geç gelebilirlermiş,] çıkmayız.
'We won't go out [until Ahmet and his friends come] (*and* apparently they may be late).'

Following an adverbial clause of time, the demonstrative in the *ki* clause may either be a pronoun or a time adverbial such as *o zaman* 'then', reiterating the time expressed by the adverbial clause:

(117) [Uçağa bindiğimiz zaman,] [**ki *ona*** daha iki saat var,] rahatlayacağım.
'[When we get on the plane,] [*and that* is still two hours away], I shall relax.'

(118) [Buraya taşındığımızda,] [**ki** ben ***o zaman*** sekiz yaşındaydım,] etrafta başka hiç ev yoktu.
'[When we moved here,] [*and* I was *then* eight years old,] there were no other houses in the vicinity.'

See 11.1.1.4 for other functions of *ki*.

Chapter 26

Adverbial clauses

Adverbial clauses are subordinate clauses that perform an adverbial function (Chapter 16) within another clause. In Turkish, adverbial clauses can be finite or non-finite (12.3) but the non-finite forms are much more numerous and more widely used.

Finite adverbial clauses (26.1) are all marked by some item that serves as a subordinator. Those which are introduced by *ki* or a compound of it are structurally similar to Indo-European-type adverbial clauses:

(1) Koca-sın-a düşkün ol-malı [**ki**
husband-3SG.POSS-DAT very.fond be-OBLG SUB

masa-sın-da o-nun üç tane resm-i var].
desk-3SG.POSS-LOC he-GEN three ENUM picture-3SG.POSS existent

'She must be very fond of her husband, [*because* there are three pictures of him on her desk.]'

Non-finite adverbial clauses have subordinating suffixes on the verb and in some cases the verb is also followed by a postposition or noun phrase, usually with oblique case marking:

(2) [Masa-sın-da koca-sı-nın üç tane
desk-3SG.POSS-LOC husband-3SG.POSS-GEN three ENUM

resm-i ol-**duğ-un-a göre**]
picture-3SG.POSS BE-CV-3SG.POSS-DAT seeing.that

on-a düşkün ol-malı.
he-DAT very.fond be-OBLG

'[*Seeing that* there are three pictures of her husband on her desk,] she must be very fond of him.'

DOI: 10.4324/9780429435836-29

The subordinate verb forms that occur in non-finite adverbial clauses are called **converbs** (8.5). More information about the structural features of these clauses is given in 26.2. Section 26.3 is devoted to a discussion of the functions of specific converbs, classified according to meaning.

Conditional clauses, which are also adverbial in function, have a different structure from other adverbial clauses and are discussed separately in Chapter 27.

26.1 Finite adverbial clauses

These clauses are formed with *diye, ki, madem(ki), nasıl ki, (sanki)… -mIş/-(y)mIş gibi, -DI mI, dA, -(y)Adursun, -mAsIn, -mAyAgörsün.* The last two are discussed in 20.8. It should be noted that those formed with *ki, madem(ki), nasıl ki, -DI mI* and *-(y)Adursun* can only modify the main clause of a sentence.

26.1.1 Clauses formed with diye

Diye (11.1.1.3), the *-(y)A* converbial form of the verb *de-* 'say', marks both noun clauses (24.3.1) and adverbial clauses in its function as a subordinator. It always stands at the end of its clause:

(3) [Çocukları getir-**ir-ler diye**] porselen eşyayı ortadan kaldırmıştı.
    bring-AOR-3PL SUB
    '[*Thinking* they would bring the children], she had put the china pieces away.'

Adverbial clauses with *diye* are used in relatively informal registers to express reason, purpose, precaution, or understanding, as explained in the following sections. The sense of 'saying' or more usually, 'thinking' (24.2.1 (iii)) embodied in the component *de-* is detectable in all of them, which gives them a subjective tone not found in their non-finite counterparts.

26.1.1.1 Reason

The kind of reason expressed by a *diye* clause is one which exists in the perception of the subject of the main verb.

(4) [Kalabalık olacağız **diye**] bir ekmek daha almıştım.
    (i) '[*As* there were going to be a lot of us], I had bought another loaf.'
    (ii) '[*Thinking* there were going to be a lot of us], I had bought another loaf.'

As indicated by (ii) above, the speaker may be aware that this perception is or was incorrect. This element of meaning differentiates reason clauses expressed with *diye* from those expressed by non-finite means (26.3.14). A form such as *olacağımız için* could not be substituted for *olacağız diye* in (4) if interpretation (ii) was intended.

26.1.1.2 Purpose

In this meaning the verb in the subordinate clause is always in the optative form (8.2.3.3, 8.4.3):

(5) [Kışın üşü-me-***ye-lim* diye**] kalorifer yaptırdık. (cf. (11), (90))
      be.cold NEG-OPT-1PL
    'We've had central heating installed [*so that* we won't be cold in winter].'

(6) [Kolay oku-n-***sun* diye**] büyük harflerle yazdım.
      read-PASS-3SG
    'I wrote [it] in large letters [*so that* it would be easy to read].'

26.1.1.3 Precaution

In this meaning (equivalent to English 'in case…'), the predicate of the subordinate clause takes the form of an open or knowable condition (27.2.1.1, 27.3), involving the conditional copula *-(y)sA*:

(7) [Bir daha görüş-e-me-***z-se-k* diye**] anahtarları
      see.each.other-PSB-NEG-NEG.AOR-COND.COP-1PL SUB

    sana şimdiden veriyorum.

    '[*In case* we don't have the chance to see each other again], I'm giving you the keys now.'

(8) [Evde meyva kal-ma-***mış-sa* diye**] buradan bir şeyler alalım mı?
      be.left-NEG-EV/PF-COND.COP
    '[In case there's no fruit left at home] shall we buy something here?'

26.1.1.4 Understanding

This type of *diye* clause expresses how the subject of the main clause understands a situation that is relevant to the performance of the action in the main clause:

(9) Ali o işe [geceleri çalışılmıyor **diye**] girmişti.
    'Ali had gone into that job [*on the understanding that* there was no night working].'

Where the subject is plural, this understanding may represent an agreement made between the people referred to (cf. *diye* clauses as object of *konuş-*, 24.3.1(i) and non-finite adverbial clauses with *-mAk üzere*, 26.3.2 (61)).

(10) [[Tülin İstanbul'a gelince] yeniden buluşuruz **diye**] ayrılmışlar o gün.
'Apparently, they had parted that day [*on the understanding that* they would meet again [when Tülin came to Istanbul]].'

26.1.2 Clauses formed with ki

Adverbial clauses formed with *ki* (11.1.1.4) share two basic structural features with noun clauses (24.3.2) and relative clauses (25.6) formed with this subordinator: (i) they always *follow* the main clause, and (ii) *ki* itself always stands at the beginning of its clause. (Note that clauses formed with *madem(ki)* and *nasıl ki* usually precede the main clause (26.1.3-4))

(11) Kalorifer yaptırdık [**ki** kışın üşü-me-ye-lim]. (cf. (5), (90))
    SUB in.winter be.COLD-NEG-OPT-1PL
'We've had central heating installed [*so that* we shan't be cold in winter].'

There are four main types of adverbial *ki* clause, expressing respectively location in time, purpose, result, and the basis for a deduction:

26.1.2.1 Location in time

In this type of clause, *ki* is equivalent to 'when'. The verb in the main clause is marked by *-(I)yordu* (21.3.2), *-mAktAydI* (21.3.2) or *-mIştI* (21.2.1), and the verb in the *ki* clause is marked perfectively by *-DI*. The reversal of the more usual order of time clause followed by main clause, and the special phonological properties of *ki* (4.3.2.1, 24.3.2) give these sentences a much more dramatic quality than equivalent constructions involving non-finite adverbial clauses of time. This is often reinforced by the use of the adverb *tam* 'just' (16.7.3) or *yeni* '(only) just' (16.1.2):

(12) ***Tam*** yemeğ-e otur-**uyor-du**-k
    just meal-DAT sit-IMPF-P.COP-1PL

[**ki** bangır bangır kapı vur-ul-du].
SUB violently door knock-PASS-PF

'We were *just* sitting down to [our] meal [*when* there was a violent banging on the door].'

26.1.2.2 Purpose

As in the corresponding construction with *diye* (26.1.1.2), the verb in purpose clauses with *ki* is always in the optative form. Some speakers add *diye* itself to the end of this type of *ki* clause:

(13) Çantamı dolaba koydum [**ki** kimse al-ma-**sın** (*diye*)].
                                          SUB no.one take-NEG-3SG.OPT
     'I've put my bag in the cupboard, [*so that* no one will take it].'

26.1.2.3 Result

Result clauses introduced by *ki* follow a main clause in which one of the following is present: *öyle (bir)* 'so', 'such', *öylesine* 'so', 'such', *o kadar*, 'so (much)' (15.6.1 (iv), 16.5):

(14) Onlar hakkında ***öyle*** şeyler anlatılıyor [**ki** aklınız durur].
     '*Such* things are being said about them [*that* you would be astonished].'

(15) Ali'nin odası ***o kadar*** dağınıktı [**ki** oturacak yer bulamadık].
     'Ali's room was *so* untidy [*that* we couldn't find anywhere to sit down].'

(16) ***Öylesine*** şaşırdım [**ki** ne söyleyeceğimi bilemedim].
     'I was *so* astonished [*that* I didn't know what to say].'

In this type of construction, the content of the *ki* clause can be deleted, leaving an exclamatory sentence of the pattern *o kadar/öyle(sine)* . . . *ki* (12.4 (112):

(17) ***Öyle bir*** öksürdü [**ki** (bayılacak sandım)].
     'S/he coughed *so* badly [(*that* I though s/he might faint)].

Another way of expressing the above sentence in an informal context is by using *bir* 'so', 'such'. This construction is made of two juxtaposed sentences without a subordinator:

(18) **Bir** öksürdü, bayılacak sandım.
     'S/he coughed *so very* badly, [and] I though s/he might faint.'

26.1.2.4 Basis for deduction

This type of *ki* clause follows a deduction expressed by the obligative form of the auxiliary/copular *ol-*, *olmalı* (21.4.1.4 (vii). It expresses the evidence upon which the deduction is based:

(19) Korkut gitmiş **olmalı** [**ki** odasında hiçbir şey kalmamış].
'Korkut *must* have gone, [*because* there's nothing left in his room].'

For another example, see (1) above.

26.1.3 Clauses formed with madem(ki)

madem, or its alternative form *mademki*, expresses the piece of information upon which the speaker bases the question or modalized utterance (21.4) contained in the main clause:

(20) [**Madem** biliyordun] neden söylemedin?
'[*Since* you knew] why didn't you say?'

(21) [**Mademki** seksen yaşındaki komşum bilgisayar kullanmayı öğrenmiş], ben de öğrenebilirim.
'[*Seeing that* my eighty-year-old neighbour has learned to use a computer], I can learn too.'

In informal discourse, *madem(ki)* can be placed in the postpredicate area (23.3.2) within its clause:

(22) [Gelemeyecektin **madem**], keşke bizi iki saat bekletmeseydin.
'[*As* you weren't going to be able to come], you needn't have kept us waiting for two hours.'
(lit. '...if only you hadn't...')

26.1.4 Clauses formed with nasıl ki

Clauses introduced by *nasıl ki* express a similarity between the situation described in the subordinate clause and that described by the superordinate clause. They are synonymous with one of the types of clause described in 27.5. The example below is a modified version of (94) in 27.5, with the addition of *ki* and the deletion of the conditional copular marker:

(23) [**Nasıl ki** Hakan akşamları garsonluk yapıyor], sen de derslerine engel olmayacak bir iş bulabilirsin.
'[*Just as* Hakan works in the evenings as a waiter], you too could find a job that wouldn't interfere with your academic commitments.'

26.1.5 Clauses formed with (sanki)...-mIş/-(y)mIş gibi

Finite adverbial clauses ending in the postposition *gibi* (17.2.1 (i)) express the manner in which an event occurs, an action is performed, or a person behaves, either by comparison with another (imagined) event or action or by suggesting an underlying motivation or emotion. The verb in the subordinate clause is marked with the evidential perfective suffix *-mIş* or the evidential copular marker *-(y)mIş*. The optional addition of the subordinating conjunction *sanki* 'as if' at the beginning of the clause provides early warning to the addressee of the non-factual status of the content of the clause.

(24) Adam [hayalet gör-*müş* gibi] sapsarı kesil-di.
man ghost see-EV/PF like very.pale become-PF
'The man turned very pale, [*as if* he had seen a ghost].'

(25) Ertan küskün duruyor,

[(**sanki**) biz on-a kötü davran-ıyor-*muş*-uz **gibi**].
(as.if) we he-DAT bad behave-IMPF-EV.COP-1PL like

'Ertan is looking resentful, [*as if* we were treating him badly].'

In such sentences, person marking on the verb in the *gibi* clause is optional:

(26) *Sen* o anda [hayalet gör-**müş**(-**sün**) gibi] sapsarı kesil-di-**n**.
you ghost see-EV/PF(-2SG) like pale become-PF-2SG
'*You* went very pale at that moment, [*as if* you'd seen a ghost].'

This structural variability of *-mIş gibi* places it in a borderline category between finite and non-finite (cf. *-(A/I)r/z gibi*, 26.3.8 (ii)).

For *gibi dur-/gibi görün-/gibi gözük-* 'seem', 'appear' and *gibi yap-* 'pretend', see 24.5.3 (160)–(161).

26.1.6 Clauses formed with -DI mI

Adverbial clauses formed with the perfective *-DI* form of a verb (8.2.3.3) followed by the interrogative clitic *mI* (11.1.1.5) have either temporal or conditional meaning (for the latter, see 27.6.2). In its temporal meaning, this construction is equivalent to 'as soon as' and can be used in sentences that have either future or habitual time reference:

(27) [Köşeyi dön-**dü**-nüz **mü**] sinemayı göreceksiniz.
turn-PF-2PL INT
'[*As soon as* you turn the corner] you'll see the cinema.'

(28) [Kapılar açıl**dı mı**] kalabalık içeri dalar.
'[*As soon as* the doors open] the crowd surges in.'

26.1.7 Clauses formed with dA

An adverbial clause in which a finite verb is followed by the clitic *dA* (11.1.1.2) is used to draw attention to the fact that the action it expresses *precedes/preceded* that expressed by the main clause:

(29) [Yemek yeDİM **de**] geldim.
'I came [having *already* eaten].'

A subordinate clause marked by *dA* always precedes the main verb of the sentence and is the stressed constituent. For *-(y)Ip dA,* see 28.2 (13).

26.1.8 Clauses formed with -(y)Adursun

-(y)Adursun is the 3rd person optative of the compound verb form *-(y)Adur-* (13.3.1.1). In its subordinator function, it points a contrast roughly equivalent to 'while' or 'however much' in English:

(30) [Çalışma Bakanı [ülkemizde işsizlik olmadığın]-ı söyle**yedursun**], resmi rakamlar bile bambaşka bir tablo gösteriyor.
'[*However much* the Minister of Labour says [there is no unemployment in our country]], even the official figures show quite a different picture.'

For clauses formed with *-mAsIn* and *-mAyAgörsün* see 20.8.

26.2 Non-finite adverbial clauses: structural characteristics

The verbal marking of non-finite adverbial clauses takes widely differing forms. In some cases (e.g. *-(y)ArAk, -(y)IncA*), a distinctively converbial suffix is added directly to the verb (8.5.2.2). In other cases (e.g *-mAsI için, -DIkçA, -DIğI zaman*), the converbial marker is composite, consisting of one of the multi-functional subordinators, such as *-mA* or *-DIK*, followed by inflectional suffixes and/or an additional lexical item (8.5.1).

The most important structural distinction among converbs is between those that are marked for person and those that are not. Only those formed with the suffixes *-DIK/-(y)AcAK* and *-mA* can be marked for person (i.e. possessive suffixes, 8.1.2), and this is obligatory except in the cases of *-DIkçA* and *-DIktAn sonra*:

(31) çalış-**ma**-*mız* **için**
work-CV-1PL.POSS for
'in order for *us* to work'

(32) telefon et-**tiğ-*in* sıra-da**
 telephone AUX-CV-2SG.POSS time-LOC
 'at the time *you* ring/rang'

(33) otel-den ayrıl-**acağ-*ınız* zaman**
 hotel-ABL leave-CV-2PL.POSS time
 'when *you* are/were about to leave the hotel'

The form *-mAdAn önce* can optionally occur with person marking where the converb has a separate subject. This affects the position of stress (26.3.16 (vi)).

Converbial forms that obligatorily include a possessive suffix are conventionally cited in the 3rd person singular form, e.g. *-mAsI için, -DIğI halde*.

26.2.1 Genitive case marking or its absence in the subject of a non-finite adverbial clause

The overt subject of most kinds of non-finite adverbial clause is non-case-marked:

(34) [***Zehra*** torununu görmek iste-**diğ-i için**] Bursa'ya uğradık.
 Zehra want-CV-3SG.POSS for
 '[*Because Zehra* wanted to see her grandchild] we stopped off in Bursa.'

In the following types, however, the subject receives genitive case marking:

(i) Clauses that have the subordinator *-mA*:

(35) [***Zehra-nın*** torununu gör-ebil-**me-si için**] ne yapabiliriz?
 Zehra-GEN see-PSB-CV-3SG.POSS for
 'What can we do [*in order for Zehra* to be able to see her grandchild]?'

(ii) Clauses formed with *-DIğI/-(y)AcAğI gibi* expressing manner (26.3.8 (iii)) or used adjectivally (26.4)
(iii) Clauses formed with *-DIğI/-(y)AcAğI kadar* (26.3.13 (ii), 26.4)

The absence of subject case marking differentiates (most) adverbial clauses with *-DIK/-(y)AcAK* from relative clauses (25.1.1.2–3) and most noun clauses (24.4.3, 24.4.6) formed with the same subordinators.

26.2.2 Possibility of the adverbial clause having a separate subject from that of the superordinate clause

In most converbial constructions, there is complete freedom for the subjects of the subordinate and superordinate clauses to be either the same or different:

(36) Makine [tamir ed-il-**dikten sonra**] yeniden bozul-du.
machine repair AUX-PASS-CV after again break.down-PF
'[*After* being repaired], the machine broke down again.'

(37) [Makine tamir ed-il-**dikten sonra**] iş-e yeniden başla-dı-k.
machine repair AUX-PASS-CV after job-DAT again begin-PF-1PL.
'[*After* the machine was repaired] *we* began the job again.'

(38) [Haberi duy**duğunuz sırada**] burada mıydınız?
'Were you here [*at the time you* heard the news]?'

(39) [Haberi duy**duğunuz sırada**] *Filiz* burada mıydı?
'Was *Filiz* here [*at the time you* heard the news]?'

There are, however, certain exceptions to this general rule:

(i) Adverbial clauses whose converb includes the subordinator *-mAK* cannot contain within them an overtly expressed subject. Their understood subject is, in the majority of cases, identical with the subject of the superordinate clause:

(40) *Çocuk*, [dondurma al-**mak için**] biz-den para iste-di.
child ice.cream buy-CV for we-ABL money ask.for-PF
'*The child* asked us for money [to buy an ice cream].'

However, in the case of purpose clauses expressed with *-mAk için/üzere* (26.3.12), some speakers use a noun phrase occurring in a non-subject role in the superordinate clause as the understood subject:

(41) *Çocuğa* [dondurma al-**mak için**] para ver-di-k.
child-DAT ice.cream buy-CV for money give-PF-1PL.
'We gave *the child* money [to buy an ice cream].'

(ii) Converbs formed with *-mAsI için*, also expressing purpose, are used with a subject *different from* that of the superordinate verb. The person-marked converb in (42) would therefore be an acceptable alternative in (41) but not normally in (40):

(42) *Çocuğa* [dondurma al**ması için**] para verdik.
'We gave *the child* money [for *him/her* to buy an ice cream].'

(iii) The use of the conjunctive converb *-(y)Ip* (26.3.5, 28.2) with a subject different from that of the superordinate clause is possible but relatively unusual.

(iv) The manner converbs *-(y)A... -(y)A* and *-(y)ArAk* (26.3.8) similarly do not often occur with a subject different from that of the superordinate verb. Where they do, it is usually in contexts where the subject of the adverbial clause includes a possessive suffix referring to the subject of the superordinate clause:

(43) [Palto-*su*-nun etek-ler-i yer-ler-e sürün-**erek**] yürüyordu.
coat-3SG.POSS-GEN skirt-PL-3SG.POSS ground-PL-DAT trail-CV
'S/he was walking [with the tail of *his/her* coat trailing along the ground].'

For another type of example, see Chapter 28 (14).

Where the subject of a non-finite adverbial clause is the same as that of the superordinate clause, it does not receive separate overt expression (18.1.5):

(44) *Ahmet* [yeni eve geçtik**ten sonra**] daha rahat olacak.
'*Ahmet* will be more comfortable [*after* moving/*after he* moves to the new house].'

26.2.3 Tense and aspect marking in non-finite adverbial clauses

The extent to which tense and aspect are marked in non-finite adverbial clauses varies from one type to another. For example, such marking is far less usual in clauses of manner and time than in clauses expressing concession or reason.

Any tense marking in non-finite adverbial clauses is interpreted in the light of the semantic relationship between the subordinate and superordinate clauses. It may be relative either to the time of utterance or to some other point in time.

Four different kinds of tense/aspect marking occur:

(i) In some converbial forms, there is a choice between *-DIK* and *-(y)AcAK*, the former expressing relative past or present, the latter relative future tense:

(45) Sen [cumartesi burada ol-ma-*dığ-ın* **için**]
you Saturday here be-NEG-CV-2SG.POSS for

Mehmet'le tanış-a-ma-dı-n.
Mehmet-COM meet-NEG-PSB-PF-2SG

'[*As* you *were* not here on Saturday] you weren't able to meet Mehmet.'

(46) Sen [cumartesi-ler-i burada ol-ma-*dığ-ın* **için**]
Saturday-PL-NCM here be-NEG-CV-2SG.POSS for

Mehmet'le henüz tanışamadın.

'[*As* you *are*n't here on Saturdays] you haven't been able to meet Mehmet yet.'

(47) [Sen cumartesi burada ol-ma-***yacağ-ın*** için]
    be-NEG-CV-2SG.POSS for

Mehmet pazar günü gelmeyi kabul etti.

(i) '[*As* you *won't* be here on Saturday] Mehmet has agreed to come on Sunday.'
(ii) '[*As* you *were* not *going to* be here on Saturday] Mehmet agreed to come on Sunday.'

For the modal differences between *-DIK* and *-(y)AcAK* in subordinate clauses expressing possibility, see 21.4.2.1.

(ii) In temporal clauses (26.3.16), *-(y)AcAK* has a much more restricted function than in other types of non-finite adverbial clause. It is used only in cases where the situation expressed by the adverbial clause is in the future with respect to the time of the situation expressed by the *superordinate clause*:

(48) [Misafir gel**eceği zaman(lar)**] Fatma Hanım çok telaşlanıyor.
    'Fatma Hanım gets very agitated [*when* guests *are going to* come].'

In the much more usual case where, of two situations in the future, the one expressed by the temporal clause either precedes or is contemporaneous with the other, *-DIK* is used:

(49) [Misafirler gel**diği zaman**] onlara önce kahve ikram edeceğiz.
    '[*When* the guests come] we shall first offer them coffee.'

(50) [Misafirler gel**diği zaman**] çocuklar evde olmayacak.
    'The children will not be at home [*when* the guests come].'

(iii) Adverbial clauses involving converbs based on *-mA, -mAk* or *-DIK/-(y)AcAK* can also be marked for relative tense or for aspect by the use of compound verb forms incorporating the auxiliary *ol-* (13.3.1.2) as in noun clauses (24.4.7) and relative clauses (25.4.1).

The following tense and aspect markers are attached to the lexical verb while the subordinating suffixes are added to the auxiliary *ol-*:

PERFECTIVE/PAST: *-mIş*
FUTURE: *-(y)AcAK*
PROGRESSIVE/HABITUAL: *-mAktA* and *-(I)yor*
HABITUAL: *-(A/I)r/-z*

(51) [Hiçbir yanlışlığı göz ardı et**miş o**lmamak için] metni dört kişiye ayrı ayrı denetlettik.
'In order not to *have* overlook*ed* a single mistake] we got four people separately to check through the text.'

(52) Musa [gece geç vakte kadar çalış***mış o**lacağı için] sabah erken kalkamaz.
'[*As* Musa *will have* work*ed* late into the night] he won't be able to get up early in the morning.'

(53) Musa [dün bütün gün çalış***ıyor o**lduğu için] bizimle plaja gelemedi. '[*Because* Musa *was* working all day yesterday] he couldn't come to the beach with us.'

For a full discussion of tense and aspect, see 21.2–3. For compound verb forms with *ol-* in finite clauses, see 21.5.

(iv) In the case of *-(y)ken* (8.5.2.2, 26.3.16 (iii)), the converbial suffix incorporates the copula *-(y)-* and can therefore be suffixed to a range of tense/aspect/modality markers in Position 3 on the verb (8.2.3.3), as well as to non-verbal subject complements. *-(y)ken* is itself tense/aspect-neutral, and produces converbs whose meaning in terms of relative tense and aspect is determined by what precedes the suffix.

When suffixed to an aorist-marked stem (less commonly *-(I)yor*) or to a nominal, a converb with *-(y)ken* expresses a situation that is either coterminous with, or temporally includes, the time of the situation expressed by the superordinate clause. This is by far the most common function of *-(y)ken*:

(54) [Çalış-***ır*-ken**] radyoyu hep açık tutarım.
work-AOR-CV
'I always keep the radio on [*while/when (I am)* work*ing*]'.

(55) [Ahmet Türkiye'de**yken**] Londra'daki evine hırsız girmiş.
'Apparently, [*while* Ahmet *was* in Turkey] his house in London was burgled.'

A converb in which *-(y)ken* is suffixed to the perfective marker *-mIş* expresses a situation that is/was completed prior to the time referred to by the superordinate clause:

(56) [Bunca çaba göster***miş*ken**] projeden kolay kolay vazgeçemiyorlar tabii.
'[*Having* put in so much effort], they naturally can't give up the project easily.'

The combination of *-(y)ken* with *-(y)AcAk*, on the other hand, marks the verb in the subordinate clause as referring to a situation that has/had not yet occurred (but is/was expected or planned to occur) at some time understood from the context. The superordinate clause often expresses the non-realization of the expectation or plan:

(57) [Deniz otobüsüyle gel-***ecek***-ler-***ken***] fırtınadan dolayı arabayla
              come-FUT-3PL-CV
gelmek zorunda kaldılar.
['*Although they were going to* (*have*) *come by hydrofoil*], because of the storm they had to come by car.'

26.3 Non-finite adverbial clauses: semantic classification

In this section, we present specific converbs in sixteen categories determined by meaning.

26.3.1 Addition

Converbs formed with *-mAktAn başka* (much less commonly *-DIktAn başka* or the more informal *-mAktAn gayrı*) mean 'apart from', 'in addition to'. These constructions are based on the postpositions *başka/gayrı* 'apart from' (17.2.3). A near synonym is *-mAktAn öte* 'beyond'.

(58) Hakan [beni sinirlendir**mekten başka**] bir de çalışmamı engelliyordu.
'[*Apart from* irritating me], Hakan was also hindering my work.'

Where the subject of the adverbial clause is different from that of the superordinate clause, the form *-mAsındAn başka* has to be used:

(59) [Hakan'***ın*** çene çal**masından başka**] [çocukların koşuşması] da
beni deli ediyordu.
'[*Apart from* Hakan's chattering], [the children's dashing around] was also driving me mad.'

The construction *-DIğI/-(y)AcAğI gibi* can be used additively in the sense of 'not only…(but also)'. In this case, the superordinate clause always includes an additive connective (28.3.1), such as *dA* in the example below:

(60) [Araba sat-ıl-**dığ-ı gibi**] ev *de* ipotek ed-il-miş.
        SELL-PASS-CV-3SG.POSS just.as
'*Not only* has the car been sold, the house has been mortgaged as well.'

26.3.2 Agreement

-mAk üzere (see also 26.3.12) is used to express the substance of a planned action agreed upon by two or more parties:

(61) [[Tülin İstanbul'a gelince] yeniden buluş**mak üzere**] ayrılmışlar o gün. (cf. (10))
'Apparently, they had parted that day [*on the understanding that* they would meet again when Tülin came to Istanbul].'

26.3.3 Concession

The two concessive converbial forms in most frequent use are those marked with *-DIğI/-(y)AcAğI halde* 'although' and *-mAsIna rağmen/karşın* 'in spite of the fact that', the latter being based on the postpositions *rağmen/karşın* 'in spite of' (17.2.2):

(62) Osman, [[Ali'ye yardım et-me-si] gerek-**tiğ-i halde**]
help AUX-VN-3SG.POSS be.necessary-CV-3SG.POSS although

hiçbir şey yapmadı.

'[*Although* Osman should have helped Ali], he did nothing.'

(63) [Hayatında bazı çok kötü şeyler

yap-mış ol-**ma-sın-a rağmen**] Şule'yi severim.
do-PF AUX-CV-3SG.POSS-DAT despite

'[*Despite the fact that* she has done some very bad things in her life], I like Şule.'

Where the subject is the same as that of the superordinate clause, *-mAklA birlikte/beraber* is occasionally used, mainly with verbs denoting states rather than events:

(64) [Ahmet bu konuda çok şey bil**mekle birlikte**] bütün ayrıntıları anlamış değil.
'[*Although* Ahmet knows a lot about this issue], he doesn't understand all the details.'

The converb marker *-(y)ken* 'while', which has a primarily temporal function (26.3.16 (iii)), is sometimes used to draw a contrast between two situations:

(65) [Herkes Nazlı'nın son resimlerine bayıl-*ır*-**ken**] ben onları ruhsuz
                                             adore-AOR-CV
buldum.

'[*While* everyone [else] was in raptures about Nazlı's latest paintings], I found them lifeless.'

26.3.4 Condition

Converbs marked with *-DIğI takdirde* 'in the event that' and *-mAsI halinde/ durumunda* 'in the case of' form clauses with conditional meaning equivalent to those formed with the suffixes *-sA/-(y)sA*. For examples, see 27.6.1. The converb marker *-mAk/-mAsI şartıyla* 'on condition that' expresses the kind of condition that one party to a transaction may impose on the other:

(66) Biz size [iki ay içinde geri öde**mek şartıyla**] on milyarlık
borç verebiliriz.
'We can give you a loan of ten billion [lira], [*on condition that* [you] pay it back within two months].'

26.3.5 Conjunction

The converbial suffix *-(y)Ip* has a conjunctive rather than a modifying function. It conjoins two clauses that are semantically of equal status in the sentence and its use is discussed in 28.2, along with the conjunctive use of *-(y)ArAk*, a suffix that also marks adverbial clauses of manner (26.3.8).

26.3.6 Dismissal

The suffix *-mAsInA* is used only in association with a finite form of the same verb, which may either precede or follow the converb but must stand immediately adjacent to it. *-mAsInA* indicates that the action expressed by the main verb is regarded as abortive or likely to be so. The use of this converb is generally triggered by a prompt or enquiry from another speaker, and the whole construction is usually linked to the following sentence by an adversative conjunction such as *ama, dA, ya* (28.3.4):

(67) A. Bugün Hüseyin doktora gidecekti galiba.
      'I think Hüseyin was going to go to the doctor today.'

     B. Gitmiş [git**mesine**], **ama** doktor gelmemiş.
      'I gather he did go, *but* the doctor didn't come.'

(68) A. Fatma'yla konuşacak mısın?
      'Are you going to talk to Fatma?'

B. [Konuşmasına] konuşacağım **da**, bakalım o dinleyecek mi?
'Yes, I'm going to talk to her, *but* let's see if she'll listen.'

26.3.7 Information base for an utterance

The forms *-DIğInA/-(y)AcAğInA göre* 'since', 'in view of the fact that' have a function somewhat similar to that of *madem(ki)* (26.1.3), in that they express the information upon which the utterance contained in the main clause is based. The main clause can express the following types of utterance:

A deduction

(69) [Ali Antalya'ya gitmek isteme**diğine göre**] başka bir planı var **demek.**
'[*Since* Ali doesn't want to go to Antalya], *that means* he's got some other plan.'

A modalized utterance (21.4)

(70) [Ali Antalya'ya gitmek isteme**diğine göre**] başka bir yer düşün**meli**yiz.
'[*In view of the fact that* Ali doesn't want to go to Antalya], we'll *have to* think of somewhere else.'

A question

(71) [Bayramda ofis kapalı ol**acağına göre**] sen bu işi *nasıl* bitireceksin?
'[*As* the office will be closed during the public holiday], *how* are you going to finish this job?'

26.3.8 Manner

Converbs expressing the manner of an action may be divided into four groups:

(i) *-(y)ArAk* and *-(y)A...-(y)A* express manner directly, in terms of an accompanying action or state:

(72) Çocuklar [koş**arak**] içeri girdiler.
'The children came [runn*ing*] in.'

The construction *-(y)A... -(y)A* occurs either with identical verb stems or different ones, usually with similar or contrasting meanings. Its use is less widespread than that of *-(y)ArAk*, and its meaning is more emphatic, stressing the continuous or repeated nature of the action it expresses. The forms involving two different verb stems are for the most part lexicalized pairs.

(73) Genç kadın [ağlaya ağlaya] hikayesini anlattı.
'The young woman wept continually as she told her story.'
(lit. '…told her story, [weep*ing continually*]')

(74) Adam [ite kaka] öne geçmeye çalışıyordu.
'[Push*ing* and shov*ing*], the man was trying to get to the front.'

This type of doubling is also used informally in contexts where the speaker belittles or derides a particular action:

(75) [Yaza yaza] bu haberi mi yazdın?
'Is this bit of news all you've managed to write?'

(ii) The forms *-(A/I)r/-z gibi, -(A/I)rcAsInA, -(y)AcAk gibi -mIş gibi, -(y)mIş gibi, mIşçAsInA, -(y)mIşçAsInA* 'as if' express manner by evoking similarity with another, purely imagined, action or by suggesting an underlying motivation or emotion. These forms produce clauses that have the same function as the finite *gibi* clauses (26.1.5) and like them can be reinforced by *sanki* 'as if':

(76) [(Sanki) uykuda gez*er* **gibi**] dolaştım birkaç gün.
'For several days I wandered around [*as if* sleepwalking].'

(77) [Hiçbir şey anlama**mış gibi**] konuşuyorsun.
'You're talking [*as if* you haven't understood anything at all].'

(78) Demet [dediklerimi duyma**mışçasına**] konuşup duruyordu.
'Demet kept on talking [*as if* she hadn't heard a word I said].'

Unlike finite *gibi* clauses, the forms discussed here can head clauses that modify adverbs (17.4.1):

(79) [Beni azarlar**casına**] *yüksek* sesle konuşuyordu.
'S/he was speaking in a voice *raised* [*as if* reprimanding me].'

(iii) *-DIğI/-(y)AcAğI/-mAsI gibi*:

a. The constructions *-DIğI/-(y)AcAğI gibi* and (much less commonly) *-DIğIncA/-(y)AcAğIncA* express manner in terms of conformity to another known action or psychological state. The subject of this type of clause, if articulated within the clause itself, takes genitive case marking:

(80) Pastayı [anne-m-*in* anlat-**tığ-ı gibi**] yapmaya çalıştım.
                 mother-1SG.POSS-GEN describe-CV-3SG.POSS as
'I tried to make the cake [*the way* my mother had described].'

b. The constructions -*DIğI/(y)AcAğI/-mAsI gibi* can also draw attention to a similarity between two situations:

(81) [Turhan'*ın* kızıp ofisi birbirine kat**ması gibi**] Ahmet de [düşünmeden] istifa etmişti.
'[*Just as* Turhan became irate and caused havoc in the office], Ahmet had resigned [without thinking].'

This structure produces the same meaning as finite clauses introduced by *nasıl ki* (26.1.4). For the use of *nasıl* 'how' in clauses containing the conditional suffix in the same function, see 27.5.

(iv) Converbs formed with *-mAdAn* or *-mAksIzIn*, both meaning 'without', express manner negatively in terms of what is not done. Note that the *-mA* in *-mAdAn* is the negative marker, and generates stress on the preceding syllable (8.5.2.2 (i)):

(82) Çocuklar, [baĞIR**madan**] oynayın!
'Children, play [*without* shouting]!'

(83) Kemal Bey bütün bir günü [televizyon seyRET**meden**] geçirebilmiş.
'It seems that Kemal Bey has managed to spend a whole day [*without* watching television].'

The form *-mAksIzIn* is rare except in relatively formal registers.

26.3.9 Means

The means by which some goal is sought or result achieved can be expressed by *-(y)ArAk* (26.3.8 (i)) or more formally by *-mAk suretiyle/ yoluyla* 'by (means of)':

(84) Ayten [her gün yürüyüş yap**arak**/yap**mak** suretiyle] kilo verdi.
'Ayten lost weight [*by* going for a walk every day].'

The form *-mAklA* can express a similar meaning at a more generalized level:

(85) Sadece [yürüyüş yap-**makla**] kilo ver-il-me-z.
simply walk do-CV weight lose-PASS-NEG-NEG.AOR
'One can't lose weight simply [*by* walking].'

-mAklA also expresses an action by the performance of which a certain result was produced, whether intentionally or not:

(86) [Öyle söyle-**mekle**] bana hakaret et-miş ol-uyor-sun.
thus say-CV I.DAT insult AUX-PF AUX-IMPF-2SG
'You insult me [*by* saying that].'

26.3.10 Preference

Adverbial clauses marked with *-mAktAnsA* 'rather than' are used in sentences expressing preference:

(87) [Kimsenin beğenmediği bir filmi seyret**mektense**] evde kalmayı tercih ederim.
'I'd prefer to stay at home [*rather than* watch a film that no one likes].'

26.3.11 Proportionality

One of the functions of the converbial suffix *-DIkçA* is to indicate that one event happens in proportion to the occurrence of another:

(88) [Çikolata ye**dikçe**] kilo alırsın.
'[*The more* chocolate you eat], *the more* you'll put on weight.'

For *-DIkçA* in the sense of 'whenever', see 26.3.16 (viii). More formal means of expressing proportionality are *-DIğI nispette*, *-DIğI oranda* and *-DIğI ölçüde*:

(89) İnsanlar [sağlıklarına dikkat et-**tik-leri oran-da**] uzun yaşarlar.
                                      care-AUX-CV-3PL.POSS proportion-LOC
'[*The more* people take care of their health], *the longer* they live.

26.3.12 Purpose

Where the subject of a non-finite clause expressing purpose is the same as that of the superordinate clause, the converbial marker *-mAk için* 'in order to' is used. *-mAk için* has a formal counterpart *-mAk üzere* that is used in some contexts, and interchangeable by its more recent and widely used counterpart *-mAk adına*:

(90) [Kışın üşü-me-**mek için/adına**] kalorifer yaptırdık. (cf. (5), (11))
     in.winter be.cold-NEG-CV for
'We've had central heating installed [*so as* not to be cold in winter].'

As explained in 26.2.2 (i), this converb can also be used where the *understood* subject of the purpose clause is a noun phrase occurring in a non-subject role in the superordinate clause. However, where the purpose clause has an overt separate subject, *-mAsI için* 'in order that/for', 'so that' is used:

(91) [***Anne-m-in*** kışın üşü-me-**me-si için**] acaba ne yapabiliriz?
     mother-1SG.POSS-GEN in.winter be.cold-NEG-CV-3SG.POSS for
'I wonder what we can do [*so that* my mother won't be cold in winter]?'

In same-subject contexts where the superordinate verb is *git-* 'go' or *gel-* 'come', *-mAk için* is usually replaced by the dative-marked form of *-mAk*, namely *-mAyA* (8.5.1.2):

(92) Ayşe [kızını gör**mey**]**-e** gitti.
'Ayşe has gone [*to* see her daughter].'

26.3.13 Quantity or degree

Like simple adverbials of quantity or degree (16.5), this type of adverbial clause expresses either (i) the quantity in which an event happens, or (ii) the degree to which the quality expressed by an adjective, or the manner expressed by an adverb, applies.

(i) *-(y)AcAk kadar/derecede* 'enough to':
This construction can express the fact that the degree of the event or state in the superordinate clause is sufficient to produce a certain result (intended or not). The version with *derecede* is relatively uncommon and rather formal:

(93) Bu işi [para kazanabil**ecek kadar**] öğrenmedim henüz.
'I haven't yet learned this job [sufficiently to be able to earn money [from it]].'

(94) Sevim [hepimizi şaşırt**acak derecede**] güzel konuştu.
'Sevim spoke *so* well [*that* she surprised us all].'

Some constructions of this type (notably *şaşılacak kadar* 'amazingly' and *inanıl(a)mayacak kadar* 'incredibly') are semi-lexicalized as modifiers of adjectives and adverbs (for examples, see 15.4.1.2, 16.8).

(ii) *-DIğI/-(y)AcAğI kadar* 'as much as', 'enough for (s.t. to happen)':
This construction specifies the quantity or degree of the event or state in the superordinate clause in terms of commensurability with another event or state:

(95) Burada [iste**diğin kadar**] kalabilirsin.
'You can stay here [*as long as* you like].'

In this type of clause, if the subject is different from that of the superordinate clause and is expressed by a noun phrase, that noun phrase takes genitive case marking:

(96) Su [herkes-*in* güven-le kullan-abil-**eceğ-i kadar**]
water everyone-GEN confidence-COM use-PSB-CV-3SG.POSS as.much.as

temiz ol-malı.
clean be-OBLG

'The water must be clean [*enough for* everyone to be able to use with confidence].'

26.3.14 Reason

By far the most commonly occurring converbial marker expressing reason or cause is *-DIğI/-(y)AcAğI için* 'because', 'as':

(97) [Bana kız**dığın için**] öyle söylüyorsun.
'You're saying that [*because* you're angry with me].'

(98) [Bu para yetme**yeceği için**] Gürkan'dan borç isteyeceğim.
'[*As* this money won't be enough] I'm going to ask Gürkan for a loan.'

Other forms with more or less identical meaning are *-DIğIndAn/ -(y)AcAğIndAn (dolayı/ötürü), -mAsIndAn dolayı, -mAsI yüzünden*.

26.3.15 Substitution

-(y)AcAğInA, -(y)Acak yerde, -mAk yerine all mean 'instead of':

(99) Seni [azarla**yacağına**/azarla**yacak yerde**] rahatlatmaya çalışmalıydı.
'[*Instead of* scolding you] s/he should have tried to reassure [you].'

(100) [[Düzenli yemek ye**mek yerine**] durmadan atıştırmak] hiç akıl işi değil.
'[Eating snacks all the time [*instead of* having regular meals]] is not at all sensible.'

For the postposition *yerine*, see 17.3.2.

26.3.16 Time

Temporal clauses specify the time of the situation expressed by the superordinate clause by reference to how it relates to the time of some other situation (event or state). The number of converbial forms in this class far exceeds that in any other, permitting a wide range of temporal relations to be expressed.

(i) *-(y)IncA* 'when' expresses a sequential relation between two events:

  (101) [Yağmur yağmaya baş**layınca**] içeri girdik.
  '[*When* it began to rain] we went inside.'

  Similar in meaning, but confined to rather formal usage, is *-mAsI üzerine*, which requires its subject to be different from that of the superordinate clause:

  (102) [Meclis**in** tatile gir**mesi üzerine**] başkentteki faaliyet azaldı.
  '[*When* parliament went into recess], activity in the capital decreased.'

(ii) Although *-DIğIndA* and *-DIğI zaman* 'when' are sometimes used interchangeably with *-(y)IncA*, their more characteristic function is to indicate that the situation described by the superordinate clause is/was ongoing at the time of the event expressed by the adverbial clause:

  (103) [Uçaktan indiğimiz**de**/indiğimiz **zaman**] kar yağ-*ıyor-du*.
  snow FALL-IMPF-P.COP
  '[*When* we came out of the plane] it *was* snow*ing*.'

  Virtually synonymous with the above two forms is *-DIğI sırada* 'at the time (that...)'. For the restricted use of future tense marking in temporal converbs, see 26.2.3 (iv).

(iii) *-(y)ken* 'while', 'as', 'when' is usually attached to the aorist suffix or to a subject complement, although other tense/aspect markings are possible, as explained in 26.2.3 (ii) above. The combinations *-(A/I)rken-/-mAzken*, as also the combination of *-(y)ken* with a non-verbal predicate, express a situation that is ongoing. The temporal relationship between the two clauses may be of two kinds, according to whether the predicate of the superordinate clause is perfective or imperfective:

  a. If the superordinate clause has a perfective predicate, it expresses an event which takes place (and is completed) during the period of continuance of the situation in the clause marked by *-(y)ken*:

   (104) [Orman-da dolaş-**ır-ken**] bir tilki gör-*dü*-m.
   forest-LOC walk.about-AOR-CV a fox see-PF-1SG
   '[*While* walking in the forest] I *saw* a fox.'

   (105) Ahmet o kitabı [öğrenci-**yken**] oku-*muş*.
   student- CV read-EV/PF
   'Apparently, Ahmet *read* that book [*when* he was a student].'

b. If the superordinate clause has an imperfective predicate, it expresses a situation which is ongoing during the period of continuance of the situation in the clause marked by -(y)ken:

(106) [Sen ormanda onu ara**rken**] Bahri burada-*ydı*.
　　　　　　　　　　　　　　　　　　　　here-P.COP
'[*While* you were looking for him in the forest], Bahri *was* here.'

(107) [Adana'da**yken**] Şule ile sık sık görüş-*ür-dü*-k.
　　　　　　　　　　　　　　　　　　see.each.other-AOR-P.COP-1PL
'[*When* (I was/we were) in Adana] I/we used to see Şule often.'
(or '[…] Şule and I/we used to see each other often.')

(iv) The juxtaposition of the positive and negative aorist stems of the same verb in the converb *-(A/I)r... -mAz* gives the meaning 'as soon as':

(108) [Su kayna-**r** kayna-**ma-z**] altını kıs.
　　　　　boil-AOR boil-NEG-NEG.AOR
'[*As soon as* the water boils] turn down the heat (under it).'

-DIğI gibi (26.3.1, 26.3.8 (iii)) also sometimes occurs in the temporal sense of 'as soon as', indicating haste. Another near synonym is *-DIğI anda* 'at the moment that'.

(v) The form *-DIğIndAn beri* 'since' and its colloquial counterpart *-(y)All (beri)* are the clausal equivalents of postpositional phrases with *beri* 'since' (17.2.3 (ii)) and the tense/aspect marking of the superordinate clause (if finite) has the same pattern as described there.

(109) [Kocası öl-**eli** (**beri**)/öl-**düğ-ün-den beri**]
　　　　　die-CV since/die-CV-3SG.POSS-ABL since

　　　ablasının yanında kal-*ıyor*.
　　　　　　　　　　　stay-IMPF

'She*'s been* stay*ing* with her sister [*since* her husband died].'

(110) [Çiğdem Almanya'ya taşın-**dığ-ın-dan beri**] ondan bir haber
　　　　　　　　　　　　　　　move-CV-3SG.POSS-ABL since
　　　al-a-*ma-dı*-m.
　　　get-PSB-NEG-PF-1SG

'[*Since* Çiğdem moved to Germany] I *haven't* had any news from her.'

Colloquially, greater emphasis can be given to the temporal relationship between the two situations by doubling the verb in the subordinate clause and marking the first verb with -*DI* and the appropriate person marker. The sequence -*DI*...-*(y)AlI*, used in colloquial speech, is roughly equivalent to 'ever since':

(111) [O köpeği al-**dı-k** al-**alı**] hiç rahat yüzü görmedik.
            buy-PF-1PL buy-CV
       '[*Ever since* we bought that dog] we've had no peace.'

Another usage that occurs with -*(y)AlI (beri)* is the addition of the negative marker to the verb stem. This refers to a period of non-occurrence of a previously recurrent event. Adverbial clauses with -*mA-yAlI* typically occur in sentences where the main clause is affirmative:

(112) [Onlar-la görüş-**meyeli**] dört beş hafta oluyor.
            they-com   NEG-CV
       'It's been four or five weeks [since we (I/we and they) *last* saw each other].'

(vi) -*mAdAn (önce/evvel)* and -*DIktAn sonra* are the converbial counterparts of the postpositions *önce* 'before' and *sonra* 'after' (17.2.3). As in the case of -*mAdAn* 'without' (26.3.8 (iv)), the stress in -*mAdAn (önce)* falls on the syllable before -*mA*.

(113) Sorunlar [ben GEL**meden (önce)**] başlamış.
       'The problems seem to have started [*before* I came].'

(114) Sorunlar [sen git**tikTEN sonra**] başladı.
       'The problems began [*after* you left].'

Just as in their postpositional function, *önce* and *sonra* in these converbial constructions can be modified by an adverbial of quantity (16.5) or an expression denoting a period of time:

(115) Ali, [babası öl**dükten *iki ay* sonra**] doğdu.
       'Ali was born [*two months after* his father died].'

Where the adverbial clause has a separate subject, the person-marked forms -*mAsIndAn önce/sonra* are sometimes used instead of the forms shown above. In this case the subject takes genitive marking (26.2.1). Note that while the converbial marker -*meden önce* below is pre-stressing (116a), -*mesinden önce* which contains the verbal noun marker -*mA* (24.4.2) has no stress-producing effect (116b):

(116) a. Bu haber-i [baba-m GEL-**meden (önce)**] almıştım.
this news-ACC father-1SG.POSS come-CV (before)

b. Bu haber-i
this news-ACC

[babam-*ın* gel-**me-sin-DEN önce**] almıştım.
father-1SG.POSS-GEN come-CV-3SG.POSS-ABL before

'I had received this news [*before* my father arrived].'

A formal alternative to -*mAsındAn sonra*, in contexts where the superordinate clause expresses a durative situation rather than a single event, is -*mAsındAn itibaren* 'from the time that', based on the postposition *itibaren* (17.2.3):

(117) [Yeni sistemin yürürlüğe gir**mesinden sonra/itibaren**] bu sorunlar yaşanmayacaktır.
'[*After/From the time that* the new system goes into operation], these problems will not arise.'

(vii) The forms -*(y)IncAyA kadar/değin/dek* and the colloquial -*(y)AnA kadar* have two meanings, both involving a terminal point:

a. 'until'

(118) Fatma artık [[öl**ünceye kadar/dek**] burada kalmak] istiyordu.
'Fatma now wanted to stay here [*until* she died].'

b. 'by the time (that . . .)'

(119) [Bu iş bit**inceye kadar/dek**] hepimiz yaşlanmış olacağız.
'We shall all have grown old [*by the time* this work is finished].'

kadar is in more frequent use in these constructions than *değin* or *dek*.

(viii) The converb -*DIkçA*, in addition to its proportionality meaning (26.3.11), can mean 'whenever':

(120) [Osman'a kaza hakkında bir şeyler sorul**dukça**] kafası daha da karışıyordu.
'[*Whenever* Osman was asked (things) about the accident], he would become even more confused.'

'Whenever' can also be expressed by a clause containing a conditional suffix (27.5).

(ix) The converbial forms -*DIğI sürece/müddetçe* mean 'throughout the time (that)':

(121) [O evde kal**dığım sürece**] kimse benimle tek kelime konuşmadı.
'[*Throughout the time* I stayed in that house] no one said a word to me.'

26.4 Converbial clauses used adjectivally

Among the kinds of converbial clauses discussed in 26.3, those that contain *gibi* or *kadar* can (like postpositional phrases headed by these same items, 17.4) function adjectivally as well as adverbially. As with adjectivals in general (15.1), such clauses can be used attributively or predicatively.

26.4.1 Attributive function

(i) Clauses headed by *-(A/I)r-z gibi*, *-mIş gibi*, *-(y)mIş gibi*, all meaning 'as if', usually modify an indefinite singular noun phrase with abstract meaning:

(122) Yüzünde [[yaptıklarımız]-ı beğenmiyor**muş gibi**] *bir ifade* vardı.
'On his/her face there was *an expression* [*suggesting that* s/he didn't like what we had done/were doing].'

The converb takes person marking if its subject is 1st or 2nd person:

(123) [Öl-ecek-**miş**-*im* gibi] *bir korku* hissetmeye başladım.
die-FUT-EV.COP-1SG as.if a fear
'I began to feel *a fear* [*that* I was going to die].'
(lit. '...as if...')

(ii) Clauses headed by *-DIğI/-(y)AcAğI gibi* (meaning roughly 'of the sort that') can modify concrete as well as abstract noun phrases, again with indefinite status. The subject of the clause, if articulated by a noun phrase occurring within the clause itself, takes genitive case marking:

(124) [Tam eş-im-in rahat ol-abil-**eceğ-i gibi**]
just partner-1SG.POSS-GEN comfortable be-PSB-CV-3SG.POSS as

bir bahçe bu.
a garden this

'This is just the sort of garden my partner/wife/husband can be happy in' (lit. '...exactly as s/he will be comfortable [in]').

(125) [İste**diğiniz gibi**] *bir araba* bulamadınız mı?
'Have you not been able to find a car of the sort you want?'

Rarely, the form *-DIğIncA* occurs in the same sense:

(126) Herkes [kendi iste-**diğince**] *bir eş* seçebilmelidir.
own want-CV
'Everyone should be able to choose a partner/wife/husband [in accordance with/of a kind to suit their own wishes].'

(iii) Clauses headed by *-(y)AcAk kadar* 'enough ... to' modify an indefinite or categorial noun phrase in respect of sufficiency to produce a certain result:

(127) [Komşu-lar-ı uyu-t-ma-**yacak kadar**] *gürültü* yapıyorlardı.
neighbour-PL-ACC sleep-CAUS-NEG-CV as.much.as noise
'They were making *enough noise* [*to* keep the neighbours awake].'

(iv) Clauses headed by *-DIğI/-(y)AcAğI kadar* 'as much as' modify a non-definite noun phrase quantitatively by comparison to some action or state of affairs:

(128) Yıllık zam olarak [her hafta yiyeceğe harca**dığımız kadar**] *bir para* teklif ediyorlar.
'They are offering [us] as an annual increase *a sum* [*equivalent to* what we spend each week on food].'

(129) Mustafa [herkes*in* bir günde yapa**bildiği kadar**] *işi* birkaç saatte yapar.
'Mustafa does in a few hours *as much work* [*as* everyone [else] is [only] able to get through in a day].'

26.4.2 Predicative function

Some of the converbial forms identified in 26.4.1 as being available for use as attributive adjectivals also occur predicatively, that is, as subject complements in nominal sentences (12.1.1.2):

(i) *-DI gibi/-mIş gibi/-(y)mIş gibi/-Iyor gibi* 'as if':

(130) Lale [yaşlan**mış gibi (sanki)**].
'It's *as if* Lale has aged.' / 'Lale seems to have aged.'

(ii) *-DIğI/-(y)AcAğI gibi* 'as':

(131) Burası [Hasan'*ın* anlat**tığı gibi**] değil.
'This (place) is not *as* Hasan described it.'

(132) Sonuçlar [tam bekle**diğimiz gibi**] oldu.
'The results were exactly *as* we (had) expected/were expecting.'

(iii) *-(y)Acak gibi* '(almost) about to...':
This particular combination with *gibi*, which is confined to the predicative function, expresses that an event is about to happen, often with the implication that it then does not.

(133) İkide birde [düşecek gibi] oluyordum.
'I kept on *nearly* falling over.'

(iv) *-(y)Acak kadar* 'enough to...':

(134) Zaman zaman karsılaştıkları aksilikler [onları caydıracak kadar] değildi.
'The setbacks that they encountered from time to time were not [*sufficient to* deter them].'

(v) *-DIğI/-(y)AcAğI kadar* 'as much as':

(135) Elimizde kalan para [sen*in* tahmin et**tiğin kadar**] olmayacak.
'The money we are left with will not be [*as much as* you predicted].'

Chapter 27

Conditional sentences

From the functional point of view, conditional clauses are a sub-type of adverbial clauses (Chapter 26). However, their expression differs from that of other adverbial clauses in that the subordinating verb forms they contain are more closely related to finite verb forms than to converbs. Person marking of the predicate of a conditional clause is Group 1 of the person markers used in finite predicates (8.4.1):

(1) [Şura-da otur-**sa-k**]
here-LOC sit-COND-2PL

ekran-ı daha rahat gör-ebil-ir-iz.
screen-ACC more comfortable see-POSS-AOR-1PL

'[*If we* sat over there] we'd be able to see the screen more comfortably.'

(2) [Öykü-yü bitir-me-di-***niz*-se**]
story-ACC finish-NEG-PF-2PL-COND.COP

daha sonra da oku-yabil-ir-im.
later also read-PSB-AOR-1SG

'[*If you* haven't finished [writing] the story yet] I can read it later.'

This chapter begins with a brief review of the grammatical marking of conditional clauses, devoting most attention to the suffixes -*sA* and -*(y)sA* and their distribution (27.1). Since the choice of conditional marker depends upon the function of the conditional clause in relation to the sentence as a whole, we proceed to discuss three main functional types of conditional sentence. **Predictive conditionals**, which express a predictable relation between two situations, are explained in 27.2. Then in 27.3, we look at **knowable conditions**, which usually serve as background for an inference, a question, or some kind of volitional utterance (e.g. a command or request). Section 27.4 deals with further uses of -*sA* and -*(y)sA* as subordinators,

DOI: 10.4324/9780429435836-30

including concessive forms with *dA* and *bile*, and 27.5 discusses clauses which contain a question phrase in addition to a conditional marker. Finally, in 27.6 we review alternative types of conditional construction which do not involve conditional suffixes.

27.1 The grammatical marking of conditional clauses

27.1.1 The verbal suffix -sA and the copular marker -(y)sA (or ise)

We use the term 'conditional clause' to denote the subordinate clause in a conditional sentence, that is the one corresponding to the 'if' clause in an English conditional sentence. With the exception of the constructions described in 27.6, all conditional clauses are marked in one of two ways:

(i) The attachment of the suffix *-sA* (8.2.3.3) to a verb:

   (3) [Biraz erken gel-**se**-n] iyi ol-ur.
      a. bit early come-COND-2SG good be-AOR
      'It would be good [*if* you came a bit early].'

   (4) [Telefon et-**se**-ydi-k] belki bekle-r-ler-di.
      phone AUX-COND-P.COP-1PL perhaps wait-AOR-3PL-P.COP '
      [*If* we had phoned] perhaps they would have waited.'

(ii) The use of the copular marker *-(y)sA*, or its free-standing alternate *ise* (11.1.1.7) following (a) one of the Position 3 tense/aspect/modality markers (8.2.3.3), (b) a subject complement (12.1.1.2), (c) the negative word *değil* 'not' (20.2), (d) one of the existential expressions *var/yok* (12.1.1.2), or (e) one of the copular markers *-(y)DI* or *-(y)mIş* (8.3.2). For a fuller explanation of the attachment properties of *-(y)sA,* see also 8.4.1.

   (5) [Yabancı bir dil öğren-ir-**se**-niz]
      foreign a language learn-AOR-COND.COP-2PL

      dünya-nız genişle-r.
      world-2PL.POSS expand-AOR

      '[*If* you learn a foreign language] your world will expand.'

   (6) [Yorgun-lar-**sa**] yarın-a bırak-abil-ir-iz.
      tired-3PL-COND.COP tomorrow-DAT leave-PSB-AOR-1PL
      '[*If* they're tired] we can leave [it] till tomorrow.'

Note that the attachment of *-(y)sA* to the past copula *-(y)DI* in nominal predicates is a usage accepted by some speakers:

(7) [Para-sı var-dı-**ysa**]
money-3SG.POSS existent-P.COP-COND.COP

çalışan-lar-a neden o kadar az para ver-iyor-du?
employee-PL-DAT why so little money give-IMPF-P.COP

'[*If* s/he had money], why did s/he pay her/his employees so little?'

The use of the non-suffixed copular form *ise* is nowadays rare in ordinary conditional sentences, particularly in those where the conditional clause contains a verb. However, it is quite often used for purposes of emphasis in the type of concessive clause discussed in 27.4.2.2, where the conditional copula is followed by *dA*.

The two conditional suffixes differ not only in the kind of stem to which they can be attached, but also in their stressability. *-sA* is a regular stressable suffix (4.3.1), whereas *-(y)sA*, like all the copular markers, is unstressable (4.3.2).

(8) [Arabayı sat-**SA**] hepimiz rahatLArız.
    sell-COND
'[*If* s/he sold the car] it would be a relief to all of us.'

(9) [Arabayı sat-**AR-sa**] hepimiz rahatLArız.
    sell-AOR-COND.COP
'[*If* s/he sells the car] it will be a relief to all of us.'

-sA occurs only in the predictive type of conditional. *-(y)sA*, on the other hand, occurs in both predictive and knowable conditional sentences. For the use of *-(y)sA/ise* as a topic shifter see 23.3.3.1 (ii).

27.1.2 The conditional conjunctions eğer and şayet

These two conjunctions, both of Persian origin, are grammatically redundant in Turkish conditional clauses but are sometimes added for emphasis or, particularly at the beginning of a long and complex sentence containing other subordinate clauses, to signal at an early point the conditionality of what is being said. Of the two, *eğer* is much the more common and is neutral in terms of the type of conditionality it expresses, like 'if' in English. It therefore appears in all kinds of conditional clauses but is extremely rare with *-sA*, except where this is affixed with *-ydI*:

(10) [*Eğer* yaşa-**sa-ydı**] çok iyi bir mimar olacaktı.
     live-COND-P.COP
'[*If* s/he *had* lived] s/he would have been a very good architect.'

In colloquial speech *eğer* can occur at the end of its clause:

(11) [Hasan bu mektubu okuduy**sa** *eğer*], çok kötü olmuştur.
'[*If* Hasan *has* read this letter] he must be feeling terrible.'

The word *şayet* is more tentative, meaning something like 'if by any chance'. It occurs only with *-(y)sA*:

(12) [*Şayet* o kadar uzak bir semti düşünebiliyor**sanız**], Kartal'da güzel bir ev gördüm geçen gün.
'[*If by any chance* you can contemplate such a remote district], I saw a nice place in Kartal the other day.'

27.2 Predictive conditionals

The predictive type of conditional sentence asserts that if one event takes (or took) place another will (or would) follow it. The first event is presented as causing or making possible the second. There are four possible markings for the subordinate clause of a predictive conditional:

(i) *-(y)sA*
(ii) *-sA*
(iii) *-sAydI* (*-sA* + past copula)
(iv) *-sAymIş* (*-sA* + evidential copula).

Although there are clear differences in meaning between some of these forms, there are also areas of overlap. (i) expresses a condition deemed capable of fulfilment, (iii) expresses a condition known to be incapable of fulfilment, while (ii) and (iv) are ambiguous in this regard. We shall discuss each form in turn and the kinds of contexts in which they occur.

27.2.1 Aorist + -(y)sA

Conditional clauses with the aorist are of two types. The first, which is more obviously 'predictive', is called an **open** conditional. In this type both the condition expressed and its consequence are in the future. The second type embraces within it two closely related kinds of statement, **generic** and **habitual**. In this type, the predictability relates not to the relationship between a pair of future events but to that in a recurrent *pattern* of events. Where the verb in the main clause is also in the aorist form, there is potential ambiguity between 'open' and 'habitual' readings:

(13) [Mehmet geç yat-**ar-sa**] zor kalk-**ar**.
Mehmet late go.to.bed-AOR-COND.COP difficult get.up-AOR
(i) '[*If* Mehmet *goes* to bed late] he *will have* difficulty getting up.'
(Open)
(ii) '[*If* Mehmet *goes* to bed late] he *has* difficulty getting up.'
(Habitual)

Note that it is rare for conditional clauses involving the aorist to be evidentially marked, even if the main clause is:

(14) [Hava kötü ol**ursa**] Cemil gelmeyecek*miş*.
'*Apparently*, Cemil's not going to come [*if* the weather'*s* bad].'

27.2.1.1 Open conditionals

In open conditionals, the speaker does not know whether or not the condition will be fulfilled but treats it as a real possibility rather than a merely hypothetical one. When the main clause expresses a statement, its verb is marked by either *-(y)AcAK* or the aorist. *-(y)AcAK* is used if the event is regarded as certain to follow the fulfilment of the condition, perhaps because of some prior decision (21.2.3):

(15) [Kayıt-lar onbeş-i bul-**ma-z-sa**]
registration-PL fifteen-ACC reach-NEG-NEG.AOR-COND.COP

ders aç-ıl-ma-*yacak*.
course open-PASS-NEG-FUT

'[*If* registrations *do not* reach fifteen] the course *will* not be run.'

The use of the aorist in the main clause, on the other hand, presents the consequence of the fulfilment of the condition more as an assumption or probability (21.4.1.4):

(16) [8-de-ki otobüs-e bin-**er-se**]
8-LOC-ADJ bus-DAT take-AOR-COND.COP

uçağ-a rahat rahat yetiş-*ir*.
plane-DAT comfortably catch-AOR

'[If s/he takes the 8 o'clock bus] s/he'll catch the plane comfortably.'

Whereas in other predictive conditionals the main clause has to be either a statement or a question, in open conditionals the main clause can also be a volitional utterance (12.4 (iii), 21.4.4):

(17) [Engin'i gör**ürse**n] benden selam söyle.
say.IMP.2SG
'[If you *see* Engin], *say* hello [to him] from me.'

(18) [Kezban gel**mezse**] onu bir daha çağır-ma-*ya-lım*.
invite-NEG-OPT-1PL
'[If Kezban *doesn't* come], *let's* not invite her again.'

When an open conditional construction occurs in the course of a narrative, reflecting a situation that was in the future at that particular point in the story, the past copula -*(y)DI* is added to the main clause:

(19) Hüseyin zor durumdaydı. [Amerika'ya gid**erse**] Jale onunla gitmeyebilir**di**.
'Hüseyin found himself in a difficult situation. [If he *went* to America], Jale *might* not go with him.'

27.2.1.2 Generic and habitual conditionals

(i) Generic conditionals:
Generic statements concern the characteristic qualities or behaviour of a class of entities and are regularly expressed with the aorist (21.4.1.1). In conditional sentences, there can be ambiguity between a generic and an open predictive reading. In the example below, *kedi* 'cat' and *köpek* 'dog' are understood generically in (i), whereas in (ii) they are understood as referring to a specific cat and dog.

(20) [Kedi-yle köpek bir arada büyüt-ül-**ür**-ler-**se**]
cat-CONJ dog together bring.up-PASS-AOR-3PL-COND.COP

dövüş-**me**-z-ler.
fight-NEG-NEG.AOR-3PL

(i) '[*If* a cat and a dog are brought up together] they *don't* fight.'
(Generic)
(ii) '[*If* the cat and the dog are brought up together] they *won't* fight.'
(Open)

(ii) Habitual conditionals:
While generics generalize about the behaviour or qualities of a whole class, habituals generalize about the behaviour or qualities of specific entities or groups. Non-past habituals usually have -*(I)yor* in the main clause (21.3.2), which entirely disambiguates them from open predictive conditionals:

(21) [Ahmet evliliklerinin yıldönümünü unut**ursa**] Şebnem çok kız**ıyor**.
'Şebnem goes into a temper [*if* Ahmet forgets their wedding anniversary].'

(22) [Vaktim ol**ursa**] okula kadar yürü**yor**um.
'[*If* I *have* time] I walk to school.'

Where a habitual conditional sentence has past time reference, the main clause receives past tense marking, whereas the conditional clause does not:

(23) Padişah [bir vezirinden memnun kal**mazsa**]
onu idam et-tir-ir-***di***.

   execution AUX-CAUS-AOR-P.COP
   '[*If* the sultan *was* not pleased with one of his viziers] he would have him executed.'

(24) [Sınavdaki puan ortalaması düşük çık**arsa**] bir ayarlama
yap-ıl-abil-iyor-***du***.

   make-PASS-PSB-IMPF-P.COP
   '[*If* the average mark in the exam turn*ed* out low], an adjustment could be made.'

27.2.1.3 Compound forms with olursa

Compound verb forms in conditional clauses are generally analogous in terms of their relative tense and aspect values to their counterparts in finite clauses (21.5).

(i) In open conditionals:
The combination *-mIş olursa* indicates that the event in the conditional clause is envisaged as being completed *before* a specified reference point:

(25) [O zaman-a kadar anne-leri
that time-DAT by mother-3PL.POSS

   gel-me-**miş ol-ur-sa**]
   come-NEG-PF AUX-AOR- COND.COP

   siz çocuk-lar-la kal-abil-ir mi-siniz?
   you child-PL-COM stay-PSB-AOR INT-2PL

   '[*If* their mother *has*n't come back by then], would you be able to stay with the children?'

-(I)yor olursa presents the event as being *ongoing* at a certain reference point:

(26) [Saat 5'te toplantı hâlâ sür**üyor olursa**] sessizce kalkıp giderim.
   '[*If* the meeting *is* still go*ing* on at 5 o'clock] I'll quietly get up and go.'

The combination of *-(y)AcAk* with *olursa* has two different functions in open conditions. Its less common function is analogous to that of the two preceding combinations, postulating a situation in which an event is *about to happen*. In such cases, the event expressed by the main clause is envisaged as taking place *before* the conditional event:

(27) [Ev-in-i sat-**acak ol-ur-sa**-n]
house-2SG.POSS-ACC sell-FUT AUX-AOR-COND.COP-2SG

bana haber ver.
I.DAT news give.IMP.2SG

'[If you *are* [*ever*] *intending to* sell your house], let me know.'

More commonly, however, *-(y)AcAk olursa* is used in a sense close to that of the simple aorist + *-(y)sA* but is more tentative. In this type of sentence, the chronological sequence of *main clause event following conditional event* is the same as in sentences with aorist + *-(y)sA*:

(28) [Mustafa fikrini sonra değiştir**ecek olursa**] hoş karşılamalıyız.
'[*If* Mustafa *should* subsequently change his mind], we must accept [that].'

(ii) In habitual conditionals:
In this type of conditional the functions of *-mIş*, *-(I)yor* and *-(y)AcAk olursa* are fully transparent. The 'tentative-making' function of *-(y)AcAk olursa* does not occur:

(29) [Yemeği Turgut yap**mış olursa**] bulaşığı Lale yıkıyor**du**.
'[*If* Turgut *had* cooked the meal], Lale *would do* the washing up.'

(30) [Geç vakit çalış**ıyor olursa**k] pizza, kebap falan getirtiyoruz.
'[*If* we'*re* work*ing* late] we order pizza, kebab or something.'

(31) [Remziye işten sonra arkadaşlarıyla buluş**acak olursa**] yanına başka giysiler alıyor.
'[*If* Remziye *is going to* meet up with friends after work], she takes other clothes with her.'

27.2.2 Open and habitual conditionals expressed without aorist marking

Certain kinds of open or habitual conditional clauses can be expressed without the use of the aorist:

(i) Where the conditional clause has a nominal predicate, the conditional copula may be attached directly to this predicate without recourse to the copular verb *ol-*. Thus, the following forms are interchangeable:

olursa   -(y)sA/varsa
olmazsa   değilse/yoksa

Open conditionals

(32) Yarın [ev fazla soğuk
     tomorrow house too cold

ol-ma-z-sa/değil-se]
be-NEG-NEg.AOR-COND.COP/not-COND.COP

burada çalış-abil-ir-iz.
here work-PSB-AOR-1PL

'Tomorrow [*if* the house *is* not too cold] we can work here.'

(33) [Başka işim **olmazsa/yoksa**] gelirim.
'I'll come [*if* I have no other commitments].'

Habitual conditionals

(34) [Yorgun **ol-ur-sa**-m/yorgun-**sa**-m]
tired be-AOR-COND.COP-1SG/tired-COND.COP-1SG

yemek yap-mı-yor-um.
food cook-NEG-IMPF-1SG

'[*If I'm* tired] I don't cook.'

(iii) Where the conditional clause has a verbal predicate marked with -*mIş* or -*(I)yor*, the conditional copula may be attached directly to this predicate, without creating a compound verb form as described in 27.2.1.3.

Open conditionals

(35) [Kırmızı satıl**mış olursa**/satıl**mışsa**] maviyi alırım.
'[*If* the red (one) *has* been sold], I'll buy the blue (one).'

(36) [Oraya gittiğim zaman çalış**ıyor olursa**/çalış**ıyorsa**] bir merhaba deyip dönerim.
'[*If* s/he's work*ing* when I get there], I'll just say hello and come back.'

Habitual conditionals

(37) Her yazdığımızı Mustafa Bey'e sunuyorduk. [Eğer herhangi bir şeyi yanlış yazmış **olursak**/yazmış**sak**] o düzeltiyordu.
'We would submit everything we wrote to Mustafa Bey. [*If* we *had* got anything wrong] he would correct it.'

27.2.3 -sA

27.2.3.1 -sA used without past copular marking of the main clause

The distribution and the range of meanings of the verbal suffix -*sA* in conditional clauses is somewhat complex. For its main-clause functions, see 21.4.4.1 and

21.4.4.4. The key to its interpretation in any particular conditional sentence lies in whether or not the main clause is marked by the past copula -*(y)DI*. If the main clause does not contain -*(y)DI*, the condition expressed in the subordinate clause is understood to be capable of fulfilment but is presented more as a hypothetical possibility than as one which the speaker locates in the 'real' future. For this reason, the verb in the main clause of such sentences is almost always in the aorist form (see also 21.4.1.3).

-*sA* is often used when talking about an action that is being considered in a detached or abstract way (compare the 'deliberative' sense of the conditional interrogative in main clauses, 21.4.4.4). (38) could represent an early contribution to a discussion about how to get to the airport in time for a particular flight:

(38) [9-da-ki otobüs-e bin-**se**-k]
9-LOC-ADJ bus-DAT take-COND-1PL

uçağ-a yetiş-ir mi-yiz acaba?
plane-DAT catch-AOR INT-1PL I.wonder

'Would we, I wonder, catch the plane [*if* we took the 9 o'clock bus]?'

-*sA* is also used where the utterance challenges the validity of something that has been said or assumed, or the appropriateness of an action intended or in progress:

(39) [9.30'daki otobüse bin**se**k] uçağa yetişmez miyiz?
'Wouldn't we catch the plane [*if* we took the 9.30 bus]?'

(40) [İğneyi şöyle tut**san**] dikişler bu kadar göze batmaz.
'[*If* you held the needle this way] the stitches wouldn't be so obvious.'

Another very widespread use of the -*sA* conditional is to express an evaluation (usually positive) of a certain possible action, often with the strong implication that the speaker wants or expects this action to be performed:

(41) [Bugün burada temizlik yap-ıl-**sa**] iyi ol-ur.
today here cleaning do-PASS-COND good be-AOR
'It would be good [*if* some cleaning were done here today].'

This usage is semantically close to the main clause use of -*sA* to express wishes (21.4.4.1).

27.2.3.2 -sA used with past copular marking of the main clause

In sentences where the conditional clause is marked by -*sA* and the verb in the main clause contains the past copula -*(y)DI*, the sentence has counter-factual meaning, that is, it expresses a situation that is contrary to the actual state of affairs. Note that in this modal function as a marker of counterfactuality *-(y)DI* does not necessarily refer to past time, as shown in the first example below:

(42) [Vakt-im ol-**sa**]
time-1SG.POSS be-COND

ben de yarın siz-ler-e katıl-ır-*dı*-m.
I also tomorrow you-PL-DAT join-AOR-P.COP-1SG

'[*If* I had time] I *would* join you tomorrow.' (But I don't, and therefore I won't.)

(43) Ali [[çocuğun kötü bir şey yaptığın]-ı bil**se**] bana söyler*di*.
'[*If* Ali knew [the child had done something bad]], he *would have* told me.' (Therefore, I assume that he didn't know.)

The counterfactual use of *-sA* occurs mainly with verbs expressing states, such as *ol-* 'be', 'exist' or *bil-* 'know'. With event verbs, counterfactuality is usually expressed either by *-sAydI* (27.2.4) or by compound forms with *olsa* (27.2.6). However, where the main clause is of the evaluative kind (27.2.3.1), event verbs can also occur in this pattern. In such utterances the counterfactuality is less absolute than in identical sentences with *-sAydI*. The possibility that the desired event might still happen in the future is not completely excluded.

(44) [Ahmet de gel-**se**] ne iyi ol-ur-*du*.
Ahmet too come-COND how nice be-AOR-P.COP
'How nice it would be/have been [*if* Ahmet came/had come too].'

(45) [Buraya birkaç ağaç dikil**se**] çok fark eder*di*.
'It would make/have made a lot of difference [*if* a few trees were/had been planted here].'

27.2.4 -sAydI

Conditional clauses marked with *-sAydI* always have counterfactual meaning, and therefore always have the past copula in their main clauses.

(46) [9.30-da-ki otobüs-e bin-**se-ydi**-n]
9.30-LOC-ADJ bus-DAT take-COND-P.COP-2SG

uçağ-a yetiş-me-z-**di**-n. (cf. (38)-(39))
plane-DAT catch-NEG-NEG.AOR-P.COP-2SG

'[*If* you *had* taken the 9.30 bus] you wouldn't have caught the plane.'

As in the case of *-(y)DI* in counterfactual main clauses, a conditional clause marked with *-sAydI* does not necessarily refer to past time:

(47) [Vaktim ol**saydı**] ben de yarın sizlere katılırdım. (cf. (42))
'[*If* I had had time] I would have joined you tomorrow.'

Although the main clause of a counterfactual conditional is most commonly marked by *-(A/I)rdI* or its negative counterpart *-mAzdI*, the form *-(y)AcAktI* is also possible where reference is being made to a firmly planned action, a scheduled event, or a situation regarded for some other reason as certain to have resulted if the condition had been fulfilled:

(48) [Temmuz-da gel-ebil-**se**-ler-**di**]
July-LOC come-PSB-COND-3PL-P.COP

biz onlar-ı bir hafta gezdir-***ecek-ti***-k.
we they-ACC one week take.sightseeing-FUT-P.COP-1PL

'[*If* they had been able to come in July], we *were going to* take them sightseeing for a week.'

27.2.5 -sAymIş

The form *-sAymIş* is a combination of *-sA* and the evidential copula *-(y)mIş*, the use of which in main clauses is explained in 21.4.3. A conditional clause marked with *-sAymIş* is always followed by a main clause also marked with *-(y)mIş*:

(49) [Dişçi-ye birkaç ay önce git-**se-ymiş**-im]
dentist-DAT a.few month earlier go-COND-EV.COP-1SG

diş-im-i kurtar-abil-ecek-***miş***.
tooth-1SG.POSS-ACC save-PSB-FUT-EV.COP

'*Apparently*, [*if* I *had* gone to the dentist a few months earlier] s/he *would have* been able to save my tooth.'

The ambiguity of tense reference which is a feature of all sentences marked with *-(y)mIş* is seen in these conditionals also:

(50) [Filiz Türkiye'de ol**saymış**] nikahınıza gelir***miş***.
(i) 'Filiz *says that* [*if* she *were* in Turkey] she would come to your wedding.'
(ii) 'Filiz *says that* [*if* she *had been* in Turkey] she would *have* come to your wedding.'

27.2.6 Compound verb forms with olsa/olsaydı/olsaymış

Compound forms with *olsa-* are analogous in terms of their relative tense and aspect values to their counterparts with *olursa* (27.2.1.3). They can occur in either hypothetical or counterfactual contexts. The counterfactual versions are differentiated from the hypothetical by past copular marking of the main clause as in (51b–c) and by the interchangeability of *olsa* and *olsaydı* in the conditional clause.

The three sentences below illustrate the combinations with *-mIş* and the semantic spectrum they cover. (51a) might be uttered in the course of planning a conference. (51c) could only be uttered after the conference had ended. (51b) could be used in either situation, but if uttered in the planning stage, this would be as an argument against a decision that had already been taken.

(51) a. [Kongre öğle zamanı bit-**miş ol-sa**]
conference noon end-PF AUX-COND

katılan-lar-ın çoğ-u aynı gün
participant-PL-GEN most-3SG.POSS same day

ev-e dön-ebil-*ir*.
home-DAT return-PSB-AOR

'[*If* the conference *had* ended at noon], most of the participants *would* be able to get home the same day.'

b. [Kongre öğle zamanı bit**miş olsa**] katılanların çoğu aynı gün eve dönebil-*ir-di*.
AOR-P.COP
'[*If* the conference *had* ended at noon], most of the participants *would have* been able to get home the same day.'

c. [Kongre öğle zamanı bit-**miş ol-sa-ydı**]
PF AUX-COND-P.COP
katılanların çoğu aynı gün eve dön-ebil-*ir-di*.
'[*If* the conference *had* ended at noon], most of the participants *would have* been able to get home the same day.'

A similar gradation of meaning occurs in the case of sentences with *-(I)yor ol-*:

(52) a. [İstanbul'da otur**uyor olsa**m] her akşam tiyatro ya da konsere gidebil*ir*im.
'[*If* I *were* liv*ing*/liv*ed* in Istanbul] I *would* be able to go to a theatre or concert every evening.'

b. [İstanbul'da otur**uyor olsa**m] her akşam tiyatro ya da konsere gidebil*irdi*m.
'[*If* I *were/had been* liv*ing* in Istanbul], I *would* be/*have* been able to go to a theatre or concert every evening.'

c. [İstanbul'da otur**uyor olsaydı**m] her akşam tiyatro ya da konsere gidebil*irdi*m.
'[*If* I *had been* liv*ing* in Istanbul], I *would have* been able to go to a theatre or concert every evening.'

The relative-future meaning of *-(y)AcAk ol-* is seen in the next trio of sentences:

(53) a. [Herhangi bir gün geleme**yecek olsa**m] size önceden bildir*iri*m.
'[If on any day I *were* not *going to* be able to come] I *would* let you know in advance.'

b. [Herhangi bir gün geleme**yecek olsa**m] size önceden bildir*irdi*m.
'[If on any day I *were* not *going to* be able to come] I *would have* let you know in advance.'

c. [Herhangi bir gün geleme**yecek olsaydı**m] size önceden bildir*irdi*m.
'[If on any day I *had* not *been going to* be able to come] I *would have* let you know in advance.'

For some speakers, the form *-(y)AcAk olsa* has another function, parallel to the 'tentative' use of *-(y)AcAk olursa* (27.2.1.3), in which the event expressed by the conditional clause is not subsequent to that of the main clause. In this case the tentativeness is compounded by the hypotheticality of the conditional element *olsa*:

(54) [[Sözleşme imzalandıktan sonra] arkadaşın çekil**ecek olsa**] sen yanarsın.
'[*If* your friend *were to* pull out [after the contract is signed]], you'd be ruined.'

The form *-mIş olsaydı* is often used synonymously with *-sAydI*, to express a counterfactual condition without any 'relative tense' component in its meaning:

(55) [Mehmet üniversiteyi kazan**saydı**/kazan**mış olsaydı**] babası ona Ankara'da ev tutacaktı.
'[*If* Mehmet had got into university] his father was going to rent/have rented a flat for him in Ankara.'

The evidentially marked *olsaymış* can occur in all compound forms where the context requires it (27.2.5):

(56) [Ben şapka giy-**ecek ol-sa-ymış**-ım]
I hat wear-FUT AUX-COND-EV.COP-1SG

o da giy-ecek-miş.
s/he also wear-FUT-EV.COP

'*Apparently,* s/he would have worn a hat [*if I was going to*].'

27.3 Knowable conditions

The potential for fulfilment of the condition expressed by a predictive conditional clause is 'unknowable' in that the condition refers to the unforeseeable future, or to a hypothetical world, or to an event that is known *not* to have happened. The knowable type of condition, on the other hand, is one about whose fulfilment or non-fulfilment information is in principle available because it refers either to present or past time or to planned or scheduled future events.

The conditional marker in a knowable condition is always the conditional copula, attached to one of the following:

(i) A Position 3 tense/aspect/modality suffix (8.2.3.3) (not the aorist)
(ii) Any constituent functioning as a subject complement (12.1.1.2)
(iii) The negative word *değil* 'not' (20.2)
(iv) One of the existential expressions *var/yok* (12.1.12)
(v) The past or evidential copula (8.3.2)

Present tense

(57) [Tanju futbol oyn-**uyor-sa**] iyileş-miş ol-malı.
Tanju football play-IMPF-COND.COP get.better-PF AUX-OBLG
'[*If* Tanju *is* playing football], he must be better.'
(lit. '...must have got...')

(58) [Meşgul-**se**-niz] rahatsız etmeyeyim.
busy-COND.COP-2PL
'[*If* you'*re* busy] let me not disturb [you].'

(59) [Para-sı yok-**muş-sa**] neden ev almaya kalkmış?
money-POSS.3SG non-existent-EV.COP-COND.COP
'[*If* (as is claimed) he *has* no money], why has he taken it into his head to buy a flat?'

Past tense

(60) Fasulye [yarım saat piş-**ti-yse**] ol-muş-tur artık.
beans half hour cook-PF-COND.COP be.done-PF-GM by.now
'[*If* the beans *have* cook*ed* for half an hour], they'll be done by now.'

(61) [Ali o sırada burada **idi-yse**] neden ondan yardım istemedin?
here P.COP-COND.COP
'[*If* Ali *was* here then], why didn't you ask him for help?'

(62) Meryem [[bunu Sevgi'nin yaptığın]-ı bil-**iyor-du-ysa**]
know-IMPF-P.COP-COND.COP
bize söylemeliydi.
'[*If* Meryem *knew* [it was Sevgi who did this]], she should have told us.'

Future tense (planned, firmly expected or scheduled events)

(63) [Şükrü gel-me-**yecek-se**]
Şükrü come-NEG-FUT-COND.COP

bir yedek bilet-imiz var demek.
a spare ticket-1PL.POSS existent it.means

'[*If* Şükrü's not *going to* come], that means we've got a spare ticket.'

(64) Bu fiyatlar bugünden sonra değiş-**ecek-miş-se** bence
change-FUT-EV.COP-COND.COP
hemen bir makine seçip almalıyız.

'[*If* (as they are claiming) these prices *are going* to change after tomorrow], I think we should choose a machine and buy it straight away.'

(65) [Uçak 17.00'de kalkıyorsa] 15.00'te havaalanında olmamız lazım.
'[*If* the plane *is* taking off at 17.00], we have to be the airport at 15.00.'

Some knowable conditions do not imply any knowledge on the part of the speaker as to whether the reality of the situation fulfils the condition. This is particularly the case where the condition relates to a present tense situation:

(66) [Vaktiniz varsa] biraz deniz kenarında yürüyelim.
'[*If* you have time], let's go for a little walk along the seashore.'

(67) [Ahmet çalışıyor**sa**] rahatsız edilmek istemez.
'[*If* Ahmet's working], he won't want to be disturbed.'

This type of knowable condition has the same kind of relation to the situation in the main clause (causing or enabling it) as that which is found in open conditionals (27.2.1.1).

In most knowable conditions, however, the relation between the two clauses is different and much freer. The conditional clause expresses some information that the speaker has newly acquired, either from another participant in the conversation or from some other source within the shared situation of the speech participants. Such a condition is more or less known to be already or soon to be fulfilled. It is presented as a working assumption and as the background to what the speaker says in the main clause.

Certain kinds of utterance occur frequently in the main clause of a knowable condition: an inference, as in (57), (60), (63); a suggestion, request, or other volitional utterance, as in (58), (66); an expression of obligation, as in (62), (65); or a question, as in (59), (61). Questions following conditions that are presented as working assumptions are usually, as in these last two examples, reproachful in tone, pointing to an incongruity between the situation assumed in the conditional clause and some observed behaviour or action.

27.4 Further uses of -sA and -(y)sA as subordinators

Subordinate clauses marked with *-sA* or *-(y)sA* do not always express conditional meaning. In this section we look at some other ways in which these suffixes are used.

27.4.1 -sA...-sA

The doubled use of the *-sA* form of the same verb, with the same person marker, produces a special kind of **concessive conditional** clause which restricts the potential applicability of the main predicate to the constituent immediately preceding it, at the same time expressing the likelihood of non-occurrence of even this event. The main predicate is always from the same root as the conditional verbs, and marked for the same person. It is usually in the aorist form, expressing a generalization (21.4.1.1) or assumption (21.4.1.4).

(68) Sabah-lar-ı [ye-se-m ye-se-m]
morning-PL-3SG.POSS eat-COND-1SG eat-COND-1SG

bir dilim ekmek ye-r-im.
a slice bread eat-AOR-1SG

'[*If I eat anything* in the mornings], it's just a slice of bread.'

(69) Bun-u [**yap-sa yap-sa**] Gürkan yap-ar.
   this-ACC do-COND do-COND Gürkan do-AOR
   '[If anyone can do this], it'll be Gürkan.'

The form *olsa olsa* has been lexicalized as an adverbial, meaning 'if anyone', 'if anything' or 'if at all'. It can be substituted for the verbal *-sA* forms in sentences like (68) and (69), and also has more general application, as in:

(70) Nazan **olsa olsa** cumartesi sabahı gelebilirmiş.
   'Apparently, the only time that Nazan could possibly come would be Saturday morning.'

27.4.2 -sA and -(y)sA/ise with dA

27.4.2.1 -sA with dA

The combination of *-sA* with the clitic *dA* (11.1.1.2) in a subordinate clause can have one of three different functions:

(i) A single occurrence of *-sA* or *-sAydI* with *dA* has the **concessive conditional** meaning 'even if':

(71) Ahmet artık [çalı**ssa da**] sınavı geçemez.
   'Now [*even if* Ahmet works], he won't be able to pass the exam.'

(72) [Beni çağırma**salardı da**] gidecektim.
   'I was going to go [*even if* they hadn't invited me].'

The clitic *bile* 'even' (28.3.1.1 (iv)) is interchangeable with *dA* in this function:

(73) Ahmet artık [çalı**ssa bile**] sınavı geçemez.
   'Now [*even if* Ahmet works], he won't be able to pass the exam.'

Where there is a compound verb form, the clitic can be placed between the two components:

(74) [O zamana kadar üniversiteyi bitirmiş **de** olsan/bitirmiş ol**san da**] Ankara'da kalacak bir yere ihtiyacın olabilir.
   '[*Even if* you have finished university by that time], you may need a place to stay in Ankara.'

(75) [Borca girecek **bile** olsam/girecek ol**sam bile**] o arsayı almaya kararlıyım.
   '[*Even if* it means going into debt] I am determined to buy that piece of land.'

It can also be placed after a non-verbal focused constituent (23.3.1):

(76) [Beni *yurt dışına* **da/bile** gönder**seler**] bu şirketten ayrılmayı düşünmüyorum.
'[*Even if* they send me *abroad*, I'm not thinking of leaving this company.'

The distinction that was noted in connection with predictive conditionals (27.2) between an open condition expressed by aorist + *-(y)sA* and a hypothetical condition expressed by *-sA* attached directly to the verb stem is neutralized in concessive conditionals, as is reflected in the translations of (71)–(76). It is also possible for *-sA dA* to occur in the (factual) concessive meaning more typical of *-(y)sA dA* (27.4.2.2):

(77) [[Ölen adamın silahlı olduğu] iddia edil**se de**] gösterilen kanıtlar hiç inandırıcı değildi.
'*Although* it was claimed that the man who died was armed, the evidence adduced was not at all convincing.'

(ii) With *olur* 'it will be all right' as the main clause, the combination of *-sA* and *dA* expresses the possibility or acceptability of an alternative course of action:

(78) [Sen gelme**sen de**] olur.
'It's not essential for you to come.'
(lit. 'It will be all right [if you don't come].')

(79) [Raporu pazartesi **de** ver**sek**] olurmuş.
'Apparently, it will be all right [if we hand the report in on Monday].'
(as opposed to a previously mentioned earlier time)

(iii) *dA* can mark each of two alternative conditions in a predictive conditional sentence ('whether ... or'), indicating that the outcome will be the same whichever of them is fulfilled (28.3.2):

(80) Ahmet artık [çalış**sa da** çalışma**sa da**] sınavı geçemez. (cf. (71))
'Now [*whether* Ahmet works *or* not], he won't be able to pass the exam.'

(81) [Evde **de** otur**sam** sokağa **da** çık**sam**] hep içimde o acı var.
'[*Whether* I sit at home *or* I go out], there is always that pain inside me.'

27.4.2.2 -(y)sA/ise with dA

A subordinate predicate marked by the conditional copula *-(y)sA* can be followed by the clitic *dA* to produce a **concessive** clause, equivalent to an English clause introduced by 'although'. The meaning produced by this construction is *factual* and not conditional. (Note, however, that combinations of the aorist-conditional forms *-(A/I)rsA/-mAzsA* with *dA*, mean 'even if', not 'although'.)

(82) Banu [toplantılarımıza gel-**iyor-sa da**] pek bir şey söylemiyor.
come-IMPF-COND.COP
'[*Although* Banu comes to our meetings], she doesn't say much.'

(83) [Mehmet'i birkaç defa sokakta

gör-**dü-m-se de**/gör-**dü-yse**-m **de**]
see-PF-1SG-COND.COP *dA*/see- PF-COND.COP-1SG *dA*

konuşmadık.

'[*Although* I've seen/I saw Mehmet in the street a few times], we haven't spoken/didn't speak.'

(84) [Parası var**sa da**/var **ise de**] harcamak istemiyor.
'Although s/he's got money, s/he doesn't want to spend [it].'

It is possible for clauses marked with *-(y)sA dA* to be introduced by *(her) ne kadar* (27.5). Although this adds nothing to the meaning, it enables the speaker to signal at the beginning of the sentence that the message of the first clause is subsequently going to be overridden by a conflicting or contrasting statement to come in the main clause:

(85) [***Her ne kadar*** Banu toplantılarımıza gel**iyorsa da**] pek bir şey söylemiyor.
'*Although* Banu sometimes comes to our meetings, she doesn't say much.'

27.5 Clauses with wh-phrases and conditional marking

Where a clause contains a wh-phrase (19.2) and conditional marking, its meaning is equivalent to a clause with 'whoever', 'wherever', etc. in English, signalling a sense of universality. A striking feature of these clauses is that *-sA* occurs interchangeably with various verbal *-(y)sA* combinations and they are somewhat removed from a conditional meaning:

(86) [***Kim***e sor-du-k-**sa**/sor-**sa**-k]
who-DAT ask-PF-1PL-COND.COP/ask-COND-1PL

aynı cevab-ı al-dı-k.
same answer-ACC get-PF-1PL

'[Whoever we asked], we got the same answer.'

(87) Hayriye Hanım [*nereye* giderse/gitse] köpeğini de yanında götürüyordu.
'[*Wherever* Hayriye Hanım went], she took her dog with her too.'

(88) [Bu resimlerden *hangi*sini seçerseniz/seçseniz] hemen çerçeveletiriz.
'[*Whichever* of these pictures you choose], we'll get [it] framed straight away.'

(89) Necla [*ne zaman* sınava girerse/girse] heyecan çekiyor.
'[*Whenever* Necla takes an exam], she gets nervous.'

Occasionally the wh-phrase in the subordinate clause is echoed by a resumptive pronoun in the main clause:

(90) [***Kim**e* sorduksa/sorsak] (*hepsin-den*) aynı cevabı aldık. (cf. (86))
    all.of.them-ABL
'[*Whoever* we asked], we got the same answer from *all of them*.'

(91) Hayriye Hanım [*nereye* giderse/gitse] köpeğini de (*oraya*) yanında götürüyordu. (cf. (87))
'[*Wherever* Hayriye Hanım went], she took her dog *there* with her.'

(92) [Bu resimlerden *hangi*sini seçerseniz/seçseniz] hemen çerçeveletiriz (*onu*). (cf. (88))
'[*Whichever* of these pictures you choose], we'll get *it* framed straight away.'

Alternatively, the idea of universality can be reinforced by placing *her* 'every' before the question phrase:

(93) Hayriye Hanım [**her** *nereye* giderse] köpeğini de yanında götürüyordu.

Conditional marking in a clause with *nasıl* 'how' expresses a sense removed from any kind of conditionality, to express simply a similarity between two situations:

(94) [*Nasıl* Hakan akşamları garsonluk yapıyorsa] sen de derslerine engel olmayacak bir iş bulabilirsin. (cf. Chapter 26 (23))
'[*Just as* Hakan works in the evenings as a waiter], you too could find a job that wouldn't interfere with your academic commitments.'

If, on the other hand, *nasıl* actually modifies the verb in the subordinate clause, it is echoed by *öyle* 'so', 'in that way' in the main clause:

(95) [Bir baba çocuklarını *nasıl* severse] Mustafa da köpeklerini *öyle* seviyor.
'Mustafa loves his dogs [*in the same way that* a father loves his children].'

27.5.1 Concessives

Many constructions with conditional marking and a wh-phrase express a concessive relation, particularly the failure (predicted or actual) to achieve an objective in spite of the efforts expressed in the conditional clause. Two alternative strategies may optionally be used to reinforce this concessive meaning:

(i) *dA* may be placed after the conditional verb:

(96) [Bu konuda **ne kadar** iyi bir kitap yazsan (*da*)] seni meşhur edemez.
'[*However* good a book you write on this subject], it won't make you famous.'

(97) Adam [**ne** söylediyse (*de*)] karısını suçsuz olduğuna inandıramadı.
'[*Whatever* the man said], he couldn't convince his wife that he was innocent.'

(98) [Kemal bana **kaç** defa anlatsa (*da*)] gene anlamayacaktım.
'[*However,* many times Kemal explained [it] to me], I still wouldn't have understood.'

Note that *dA* is generally not used where the verb in the conditional clause has aorist marking.

(ii) If the conditional clause is in the form aorist + -*(y)sA*, the imperative or optative form of the same verb (in the same grammatical person) may be inserted immediately after the conditional form. This additional verb form serves to reinforce the meaning of the clause with conditional marking.

(99) [[**Ne kadar** konuş-**ur**-lar-**sa**] konuş-*sun*-lar]
what amount talk-AOR-3PL-COND.COP talk-IMP.3PL

hiçbir zaman anlaşamayacaklar.
'*However long* they go on talking, (let them talk;) they're never going to be able to agree.'

(100) [[**Nere-ye** gid-er-se-niz] gid-*in*]
where-DAT go-AOR-COND.COP-2PL go-IMP.2PL

bu fiyata bu kadar güzel bir kanepe bulamazsınız.
'*No matter where* you go, (go); you won't find such a fine sofa at this price.'

As noted in 27.4.2.2, *(her) ne kadar* in a conditional-marked clause does not always mean 'however much/long', as it has become lexicalized as a general marker of concessive clauses with *-(y)sA dA*.

27.6 Conditional constructions without conditional suffixes

There are a number of constructions that express the same meaning as aorist + *-(y)sA*, that is, predictive open and habitual conditional clauses (27.2.1.1–2), without the use of either of the conditional suffixes.

27.6.1 *-DIğI takdirde, -mAsI durumunda/halinde*

Conditional clauses whose verbs are marked with these forms structurally resemble the other non-finite adverbial constructions discussed in 26.3. They are characteristic of relatively formal styles, and approximate to 'in the event of/that'.

(101) [Aday-lar-dan hiçbir-i çoğunluk
candidate-PL-ABL none-3SG.POSS majority

sağla-ya-ma-**dığ-ı takdirde**] ikinci tur-a
secure-PSB-NEG-CV-3SG.POSS *takdirde* second round-DAT

geç-il-ecek-tir.
move-PASS-FUT-GM

'[*In the event of* none of the candidates being able to secure a majority], [the process] will continue into a second round.'

(102) [Yapılaşmanın denetim altına alınma**ması durumunda/halinde**] kıyı bölgeleri kısa zamanda bozulmaktadır.
'[If building development is not brought under control], coastal regions are rapidly spoilt.'

27.6.2 *-DI mI*

By contrast, *-DI mI* (the perfective verb form (8.2.3.3) followed by the interrogative clitic (11.1.1.5)) is a colloquial alternative to the aorist conditional. It is used only where speaker wishes to impart a rather dramatic tone to a conditional utterance:

(103) [O kağıdı imzaladık **mı**] artık yakamızı hiç kurtaramayız.
'[If we once sign that piece of paper], we'll never be able to escape.'

Subordinate clauses with *-dI mI* also occur with temporal meaning (26.1.6).

Chapter 28

Conjunctions, co-ordination and discourse connection

In Turkish, a number of devices are used for co-ordinating phrases and/or sentences:

(i) The juxtaposition of two or more constituents (28.1)
(ii) The subordinating suffixes *-(y)Ip* and *-(y)ArAk* (28.2)
(iii) Conjunctions and connectives (28.3)

Certain items may be omitted when two or more phrases or clauses are conjoined. These are discussed in 28.4.

28.1 The juxtaposition of two or more constituents

One of the most common methods of co-ordinating two or more phrases or sentences is simply to list them without using an overt co-ordinator. Note that Turkish uses simple juxtaposition in many cases where English uses 'and' or 'or':

(1) **siyah beyaz** bir film
    'a black [*and*] white film'

(2) Öğleyin **peynir ekmek** yedim.
    'I had bread [*and*] cheese at lunch time.'

(3) **Gece gündüz** çalışıyoruz.
    'We're working night [*and*] day.'

Apart from semi-lexicalized pairs such as those shown in (1)–(3), and juxtaposed numeral pairs such as *iki üç* 'two [or] three' (15.7.1), constituents co-ordinated in this way are sometimes separated by a pause in speech, and all but the last of the conjoined items have rising intonation at the end (5.1 (iii.b)). In writing, listing in this manner requires a comma:

(4) güzel, büyük, deniz manzaralı bir oda
    'a beautiful, large room with a view of the sea'

(5) Ziya pabuçlarını, paltosunu giydi, eline şemsiyesini aldı, işe gitti.
'Ziya put on his shoes [*and*] coat, picked up his umbrella [*and*] left for work.'

28.2 The subordinating suffixes -(y)Ip and -(y)ArAk

-(y)Ip (8.5.2.2) is a regular means of conjoining clauses which are semantically of equal status with respect to tense/aspect/modality. *-(y)ArAk* (8.5.2.2 and 26.3) can also be used for the same purpose. These suffixes are attached to all verbs but the last in a series of conjuncts, in place of any of the tense/aspect/modality suffixes in Position 2 (8.2.3.2) and the suffixes following them:

(6) Sinemaya gid**ip** güzel bir film seyred**ebilsek**.
(crs. Sinemaya git**ebilsek ve** ...)
'It would be nice if we could go to the cinema *and* watch a good film.'

(7) Başbakan İzmir'e gid**erek** bazı işadamlarıyla görüştü.
(crs. İzmir'e git**ti ve** ...)
'The Prime Minister went to Izmir *and* met some businessmen.'

In (6), *-(y)Ip* the possibility suffix, the conditional copula and the person marker. In (7), it replaces the perfective suffix.

In subordinate clauses, *-(y)Ip* and *-(y)ArAk* replace other subordinating suffixes (8.5) and any other suffixes that follow them:

(8) [Kendin gel**ip** gör**ünce**] anlayacaksın.
(crs. gel**ince ve** ...)
'[When you come *and* see for yourself], you will understand.'

(9) [Konuyu bil**ip** fark ettirme**diğin**]**-i** tahmin ediyorum.
(crs. bil**diğini fakat**...)
'I have a feeling [that you know about the matter *but* you're not giving it away].'

Where the verb in the superordinate clause contains the negative marker, the verb containing *-(y)Ip* is also typically understood to have negative meaning:

(10) Bu havada herhalde evde otur-**up** televizyon seyret-**me-yeceğ-iz**!
                                    stay-CONJ   watch-NEG-FUT-1PL

(crs. evde otur-**ma-yacağ-ız** ve...)
(stay-NEG-FUT-1PL and...)

'We'll hardly be staying indoors *and* watching the telly in this weather!'

It is also possible, however, for the verb containing -*(y)Ip* to have affirmative meaning despite negative marking of the superordinate verb, as in (9). If the clitic *dA* follows -*(y)Ip* in such contexts it serves to emphasize an adversative relation between the two verbs (28.3.4.5):

> (11) Ahmet mesajı bul-up **da** anla-*ma*-mış mı acaba?
>   find-CONJ *dA* understand-NEG-EV/PF
>   'I wonder if Ahmet found the message *but* didn't understand [it]?'

The verb containing -*(y)Ip* can itself be negative-marked only where the superordinate verb is not:

> (12) Bu havada evde otur-**ma-yıp** yürüyüşe çık-malı-yız.
>   stay-NEG-CONJ   go.out-OBLG-1PL
>   'In this weather we must not stay indoors *but* go out for a walk.'

Where a verb containing -*(y)Ip* is followed by *dA* and is *stressed*, the clause in which it occurs is exactly equivalent to a finite subordinate clause marked by *dA* (26.1.7), that is, it emphasizes the fact that the action it expresses *precedes/preceded* that articulated by the main clause:

> (13) [Yemek yi**YİP** de] geldim. (cf. Chapter 26 (29))
>   'I came [having [already] eaten].'

Some speakers use -*(y)Ip* when conjoining clauses with different subjects, especially when they both have 3rd person subjects:

> (14) Tam o saat-te Semra iş-i bırak-**ıp**
>   exactly that time-LOC Semra work-ACC leave-CONJ
>
>   Ahmet işbaşı yap-**ıyor**.
>   Ahmet clocking.on do-IMPF
>
>   'At exactly that time, Semra leaves work and Ahmet goes on duty.'

For the -*(y)(I)p...-mA* 'whether/if...(or not)' construction that involves identical verb stems in noun clauses, see 20.1.3.

28.3 Conjunctions and discourse connectives

Conjunctions are expressions such as *ve* 'and', *fakat* 'but', and *ya da* 'or', which join two or more items that have the same syntactic function. These conjoined items can be single words, phrases, subordinate clauses or sentences. The conjoining function of **discourse connectives**, on the other hand, is minimally to join two sentences. Discourse connectives such as *aksine* 'on the contrary', *üstelik* 'moreover' and *sonuç olarak* 'as a result' can be used for purposes of forming a cohesive link between concepts expressed by entire groups of sentences. Another difference between the two classes is that while a conjunction always joins two or more linguistic items, this is not always the case with discourse connectives, which can sometimes be used on their own if the context presents a situation (e.g. a recent experience shared by speaker and addressee) to which a cohesive link can be made.

The various semantic functions of Turkish conjunctions and discourse connectives are explained below. Some expressions (e.g. *yoksa* 'or', 'otherwise') can function both as conjunctions and as discourse connectives, and some fulfil more than one role even as discourse connectives. For example, *dA* (11.1.1.2) has additive, enumerative and adversative functions, all of which are discussed under different subsections below. Quite a number of discourse connectives are adverbial in form and function. For example, those such as *bununla birlikte* 'in spite of this' or *onun için* 'for that reason' consist of a postpositional phrase with a demonstrative pronoun as its complement. From the point of view of their function, most of the discourse connectives are modal adverbs and some of them are mentioned in 16.3.

28.3.1 Additive

The common characteristic of the items in this group is that they signal the addition of a new item without changing the direction of the discourse.

28.3.1.1 ve, -(y)lA/ile, dA 'and', dA 'too', bile 'even', ve de 'and what's more', bir de 'and also', ya 'and [...]?'

(i) *ve*, a word borrowed from Arabic, conjoins all types of phrases and clauses, and can function both as a conjunction and as a discourse connective.

    (15) Arapça **ve** Farsça
           'Arabic *and* Persian'

    (16) [Paris'e gittiğin]-e **ve** [müzeleri gezdiğin]-e çok seviniyor.
           'S/he is very happy [that s/he went to Paris *and* visited the museums].'

In its function of conjoining two clauses, *ve* is often replaced by *-(y)Ip* or (less commonly) by *-(y)ArAK* (28.2).

(ii) The clitic *ile* and its suffixal counterpart *-(y)lA* (8.1.4), unlike *ve*, attach only to non-case-marked noun phrases and to noun clauses formed with *-mAK* (24.4.1) and *-mA* (24.4.2). They cannot occur as discourse connectives.

    (17) Arapça'**yla** Farsça
           'Arabic *and* Persian'

(18) [Ahmet'in bu kitabı okuması]-**yla** [okumaması] arasında bir fark olacağını sanmıyorum.
'I don't believe there will be a difference between [Ahmet's reading this book] *and* [his not reading [it]].'

Another difference between *ve* and *-(y)lA/ile* is that *ve* is exclusive, whereas *-(y)lA/ile* can be either exclusive or inclusive. Where the conjunction is *ve*, a plural pronoun (such as *biz* 'we' below) does not include within its reference the noun phrase conjoined to it:

(19) **Zehra ve biz** kolay anlaşıyoruz.
'*We and Zehra* get along well.'

-(y)lA/ile, on the other hand, can be either inclusive or exclusive, that is, the conjoined noun phrase may or may not denote a member of the group that the plural pronoun refers to:

(20) **Zehra'yla biz** eve gidiyoruz.
   (i) '*Zehra and I* are going home.'
  (ii) '*We and Zehra* are going home.' (*We* are going home *with Zehra*.)

For subjects conjoined by *ve* or *-(y)lA/ile,* see 12.2.2.4, 13.2.3.2, and for *-(y)lA* as a postposition, see 17.2.1 (iii).

(iii) In its additive usages, the clitic *dA* (11.1.1.2) is a discourse connective occurring in the second conjunct (cf. the usages described in 26.1.7, 28.3.4.5 (i)). It has different functions according to the type of constituent it is attached to. It can be attached either to a non-focused constituent or to a focused one.

  a. *dA* attached to a non-focused (i.e. unstressed) constituent:
A non-focused constituent to which *dA* is attached is usually the first constituent in a sentence. In this case, *dA* has a primarily continuative function, indicating that the events or states described in successive sentences are connected, but it may also signal a change in topic (23.3.3.1 (i), as in the case of *Semra'ya* in (21)). In this usage, *dA* corresponds to 'and':

(21)   Sana bugün iki mektup geldi. *Semra'ya* **da** bir paKET.
     'Two letters arrived for you today. *And* a package for Semra.'

(22)   Balığı kızarttım. Biraz sonra **da** yiyeCEğim.
     'I have fried the fish *and* will eat [it] in a few minutes.'

  b. *da* attached to a focused (i.e. stressed) constituent:
This can be any constituent in the sentence, including the predicate. In this function, *dA* corresponds to 'too', 'also':

(23) Kışın ortasında Bodrum'a gitti, deniZE **de** girdi.
'S/he went to Bodrum in the middle of winter, [*and*] swam in the sea, *too*.'

(24) Hep İzlanda'ya gitmek isterdi, sonunda gitTİ **de**.
'S/he always wanted to go to Iceland, [*and*] in the end s/he went, *too*.'

dA can sometimes attach to the stressed constituent within a phrase:

(25) Bebek ne tatlı. ÇOK **da** uslu maşallah.
'The baby is so sweet. And *very* well-behaved, *too!*'

See 28.3.4.5 (i) for the adversative function of *dA*, 27.4.2.1-2 for combinations of *dA* with the conditional markers *-sA* and *-(y)sA*, 26.1.7 for *dA* as a subordinator, and 28.3.2 for enumerating *dA... dA*.

(iv) *bile* 'even', 'already' attaches to any constituent that can receive stress and interacts with focus:

(26) Nuri, **sokaĞA** *bile* **çıkmak** istemiyor.
'Nuri doesn't *even* want to go out [of the house].'

The implication here is that in addition to not wanting other things, Nuri also doesn't want to go out.

When *bile* attaches to a predicate in a finite clause, it can mean 'even', but more often corresponds to 'already':

(27) Bazen o pis köpeği okŞUyor **bile**.
'Sometimes s/he *even* strokes that filthy dog.'

(28) O filmi görDÜM **bile**.
'I have *already* seen that film.'

(v) *ve de* is an emphatic form of *ve*, mostly in its function as a sentence co-ordinator, and is used mainly to highlight the significance of the comment that follows:

(29) 80 yaşında Almanca öğrenmeye başladı **ve de** bundan çok memnun.
'S/he has started learning German at 80, *and what's more* s/he's very happy about it.'

(vi) *bir de* can follow or precede the second conjunct. It sometimes signals that the item it introduces is an afterthought:

(30) Evde tuz kalmamış, **bir de** süt.
'We are out of salt...*and* milk.'

(31) İtalya'ya gitmek istiyorum, İspanya'ya **bir de**.
'I want to go to Italy...*also* to Spain.'

(vii) *ya* as an additive is a discourse connective introducing a question:

(32) A. Tatile giderken köpeği yanlarına alacaklar.
'They will take the dog with them on their holiday.'

B. Ya kedileri?
'(And) what about the cats?'

Such questions are usually speculative. They can involve a conditional clause in which case the predicate is marked with one of the conditional suffixes *-sA* or *-(y)sA* (Chapter 27). There may or may not be a main clause in the question. The ones with main clauses correspond to questions expressed with '(And) what if...' in English:

(33) **Ya** bir kazaya uğrad**ıysa**?
'(And) what if s/he's had an accident?'

(34) **Ya** [ben evde olma**saydım**] seni *kim* kurtaracaktı?
'(And) who would have rescued you [*if* I hadn't been at home]?'

28.3.1.2 *üstelik, üstüne üstlük, hem, hem (de), buna ek olarak, ayrıca, kaldı ki* 'and (what's more)', 'also', *sonra* 'and then'

These connectives do not merely conjoin two sentences, they also draw attention to the speaker's conscious decision to add something to what has already been said. As seen in the examples below, they are often combined with *dA*. They can be situated at the beginning or at the end of the second sentence:

(35) Nota okumayı sevmiyormuş. **Üstelik** piyanist!
'S/he doesn't like reading scores. *And* she's a pianist!'

(36) Erken buluşalım. **Hem bir çay kahve de** içeriz.
'Let's meet early. *Then* we could have some tea or coffee *as well*.'

28.3.1.3 *hatta, dahası* 'even', 'indeed'

These discourse connectives introduce a statement that reinforces the previous statement, usually by making an even more convincing point. They usually occur at the beginning of the second conjunct, and are often combined with *bile* (28.3.1.1 (iv)):

(37) Akşam kurslarına gitti. **Dahası** tatillerde *bile* ders çalıştı.
'S/he went to evening classes. S/he *even* studied in the holidays.'

(38) [Erol'un Korkut'u sevmediği] belli. Bunu açıkça söylüyor **hatta**.
'It's obvious [that Erol doesn't like Korkut]. *Indeed*, he says so quite openly.'

hatta also occurs as a conjunction:

(39) [Sıcaktan bayılanlar], **hatta** [ölenler] olmuş.
'Apparently there were [people who fainted from the heat], *and even* [some who died].'

28.3.1.4 *şöyle dursun/bir yana/bırak(ın) 'let alone'*

These expressions, which function as conjunctions, occur only in negative sentences and are placed at the end of the first conjunct. Their effect is to reinforce the negativity of the assertion involving the first conjunct by drawing a comparison with the negativity of another situation regarded as inherently more realizable. The second conjunct almost always includes *bile* 'even' (28.3.1.1 (iv)). Note that if the comparison is between two clauses (rather than two noun phrases), the first is expressed as a *-mAk* clause (24.4.1.1-2):

(40) Diplomasını almak **şöyle dursun/bir yana**, tezini **bile** daha yazmamış.
'S/he hasn't *even* written her thesis yet, *let alone* received his/her degree.'

(41) **Bırak(ın)** diplomasını almayı, tezini **bile** daha yazmamış.
'S/he hasn't *even* written her thesis yet, *let alone* received his/her degree.'

In (41) the noun clause *diplomasını almayı* has accusative marking as it is the direct object of the verb *bırak-* 'leave'.

For the use of the negative word *değil* 'not' in a similar function, see 20.2.3.

28.3.2 Enumerating

This group contains *dA...dA*, *hem...hem*, *gerek...(ve) gerek(se de)* '(both)...and', *bir...bir* 'one moment...the next moment'

All the items in this group of reduplicated conjunctions except for *bir...bir* 'one moment...the next moment' emphasize the equal status and function in an utterance of two or more persons, things or events. *dA* is attached to the end of each of the phrases involved, whereas *hem* and *gerek* precede the phrases or clauses they connect:

(42) Dünya Kupasında **Güney Kore** *de* **Türkiye** *de* yarı finale kaldı.
'*Both* South Korea *and* Turkey have reached the semi-finals of the World Cup.'

(43) Necla *hem* **Boğaziçi Üniversitesi**, *hem* **Sabancı**, *hem de* **Bilkent**'e girebiliyormuş.
'Necla has been admitted to Boğaziçi University, Sabancı *and* Bilkent.'

In the last occurrence of *hem*, *dA* can be used for emphasis, as in (43). The last occurrence of *gerek* can be replaced by *gerekse, gerekse de* or *ve gerekse de*:

(44) *Gerek* **İngiliz takımı**, *gerekse (de)* **Fransızlar**, bu Dünya Kupası yarışmasına iddialı giriyorlar.
'*Both* the English team *and* the French are entering this World Cup competition with high hopes.'

Where *dA... dA, hem... hem* or *gerek...(ve) gerek (se de)* are used in sentences with a negative predicate they correspond to *ne...ne* 'neither...nor' (20.4).

bir...bir is used colloquially for expressing repeated sequential activities or states that contrast with each other:

(45) **Bir** hasta, **bir** iyi.
'*One moment* s/he's ill, *the next*, s/he's well again.

(46) **Bir** yağmur yağıyor, **bir** güneş açıyordu.
'*One moment* it would be raining, *the next* the sun would come out.'

28.3.3 Alternative

This group of items conjoins phrases, clauses or sentences that express objects, persons, events or situations presented as alternatives. Some such alternatives are semi-lexicalized, as in the usage of *çay kahve* 'tea or coffee' in (36) above.

28.3.3.1 ya da, veya, (ve) yahut (da), yoksa 'or', ya...ya (da) '(either...) or'

Of the various terms expressing 'or' in Turkish, *ya da, veya* and *(ve) yahut (da)* are interchangeable in most contexts, both as conjunctions and as discourse connectives:

(47) Evde meyva **veya/ya da** tatlı var mı?
'Is there any fruit *or* any [sort of] sweet in the house?'

When *ya da* is used as a discourse connective it can be placed after the second conjunct:

(48) Necla sinemaya gitmek istemiyor. **Ya da** öyle söylüyor./
Öyle söylüyor **ya da**.
'Necla doesn't want to go to the cinema. *Or* that's what she says.'

When used as a conjunction, *ya da* can occur either on its own, as in (49), or with another *ya* preceding the first conjunct:

(50) O konuyu (**ya**) Ahmet('le) **ya da** karısıyla konuşabilirsin.
'You can discuss that matter (*either*) with Ahmet *or* with his wife.'

In such 'either...or' constructions, where the first conjunct is preceded by *ya, da* is optional before the second conjunct (and any others):

(51) Her yaz **ya** Fransa, **ya** (**da**) İtalya, **ya** (**da**) İspanya'ya gidiyorlardı.
'Every summer they would go to either France, Italy or Spain.'

Note that *ya* used on its own can function as an additive connective introducing conditional questions (28.3.1.1 (vii), an adversative connective (28.3.4.5 (ii), 28.3.4.7), or a reminding connective (28.3.12).

yoksa as an alternative conjunction occurs only in alternative questions (19.1.2). As a discourse connective, it can introduce a question expressing surprise at an inference drawn (19.5.3), or it can have the conditional sense of 'otherwise' (28.3.9).

28.3.3.2 *ister...ister, olsun...olsun, ha...ha, ama...ama* 'whether...or'

These reduplicated conjunctions indicate the speaker's indifference towards the alternatives mentioned.

(i) *ister...ister* conjoins imperative or optative verb forms (8.3, 8.4.3, 4.4.2–3), or nominal predicates. Each conjunction is placed before the constituent it conjoins:

(52) **İster** kal, **ister** git, yeter ki bugün şu işi bitir.
'*Whether* you stay *or* leave, make sure you finish off the job today.'

(53) Nazlı **ister** kursa yazılsın **ister** yazılmasın, bir şekilde Fransızca öğrenmesi gerekiyor.
'*Whether* she joins a class *or not*, Nazlı has to learn French somehow.'

(ii) *olsun...olsun*, which is a combination of the copular verb *ol-* 'be' (12.1.1.3) and the 3rd person optative form (8.4), is used with nominal predicates. Each conjunction is placed after the constituent it conjoins:

(54) Büyük **olsun** küçük **olsun**, evlerin sorunları bitmiyor.
'Big *or* small, houses always have problems.'

ister... ister can occur with *olsun...olsun*:

(55) **İster** büyük **olsun**, **ister** küçük (**olsun**), evlerin sorunları bitmiyor.
'Whether big *or* small, houses always have problems.'

(iii) *ha...ha* and *ama...ama* are both colloquial conjunctions which precede the constituents they conjoin:

(56) **Ha** Boğaziçi'ne gitmişsin **ha** Bilkent'e. İkisi de iyi üniversite.
'*It doesn't matter whether* you go to Boğaziçi *or* to Bilkent. They are both good universities.'

(57) Bu tip fırınlarda genellikle ızgara olmuyor, **ama** yerli **ama** yabancı.
'*Whether* they are made in Turkey *or* imported, these ovens don't usually have grills.'
(lit. '*Whether* they are made locally...')

28.3.4 Adversative

Adversative conjunctions signal a turning of the discourse in a direction contrary to what has been previously established.

28.3.4.1 ama, fakat, ancak, yalnız 'but'

fakat and *ama* are interchangeable. They conjoin clauses whose combined content expresses some kind of conflict or contradiction:

(58) Semra hep gezmek istiyor **ama/fakat** zamanı yok.   (Conflict)
'Semra always wants to travel, *but* she doesn't have the time.'

(59) Sonbahar geldi **ama/fakat** ağaçlar hâlâ yeşil.   (Contradiction)
'Autumn is here, *but* the trees are still green.'

When *ama* is used as a discourse connective, in other words when the second conjunct is uttered as a separate statement from the first, *ama* can also be placed at the end of the second conjunct:

(60) Kitabı hevesle satın aldım. Okuyamadım **ama**.
'I bought the book with great enthusiasm. I haven't managed to read it, *though*.'

ama and *fakat* can also conjoin adjectival constructions:

(61) Sıcak **ama** [bunaltıcı olmayan] bir havası var Ankara'nın.
'The weather in Ankara is hot *but* not suffocating.'
(lit. 'Ankara has a hot but not suffocating climate.')

ancak and *yalnız* (which as adverbials mean 'only' (16.7)) are slightly more restricted in their occurrence as adversative connectives than *ama* or *fakat*. They are used mainly to introduce a sentence expressing inability, failure, obligation, or some other disadvantageous situation:

(62) Ahmet aslında çok iyi bir mimar. **Ancak/Yalnız** aksiliği yüzünden müşterileri kaçırıyor.
'Ahmet is actually a very good architect. *But* he loses customers because of his bad temper.'

28.3.4.2 gene (de)/yine (de) '(and) yet', '(and) still', bununla birlikte/ beraber, buna karşın/rağmen 'despite this', 'nevertheless'

These discourse connectives are more emphatic as adversatives than those in 28.3.4.1. *gene de/yine de* are often used together with *ama* or *fakat* (for an example see (72) below). *gene/yine* also occur as adverbials meaning 'again' and the addition of *de* eliminates potential ambiguity.

(63) Rusça çok zor bir dilmiş, **gene de** onu öğrenmeye kararlıyım.
'Russian is said to be a very difficult language, *yet* I am determined to learn it.'

(64) Ahmet nezle olmuş. **Buna rağmen** yüzmek istiyor.
'Ahmet's got a cold. *Despite this*, he wants to go swimming.'

28.3.4.3 ne (var) ki, gelgelelim, gel gör ki, mamafih 'however'

These items are confined to rather formal registers, and highlight the speaker's conscious intention to articulate a conflictual or contradictory state of affairs:

(65) İlköğretimi tamamlayanların sayısında önemli bir artış olmuş. **Ne var ki/ gelgelelim** rakamlara ayrıntılı bakıldığında bölgesel farklılaşma da dikkat çekmektedir.
'There has evidently been a significant increase in the number of those completing primary education. *However*, when one looks at the figures in detail, one is also struck by regional differentiation.'

28.3.4.4 halbuki/oysa (ki), 'whereas', 'however'

The discourse connectives *halbuki/oysa (ki)* sometimes merely point to a contrast between two states of affairs:

(66) Sen [bütün duvarların düz beyaz kalmasın]-ı istersin, **oysa** ben
[bazı odalarda değişik renkler olsun] isterim.
'You want [all the walls to stay plain white], *whereas* I want [there to be different colours in some rooms].'

In this function, a sentence with *halbuki/oysa (ki)* could be paraphrased with *-(y)sA* (23.3.3.1 (ii)). The more distinctive function of *halbuki* and *oysa (ki)* is to signal a contradiction between a *factual* state of affairs and a *belief* or *claim* concerning it. The connective always appears at the beginning (or end) of the second conjunct, but this may be the one expressing either the factual or the supposed state of affairs:

(67) a. Necla [evini sattığında] bunalıma girdi. **Halbuki/Oysa (ki)**
[bu fikre çoktandır alıştı] sanıyordum.
'Necla became very depressed [when she sold her house].
Whereas I thought [she had got used to the idea].'

b. Necla [evini satma fikrine alıştı] sanıyordum. **Halbuki/Oysa (ki)**
[bir alıcı çıktığında] bunalıma girdi.
'I thought [Necla had got used to the idea of selling her house].
However, [when a buyer appeared] she became very depressed.'

For *meğer*, see 16.3 (iv).

28.3.4.5 dA, ya 'but', -(y)sA/ise 'as for', 'whereas'

These are conjunctions which contrast a situation presented in the second conjunct to the situation presented in the first one.

(i) *dA* is placed after the predicate of the first conjunct, and produces stress on the last syllable of the predicate, even if this position is not the normally stressable position of that word (11.1.1.2 (iii)):

(68) Öğrencilerin hepsinin adlarını bilmiyoRUM **da** yüzlerini tanıyorum.
'I don't know the names of all the students, *but* I know their faces.'

(69) Sen GİT **de** ben gelmeyeceğim.
'You go, *but* I'm not coming.'

Note that adversative *dA* does not necessarily produce primary stress on *-(y)Ip* (28.2):

(70) Ahmet mesajı bul**up da** yanLIŞ anlamış meğerse.
'It turns out that Ahmet had found the message *but* misunderstood [it].'

(ii) *ya* is used in colloquial speech as a contrastive adversative conjunction:

(71) Toplantıya katılırım **ya** [ne diyeceğim]-i bilemem.
'I'll join the meeting, *but* I won't know [what to say].'

(iii) The contrastive function of *-(y)sA/ise* (11.1.1.7) is to switch the attention of the speaker to a new topic (23.3.3.1 (ii).

28.3.4.6 gerçi/hoş 'it's true that', 'admittedly', 'actually', aslında/esasında 'actually'

The function of this group of adversative discourse connectives is concessive. While marking the statement they introduce as contradictory to what has previously been said, they also signal that the speaker regards this contradiction as illusory, reparable or otherwise tolerable. *gerçi* arouses an expectation that the statement it introduces will be followed by another, introduced by a conflictive adversative (such as *ama* 'but'), which will coun-terbalance the concession made and cancel out its effect:

(72) Uludağ'a gidiyorlarmış. **Gerçi** Ziya kayak yapmayı sevmez **ama yine de** gidecekmiş.
'They are going to Uludağ. *Actually*, Ziya doesn't like skiing, *but* he is still going.'

hoş is used in the same way as *gerçi* but is a slightly dated expression, used only in colloquial speech. As for the very common expression *aslında* 'actually', this can be used either in the same way as *gerçi* or on its own, as in (62), leaving the concession unrepaired:

(73) [Bakkala gittiğinde] gazete de alır mısın? **Aslında** birazdan ben de çıkacağım.
'Can you buy a paper as well [when you go to the corner shop]?
Actually, I shall be going out soon, too.'

28.3.4.7 ki and ya

As adversative connectives, the clitics *ki* and *ya* have a repudiative function. Both challenge the previous statement or question, or the presupposition of the previous speaker. For some speakers, *ki* and *ya* complement each other: *ki* is used in negative statements and in questions and *ya* only in affirmative statements as a repudiator. For other speakers, they can be used interchangeably as repudiative connectives in affirmative and negative statements. Both clitics occur after the predicate and usually at the end of a sentence, placing stress on the preceding syllable, even where this position is not normally the stressable syllable of a word (11.2.2):

(74) Ahmet gezide fotoğraf çekecekti **ama** makinasını yanına almaMIŞ **ki/ya**!
'Ahmet was supposed to take photographs on the trip, *but* apparently he hadn't taken his camera with him!'

(75) A. Sana [bu sabunu kullan] demedim mi?
'Didn't I tell you [to use this soap]?'

B. KullanDIM **ya/ki**!
'*But* I did!'

(76) A. Hasan artık burada kalamaz.
'Hasan can't stay here any longer.'

B. Başka nereye gidebilir *ki*?
'*But* where else can he go?

The discourse connective function of *ki* described here is related to one of its subordinating functions in which it introduces clauses expressing purpose (26.1.2.2). For this reason, repudiative *ki* can be followed by an optative-marked verb (8.3, 8.4.3):

(77) A. Hani alışverişe gidecektin?
'I thought you were going to go shopping?'

B. Dükkanlar daha açıl**mam**ışTIR ki (gideyim).
'*But* the shops won't be open yet.'

For the various other functions of *ki* and *ya* see 11.1.1.4 and 11.1.1.6.

28.3.4.8 *peki* 'but'

The most common function of *peki* is to express the speaker's agreement with a proposal or instruction articulated by the addressee. In this usage, it means 'all right' and can stand on its own as a complete utterance. As a discourse connective, *peki* is used only in questions, and indicates that the speaker is not satisfied with the information conveyed in a previous statement and requires more information:

(78) A. Bütün yazı çalışarak geçirmem gerekiyor.
'I have to spend the whole summer working'.

B. **Peki**, sen bu yaz evini satmayacak mıydın?
'*But* weren't you planning to sell your house this summer?'

28.3.4.9 yok 'but'

Yok (20.3) can be used as an adversative discourse connective in the second of two consecutive conditional sentences. In each sentence, the conditional verb is marked with *-(y)sA* (27.1–3), and the two conditions expressed are mutually exclusive. *Yok* is placed at the beginning of the second sentence, and may optionally be followed by the conditional conjunction *eğer* 'if':

(79) [Mehmet ikiye kadar geli**rse**] iyi. [**Yok (eğer)** o saate kadar gelmemi**şse**] daha fazla bekleyemeyiz.
'[If Mehmet arrives by two o'clock], that's fine. [*But* if he hasn't come by that time], we won't be able to wait any longer.'

28.3.5 Expansive

This group of conjunctions and connectives are used to signal an expansion of the speaker's statement. Expansion may take the form of exemplification, particularization, analogy, explanation, justification, correction or, in the case of a negative statement, amplification. *Şöyle ki* always precedes the comment it introduces. The others, with the exception of the expansive suffixes in (ii), are likewise often placed at the beginning of the second conjunct but in colloquial speech they can also follow the second conjunct or or can occur in some position within it.

(i) *örneğin/mesela/sözgelişi/sözgelimi* 'for example' *örneğin* and its Arabic synonym *mesela* are the most frequently used expressions in this group:

(80) Nane bazı şeylerle çok iyi gidiyor, **örneğin** mercimekle.
'Mint goes very well with some things. With lentils, *for example*.'

(ii) *-(y)DI... -(y)DI, -(y)mIş ...-(y)mIş, yok ...yok* '...and the like', 'etc.':
In colloquial usage, these reduplicative forms perform another kind of exemplifying function, listing some of the possible items in a set. Two of the connectives in this group are the copular markers *-(y)DI* and *-(y)mIş* (8.3.2). The listed items marked in this manner usually precede the general term (indicated by italics below) referring to them:

(81) Yanına **kağıttı, kalemdi**, *sınav için ne gerekliyse* al.
'Take with you *all that you need for the exam, paper, pencils and what have you.*'

(82) **Koşmakmış, yüzmekmiş**, hiç öyle *spor*la filan uğraştığı yok.
'S/he is not interested in *sports* at all, like running, swimming, etc.'

Reduplicated *yok*, also a colloquial way of listing items, is used in a different way. It allows the speaker to express his/her frustration with a particular situation. Each statement that follows *yok* is presented by the speaker as an untenable excuse or an unrealistic wish. These statements often contain the evidential copula *-(y)mIş*.

(83) Hep bir bahanesi var. **Yok** hava kötü**ymüş**, **yok** parası yetmez**miş**, **yok** vakti yok**muş**...Yani anlayacağın, bizimle tatile gitmemek için elinden geleni yapıyor.
'S/he always has an excuse . . . *Either* the weather is bad, *or* s/he doesn't have enough money, *or* s/he doesn't have time...In short, s/he does whatever s/he can to avoid going on holiday with us.'

(iii) *hele (hele)* 'in particular', 'above all' and *özellikle/bilhassa* 'particularly', 'especially' single out one of the alternatives within a set (see also 16.7.2):

(84) Nimet Hanım torunlarını çok seviyor. En küçüğe **hele** bayılıyor.
'Nimet loves her grandchildren. She *particularly* adores the youngest one.'

(85) Annem Afrika'yı, **özellikle** güney Afrika'yı çok seviyor.
'My mother loves Africa, *especially* southern Africa.'

hele hele is an emphatic version of *hele*, placed usually at the beginning of a sentence.

(iv) *nitekim/nasıl ki* 'just as', 'similarly' expand by way of analogy:

(86) Her yıl okullarımızda büyük bir öğretmen sıkıntısı yaşanıyor, **nitekim** hastanelerimizdeki sağlık personelinin sayısı da yetersiz.
'Every year there is a great shortage of teachers in our schools, *just as* the number of health professionals in our hospitals is insufficient.'

(v) *başka bir deyişle* 'in other words', *yani* 'I mean', 'in other words', 'that is to say': These explanatory conjunctions/connectives introduce a phrase, clause or sentence in which the speaker reformulates his/her message in a different way. *başka bir deyişle* is used in formal contexts, and is limited to introducing a straightforward paraphrase:

(87) Babıali, **başka bir deyişle** Osmanlı hükümeti, ...
'The Sublime Porte, *in other words* the Ottoman government...'

yani, on the other hand, which is in much more general use, may introduce any kind of paraphrase or explanation, including the provision of further information:

(88) Seninle salı günü, **yani *bu iş bittikten sonra*** görüşebiliriz.
'You and I can get together on Tuesday, *that is, after this job is finished.*'

yani is a very common expression in conversation. Speakers often use it as a filler when they have not yet found the appropriate words to use:

(89) Evden hiç çıkmak istemiyor. **Yani** ...ne bileyim...
'S/he doesn't want to leave the house. *Well*... I don't know...'

(vi) *şöyle ki* '[the situation is] as follows':
şöyle ki is used in formal contexts, and generally introduces a sequence of sentences which as a whole expand on the previous remark of the same speaker.

(vii) *bir kere* 'for one thing', *sonra* 'for another thing', 'and then (again)':
These discourse connectives introduce statements which expand on the speaker's previous statement in terms of providing justification for the attitude or opinion expressed. If just one justificatory point is made, *bir kere* is used:

(90) Necla'ya güvenemem. **Bir kere** doktor değil.
'I can't trust Necla. *For one thing*, she's not a doctor.'

If a further point is added this is introduced by *sonra*:

(91) Bence başkanlığı en iyi Osman yapar. **Bir kere** herkes ona güveniyor, **sonra** bilgi ve deneyimi var.
'In my view, Osman would be the best chairman. *For one thing* everyone trusts him, *for another* he has the knowledge and experience.'

(viii) *daha doğrusu* 'or rather':
The conjunction/discourse connective *daha doğrusu* has a corrective function. It is used when the speaker wants to reformulate a phrase, clause or sentence that s/he has uttered, and wants the addressee to disregard all or part of the first conjunct:

(92) Yusuf pilavı çok sever. **Daha doğrusu** annesinin yaptığı pilavı sever.
'Yusuf loves rice, *or rather* the rice that his mother cooks.'

(ix) *aksine, tersine, bilakis* 'on the contrary':
These connectives introduce a statement that amplifies the statement in the first conjunct, which is always negative:

(93) Erol, Semra'yı görmek iste**mi**yor. **Aksine**, görecek diye ödü kopuyor.
'Erol doesn't want to see Semra. *On the contrary*, he dreads seeing [her].'

28.3.6 Causal

These connectives link two statements that are connected to each other by a causal link.

(i) *çünkü/zira* 'because':
Situated either at the beginning or (*çünkü* only) at the end of the second conjunct, these connectives present the cause of an event or state expressed by the first conjunct.

(94) Partiye gelmek istemiyor, **çünkü** kimseyi tanımıyormuş.
'S/he doesn't want to come to the party, *because* s/he says s/he doesn't know anyone.'

(95) Antalya'ya gidemedim. Param yoktu **çünkü**.
'I wasn't able to go to Antalya. *Because* I didn't have any money.'

As a strategy for expressing the cause of a situation, the use of *çünkü/zira* is mainly confined to informal registers. In more formal styles, the use of a non-finite causal clause (26.3.14), which places the cause before the result, is generally preferred. Informally also, adverbial clauses, whether finite (with *diye*, 26.1.1.1) or non-finite, are regularly used for the expression of reason. The use of a separate sentence introduced by *çünkü* is preferred where either the reason is added as an afterthought or where the reason is a fact not known to the addressee, to which the speaker wishes to give as much informational value as to the resultant event or state.

(ii) *bunun için/onun için/bundan dolayı/dolayısıyla/bu nedenle/bu yüzden/sonuç olarak* 'because of this/that', 'as a result':
This group of discourse connectives presents the result of a state of affairs described in the preceding sentence(s):

(96) Ahmet'in ehliyeti yok. **Dolayısıyla** araba kullanamaz.
'Ahmet doesn't have a driving licence. *As a result,* he is not allowed to drive.'

For *dolayı* as a postposition, see 17.2.3 (iv).

28.3.7 Inferential

demek (ki) 'that means', 'so' stands at either the beginning or the end of the sentence in which it is located, and indicates that this sentence expresses an inference drawn from what has been said previously:

(97) Görgü şahidi olarak mahkemeye çağırılmışsın. **Demek** sen de kaza yerindeydin!
'I hear you've been summoned as an eyewitness. *So*, you were at the scene of the accident as well!'

(98) Orhan artık Amerika'ya iyice alışmış **demek ki**.
'*So* Orhan now feels well and truly settled in America, it seems.'

e(ee) is a connective used in colloquial speech. It is placed at the beginning of a sentence to challenge the addressee to explain a situation that is different than what had been promised, or what should have been the case. It may also have an adversative flavour:

(99) E(ee) sen daha işe gitmedin mi?
'Haven't you been to work yet?'

28.3.8 Temporal

This group of discourse connectives includes *daha sonra* 'later', *ondan/bundan sonra* 'then', *onun/bunun üzerine* 'upon this/that', *derken* 'just then':

(100) Ücretlerinde bir artış olmadı. Onlar da **bunun üzerine** grev yapmaya karar verdiler.
'They got no pay increase, *upon which* they decided to go on strike.'

The colloquial connective *derken* introduces an event that comes as the climax of a process or series, or a situation that creeps up on someone without their realizing it:

(101) Bütün gün ev baktık. Osmanbey, Şişli, Mecidiyeköy, Beşiktaş'ta dolaşıp durduk. **Derken** saat beş olmuş.
'We spent all day looking at flats. We went round and round Osmanbey, Şişli, Mecidiyeköy [and] Beşiktaş. *And suddenly* it was five o'clock.'

For a fuller discussion of temporal adverbials, see 16.4.1, and for *önce* and *sonra* as postpositions, see 17.2.3 (vi-vii).

28.3.9 Conditional

The discourse connectives in this group express what conditionality, if any, attaches to one or other of the conjuncts.

(i) *yeter ki* 'all that is needed is…', introducing the second conjunct, expresses a condition that needs to be fulfilled in order for the state of affairs described in the *first* conjunct to be fully realized:

(102) Sana iş bulacağım. **Yeter ki** sen bulduğum işi beğen.
'I will find you a job. *All that is needed is* for you to like the job I find.'

(ii) Other connectives perform the opposite function, of specifying the conditionality (or lack of it) of the *second* conjunct. They fall into three groups:

a. *o halde/öyleyse* 'in that case' and *o zaman* 'then' treat the content of the first conjunct as a **knowable condition** (27.3), which is assumed to be fulfilled:

(103) A. Dükkanlar saat 5'te kapanıyormuş.
    'Apparently the shops close at 5 o'clock.'

  B. **O halde** bugün alışveriş yapamayacağız.
    '*In that case* we won't be able to do any shopping today.'

b. *yoksa, aksi halde/takdirde, olmadı, olmazsa,* and *sonra* 'otherwise', by contrast, treat the relation between the two sentences as a **predictive conditional** (27.2) in which the second conjunct predicts what the consequence would be if the state of affairs were *other than* what is described in the first conjunct:

(104) Herhalde evde oturmaktan çok sıkıldı. **Yoksa** bu soğukta sokağa çıkmazdı.
    'S/he must have got very bored staying indoors. *Otherwise,* s/he would never have gone outside in this cold weather.'

aksi takdirde is formal. On the other hand, *sonra* in this usage is colloquial, and the sentence that it marks usually follows a command:

(105) Haydi ceketini giy. Üşürsün **sonra**.
    'Come on now, put your jacket on. *Otherwise,* you'll get cold.'

olmadı and *olmazsa* are usually used with the aorist (-(A/I)r/-z) or the future marker (-(y)AcAK):

(106) Normalde paketi eve yolluyorlar. **Olmadı/olmazsa** kendin gidip alırsın.
    'They normally send the package to your house. Otherwise, you can go and get it yourself.'

c. *nasılsa/nasıl olsa/zaten* 'in any case', 'anyway':
These items indicate that the statement to which they are attached is independent of *any* conditionality:

(107) A. Benim yüzümden boş yere para harcadın diye üzülüyorum.
    'I feel bad about you spending money unnecessarily on my account.'

  B. Yok canım, ben **ZAten/NAsılsa** yeni bir bavul alacaktım.
    'That's nonsense; I was going to buy a new suitcase *anyway.*'

These items are usually stressed. For unstressed *zaten,* see 28.3.11.

d. The expression *ne de olsa* 'after all' has concessive meaning (27.5.1):

(108) Sevil'in bunu bilmesi gerekir. **Ne de olsa** fizikçi.
'Sevil ought to know this. *After all*, she is a physicist.'

28.3.10 Organizational

This class of connectives provides organizational clues as to how an utterance is to be understood.

(i) *işte* has a resumptive or summarizing function. It very often co-occurs with one of the demonstratives (e.g. *bu* 'this' (18.2) or their derivatives (e.g. *böyle* 'like this'). It is used for linking some previously mentioned item to the speaker's present statement, which may be a summary of a longer utterance:

(109) Ortalık karmakarışıktı. Yerlerde gazete kağıtları, kitaplar. Bir gün önce de evde kızkardeşimin doğum gününü kutlamıştık. Bulaşık bile daha yıkanmamıştı. **İşte** karışıklık derken **bundan** söz ediyorum.
'The place was in a real mess. Newspapers and books were strewn all over the floor. The previous day we had celebrated my sister's birthday in the flat. Even the dishes hadn't been washed yet. *Now this* is what I mean by a mess.'
(lit. '*So* when I say a mess, *it's this* that I'm talking about.')

In the spoken language, the cohesive link provided by *işte* is often to the visual environment of the speech situation:

(110) **İşte** cuma akşamları toplandığımız yer **orası**.
'*That* is the place [*that I mentioned earlier*] where we gather on Friday evenings.'

Another function of *işte* can be to indicate that the speaker does not wish to continue discussion of the topic in question:

(111) Gitmek istemiyorum **işte**.
'*Well*, I don't want to go.' (As I have already told you.)

(ii) The expressions *velhasıl/kısaca(sı)/özetle/özet olarak* 'in short' introduce a summary of what the speaker has been saying, without the resumptive dimension given by *işte*:

(112) Karısı yemeklerini yapıyor, çamaşırını yıkayıp ütülüyor, telefonlarına bakıyor, **kısacası** hayatını kolaylaştırmak için her şeyi yapıyor.
'His wife cooks his meals, does his washing and ironing, answers the phone for him, *in short* does everything to make his life easy.'

özetlersek/özetleyecek olursak 'to sum up' are much more formal alternatives.

(iii) *konumuza dönersek/dönecek olursak* 'to return to our topic' is used to indicate the end of a digression, or the intention of bringing the discussion back to what the speaker wants to talk about.

(iv) As an organizational connective the colloquial expression *neyse* 'well anyway', 'oh well' expresses the speaker's feeling that discussion (of a certain topic, or in total) has gone on long enough and should be concluded:

(113) Sabah erkenden trene yetişmem gerekiyordu. Kalktım, ortalığı topladım. Bu arada kediler de yemek bekliyorlardı. Bir ara kapıya birisi geldi. Meğer postacıymış. İmza gerektiren bir paket varmış. **Neyse**, 8.50 trenine yetişebildim.
'I had to catch an early train. I got up and tidied the house. Meanwhile the cats were waiting to be fed. Then someone came to the door. It turned out to be the postman. There was a packet that had to be signed for. *To cut a long story short*, I did manage to catch the 8.50.'

(114) **Neyse**, ben gitmeliyim artık.
'*Well anyway*, I must be going now.'

For another function of *neyse,* see 28.3.13.

28.3.11 Corroborative

zaten 'in any case', 'well' occurs at the beginning or end of the second conjunct, and presents a statement which makes the first conjunct predictable, thus corroborating or overriding it:

(115) Oraya trenle gidemezsin. **Zaten** bugün trenler çalışmıyor.
'You can't go there by train. *In any case*, the trains aren't running today.'

(116) A. Ben o kadar aç değilim.
'I'm not all that hungry.'

B. Sen yemek yemiştin **zaten**.
'*Well*, you had [already] eaten.'

Note that in this usage *zaten* is usually unstressed. For stressed *zaten* see 28.3.9.

28.3.12 Reminding

The discourse connectives in this group occur in the first of the two conjuncts. They are used by the speaker to remind the addressee of a person, thing or situation within their shared knowledge, in order that the speaker may go on to say something on that topic. The expressions in question are as follows:

(i) For recalling an event or state: *(hani)...ya* (most commonly used with *ya* placed immediately after the predicate)
(ii) For recalling people or things: *(hani)... var ya/yok mu*

All of these correspond to phrases such as 'you know' and 'remember' in English:

(117) (**Hani**) geçen gün okula gitmemiştim **ya**, meğer okul zaten tatilmiş.
'*Remember* I didn't go to school the other day? Well, it turns out it was a holiday anyway.'

(118) (**Hani**) şu marangoz İbrahim **var ya/yok mu**? İşte onun dükkanından söz ediyorum.
'*You know* İbrahim the joiner? It's his shop I'm talking about.'

hani can also introduce a sentence as an afterthought:

(119) Beyaz Fırın... (**hani**) geçen gün gitmiştik (**ya**).
'Beyaz Fırın...*you know*, we went there the other day...'

For *hani* as a modal adverb used in questions, see 19.5.1.

28.3.13 Constructive

The function of this group of discourse connectives is to present constructive interpretations of, or responses to, undesirable situations that have been described, or which are part of the shared knowledge of the speaker and addressee:

(i) *neyse* 'oh well' has two constructive functions:
   a. It points to a redeeming feature of a seemingly undesirable state of affairs:

   (120) Hafta sonunda hep yağmur yağdı. **Neyse**, okuduğum romanı bitirebildim.
   'It rained all weekend. *Oh well*, I was able to finish the novel I was reading.'

   b. It expresses acceptance or resignation:

   (121) **Neyse**, bizim yapabileceğimiz bir şey yok.
   '*Oh well*, there's nothing we can do.'

(ii) For *bari, oldu olacak en azından, hiç olmazsa, hiç değilse* 'at least' *keşke* 'if only' see 16.3 (v).

28.4 The effects of co-ordination and discourse connection

When identical items occur in co-ordinated constructions all but one of them may be omitted to avoid repetition. This kind of omission is called **ellipsis**. In Turkish, suffixes and clitics can be elided (28.4.1) as well as phrases (28.4.2). Ellipsis of noun phrases can also occur across sentence boundaries where a referent can be identified by the addressee from previous mention (28.4.3). For ellipsis as a result of *değil* 'not', see 20.2.3.

28.4.1 The elision of suffixes and clitics in co-ordinated constructions

If a series of conjoined phrases or clauses contain certain identical suffixes and/or clitics, these may be omitted in all of the conjuncts except the last one. For example, in (122) the copular marker *-(y)DI*, which appears on *giderdi*, can be omitted in the first two predicates, leaving *giyer* and *alır* as 'incomplete' forms in terms of the meaning expressed:

(122) Ziya her sabah paltosunu **giyer**(...), şemsiyesini **alır**(...) ve işe **gider*di*.**
'Every morning Ziya *would put on* his coat, *pick up* his umbrella and *leave* for work.'

This is known as 'suspended affixation'. Below we explain the most common types.

28.4.1.1 Elision of copular markers and person markers

A person marker from Group 2 (8.4.2) can be suspended if it is directly attached to one of the markers from Position 3 on the verb:

(123) Eskiden Kayseri'ye **gitmiş**(...), hatta orada **yaşamış*lar*.**
'*Apparently* at one time *they went* to Kayseri and even *lived* there.'

If the predicate contains a copular marker (8.3.2) and/or the generalizing modality marker *-DIr* (8.3.3), these can only be omitted together with any person marker that is present. The conjunct which is 'incomplete' can be either a subject complement, as in (124), or a verb inflected with one of the Position 3 suffixes, as in (125):

(124) **Öğretmen**(...) ve **bilim insanı-*ymış*.**
teacher and scientist-EV.COP
'*Apparently* s/he *is*/*was* a teacher and *a scientist*.'

(125) Hem sinema-ya **git-miş**(...) hem de biraz **gez-miş-*ti-m*.**
both cinema-DAT go-PF both also a.little go.around-PF-P.COP-1SG
'*I had* both *gone* to the cinema and *walked around* a bit.'

In alternative questions (19.1.2) which contain the combination copular marker + person marker, usually the suffixes in the *last* conjunct are omitted:

(126) Öğretmen **mi***ydiniz* (yoksa) öğrenci *mi*(…)?
'*Were you* a teacher, or a student?'

Of the Position 3 suffixes, those which can occur in suspended affixation constructions are *-(I)yor*, *-mIş*, *-(A/I)r/-z*, *-(y)AcAk*, *-mAlI* and *-mAktA*. Note that in 1st person negative aorist verb forms (which do not contain an aorist suffix (8.2.3.3 (iv)), e.g. *oyna-ma-m* (play-NEG-1SG) 'I don't/won't play') suspended affixation is not possible, and these have to appear in their full form in conjoined constructions.

28.4.1.2 Elision of nominal inflectional markers

In noun phrases, the following suffixes can be omitted:

(i) The plural suffix (8.1.1) can be omitted but only together with any other suffixes following it:

(127) bütün kitap(…) ve defter**lerimiz**
'all *our* book*s* and notebook*s*'

(ii) Case markers (8.1.3), the comitative/instrumental marker *-(y)lA/ile* (8.1.4), the suffix *-slz* 'without' (7.2.2.2), adjectival *-ki* (15.3.6-7) and pronominal *-ki* (18.5) can each be omitted on its own:

(128) Vapur hem Napoli(…) hem Venedik'**e** uğruyormuş.
'Apparently the boat stops *at* both Naples and Venice.'

(129) kitap(…) ya da defter**siz**
'*without* books or notebooks'

(130) öğretmen-ler(…) ve öğrenci-ler-**le**
teacher-PL and student-PL-COM
'*with* (the) teachers and (the) students'

If one of these suffixes occurs with the plural marker and a possessive suffix, all three can be omitted:

(131) köy(…), kasaba(…) ve kent**lerimizden**
'*from our* village*s*, small town*s* and citie*s*'

(iii) *-ki* can sometimes be omitted either on its own or with a preceding locative or genitive marker:

(132) ağaçta(…) ve yerde**ki** erikler
'(the) plums *that are* on the tree and on the ground'

(133) bilgisayar(…) ve yazıcınınki
'*the one belonging to* the computer and printer'

The omission of suffixes can create ambiguity:

(134) öğretmen(…) ve öğrencilerle
(i) 'with the teacher and the students'
(ii) 'with the teachers and the students'

28.4.1.3 Elision of other items: -(y)ken, bile, ml, (subordinator) ki

The following can also be omitted from all but the final conjunct:

(i) The adverbial marker -*(y)ken* (26.3.16 (iii)):

(135)   insanlar küçük(…) ve daha konuşmaz-***ken***
'*when* people are small and can't yet talk'

(ii) The connective *bile* 'even' (28.3.1.1 (iv)):

(136)   Dersini çalış-mış(…) ve odanı topla-mış-***sa-n bile*** sokağa çıkamazsın.
'You can't go out *even if you* have done your homework and tidied your room.'

(iii) The interrogative marker *ml* (11.1.1.5):

(137)   Gittin (…) ve gördün ***mü***?
'Have you gone and seen (it)?'

(iv) The subordinator *ki* (11.1.1.4):

(138)   Gördüm (…) ve biliyorum ***ki***…
'I have seen and know *that* .. .'

28.4.2 The elision of phrases in co-ordinated constructions

The following constituents can be elided when they are in co-ordinated constructions within the sentence:

(i) Determiners and adjectives:

(139) **yeşil bir** atkı ya da (…) şapka
'*a green* hat or (*a green*) scarf'

(ii) Adverbs and modifiers of adjectives and adverbs:

(140) **yavaşça** oturup (…) kalk-
'sit down (*slowly*) and get up *slowly*'

(141) **çok** şeker ve (...) cana yakın bir çocuk
'a *very* sweet and (*very*) lovable child'

(iii) Postpositions:

(142) karısı (...) ve kendisi **için**
'*for* his wife and (*for*) himself'

(iv) Verbs and verb phrases (see also 20.2.3):

(143) a. Ali odayı (...), Mehmet balkonu **temizledi**./
Ali odayı **temizledi**, Mehmet balkonu (...).
'Ali *cleaned* the room and Mehmet (*cleaned*) the balcony.'

b. Ali **odayı temizledi**, Mehmet de (...).
'Ali *cleaned* the room, and so [*did*] Mehmet.'

(144) Ali annesinin (...), Büşra babasının **evinde yaşıyor**.
'Ali *lives at his mother's house* and Büşra at her father's.'

Notice that the elided parts in Turkish and in the English translation belong to different conjuncts.

28.4.2.1 The elision of noun phrases in co-ordinated constructions

Noun phrases in subject, complement and possessor-modifier functions can be elided in co-ordinated constructions within the sentence and the use of pronouns is usually avoided:

(i) Subjects (see 18.1.5 for details):

(145) **Nuri** geldi ve (...) karşıma oturdu.
'*Nuri* came and sat opposite me.'

(ii) Complements:
Elision of complement noun phrases occurs regularly where they have identical referents and case markers.

(146) Zeki **köpekten** hem nefret ediyor, hem de (...) korkuyor.
(Oblique object)
'Zeki both hates and fears *dogs*.'

Where the referent is specific, a pronoun can be used in the place of the elided noun phrase:

(147) **Semra'yı** tanıdım ve (**onu**) çok sevdim.   (Direct object)
       'I got to know *Semra* and liked [*her*] very much.'

If the second or subsequent occurrence of a complement requires a different case marker from that used on its first occurrence, then a pronoun with the appropriate case marker is usually used. For example, *Semra* below is in the accusative case when it first occurs, but since the verb *hayran kal-* 'admire' requires a dative-marked noun phrase, the form *ona* 'for her' is likely to be used in the second conjunct:

(148) **Semra'yı** tanıdım ve (**ona**) hayran kaldım.
       'I got to know *Semra* and became full of admiration for *her*.'

(iii) Genitive and ablative modifiers (see also Chapter 14 (150)):

(149) **Esra'nın** anne(si) ve (…) babası
       'Esra's mother and father'

(150) Ali Zehra'nın mobilyalarını satın aldı, Büşra (…) kitaplarını (…)
       'Ali bought Zehra's furniture, Büşra her books.

28.4.3 The elision of noun phrases in other contexts

Unlike other types of phrase, noun phrases are regularly omitted in contexts other than co-ordinated constructions, wherever (i) the identity of the referent is unambiguous, and (ii) (in the case of subjects or possessors) no contrast is involved or emphasis required:

(151) Bugün **Ayşe**'yi gördüm. (…) Sana selam söyledi.
       'I saw *Ayşe* today. *She* sent you her love.'

For the conditions governing the omission of subject pronouns, and of genitive-marked pronouns expressing possessor-modifiers see 18.1.5.

Direct object noun phrases are also regularly omitted after their first mention, for as long as the identity of the referent can still be assumed to be unambiguously identifiable by the addressee:

(152) *Tante Rosa*'yı ilk defa 1970'lerde okudum ve (…) çok sevdim. Geçen hafta [Handan (…) bana verince] (…) yeniden okudum.
       'I first read *Tante Rosa* in the 1970s and liked [*it*] very much. Last week [when Handan gave [*it*] to me] I read [*it*] again.'

Noun phrase ellipsis also crosses the boundary between the utterances of different speakers, and occurs regularly in answers to questions:

(153) A. **Kitabını** buldun mu?
       'Have you found *your book*?'

      B. (…) Aramadım ki.
      'I haven't looked for [*it*].'

Another context in which noun phrase ellipsis occurs is where the referent is identified by non-linguistic means:

(154) A. (pointing at something) (…) Gördün mü?
      'See?'
      (lit. 'Have you seen [*that*]?')

      B. Tabii. İlk ben (…) farkettim.
      'Sure. I was the one who first noticed [*it*].'

Appendix 1: Reduplicated stems

List of emphatically reduplicated stems (9.1) starting with a consonant (all stems starting with a vowel are reduplicated with 'p'):

başka	bambaşka
bayağı	basbayağı
bedava	besbedava
belli	besbelli
beter	besbeter
beyaz	bembeyaz
boş	bomboş
bok	bombok
buruşuk	bumburuşuk
bütün	büsbütün
canlı	capcanlı, capacanlı
cavlak	cascavlak
cıbıldak	cıscıbıldak
cıvık	cıscıvık
çabuk	çarçabuk
çevre	çepçevre, çepeçevre
çıplak	çırçıplak, çırılçıplak
dar	dapdar
daracık	dapdaracık
derin	depderin
dik	dimdik
diri	dipdiri
doğru	dosdoğru
dolu	dopdolu
duru	dupduru
düz	dümdüz, düpedüz
düzgün	düpdüzgün
genç	gepgenç/gepegenç

geniş	gepgeniş
gündüz	güpegündüz
güzel	güpgüzel
kalın	kapkalın
kara	kapkara
karanlık	kapkaranlık
katı	kaskatı
kırmızı	kıpkırmızı
kısa	kıpkısa
kıvrak	kıskıvrak
kızıl	kıpkızıl
kirli	kipkirli
koca	koskoca
kocaman	koskocaman
kötürüm	köskötürüm
koyu	kopkoyu
kuru	kupkuru
mavi	masmavi
mor	mosmor
parça	paramparça
pembe	pespembe
perişan	perperişan
sağlam	sapasağlam
sarı	sapsarı
sebil	sersebil
sefil	sersefil
serin	sepserin
sıcacık	sımsıcacık
sıcak	sımsıcak
sıkı	sımsıkı
silik	sipsilik
sivri	sipsivri
siyah	simsiyah
soğuk	sopsoğuk
şirin	şipşirin
tamam	tastamam
taze	taptaze
temiz	tertemiz
toparlak	tostoparlak
yanlış	yapyanlış, yapayanlış
yalnız	yapayalnız
yassı	yamyassı
yaş	yamyaş
yeni	yepyeni

yeşil	yemyeşil
yumru	yusyumru
yuvarlak	yusyuvarlak
zayıf	zapzayıf

Appendix 2: Tense, aspect and modality markers

The following list shows all the suffixes used in Turkish to express tense, aspect and/or modality (Chapter 21), together with a brief indication of their meanings. Except where otherwise shown (by 'or' or the use of roman numerals), the various elements of meaning shown for each suffix are present simultaneously in every usage of that form. For example, every usage of -*DI* involves past tense, perfective aspect and factual modality. Individual occurrences of -*(A/I)r/-z*, on the other hand, while they may be open to more than one interpretation, may also fall into just one of the three patterns of meaning shown.

Verbal tense, aspect and modality suffixes (8.2.3)

-(y)Abil
Possibility (21.4.2.1)

(1) Hasan Fransızca oku-**yabil**-iyor.
    'Hasan can read French.'

(2) Yağmur yağ-**abil**-ir.
    'It may rain.'

-(y)AmAz
Negative possibility (21.4.2.1)

(3) Oraya gid-**e-me-z**-sin.
    'You can't go there.'

-DI
Past tense (21.2.1)
Perfective aspect (21.3, 21.3.1)
Neutral modality (direct knowledge) (21.4)

(4) Arabamı sat-**tı**-m.
   'I sold/have sold my car.'

-mIş
Relative past tense (21.2.1)
Perfective aspect (21.3, 21.3.1)
Evidential modality (indirect knowledge) (21.4.3)

(5) Burada yağmur yağ-**mış**.
   'Apparently, it rained/It seems to have rained here.'

The modality component of the meaning of *-mIş* is neutralized when the past copula *-(y)DI* is added, or the auxiliary verb *ol-* follows:

(6) O hafta çok yağmur yağ-**mış**-*tı*.
   'It had rained a lot that week.'

-(I)yor

(i) Imperfective aspect (progressive or habitual) (21.3.1–2)

Progressive

(7) Şu anda Ahmet futbol oyn-**uyor**.
   'Ahmet is playing football at the moment.'

(8) Sen telefon ettiğinde Ahmet futbol oyn-**uyor**-*du*.
   'Ahmet was playing football when you rang.'

Habitual

(9) Cumartesileri Ahmet futbol oyn-**uyor**(-*du*).
   'On Saturdays Ahmet plays (used to play) football.'

(ii) Scheduled future tense:

(10) Yarın Paris'e gid-**iyor**-uz.
    'We're going to Paris tomorrow.'

-mAktA
Imperfective aspect (progressive or habitual) (21.3.1–2)

Progressive

    (11) Şu sıralarda konferansımı hazırla-**makta**-yım.
         'At the moment, I'm preparing my lecture.'

Habitual

    (12) Cep telefonlarının kullanımı uçağın iletişim sistemini kötü yönde etkile-**mekte**-dir.
         'The use of mobile phones adversely affects the plane's communication system.'

-(y)AcAK

  (i) Relative future tense (21.2.3):

    (13) Burada dört ev yap-ıl-**acak**(*-tı*).
         'Four houses are/were going to be built here.'

  (ii) Non-fact modality (assumption) (*ol-* only) (21.4.1.4):

    (14) Kapı çaldı, Hasan ol-**acak**.
         'The door bell rang, that'll be Hasan.'

  (iii) Volitional modality (command) (21.4.4.2 (iv)):

    (15) Herkes saat ikide burada ol-**acak**, anlaşıldı mı?
         'Everyone is to be here at two o'clock, is that clear?'

-(A/I)r/-z (Aorist)

  (i) Imperfective (habitual) aspect (21.3.2) + generalizing modality (21.4.1.1):

    (16) Burada çok yağmur yağ-**ar**.
         'It rains a lot here.'

    (17) Para mutluluk getir-**mez**.
         'Money doesn't bring happiness.'

    (18) Öğrenciler çok kahve iç-**er**.
         '(The) students drink a lot of coffee.'

  (ii) Hypothetical modality (21.4.1.3):

    (19) Sen oradaki havayı beğen-**mez**-sin.
         'You wouldn't like the atmosphere there.'

  (iii) Future tense + non-fact modality (assumption) (21.4.1.4):

    (20) Oradan iki saatte gel-**ir**-siniz.
         'From there you'll get here in two hours.'

(iv) Volitional modality (21.4.4.5–6):

    (21) Bana yardım ed-**er** misiniz?   (Request)
         'Would you [please] help me?'

    (22) Bunu kimseye söyle-**me**-m.   (Promise)
         'I won't tell anyone about this.'

-mAlI

(i) Speaker-generated obligation (21.4.2.2):

    (23) Artık git-**meli**-yim.
         'I must go now.'

(ii) Non-fact modality (deduction) (*ol-* only) (21.4.1.4):

    (24) Bu ceket senin ol-**malı**.
         'This jacket must be yours.'

-sA

(i) Volitional modality (wish) (21.4.4.1):

    (25) Daha büyük bir arabamız ol-**sa**.
         'If only we had a bigger car.'

-sAm/-sAk

(ii) (1st person forms only, in questions) volitional modality (deliberation) (21.4.4.4):

    (26) Bu akşam ne yap-**sa**-k acaba?
         'What should we do this evening, I wonder?'

(zero), *-(y)In(Iz)*, *-sIn(lAr)* (Imperative) (8.4.4)

Volitional modality (command) (21.4.4.2 (i), (ii)):

    (27) Bu parayı Kaya'ya ver.
         'Give this money to Kaya.'

    (28) Düğmeye bas-**ın**-(ız).
         'Press the button.'

    (29) Ayşe bu akşam bana telefon et-**sin**.
         'I want/Tell Ayşe to ring me this evening.'

-(y)AyIm, *-(y)AlIm* (Optative, 1st person forms) (8.4.3)

Volitional modality (suggestion) (21.4.4.3):

    (30) Sana yardım ed-**eyim**.
         'Let me help you.'

(31) Biraz otur-**alım** mı?
'Shall we sit down for a while?'

Copular markers (used in nominal and verbal sentences) (8.3.2)
-(y)DI

(i) Past tense (21.2.1):

(32) Herkes bahçe-de-**ydi**.
'Everyone was in the garden.'

(33) Eğ len-iyor-**du**-k.
'We were having a good time.'

(ii) Counterfactual modality:

(34) Sen bu işi daha güzel yapar-**dı**-n.
'You would have done this job better.'

(35) Baştan söyle-**se-ydi**-n.
'If only you had said [so] at the start.'

-(y)mIş
Evidential modality (indirectly or newly acquired knowledge) (21.4.3):

(36) Aysel'in babası mühendis-**miş**.
'Apparently, Aysel's father is/was an engineer.'

(37) Her yaz Amerika'ya gid-iyor-lar-**mış**.
'It seems they go/went to America every summer.'

(38) Burası gerçekten güzel-**miş**.
'This really is a beautiful place.'

The generalizing modality marker *-DIr* (*8.3.3*)

(i) Generalizing modality (21.4.1.1–2):

(39) Demir ağır-**dır**.
'Iron is heavy.'

(40) İnsanlar tembel-**dir**.
'People are lazy.'

(ii) Non-fact modality (assumption) (21.4.1.4):

(41) Yorgun-sun-**dur**.
'You must be tired.'

(42) Toplantı artık bit-miş-**tir**.
'The meeting will have finished by now.'

Glossary of grammatical terms

ablative	one of the five **case markers** (*-DAn*), often expressing concepts such as *from, out of, through*
accusative	one of the five **case markers** (*-(y)I*), indicating a **direct object** which is **definite** or **specific**
active	(of a verb form or sentence) which expresses the concept of someone or something performing an action: *Peter Smith wrote a book*; opposed to **passive**
addressee	the person to whom a speaker is speaking, also called the hearer
adjectival (construction)	any linguistic structure that performs the function of an adjective
adjective	a word that ascribes some property, quality or status to the entity denoted by a noun (e.g. *blue, good, democratic, imaginary*)
adverb	a word that modifies (i.e. further specifies the meaning of) a verb, an adjective, another adverb, or a whole sentence (e.g. *easily, very, now, probably*)
adverbial (phrase)	any linguistic structure that performs the function of an adverb
adverbial clause	a finite or non-finite subordinate clause that performs an adverbial function in relation to its superordinate clause
affirmative	not negative
affricate	(consonant) produced by the gradual opening of the vocal tract after complete closure
agent	the item expressing the person(s) or thing(s) that perform the action of the verb; identical with the **subject** in an **active** sentence, but either suppressed or expressed as an optional constituent in a **passive** sentence
agreement	the requirement for the **predicate** to be marked

	for **person** and **number** in accordance with the person and number of the **subject**
allophone	a variant form of pronunciation of a **phonological unit**
alveolar	articulated with the tip or blade of the tongue against the alveolar ridge (the bony ridged area just behind the upper front teeth)
antecedent	a linguistic item (usually a noun phrase) which identifies the person(s) or thing(s) referred to by a pronoun
aorist	a **finite verb form** marked by the suffix *-(A/I)r* (or its negative counterpart *-z*); the aorist expresses either habitual aspect or various kinds of modality: generalizing, hypothetical, presumptive (with future time reference) or volitional
approximant	(here) a sound produced by bringing the tip of the tongue towards the alveolar ridge or hard palate
aspect	the temporal viewpoint from which an event is presented; see **perfective** and **imperfective**
aspirated	(of a **voiceless consonant**) whose articulation is followed by an escape of breath
attributive	(of an adjectival) occurring as part of a **noun phrase** (e.g. *pahalı bir araba* 'an *expensive* car'); cf. **predicative**
auxiliary verb	a verb that cannot stand on its own, but occurs either suffixed to another verb (bound auxiliary) or compounded with another verb or a nominal (free auxiliary)
back	(of a vowel) articulated with the tongue positioned at the back of the oral cavity
bilabial	(consonant) articulated by bringing both lips together
case marker/suffix	a nominal inflectional suffix attached to the **head** of a **noun phrase** to indicate the relationship of that noun phrase to other constituents of the sentence *ay-a bak* 'look *at* the moon'
categorial	the status of a noun phrase that is not marked for number (i.e. is **transnumeral**), and denotes an unspecified quantity/number from a designated class of persons or things
causative suffix	a suffix that turns an **intransitive** verb into a **transitive** one (e.g. *öl-* 'die', *öl-dür-* 'kill') or that expresses the concept of causing, securing or allowing the performance of the action of the verbal root; a clause in which the verb is marked with a **causative suffix**

causee	in a causative construction, the noun phrase expressing the person (or machine, etc.) that is made to perform the action expressed by the verbal root
clause	a syntactic structure that is either grammatically a *complete* sentence, or resembles a sentence in having a subject (overt or implied) and a predicate
clitic	a linguistic item which (although in most cases written as a separate word) cannot stand on its own, is dependent on the phrase that it follows (in Turkish), and is unstressed (e.g. the interrogative particle *mI*)
comitative	expressing the concept *(together) with/in the company of*
comitative/ instrumental marker	the suffix *-(y)lA* or its free-standing counterpart *ile*
complement	a noun phrase that 'completes' the meaning of another constituent, e.g. a verb (as in **Filmden hoşlandım** 'I enjoyed *the film*'), an adjective (as in **spora meraklı** 'interested *in sport*') or a postposition (*o günden beri* 'since *that day*'); see also **subject complement**
complex sentence	a sentence which, in addition to its **main clause**, contains at least one **subordinate clause**
compound verb form	composite verb form in which a **lexical verb** marked for relative tense or aspect is followed by one of the free **auxiliary verbs** *ol-* or *bulun-*, the auxiliary verb carrying either supplementary tense/aspect/modality marking or a **subordinating suffix**
concessive	(of an adverbial clause) expressing a situation that is in apparent contradiction to the superordinate clause (expressing the concept *although*); (of a discourse connective) marking the speaker's recognition that s/he is making an observation that appears to contradict what has been said before, but not irreparably (e.g. *actually*, *admittedly*)
conditional clause	an adverbial clause expressing the concept *if*
conjunct	one of the items joined by a conjunction
conjunction	a word that joins two or more items that have the same syntactic function (e.g. *and*, *or*, *but*)
connective	see **discourse connective**
constituent	any linguistic unit viewed as part of a larger construction
converb	the non-finite verb of an **adverbial clause**
co-ordination	the linking of two or more phrases or clauses that

	are equivalent to each other in terms of syntactic function (e.g. **Londra** ve **Paris** '*London* and *Paris*', **ucuz** ama **iyi** bir otel '*a cheap* but *good hotel*')
copula	forms which express the concept *be* (see 8.3.1)
copular markers	markers that contain the *-y-* form of the copula: the unstressable suffixes *-(y)DI*, *-(y)mIş* and *-(y)sA*
counterfactual	(of a conditional clause or a main clause that implies the fulfilment of a condition) expressing what is known not to have happened, or not to be the case (e.g. *(If you had told me) I would have come)*
dative	one of the five **case markers** (*-(y)A*), often expressing concepts such as *to*, *into*, *on to*
definite	the status of a noun phrase that refers to a specific entity or entities which the speaker assumes to be unambiguously identifiable by the addressee(s) (e.g. *France, the first house, these plates*)
demonstrative	a **determiner** or **pronoun** that has (literally or figuratively) a 'pointing' function (e.g. *this, those*)
dental	articulated with the tip of the tongue against the upper front teeth
denti-alveolar	articulated with the tip or blade of the tongue at the junction between the top teeth and the alveolar ridge
derivation	the creation of a new **lexical item**, by suffixation (e.g. *iyileş-* 'get better', *tuzlu* 'salty'), compounding (e.g. *karabiber* 'black pepper, *futbol takımı* 'football team') or reduplication *(simsiyah* 'jet black')
derivational suffix	a suffix which, when added to a stem, produces a new **lexical item** whose meaning is connected to that of the stem (e.g. *-lAş-* 'become', *-lI* 'having', 'characterized by')
derived	(of a word) that contains one or more (usually derivational) suffixes in addition to the root
desiderative	a modality that indicates intention, inclination, or temptation to perform an action.
determiner	a word whose function is to specify the limitation (or lack of limitation) of the potential referent of a noun phrase (e.g. **this** *city*, **some** *daily newspapers*, **every** *university student*)
direct object	the **complement** of a **transitive** verb, as in *John is building **a boat**, I've finished **my work***
discourse connective	a word or phrase which provides a cohesive link between two sentences or larger pieces of discourse, indicating how the content of what is newly uttered

	relates to what has gone before (e.g. *what's more, however, or rather, in short*); sometimes just called a **connective**
distributive numeral	a form of numeral expressing *one each, two each*, etc.
echo question	a question which partly (or in full) repeats a statement just made by another speaker, e.g. A: *John's bought a crocodile.* B: *He's bought what?/John's bought a crocodile?*
ellipsis (or elision)	the omission of a linguistic item that is readily identifiable from the context, e.g. *our* in *our friends and (. . .) neighbours*) or *I'm* in *Where are you? (. . .) Here.*
epenthetic vowel	a **high** vowel that appears in the last syllable of certain nouns, only in the **root** form or when a suffix beginning with a consonant is added (e.g. *resmi* 'his/her picture', but *resim* 'picture', *resimler* 'pictures')
evidential	a type of **modal** marking (with *-mIş* or *-(y)mIş*) which indicates that a statement is based upon knowledge acquired by the speaker indirectly
existential sentence	a **nominal sentence** which asserts (or, in the negative, denies) the existence or presence of some entity or entities; there are two types: **locative**, expressing the basic notion *there is an x (in y)*, and **possessive**, expressing the basic notion *x has y* (where *is* and *has* stand for any form of the verbs *be* and *have* respectively)
finite clause	a clause whose predicate is either a **finite verb** or identical in form to a **nominal sentence**
finite verb form	a verb form that can occur in a **simple sentence** or **main clause**
focused	(of a sentence constituent) emphasized by being pronounced with heavy stress
fricative	(consonant) produced through friction in the vocal tract resulting from two organs (e.g. tongue and teeth) coming very close together
front(ed)	(of a vowel) articulated with the tongue positioned at the front of the oral cavity
generic	the status of a noun phrase that (in any given utterance) is used with a generalizing function, to refer to an entire class of entities, or to a(ny) typical member of that class (e.g. *drugs* in *Drugs can kill* or *the tiger* in *The tiger is a carnivore*)

genitive	one of the five **case markers** (*-(n)In*), marking a noun phrase either as the possessor of another entity expressed in the sentence, or as the **subject** of certain types of **subordinate clause**
genitive-attracting pronouns	a set of pronouns which, when not plural-marked, require genitive case marking with certain post-positions
genitive-possessive construction	a composite **noun phrase** consisting of a **genitive-**marked noun phrase followed by a noun phrase marked with a **possessive suffix**: *ben-im ad-ım* 'my name', *kitab-ın fiyat-ı* 'the price of the book'
glide	a consonant whose articulation does not involve any closure or friction, also called a semi-vowel
glottal stop	consonantal sound produced by the audible release of a complete closure at the glottis (the aperture in the larynx between the vocal cords)
habitual	(of an **imperfective** verb form) presenting a situation as part of a recurring pattern
hard palate	the hard bony area in the roof of the mouth between the **alveolar** ridge and the **velum**
head	(i) the obligatory constituent (cf. **modifier**) of certain types of phrase: in particular, the verb in a **verb phrase** and the constituent furthest to the right in a **noun phrase**; (ii) the last constituent of a **noun compound**
high vowel	a vowel produced by raising the tongue above its neutral position
imperative	a **finite verb form** expressing a command
imperfective	(of a verb form) expressing a situation from an internal temporal **aspect**, as being in some sense incomplete and ongoing (e.g. *gidiyordum* 'I was going', 'I used to go'); see **progressive** and **habitual**
impersonal passive	a form that occurs in Turkish but not in English, namely the **passive** form of an **intransitive** verb (e.g. *sevinilir* 'one is pleased', 'people are pleased')
indefinite	the status of a noun phrase that either (i) refers to a **specific** entity (or set of entities) known to the speaker, but assumed not to be familiar to, or identifiable by, the addressee(s) (e.g. *a tiger* in *we saw a tiger today*) or (ii) denotes a **non-specific** entity (or set of entities), whose identity is unknown or unknowable to the speaker (e.g. *a tiger* in *I've never seen a tiger*)
indirect command	a noun clause whose content would, if converted

	into an independent sentence, express a command (e.g. *to wait there* in *They told me to wait there*)
indirect question	a noun clause whose content would, if converted into an independent sentence, express a question (e.g. *where Louise is* in *I don't know where Louise is*)
indirect statement	a noun clause whose content would, if converted into an independent sentence, express a statement (e.g. *you're right* in *I know you're right*)
inflected	(of a word) that contains at least one inflectional suffix
inflection	alteration of the grammatical form of a word by the addition (to the lexical form) of one or more **inflectional suffixes**
inflectional suffix	a suffix which changes the grammatical form of a word; in verbs, inflectional suffixes express categories such as voice, negation, tense, aspect, modality and person/number; in nominals they express categories such as number, possession and case
instrumental	the concept *with* denoting use of an instrument, or *by* denoting use of a means of transport or communication
intonational phrase	a unit of speech (one, or more usually, several words) containing one **primary stress** and a single
intonation contour	one of a number of distinctive patterns of rise and fall in the pitch of the voice
intransitive verb	a verb that either takes no complement (e.g. *laugh, walk, sleep*), or takes an **oblique object** (expressed in English using a preposition, e.g. *look (at/after/for)*
labio-dental	(consonant) articulated with the lower lip against the upper front teeth
lateral	(consonant) produced by air flowing around a complete closure formed in the mouth
lexical item	a linguistic form that one would expect to find as an item in a dictionary of the language; normally the uninflected form of a word
lexicalized stem	a term applied to an **inflected, derived, or compounded** form which, through usage, has acquired the status of a **lexical item** (e.g. *di-ye, karşı-lık* 'response', *üç beş* 'a few')
lexical verb	in a **compound verb form,** the first of the two verbs, and the one that provides the lexical (dictionary) meaning

linking sentence	a **nominal sentence** expressing the basic notion *x is y* (or, in the negative, *x is not y* (where *is* stands for any form of the verb *be*)
locative	one of the five **case markers** (-*DA*), expressing spatial, temporal or abstract location (*in, on, at*)
locative existential	see existential sentence
low vowel	a vowel produced by lowering the tongue below its neutral position
main clause	in a **complex sentence**, the clause which includes, and is **superordinate** to, all the others
mid vowel	a vowel produced with the tongue at a level intermediate between **high** and **low**
modal adverbial	an adverbial expressing e speaker's stance towards the utterance that is being made (e.g. *belki* 'perhaps', *maalesef* 'unfortunately')
modality	a grammatical category whose expression is linked with that of **tense** and **aspect**, and which concerns the speaker's degree of commitment to the truth of a statement, the speaker's attitude towards the potential occurrence of an event, or general notions of possibility or necessity
modifier	a non-obligatory constituent of certain types of phrase, which 'modifies' (i.e. makes more specific) the meaning of the **head**; nouns and noun compounds can be modified by determiners, numerals and adjectivals (*o dört büyük ağaç* 'those four big trees'), while verbs, adjectives and adverbs can be modified by adverbials *(erken gel-* 'come *early*', *fazla büyük* 'too big', *fazla erken* 'too early')
nasal	(sound) produced while the **velum** is lowered to allow the audible escape of air through the nose; in the case of nasal consonants, such as /m/ and /n/, there is complete closure of the oral cavity
nominal	a word belonging to one of the following (related) classes: noun, pronoun, adjective and adverb
nominal sentence	a sentence whose main or only clause either contains no verb or whose verb is one of the forms of the **copula**; the two types of nominal sentence are **linking sentences** and **existential sentences**
nominalized forms	forms derived from verbs by means of a **subordinating suffix** (such as -*DIK* or -*mA*), and functioning as nominals
nominal-verb	a **lexical item** functioning as a **verb**, which is

compound	formed by the combination of a nominal with a verb used as a free **auxiliary** (e.g. *mücadele et-*'fight', e.g. *karşı çık-* 'oppose')
non-definite	**indefinite or indefinite or categorial**
non-finite clause	a **subordinate clause** in which the verb is non-finite, i.e. marked with a **subordinating suffix**
non-specific	see under **indefinite**; also used as a cover term for **categorial and generic**
noun	a word that denotes a class of things or persons, a member of such a class, a substance, an abstract concept, or the proper name of a person or place (e.g. *table, girl, water, knowledge, Ahmet, Turkey*)
noun clause	a finite or non-finite subordinate clause that performs the function of a **noun phrase** within its superordinate clause
noun compound	a word-like unit which is made up of two nouns (e.g. *kız kardeş* 'sister', *balık lokantası* 'fish restau- rant)' or an adjective and a noun (e.g. *ilkbahar* 'spring'); the majority of noun compounds in Turkish are *-(s)I* compounds
noun phrase	any word or sequence of words that can function as the subject or object in a sentence (e.g. *it, the others, a very loud noise, Mary's uncle, the car you usually drive*); the **head** of a noun phrase may be a **noun**, a **noun compound**, or a **pronoun**
number	the distinction between singular and plural
object	see **direct object, oblique object**
oblique case markers	this term is applied to the dative, locative and ablative case markers, and sometimes also to the comitative/instrumental marker
oblique object	the **complement** of an **intransitive** verb, marked in Turkish by one of the **oblique case** markers, or by the **comitative/instrumental marker**: *Bun-a çok sevindim* 'I'm very pleased *about this*', *Mehmet'le alay ettiler* 'They made fun *of Mehmet*'
optative	a **finite** verb form expressing the speaker's (or, in questions, the hearer's) will or desire
ordinal numeral	a numeral which indicates an ordered position in a series (*first, second*, etc.)
palatal	(consonant) articulated with the blade of the tongue against the **hard palate**
palatalization	the pronunciation of a consonant as palatal in a

front-vowel environment, or the pronunciation of a back vowel in a relatively fronted position in the environment of certain palatal consonants

participle the non-finite verb of a **relative clause**

partitive construction a composite **noun phrase** (made up of a modifier noun phrase followed by a head noun phrase) used to express part of a whole, or to select one or more items from a type or set; the modifier has either **ablative** or **genitive** case marking, and the head may or may not have a 3rd person **possessive suffix**

passive (a verb form) which expresses that an action *is (or was) done* rather than that someone or something *does (or did)* it (although an **agent** may optionally be expressed within the clause): *A book **was written** (by Peter Smith)*

perfective (of a verb form) expressing an event from an external temporal **aspect**, as a completed whole (e.g. git**tim** 'I went')

person in a grammatical context this term refers to the distinction between 1st person (referring to the speaker or a group including the speaker), 2nd person (referring to the addressee(s)), and 3rd person (referring to other entities)

person marker a suffix attached to the predicate to indicate the **person** of the **subject**

phonological unit any one of the consonants and vowels that can be distinguished functionally (i.e. in terms of creating differences of meaning) in a particular language

phrase a syntactic unit (word group) that is less than a **clause**; the name of a particular type of phrase indicates either the class of word that constitutes its **head** (as in **verb phrase**, **postpositional phrase**), or the function of the phrase as a whole within the sentence (as in **adjectival phrase**, **adverbial phrase**), or it may include both of these meanings (as in **noun phrase**)

plosive (consonant) produced by the sudden opening of the vocal tract after complete closure

possessive existential see existential sentence

possessive suffix one of a set of nominal inflectional suffixes attached to the **head** of a **noun phrase**; while the 3rd person singular possessive suffix has other additional functions, the function shared by all possessive suffixes is to indicate the grammatical person (1st, 2nd, 3rd,

	singular/plural) of the possessor of the entity denoted by the noun phrase: *evimiz* 'our house', *kapısı* 'his/her/its door'
post-alveolar	(consonant) articulated towards the back of the alveolar ridge (see **alveolar**)
postposition	a word which, together with the noun phrase complement that it follows, forms a phrase with an adverbial or adjectival function: *bütün bunlardan sonra* '*after* all this', *dolabın üstünde* '*on top of* the cupboard'; Turkish postpositions usually correspond to prepositions in English
predicate	in a verbal sentence or subordinate clause, the **verb**; in a nominal sentence or non-verbal small clause, the **subject complement** plus (if present) the **copula**
predicative	occurring as (part of) a nominal **predicate**, i.e. as a **subject complement**
primary stress	the acoustically most prominent syllable in an **intonational phrase**
productive	(of a suffix) that regularly has a particular meaning and can be used freely with a particular type of stem
progressive	(of an **imperfective** verb form) expressing an event or state as ongoing at a specific reference point
pronoun	an expression used when referring to persons or things that have previously been mentioned, whose referents are obvious from the context or whose content is only partially specified (e.g. *he, those, I, herself, someone, anything*)
proposition	the content of a sentence
quantifier	**determiner** or **pronoun** that expresses quantity in non-numerical terms (e.g. *many, much, some, all; someone, everything*)
reduplication	the repetition of a word or part of a word, as a lexical or grammatical process (e.g. *bambaşka* 'quite different', *birer birer* 'one by one', *rahat rahat* 'comfortably')
referent	the person(s) or thing(s) referred to by a speaker in a particular instance of the use of a noun phrase
referential status	the status of a **noun phrase**, on any particular occasion of its use, in terms of the type of reference it makes to entities in the world; see **definite, indefinite, categorial, specific, generic**
register	a variety of language defined by its use in particular social situations or text types (e.g. colloquial, formal, legal)

relative clause	a finite or non-finite subordinate clause that performs an **adjectival** or, in the case of headless relative clauses, a pronominal function within its superordinate clause
relative tense	**tense** marking that locates an event as prior to, simultaneous with, or subsequent to, any refer-ence point established by the context
resumptive pronoun	a pronoun referring (i) in sentences with certain types of relative clause, to the head of the noun phrase qualified by the relative clause, and (ii) in the superordinate clause of a universal conditional clause, to the entity or class defined by the conditional clause
root	the minimal form of a word, not including any suffixes, whether derivational or inflectional
round(ed)	(of a vowel) produced with the lips in a rounded position
-(s)I compound	a **noun compound** consisting minimally of two juxtaposed nouns, the second of which (the **head**) is marked with the 3rd person possessive suffix *-(s)I* (e.g. *otobüs durağı* 'bus stop')
simple sentence	a sentence consisting of just one clause (a **main clause**)
small clause	a type of **finite noun clause** whose subject is also the subject or object of the **main clause**
specific	a term encompassing both **definite** and one of the two types of **indefinite**; see also **non-specific**
stem	any linguistic item to which suffixes can be added, whether a simple root or a combination of a root plus suffix(es)
stress	the high pitch and loudness with which a syllable is uttered relative to others in the same word or sequence of words
subject	in an **active** sentence or clause, the item expressing the person(s) or thing(s) that perform the action of the verb: *Susan plays tennis*, or are described by the **predicate**: *The children are happy*; in a **passive** sentence or clause, the item expressing the person(s) or thing(s) that undergo the action of the verb: *Susan was beaten in today's match*
subject complement	a noun phrase or adjectival phrase that forms (part of) the **predicate** of a **linking sentence** (e.g. *Siz komşumsunuz* 'You are *my neighbour*') or of a

	small clause (*Sizi komşu sayıyorum* 'I consider you a neighbour')
subordinate clause	a clause which forms a constituent within a **complex sentence**; there are three functional types: **noun clauses**, **relative clauses**, and **adverbial clauses**
subordinating suffix	one of a range of suffixes (e.g. *-mAK, -(y)An, -(y)ken*) that mark a predicate as **non-finite**, and thus the clause in which it occurs as a **subordinate clause**; apart from *-(y)ken* and the conditional copula marker *-(y)sA*, subordinating suffixes can be attached only to verbal predicates
subordinator	any linguistic item that marks a **subordinate clause**, whether a separate word such as *diye* or *ki*, or a **subordinating suffix**
suffix	a linguistic item that cannot stand on its own, but is added to a **root** or **stem** to form part of the same word; see **derivational suffix** and **inflectional suffix**
superordinate clause	the clause within which a **subordinate clause** occurs; this may be either the main clause of the sentence or another subordinate clause
tap	consonant produced by a single rapid contact between the tongue and the roof of the mouth
tense	the grammatical marking of location in time: past, present or future (see also **relative tense**)
topic	a constituent taken as indicating what the sentence is 'about'; this usually occurs at the beginning of the sentence, but if marked by the topic-shifter *dA* it can occur in other positions also
topic shifter	a linguistic item which marks a change of **topic**
transitive verb	a verb (such as *al-* 'take', *iste-* 'want') that requires to be complemented by a **direct object** expressing an entity or entities directly affected by its action; the direct object can be omitted in Turkish if it is obvious from the context
transnumeral	(of a noun phrase) neutral with regard to **number**
universal conditional clause	a Turkish conditional clause that includes a **wh-phrase**; such clauses express the concepts *whoever*, *wherever*, etc.
universal quantifier	**quantifier** denoting an entire class (e.g. *all*, *each*, *everyone*)
unmarked order sentence	(a sentence with) the most neutral order of constituents found in contexts in which no information is presupposed, and no constituent is given special emphasis

velar	(consonant) articulated with the back of the tongue against the **velum**
velum	the mobile fleshy area at the back of the mouth, behind the hard palate; also known as the soft palate
verb	a word that expresses an action, event, process or state, and which, in Turkish, takes verbal suffixes, such as the infinitive suffix *-mAk* or the imperfective suffix *-(I)yor*: *yaz-* 'write', *düş-* 'fall', *eri-* 'melt', *görün-* 'seem'
verbal noun	the non-finite verb of a **noun clause**
verbal sentence	a sentence whose main or only clause has a finite verb (other than *ol-* in its copular function) as its predicate
verb phrase	that part of a clause which consists of the verb together with its complement(s) and any modifying adverbials
voiced consonant	a consonant pronounced while the vocal cords are vibrating (e.g. /b/, /d/, /g/, /z/)
voiceless consonant	a consonant pronounced while the vocal cords are not vibrating (e.g. /p/, /t/, /k/, /s/)
voice suffix	collective term for the **causative**, **passive**, reflexive and reciprocal suffixes, which precede all other inflectional suffixes on the verb stem
volitional utterance	a type of sentence (distinguished from statements and questions) which expresses the speaker's (or in interrogative forms the hearer's) will or desire (e.g. *Buraya gel!* 'Come here!' *Gidelim mi?* 'Shall we go?')
wh-phrase	a questioning expression used in questions other than yes/no questions or alternative questions; so named because most of the Engish expressions in this class (*who*, *where*, *which*, etc.) begin with *wh-*

Bibliography

Akar, D. (1988) Some syntactic properties of Turkish interjections, in S. Koç (ed.) *Studies on Turkish linguistics: Proceedings of the Fourth International Conference on Turkish Linguistics*, 265–74. Ankara: METU.
Atalay, B. (1942) *Türk Dilinde Ekler ve Kökler üzerine bir Deneme*. İstanbul: Matbaai Ebüzziya.
Aygen, G. (2002) Finiteness, case and clausal architecture. Doctoral dissertation, Harvard University.
Bainbridge, M. (1980–1987) *A Comprehensive Turkish Course* (in four stages, each consisting of five books plus cassettes). SOAS, University of London.
Banguoğlu, T. (1974) *Türkçenin Grameri*. İstanbul: Baha Matbaası.
Bozşahin, C. (2003) Gapping and word order in Turkish, in A. S. Özsoy, D. Akar, M. Nakipoğlu-Demiralp, E.E. Erguvanlı-Taylan and A. Aksu-Koç (eds.) *Studies in Turkish Linguistics: Proceedings of the Tenth International Conference on Turkish Linguistics*, 95–104. İstanbul: Boğaziçi Üniversitesi Yayınevi.
Bussmann, H. (1996) *Routledge Dictionary of Language and Linguistics* (translated and edited by G. P. Trauth and K. Kazzazi). London: Routledge.
Cevat, M. [Emre] (1931) *Yeni bir Gramer Metodu Hakkında Layıha*, vol. 1. İstanbul: Devlet Matbaası.
Charette, M. (2004) Defining the structure of Turkish words, in A. Bellem and K. Rowan (eds.) *SOAS Working Papers in Linguistics* 13, 49–79. London: SOAS.
Charette, M. and Göksel, A. (1998) Licensing constraints and vowel harmony in Turkic languages, in E. Cyran (ed.) *Structure and Interpretation: Studies in Phonology*, 65–88. Lublin: Folium.
Crystal, D. (1991) *A Dictionary of Linguistics and Phonetics* (3rd edition). Oxford: Blackwell.
Demiray, K. (1994) *Temel Türkçe Sözlük* (3rd edition). İstanbul: İnkılâp Kitabevi.
Demircan, Ö. (1978) *Türkiye Türkçesinin Ses Düzeni, Türkiye Türkçesinde Sesler*. Ankara: Türk Dil Kurumu Yayınları.
Demircan, Ö. (2000) *Türkçenin Ezgisi*. İstanbul: Yıldız Teknik Üniversitesi Vakfı Yayınları.
Demirok, Ö (2017). A Compositional Semantics for Turkish Correlatives, in Aaron Kaplan, Abby Kaplan, M. K. McCarvel, and E. J. Rubin (eds.) *Proceedings of the 34th West Coast*

Conference on Formal Linguistics, 159–166. Somerville, MA: Cascadilla Proceedings Project.

Denwood, A. (2002) K~Ø: Morpho-phonology in Turkish, in C. Colella and S. Hellmuth (eds.) *SOAS Working Papers in Linguistics* 12. London: SOAS.

Deny, J. (1921) *Grammaire de langue turque (dialecte osmanli)*. Paris: Leroux.

Dizdaroğlu, H. (1976) *Tümcebilgisi*. Ankara: Türk Dil Kurumu Yayınları. Ediskun, H. (1963) *Yeni Türk Dilbilgisi*. İstanbul: Remzi Kitabevi.

Ediskun. H. (1985) *Türk Dilbilgisi*. İstanbul: Remzi Kitabevi.

Elöve, A. U. (1941) *Türk Dili Grameri (Osmanlı Lehçesi)*. İstanbul: Maarif Matbaası. [Turkish translation of Deny 1921, with additional notes.] Emre, A. C. (1945) *Türk Dilbilgisi*. Ankara: Türk Dil Kurumu Yayınları.

Enç, M. (1986) Topic switching and pronominal subjects in Turkish, in D. I. Slobin and K. Zimmer (eds.) *Studies in Turkish Linguistics*, 195–208. Amsterdam: John Benjamins.

Enç, M. (1991) The semantics of specificity. *Linguistic Inquiry* 22.1: 1–25.

Erdal, M. (1998) On the verbal noun in *-(y)Iş*, in *Doğan Aksan Armağanı*, 53–68. Ankara: Ankara Üniversitesi Basımevi.

Erdal, M. (2000) Clitics in Turkish, in A. Göksel and C. Kerslake (eds.) *Studies on Turkish and Turkic Languages; Proceedings of the Ninth International Conference on Turkish Linguistics*, 41–55. Wiesbaden: Harrassowitz Verlag.

Ergin, M. (1989) *Türk Dil Bilgisi*. İstanbul: Bayrak Basım-Yayın-Tanıtım.

Erguvanlı, E. E. (1984) *The Function of Word Order in Turkish Grammar*. Berkeley: University of California Press.

Erguvanlı-Taylan, E. (1986) An odd case in the causative construction in Turkish. Papers from the 15th Annual Regional Meeting of the Chicago Linguistics Society. Chicago: University of Chicago Press.

Erguvanlı-Taylan, E. (2015) *The Phonology and Morphology of Turkish*. İstanbul: Boğaziçi Üniversitesi Yayınevi.

Erkman-Akerson, F. and Ozil, Ş. (1998) *Türkçe'de Niteleme: Sıfat İşlevli Yan Tümceler*. İstanbul: Simurg Yayınları.

Gencan, T. N. (1971) *Dilbilgisi* (2nd edition). Ankara: Türk Dil Kurumu Yayınları.

Golstein, B. (1999) *Grammaire du Turc: Ouvrage pratique à l'usage des francophones* (2nd edition). Paris and Montreal: L'Harmattan.

Göknel, Y. (date not indicated) *Modern Türkçe Dilbilgisi*. İzmir: Hür Efe Matbaası.

Göksel, A. (1993) Levels of representation and argument structure in Turkish. Doctoral dissertation, SOAS, University of London.

Göksel, A. (1998) Linearity, focus and the postverbal position in Turkish, in L. Johanson with É. Á. Csató, V. Locke, A. Menz and D. Winterling (eds.) *The Mainz Meeting*, 85–106. Wiesbaden: Harrossowitz Verlag.

Göksel, A. and Özsoy, A. S. (2000) Is there a focus position in Turkish?, in A. Göksel and C. Kerslake (eds.) *Studies on Turkish and Turkic Languages; Proceedings of the Ninth International Conference on Turkish Linguistics*, 219–28. Wiesbaden: Harrassowitz Verlag.

Göksel, A. and Özsoy, A. S. (2003) *dA*: a focus/topic associated clitic in Turkish'. *Lingua* 113, no.11: 1143–67.

Görgülü, E. (2006) Variable wh-words in Turkish. MA thesis, Boğaziçi University

Griffiths, J. and Güneş, G. (2015) Ki Issues in Turkish, in M. Kluck, D. Ott and M. de Vries (eds.) *Parenthesis and Ellipsis; Cross-Linguistic and Theoretical Perspectives*, 173–217. Berlin: De Gruyter Mouton.

Haig, G. (1997) *Relative Constructions in Turkish*. Wiesbaden: Harrassowitz Verlag.
Hankamer, J. (1986) Finite state morphology and left to right phonology. *Proceedings of the West Coast Conference on Formal Linguistics* 5: 41–52.
Hankamer, J. and Knecht, L. (1976) The role of the subject/non-subject distinction in determining the choice of relative clause participle in Turkish. *Harvard Studies in Syntax and Semantics* 2: 197–219.
Hazai, G. (1978) *Kurze Einführung in das Studium der türkischen Sprache*. Budapest: Akadémiai Kiadó.
Hengirmen, M. (1995) *Türkçe Dilbilgisi*. Ankara: Engin Yayınevi.
Iatridou, S. (2013). Looking for Free Relatives in Turkish (and the unexpected places this leads to), in U. Özge (ed.) *Proceedings of Workshop on Altaic Formal Linguistics*, 129–152. Cambridge, MA: MIT Working Papers in Linguistics.
İnce, Atakan 2009. Dimensions of ellipsis: Investigations in Turkish 2009. PhD dissertation. University of Maryland.
Inkelas, S. (1996) The interaction of phrase and word rules in Turkish. *Linguistic Review* 13: 193–217.
Inkelas, S. (1999) The exceptional stress-attracting suffixes in Turkish: Representations versus the grammar, in R. Kager, H. van der Hulst and V. Zonneveld (eds.) *The Prosody-Morphology Interface*, 134–87. Cambridge: Cambridge University Press.
Inkelas, S. and Orgun, O. (1995) Level ordering and economy in the lexical phonology of Turkish. *Language* 71: 763–93.
Johanson, L. (1990) Studien zur türkeitürkischen Grammatik, in G. Hazai (ed.) *Handbuch der Türkischen Sprachwissenschaft* Teil I: 146–301. Wiesbaden: Otto Harrassowitz.
Kabak, Barış. (2007). Turkish suspended affixation. *Linguistics* 45 (2): 311–347.
Kabak, B. and Vogel, I. (2001) 'The phonological word and stress assignment in Turkish'. *Phonology* 18: 315–360.
Kelepir, M. (2000) To be or not to be faithful, in A. Göksel and C. Kerslake (eds.) *Studies on Turkish and Turkic Languages: Proceedings of the Ninth International Conference on Turkish Linguistics*, 11–18. Wiesbaden: Harrassowitz.
Kelepir, M. (2001) Topics in Turkish syntax: clausal structure and scope. Doctoral dissertation, MIT.
Kerslake, C. (1998) Ottoman Turkish, in L. Johanson and É. Á. Csató (eds.) *The Turkic Languages*, 179–202. London: Routledge.
Kerslake, C. (2001) 'Does Turkish prefer events to states?' *Turkic Languages* 5: 198–215.
Kerslake, C. (2003) 'A new look at conditional constructions in Turkish', in A. S. Özsoy, D. Akar, M. Nakipoğlu-Demiralp, E. E. Erguvanlı-Taylan, A. Aksu-Koç (eds.) *Studies in Turkish Linguistics*, 215–26. İstanbul: Boğaziçi Üniversitesi Yayınevi.
Kılıçaslan, Y. (2003) Syntax of information structure in Turkish. *Linguistics* 42/4: 717–65.
Kissling, H. J. (1960) *Osmanisch-türkische Grammatik*. Wiesbaden: Otto Harrassowitz.
Kononov, A. N. (1956) *Grammatika Sovremennogo Tureckogo Literaturnogo Jazika*. Moskva: Izdatel'stvo Akademii Nauk SSSR.
Kornfilt, J. (1996) On copular clitic forms in Turkish, in A. Alexiadou, N. Fuhrkop, P. Law and S. Löhken (eds.) *ZAS Papers in Linguistics* 6: 96–114. Berlin: Zentrum für Allgemeine Sprachwissenschaft.
Kornfilt, J. (1997) *Turkish*. London: Routledge.
Kornfilt, Jaklin (2005). Free Relatives as Light-headed Relatives in Turkish, in H. Broekhuis, N. Corver, R. Huybregts, U. Kleinhenz and J. Koster (eds.) *Organizing Grammar: Studies in Honor of Henk van Riemsdijk*, 340–349. Berlin: Mouton de Gruyter.

Kural, M. (1994) Scrambling in Turkish. UCLA ms.
Kural, M. (1997) Postverbal constituents in Turkish and the linear correspondence axiom. *Linguistic Inquiry* 28: 498–521.
Lees, R. B. (1961) *The Phonology of Modern Standard Turkish*. Uralic and Altaic Series 6. Bloomington: Indiana University.
Lewis, G. (1999) *The Turkish Language Reform: A Catastrophic Success*. Oxford: Oxford University Press.
Lewis, G. (2000) *Turkish Grammar* (2nd edition). Oxford: Oxford University Press.
Matthews, P. H. (1997) *The Concise Oxford Dictionary of Linguistics*. Oxford: Oxford University Press.
Moser-Weithmann, B. (2001) *Türkische Grammatik*. Hamburg: Helmut Buske Verlag.
Nakipoğlu, M. (2009) The semantics of the Turkish accusative marked definites and the relation between prosodic structure and information structure. *Lingua* 119: 1253–1280.
Nash, R. (1973) *Turkish Intonation; An Instrumental Study*. The Hague: Mouton.
Özbek, N. (2000) *Yani, işte, şey, ya*: interactional markers of Turkish, in A. Göksel and C. Kerslake (eds.) *Studies on Turkish and Turkic Languages; Proceedings of the Ninth International Conference on Turkish Linguistics*, 393–401. Wiesbaden: Harrassowitz Verlag.
Özel, S. (1977) *Türkiye Türkçesinde Sözcük Türetme ve Bileştirme*. Ankara: Türk Dil Kurumu Yayınları.
Özge, U. (2003) A tune-based account of Turkish information structure. M.Sc. thesis, Middle East Technical University.
Özsoy, A. S. (1999) *Türkçe*. İstanbul: Boğaziçi Üniversitesi Yayınları.
Özsoy, A. S. (2002) On "small clauses", other "bare" verbal complements and feature checking, in E. E. Erguvanlı-Taylan (ed.) *The Verb in Turkish*, 213–38. Amsterdam: John Benjamins.
Özsoy, A. S. (2004) *Türkçe'nin Yapısı - I; Sesbilim*. İstanbul: Boğaziçi Üniversitesi Yayınları.
Öztürk, B. (1999) Turkish as a non-pro-drop language, in E. E. Erguvanlı- Taylan (ed.) *The Verb in Turkish*, 239–59. Amsterdam: John Benjamins.
The Redhouse Turkish-English Dictionary (1999). İstanbul: SEV Matbaacılık ve Yayıncılık A. Ş.
Rona, B. (1972) Lectures given on the structure of Modern Turkish at Boğaziçi University, İstanbul.
Schroeder, C. (1997) "Relative" *ki*-clauses and the structure of spoken Turkish', in K. İmer and N.E. Uzun (eds.) *Proceedings of the VIIIth International Conference on Turkish Linguistics*, 347–362. Ankara:Ankara Üniversitesi Basımevi.
Schroeder, C. (1999) *The Turkish Nominal Phrase in Spoken Discourse*. Wiesbaden: Harrassowitz Verlag.
Sebüktekin, H. (1971) *Turkish-English Contrastive Analysis*. The Hague: Mouton.
Sebüktekin, H. (1975) *An Outline of English-Turkish Contrastive Phonology: Segmental Phonemes*. İstanbul: Boğaziçi Üniversitesi.
Sebüktekin, H. (1997) *Turkish for Foreigners/Yabancılar için Türkçe*, vols. 1–2 (2nd edition). İstanbul: Boğaziçi Üniversitesi Yayınları.
Sezer, E. (1986) An autosegmental analysis of compensatory lengthening in Turkish, in L. Wetzels and E. Sezer (eds.) *Studies in Compensatory Lengthening*, 227–50. Dordrecht: Foris.

Sezer, E. (1978) Eylemlerin çoğul öznelere uyumu. *Genel Dilbilim Dergisi*, 25–32. Ankara: Ankara Dilbilim Çevresi Derneği.
Sezer, E. (2002) Finite inflection in Turkish, in E. E. Erguvanlı-Taylan (ed.) *The Verb in Turkish*, 1–46. Amsterdam: John Benjamins.
Slobin, D. I. and Aksu, A. A. (1982) Tense, aspect and modality in the use of the Turkish evidential, in P. J. Hopper (ed.) *Tense-Aspect: Between Semantics and Pragmatics*, 185–200. Amsterdam: John Benjamins.
Swift, L. B. (1963) *A Reference Grammar of Modern Turkish*. The Hague: Mouton.
Şener, S. and İşsever, S. (2003) The interaction of negation with focus: *ne...ne...* phrases in Turkish. *Lingua* 113/11: 1089–117.
Tansu, M. (1963) *Durgun Genel Ses Bilgisi ve Türkçe*. Ankara: Türk Tarih Kurumu Basımevi.
Tekin, T. (2000) *Orhun Türkçesi Grameri*. (Türk Dilleri Araştırmaları Dizisi 9.) Ankara: Yayınları.
Underhill, R. (1976) *Turkish Grammar*. Cambridge, MA: MIT Press. Underhill, R. (1986) Bibliography of modern linguistic work on Turkish, in D. I. Slobin and K. Zimmer (eds.) *Studies in Turkish Linguistics*, 23–51. Amsterdam: John Benjamins.
Underhill, R. (1988) A lexical account of Turkish accent, in A. Sezer (ed.) *Studies on Turkish Linguistics*. Ankara: Middle East Technical University.
Uygun, D. B. (2000) The question particle and movement in Turkish. MA dissertation, Boğazici University, İstanbul.
van Schaaik, G. (1999) The order of nominalizations in Turkish. *Turkic Languages* 3: 87–120.
van Schaaik, G. (2000) Higher order compounds in Turkish: some observations, in A. Göksel and C. Kerslake (eds.) *Studies on Turkish and Turkic Languages, Proceedings of the Ninth International Conference on Turkish Linguistics*, 113–120. Wiesbaden: Harrassowitz Verlag.
van Schaaik, G. (2020) Turkish. Oxford: Oxford University Press.
von Gabain, A. (1988) *Eski Türkçe'nin Grameri* (translated by M. Akalın). Ankara: Türk Tarih Kurumu Basımevi.
Zimmer, K. and Orgun, O. (1999) Turkish, in *Handbook of the International Phonetic Association*, 154–6. Cambridge: Cambridge University Press.

Index

The index is arranged according to the Turkish alphabet for which see pp. xliii–xliv. Any parts of a suffix that are subject to variation are shown in capital letters, e.g. *-lAr, -sIn, -DI* (pp. 41–42).

As explained in the text (pp. 42–43), many suffixes have an initial vowel or consonant that is omitted in certain contexts; these are shown in brackets, e.g. *-(A)l, -(y)AcAK*. Such entries are listed according to the letter which appears in the brackets. As a result, e.g. the 2nd person plural possessive suffix *-(I)nIz* appears under 'I', and the 2nd person plural imperative suffix *-(y)In(Iz)* appears under 'Y'.

We indicate the grammatical category of an entry only where there may be potential ambiguity or confusion. In entries with a large number of references, we use bold to indicate the most prominent one.

A (interjection) 51, 55
-*A* 51, 55
ablative case marker *see* -*DAn*
ablative-marked noun phrase **184–5**; as adjectival 198, 213; as adverbial 148, 234, 239–40; as complement/modifier **147**, 184, 190–3, 205, 219, 430, 439; as object of comparison 202–4
acaba 316, 372–3
-*(A)C* 51, 57
-*(A)cAn* 51
accusative case marker *see* -*(y)I*
accusative-marked noun phrase **187**, 384, 393–4, 429; as subject of small clause 447–9; position of 404–5; *see also* direct object
adına 33; 'for', 'in order to', 498; 'in the name of', 'on behalf of' 263
adjective/adjectival 48, **Ch. 15**, **Ch. 25**; as attributive/modifier 102, 105, 196; comparative 202–4; complement of 205; as compound 103; dislocated 415; doubled 98; intensive forms/intensification 95–6, 98, 197, **561–3**; modification of 201–2; noun compound 102; predicative 196; pronominalized 288; reduplicated 95–6, 98, 561–3;
and stress 32; superlative 204–5; used adverbially 149; and word order 108, 168; *see also* relative clause
adverb(ial) 48–9, 148–9, **Ch. 16**, as modifier 201–2, 222–3; and stress/intonation 27, 35; and word order 399–402; *see also* adverbial/converbial clause; demonstrative, directional, manner, modal, place, time adverbials
adverbial/converbial clause **Ch. 26**; questioning part of 314–5
agent 153–9, 219, 462
agreement: subject-predicate 132–9; possessor-possessed 187–9; in small clauses 449–50
-*AğAn/-AgAn* 51
-*(A/I)cIK see -CAK₁*
-*(A/I)klA* 55
-*(A/I)r* (der.) 52, 475
-*(A/I)r/-z* (aor.) 75, **78–9**, **341–344**, 566–7; in generalizations 349–50, 396; in conditional clauses 511–14; and referential status 395–6; ___ *gibi* 93, 496; -*(A/I)rcAsInA* 93, -*(A/I)r...-mAz* 94, 502; *see also* compound verb forms
-*(A)K* 51, 56

aksine 548
-(A)l 52, 56
-AlA 55
-(A)m 52
ama 541–2; *ama...ama* 541
-(A)mAK 52
-(A)n 57
-(A)nAK 52
ancak 236, 245–6, 541–2
ane- 57
animacy: of agent 154; of causee 150; in compounds 99; of direct object 393; of *kendi* 270–2; of subject 133, **134–5**, 399; and *tane* 289
anlaşılan 223–4
aorist see *-(A/I)r/-z*
apostrophe xliv, xlv
approximations 60, 173, 209
-Ar/-Art (caus.) 56, 150–3, 159–60
Arabic xxx–xxxiv, xxxvii, xliv, 10, 12, 15, 17–18, 27, 51, 57, 60–1, 63–4, 534, 546
-(A)rI 57
artık 236, 328
asıl 245
asla 331
aslında 554
aspect **Ch. 21**, **341–8**, **564–8**; habitual **342–4**, **346–7**, 374–5, 470–3, 513–14; imperfective 341; markers 75–81; in nominal sentences 130, **345–7**; perfective 130, **341**; in non-finite clauses 445–7, 449–50, 468–73, 489–92; progressive 338, **342–5**; and referential status 395–7; see also compound verb forms
aspiration 4
assumptions 352, 356, 375
-(A)ş 56
aşırı 243
-(A)t 57
auxiliary verb 160–4; see also *bulun-, -ol-*
-(A)v 52
axioms (universal truths) 349
-(A)y 52, 57
aynı 207; ___*-sı* 289
ayrıca 537
az 204; ___ *daha/kalsın* 243, 357

background information/backgrounding 408, 41012
bakalım 317
bakarsın 223, 420

bari 225–6, 369
başta 222
-baz 58
bazı 206; ___*-sı*; 38, 136–7, 192
belki 224
beneficiary 148, **151–2**, 159, 181
beri 235, 254–5, 288
bil-: 'know' 161, 322, 420, 438; 'think' 320, 447–50; and stress 439
bilabial(ization) 4, 5, 7–9
bile 325, 391, **410**, 475, 534, 537–8; and stress 119–20, 325, 535
biliyorsun 224, 420
bir: (adv.) 483; ___ *an önce* 237; ___ *daha* 237, 328; ___ *de* 534; ___ *kere* 548; ___ *yana* 538; a(n) (det.) 169–70, 171–2, 206, 383, 391–2; ___ *şey* 291–2; (one) 208, 212–13; *bir... bir* (conj.) 539
biraz 169, 206, 243, 256
birbir- (pronoun)158, **278–9**
birçok 169, 171; *birçoğu* 137
biri(si) 289, 291
birkaç 289; ___*-ı* 38, 136–7, 192
birtakım 206
biz(ler) 269–70
body-part-denoting nouns 99
böyle: (adv.) **240–1**, 243; (det.) ___ *(bir)* 207, 391; ___ *-si* 289; ___ *-sine* 243
bu: (adv.) 242–3; (det.) 207; (pronoun) 285–6; ___ *gibi* 207; ___ *kadar(ı)* 142, 192, 206, 289; ___*-nun üzerine* 550; ___ *yana* 255; ___ *yüzden* 549; see also demonstrative pronouns
buçuk 208, 227
buffer: consonant 42; stem 162
bulun-: (aux.) 124, **162–3**, 320, 454; (as main verb) 129
bura- 239, 286–7
bütün 170, 207; ___*-ü* 193

-C/-InC 52
-CA₁ **44**, 58, 240, 244, 256, 262; *-CA₂* 58; *-CA₃* 58
-CAcIK 58
-CAğız 58
-CAK₁ 58; *-CAK₂* 58–9
case marker/suffix 178–86; as time adverbial 233–4; omission of 556; see also ablative, accusative, dative, locative, genitive, oblique
-CAnA 59
-CAsI(nA) 59, 93, 496; and stress 31

causative 73, 149–50, **150–3**, 159–60
causee 150–2, 159, 183
-*CI* 54–5, 59, 304
-*CIK* 58; *see also CAK₁*
-*CIl* 59
circumflex xliv
clitics **Ch. 11**; and compound verb forms 164, 298; and negative marker 120; and stress 118–20, 27; and vowel harmony 25; position of 45–46, 117–8, 404
comitative/instrumental marker *see -(y)lA/ile*
comitative/instrumental-marked noun phrase **68–9**, 178; as adverbial 158, **251**; as complement **147–8**; as conjunction 534–5; 556
commands 317, **370–1**, 434–5
comment (clauses) 113, 478–9
comparison 202–4, 251–2, 288
complement: of adjective 205; of postposition 249–54; of verb 143, 145–6; and stress 32–3; *see also* direct object, oblique object, subject complement
compounds *see* compound verb forms, nominal-verb compounds, noun compounds
compound verb forms/compound forms 161–4, 514–16; and negation 320–2; and tense/aspect/modality 374–9, 445–6; *see also bulun, -ol-*
concessive 493–4; (clause) 524–6, 529–30, 544, 552
conditional clauses **Ch. 27**; concessive 524–6; counterfactual 518–21; hypothetical 517, 520–2; and intonation 35; with wh-phrases 527–9; without conditional markers 530
conditional copula *see -(y)sA*
conditional suffix *see -sA*
conjunctions 49, 510–11, **Ch. 28**
consonants **3–10**; alternation 14–15, 17; deletable 42–3; doubled 5, 17
converb **88–94**, 486–507
co-ordination **Ch. 28**; and intonation 35
copula 'be' **81–3**, 124, 129–131, 345–7
copular markers **82–3**, 125; with interrogative *ml* 113–4; *see also -(y)DI, -(y)mIş, -(y)sA*
counterfactuals 348–9, **351–2**, 356–7, 360, 364, 369, 379; *see also* conditional clause

çeyrek 208, 227
çok: (adv.) 201–2, 242–3, 246; (det.) 171, 206; *çoğu* 137, 206, 289
çünkü 549

-*DA* (der.) 59
-*DA* (loc.) 68, **183–4**; *see also* locative-marked noun phrase
dA **110–11**; 'and', 'too' 413–14, 535–6; 'but' 521, 543; and definiteness 211–12, 289; and stress 118–20; as subordinator 486; with -*sA* 525–6; with -*(y)Ip* 533; *dA...dA* 138–9; 538–9
daha: comparative 202–4; time adverbial 232, 237; ___ *çok* 246; ___ -*sı* 537
-*DAm* 60
-*DAn* (abl.) 68; **184–5**; *see also* ablative-marked noun phrase
-*DAn* (der.) 60
-*DA(n)* (der.) 56
-*dan* (der.) 60
-*dar* 60
-*DAş/-Deş* 60
dates 104–5, 227–8
dative case marker *see -(y)A*
dative-marked noun phrase **182–4**; as adverbial 148, 233, 238–9; as causee 150–2; as complement 146, 148, 205 252–4, 449
de- 'say' 20, 418–20, 423
decimals 209
deduction 354, **482–4**, 495, 567
deference (in 3rd person forms) 133, 276–7
değil 125–6, **322–4**; (conj.) 325; in elliptical constructions 324–5; ___ *mi* 295–7
dek 253
demek ki 549
demonstrative: (adv.) 240; (det.) 207; (pronoun) 285–6
derhal 238
derivation 42, 47, **Ch. 7**
derken: (adv.) 550; in echo questions 314
desen(iz) 414–15
desiderative *see -(y)AsI*
determiners 168, 206; and agreement 135–6; definite 207; indefinite 171, 206, 391–2; pronominalized 136–7, 289–90; quantifying 171, 206
-*DI* (der.) 52

-*DI* (pf.) 75, 77, **564–5**; neutral modality (direct knowledge) 348, 564–5; past tense 337–8; perfective aspect 341; and referential status 395; ___ *mI* 485, 530;
-*DI*...-*(y)AlI* 94, 503
-*DIğI*: ___ *gibi* 493, 497, 502; ___ *halde* 242, 487, 493; ___ *için* 500;___ *kadar* 507; ___ *nispette/oranda/ölçüde* 498; ___ *sırada/anda* 501; ___ *taktirde* 494, 530; ___ *zaman* 490, 501
-*DIğInA göre* 89, 495
-*DIğIncA* 496
-*DIğIndA* 89, 501
-*DIğIndAn* 89, 500; ___ *beri* 502; ___ *dolayı/ötürü* 500
-*DIK* (der.) 52
-*DIK*: (sub.) 88–90, 437–44, 458–63
-*DIkçA* 89, 498, 504
-*DIktAn*: *başka* 89, 492; ___ *sonra* 89, 503
-*DIr* (adv.) 83–4, 235
-*DIr* (caus.) 56, 150–3, 159–60
-*DIr* (generalizing modality marker) 75, **83–4**, 350–1; modality 224; and referential status 396; and stress 83, 114
diğer 207; ___-*i*; 289, 383
diminutive 27, 58
direct object **145–6**, 153; and case marking 180–1; categorial 145, 179–80, 385, 40; generic 391–2; indefinite 179–81, 384; non-case-marked 164–5; omission of 144–5, 558–9; and referential status 145–6, 216, 303–4, 393–4; and word order 218, 400, 404–5
direct speech 419, 421, 423
directional: (adv.) 239–40; (pronoun) 287–8
discourse connectives **Ch. 28**
dislocation 415–6
distributive numerals **210**; *see also* -*(ş)Ar*
diye **111–12**; adjectival function 200–1; in adverbial clauses 480–2; in noun clauses 421–2
dolayı 255
dolusu 211
doubling **97–9**, 495, 503
dur- *see* -*(y)Adur*

e(ee) 550
echo questions 313–14
eğer 510
ellipsis 324–5, 555–60
emphasis 95–6, 272–4; *see also* focus

-*en* 60
en 32, **204–5**, 346; position of 212, 214; ___ *çok* 245; ___ *azından* 224–6, 554
-*engiz* 60
enumerators 210–11; pronominalized 288–9
epenthetic vowels 17–18
et- 17, 29, 164
events (versus states) 342–5
evidential: copula *see* -*(y)mIş*; modality 225, **365–8**, 519; suffix *see* -*mIş*
exclamations 112, 142, 331
existential sentence 126; locative 126–9; negation in 325–6; possessive 127–9; word order in 139, 399, 402–4, 407–8

fact (neutral modality) markers 348
fakat 541
falan/filan 169; ___-*ca/*___-*ca* 207
fazla(sıyla) 171, 206, 243, **246–7**, **331–2**
final devoicing 14–17
finite: as main clause **Ch. 12**; as subordinate clause; 424–6, 475–7, 480–92; predicate 123–4; verb forms 71–2, 75–6, 564–8
focus 244, 406–8, **409–10**; and discourse connectives 535–6; and personal pronouns 282, 283, 284; ___-sensitive adverbials 244–6
fractions 208–9
future suffix *see* -*(y)AcAK*

-*GA*/-*(A)lga* 52
-*GAC* 52
galiba 224
-*GAn* 52
geçe- 227
gel gör ki 542
gelgelelim 542
gelince 414–15
-*gen* 60
generalizations 348–51, 390–4, 419, 513
generalizing modality marker *see* -*DIr*
genitive case marker *see* -*(n)In*
genitive-marked noun phrase **185–6**, as complement of postposition 249–52, 258, 260–4; in noun clause 432–3, 437, 440; in partitive construction 193–4; as subject 418, 444–5
genitive-possessive construction **186–9**, 193–4, in existential sentences 127–9, 402–3; and dislocation 415–6

geopolitical terms 104–6
gerçi 544
gerek: (necessary) 353, 361; *gerek-* (be necessary) 365, 445; *olsa* ___ 374–5, 378; *gerek...(ve) gerek(se de)* 538–9; subjects conjoined by 138
-GI 52
-GIC 52
-GIn 52
-GIr 56
gibi 241, **249–50**; (sub.) 425–6; *see also bu/şu/o gibi, -DIğI/-(y)AcAğI gibi, -mAsI gibi, ne gibi*
gibi dur-/görün-/gözük- 426, 449–50
gibi gel- 425–6, 450
gil- 60
glottal stop 10
göre **252**, 266; *see also –DIğInA/-(y)AcAğInA göre*

ğ (soft 'g') 7–8, 14, 16–17, 43

habitual *see* aspect
ha...ha 541
hâlâ xliv, 238
halbuki 542–3
-(h)ane 60
hangi 306; ___*-si* 289
hani 301, 315–16, 545, 554
hatta 537–8
hazır 238
hele (hele) 547
hem (de) 138, 537; *hem...hem* 538–9
hemen 238; *hemen hemen* 211
henüz 232, 237, 328
hep 235; *hepsi* 137, 193–4, 290
her 171, 193, 207; ___ *biri* 193; ___ *ne kadar* 527, 530; ___ *şey* 291, 383; ___ *yer* 240; ___ *zaman* 235
herhalde 223–4
herhangi bir 205, 329, 391–2; ___*-i(-si)* 289
herkes 291, 383
hiç 236, **328–9**; ___ *değilse/olmazsa* 224–6, 554
hiçbir 328–9; ___ *şey/yer/zaman* 329; ___*-i(si)* 136, 289, 328–9
hypothetical modality 348–9, **351–2**, 356–7, 385–7, 566; *see also* conditional clauses

-I 60
-(I)K 53, 56
-II (pass.) 73–4, 153
-(I)lI 53
-(I)m: (1sg. poss.) 67; (der.) 60
-(I)mIz (1pl. poss.) 67
-(I)msA 56
-(I)msAr 60
-(I)msI 60
-(I)mtraK 60
-(I)n: (2sg. poss.) 67; (der.) 53, 55; (ref.) 74, 176, 188
-In (pass.) 73–4, 153
-InC see -C
-(I)ncI 61, 209
-(I)nIz (2pl. poss.) 67
-(I)ntI 53
-(I)r (caus.) 56, 150–3, 159–60
-(I)r (der.) 53
-(I)ş: (der.) 55; (rec.) 74
-(I)ştIr 55
-(I)t (der.) 53, 61
-(I)t (caus.) 56, 150–3
-(I)yor 75, **80**, **341–4**; effect on previous vowel 20, 80; neutral modality (direct knowledge) 348; future reference 339–40; present tense 338–9; and referential status 396; and stress 31; ___ *gibi* 93; *see also* compound verb forms
-(I)z 61

-i (der.) *see -(v)i*
i- (cop.) 81–2
için 235, **248–50**; *see also -DIğI için, -mAk için, -mAsI için, -(y)AcAğı için*
-idi 82–3; *see also -(y)DI*
iken see -(y)ken
ile 68–9; *see also -(y)lA*
ilk 207, 209, 213, 233, 346; ___*-i*, 289 ___ *önce* 231
imiş 82–3; *see also -(y)mIş*
imperative 87, 369–70
imperfective *see* aspect
impersonal construction 155–6, 160, 318, 362, 428, 433, 437, 462
indirect: question 440–1; statement 438–40
infinitive *see -mAk* (sub.)
inflectional suffixes 43, **Ch. 8**
insan 292
interjections 49–50, 87
intonation **Ch. 5**; in questions **Ch. 19**
ise: (cond.) 82; (conj.) 543; *see also -(y)sA*
-istan 61

Index   593

iste- 'want' **420, 425**, 427; (pass.) ___*-n* 431, 434–5; in small clauses 447–50
ister...ister 540–1
işte 552
-iye 61
-iyet 61

juxtaposition 340, 502, 531

-k 85
kaç 169, 171, **306–7**; ___*-ı* 192, 289
kadar: 'as…as' 202, **251–2**; 'until' 253; *see also bu/şu/o/ne kadar*, *-DIğI/-(y)AcAğI kadar*
kal- see *-(y)AkAl*
kala 227
kaldı ki 537
-kâr 61
karşı 253, 258
karşın 254, 493, 542
kendi (adj. modifier) 271
kendi- 157, 272–7; *kendi kendi-* 157, 277–8; *(kendi)* ___*-si/-leri 276*; *see also* resumptive pronoun
keşke 225–6, 369
-ki see -ki(n)
ki (sentence-final) **112–13**, 142, 544–5; and stress 120
ki (sub.) **112–13**, 140; in adverbial clauses 482–4; in comment clauses 477–8; in noun clauses 422–5; in relative clauses 475–7
kim(ler) 170, 303
kimi (det.) 170, 206, 213; ___*(si)* (pronoun) 136–7, 192, 289
kimse 328, **330**, 332–3; ___*-cikler* 330
-ki(n) 44, **69–70**; adjectival 200, 214–15; pronominal 290–1; omission of 556–7

-lA 56, 61
-lAm 61
-lAmA 61
-lAn 56, 149
-lAr (nominal plural marker) 67, **170–4**; and *bir* 172–3; definite status 388–9; and generic reference 392–3; indefinite status 384; in recurrent time locations 234
-lAr (3pl.) 84–5, 87–8, 134–5
-lArI(n) (der.) 61, 234
-lArI(n) (3pl. poss.) **67–8**, 176–7, 188
-lAş 56–7, 149
-lAt 57, 149

lazım see gerek (necessary)
-leyin 61, 231
-lI 61–2, 199, 213–14
-lIğInA 62, 235
-lIk **62**, 197, 199, 213
-lIm (1pl. opt.) *see -(y)AlIm*
linking sentence 125–6; negation in 322–3; word order and stress in 399, 402
loanwords xxxii, 6–13, 15, 24, 50, 65; *see also* Arabic, Persian
locative case marker *see -DA*
locative-marked noun phrase **183–4**; as adjectival 198, 200, 214; as adverbial 148, 219, 233–4, 238–9, 258; as complement **146**, 205, 430
long vowels *see* vowel length

-m (1sg.) 85
-mA (der.) 53
-mA (neg.) **74–5**, 92, **319–21**; and clitics 120; irregular combinations 79–80; and stress 120
-mA (sub.) **90–2, 432–7**; in converbs 486–7, 493, 498, 501, 504; in expressions of necessity 361, 363–4; interchangeability with *-DIK/-(y)AcAK/-(y)Iş* 442–4
-mAC 53
-mAcA 53
-mAdAn 497; ___*önce* 487, 503–4
madem ki 482, 484
-mAdIk (der.) 53
-mAK (der.) 53
-mAk (sbu.) 90–1, 429–31; ___*adına* 498; *-mAk* ___*için* 489–9; ___*üzere* 493, 498–9; *yerine* 498–9; ___*-sIzIn* 91, 497; ___*-tansa* 91, 498; ___*yerine* 500
-mAktA 75, **81**, 565–6; imperfective aspect 342–3; modality 348, 355; present tense 338; *see also* compound verb forms
-mAlI 80–1, 351, **362**, 364, 556
-mAn 53, 63
manner: (adv.) 240–1, 401; clause 495–7
-mAsI: durumunda/halinde 530; ___*gibi* 497; ___*için* 486; ___*üzerine* 501; ___*yüzünden* 500; ___*-nA* 494
-mAyAgör 162, 334
-mAz (der.) 53
-mA-z (neg. + aor.) 79, 564; *see also -(A/I)r/-z*
-mAzdAn 92; ___*(/-mAmAzlIktAn/-mAzlIktAn) gel* 164
-mAz ol- 379, 447, 467

measure/type terms 191, **210–11**; doubled 98; pronominalized 288–9
meğer(se) 225
mI **113–16**, **293–302**; in alternative questions 297; in echo questions 313–14; in indirect questions 440; as intensifier 98; in rhetorical questions 317–8; and stress/intonation 35, 294–7, 298, 300–1; in tag questions 295–7; with wh-phrase 313–4; *see also -DI mI*
-mIK 53
-mIş (der.) 53
-mIş (ev./pf.) 75, **77**, 565; evidential modality **365–8**, 519; past tense 337–8; perfective aspect 341; in truncated relative clauses 473–5; -___ *çAsInA* 93, 496; ___ *gibi* 93, 496; *see also* compound verb forms
modal adverb(ial)s 31–6, **223–6**, 352–3; in questions 315; and word order 399, 403–4
modality **Ch. 21**, **348–80**, **564–8**; markers 75–81; and referential status 395–7; *see also* assumptions, commands, compound verb forms, counterfactual, evidential, hypothetical, necessity, possibility, requests, suggestions, volitional utterances, wishes
m-reduplication 96–7

-n (pass.) 73
-n (2sg.) 85
n (buffer) 43–4
nasıl **309–10**, 275; ___ *bir* 207; ___ *ki* 480, 482, **484**, 547; ___ *-sa*/___ *olsa* 551
nationality terms 105–6
ne 303–4; in statements 318; ___ *de olsa* 552; ___ *gibi (bir)* 206–7, 309–10; ___ *kadar* 191, 307–9; ___ *...ne* 138, 326–7 ___ *var ki* 542; ___ *...-si* 318
necessity/obligation 360–5, 379, 434, 462, 524, 542
neden/niçin/niye 309
negation **Ch. 20**; *see also* nominal sentences, verbal sentences, *-mA*, *ne...ne*, *değil*, *yok*
nere- 304–5; ___ *-si* 287
neredeyse 238, 243, 357
neyse 553–4
ne zaman 309; ___ *ki* 140
-(n)In (gen.) 68, **185–6**; omission of 444–5; *see also* genitive-marked noun phrase

-nIz (2pl.) 85
nitekim 547
nominal predicate/sentence **124**, 125–9; negation in 322–3; person marking in 86–7, 136; and referential status 396–7; of subordinate clause 130, 473–5; and tense/aspect/modality 129–31, **345–8**; and word order 402–3; *see also -DIr*; existential sentence, linking sentence
nominal-verb compounds 18–19, **164–5**, 298, 389
non-case-marked noun phrase **178–80**, 233, 386, **428–9**; as adverbial 219, 233, 235; as complement of postposition 249–50, 259–60; as direct object 145, *179*, 384; as subject **178**, 448–9, 487; as subject complement 125, 179; and word order 311, 384, 393, 399–400, **404**
non-finite verb form 72, 76, **140–1**; *see also* converb, participle, verbal noun
non-finite clause 139–41; negation in 320–1; *see also* adverbial clause, noun clause, relative clause
noun 48; countable/uncountable 168–9; doubled 97; as head of noun phrase 167–8; proper (name) xliv, xlv, 171, 190, 262, 465
noun clause **Ch. 24**; dislocation 416; inside relative clause 463–4; as modifier in compounds 450–2; questioning part of 314; stress in 439
noun compounds **Ch. 10**; as head of noun phrase 168; stress in 29; *see also -(s)I* compounds
noun phrase **Ch. 14**; categorial 388–90; definite 394, 395; generic 390–4; (in)animate 135, 399 (*see also* animacy); elision of 558–60; indefinite **383–7**, 391–2, 395; inflection **66–71**, **170–86**; modification of 168, **Ch. 15**; and position of determiners and numerals 211–15; stress in 32; *see also* accusative-marked ___, non-case-marked ___, noun clause, oblique-marked ___, plural marking, possessive
number 66–7, 170–5; *see also -lAr*, plural marking
numerals 48, **207–10**; and agreement (subject-predicate) 133–4; and countability 169; and *-lAr* 171; position of 211–12; pronominalized 288–9; with *-(s)I* 192–3

o: (adv.) 242–3; (det.) 207; (pronoun) 268, 285–6; ___ *gibi* 207, ___ *kadar(ı)* 112, 142, 192, 206, 289, ___ *-nun üzerine* 550; ___ *zaman* 551; *see also* demonstrative pronouns, resumptive pronouns
object *see* direct object, oblique object
oblique case-marked noun phrase 219, 256, 263, 287, 429–31, 479, and relativization, 458–9; *see also* oblique object, and ablative-marked, dative-marked, locative-marked, comitative/instrumental-marked noun phrase
oblique object **146–8**, 428, **429–30**, **436–9**, 443–4; omission of 558–9; referential status of 259–60; relativization of 461, 463; and word order 311, 399, 401, 404–5;
offers 373
-oğlu 45
o halde 551
ol-: (aux.) 160, **162–3**, 445, **469–73**; (cop.) 124, 127, 345; (main verb) **129–31**, 44; *see also -mAz ol-*
oldu olacak 224–6
olmak üzere 221–2
olsa olsa 525
olsun...olsun 540–1
onca 44
onomatopoeic stems 56, 64
optative **87**, 333–4, 372–3, 376, 567; with discourse connectives 529, 540, 541, 545; negative forms 317, 476; in subordinate clauses 419–20, 424–5, 481, 483, 486; *see also -sA, sakın*
ora- 239, 286–7
oysa (ki) 117, 542–3

öbür; ___ *-ü* 289, 383
önce(den) 232, 234, **256**, 503–4
öte(si) 240, 288
öteki 207
öyle: (adv.) **240–1**, 243, 424; (det.) ___ *(bir)* 207, 391; ___ *ki* 548; ___ *mi* 295–7; ___ *-sine* 112, 142; ___ *-yse* 551
özellikle 245, 547

palatal(ization) xliv, 4, 6, 8–12, 24, 577
participle **88–92**, 453–63
partitive construction 134, 185, **189–94**
passive 73–4, 149–50, 153–6, 159–60
past copula, *see -(y)DI*
pek (de) 142, 236, 243, 331–2

peki 545
perfective *see* aspect
Persian xxx–xxxii, xxxiv, xliv, 7, 10, 12, 15, 17, 28, 51, 57, 140
person marking **84–7**; in finite predicates **132–9**, 280; in adverbial clauses 486–7; elision of 555–6; with *mI* 114–16; in noun clauses 418–23; in relative clauses 458–60; in noun phrases 175–7; in compounds 177–80; in postpositions 256–7, 262, 262; in pronouns 271–77; in small clauses 449–50
phrasal compound 450–2
place: (adv.) 183, **238–40**; ___ name 28, 30, 105–6; reference to 305
plural marking: of noun 170–4; of predicate 132–9; *see also -lAr*
politeness strategies 224–5
possessor *see* genitive-marked noun phrase
possessive: ___ -marked noun phrase 90, 174, **186–9**, 458–9; ___ -marked postposition 259; suffixes **67**, **175–6**, 432–5, 458–61; omission of 188–9; *see also* person marking
possibility 354–360
postpositions 49; bare 249–56; possessive-marked 256–65
postpositional phrase **Ch. 17**; adjectival 266; adverbial 220, 266; predicative 267; in stress 33
postpredicate area 410–11
predicate 123–4; finite 71–2 focused/stressed 411; nominal 124–127; non-finite 72; verbal 124
predictions 353
prefixation 65, 95–97, 561–3; *see also m-*reduplication
prepredicate area/position 384, **409–10**
prescriptive statements 349
preverbal area/position 217–8, 232, 240 **400–1**, 412; and referential status 386–7, 394
progressive *see* aspect
prohibitions 333, 349, 357
pronouns 48 **Ch. 18**; agreement with predicate 131–2; antecedent of 270–79, 414; genitive-attracting 249–52; locative 286; omission/usage of 280–5; personal 268–70; *see also birbir-*, demonstrative pronouns, *kendi-*, resumptive pronouns
proportion(al relation/expression) 193–4, 221; proportionality 498, 504
purpose clauses 483

quantifier/determiner 32, 169–70, 191, **206–7**, 236; pronominal 194, **291–2**, 328–30, 383
questions 141, **Ch. 19**; alternative 297, 440–1; consultative/deliberative 372–3; indirect 440–1; intonation in 35, 294–7, 300–2; wh-questions 301–10, yes/no questions 393–5; *see also* mI

-*rA* 63
rağmen see karşın
recipient *see* beneficiary
reciprocal 74, 158, 160; pronoun 158, 278–9
reduplication **Ch. 9**, 28, 538, 540, 546, 561; *see also* doubling
reflexive 74, 156–7; pronoun 274
relative clause **Ch. 25**; pronominal 466–8; questioning part of 314; truncated 473–5
requests 357, **373**, 434–5, 524
result clauses 483
resumptive pronouns 270, **277**, 459, 476–7, 528
root 13, 16, 50–1; vowel harmony in 24

-*sA* (der.) 57
-*sA* (cond.) 75, **78**, **509–10**, **516–18**, 527–9, 567; in deliberative questions 372–3, 517; in wishes 369; ___ *dA* 525–6; -*sA..-sA* 524–5
-*sAK* 53, 63
sakın 333–4
-*sAl* 53, 63
san- 'think' 420, 438–9, 447–50
-*sAnA* 31, 87, 371
-*sAnIzA* 31, 87, 371
sanki 224, 480, 484–5, 496, 506
scrambling **Ch. 23**, 406–412
secondary predication 448
sentence/clause **Ch 12**, **Ch. 23**, complex 139–41; functional 141–2; stress **Ch. 5**; *see also* existential, linking, nominal, verbal sentence/clause
sentential complement *see* noun clause
-*sI* (der.) 54, 63
-(*s*)*I* (3sg. poss.) *see* -(*s*)*I(n)*
-(*s*)*I* compounds 29, **103–6**, 177–8, 198, 228, **450–2**
-*sII* 64
-*sIn* (stressable, 3sg. opt./imp.) 87; *see also* optative
-*sIn*: (unstressable, 2sg.) 86; (2sg. opt.) 87

-(*s*)*I(n)* (3sg. poss.) 67; in impersonal verbal nouns 429; omission of 272; in pronominalized forms 287; *see also* -(*s*)*I* compound
-(*s*)*InA* 64
-*sInIz* (2pl.) 86; (2pl. opt.) 87
-*sInIAr* (3pl. opt./imp.) 87
-*sIz* (der.) 64
siz(ler) 269–70
small clause 179, 186, **447–50**; negation 320; word order 400
'soft g' *see* ğ
son 207, 213, 233; ___-*uncu* 346; ___-*uncusu* 289
sonra(dan) 232–3, 234, 256, 266, 308, **256**, 503–4
sözde 224, 367
space-denoting nouns 99
spatial meaning/nominal/relation 33, 102, 179, 184, 219, 239, 253, **257**
statements 141
states (versus events) 342–5; entry into 344–5, 377
stem 41–4, **Chs. 6–7**
stress **Chs. 4–5, 11**; in clitics 118–20; in noun phrases 32; in postpositional phrases 33; primary 36–7; and referential status 395; secondary 37–8; in verb phrases 32; in words 26–9
subject 123, 128–9; of adverbial clause 487; and agreement 133–9; animate/inanimate 133, 135, 399; categorial 456; conjoined 137–9; of existential sentence 126–127; genitive-marked **186**, 487; indefinite 456, 461; non-case-marked 178, 274, 448; of noun clause 279–80, 428; omission of 280–1; of relative clause 455–7; of small clause 447–9; and word order 394, 403–4
subject complement **125–6**, 138, 179, 400
subjunctive *see* optative
subordinate clause 139–41; questioning part of 314–5
subordinating suffixes **87–94**, 426–42
subordinator *see* converb, *diye*, *ki*, participle, verbal noun
suffixation **Chs. 6–8**
suffixes: A-type 23; consonant alternation in 42; derivational **Ch. 7**; elision of 555–7; I-type 22–3; inflectional **Ch. 8**; non-harmonic 24–5; ordering of 45–6, 75; stressable 30–1; unstressable 31

suggestions 87, 141, **372**
syllable xiv, 13
superlative *see en*
suspended affixation 555–7

-(ş)Ar 64
şart 353, 361
şeklinde (sub.) 421
şey 292
şimdi 231–2; ___ *-den* 234
şöyle: (adv.) **240–1**, 243; (det.) ___ *(bir)* 207, 391; ___ *ki* 546; ___ *dursun* 538; *see also* demonstrative pronouns
şu: (adv.) 242–3; (det.) 207; (pronoun) 285–6; ___ *gibi* 207, ___ *kadar(ı)* 142, 192, 206, 289
şura- 239, 286–7

-t 56, 150–3, 159–60
ta 253
tag questions 295–7
tam 245–6
tane 192–3, 210–11; ___ *-si* 288–9
tarafından 153–4
-tay 54, 64
tek 244–5
tense **Ch. 21**, **336–40**, **564–8**; future 339–40; markers 75–81; in nominal sentences 129; in non-finite clauses 445–7, 449–50, 468–73, 489–92; past 337–8; present 338–9; and referential status 395–7; *see also* compound verb forms
-tI 54, 64
tıpkı 250
time adverbials **227–38**, 366–7, 468
topicalization 408, **412–15**; of pronouns 283; of subject 127
topic shifters 35, 413–15; and intonation 35
topographical entities 104–5
transitivity 149–50
transitivizer *see* causative
transnumeral meaning 174–5
truncated relative clause 222–3, 473–5

üzere 260
üzerine 260, 550

var **126–31**, 345–6, 509–10; ___ *ya* 554
-vari 64
ve 138, 262, 534–5; ___ *de* 536

verb: **49**, 73–4, **143–60**, 447–9; of communication 421; of emotion 182, 184, 205, 344–5, **421–2**, 436, 443–4, 468; of perception/cognition **421–2**, 344–5, 421–5, 443–4, 447; ___ -verb compounds 103; *see also bil-, de-, iste-, san-*, compound verb forms, nominal-verb compounds
verb phrase **Ch. 13**; stress in 32
verbal noun **88–92**, 426–42
verbal predicate/sentence 124, **Ch. 13**; and negation 319–21, 323–4; and word order and stress **Ch. 23**, 398–402
veya 138, 539–40
-(v)i 64
vocative 26–7
voice 149–50; ___ suffixes 72–4
volitional utterances 141–2, **369–70**
vowel **10–13**; alternation 17–20; deletable 22–23
vowel harmony **Ch 3**; fronting harmony 21–2, 24; rounding harmony 22–4
vowel length/long vowels 12–13; caused by 'ğ' 7–8; caused by 'h' 8–9; occurring under suffixation 18–19

wh-phrase 301–2, **302–10**, and conditional marking 527–9; in echo questions 313–14
wh-questions *see* questions
wishes 369–70, 423
word order **Ch. 23**; and referential status 394

'*y*' (buffer) 42, 45
-(y)- (cop.) **81–2**, 124, 129–30
-(y)A (cv.) 93
-(y)A (dat.) 68, **181–3**; *see also* dative-marked noun phrase
-(y)A₁ (der.) 64
-(y)A₂ (der.) 64
-(y)A (opt.) 75, **81**
-(y)A (psb.) 75, **76–7**
-(y)A...-(y)A 94, 495
ya (clitic, sentence-final) 116, 537, **544–5**
ya ...ya (da) 540; subjects conjoined by 138
-(y)Abil 24–5, 31, 46, **77**, 160–1, **564**; modality 348, **354–60**
-(y)AcağInA 89, 500; ___ *göre* 495
-(y)AcağIndAn (dolayı/ötürü) 89, 500

-(y)AcAK (der.) 54
-(y)AcAK (fut.) 75, **79**, 566; imperative usage 371; modality 348, 352–3, 359, 363–4; in relative clauses 461–2; ___ *gibi* 93; ___ *kadar/derecede* 506, ___ *ol-* 521; *see also* compound verb forms
-(y)AcAK (sub.) 88–9; *-(y)AcAğı*: ___ *gibi* 487, 496, 505–6; ___ *halde* 493; ___ *için* 500; ___ *kadar* 499, 506–7; ___ *sırada/anda* 501; ___ *zaman* 490
-(y)Adur 24–5, 31, **77**, 160–2
-(y)Agel 24–5, 31, **77**, 160–1
-(y)Akal 24–5, 31, **77**, 160–2
-(y)AlI (beri) 93, 502
-(y)AlIm 87, 372, 419, 567
-(y)An (der.) 54
-(y)An (part.) **92**, **455–8**, 461, 463
-(y)An...-(y)AnA 94
-(y)AnA kadar 93, 504
yani 547–8
-(y)ArAk 93, 495
yarı 242–3; ___ *-sı* 193
yarım 208, 227
-(y)AsI 75, **81**, 378; ___ *-cA* 54; ___ *-yA* 54
-(y)at 64
-(y)Ayaz 24–5, 31, **77**, 160–1
-(y)DI 75, **82–3**, 568; neutral modality (direct knowledge) 348; imperfective aspect 341; past tense 337–8; *-(y)DI...-(y)DI* 546–7
yes/no questions *see* questions
yeter ki 550
-(y)I: (cv.) 93; (der.) 54

-(y)I (acc.) 68, **180–1**; *see also* accusative-marked noun phrase
-(y)IcI 54
-(y)Im: (1sg.) 86; (der.) 55
-yIm (1sg. opt.) 87, 372, 419, 567
-(y)In (der.) 64
-(y)IncA 93, 501; ___ *-yA kadar/değin/dek* 504
-(y)In(Iz) (2pl. imp.) 87, 370
-(y)Ip 93, 333, 532–4; *-(y)Ip...-mA* 322, 440
-(y)Iş: (der.) 55; (sub.) 92
-(y)Iver 24–5, 31, 46, **77**, 160–1
-(y)Iz (1pl.) 86, 117
yeni (time adv.) 232
-(y)ken 93–4, 501–2
-(y)lA/ile: (com./ins.) 68–9, 262, 303; (conj.) 261–2, 534–5; as postposition 251
-(y)mIş 75, **83**, **365–8**, 505–6, 568; and conditional marker 519; evidential modality 365–8; ___ *-çAsInA* 93, 496; ___ *gibi* 93, 484–5, 496; *-(y)mIş...-(y)mIş* 546–7
yok **126–31**, 325–6, 509–10; ___ *mu* 554; (conj.) 546–7; *yok...yok* 546–7
yoksa 297, 316–7, 440, 539
-(y)sA/ise 75, **83**, **116–17**, **509–10**; (con.cop./conj./sub.) 526–7, 543–4; (topic shifter) 413–14; ___ *da* 526–7

-z (aor.) *see -mA-z*
zaten 551, 553
-zade 65
-zede 65

Printed in the United States
by Baker & Taylor Publisher Services